AUTHOR Dedicated to discovering and sharing knowledge
and creative vision, authors and scholars have endowed
this imprint to perpetuate scholarship of the highest caliber.

*Scholarship is to be created ... by awakening a pure interest in knowledge.*

—Ralph Waldo Emerson

The publisher gratefully acknowledges the generous support of the Authors Imprint Endowment Fund of the University of California Press Foundation, which was established to support exceptional scholarship by first-time authors.

From the Indian Ocean to the Mediterranean

# THE CALIFORNIA WORLD HISTORY LIBRARY

Edited by Edmund Burke III, Kenneth Pomeranz, and Patricia Seed

# From the Indian Ocean
# to the Mediterranean

*The Global Trade Networks
of Armenian Merchants from New Julfa*

———

Sebouh David Aslanian

UNIVERSITY OF CALIFORNIA PRESS

*Berkeley   New York   London*

University of California Press, one of the most distinguished university presses in the United states, enriches lives around the world by advancing scholarship in the humanities, social sciences, and natural sciences. Its activities are supported by the UC Press Foundation and by philanthropic contributions from individuals and institutions. For more information, visit www.ucpress.edu.

University of California Press
berkeley and los Angeles, California

University of California Press, ltd.
london, England

library of Congress Cataloging-in-Publication data

Aslanian, sebouh david.
   From the Indian Ocean to the Mediterranean : the global trade networks of Armenian merchants from new Julfa / by sebouh david Aslanian.
      p.  cm. — (The California world history library ; 17)
   Includes bibliographical references and index.
   isbn 978-0-520-26687-2 (cloth, alk. paper)
   1. Julfa (Isfahan, Iran)—Commerce—history—sources.
2. Merchants—Armenia—history—sources.  I. Title.
HF3770.2.Z9J853   2010
382.089'9199205595—dc22            2010023440

Manufactured in the United states of America

19   18   17   16   15   14   13   12   11
10  9  8  7  6  5  4  3  2  1

*For Houri, my home in this world*

# CONTENTS

# ILLUSTRATIONS

## FIGURES

## MAPS

## TABLES

# ACKNOWLEDGMENTS

It is not possible to thank all the individuals who have given so generously of their time and expertise. I would like to single out for special mention those whose help was indispensable during the writing of this book. I am grateful for the patience and expert guidance of my advisers and mentors while this book was in its dissertation stage: Francesca Trivellato, Rudi Matthee, Nader Sohrabi, and Partha Chatterjee. Francesca's mentorship in matters pertaining to long-distance trade and economic history gave shape to this project from very early on. Most of what is good in this book is a reflection of her friendship and professional advice. Rudi offered the same by sharing with me his unrivaled knowledge of Safavid history and political economy. I owe Nader a special debt for unceremoniously rejecting my initial proposal and compelling me to restructure my inquiry along lines of historical sociology. Though I did not appreciate what seemed to me a rather harsh intervention at the time, I am deeply thankful to him for launching me on the path that I took. I am grateful to Partha for hosting and assisting me during my research trip to Calcutta. Marc Nichanian, though not directly involved in my project, played an important role in luring me back to graduate school, and for that I am grateful to him. In India, I would like to thank Michael Stephen, the warden of the Armenian church of Madras, for his kind hospitality and for his help in 2003 in locating various documents stored at the church. Sonia John of Calcutta was also a generous host, as were Professor Partha Chatterjee and the staff of the Center for Social Studies in Calcutta, especially Lakshmi Subramanian. In Yerevan, I would like to acknowledge the support and guidance of Shushanik Khachikian at the Matenadaran State Repository of Ancient Manuscripts, who generously helped me decipher some of the documents in my possession. Her pioneering work on the

Julfa merchants has been a source of inspiration, and she has been a mentor and a good friend. I also would like to thank Pavel Chobanyan, of the Armenian Academy of Sciences, and Meroujan Karapetyan for teaching me most of what I know about the onerous task of deciphering and understanding the Julfa dialect. Special acknowledgment is also due to the staff at the Mashtots Matenadaran, including Gevorg Ter Vardanyan, for enabling me to consult many hard-to-find books and manuscripts. In the same vein, I owe a debt to archivists in Italy and Spain, especially Manuel Ravina Martin, the director of the Archivo Histórico Provincial de Cádiz, for bringing the Armenian-related material to my attention, as well as for kindly sending copies of some documents that I had neglected to photograph while there. Giovanni Caniato of the Archivio di Stato di Venezia was also extremely generous with his help in various matters, as was Abbot Yeghia Kilaghbian at San Lazzaro. Likewise, I would like to thank Monsignor Gugerotti, whom I have never met, for kindly putting me in touch with the archivist at the Archivio di Istituto Don Nicola Mazza in Verona, Signor Graziano Costa, whom I also thank heartily for being an incredibly generous host during my visits to Verona in the summer of 2008. In London, my chance encounter with Gagan Sood, which led to my discovery of some of the documents used in this book, was a decisive moment in sparking a new research interest. My heartfelt thanks go to all those who made my trip to New Julfa possible, memorable, and rewarding, especially the Primate of New Julfa, Srpazan Papken Charian; Tatul Ohanian; Sona Baghoomian; Ani Babayan; Archbishop Goriun Babian; and the Diocesan Council for their warm hospitality and kindness. Without their generous support, this book could not have been written.

The following individuals have been particularly influential throughout my journey: Claude Markovits, Jerry Bentley, Willem Floor, William Clarence-Smith, Lakshmi Subramanian, Sanjay Subrahmanyam, Jack Wills, Kéram Kévonian, Amy Landau, Raymond Kevorkian, Scott Levi, Peter Cowe, Boghos Levon Zekiyan, Arash Khazeni, Dickran Kouymjian, Tatiana Seijas, Richard Hovannisian, Razmik Panossian, Ramzi Rouighi, Sarah Abrevaya Stein, Aron Rodrigue, and Karen Leonard. Many friends and colleagues have also been part of the writing of this book in one way or another and deserve special mention: Taline Voskeritchian, Loretta Nasser, Anny Bakalian, Elyse Semerdjian, Rachel Goshgarian, Tim Keirn (who was the first to introduce me to world history), Holly Shissler, Afshin Matin-asgari, Jasamin Rostam-Kolayi, Kathryn Babayan, Muge Gocek, Mehrdad Amanat, Ron Suny, Richard Antaramian, Mana Kia, Eric Beverley Lewis, Patricia Cleary, Claire Martin, Ali İğmen, Sean Smith, Vincent Del Casino, Vartan Karapetian, Helin Avedissian, Barlow Der Mguerdichian, and particularly Gabriella Djerrahian. I am most grateful to Engseng Ho and Khachig Tölölyan for their advice and comments, the latter for his indirect involvement, in providing sage advice and inspiration, the former for reading and commenting on the entire manuscript. This book would have fewer errors than it does had I listened more attentively to their suggestions and especially to those of Willem Floor, who also read the entire manuscript and offered many useful suggestions. I am very grateful to Ned Alpers and Edmund Herzig for their detailed comments at an early stage of the manuscript of this book. Edmund's pioneering dissertation on Julfa and his mentoring from across the ocean have made my modest accomplishments possible. Olivier Raveux deserves my special gratitude not only for carefully reading the entire manuscript and offering detailed suggestions but also for his friendship and generosity in putting at my disposal many of his own findings; my debt to him will become apparent in the endnotes of the book. I especially thank my friends Danny Beylerian and Bedross Der Matossian for their constant support and interest in my work and for providing much-needed emotional and intellectual recharging throughout the process of research and writing. Several colleagues have consistently been responsive to my unending list of queries and requests. They are Bert Vaux, Kapil Raj, Levon Avdoyan, Ara Sanjian, Aram Arkun, Lise Sedrez, Vartan Matiossian, Vrej Nersessian, Margaret Makepeace, Tatiana Seijas, and Kevork Bardakjian. I am grateful to Tamar Salibian for preparing the image of the map that graces the cover of this book and to Liz Chater for providing a family tree of the Minasian family, which served as a basis for figure 16 in chapter 6. I could not have embarked on my journey without the generous financial support of the Tavitian Foundation and the Dolores Zohrab-Liebman Fund at Columbia University. A Manoogian postdoctoral fellowship in the Department of History at the University of Michigan in 2007–2008 and a Mellon Foundation postdoctoral fellowship in world history at Cornell University in 2009 afforded me the time to revise my manuscript and benefit from the company of learned colleagues and friends. I am extremely grateful to Gerard Libaridian at the University of Michigan for being a pillar of support and to Ruth Mas, Mary Jacobus, and Peter Dear at the Society for the Humanities, Cornell University, for their encouragement and useful comments. I am also appreciative of the collegiality and friendship of Robert Travers, Eric Tagliacozzo, Duane Corpis, and others in the Department of History at Cornell University. Discussions with my students at Michigan and Cornell (especially Kenneth C. Kowren) were also useful in bringing this project to a conclusion. Niels Hooper, Cindy Fulton, and Eric Schmidt at UC Press deserve special gratitude for their professionalism and for having confidence in my book, as does Marian Rogers for her painstaking work in copy-editing the manuscript.

Last but certainly not least, the constant support and love of my family, particularly my mother, father, sister, and grandmother (who sadly did not live long enough to see the publication of my book), have been vital in the completion of this book. Most importantly, I am certain I would not have finished this work had I not been fortunate enough to meet my irreplaceable soul mate, my wife, Houri Berberian, whose multiple intellectual and emotional interventions in my life have brought new meaning to my work and even more so to my life. Her unfailing love, exuberant joie de vivre, Job-like patience, and constant companionship have transformed me as a human being and propelled me to new horizons. In that sense, I owe her much more than the dedication of this book can ever express.

# PREFACE

*For some scholars, no doubt, archival work is logistically too difficult or temperamentally uncongenial. Such must survive by their theorizing, and hope to invent a concept which catches on. But history is too important to be left to stay-at-home theorists.*[1]

Some studies are idea-driven; at their inception is a notion or theory about a process of historical development. The writer usually begins with an insight that may help pull together certain relatively well-known historic facts or events into a coherent whole. Others are archive-driven. In this case, the work in question begins not with a theoretical insight; rather, it is propelled by the discovery of a mass of archival documents heretofore neglected or overlooked by other scholars. Theoretical insights and generalizations certainly may play an important role in works of this sort, but mostly after the documents have been carefully gathered, laid out from beginning to end, scrupulously mined for the information they possess, and interpreted for the answers they may hold to the kinds of big questions historians are in the habit of posing.

This book, which began its career as a Columbia University doctoral dissertation, falls into the second camp. The idea of writing it took shape in my mind after the serendipitous discovery of archival material in the spring of 2003 while I was doing dissertation research in London. At the time, I had already begun work on another topic dealing with the role of Armenian merchants in the "origins" of Armenian nationalism and the flowering of Armenian culture in the late eighteenth-century Armenian diasporic settlements of Europe and India. Based on the secondary literature I had read, I had decided to focus my study on the patronage activities of a group of merchants from New Julfa, an Armenian commercial suburb of the Safavid capital of Isfahan, who were for the most part residing in Madras, India. This Perso-Armenian community of merchants in India provided the social and economic foundations for what has come to be known in Armenian historiography as the "national revival movement" in the diaspora. They bankrolled the nascent craft of Armenian printing in places like Venice, Amsterdam, Livorno, Madras, Calcutta, Lvov (now in the Ukraine), and New Julfa. They were also behind the revival of letters then spearheaded by a small band of Armenian Catholic missionaries known as the Mkhitarist Order, based on the island of San Lazzaro in Venice; they supported the establishment of schools of higher education in Venice, Paris, New Julfa, Moscow, and Calcutta. In addition to their financial patronage, some members of the Julfan merchant community became cultural and intellectual producers in their own right, as in the case of Shahamir Shahamirian, the wealthiest Armenian merchant in Madras during the second half of the eighteenth century.

After conducting research in Venice and Vienna during 2001–2002, thanks to a Columbia University Dissertation Travel Fellowship, I realized that the theoretical insights that had led me to formulate some ideas concerning the Armenian "revival movement" were inadequate in themselves to the task at hand. In order to write a thickly described and analytically informed historical narrative of the "revival" movement, I needed fresh archival evidence. Such evidence, however, was hard to come by. The most likely repository of Armenian documents pertaining to the cultural activities of Armenians in the seventeenth and eighteenth centuries was the archive of the cultural producers themselves, namely, the Mkhitarist Congregation on San Lazzaro, as well as the archives of the Armenian churches in Calcutta and Madras.

Unfortunately, my one-year research stint in Venice proved to be fruitless in this regard. The Mkhitarist archives were not open to most noncongregationists and have largely remained so to the present. This was a great disappointment, since these archival collections are among the richest repositories of documents pertaining to Armenian history in the early modern period (1500–1800). To remedy the situation, in the spring of 2003 I traveled to London, where I worked for three months examining some of the East India Company's papers at the India Office Records (IOR) stored in the British Library, in the hope of discovering material on some of the Madras-based Armenian merchants whose patronage activities I had been studying. Though I did not come across important material on these merchants and their cultural activities, I did stumble upon a collection of mercantile papers relating to an Armenian-freighted ship called the *Santa Catharina,* which was confiscated in India by the British navy in 1748. This collection of about 330 mercantile documents (in Lansdowne MSS 1047 and 1048) had been extensively examined by scholars of Armenian trade. What led me to them was the hope that mingled among these commercial documents would be some papers relating to cultural history. An analysis of these papers led me on a long paper chase through a number of archives in search of the original set from which these 330 documents, at some point, had been separated. After weeks of searching, I stumbled upon the original trove of documents in a London archive from which the Lansdowne papers at the British Library had been separated sometime in the eighteenth century. This trove, which serves as one of the bases of the present study, consists of some 1,700 mercantile documents from the 1740s. Mostly letters and business correspondence, these documents were written by Armenian merchants at their trading headquarters in New Julfa/Isfahan (Iran) to their agents and correspondents in India. I was later to find out that these papers were originally part of the cargo of the *Santa Catharina* and were confiscated by the British navy and shipped to London in 1748 to serve as exhibits in a high-stakes trial on the fate of the ship and its cargo.[2]

When I left London for India later in the spring of 2003, I still had hopes of salvaging my initial topic by discovering some new material on the Madras-based Armenian merchants and their cultural activities. After a two-month stay in Madras and Calcutta, I was disappointed once again to discover that the Armenian churches of both cities had failed to preserve much documentation from their once-illustrious communities in the seventeenth and eighteenth centuries. Sadly, bureaucratic obstacles at the local Indian archives made it impossible for me to work there. It was against this backdrop of frustration and disappointment as well my earlier discovery that I decided to abandon my initial topic and focus on the mercantile material I had found in London.

An opportunity to present my preliminary findings at a UCLA conference on New Julfa in the fall of 2003 compelled me to sift through the collection of *Santa Catharina* documents that I had photographed with a digital camera. A year of research in Yerevan, Republic of Armenia, enabled me to work on some of the documents and to study the obscure mercantile dialect of Julfa in which they are written.

Several more archival trips between 2004 and 2010 enabled me to collect more Julfa material from archives in Europe, Armenia, Iran, and North America. A four-month stay in Venice during the spring and early summer of 2005 made it possible for me to gather several thousand pages of Julfa documents from the Archivio di Stato di Venezia, the Archivio della Biblioteca di Museo Correr, and the Archivio Patriarchale. During my stay in Italy, I was also able to visit and work at the Archivio di Stato di Livorno, the Archivio Storico, Congregazione per l'Evangelizzazione dei Popoli o "de Propaganda Fide," and the Archivio di Stato di Firenze. In the Archivo de Indias in Seville, Spain, I was fortunate to find many papers relating to the Julfan community in Manila (the Philippines). The Archivo Histórico Provincial de Cádiz also yielded an unexpected find on the seventeenth-century Julfan community of Cadiz. By far my most important archival trip was to New Julfa/Isfahan in January 2005. The All Savior's Monastery Archive in New Julfa (ASMA) had last been systematically examined in the second half of the nineteenth century, and no scholar working on Julfan trade had managed to consult this important repository. I was very fortunate to receive encouragement and support of my interest in Julfan history from a number of leading personalities in the Armenian community there who have all been heartily thanked in the acknowledgments. Armed with a state-of-the-art digital camera, I was able to photograph most of the ASMA documents dating from 1595–1800, thus accomplishing in three weeks what would otherwise have taken several years. This book is the result of long hours of reading hard-to-decipher documents, listening to their stories, gaining an understanding of the global community that produced the documents, and finally retelling their stories in novel ways.

While considering the value of data contained in an ocean of Julfan letters, contracts, accounting ledgers, notarized court papers, and so on, I have often found myself face to face with what the great historian William H. McNeill once described as one of the cardinal tasks of the historian: "pattern recognition." As McNeill astutely observed in his essay "Mythistory," such pattern recognition involves

> paying selective attention to the total input of stimuli that perpetually swarm in upon our consciousness. Only by leaving things out, that is, relegating them to the status of background noise deserving only to be disregarded, can what matters most in a given situation become recognizable. Pattern recognition is . . . what historians have always done, whether they knew it or not. Only some facts matter for any given pattern to emerge. Otherwise, useless clutter will obscure what we are after: perceptible relationships among important facts. That and that alone constitutes an intelligible pattern, giving meaning to the world.[3]

This book is an attempt to give meaning to the global history created by a small community of Armenian merchants from Iran by sorting through and analyzing documents they left behind and looking for intelligible patterns and "perceptible relationships among facts." What has interested me most is to recognize patterns that might shed important light on how merchants of this community structured their social lives, how their trading habits and practices sustaining a global network of settlements scattered halfway around the world also shaped and structured their community life and most of all dictated how they related to each other and to noncommunity members in commercial matters requiring "trust" relations and business cooperation. In my quest to discern recognizable shapes and patterns in documents stored in thirty-one archives around the world, I may have selectively focused on some facts and valorized some documents over others I neglected to examine or implicitly regarded as "background noise" or "useless clutter"; I recognize that others might consider them valuable in the service of a differently focused pursuit. Some of the patterns I have discerned in this book, no doubt, are provisional in nature and will be qualified and improved upon by further research and study. Until then, I adhere to the caveat of another great historian, Niels Steensgaard: "I can only hope that I have substantiated my conclusions or, if I have erred, that my errors may prove useful."[4]

In general, I have utilized the Armenian script in the notes to transcribe longer passages from archival documents. Shorter passages in the body of the text as well as titles of works originally written in Armenian have been transliterated using the scheme of the *Journal of the Society of Armenian Studies (JSAS)*. Based on the system developed by the Library of Congress, the *JSAS* transliteration scheme relies on the pronunciation of Classical Armenian and Standard Eastern Armenian.

|  |  |
|---|---|
| Ա ա | A a |
| Բ բ | B b |
| Գ գ | G g |
| Դ դ | D d |
| Ե ե | E e |
| Զ զ | Z z |
| Է է | Ē ē |
| Ը ը | Ĕ ĕ |
| Թ թ | Tʻ tʻ |
| Ժ ժ | Zh zh |
| Ի ի | I i |
| Լ լ | L l |
| Խ խ | Kh kh |
| Ծ ծ | Ts ts |
| Կ կ | K k |
| Հ հ | H h |
| Ձ ձ | Dz dz |

| Ղ ղ | Gh gh |
| Ճ ճ | Ch ch |
| Մ մ | M m |
| Յ յ | Y y |
| Ն ն | N n |
| Շ շ | Sh sh |
| Ո ո | O o |
| Չ չ | Ch' ch' |
| Պ պ | P p |
| Ջ ջ | J j |
| Ռ ռ | Ṙ ṙ |
| Ս ս | S s |
| Վ վ | V v |
| Տ տ | T t |
| Ր ր | R r |
| Ց ց | Ts' ts' |
| Ւ ւ | W w |
| Փ փ | P' p' |
| Ք ք | K' k' |
| Եւ եւ | Ew ew |
| Օ օ | Ō ō |
| Ֆ ֆ | F f |

For the most part, Armenian proper names have been transliterated according to the above scheme except in cases where common usage differs (e.g., Sebouh Aslanian as opposed to Sepuh Aslanean or Gilanentz as opposed to Gilanents'). Reformed Eastern Armenian orthography has been transliterated in accordance with the same scheme (e.g., Patmut'yun as opposed to Patmut'iwn for works published in Soviet and post-Soviet Armenia). All the Julfa dialect passages transcribed in this book have been reproduced in their original orthographic state; in the interest of making the passages more easily readable, I have placed brackets around vowels and consonants that were condensed or suppressed in the original. Readers interested in the peculiar grammar of the Julfa dialect or in a glossary of most commonly used expressions or terms may consult the appendix in Aslanian 2007b.

# From Trade Diasporas
# to Circulation Societies

During the Safavid-Ottoman wars of 1603–1605, the Safavid monarch Shah ʿAbbas I (r. 1587–1629) practiced "scorched earth" tactics, laying waste to the frontier regions of his empire, deporting up to 300,000 Armenians and others from the frontier territories, and resettling them in the interior of his realm.[1] While many of the deportees suffered from their brutal displacement and perished during their deportation to Iran, the population from the small mercantile town of Old Julfa on the banks of the Aras River was given relatively privileged treatment by the Safavid ruler. After their town was razed to the ground in the autumn of 1604, the Julfans were driven to the Iranian capital of Isfahan, where ʿAbbas I granted them land across the Zayandarud River and permitted them to build their own suburb, named New Julfa, in memory of their abandoned home. Though ʿAbbas I does not seem to have had a "conscious policy" or blueprint for resettling the population of Old Julfa, he was clearly aware of the mercantile reputation of the town's merchants.

Soon after resettling the Julfans in an exclusive suburb of his capital, ʿAbbas I granted them a number of privileges, including broad administrative and religious autonomy that went well beyond the rights usually associated with *dhimmi* communities residing under Muslim-ruled polities. As rootless aliens in a land where they were strangers, the Julfan Armenians were ideal "servants of power" for the centralizing Safavid monarch.[2] That they were "stateless" and owed their safety and prosperity to ʿAbbas I meant that the shah could trust them without significant fear of threat to his power in ways that he could not do with his other subjects. Because they were "service nomads" with special skills to offer,[3] the Julfans were also ideal for the shah's policies of state centralization, which hinged on reformist measures aimed at promoting Iran's international silk trade. The Julfans had extensive experience as purveyors of Iranian silk to European merchants dating back several decades before their deportation. They were also known for their international connections and network of contacts in markets as far away as Aleppo, Venice, and possibly Mughal India. Moreover, they were well versed in numerous languages and were a Christian minority, traits that increased their mobility and contributed to their commercial success. Their Christian status was particularly advantageous because it meant that they were often perceived as "neutrals" in the largely "Sunni versus Shi'a"–colored Ottoman-Safavid rivalry during the sixteenth and seventeenth centuries. As such, the Julfans were able to travel across Ottoman territory to the Mediterranean markets in times of conflict while transit rights were generally denied to Shi'a merchants. All these attributes, coupled with the Julfans' status as rootless outsiders with no prior relations with potentially fractious elements in Iranian society, allowed Safavid monarchs, and especially 'Abbas I, to lavish on them a number of privileges, in exchange for using their skills in much the same manner as the Habsburg emperors relied on the services of their "court Jews."[4]

After winning a public auction in 1619 for the right to export Iranian silk, the Julfans became the principal exporters of Iranian silk, and they held on to their privileged position even after the silk industry was deregulated under 'Abbas I's successor Shah Safi (r. 1629–1642). As a result of its lucrative hold on Iran's silk exports to Europe, the small suburb of New Julfa grew throughout the seventeenth century to become one of the most important mercantile centers in Eurasia. Its Armenian merchants experienced unparalleled economic prosperity as purveyors of Iranian raw silk, then one of the most important commodities in world trade; during the late seventeenth and early eighteenth centuries, New Julfa's Armenian merchants diversified their portfolios and traded in Indian textiles as well as gems. Within decades of their deportation and exile from Old Julfa, the Julfan Armenians were able to build one of the greatest trade networks of the early modern period. This network, consisting of a cluster of trade settlements, grew as four interconnected, and to some extent overlapping, circuits around what I refer to as the "nodal center" of the New Julfan suburb. The most important of these circuits was established in the Indian Ocean, extending out from Julfa by way of the nearby ports on the Persian Gulf (Basra, Bandar Kung, and Bandar 'Abbas) and reaching out to Mughal India, then Southeast Asia, and, by the turn of the seventeenth century, to Canton and all the way to Manila and Acapulco in the New World. This Indian Ocean circuit of settlements was the first region to be extensively settled by Julfan merchants and served as the hub of Julfan trade activity. A second circuit of settlements was in the Mediterranean zone, encompassing mostly port settlements on the Mediterranean littoral, such as Aleppo (ideally situated near the port of Iskenderun/Alexandretta), Izmir, Venice, Livorno, Marseilles, and Cadiz on the Atlantic. These settlements were important because they provided access to the northern European markets in Amsterdam and London, where raw Iranian silk was a much sought-after commodity and where silver currency was readily available. In the course of the seventeenth century, the Julfans established trade settlements in a third circuit overlapping parts of northwestern Europe and including settlements in Amsterdam and London. A fourth circuit was located north of Julfa, on the Eurasian landmass crossing the Russian Empire and leading to the ports on the Baltic and White seas. Settlements in Astrakhan, Moscow, St. Petersburg, Archangel, and the Baltic region served as relay stations connecting the Russian circuit to that in northwestern Europe, and especially to the markets of Amsterdam and London via the Baltic region.

The Julfan merchants are of interest to scholars of international trade and to world historians for at least two reasons. First, they were arguably the only Eurasian community of merchants to operate simultaneously and successfully across all the major empires of the early modern period, including the three "gunpowder empires" of Islamicate Eurasia (Mughal, Ottoman, and Safavid), Muscovite Russia, Qing China, and all the major European seaborne empires (the Portuguese, Spanish, British, Dutch, and French).[5] The Julfan mercantile network, as we shall see, expanded and flourished in a proto-globalized space in early modern Eurasia during the seventeenth and eighteenth centuries that interconnected the regional world-economies of Islamic Eurasia to their counterparts in the Christian Mediterranean and northwestern Europe. The conjuncture of several early modern global processes and developments helped create the interconnected world of Eurasia that facilitated Julfan expansion.[6] Of these, the most important was arguably the development of four large centralized and stable Eurasian states or empires (Safavid Iran, Mughal India, Ottoman Empire, and Muscovite Russia) that promoted long-distance trade by establishing an infrastructure of transportation and patronizing mercantile communities. H. R. Roemer's remarks on the role of the most important Safavid ruler, Shah 'Abbas I, help contextualize the subsequent rise of the Julfa merchants and their global networks:

> At the end of the 10th/16th and the beginning of the 12/17th century, Shah 'Abbas had mastered the crises which had shaken his country at the time of his accession. . . . After security had been restored in the country 'Abbas turned his attention to establishing an effective administration. In the development of transport routes, which he pursued with energy, particularly noteworthy is the network of caravansarais he created. . . . These and other measures invigorated trade and industry.[7]

The same can be said of Akbar in restructuring the infrastructure of the Mughal Empire during the second half of the sixteenth century, and of contemporaneous rulers in the Ottoman and Muscovite empires. All four empires, pivotal to Julfan success, were successors of the Mongol-Timurid empires that stretched across Eurasia in the fourteenth and fifteenth centuries, and in each case the centralization and expansion of each empire/state during the early modern period helped promote Julfan expansion and commercial prosperity.[8] The simultaneous growth of European maritime networks, beginning with the Portuguese expansion into the Indian Ocean and followed by English, Dutch, and French expansion into the same space, where the Julfans were already operating for the most part, also helped integrate the early modern Indian Ocean with the Mediterranean and other parts of Europe. In doing so it also facilitated the further expansion of the Julfan network. The Julfans can thus be seen as an emblematic early modern mercantile community and trade network that both contributed to and benefited from the forces of what Chris Bayly has called "archaic" and "proto"-globalization,[9] integrating and connecting the diverse parts of the early modern world stretching from the Mediterranean to the far recesses of eastern Eurasia.

As a community with a global network, the Julfans were also important "go-betweens," or cross-cultural brokers adept at "articulat[ing] relationships between disparate worlds or cultures by being able to translate between them."[10] As we shall see in chapter 4, the role of their Eurasian network as a conduit for technology transfers from the East to the West and vice versa is illustrated by the transmission of South Asian calico printing techniques to Marseilles and other European cities in the seventeenth century, as well as by the transfer of printing technology and European artistic motifs and "visual culture" first to Safavid Iran, followed by Muscovite Russia, also during the seventeenth century.[11] In South Asia, the "Armenians [read: Julfans] were to play a central role in diplomatic and financial negotiations with the Mughal and Safavid authorities on behalf of the British and thus counted as indispensable go-betweens for their continued existence in the region until the middle of the 18th century."[12] For instance, in 1698 the Julfan merchant-diplomat Khwaja Israel di Sarhat acted as a "go-between" for the English East India Company by helping the company attain *taluqdari* (rent farming) rights over a region that later developed into modern Calcutta, in addition to the famous Mughal *farman* (royal edict) of 1715 giving the English trading privileges and the right to build fortifications around their settlement.[13] Another merchant-diplomat, Martin di Marcara Avachintz, served as a regional director for the newly established French Compagnie des Indes in the 1660s and secured a *farman* through his contacts with the ruler of Golconda granting the French company the right to establish a settlement in the South Indian coastal city of Masulipatam.[14]

The second reason a study of Julfan history should be of interest to global historians and economic historians of Eurasia and the Indian Ocean in particular is that of all the Asian communities of merchants operating across the Indian Ocean, the Julfans are possibly the only Asian community to have left a trail of documentation, stretching east from London to Isfahan, written by themselves and in their own obscure and now extinct dialect.[15] Not only are these sources important for scholars studying other Asian mercantile communities (where local sources are, for the most part, lacking), but they can also be a healthy corrective to decades of scholarship on Indian Ocean history, much of which has been centered almost exclusively on documents produced by the bureaucracies of various European East India Companies, thus giving the Eurocentric impression that the "driving force of the Indian Ocean has been the crusading Europeans."[16]As Denys Lombard put it in the introduction to an important collection of essays on Asian merchants in the Indian Ocean world,

> The immense body of Western sources, which are both precise and lend themselves to quantitative treatment, as also the colonial perspective, itself well-established from the end of the nineteenth century, have created a situation in which all exchanges are seen through the prism of a periodization whose pulse is to be found in Lisbon, London, or Amsterdam.[17]

Holden Furber, another eminent scholar of the Indian Ocean, expressed similar concerns about the difficulty of escaping from a "Europe-centeredness" in historians' accounts of the Indian Ocean, given the fact that

> the bulk of the Asian sources for the maritime and commercial history of the Indian and China seas has in large part perished, a victim of tropical climate and paucity of family and business archives. . . . Paradoxically the European records of maritime, commercial, and political contact with the East are bulk, but anyone who delves among them even cursorily will at once become aware that they represent, as concerns Asian life, only the tip of an iceberg, a tip seen almost wholly through European eyes.[18]

Use of Julfan sources thus can provide unprecedented insight into the inner workings of an important Eurasian mercantile community and in doing so help reorient our focus on the dynamics of Eurasian trade away from the citadels of Lisbon, London, and Amsterdam to local Asian actors in the Indian Ocean.

This book examines the emergence and growth of the global trade network of Armenian merchants from New Julfa from the founding of the suburb in 1605 to roughly 1747, when the suburb was looted and largely destroyed by the post-Safavid ruler Nadir Shah Afshar (r. 1736–1747). Unlike other works on the Julfa merchants, the primary focus of this book is not the communal history of New Julfa,[19] the international trade of Iranian silk or the trade of Indian textiles or gems and their modes of operation,[20] nor is its aim to analyze Julfan merchants' relationships with Armenian merchants from other communities or with "state power" represented by either the Safavid state or the European trading companies.[21] These issues are touched upon in the first part of the book and periodically crop up in other places where they help to illuminate matters connected to the sociological aspects of Julfan society and economy, such as the impact of long-distance trade on the organization of community life, to which I give privileged treatment. In tracing Julfan settlements and trade in the Indian Ocean, the Mediterranean, and northwestern Europe and Russia, my aim is not to focus on the types of commodities the merchants traded but to explore the ways in which they were able to travel across these settlements and create a hybrid and syncretic identity that I call transimperial cosmopolitanism. Relying on economic sociology, this book also explores the creation of networks of trust between long-distance merchants. Through the rigorous use of thousands of pieces of mercantile correspondence, most of which are consulted here for the first time, this book seeks to recreate the ethos of trust and cooperation between merchants of the same community. From the perspective of economic history, the book also explores particular types of economic institutions, such as the *commenda* contract and the family firm, and their uses in the context of the Islamicate world of Eurasia.

Another aim of this book is to demonstrate the importance of information networks and communication in the workings of early modern long-distance merchant communities. Through the study of the art of Julfan business correspondence across early modern Eurasia and the Mediterranean, I argue that information sharing was important not only for merchants in their daily commercial affairs, but also for maintaining the social and cultural integrity of merchant networks as a whole. In the context of the Julfan mercantile community, letter writing connected far away *commenda* agents to their masters in New Julfa and also unified the trade settlements on the periphery to the nodal center of the entire network in New Julfa. Finally, the book examines the Julfan network in a comparative context with two other early modern long-distance trading networks, the Multani and the Sephardic. By placing the Julfan network in a comparative context, the book probes the Julfan network for possible structural flaws and argues that one such flaw was the high premium the Julfans placed on trust in their network, which compelled them to hire *commenda* agents almost exclusively from within their coalition, limiting their ability to expand and diversify into new markets.

Many scholars of early modern merchant communities specializing in long-distance trade have studied merchant communities using the theoretical literature of "trade diasporas," broadly defined as nations of "socially interdependent but spatially dispersed communities."[22] Invented in the 1960s and 1970s, the trade diaspora paradigm has been widely used by scholars of early modern trade and indiscriminately applied to such communities as Sephardic Jews, the Chinese, Parsies, Lebanese in West Africa, officials of the powerful European East India Companies in the Indian Ocean, and especially the Julfan Armenians. The use of this paradigm has gained momentum in recent decades and infiltrated work in the discipline of world history, where scholarship on trade diasporas has come to be seen as an ideal counterpart to the narrowly parochial concerns of national(ist) historiography. Despite its popular appeal, however, the trade diaspora school of scholarship has yet to formulate an analytically thorough definition of the concept. Much of the work in this field suffers from an absence of theoretical and analytical rigor when it comes to the use of the label as a central category of analysis. My book breaks from this tradition of scholarship and argues that the ubiquitous category of "trade diaspora" is at best a *descriptive* label rather than an *analytical* category. Given the widespread and uncritical use of the label, it is important to revisit the trade diaspora paradigm and take stock of its principal weaknesses before proposing an alternative paradigm that may be more useful for the study of certain types of long-distance merchant communities, such as the Julfan community.

## THE CONCEPT OF "TRADE DIASPORA": CRITIQUE OF A PARADIGM

One of the first attested uses of the term *diaspora* in connection with trade or commerce occurs in Fernand Braudel's classic work, *The Mediterranean and the Mediterranean World in the Age of Philip II,* first published in 1949. In a part of this work discussing civilizations, the French historian devotes a whole section to the Jews and famously refers to them as a "civilization of the diaspora type." Further describing the Jewish experience, he writes:

> The matter of this civilization was dispersed, scattered, like tiny drops of oil, over the deep waters of other civilizations, never truly blending with them yet always dependent on them. So its movements were always the movements of others, and consequently exceptionally sensitive 'indicators.' Emile-Felix Gautier, trying to find an equivalent of the Jewish diaspora, proposed as a very humble example, the history of the Mozabaites of North Africa, who were also dispersed in very small colonies. Another possible parallel is the case of the Armenians, mountain peasants who at about the time of the Renaissance in Europe were becoming international merchants from the Philippines to Amsterdam; or there are the Parsees in India or the Nestorian Christians of Asia. It is essential then to accept that there are civilizations of the diaspora type, scattering their countless islands in foreign waters, and they are more numerous than one might imagine at first sight.[23]

Braudel's discussion here is particularly noteworthy because of its urge to provide a comparative framework for future work on such "dispersed and scattered" merchant communities. Even the choice of Jews, North Africans, Armenians, and Parsees— all prominent candidates for more recent work that has aspired to create a model for comparative history—is prescient. Braudel's invitation to study these groups from a comparative perspective went unheeded for several decades. Scholars working on communities that would otherwise seem to fall into Braudel's general category chose to study them using different paradigms, such as that of "middlemen minorities."[24] In 1968, Abner Cohen, an economic anthropologist specializing in North African trade, became the first scholar to coin the term "trade diaspora." In a programmatic essay on the West African Hausa merchant communities, Cohen explicitly formulated his new category in opposition to the notion of "network,"[25] defining "trade diaspora" as a distinct . . . type of social grouping in its culture and structure. Its members are culturally distinct from both their society of origin and from the societies among which they live. Its organization combines stability of structure but allows a high degree of mobility of personnel. It has an informal political organization of its own which takes care of stability of structure but allows for a high degree of mobility of personnel. It has an informal political organization of its own which takes care of stability of order within one community, and the co-ordination of the activities of its various member communities in their perpetual struggle against external pressure. It tends to be autonomous in its judicial organization. Its members form a moral community which constrains the behavior of the individual and ensures a large measure of conformity with common values and principles. It also has its own institutions of general welfare and social security. In short a diaspora is a nation of socially interdependent, but spatially dispersed, communities.[26]

A decade later, Cohen's new label was picked up and popularized by Philip Curtin, another historian specializing in African trade. In Curtin's landmark study, *Cross-Cultural Trade in World History*, "trade diaspora" became a capacious category that embraced a variety of merchant communities, from the "stateless" Armenians and Jews to the empire-building European East India Companies whose members shared the hallmark of being dispersed across vast spaces, yet being "socially interdependent" through complex networks. Unlike Cohen's relatively nuanced treatment of the concept, which devoted sufficient attention to raising though not necessarily resolving important questions about such matters as the role of communication and "trust relations" among members of a trade diaspora, Curtin's reworking of it is largely lacking such concerns. To accommodate a broad sweep of world history beginning with the Phoenicians and ending with the European seaborne empires and the onset of the Industrial Revolution in the nineteenth century, Curtin felt it necessary to embed his newly adopted term within the theory of "trade settlements" adumbrated by work of economic and social theorist Karl Polanyi. In this connection, Curtin described the emergence of trade diasporas as follows:

Commercial specialists would remove themselves physically from the home community and go to live as aliens in another town, usually not a fringe town, but a town important in the life of the host community. There, the stranger merchants could settle down and learn the language, the customs and the commercial ways of their hosts. They could then serve as cross-cultural brokers helping and encouraging trade between the host society and people of their own origin who moved along the trade routes. At this stage, a distinction appeared between the merchants who moved and settled and those who continued to move back and forth. What might have begun as a single settlement soon became more complex. The merchants who might have begun with a single settlement abroad tended to set up a whole series of trade settlements in alien towns. The result was an interrelated net of commercial communities, forming a trade network, or trade diaspora—a term that comes from the Greek word for scattering, as in the sowing of grain.[27]

Curtin's theoretical intervention was very timely; it came at a conjuncture in modern history when the auxiliary and even more capacious category of "Diaspora" was entering a period of wide acceptance and circulation.[28] The timing for Curtin's intervention also coincided with the increasing interest in world history and the concern among historians to move away from the rigid and artificial boundaries imposed by the near-hegemonic grip of "nation-statist historiography" on the historical imagination during the nineteenth and twentieth centuries as well as on their discipline. In this scheme, the trade diaspora paradigm, enthusiastically endorsed by Curtin and his students, naturally appeared as an auxiliary field for the rapidly rising subdiscipline of world history. The concept's popularity can be seen in its use by an increasing number of historians working on merchant communities, as well as by some anthropologists and cultural theorists, who use the concept often without the need to qualify it or critically engage with its theoretical underpinnings.[29]

Robin Cohen, a sociologist of migration, picked up the term in his book *Global Diasporas,* where he employed Curtin's formulation alongside other typologies of his own making, such as "victim diasporas" and "cultural diasporas."[30] While Cohen's discussion introduced some helpful distinctions to the emergent field of "diaspora studies" and is welcome as an attempt to theorize critically and refine the trade diaspora concept, it fell short of a wholesale critique of the category, which was now supplemented by a variety of diaspora typologies, some of which are hardly distinguishable from Curtin's original usage.

Several assumptions underlie Curtin's use of the trade diaspora category. A critical assessment of Curtin will enable us to assess the general use of the term and to reconsider what role, if any, the category of trade diaspora should play in our examination of the Julfan Armenian merchant community in the seventeenth and eighteenth centuries.

A trade diaspora for Curtin is characterized by the following traits or hallmarks:

1. It begins to take shape when "commercial specialists . . . remove themselves physically from the home community and go to live as aliens in another town, usually not a fringe town, but a town important in the life of the host community."[31] Once they settle and begin to learn the cultural ways of their host community and encourage trade between their hosts and merchants belonging to their home community, a whole range of similar settlements begins to appear, thus creating a network of settlements, which Curtin labels a "trade diaspora."
2. It consists of "a nation of socially interdependent, but *spatially* dispersed communities."[32] Here the key trait is spatial dispersion, since *all* communities of merchants as such are to some degree "socially interdependent."
3. It is, or strictly speaking should be, a "stateless" community, as the sobriquet "diaspora" implies, though many of the examples used by Curtin ("Banians," Chinese, European East India Companies, etc.) fail to meet this criterion.

4.  It is "culturally distinct" from its host society as well as its society of origin. The idea of cultural distinction, as problematic as it is, is central to Curtin's definition because it allows him to treat trade diasporas as "cultural brokers" in world trade. Trade diasporas are "swept away" from the historical stage at the onset of the Industrial Revolution, which does away with their function of cultural brokerage.

5.  Members of a trade diaspora come into existence to fill a niche in the economies of their host societies. Their presence is determined by a kind of (ethnic) division of labor. This is so because according to Curtin trade diasporas monopolize or specialize in a particular commodity or fill a space in a particular sector of the economy left vacant by the host society.

6.  Finally and most importantly, a trade diaspora is a politically *neutral* and marginalized social formation. Curtin treats its members as *apolitical* actors in the host society's economy and polity. They do not, as a rule, mix politics with business but rather remain on the political margins. As Sanjay Subrahmanyam has pointed out, this detail is pivotal for Curtin's definition.[33]

As we shall see, each of these postulates is problematic in its own way, not only for the Armenian case, which occupies a central place in Curtin's overall framework, but also for the broader comparative framework that lies behind his general project. Therefore, as K. N. Chaudhuri counseled many years ago, "some caution is needed in using the term 'trading diasporas' as an analytical tool."[34] What are some of the flaws in Curtin's category?

As for the first postulate, regarding the "origins" of trade diasporas, the notion that trade diaspora settlements begin with commercial specialists "moving and re-settling" in a foreign community does not correspond to the historical experience of many of the communities discussed by Curtin. This is particularly the case with the Armenians, whose "diasporic" migrations were not characterized by commercial motives alone. Here we are well advised to resuscitate the once fashionable "push-pull" theory used by migration theorists.[35] In most cases such as the Armenian one, merchants moved away from their home because they were "pushed" out, for instance, by being uprooted and forcibly transplanted elsewhere, as was the case with Julfa merchants at the turn of the seventeenth century, when they established a new home near the Safavid capital of Isfahan. In other cases, they moved because they were "pushed" by unfavorable economic or political conditions at "home," or conversely because they were "pulled" by more favorable conditions abroad. This was the case with the Julfan migration out of Julfa in the middle of the eighteenth century, when political chaos and attendant economic collapse in Nadir Shah's Iran pushed them to relocate their base to India, Russia, or the Mediterranean, depending on what they perceived to be the alluring "pulls" of each of these prospective homes. In this connection, Robin Cohen's more recent attempt to distinguish between "victim" and "trade" diasporas is somewhat helpful in terms of pointing out their fundamental difference as far as the origins of these distinct typologies of "diaspora" are concerned. The problem with Cohen, however, is that he uncritically embraces Curtin's trade diaspora concept, leaving it practically untouched.[36]

The postulate concerning dispersion as the hallmark of the trade diaspora condition is also problematic, because all communities of merchants in the early modern period were by definition dispersed. After all, one has to be dispersed in space to conduct commerce; so making dispersion a defining feature of trade diasporas invalidates it "by epistemological reason alone."[37] Moreover, using dispersion as a marker for trade diaspora status runs the danger of lumping together merchant communities that had little in common except the universal attribute of being dispersed. Thus in his attempt at writing a global and comparative history, Curtin groups together under the rubric "trade diaspora" such diverse communities as the members of the powerful East India Companies, the stateless Armenians, and others, such as the "Banians" in East Africa and Chinese merchants in Southeast Asia.

As we have seen, Curtin does not make "statelessness" part of his core definition of "trade diaspora" because doing so would severely restrict the comparative dimension of his work. It should be noted here that the Greek term *diaspora* (derived from the Greek verb *sperein:* to scatter, as in the sowing of seeds)[38] has embedded in it two essential attributes: (a) that of a community that is uprooted from its "homeland" and thereby bereft of a state of its own (as is the case with the two "classic diasporas," namely, the Jews and the Armenians); and (b) that of being physically dispersed or scattered into far-flung colonies (the trait of the other classic diaspora, i.e., the Greeks). The two attributes are not mutually exclusive, but until the late twentieth century, the term *diaspora* carried with it the connotation of statelessness. In his definition, Curtin chooses to focus on the attribute of dispersion and fails to address diaspora's other hallmark, namely, statelessness. This is evident from the field of candidates marshaled in his book as case studies of trade diasporas. Of such communities covered in *Cross-cultural Trade in World History,* only the Armenians are cited as an example of stateless merchants; one cannot aspire to write comparative history if one's field of examples consists of one seemingly unique case.

Postulates 4, 5, and 6 are also untenable for theoretical as well as empirical reasons. The idea that trade diasporas were culturally distinct from their host communities is only partially true and moreover accepts the notion of "culture" as a phenomenon hermetically sealed by "cultural" boundaries—a notion that is no longer acceptable in much of current anthropological literature on the subject.[39] Furthermore, Curtin's implicit assumption that as culturally distinct groups, trade diasporas acted as cross-cultural brokers and were *apolitical* participants in their host countries' societies is empirically unsubstantiated. For many merchant communities in Asia in the seventeenth to nineteenth centuries trade and politics often mixed, as Subrahmanyam's studies have pointed out. This was not only the case for the Iranian merchant community dispersed across Mughal India in the sixteenth to eighteenth centuries, but, for Julfan Armenian merchants in Iran, India, Burma, and elsewhere in the Indian Ocean during the same period. In short, the assumption that trade diasporas are by definition uninterested in politics prevents us from examining the important role of what Subrahmanyam and Bayly have called "portfolio capitalists."[40]

Apart from these flaws, the concept of "trade diaspora" as formulated by Curtin and his students and applied to the Armenian and other cases has been a *descriptive* as opposed to an *analytical* category. It has been useful in terms of helping us paint a broad picture of the Armenian and other merchant communities of the early modern period, but weak in terms of helping us understand *analytically* how this and other merchant communities actually operated. How did merchants belonging to these dispersed communities communicate with one another? What kind of institutional mechanisms did members of such merchant communities rely upon to generate networks of trust and solidarity across the great spaces covered by their communities? This question is particularly relevant in the context of the absence of formal institutions such as courts and other trust-generating institutions without which it would be difficult to imagine the smooth conduct of any economic activity. If these merchants were "stateless," as the concept of trade diaspora implies, then what (if any) forms of "stateless power" peculiar to their social formation did they foster in order to compete and often succeed against rival networks of trade?[41] Again, this is an important question that needs to be addressed in the context of the recent literature on Indian Ocean maritime historiography, which has been trying to reassess the relationship between Asian merchants and the European trade companies that appeared in the world of the Indian Ocean with the backing of powerful national states with increasingly territorial ambitions. Finally, did merchants belonging to "trade diasporas" coordinate their business decisions (in terms of making sound market investments and so on) with other merchants belonging to their network, or did they operate merely as "peddlers," devoid of economic rationality and collective action, the hallmarks (according to Niels Steensgaard) of European merchants?[42] If the trading habits of such merchants demonstrate the presence of a sophisticated transimperial network of coordination and cooperation, then how was this made possible? The current model of "trade diaspora" does not help us answer any of these questions. A recent attempt at reviving the concept of trade diaspora by merely renaming it "diaspora entrepreneurial networks" does not bring us any closer to conceptual clarity or analytical rigor.[43]

As we have seen, the trade diaspora paradigm was invented by Abner Cohen in the late 1960s in conscious opposition to the concept of network. Instead of contributing to greater analytical clarity, the abandonment of the notion of network has contributed to a significant weakening of the new paradigm, thus prompting us to revisit the idea of trade network, which seems to have been too hastily discarded.

## THE CONCEPT OF "TRADE NETWORK"
## AND THE LOGIC OF CIRCULATION SOCIETIES

The central analytical framework of this book is to reconceptualize "trade diasporas" of the early modern period as "circulation societies" with their peculiar networks. As we shall see, the notion of "circulation society" and its corollary "circulatory regimes" that I shall outline below provide us with a better analytical framework to conceptualize the workings of what have traditionally been termed trade diaspora networks.

I have borrowed the notion of "circulation" from the influential work of Claude Markovits, who applies it to the study of a North Indian trade network in the eighteenth and nineteenth centuries.[44] According to Markovits, a trade network is a circuit that consists of what I shall call a "nodal center" and a cluster of dispersed nodes around it, connected both to each other and to the center. These nodes are settlements where merchants from the nodal center reside either ephemerally or for longer stretches of time. Where a significant number of such merchants exist, they erect ethno-religious institutions such as churches, synagogues, mosques, or temples, as well as institutions that serve to transmit their identity (schools, printing presses, cultural societies, etc.). These nodes or settlements are connected to each other and to the center through what Markovits calls the "circulation of men and things."[45] Markovits argues that there are at least five things that circulate along such circuits or networks: merchants, credit, goods, information (about market conditions, "the secrets of the trade," and so on), and women. An important element of circulation missing in Markovits's account and one that is the strong suit of the trade diaspora paradigm has to do with culture and identity. To compensate for this absence, I include the circulation of priests in my account of the Julfan network. Of the six things circulating in a given network, only women, information, and priests tend to circulate exclusively *within* the network. The others tend to circulate both within a given network and in other coexisting networks. The reasons for this are easy to understand: merchants, commodities, and credit, for instance, *need* to circulate and mingle with coexisting networks (even rival ones) due to the exigencies of commercial life and its rules. Otherwise, as Markovits explains, there would be no exchange. Priests, women, and especially information, on the other hand, are crucial to the maintenance of the identity/integrity of the network and are thus jealously guarded possessions.

What is interesting to note about this model of circulation is that the objects that travel through the circuit have their origin at the nodal center of the network. The center is thus not only "where capital is raised and where capitalists have their main place of residence,"[46] it is also the source of the merchants, commodities, priests, and the information that keeps the merchants apprised of the latest market conditions and of news concerning their community residing in the center. Women also originate from the center. In this connection, it was not unusual for eighteenth-century Julfan merchants to travel "home" to New Julfa often from India and Russia and even possibly from the Philippines with the intention of marrying a bride from their home community.

One of the aims of this book is to examine the trade networks of Armenian merchants from New Julfa, using the model of circulation sketched above.[47]Soon after its founding in 1605, the Armenian suburb of New Julfa, as we shall see, became a "nodal center" of a far-flung network of commercial settlements stretching from London and Amsterdam in the West to China and Manila in the East. Though not all Armenian merchants trading and residing in these dispersed trade settlements were from New Julfa, the overwhelming majority had important family and business ties to this prosperous Armenian colony in the suburbs of Isfahan and regarded it as their "home." New Julfa was thus the principal center of this trade network; it supplied the network with circulating merchants (most of whom were *commenda* agents working for their masters or *khwajas* residing at home in Julfa) and with vital information in the form of commercial correspondence, as well as with a sophisticated system of transmitting commercial knowledge (knowledge of accounting, manuals with trading itineraries, prices of commodities in various markets, etc.). It also supplied a prized commodity (i.e., Iranian raw silk especially for the Western markets) and, most importantly, capital/credit. As a leading Armenian religious center with its own diocese, New Julfa also provided the network with a retinue of circulating clerics who helped maintain the identity of the communities dispersed along the network. I refer to the community of Julfans, whether at home in Julfa or across their settlements in the Indian Ocean or Mediterranean, as a "circulation society" ruled by what Markovits calls the "logic of circulatory regimes."[48]

Long-distance mercantile networks such as the Julfan one tend to maintain their cultural and mercantile integrity for long periods, thanks in large measure to the circulatory flows emanating from their nodal centers. However, while circulation and mobility are important for sustaining networks over time, we should be careful about privileging mobility and movement over permanence and immobility. Long-distance trade networks, to quote Khachig Tölölyan writing about contemporary diasporas, "require not just migratory mobility but also a quite different form of life, the sedentary."[49] In other words, long-distance trade networks and their nodes, much like electrical circuits, also need "anchor points," not only to "fasten" them in place and endow them with permanence and stability but also to steer or route, facilitate, and channel circulatory flows of men (mostly *commenda* agents in our case), information, and capital emanating from their nodal centers, and to redirect their own flows back to their nodal centers in a reciprocal relationship to their centers. In order to function effectively, trade networks need sedentary overseas nodes or settlements to act as "routing stations."[50] As we will see in our account of the Julfan network of settlements below, not all the merchants circulating across the network from their center in Julfa were constantly on the move. Some people, including *commenda* agents, actually settled down and became "sedentary" in the nodes and resided there for varying periods of time. They were crucial sources of support for more peripatetic members of the network who happened to be passing through on their way elsewhere; they also contributed to circulating local knowledge back to the center and to other nodes through letter writing and played a crucial role in procuring local commodities from their respective regions. There were also physical buildings such as churches and printing presses that were "fixed" in some of Julfa's overseas nodes. These anchor points were important in shaping the mobility and circulation that linked these nodes to the center, which was also fixed and sedentary.

While most long-distance merchant communities have trade networks whose workings can be characterized through the "dynamic" model of circulation that is absent in the trade diaspora paradigm of merchant communities, not all follow the same "circulatory regime." At the risk of simplification, we can assert that there are at least two types of circulation societies. The first belongs to the type outlined above and consists of a "multinodal" but monocentric network where the overwhelming majority of the objects circulating through the network have their origins in one dominant "nodal center," which defines and regulates the identity and economic vitality of the network as a whole. The Julfan trade network examined in this book can be seen as a paradigmatic case of such a trade network; the Shikarpuri and Hyderabadi merchants of Sind in India examined by Markovits's book, as well as the Multani network discussed by Scott Levi and Stephen Dale and briefly analyzed in chapter 9 of this book, also fall into this typology. Similarly, an argument can be made that the Hadrami network expertly studied by Engseng Ho can also be classified as a multinodal and monocentric network driven and shaped by a strong nodal center in the town of Tarim in the Hadramaut in present-day Yemen.[51]

In contrast, the impressive Sephardic Jewish network of the early modern period studied by Francesca Trivellato and Jonathan Israel can be characterized as a synchronically "polycentric network." Unlike the Julfan Armenians, the Sephardic Jews did not have one nodal center that dominated most aspects of their lives as merchants and members of the same community. After their displacement from the Iberian Peninsula in the late fifteenth century, the Sephardic Jews operated from numerous centers, including Livorno, Amsterdam, London, Venice, Salonika, and Istanbul. One of the advantages of such a synchronically polycentric network was its agility and survival power. Not being dependent on one nodal center meant that the merchant community in question could recover and reorganize its trading activities in the event of an economic or political shock afflicting one of its centers of operation. In the case of the Julfan network, the destruction of New Julfa as a nodal center in 1747 led to the eventual collapse of the entire trade network.

## ORGANIZATION OF THIS WORK

This book is divided into two distinct but complementary parts. The first part (chapters 2–4) is descriptive in nature and provides a broad overview of the origins of the New Julfan community and the subsequent expansion of its trade network; the second part (chapters 5–9) is more analytical and discusses the social and economic institutions underpinning Julfan economy and society.

Chapter 2 provides an overview of the origins of the Julfan merchant community and the establishment of its nodal center in the suburb of the Safavid capital at Isfahan. Examining the scant documentation on the history of Old Julfa, the chapter discusses the role of Old Julfa in the international trade of Iranian raw silk in the second half of the sixteenth century, and the Safavid-Ottoman wars of 1603–1605, during which the town was razed to the ground and its mercantile and artisan population deported and resettled on the outskirts of Isfahan. Contrary to most of the literature on the deportation of the Julfans, this chapter argues that the decision to deport the Julfans was most likely made in the course of the war and was not necessarily part of a larger "conscious policy" or blueprint of economic and urban renewal by 'Abbas I.

Chapters 3–4 provide a "nuts-and-bolts" discussion of the Julfan trade network, synthesizing the available Armenian, English, Spanish, and Italian language literature on Julfan settlements in various parts of the world. Gaps in the literature are supplemented by original archival research, which in some cases provides fresh evidence from newly discovered archives for settlements that have not yet been properly studied. Thus chapter 3 examines the expansion of the Julfan trade network in the Indian Ocean and provides a settlement-by-settlement discussion of the Julfan presence in Mughal India, Southeast Asia, and the little-studied Julfan community in Spanish-controlled Manila in the Philippines, which served as a gateway to sporadic Julfan relations with Acapulco and Mexico City in the New World. Chapter 4 examines the Julfan network from the Indian Ocean to the Mediterranean. It discusses Julfan settlements in Aleppo, Izmir, Venice, Livorno, Marseilles, and Cadiz on the Atlantic rim. It also treats Julfan settlements in northwestern Europe, such as in Amsterdam and London, as well as the important settlements across the Russian Empire to the north.

Chapter 5 addresses the glue that held these settlements and the network together. It examines the circulation of what was arguably the most important commodity throughout the Julfan network: information. The chapter offers the first scholarly treatment of the art of Julfan business correspondence by examining thousands of business and family letters written by Julfan merchants in their unique dialect of mercantile Armenian. The bulk of these letters originated from the nodal center at Julfa, but a great many were written by merchants residing in Julfa's overseas nodes and as such carried a precious cargo of local knowledge back to the nodal center. In addition to analyzing the stylistic properties of Julfan correspondence and assessing the economic function of letter writing and information sharing, the chapter also addresses the role of correspondence in helping create an "imagined community" of merchants who were scattered in different parts of the world, much as print capitalism, according to Benedict Anderson, helped create modern nations as "imagined political communities."[52] The chapter also discusses the crucial role of Julfan courier networks, which acted as a private order postal system and delivered information and news to Julfan merchants and their families, thus gluing merchants in different settlements together and the settlements to their "nodal center" in New Julfa.

Chapter 6 explores another important aspect of circulation in the Julfan network, namely, the circulation of merchants and credit. It explores the legal and economic institution of the *commenda* contract among the Julfan merchants and argues that the *commenda* was the principal mechanism among Julfans for the circulation of men and credit. As a means of bringing together a principal merchant, known as a *khwaja* among the Julfans, who had ready capital and credit to invest, and a junior merchant, who usually had no capital but possessed a good reputation and professional skills in accounting and trade and was prepared to travel for periods of up to several decades to invest his master's capital in exchange for usually one-third of the total profit, the *commenda* was an economic institution of possibly Islamic origins and was widely used in the Mediterranean in the medieval period. The chapter surveys the origins and functions of the Mediterranean *commenda* and through a rigorous examination of Julfan commercial law and of surviving *commenda* contracts points out the crucial differences of this legal-commercial institution among Julfan merchants.

Chapter 7 tackles an issue at the heart of most long-distance merchant communities in the early modern period, the crucial issue of "trust" and cooperation. "Trust," or the ability of one individual to have confidence that another person "entrusted" with something (e.g., money or fulfilling an important task such as carrying out the instructions in a power of attorney) would not act in a manner detrimental to the entrusting individual, is a fundamental component in any type of economic transaction, especially in the context of early modern trade, where legal institutions capable of enforcing contracts and effectively punishing offenders were either absent or ineffective in the world of long-distance trade. The chapter argues that the tendency to take "trust" in early modern merchant communities for granted, despite its central role in the lives of such communities, is one of the hallmarks of the trade diaspora paradigm, which assumes that trade diaspora communities are naturally imbued with trustworthy members because of kinship or family ties. Rather than taking trust as a given, this chapter thus attempts to *explain* trust as a commodity created by merchants largely through rigorous monitoring of merchant behavior, rewarding individuals upholding high ethical standards, and sanctioning those who break codes of honor and betray their fellow merchants. To explain the creation of "trust" and cooperation, this chapter relies on theoretical literature in economic sociology known as "social capital theory." The theoretical model I devise to study the creation and maintenance of "trust" in the Julfan network differs from the model of "multi-lateral reputation mechanism" associated with the work of Avner Greif and the school of new economic institutionalism, which largely relies on the informal policing of reputation by purely self-interested rational actors. In contrast to Greif and his followers, my model places much more emphasis on a centralized and centralizing semiformal legal institution in Julfa known as the Assembly of Merchants and to a lesser degree the church and its network of priests. Unlike Greif and others who have attempted to explain trust in early modern merchant communities, my account does not merely take the circulation of information as a given attribute of long-distance merchant communities but embeds information flows within a detailed study of merchant correspondence and courier networks, which were vital to the proper functioning of the Julfan network.

In chapter 8, I explore the decline and collapse of the Julfan network. Examining a number of different interpretations of Julfan decline, I argue that the Julfan network collapsed in the decades following 1747 when the suburb was extensively looted and overtaxed by the predatory policies of Nadir Shah Afshar, who became the ruler of Iran in 1736 after the Afghan occupation of Isfahan and the collapse of the Safavid dynasty in 1722. Relying on fresh documentation of Nadir Shah's destructive policies in Isfahan and New Julfa in the winter of 1746–1747, the chapter argues that New Julfa as a nodal center of a vast network collapsed under excessive taxation and looting, which ruined many of the township's leading merchant families and caused a massive exodus of its population to Russia, the Mediterranean, and especially India. With the collapse of the nodal center and the financial ruin of its remaining wealthy families, the rest of the network gravitated to India, where it continued to function in a debilitated fashion for a few more decades, eventually succumbing to pressures from the rival imperializing network of the English East India Company.

The study concludes with a comparative chapter that seeks to place the Julfan network and its methods of policing trust within a larger comparative context by examining two other exemplary early modern long-distance trading networks, those of the Multani Indians and the Sephardic Jews, and assesses the particularities of the Julfan network through a larger comparative analysis. In doing so, it probes the Julfan network for possible structural flaws and argues that one such flaw was the network's privileging of the *commenda* contract over other forms of partnerships, a choice that severely limited the network's ability to expand and diversify into new markets.

## SOURCES AND INDIAN OCEAN HISTORIOGRAPHY

In his *Trade and Civilisation in the Indian Ocean,* K. N. Chaudhuri laments the "severe lack of documentation" in the context of Indian Ocean trade and its historiography:

Merchants and business organizations rarely preserve their records for the benefit of posterity. Once the practical reason for record-keeping is removed, commercial documents are either destroyed or deposited with law courts or religious foundations, according to the social usage of the time. To family inheritors, even when they were engaged in trade, the business papers of another generation made little sense. The surviving documents remain difficult to interpret to this day. Calculations of profits, before the age of double-entry book-keeping, could be carried out with ease only by contemporary participants perfectly familiar with running accounts. The obscurity and special nomenclature may have been deliberately adopted in order to discourage outside investigations. *The result of the secretive attitude of merchants in the context of the Indian Ocean trade is a severe lack of documentation on the content of commercial dealings.*[53]

Chaudhuri, of course, was not the only prominent Indian scholar to note the absence of "indigenous" documents with regard to the economic and social history of the Indian Ocean. In one of his early essays, Ashin Das Gupta, one of the founders of the field of Indian Ocean studies, also noted the fact that "the papers of Indian merchants are . . . almost totally lost."[54] With the exception of a famous diary written by Ananda Ranga Pillai, covering the period from 1736 to 1761, not much seems to have survived in terms of private papers written in "indigenous" languages left behind by Indian merchants operating in the Indian Ocean.

The ostensible absence of Asian documents in indigenous languages has prompted most scholars of Indian Ocean trade to rely on the rich mass of documentation created by the European trading companies that were later to become colonial masters. Clearly, the problems and Eurocentrism inherent in excessive reliance on European documents to write the history of Asian merchants have not been lost on scholars. Nonetheless, given the putative absence of "indigenous" sources, Das Gupta and others have argued that economic and social historians of India and the Indian Ocean could make judicious use of "the papers of the various European Companies and some private papers of their officials in India."[55] Om Prakash has even suggested that documents written by private European merchants in India may be used as a sort of "proxy" for understanding the commercial practices and mental world of Indian merchants, who do not appear to have left behind much of an archival trail.[56]

Fortunately for us "the severe lack of documentation on the content of commercial dealings" attributed to Indian and Asian merchants by Chaudhuri and others does not apply to the Julfan Armenians. Indeed, one reason the Julfans may be seen as an exemplary Indian Ocean community is precisely because over 10,000 separate documents (amounting to several 100,000 pages when fully transcribed) written by them about their own trading practices have reached us, thus allowing us to have a fairly accurate view of their customs and practices. The overwhelming majority of these documents were written in a peculiar dialect of mercantile Armenian (a dialect extinct since the late nineteenth century and understood by only a handful of scholars in the world) that was used by Julfan merchants and remains largely incomprehensible to other Armenians. Since Julfan Armenian identity and trading practices were profoundly shaped by the Islamicate world of the Indian Ocean and Eurasia in general, and since the Julfans, like the "*geniza* Jews" before them, were deeply "embedded" in the Islamic societies around them and had a common history and legal-commercial culture, their papers also mirror the shared world of common trading practices of other Asian merchants in the Indian Ocean and beyond. To paraphrase Roxani Margariti's recent thoughts on the use of Judeo-Arabic *geniza* documents, one could indeed say that Julfa dialect documents are not only useful to scholars of Armenian history but also to those studying other Asian merchants of the early modern Indian Ocean, though their precise use remains to be fully explored.[57]

The seventeenth-century English traveler John Ovington best sums up the place of the Julfans and their dialect in the Indian Ocean world of the early modern period:

> . . . *Armenians,* who above any of the rest Travel the farthest, spread themselves in all parts of *Asia,* as well as *Europe,* and are as universal Merchants as any in the World. The *Armenians* are Civil and Industrious, their Language is one of the most general in all of Asia, and they have spread themselves in vast Colonies very far, in *Anatolia, Persia,* the *Holy Land, Egypt, Russia* and *Polonia,* and range by private Persons and Families, like Jews into all parts, and like them are as subtle and diligent in their Traffick.[58]

Ovington describes "their [the Armenians'] Language" (read: the Julfa dialect) as "one the most general in all of Asia." He was right, of course, because one could find speakers of this dialect in the caravansaries of Mughal India, Lhasa, Inner China, Siam, and Manila, to name only a few places. A compelling case can be made for considering the Julfa dialect an "indigenous" language to the entire Indian Ocean, in the same sense that one considers Gujarati, Arabic, Persian, and even creolized Portuguese as indigenous to the region.[59] This means that there is little need for future historians to rely excessively on "proxy" European company documents to write Asian economic and social history.

One reason Julfa dialect documents are valuable for scholars working on Indian Ocean maritime history and may therefore contribute to the larger study of Asian trade and trading practices during this period has to do with the broad variety of mercantile practices they cover, ranging from double-entry accounting to *commenda* contracts and powers of attorney. Shushanik Khachikian and Edmund Herzig have noted the importance of this corpus of documentation in their groundbreaking investigations into Julfan history. Herzig, in particular, has pointed out the potential use of Julfan documents for scholars of Indian Ocean maritime history whose work has been hampered by the absence of "indigenous" (as opposed to European company) sources.

This study thus aims to build on the work of Khachikian and Herzig by ground-ing the analysis of the commercial and social world of Julfan merchants in a close textual reading of original Julfan documents. These sources derive from the re-markable archive of eighteenth-century documents I discovered while doing research at the Public Records Office (PRO) in London. The archive consists of approxi-mately 1,700 Julfan mercantile letters seized in the Indian Ocean in 1748 on board an Armenian-freighted ship called the *Santa Catharina*. The majority of these let-ters were carried by Armenian overland couriers across the Mediterranean littoral and Asia Minor to the Persian Gulf port city of Basra, where they were relayed to other merchant-couriers traveling by ship to Bengal to be delivered to recipients there and farther east in China. What makes this collection valuable for the present investigation is that their journey was unexpectedly cut short when the ship on which they were traveling was captured as a wartime "prize" by a British naval squadron patrolling the waters off the southern coast of India. The letters were con-fiscated along with the *Santa Catharina*'s other cargo and shipped to England to be presented as "exhibits" in a high-stakes trial in London.[60] This event not only insured their survival but also transformed them into a kind of Julfan *geniza*.[61] In addition to this vast trove of documents, I shall use several other collections of business and family correspondence and contracts and legal papers stored in the Archivio di Stato di Venezia (ASV), the Archivio di Stato di Firenze (ASFi), and the Archivio di Stato di Padua (ASP), as well as the papers of a prominent Julfan family stored in private archives in Verona and in San Lazzaro in Venice. Most im-portantly perhaps, this study is the first since the mid-nineteenth century to make extensive use of the wealth of Julfan documentation stored at the All Savior's Mon-astery Archive (ASMA) in Julfa.[62] All these collections are valuable because they contain thousands of commercial letters and other documents sent from Europe and India, the overwhelming majority of which are examined here for the first time. With the exception of a handful of *farmans* (royal edicts) stored in the ASMA in Julfa, Persian-language documents on merchants have not been used in this study, since such documentation is virtually nonexistent; as most scholars work-ing on Safavid history know, there is a dearth of Persian sources on the Safavid period because the Safavid archives appear to have been destroyed in the after-math of the Afghan conquest of Isfahan in 1722.[63] The one major collection of doc-umentation relating to the Safavid period and written by Iranian-Armenians is preserved in the Julfa dialect at the ASMA in New Julfa; it is used extensively for this study.

Work on Julfan documents remains crucial to the future advancement of schol-arship not only on Julfan commerce,[64] but also on Asian commerce in general, as the Julfans were among the very few communities to have left us a rich paper trail of documents. It is my intent to present a study that is theoretically informed and multidisciplinary in its approach, and at the same time firmly grounded in archival material. The archival material is derived from thirty-one collections in a dozen countries and seven languages, including the Julfa dialect, making this study part of a new wave of scholarship, one based on "indigenous" primary sources rather than European "proxy" documents.

# 2

# Old Julfa, the Great Deportations, and the Founding of New Julfa

In 1595, an Armenian merchant from Old Julfa named Mahdasi Aghaval wrote a will bequeathing his house on the edge of the Aras River along with his patrimonial gardens, which formed the southern perimeter of the town, to the children of his brother, Selim.[1] This will is the oldest preserved document in the All Savior's Monastery Archive in Julfa, Isfahan. It most likely would have been entirely insignificant were it not for the fact that it is at this point the sole surviving textual evidence from Old Julfa, apart from some surviving tombstone inscriptions and colophons. This is paradoxical because, by the time Mahdasi Aghaval drafted his will, the merchants of Old Julfa had already acquired international renown for their wealth and cosmopolitan connections in the Mediterranean as well as the Indian Ocean. The lack of other textual evidence (except funerary inscriptions and colophons) written by Old Julfans severely limits our knowledge of the commercial activities of the Old Julfans before the Safavid monarch Shah 'Abbas I destroyed their town in the autumn of 1604 and carried off the population to the outskirts of his capital at Isfahan, where he allowed them to build a mercantile suburb named New Julfa.[2]

This chapter explores the history of Old Julfa and focuses in particular on its destruction by Shah 'Abbas I during the Safavid-Ottoman war of 1603–1605, followed a decade later by its resurrection and reincarnation as a wealthy mercantile suburb of Isfahan named New Julfa. The first section discusses the history of Old Julfa, especially its rise to commercial fame and fortune in the second half of the sixteenth century, when its merchants began to play a dominant role in the international export of Iranian silk. The second section examines, in detail, the Safavid-Ottoman war of 1603–1605 during which the town was destroyed. The chapter concludes with a discussion of how the merchant population of Old Julfa was resettled on the outskirts of Isfahan, where 'Abbas I granted them crown lands south of the Zayan-darud River to build an Armenian mercantile suburb.

Besides the limited primary source material relating to the history of Old Julfa, there are only a handful of reliable secondary sources on the history of the town, most of which rely on the epigraphic evidence provided by gravestones in Old Julfa's cemetery and scanty references to the town and its merchants by European travelers who passed through the region before the fateful years of 1604–1605. Neither of these sources is ideal, but they are somewhat useful. Compared to the near-complete absence of documentation on the town's history before the Safavid-Ottoman wars at the turn of the seventeenth century, its destruction and the depor-tation of its mercantile and artisan population in 1604–1605, as well as its resur-rection in the form of New Julfa, is amply documented both by vital eyewitness accounts written by Armenian scribes in numerous colophons and by a variety of accounts by European travelers who observed the events from close quarters.

## OLD JULFA: A SPECTRAL PRESENCE

*At length our caravan ferried over the foresaid River, and so we arrived at* Chi-ulfal, *a town situate in the frontiers between the* Armenians *and* Atropatians, *and yet within Armenia, inhabited by Christians, partly* Armenians, *partly* Georgians: *a people rather given to the traffique of Silkes, and other sorts of wares, whereby it waxeth rich and full of money, then instructed in weapons and matters of warre. This towne consisteth of two thousand houses and ten thousand soules, being built at the foot of a great rocky mountaine in so barren a soile, that they are constrained to fetch most of their provision, only wine ex-cepted, from the City of* Nassuan, *half a days journey off. . . . The buildings of* Chiulfal *are very faire, all of hard quarry stone: and the inhabitants very cour-teous and affable. . . . It is subject and tributary to the Scepter of Persia, and contrariwise both by nature and affection great enemies of the Turke. This Towne was indangered in the warres betwixt* Amurat *the great* Turke, *and* Mahomet Codibanda *the Persian King, ready to be swallowed up by both.*[3]

The town of Old Julfa was located in the Iranian-Ottoman frontier region on the northern banks of the Aras River. Its ruins are still visible today in the Azerbaijani-controlled Nakhchivan Autonomous Republic, just north of the Iranian frontier. In the sixteenth century, when the commerce of Old Julfa was in full bloom, the town "stood on a narrow spit of land a little more than two kilometres long and four or five hundred metres wide sandwitched between the River Aras to the South and a steep mountain ridge to the north."[4] The French traveler Jean Chardin, who passed through the region in 1673, about seven decades after the town's destruction, and compared the surviving layout of Old Julfa to a "long amphiteater," remarked "that it is not possible to find another town situated in a place that is more dry and more rocky."[5] The fact that the soil around the town was barren, as both the English traveler John Cartwright and, following him, Chardin note, made it difficult if not impossible for its residents to practice agriculture and thus must have encouraged them, early on, to turn to commerce to meet their needs.[6] The town seems to have depended on the nearby region of Nakhjavan to meet its needs. Despite its inhospitable location, Old Julfa had two important advantages. First, "it was readily defensible, being protected by the high ridge and the river to the north and south, while the entrances to the gorge from East and West were closed with strong walls."[7] Second and most importantly, it was situated on an important river crossing astride the major overland routes connecting Transcaucasia and Iran with Asia Minor, Syria, and the Mediterranean.[8]

The first mention of the town is found in Movses of Khoren's *History of Armenia* (written sometime between the fifth and eighth centuries), where the founding of Julfa is ascribed to the first-century B.C.E. Armenian king Tigranes the Great. There is also a passing reference to Julfa in the late seventh-century *History* by Ghevont, an Armenian historian under Arab rule in the region. Thereafter there is a silence of several centuries until the next historical reference to the town at the time of Tamerlane's conquests in the region.[9]

Apart from these passing references, most of our knowledge of Old Julfa derives from fragmentary information recorded by a small number of European travelers who passed through the town in the last decades of the sixteenth century, shortly before its destruction. According to the London merchant John Newbery, who was in Julfa in 1581, the town had 7 churches and 3,000 houses.[10] Cartwright, who stayed in Julfa for eight days in the mid-1580s, reported 2,000 houses, or about 10,000 inhabitants.[11] Sefer Muratowics, an Armenian representative to the Polish king Sigismund III, recorded 15,000 houses or families in the town when he traveled through the region in 1601 on his way to the Safavid court, but his figure is almost certainly a scribal error.[12] Finally, a Portuguese missionary writing from Goa in India in 1607 estimated that the town had 40,000 inhabitants at the time of their deportation by 'Abbas I, but this too is an exaggerated figure.[13] Argam Aivazian's more recent estimate of between 2,000 and 4,000 houses and a population of about 15,000 seems to be the most reasonable account to date and matches the figure given by Chardin, who wrote in the seventeenth century.[14]

Our knowledge of Julfa's economic history is shrouded in even more obscurity. What we do know with certainty is that its merchants attracted international renown as purveyors of raw Iranian silk to the markets of the Mediterranean only in the second half of the sixteenth century, when they began trading with European merchants in Aleppo and Venice. To the Europeans who came into contact with them, the Julfans were known as "Chelfalynes,"[15] or as Armenians hailing from Djulfa, Giulfa, Iulfa, Zulfa, Sulfa, Diulfa, Tulfa, Iula, Chiulfa, Zugha, Usulfa, Soulpha, Chinla, and even Gilgat.[16]

As Edmund Herzig has noted, Julfa's sudden rise during the second half of the sixteenth century is puzzling for a number of reasons. First, it occurred in the midst of intense Ottoman-Safavid wars, "when much of the surrounding regions and many towns suffered serious social and economic disruption and in some cases complete destruction."[17] Old Julfa was in many ways in "the eye of the storm" during decades of fighting between the Safavids and Ottomans, when both warring factions readily resorted to "scorched-earth" strategies, destroying the land and population surrounding Julfa. In the aftermath of the stunning Ottoman victory over the Safavids at the battle of Chaldiran in 1514, the two "gunpowder empires" were chronically at war over the geopolitically prized region of eastern Anatolia and the Caucasus. After the signing of the treaty of Amasya in 1555, which left the Ottomans in control of Iraq (conquered earlier, in 1534) and parts of the Caucasus, war resumed in the 1578 during the reign of Shah Mohammad Khodabanda.[18]

According to some sources, Julfa passed into Ottoman hands in the 1580s, and its tribute to the empire appears to have gone directly to meet the expenses of the queen mother (*valide sultan*), which might explain why the Julfans survived the turbulent period of the late sixteenth century relatively unscathed. It is interesting to note that after the destruction of the town and the founding of New Julfa at Isfahan in the seventeenth century, the new settlement paid its tribute to the shah's mother.[19] While Safavid-Ottoman armies continued to clash in the borderland region until the treaty of Istanbul in 1590 left Julfa in Ottoman hands for over ten years, each time the Julfans were spared through a combination of sheer luck, important political patrons, perceived neutrality as an all-Christian town, and handsome bribes paid to keep invaders at bay. The town not only survived throughout the sixteenth century but even managed to prosper.

Geography played an important role in shaping Julfa's economic prosperity. The town's location on the Aras River was a blessing for several reasons. The Aras, as even classical writers like Strabo had noted, was notorious for its tumultuous twists and turns and unruly waves, making it impossible to ford most parts of the river.[20] Cartwright noted the "outrageous turnings and windings and [its] many rushing downfalls."[21] Though steep gorges characterized much of the river, "at Julfa the river bed and banks flatten out and become less rocky."[22]

In 1340, Ziya al-Mulk Nakhjavani built a famous stone bridge across the Aras in the vicinity of Julfa with gates and a caravansary on the northern end.[23] It was in all likelihood this bridge that Amir Timur crossed with his forces during one of his campaigns in 1396.[24] The bridge seems to have been destroyed during one of the Ottoman-Safavid wars of the 1570s or 1580s and was certainly not standing by the time 'Abbas I retreated from Julfa in 1604.[25] Until the sixteenth century, the bridge appears to have been the most significant feature of Julfa.[26]

According to Herzig, Julfa experienced a "meteoric" rise in the second half of the sixteenth century in general, and the period after 1570 in particular. A number of developments are indicative of Julfa's rise at this relatively late period in its history. First, there was a remarkable upsurge in Armenian manuscripts commissioned by wealthy Julfan merchants known as *khwajas*. This suggests that the town's merchant class was affluent enough at this time to undertake patronage activities involving the commissioning of lavish manuscripts. Interestingly, few if any of the surviving manuscripts, written before the mid-sixteenth century, bear signs of Julfan patronage. Dickran Kouymjian's work on the revival of Armenian culture in the early modern period also suggests a sudden increase in patronage activity of churches associated with Julfa's *khwaja* merchants.[27]

Another related development during this time was the "boom" in the construction of ornate tombstones known as *khatchkars* (stone crosses) in Julfa's historic cemetery.[28] Of the more than 2,000 surviving *khatchkars,* only a handful are dated earlier than 1500, the overwhelming majority belonging to *khwajas* who passed away in the last three decades of the sixteenth century and shortly before the destruction of the town.[29] The unusual decorative motifs of these gravestones distinguish them from traditional Armenian patterns and probably show traces of Islamicate influences, hinting at the rich cosmopolitan world of Julfa's long-distance merchants.[30]

Other evidence also suggests that the town's economy experienced a sudden boom during this period. For instance, the scant evidence of Julfan merchants visiting foreign markets during the last four decades of the sixteenth century is a telltale sign of intense economic prosperity. One of the first markets frequented by Julfan merchants was the bustling city of Ottoman Aleppo with its Venetian, English, and later Dutch merchants. Already in 1566, an agent of the English Moscovy Company mentions that while he was in Aleppo he encountered many Armenians actively trading Iranian raw silk with Venetian merchants.[31] Though this agent does not refer to the Armenians as Julfans, we can safely assume that most if not all the Armenian merchants he came across were from Old Julfa, since other English traders in Aleppo around the same time do refer to them as "chelfalynes."[32] Discussing Aleppo's international trade during that period, another English employee for the Moscovy Company notes that "one village of *Armenia* named *Gilgat* doth carie veerely fyve hundred, and sometime a thousande mules laden with sylke to *Halepo* in *Sorya* of *Turkye,* being foure days of iorney of *Tripoli,* where *Venetians* have their continuall abidying, and send from thence sylkes, which they returne for *English* carses and other clothes, into all partes of Christendome."[33] Another report, written in 1568, complains about the difficulty of "breaking the trade betwixt the Venetians and the whole company of Armenians," indicating that the Julfans were already the principal suppliers of Iranian silk to European merchants in Aleppo.[34] The timing of these reports coincides with the major influx of Old Julfans into Aleppo's preexisting Armenian community, making them the dominant element in social and economic life of the community. As Artavazd Surmeyan's research has confirmed, thirteen of the fourteen sixteenth-century tombstones in Aleppo's Old

Armenian cemetery belong to Julfan merchants.[35] The identification of the Old Julfans as important silk merchants as early as 1566 by English sources means that
Old Julfa must already have risen to prominence in Iran's booming silk trade at this
early date. The evidence in these sources is corroborated by Halil Inalcik's work on
the silk trade and the Ottoman city of Bursa. As Inalcik points out, Muslim Iranians are recorded in the Bursa archives as the dominant merchants of Iranian silk
during the first half of the sixteenth century, with hardly any mention of Armenians in this trade. Inalcik suggests that by the second half of the century, the situation had drastically changed in favor of the Armenians. Though he does not proffer
any explanations for this dramatic change of fortune, one possible explanation could
be the intense Ottoman-Safavid rivalry and war in the second half of the sixteenth
and early seventeenth centuries, which made it difficult for Shi'a Iranians to travel
and trade across Ottoman domains.[36]

Around the same time, Old Julfans had begun to travel directly to Venice to sell
their silk and other merchandise. According to Ghevont Alishan, the first appearance of Julfans in the archives of Venice dates from 1571.[37] Alishan notes that the
correspondence of the Venetian traveler and envoy to Iran Vincenzo degli Alessandri indicates that a number of Julfan merchants kept their agents in Venice as early
as 1571 and even had money deposited in Venice's Banco Dolfin.[38] A fairly steady
stream of documents in the Archivio di Stato of Venice related to merchants from
Old Julfa in the closing decades of the century is an indication of frequent ties and
visits between the town and the Venetian republic. A Julfan merchant named Nuri-
jan is also mentioned as residing in Rome around this time. His tombstone at the
ancient Armenian church in Rome is dated 1579. However, the most compelling
evidence for Julfa's rise during this period is the town's direct involvement in the
trade of raw Iranian silk that also began to spike at this time, a topic to which we
shall return shortly. Therefore, it comes as no surprise that this is also the period
when Julfa's name first reaches western Europe via the encounters between the town's
silk merchants and European Levant merchants in Aleppo and Venice. Though there
is no direct evidence, it seems reasonable to speculate that some of the Armenian
merchants described as hailing from Aleppo and already trading and residing in
the Mughal capital of Agra during the second half of the sixteenth century may
also have been from Old Julfa (see chapter 3). Indeed, one scholar has even suggested that the sudden increase in toll revenues in the late sixteenth century at the
Portuguese-controlled port of Hormuz, the gateway to India, might be associated
with "the contemporary development of Iran's raw silk for bullion trade in which
the Julfa merchants played such a prominent role."[39] In sum, by the last few decades
of the sixteenth century, Old Julfa's reputation had spread far beyond its borders.
In 1570, Old Julfa was literally placed on the map when it appeared in Ortelius's famous world atlas, where it was referred to as Chinla.[40]

In his groundbreaking essay on the "rise of the Julfa merchants," Herzig poses the crucial question of why this sudden rise to prosperity affected Julfa and not, for instance, another town in the same region, and why prosperity came to Julfa only in the last few decades of the 1500s. In trying to solve this puzzle, Herzig considers the "interplay" between a number of geographic, political, and regional economic factors, including: (1) Julfa's strategic location on the main trade route connecting the rich emporium of Tabriz in northern Iran to the markets of Asia Minor and the Mediterranean; (2) Julfa's ability to escape the brutal military campaigns of the Safavids and Ottomans throughout the sixteenth century; and (3) its close proximity to the regional silk-producing areas of Karabagh, Shirvan, Mazanderan, and Gilan. Herzig astutely argues that none of these factors studied in isolation can yield an explanation for Julfa's sudden prosperity. While the town was fortunate enough to be strategically located on one of the most important trade routes of the period and happened to have the only bridge, equipped with a caravansary, over the Aras River in the vicinity of the commercial center of Tabriz, a hub of European merchant presence in the region, its location and strategic value alone cannot account for Julfa's unexpected growth during the second half of the sixteenth century. The same argument holds for the town's proximity to the silk-producing regions of Iran and its near-miraculous survival from the ravages of war.

For Herzig, an explanation for Julfa's commercial takeoff must be sought in the coincidence or conjuncture of these factors with global economic developments. Although Herzig does not mention it, it would seem that his explanation hinges on the notion of "global conjuncture" deployed by world historians like Kenneth Pomeranz, John Darwin, and, on a more popular level, Robert Marks.[41] Darwin, for instance, describes the idea of "conjuncture" as "periods of time when certain general conditions in different parts of the world coincided to encourage (or check) the enlargement of trade, the expansion of empires, the exchange of ideas or the movement of people." In this scheme, an explanation of Old Julfa's sudden rise in the second half of the sixteenth century would have to account for the *interaction* or momentary overlapping of "several otherwise independent developments," simultaneously on a global and local scale, "creating a unique historical moment."[42] The most important development in this respect was the impact of the "Columbian exchange" on the global economy and the resulting inflow of American silver into the Mediterranean port cities (especially on the Italian peninsula) beginning in the 1580s.[43] As Fernand Braudel and, following him, Andre Gunder Frank and others have argued, American silver, discovered by Spanish conquistadores in the world's largest silver mine at Potosí (in present-day Bolivia) in 1545 and shipped to Europe shortly afterward, allowed Mediterranean merchants to purchase large quantities of Eastern goods, including Iranian raw silk, from the markets of the Levant, thus stimulating Iran's silk trade. Coupled with this, the Portuguese crown's "overwhelmingly dominant share" in the trade of Asian spices, and especially pepper, diverted from the overland routes to the Levant through the Cape route directly to

Lisbon and Antwerp, compelled Mediterranean traders and especially the English and the Venetians to turn to Iranian raw silk as an alternative commodity to spices beginning as early as the 1550s.[44] Parallel to this, there might have been an increase in the demand for raw silk in the Mediterranean. "These developments were obviously advantageous for anyone with raw silk to sell in Bursa or Aleppo, and particularly advantageous for the Armenians, who as Middle Eastern Christians formed natural intermediaries between Christian West and Muslim East and were generally the preferred trading partners and agents of European Levant merchants."[45] Moreover, the fact that Julfan trade depended on European demand for silk and Iranian supply of raw silk, both of which were largely independent of the military conditions on the ground, allowed Julfa to prosper at a time when most of the region around it was devastated by the ravages of war.[46]

## WAR, DESTRUCTION, AND DEPORTATION

Iran's silk trade in the late sixteenth and early seventeenth centuries and the role of the Julfan Armenians merchants in this trade were intimately tied to centralizing policies geared toward state formation pursued by the Safavid monarch Shah 'Abbas I (r.1587–1629). The examination of the Julfan role in Safavid Iran's silk policy must, therefore, be conducted within the larger context of 'Abbas's policies.

Soon after coming to power in 1587, 'Abbas undertook a number of administrative reforms aimed at strengthening his realm. Faced with the prospect of fighting the Ozbegs on the eastern front of his empire and continuing threats from the Ottomans in the northwest, the young monarch signed the humiliating treaty of Istanbul in 1590, ceding much of the territory in the northern region of his empire and especially the Caucasus to the Ottomans. With temporary respite from war, 'Abbas focused his energies on combating the Ozbegs in the East, then threatening the province of Khurasan, and in weakening the power of the *qizilbash* amirs at home. Turcoman tribes from the Ottoman-Safavid borderlands in eastern Anatolia, the *qizilbash* had played a vital role in bringing the Safavid dynasty to power at the outset of the sixteenth century.[47] The "military backbone of the Safavis," the *qizilbash* formed the bulk of the new empire's army and had been staffed in key administrative and military positions for much of the first hundred years of Safavid power.[48] As a result of their prominent status in the emerging Safavid state and as potential sharers of the Turco-Mongol concept of "corporate sovereignty," which defined early Safavid political life, they posed a threat to the dynasty's grip on power.[49] Early in Safavid rule, Shah Tahmasp had taken steps to curb the independence and power of the *qizilbash* by introducing a foreign, Caucasian element into the state.[50] Known as the *ghulam*, or royal slaves, this element consisted predominantly of Georgian and Armenian converts to Islam who played a role roughly similar to that of the Janissaries in the Ottoman Empire,[51] and that of the Persian governors whom Akbar the Great promoted to neutralize the power of the Central Asian and Afghan nobility who had brought his father to power.[52] The policy of promoting the *ghulam* into key positions of power was not systematically pursued until the reign of 'Abbas I.

One of the first steps 'Abbas took after signing the treaty of Istanbul with the Ottomans was to resume the *ghulam* policy of his predecessors and to weaken simultaneously the power of the *qizilbash* amirs. During the first years of his reign, 'Abbas thus began to promote Armenian and Georgian converts to Islam to key positions of power. He also deprived many *qizilbash* governors of their posts in the silk-producing regions of Gilan and Mazendaran on the shores of the Caspian and replaced them with officials who were personally loyal to him. As part of his larger policy of state centralization (ushering in what Kathryn Babayan refers to as the "Isfahani era of Absolutism")[53] and enhancing "the infrastructural" and "administrative" powers of his state, in 1598 'Abbas also removed his capital from Qazvin in the north to the more strategically located city of Isfahan at the center of his realm.[54] In addition, he improved the transportation networks in Iran, established caravansaries, and fixed road tolls and customs duties to facilitate commerce in his domains. Most importantly, 'Abbas deprived the *qizilbash* of their appanages, or *tiyuls*, and converted the silk-producing regions near the Caspian into *khassah*, or crown lands, thereby reserving for the crown the revenue generated from this economically lucrative area.[55]

Whether 'Abbas had a self-conscious and overarching policy of economic renewal involving silk trade, and the role of the Julfan Armenians in that trade, have been topics for scholarly discussion. In *The Politics of Trade in Safavid Iran: Silk for Silver,* Rudi Matthee deftly explores the issues at stake in this debate. To Matthee, the temptation to seek a self-conscious mercantilist policy in 'Abbas's measures runs the risk of falling into "procrustean interpretations" that fail to take into account "the mutuality between principle and practice in European mercantilism as much as [ . . . ] the embededness of Safavid economic practice in normative tradition."[56] To avoid the pitfalls of this temptation, Matthee thus proposes the following sensible approach:

> Though the multifaceted and protracted nature of [Shah 'Abbas's] measures makes it tempting to label the Shah's involvement with silk part of a concerted economic policy, it might be more appropriate to view it as consonant with his overall approach to economic issues and to analyze it as a series of interventions that reflect an acute awareness of ways in which revenue might be enhanced and *whose timing was in part determined by geopolitical considerations, in part by contingency and fortuitousness.*[57]

One of the difficulties facing historians of the Safavid silk trade is the dearth of primary source material concerning 'Abbas's economic policies and his intentionality or motives in such policies. Given the absence of evidence, historians must be cautious about their conclusions and particularly careful to avoid the temptation of reading back motives into the past based on their understanding of subsequent events.

The question of the Julfans' role in 'Abbas's policies of promoting Iran's silk trade is fraught with similar problems. Some historians, such as Roger Savory, have argued that 'Abbas had a conscious policy soon after coming to power of using the Julfans to promote his realm's economic development. According to this interpretation, the deportation of the Julfans from their town on the Aras River and their resettlement on the outskirts of Isfahan was part of a larger policy whose "purpose was to enlist the industrious and thrifty nature of the Armenian merchants in the service of the Safavid state."[58] This interpretation has been uncritically endorsed by most scholars working on the Julfans, including Ina Baghdiantz McCabe. According to her, for instance, when 'Abbas deported the Julfans he was merely following a "well-planned" or "conscious policy."[59] Baghdiantz McCabe, in fact, gives the impression that the shah had a "verbal treaty" with the Julfans to resettle them near Isfahan with promises of great economic prosperity.[60] However, in the absence of evidence, it is impossible to substantiate or verify the claim of a verbal treaty. Her argument that the Julfans "came of their own will" is a retrospective projection of intentionality into 'Abbas's plans in light of the subsequent relationship between the shah and Julfan merchants and is not supported by contemporary Armenian accounts regarding the brutal circumstances of 'Abbas's deportation of the Julfans and the destruction of their town, to which we now turn.[61]

By the spring of 1603, a number of developments in the Ottoman Empire persuaded 'Abbas to wage war against his old Ottoman enemies with the aim of recouping territories ceded to them in the treaty of Istanbul. The deployment of Ottoman forces on the European front, the Celali rebellions destabilizing much of the region of eastern Anatolia, and the growing tide of discontent against Ottoman rule in the Caucuses and the Safavid-Ottoman frontier region prompted 'Abbas to move his forces to the northwest of his realm.[62] 'Abbas took Tabriz by surprise in March of 1603 and marched north to Ottoman-controlled Nakhjavan, which surrendered to him later that spring.[63] On his way there, the shah made a brief stop at Old Julfa, where the town's local Armenian population received him with much pomp and ceremony. The Armenian chronicler Arakel of Tabriz describes how the Julfans greeted the shah:

> On the way, when they [the shah and his forces] reached the small town of Julfa, the large and diverse population of the town, who had prepared themselves earlier, came out to greet the shah as befitting a king. Old and young, dressed and equipped, robed in magnificent garments of golden cloth, walked in a procession to greet the shah. Young lads carried sweet and precious wine in golden cups. With lit candles, frankincense, and incense, and singing fine hymns, the [parish priests] walked in front and sang with beautiful voices. The shah's path was decorated: from the banks of the river

to the mansion of Khwaja Khachik,[64] the road was covered with carpets and expensive and magnificent brocades, upon which the shah marched to the house of Khwaja Khachik, In his house, Khwaja Khachik handed his son a golden tray full of golden coins, which was presented to the king. All the notables of Julfa also brought gifts, befitting a king. The shah remained there for three days, and the Julfans entertained him with magnificent, refined victuals and fragrant wines.[65]

Georg Tectander, an Austrian envoy to 'Abbas's camp, also describes the shah's friendly welcome in the town and how the flat-roofed homes there "were covered with more than fifty thousand oil lamps that burned all night long."[66] Khwaja Khachik, described in the above passage by Arakel of Tabriz as hosting the shah, was the mayor (k'aghak'apet) of Old Julfa. His son, who presented 'Abbas with gold coins, was most likely Khwaja Safar, who, as we shall see in chapter 7, later became the first kalantar (mayor) of New Julfa.

After his departure from Old Julfa, the shah marched with his forces on Nakhjavan, which quickly surrendered to him. The Ottoman garrison of Yerevan also surrendered after a grueling siege of seven and a half months.[67] Both the European and the Armenian evidence suggests that until the summer of 1604, there were no significant cases of population deportation involving Armenians. Such deportations (sürgün, the term employed at the time) did occur shortly afterward, but the decision to undertake them was made in response to rapidly unfolding events on the ground. It appears that the catalyst for the deportation of many of the region's Armenians and other populations was the news of the advancing Ottoman army under the command of Sinan Pasha or Cheghaloghlu from the West.[68]

The following account from an Armenian colophon written during the period sheds light on the effect of Sinan Pasha's advance to the East on 'Abbas's decision to practice a scorched-earth policy and the forced migration of the region's population:

But with the approach of autumn, the Turkish commander . . . mustered a large army and launched a fierce attack on King Abas in the Ararat province (gavar). When he (Abbas) saw that he could not face him (Cheghaloghlu) in battle, he fled from one place to the next, and put the country to fire, so that there would be no shelter for the Turkish forces nor food or nourishment for their beasts. Also he gave the order for his wicked troops to drive the Armenian people into Persia, as of Old Nebuchadnezzar drove ancient Israel into Babylon. With savage blows and violent haste they began to empty of inhabitants the whole area between Shirakuan [Shirakavan] and Kars provinces and Goghtn province. In the days of winter they dragged vardapet and bishop, priest and congregation, noble and commoner from their abodes and dwellings in village, city, monastery and hermitage, and drove them off with all speed before their horses, brandishing their swords aloft to spur them into greater haste, for the enemy, the Turkish army, was on their heels. Woe and alas for this calamity! Oh the sufferings, the misery and bitterness! For when they drove the people out of their homes they set fire to the houses with all their possessions in them, and the owners, looking back, saw the flames leaping up. Then they wept, uttering piercing cries, wailing loudly and pouring dust on their heads. There was no help to be found, for the King's edict was unbending. Then on the road they (the soldiers) killed some and maimed others, took babes from their mothers' arms and dashed them on the stones, so that [the women] would be lighter for the march.[69]

It was in this larger context of retreating from the advancing Ottoman army that 'Abbas ordered one of his *ghulam* officers of Armenian origin, Tahmasp-qoli Beg, to go to Julfa and deport its population. According to the account of the Armenian chronicler Arakel, Tahmasp-qoli marched on the town and gave the local population three days to evacuate their homes and march with his forces into Iran. Arakel notes that the Julfans were rushed to vacate their town. The evidence (both from Arakel and other sources) suggests that the deportation of the town was anything but orderly. The "shah's order was immediately carried out and they [the Julfans] went on their way."[70] Since the decision to deport must have come suddenly, the population "could not make advanced preparations [and] people could not find beasts of burden."[71]

The population of Julfa was ordered to cross the river hastily. Since there was no bridge standing at the time, many could have drowned. An Armenian Catholic priest from Nakhjavan, Awgostinos Bajets'i, who was probably among another group of deportees, describes the perils of the river crossing:

> We arrived at a river called Aras [arasdgh], too wide to be crossed without a boat; they pushed the multitude [into the open current], without boats or cattle [ařants' nawi ew ařants' tawari]. Some were able to cross [the river]; others were swept away by the waves, some calling in great cries for their father, some their children, their mother, brother, sister, priest. Many were drowned in the river. As for me, a sinner, I too would have been swept away by the river had I not grabbed the tail of a buffalo and been saved by the will of God.[72]

Shortly after the Julfans were forced to vacate their homes and had already been driven into Iranian territory, the shah ordered Tahmasp-qoli Beg to return to the town and raze it to the ground, so as to prevent the Julfans from eventually returning home. According to Arakel's account, 'Abbas also ordered the rounding up of any stragglers and took measures to ensure that no one evaded the deportations.[73]

In light of the above sequence of events, it is difficult to give credence to the view that the deportation of the region's population was carried out in accordance with a systematic and conscious policy pursued by 'Abbas of resettling the Julfan Armenians in Iran and making use of them to promote Iran's silk trade. Rather, the deportations appear to be the outcome of *improvised* decisions taken in response to a series of contingent events. As Herzig observes,

> The picture that emerges is of a sudden decision to deport the entire civilian population (Christian and Muslim), reached only when Abbas realized that he could not face

the superior Turkish forces in the field. The delay in initiating the evacuation meant that it had to be carried out with extreme haste and violence, and little regard for the lives, property or liberty of the evacuees. The fact that it took place in late autumn, combined with the evacuees' inability to make any preparations, increased the hardship involved.[74]

Herzig's interpretation of these events challenges the conventional wisdom, repeated in standard accounts such as those of Vazken Ghougassian and Baghdiantz McCabe, that retrospectively projects a teleology for Shah 'Abbas's "motives" and asserts that the Safavid monarch had a "conscious policy," perhaps dating back to the 1590s, of resettling the Julfans in Isfahan to make use of their skills in rebuilding the political economy of his realm.[75] As Herzig notes, the existing evidence does not support such a claim. On the contrary, the evidence suggests that the decision to deport and resettle the Julfans was made on the spur of the moment and had more to do with 'Abbas's reaction to the rapidly developing events on the ground than any long-term "conscious policy."

After the hasty crossing of the Aras River, most deportees were driven east while the Julfans were given relatively privileged treatment and taken first to Tabriz before being resettled on the outskirts of Isfahan.[76] While most European and Armenian historians give the impression that 'Abbas I intended to settle the Armenians immediately in Iran, Herzig remarks that "contemporary sources suggest that some time elapsed before he reached this decision."[77] Citing an Armenian colophon, Herzig contends that 'Abbas in fact allowed some of the evacuees from Nakhjavan to return to their homes, and even issued a decree while wintering in Tabriz in 1604–1605:

> He who wishes to settle here, let him stay here, and he who does not wish to settle here, let him go his own way, each to his own place. Then many of the Armenians and Muslims (tachik) set off on their way and travelled for two days, but the wicked Kurdish khans killed all the men and women, and took the youths captive. . . . Then compassionate and merciful God . . . instilled pity in the heart of the King, and he gave a decree, that, "The Armenians are free, but there is no order for them to leave, let them remain here until the spring." And then in March they all departed and went to Shush (Susa) which is called Aspahan (Isfahan).[78]

Based on this evidence, Herzig concludes: " 'Abbas only decided to resettle at least part of the Armenians in Iran during the winter months of 1605, when it became apparent that it would be impossible for them to return home because of the danger from Kurdish and celali marauders."[79] This seems plausible enough but overlooks the fact that, in the Julfans' case at least, 'Abbas had their town deliberately razed to the ground and ordered his men not to allow any Julfans to remain behind or to return later to what was left of their homes. Given that this was the case, it could very well be that 'Abbas actually had plans to deport and resettle the Julfans as early as 1604, when he gave the order for the deportation of the town and for its destruction, and not in the winter of 1605, as Herzig concludes. Of course, we have no way of being certain because 'Abbas's "intentions" are not recorded in any of the surviving documentation. However, it seems clear that 'Abbas had no such plans soon after coming to power in 1587, which is the impression one gets from reading Arakel of Tabriz's seventeenth-century chronicle and some of the recent Armenian scholarship influenced by his account. It is more likely that Herzig's argument for contingency is still the most persuasive account to date, but that his timing for the decision may be challenged.

## THE ESTABLISHMENT OF NEW JULFA

After a brief stay in Tabriz, the Julfans and other Armenians displaced from the war zone were relocated to the imperial capital of Isfahan. A colophon written in 1620 in New Julfa by an Armenian priest named Simeon provides the following account of events that transpired once the Armenians had arrived in Isfahan in 1605:

> And having been brought to the city of Shosh at Isfahan, upon the river Zayandarud, they remained there for three months, and then an order came from the king to settle them in the city and village and in the caravansary/hostel. And there they stayed for two or three months, and as the prophet David declares, "They mixed with the pagans and learned their ways." They were mixed with the Muslims, and the Christians were learning all the ways of the Muslims. And then they were given lands and places to live along the river. And they laid down the foundations of this town and built houses and dwellings and established twelve churches.[80]

The information contained in this source is important because it indicates that the Julfans were not immediately settled in the area south of the Zayandarud River that later became associated with the suburb of New Julfa. Rather, as this document demonstrates, the deportees were initially settled in the city of Isfahan for three months, after which they were moved into the neighboring area and a caravansary for another two or three months. Thus it was only after about five or six months, when their settlement among Muslims proved too difficult to manage, that orders were given by 'Abbas to move the Julfans to the area south of the river, where they were granted residence and land on which to build their houses. It was there that in 1606 the Julfans began constructing their own houses, and between 1606, the date of their resettlement in New Julfa, and 1620, when the above colophon was written, they also built twelve churches.[81]

A *farman* issued by 'Abbas in August/September of 1605 and stored in the All Savior's Monastery Archive in Julfa sheds light on why the decision was taken to provide the Julfans with their separate quarters south of the Zayandarud. The *farman* suggests that the newly arrived Julfans were initially settled in the Marnanan district of Isfahan alongside the Muslim population. This had resulted in discord and fighting between the immigrant Christians and the local Muslims, who must have been resentful of the new arrivals. This development had clearly angered 'Abbas, who issued the following orders in his *farman*:

> During this winter, lodging should be provided for them [i.e., the Julfans] in the Royal estates of Arsabaf, Falashan and Marbanan. For some of them you should rent the houses of peasants, who must evacuate their homes, until next year, when by God's will, they [the Armenians] will build their own houses. We order that the people of Marnanan, who have fought against them be punished severely.[82]

The information from the 1620 colophon and the 1605 *farman* casts further doubt on the planned and orderly relocation of the Julfans and their systematic incorporation into Safavid Iran's developing silk trade. On the contrary, the evidence provides additional support for Herzig's and Matthee's hypothesis that whatever plans 'Abbas had in mind regarding the use he would make of his commercially savvy Julfan subjects, they were most likely not fully conceived or premeditated before the original deportation in 1604, and possibly later. Improvisation seems to have guided 'Abbas's policies with regard to the Julfans. The fact that the Julfans were originally settled in Isfahan alongside the Muslim locals and were only later moved to the area that became New Julfa indicates that 'Abbas's tactics were off-the-cuff and shifted according to developments on the ground; they were not the outcome of a conscious decision taken years before the deportations that brought the Julfans to Isfahan. That the land south of the river Zayandarud was not earmarked for the Julfans but was chosen as their place of residence only after their settlement in Isfahan caused discord with the local Muslim population gives further support to the ad hoc nature of the Julfans' integration into the political economy of Iran.

The informal and improvised nature of 'Abbas's integration of the Julfans into the political economy of his realm also applies to other aspects of the Julfans' status in their newly built home on the outskirts of the Safavid capital. After their relocation south of the river, the Julfans were initially accorded the same rights as *dhimmis* in other Muslim-ruled lands. They were obliged to pay a poll tax in return for protection from the state and, most importantly, did not have the right to own land. This situation, too, was changed in the course of developments related to 'Abbas's changing policies with regard to his realm's silk trade, to which we shall return below. The most important development in the social status of the Julfans occurred in the fall of 1619, when 'Abbas issued another decree, this time granting the land south of the Zayandarud, where the Julfans had been residing since 1606, as a gift from the crown to the Julfans. The *farman* in 'Abbas's name, dated September 11–October 9 of the same year, states:

> At this time, due to our endless Royal benevolence and mercy towards the Armenians of Julfa, and for the betterment of their life, We decided to grant them, free of charge, the land at the bank of the river Zayandarud, in the Capital City of Isfahan,

which is part of our royal property and where they have already built houses. Honorable and great treasurer of the Chancery, delete the above mentioned land from the list of royal properties and register it in the books as a gift to the Armenians. Vazir, Kalantar and public officials of Isfahan, obey the present order and consider the said land as accorded property to the Armenians.[83]

This decision too must be understood in the context of arguably the most important decision 'Abbas took regarding Iran's silk trade. Having attracted a number of European clients eager to have a share of Iran's growing silk trade, including the English East India Company (EIC), which had sent its representatives to the shah's court in 1615, 'Abbas decided to transform the export of Iranian silk into a state monopoly whereby all purchases of silk for export would have to be made directly from the court.[84] In 1619, 'Abbas held a public auction offering the purchase of his silk to the highest bidder. Present at the auction were EIC officials, a representative of the Carmelite Order, who had no authorization from the Spanish crown to make business-related decisions, and Julfan Armenians anxious to prevent their privileges from being taken by the newly arrived Europeans.[85] According to the Italian traveler Pietro della Valle, who has left us one of the few accounts of this event, the Julfans were able to outbid the English and gain a near monopoly of the purchase of Iranian silk for export.[86] As a result of their successful bid, they were able to carry the lion's share of Iran's silk exports during the entire period of the silk monopoly. Even after the monopoly was abolished in the 1630s by 'Abbas's successor, Shah Safi, the Julfans still managed to retain their privileged position as exporters of Iranian silk, largely through their connections with powerful *ghulam* officials of Armenian origin who were in positions of power in the silk-cultivating regions near the Caspian.[87] In light of 'Abbas's promotion of the Julfans as privileged merchants for the crown, it should not come as a surprise that his decision to grant the land of New Julfa as a gift to his subjects coincided with the silk auction.

That the Julfans were seen by 'Abbas as important "service gentry," to borrow Matthee's phrase, or "service nomads," to use the more recent formulation by Yuri Slezkine, is evident even from the first years of their forced resettlement in Isfahan.[88] Indeed, within two years of Old Julfa's destruction and only as the new mercantile suburb was being built, Shah 'Abbas sent a Julfan as his personal representative and envoy to the Venetian Republic to negotiate an agreement with the Venetians against his Ottoman foes. The person he chose for this mission was a Julfan merchant by the name of Khwaja Shiosh, who left Isfahan for Venice in 1606–1607 as an agent and ambassador of the shah.[89] A few years later, 'Abbas sent a second Julfan envoy by the name of Khwaja Sefer son of Edigar (not to be confused with New Julfa's first *kalantar*/mayor or ruler, Khwaja Safar), who arrived in Venice in 1610 as part of his larger mission to Rome, Florence, and Madrid.[90] A number of other Julfans came and went around the same period according to Alishan, thus demonstrating that it did not take too long for the newly deported and resettled Julfans to be up on their feet and to revisit their old haunt in Venice.[91]

## THE GROWTH OF NEW JULFA AND
## ITS ADMINISTRATIVE STRUCTURE

The township of New Julfa initially started on a narrow sliver of land immediately south of the Zayandarud River, facing the central part of Isfahan; here the wealthiest merchants were given land to build their homes and gardens. This core region came to be called Hin Jugha (Old Julfa), not in reference to the original home of the merchants near the Aras River but to distinguish it from neighboring regions that were incorporated into the Armenian colony in the 1650s when Shah 'Abbas II (r. 1642–1666) resettled a number of Armenians originally from Yerevan, Tabriz, Nakhjavan, and Dasht or Agulis who were still residing in Isfahan after their deportation at the turn of the century. Their resettlement across the river and in areas annexed to the oldest part of New Julfa helped expand the suburb's territory and population.[92]

There are few reliable population figures for the township of New Julfa, and the few estimates made by European visitors to Isfahan are far from consistent. The English traveler Thomas Herbert, who visited Isfahan in 1626, put the figure of Julfa's population at 10,000 individuals. Father Sebastian Manrique, writing about his trip to the Safavid capital in 1642, gave a conservative estimate of Julfa's population at 6,000 people, while the French traveler Boulaye le Gouz gave an inflated figure of the township's population as 6,000 families in the 1640s, amounting to about 30,000 people.[93] Chardin, referring to the period in the 1660s, estimated around 3,500 houses or roughly 17,000 people;[94] around the same period the Catholic missionary Gabriel de Chinon estimated that there were "at least 4,000 houses" in the township, while another missionary, Father Giovanni Battista da S. Aignan, writing in 1673, provides the inflated figure of more than 50,000 inhabitants for the township.[95] In 1677, the English traveler John Fryer put the figure at "more than six thousand families" or around 30,000 people, a figure maintained by Englebert Kaempfer, who visited Isfahan in 1685 and published his account in 1712.[96]

Assessing the available data on Julfa's demographic situation, Herzig concludes that the township probably had between 5,000 and 10,000 residents after its initial foundation, and about 10,000 to 15,000 during the second quarter of the century, rising to about 20,000 after the expansion of the suburb under 'Abbas II in the 1650s, and finally peeking at around 30,000 toward the end of the seventeenth century.[97]

As confusing as these figures may seem, they all indicate a natural growth in the suburb's population in the second half of the seventeenth century, a trend commensurate with the growing prosperity of its merchants and the parallel growth of its urban landscape. During the second half of the seventeenth century, the township had experienced so much growth that Chardin referred to it as "the greatest suburb in the world,"[98] and Jean Baptiste Tavernier, writing roughly around the same time, compared it to a real city:

> Zulpha . . . is so much encreas'd for some years since, that it may now pass for a large City, being almost a League and a half long and near upon half as much broad. There are two principal Streets which contain near upon the whole length, one whereof has on each side a row of *Tchinars*, the roots whereof are refresh'd by a small Channel of Water, which by a particular order the *Armenians* bring to the City to water their gardens. The most part of the other Streets have also a row of trees, and a Channel. And for their Houses, they are generally better built, and more cheerful than those of *Isfahan*.[99]

That the new township was an exclusively Armenian colony is attested by all the available sources. The only non-Armenians mentioned as residents of New Julfa were the few Catholic missionaries who had their churches there, some Calvinist Frenchmen who were for the most part jewelers (like Tavernier), gunsmiths, or watchmakers, and a handful of Muslim Iranians who, according to Fryer, were there "as Spies rather than Inmates [i.e., residents]."[100]

Between 1606 and 1620, twelve Armenian churches were built in New Julfa, and by the middle of the century New Julfa had acquired its own diocese, initially overseeing Iran's Armenian Christian population but, with the growth of Julfan settlements in the Indian Ocean at the end of the century, extending its diocesan jurisdiction to Armenian churches and communities in India and Southeast Asia. At the center of the diocesan hierarchy in New Julfa and overseeing the churches in the East was All Savior's Monastery, the construction of which was completed in the early 1660s.[101]

The township also became an important Armenian cultural center during the seventeenth century and had its own printing press as early as 1638, when one of the township's primates, Bishop Khachatur Kesarats'i (Khachatur of Caesaria) learned the art of printing and cast his own fonts and printed several books.[102] Not satisfied with the results, Khachatur dispatched one of his own priests, Hovhannes Jughayets'i, to Europe in 1639 to perfect his study of the art of printing and to bring this valuable knowledge back to Julfa. Hovhannes traveled to Venice, Rome, and finally to Livorno, where he lived and worked for three and a half years and produced the first printed book in the city (1644) before returning to Julfa in 1646 with a press and resuming his work in his hometown.[103]

## URBAN LAYOUT AND ADMINISTRATIVE AUTONOMY

At the heart of New Julfa's urban layout was an avenue running east to west and parallel to the river. Known as Khiaban-i Nazar, or Nazar Avenue (still the main street in Julfa today), this thoroughfare was named after New Julfa's second *kalantar,* or mayor, Khwaja Nazar. Running north to south from the riverbank to Nazar Avenue were ten perpendicular streets that divided the oldest section of the suburb into ten districts known in Armenian as *tasnaks* (one-tenths), thus dividing the initial area of the township into ten neighborhoods, similarly to the division of European urban centers into "quarters." After the territory of the suburb was expanded in the 1650s to include lands farther south and west of the core area of "Old Julfa," extending from the riverbank to Nazar Avenue, the ten perpendicular streets were also extended south of Nazar Avenue, thus creating twenty *tasnaks,* or districts, ten each for the northern and southern parts of Nazar Avenue. Each *tasnak* appears to have been named after the wealthiest and most prominent family residing there.[104] These families also appointed their eldest members to become *kadkhudas,* or district heads, representing their neighborhoods and delegated with the responsibility of maintaining order in their districts.

The *kadkhudas* were not only in charge of administering their respective districts, but, more importantly, they were members of two special administrative bodies tasked with running day-to-day affairs in Julfa. As Shushanik Khachikian has pointed out, Julfa's twenty *kadkhudas* were members of the suburb's key administrative body known as the *Vacharakanats Zhoghov,* or Assembly of Merchants, which was composed of the *kalantar* and the twenty *kadkhudas,* and a second, larger body that we may call the Municipal Assembly, both of which will be discussed at length in chapter 7.[105]

The forced migration or deportation of the Julfan community of silk merchants from the town of Old Julfa on the Aras River in 1604, and their resettlement in a suburb of Isfahan two years later, set the stage for the economic prosperity of not only this community but also the Safavid Empire. The Julfans were an important community of "service nomads" for the Safavid dynasty for several reasons. First, they were already skilled merchants who had acquired considerable expertise in the long-distance trade of Iranian raw silk, then one of the most important commodities in the global economy, second only to Eastern spices. From the second half of the sixteenth century, merchants from Old Julfa had branched out and established trading connections with Aleppo, Venice, and possibly with Mughal India and other trading centers in Europe and East Asia. The fact that they were Christians and had the relevant cultural and language skills of Islamicate Eurasia made them ideal brokers between the Christian West and the Muslim East. Moreover, their religious "neutrality" as a Christian community exempted them from Ottoman restrictions against Iranian Shi'a merchants traveling over Ottoman territory to the markets on the Mediterranean. Second, and more importantly, as an alien community with no power interests in Iran and no national state of their own, the Julfans served as ideal "servants of power."[106] They embodied many of the traits that the sociologist Lewis Coser defines as "political eunuchism."[107] Like "court Jews" in the Habsburg Empire, they came as "foreigners" to the land where they were resettled; as such they did not have preexisting strong bonds with the local communities alongside whom they were resettled, which, in theory at least, prevented them from developing a power base in opposition to the centralizing monarch. Their resettlement in an exclusive Christian Julfan suburb across the river from central Isfahan, in what amounted to a privileged merchant ghetto, also ensured that they would not cultivate ties to potentially fractious interests in Safavid Iran. In sum, the rootless nature of the Julfans and their segregation from the larger community in their new "host society" made them ideally loyal servants to their chief patron, 'Abbas I. The latter, like his Austro-Hungarian centralizing counterparts in relation to their court Jews, could thus bestow his trust upon them and grant them privileges in exchange for their services as royal merchants responsible for generating much needed revenue for his centralizing projects.

That Shah 'Abbas I does not seem to have had a blueprint or "conscious policy" in relocating the Julfans from their original home in Old Julfa, as I have argued in this chapter, does not mean that he did not come to improvise a centralizing policy wherein his newly transplanted alien subjects would occupy a central role in his policies regarding Iran's booming silk trade. As Coser, echoing Émile Durkheim, notes, "The origin of a phenomenon does not explain its persistence or transformation."[108] In other words, whether or not Shah 'Abbas had a "planned policy" of making the Julfans one of the pillars of his political economy, as some observers have insisted, seems largely irrelevant to the discussion of what happened to the Julfans after their relocation to Isfahan. On the basis of the evidence of Armenian and European primary sources from the period, I have argued that there is little if any support for the claim that 'Abbas I had a "blueprint" in mind when he ordered the destruction of Old Julfa and the resettlement of its merchant population in the interior of Iran, far away from the war zone. On the contrary, the evidence suggests that the decision to promote the Julfans as pillars of Iran's developing silk trade was improvised *after* the Julfans had already been displaced from their homes near the Aras River.

The privileged treatment the Julfans received after their resettlement under the watchful eyes of Shah 'Abbas I in Isfahan allowed them to experience hitherto unparalleled heights of economic prosperity. Even after the revocation of the royal silk monopoly under Shah Safi (r. 1629–1642), the Julfans maintained their privileged status as the principal exporters of Iranian raw silk, largely through their ties to Armenian converts to Islam who served as prominent *ghulam* officials in the silk-producing regions near the Caspian. As a result of their privileged position in Safavid Iran's booming silk trade, within decades of their resettlement in

Iran the Julfans were able to expand from their new suburb of New Julfa and establish one of the greatest trade networks of the early modern period, when both colonialism and capitalism were beginning to coalesce as defining social formations in world history. In the next two chapters, we shall explore the Julfan expansion to the world of the Indian Ocean and their foray into the Mediterranean, Russian, and northwestern European circuits of world trade.

3

# The Julfan Trade Network I

## *The World of the Indian Ocean*

This chapter and the next provide a broad overview of the Julfan trade network in the early modern period to elucidate not only the trade settlements' connection to each other and to the nodal center in Julfa, Isfahan, but also the network's circulatory nature —that is, its circulation of credit, merchants, and information—which is the subject of chapters 5, 6, and 7. Thus our focus here and in chapter 4 is the cluster of trade settlements that formed four general circuits around New Julfa: Indian Ocean, Russian, Mediterranean, and northwestern European. The Indian Ocean circuit was arguably the most important of the Julfan network, extending out from Julfa by way of the nearby ports on the Persian Gulf (Basra, Bandar Kung, and Bandar 'Abbas) and reaching out to Mughal India, then East Asia, and finally all the way to Manila and Acapulco in the New World. This circuit of settlements was the first to be extensively settled by Julfan merchants. It served as the hub of Julfan trade activity and functioned as an important counterpart to the other pole of the Julfan network, the Mediterranean.

In presenting a settlement-by-settlement account of the Julfan trade network, I have aspired to devote as much attention to each settlement as possible in proportion to its overall importance to the network as a whole, and in proportion to the available data. Unfortunately, the data are not always readily and equally available. Moreover, sometimes the available data on a given settlement are not necessarily commensurate with that settlement's relative importance in the overall framework of the Julfan trade network, indicating instead the quality of the archival institutions in the settlement. Thus, while the discussion below will provide as much credible information on each community as the sources permit, its ultimate aim is to cast light on the overall structure of the Julfan network.

The survey outlined here and in chapter 4 is thus meant to provide a historical context for subsequent examination of the various types of circulatory flows characterizing the Julfan economy and society. It should be made clear at the outset that some of the settlements described below originated in the seventeenth century. In other words, their history can be directly traced to the founding of New Julfa in 1605. Others, however, were "relics" of the merchants of Old Julfa. Whenever possible I have endeavored to bring to light these older networks and to emphasize how they "were often enlarged, complemented, or given new life" after the creation of New Julfa in the seventeenth century.[1] In most cases, I have also explained why some of the communities settled by Julfan merchants expanded at certain points in history, while others waned, declined, and eventually disappeared.

The sources I have used to reconstruct the Julfan network consist mostly of travel literature from the period but also include, whenever possible, Julfan documents that have survived in the archives of their respective communities. I have also relied upon specialized community histories (mostly in Armenian, Italian, and Spanish), such as those found in monographs exploring the history of various Armenian "diaspora" communities.[2] While individual studies of some of the communities discussed below are available, a comprehensive study synthesizing them under the general umbrella of the Julfan commercial network is more or less nonexistent. The exception is a chapter in Edmund Herzig's dissertation, which, while quite comprehensive, neglects to discuss some Julfan communities (omitting, for example, Cadiz in Spain and the Manila-New World connection) and pays scant attention to others (such as those in the Indian Ocean). It is my intent not only to fill in some of the gaps in Herzig's otherwise outstanding discussion, but also to present a more detailed and accurate picture of some of the Julfan communities than has previously been provided by specialized monographs. To do so, I examine archival documents never before consulted, draw connections among communities and between communities in the network and the Julfan center, and explore the cultural and social dimensions of the Julfan commercial network, specifically, the building of churches (and the circulation of priests in the case of the Indian Ocean) and the establishment of printing presses and other community institutions where applicable. These community institutions, or "anchor points," as we shall see, were crucial for the long-term survival and smooth operation of the network as a whole.

## INDIA AND SETTLEMENTS

> . . . the Armenians, who were still in possession of the richest branch of the Indian commerce. These merchants [the Armenians] had, for a long time, been concerned with the linen trade. They had never been supplanted either by the Portuguese, who were intent only on plunder, or by the Dutch, whose attention was totally confined to the spice trade. They might, nevertheless, be appre-

> *hensive, that they should not be able to withstand the competition of a people who were equally rich, industrious, active, and frugal. The Armenians acted then as they have ever done since: they went to India, where they bought cotton, which they sent to the spinners; the cloths were manufactured under their own inspection, and carried to Gombroon, from whence they were transported to Ispahan. From thence were conveyed into the different provinces of the empire, the dominions of the Grand Signior; and into Europe, where the custom has prevailed of calling Persian manufactures, though they were never made but on the coast of Coromandel.*[3]
>
> *What would Madras be without the Armenians?*[4]

The earliest extant source on Armenian relations with India is an interesting twelfth-century Armenian itinerary of India and the neighboring islands of the Malay Archipelago entitled *Names of Cities in the Indies and on the Frontier of Persia*, published and scrupulously analyzed most recently by Kéram Kévonian.[5] This work, whose provenance can be traced to the first quarter of the twelfth century, indicates that some Armenians were already familiar with the distant lands of India and the Indian Ocean at that early date. As Kévonian remarks, "If their [i.e., the Armenians'] presence in Asian trade is known for the 16th–18th centuries, this text demonstrates that the latter was probably only a continuation of an ancient tradition that had its ups and downs."[6] Nonetheless, it is necessary to note here that although evidence suggests that individual Armenians such as the anonymous author of this geographical tract had visited India and Southeast Asia as early as the twelfth century, if not earlier, there is little evidence to indicate the presence of Armenian settlements in the Indian Subcontinent prior to the early modern era.[7]

By the early sixteenth century, Armenian merchants begin to crop up in European sources as using Hormuz on the mouth of the Persian Gulf for their transit trade with India.[8] The evidence indicates that a small number of Armenians were residing in that remote kingdom when the Portuguese occupied the area in 1515. In the 1580s, a Dutch official working for the Portuguese in Goa, Van Linschoten, reported that the Armenians were in Hormuz along with Persians, Turks, and Venetians.[9] Hormuz was important because of its strategic location as the passageway to Cambay and Diu on the Gujaratee coast of northwestern India, where Armenian maritime merchants were ensconced before and after the arrival of the Portuguese. From there, some Armenians ventured to southern port cities such as Goa, where Van Linschoten observed some of them in the closing decades of the sixteenth century.[10]

The first reliable references to Armenian communities in India date from the first quarter of the sixteenth century. When the Portuguese first appeared on the western coast of India in 1498 and shortly afterward began to assess their trading prospects in the southern region of the country, they found Armenians already living in those parts. The small town of Mylapur (later renamed San Thomé) on the outskirts of Madras had Armenian inhabitants in the first quarter of the sixteenth century. According to Portuguese sources, it was Armenian merchants residing in Pulikat (in the kingdom of Vijayanagar) who first led the Portuguese to the tomb of the apostle Saint Thomas in Mylapur where a small church had been built.[11] Later in the seventeenth century, Francois Martin, the founder of the French colony of Pondicherry, who retired in San Thomé to write his famous memoirs, noted the following about Armenian relations with the town:

It is held that the commencement of the building of San Thomé was the work of many Armenians who were frequenting there on account both of trade and also of their pious devotion to the saint whose name the town bears. When the Portuguese secured themselves in India, the members of that nation settled in all parts of the country, and a number of them in San Thomé, where they united with the Armenians who were already in residence there. They then built a town and residences by the help of their trade with other parts of India. It is assured that in former times there were families in this place whose opulence reached millions, and the trade in this place in the early days was a gold mine.[12]

In the middle of the same century, Armenian merchants are said to have been invited to settle in the Mughal capital of Agra by Emperor Akbar the Great (1556–1605).[13] Some Mughal accounts, such as the *Ain-i-Akbari* (Institutes of Akbar) and the *Tuzzuk-Jahangiri* (Memoirs of Emperor Jahangir), mention several prominent Armenians in Akbar's court, including a certain Abdul Hayy, described as Akbar's "minister of justice," and an Armenian merchant from Aleppo (possibly of Old Julfa origin) named Iskandar, one of whose sons, Mirza Zul Qarnain, was raised in Akbar's harem and later accorded a high rank as a *mansabdar* (Mughal military rank holder), governor of Bengal, and overseer of Mughal saltworks in Sambahar.[14] According to Mesrovb Seth, who has written the only detailed history of Armenian communities in India to date, an Armenian church was built in Agra in 1562.[15] Many decades later (1640), Father Manrique passed through Agra and paid a visit to the Armenian caravansary of the city.[16] The important commercial port of Surat to the north, which had risen to commercial prominence after the decline of Cambay in the mid-sixteenth century and was the first port of call in India for most visitors traveling to the East from the Persian Gulf ports of Basra and Hormuz, had also attracted Armenian merchants starting in the late sixteenth century, if we are to believe Seth. According to Seth, the earliest tombstone in Surat's old Armenian cemetery dates from 1579 and belongs to the wife of an Armenian priest.[17] Based on this evidence, the veracity of which might be doubtful, Seth concludes that there must have been a sizable community of Armenians in the city to warrant having a priest and most likely a church to meet its religious needs. According to an Armenian treatise on historical geography published in Venice in 1805, one of Surat's Muslim governors is said to have destroyed the Armenian church (if true, this event most probably occurred in the early part of the seventeenth century under Shah Jahan's rule, which was much less tolerant than that of Akbar and Jahangir) upon complaints by Muslim merchants returning from the pilgrimage to Mecca.[18] No physical or documentary remains of this early church, if it did exist, seem to have survived, though another church appears to have been built later in the seventeenth century to serve the needs of the city's growing Julfan community.[19] Several dozen tombstones from this church and other Armenian cemeteries in Surat have been preserved, the oldest of which dates from the 1690s.[20] Lahori Bandar in Sind also seems to have had a small Armenian community in the first decade of the seventeenth century.[21] At least two important manuscripts copied by Armenian priests in that port city in 1635 and 1641 have survived.[22] Both Surat in Gujarat and Lahori Bandar in Sindh were important hubs for Julfan merchants in the seventeenth century because of their proximity to textile-producing regions in northern India.[23]

Two events helped accelerate Armenian migration and settlement in India during the seventeenth century. The first and most important was the founding of New Julfa in 1605 through Shah 'Abbas's forced deportations of Armenians from Old Julfa, followed in 1622 by the transfer of Hormuz from Portuguese to Safavid control and the consequent opening of the Indian Ocean to Julfan merchants. In less than fifty years, merchants from New Julfa were already visiting the markets of Hyderabad, Golconda, and Masulipatam in southern India and Hugli, Patna, and Calcutta in the north. Like other merchants traveling to India from the West, Julfan Armenians must have traveled there on ships from the Persian Gulf. Since it was difficult to make a return trip to India from the Persian Gulf during the same year due to the monsoon regime regulating maritime travel across the Indian Ocean, merchants traveling to India usually allowed themselves up to two years to dispose of their goods and return home. This long layover probably encouraged the formation of new settlements in places not settled by Armenians before the almost sudden arrival of New Julfans in India. By the end of the seventeenth century, Julfans had crossed the Himalayas from Patna to establish a small community in Lhasa, the capital of Tibet (1680s–1717); around the same time they had settled in Spanish-ruled Manila on the outer limits of the Indian Ocean. They had also settled in the Dutch colony of Batavia by the middle of the eighteenth century.

The second event that spurred Armenian settlement in India was a trade agreement between the "English East India Company and the Armenian Nation," signed in London on June 22, 1688. For the company, the main objective of the agreement was to encourage the Armenians "to alter and invert the ancient course of their Trade to and from Europe,"[24] that is, to have the Armenians transport their silk to Europe on English company ships around the Cape of Good Hope, as opposed to the overland route across Ottoman territory. To this end, the company accorded the Armenians special privileges, such as "liberty at all times hereafter to pass and repass to and from India on any of the Company's Ships on as advantageous terms as any

Freeman whatsoever," as well as low customs fares.[25] The most important clause in the agreement, at least as far as Armenian migration and settlement in India are concerned, was the following: "That they shall have liberty to live in any of the Company's Cities, Garrisons, or Towns in India, and to buy, sell, and purchase Land or Houses, and be capable of all Civil Offices and preferments in the same manner as if they were Englishmen born, and shall always have the free and undisturbed liberty of the exercise of their Religion."[26]

In an addendum to the agreement, the company further agreed that

> whenever forty or more of the Armenian Nation shall become Inhabitants in any of the Garrisons, Cities or Towns belonging to the Company in the East Indies, the said Armenians shall not only have and enjoy the free use and exercise of their Religion, but there shall be also allotted to them a parcel of Ground to erect a Church thereon for the worship and service of God in their own way and that we will also at our own Charge, cause a convenient Church to be built with stone or other Solid Materials to their own good liking and the said Governor and Company will also allow fifty Pounds per annum during the space of Seven Years for the maintenance of such Priest or Minister as they shall choose to officiate therein.[27]

Low taxes, promises of integration within the English settlements of India, and especially religious tolerance enticed greater numbers of Julfan merchants to the shores of India in the seventeenth and eighteenth centuries and stimulated the establishment of new settlements alongside older ones.

Julfan merchants had settled in Bengal (the richest province of Mughal India) during the first half of the seventeenth century. They appear to have already established themselves in the area of Calcutta at least half a century before the English East India Company leased, through the mediation of the Armenian merchant Khwaja Sarhat di Israel, the villages of Sutanati, Govindapur, and Kalikata in 1698 and later established in Kalikata their factory (fortified trading outpost) of Fort William. This factory and the villages surrounding it became the nucleus of present-day Calcutta. It is interesting to note that the Armenian Church of Holy Nazareth in Calcutta (built in 1724 on the grounds that served as an old Armenian cemetery) has a tombstone purporting to date from 1630. Until the discovery of this tombstone in 1894, it was assumed that the English were the first foreign settlers of Calcutta.[28]

The most notable place in Bengal where Julfan Armenians settled in the seventeenth century was Chinsura (known to Julfans as Chichra from the local Chuchura),[29] a small town about twenty-eight miles north of Calcutta near the thriving port town of Hugli. According to Seth, their presence there dates from 1645.[30] Armenian merchants were attracted to Chinsura because of its access to Bengali raw silk and silk textiles, which they used for their "country trade" in the Indian Ocean, and because the nearby settlement of Hugli was the leading port in Bengal at the time and the area acted as the commercial headquarters in Bengal of first the Portuguese, followed by the Dutch and English East India Companies in 1645 and 1651, respectively.[31] Despite the importance of this community, our sources concerning its early history are quite meager until the last decade of the seventeenth century. In November of 1692, a Julfan merchant named Hovhannes of Julfa (Hovhannes Joughayetsi) visited Chinsura after his return from Tibet and noted in his commercial diary that he donated funds to an Armenian priest there for the celebration of church services.[32] Since the town's Armenian church was not built until three years after Hovhannes's visit, we may conclude that the Chinsura Armenians were probably using a private house for their religious services.[33] In 1695, a wealthy Armenian merchant originally from New Julfa named Khwaja Hovsep Marcarian (known as Joseph Demarcora, De Mark, or Demercora in European sources),[34] whose relatives were most likely among the first Armenian settlers of Chinsura in the middle of the seventeenth century,[35] provided 20,000 rupees for the construction of the Armenian Church of Saint John the Baptist, where he buried his brother Hovhannes Marcarian (known to Europeans as John Demarcora[36] or Khwaja Abnus[37] in Persianate circles).[38]

Chinsura's decline as a Julfan settlement began considerably earlier than the mid-nineteenth century date proposed by some scholars.[39] A letter written in 1727 by the parish priest of the Armenian Church of Chinsura indicates that the once prosperous Julfan merchant community of the town had been reduced to only three well-to-do merchants, the rest relying on the church for their sustenance. According to the letter, the town's wealthiest merchants had resettled in the neighboring English settlement at Calcutta, where the Armenian Church of Holy Nazareth was built in 1724.[40] Elsewhere in Bengal, in 1665 Julfan Armenians were apparently invited to settle in Saidabad, a suburb of the provincial capital of Bengal at Murshidabad.[41] In a manner reminiscent of their settlement in New Julfa, they were reportedly granted land on the outskirts of the city (through a royal *farman* from the Mughal emperor Aurangzeb) to build a predominantly Armenian commercial suburb.[42] The Armenian Church of the Virgin Mary was built in Saidabad in 1758.

Armenians were also present in other parts of India, including Portuguese Goa (where some were residing as early as the sixteenth century and in greater numbers after Julfans started arriving in the seventeenth and eighteenth centuries) and the French settlements of Pondicherry near Madras and Chandernagor near Calcutta.[43] Before its absorption into the Mughal Empire in 1687, the southern Indian city of Hyderabad/Bhagnagar in the kingdom of Golconda was home to a small Julfan Armenian community whose members appear to have been well integrated as "portfolio capitalists" into the higher echelons of power, along with other Iranians. The region's famed diamond mines and its gem markets as well as the fact that the ruling dynasty of the kingdom was originally from Iran and thus shared a Persianate cultural background with the Julfans were key factors that account for the Julfan presence there.[44] Bombay/Mumbai also had a Julfan community after the English East India Company acquired the area in 1668 and invited Julfan merchants from Surat to settle there.[45] Bombay had its own Armenian Church of Saint Peter's in the late eighteenth century. But arguably the most important Armenian settlement in India was located at Madras, where Julfan merchants had settled as early as 1666. Known to the Julfans by its old local name of *Chini p'atan* (from *chinapatinam*), Madras attracted a greater number of Julfans after the 1688 Agreement between the East India Company and the Armenian Nation promised favorable terms and granted them religious freedoms. A number of letters from *Chini p'atan* dating from the 1690s and stored in the All Savior's Archive in Julfa suggest that the town was already boasting a significant community of Julfans. That the English East India Company placed a great deal of importance on luring the Julfan Armenians to settle in Madras can be seen in the following project, formulated in a dispatch to Madras by the company's headquarters in London in 1691/92, of designating a special quarter of Madras as a Julfan settlement with its own Armenian church, and going so far as to suggest that this new area be called "Julpha":

> We have discoursed Sir John Goldsborough about enlarging our Christian town to a quadrangle so as it may be done without detriment to the Company with handsome stonebridges over the river in which designed new moyety of the city one quarter of that moyety may be set apart for the Armenian Christians to build their new church ... and convenient dwelling houses for their merchants ... that quarter so set apart you may call Julpha, that being the town from whence Shah 'Abbas the Great brought them when he conqueared Armenia.[46]

The first Armenian church in Madras dates from 1712 and was later replaced by another church in 1772. By the first half of the eighteenth century, the Julfan community was well integrated into the local colonial administrative institutions. A number of wealthy Julfans served as aldermen of the town, and an increasing number of merchants were making liberal use of the town's Mayor's Court for litigation purposes.[47] Julfans were attracted to Madras in the eighteenth century because, as Abbé Raynal's passage quoted at the outset of this section indicates, the Coromandel Coast (where Madras was located) had become an important center for cotton textiles. Madras was also an important regional hub for the markets in the eastern segment of the Indian Ocean and also happened to be in close proximity to the diamond-producing region of Golconda.

Madras was also the birthplace in India of Armenian printing; the first Armenian printing press was established in the city in 1771 and the first Armenian periodical/newspaper in the world, *Azdarar,* was published there, as was the first legal treatise containing a republican (proto-) constitution for a future Armenian state.[48] For much of the eighteenth century, Madras played the role of a "regional center" for the rest of Julfan trade network in the Indian Ocean. Most Julfans trading in Southeast Asia, as far away as Manila, and beyond there to Acapulco used Madras as their node and way station. Madras's status as a regional center is also attested by its prominent position within the complex network of diocesan jurisdiction that the Armenian Church in New Julfa was beginning to develop in the East. Despite Madras's importance as a trade settlement, its Armenian population seems to have been rather small, as was the case in most other settlements in the Julfan network, and does not appear to have exceeded 200 to 240 merchants (most of whom were originally from Julfa) at its peak in the 1770s.[49]

At the beginning of the seventeenth century, the Armenian communities in India came under the religious jurisdiction of All Savior's Monastery in Julfa. In order to maintain the ethno-religious identity of these communities and more effectively to collect taxes and donations from wealthy merchants, the religious hierarchy of All Savior's Monastery, led by the primate, periodically staffed the churches in India with Armenian priests sent from their mother colony in New Julfa.[50] Not much is known about the early history of New Julfa's network of diocesan sees in the East.[51] What is known is that by 1793 the following hierarchical system of diocesan authority had emerged. The senior priest of the church in Surat had authority over Armenian priests in Bombay, Shahjahanabad, Aurangabad, and Hyderabad; that of Madras had authority over the priests in Muchlibandar, Nagapatan, Pegu, and Batavia; while, after its establishment in 1724, the Church of Holy Nazareth in Calcutta had jurisdiction over the churches of Chinsura, Saidabad, and Dhaka.[52] The evidence suggests that throughout the eighteenth century, Armenian churches in India had two or three priests posted there at any given time. These priests maintained regular communication with their primate in New Julfa, using the same commercial mail system devised and used by Armenian merchants across New Julfa's vast commercial network. The church's own network of diocesan sees in India and Southeast Asia mirrored the commercial network of Julfan merchants in much of the Indian Ocean and, in fact, helped reinforce the commercial network by acting as a parallel conduit of information and intelligence sharing, as we shall see in chapter 5.

## TIBET AND CHINA

Virtually nothing was known about the tiny community of Julfan merchants in Tibet until 1968, when a valuable accounting ledger belonging to a Julfan merchant named Hovhannes of Julfa, who had resided in Tibet for six years in the 1690s, was discovered in the National Library in Lisbon and studied by the renowned Armenian scholars Levon Khachikian and Hakob Papazian.[53] The publication of *The Accounting Ledger of the Merchant Hovhannes Tēr Davt'yan of Julfa* in 1984 was a milestone in the study of Julfan history, not only because the document shed light on numerous aspects of Julfan commercial practice, but also because it brought to light the existence of an Armenian community in the Tibetan capital of Lhasa during the last three decades of the seventeenth century. Since little documentation on this community has come down to us, it is difficult to say when it was established. What we know with certainty is that Julfan merchants had been conducting commerce in Tibet at least since the early 1660s. It must have been sometime afterward that a small community of resident Julfan merchants settled in the remote Himalayan country.

For Julfan Armenians, Tibet seems to have been an extension of their trade networks in Bengal and northern India, as most merchants who eventually traded and resided in Lhasa traveled there by way of the region around Calcutta, Chinsura (Chichra/Hugli), and especially Patna and north across the Himalayas through Nepal (known as Bhutand in Julfan sources). This, at any rate, was the route followed by Hovhannes, as is evident from his journal. Musk, precious stones, and Chinese gold were exchanged in Tibet for Indian textiles, amber, and pearls.[54]

According to the correspondence of Italian missionaries in Tibet, there were about five wealthy Julfan mercantile families residing in Lhasa in the 1680s and 1690s.[55] Many were there with their "Christian slaves" (i.e., their agents or servants). One merchant whose name crops up on numerous occasions in *Missionari Italiani nel Tibet e nel Nepal,* a seven-volume collection of missionary reports sent to the Propaganda Fide headquarters in the Vatican, was a certain Khwaja Dawith or Davuth (David), who is said to have hosted and provided housing expenses for the first Capuchin missionaries in Lhasa, when they arrived there from India in 1706–1707.[56] This same merchant later purchased a house for the missionaries and financially supported them by building a small chapel for their use. Since the Armenian community did not have its own house of prayer in Tibet, it is probable that they relied upon the Capuchin missionaries for their religious needs and thus generously supported their mission there.[57]

The Julfan community seems to have been well integrated in its remote colony. When the first missionaries arrived in 1707, some Armenians, such as Khwaja Dawith, had already been residing in Tibet for over twenty years and were naturally well versed in the customs and languages of their host society. Their ability to straddle both local Tibetan customs and those of the European missionaries made them ideal "go-betweens" for the work of the missionaries. Indeed, Khwaja Dawith is said to have translated a book of catechism into Tibetan at the request of his missionary friends.[58] Moreover, the resident Julfans had connections with some of the elite members of Tibetan society, including the Dalai Lama of the period, and were granted special privileges, as can be seen from a "Tibetan passport from 1688" granted to an Armenian merchant traveling back to Julfa by way of northern India.[59]

One of the principal attractions of Tibet for Julfan merchants was its strategic location near the Chinese heartland. Most Julfan trading firms had agents residing in the Chinese city of Sining (Slink according to Julfan sources),[60] where silver was more prized than gold, as elsewhere in China. Interestingly, Julfan merchants were so familiar with the route to China that they were the main informants to the European missionaries who were then eager to gain access to those areas. One such missionary, Giambattista di Sarravalle, notes in his report to his superiors in Rome that Armenian merchants in Julfa and India informed him of the routes to China. He further attests that Armenian merchants were present in some of the caravansaries of China, especially in Sining.[61]

The Julfan community of Tibet did not have a long history. It seems to have come to an abrupt end in 1717, following the invasion of Tibet by the Mongolian Dsungars (Juun Ghar) and the Chinese occupation of the country in 1720, after which Tibet remained closed to foreigners until the early years of the last century.[62]

## BURMA

The history of the Burmo-Armenian community before the nineteenth century is scarcely studied, and only a single document in Armenian pertaining to this community before the nineteenth century seems to have survived.[63] There are two schools of thought on the history of Armenian settlements in Burma. One school maintains that the Armenian communities of Burma were extensions of the larger communities in India and, therefore, were established at a later period than the Armenian communities in India. Another school, however, claims that the Burmese Armenian community was actually founded around the same time if not earlier than its counterparts in India.

As sketchy as the available evidence on Armenians in Burma is, it suggests that Armenian merchants had traveled and settled there decades before the destruction of Old Julfa in 1604 by Shah 'Abbas. This places the Burmese Armenian community on the same footing as the communities in Aleppo and Venice, as we shall see in chapter 4. According to G. E. Harvey, when the southern Mon port city of Martaban fell to the forces of the Burmese Toungoa dynasty in 1541 and suffered three days of looting, an immense booty was taken from the warehouses of merchants of many "races," including Iranians, Armenians, Abyssinians, and Jews.[64] Another source notes the presence of Armenians as mercenaries in the Burmese army in 1545.[65] These two references are notable because of their relatively early date, indicating the possible presence of Armenian merchants in Burma well before the destruction of Old Julfa. The mercenary connection is also intriguing because it suggests that Armenian resident merchants in Burma were not simply "trade diaspora" merchants devoid of political interests, but integrated into the military and political establishment of their host society, a trait that seems to have been prominent in the Julfan-Burmese community in the eighteenth and nineteenth centuries.[66]

In the seventeenth century, less than a decade after the founding of New Julfa, Armenian merchants had settled in Syriam, the leading port of Burma in the seventeenth and early eighteenth centuries. Harvey, apparently consulting documents in the archives of the Armenian Church of Rangoon, claims that the Armenians first settled in Syriam in 1612.[67] The English traveler Alexander Hamilton, who visited the country in the early 1700s, noted: "There are some Christians in Syrian [read: Syriam] of the *Portuguese* offspring and some *Armenians*."[68] He further remarks that "the town [of Syriam] drives a good trade with *Armenians, Portuguese, Moors,* and *Gentows* [Hindu Indians] and some English . . . but the *Armenians* have got the Monopoly of the Rubies, which turns to a good Account in their trade."[69]

According to Hamilton, by the late 1690s, the Armenians of Madras had wrested control of the town's maritime trade with Pegu from the English.[70] Given the extensive nature of Armenian trade relations with Burma, it should not come as a surprise that Pegu had a resident Armenian community, with a solid Julfan majority, beginning in the second half of the seventeenth century. We know from a letter stored in the Archivio di Stato of Venice that the Sceriman (Shahrimanian) family of Armenian Catholics who had left Julfa in the seventeenth century to settle in Livorno and Venice (see chapter 6) also had a family member or factor residing in Pegu in 1676, which is when the above-noted letter was sent to them in Livorno.[71] We learn that about a decade later a wealthy Armenian merchant residing in Hyderabad in the kingdom of Golconda in southern India had moved to Pegu with his wife and children.[72]

The Julfan community in Burma seems to have been connected to the nodal center of the Julfan network in New Julfa not only through the circulation of merchants, but also through that of priests. According to the scant sources on the Armenian communities in Burma, there were Armenian churches in the following cities in the kingdom: Ava (built sometime in the seventeenth century); Syriam[73] (pre-1743 and 1756);[74] Mandalay (1863); Rangoon (1769, renovated in 1844?).[75] The communities in Burma were under the religious jurisdiction of All Savior's Monastery in Julfa, which periodically used to dispatch priests to Julfan settlements in the East to meet their religious and cultural needs. This circulation of priests from Julfa to Burma must have existed as early as the last decades of the seventeenth century, but at some point in the early part of the next century ties appear to have broken down, for we read the following reminder concerning the need for new priests in the East in a 1711 letter sent by an Armenian priest in Madras to the primate of Julfa: "I beg your eminence to send us three fine priests during the next monsoon, two of them for Madras, and one for Pegu; our community in Pegu has been begging me of late, saying that they have been left without a priest for some time."[76]

Julfans had also settled in Rangoon in the eighteenth century, where they played an important role both as merchants and as diplomatic go-betweens (political advisers and ministers) to various Burmese kings, thus embodying what Sanjay Subrahmanyam and C. A. Bayly have called "portfolio capitalists."[77] As Victor Lieberman puts it, at "various times between 1685 and 1737, Armenian traders are said to have enjoyed considerable influence in official circles at both Ava and Syriam."[78] Their go-between role as translators and as a crucial source of information to the

British (with whom they had an ambivalent relationship) continued into the nine-teenth century, as is attested by Bayly.[79] A legal document written in the Julfa dialect by several Julfan merchants residing in Rangoon in 1757 and preserved in the private papers of Dutch merchant Baron Van Heck suggests that a small community of Julfans was settled in Rangoon in the mid-eighteenth century and was active in the maritime trade of the region.[80]

## MARITIME SOUTHEAST ASIA

In his famous manual of trade written as a textbook for the education of young Julfan merchants in the 1680s, Constant Jughayetsi provides the following itinerary of emporia and towns in the world of the Indian Ocean where Julfan merchants were plying their trade in the second half of the seventeenth century:

> In moving from the East to the West, we come first to Multan; 2) Lahor; 3) Sehrend; 4) Janapat [Shahjahanabad?]; 5) Akparapad [Akbarabad], which is Egra; 6) Khurja and Hntvan; 7) Bangala; 8) Bihar Patana; 9) Benares; 10) Movn; 11) Ghazipur; 12) Jaralpur [??]; 13) Shahzadapur; 14) Kherapat [Heirabad?]; 15) Gariyapat [?]; 16) Dovlatapat; 17) Srhenjn [Sironj?], from which one enters Purupna [??]; 18) Beran-pur; 19) Surat; 20) Gujarat; 21)Avrankapat; 22) Shakar [?], from which one enters Pu-rupna [vor esdonk dakhil i purupna ???!!]; 23) Heytarapat; 24) Muchlibandar; 25) Pegu and Ava, which is under the dominion of the king of Pegu [or e Pegva takavorin Payi takht'n]; 26) Butand; 27) Khata and Khuta; 28) Zirpat; 29) Cochin; 30) Selan [Ceylon]; 31) Malaka; 32) Jakatra *[sic]*, which some call Batavia; 33) T'rnati; 34) Ambun [Am-boin]; 35) Mukasar (Maccasar); 36) Timur [Timor]; 37) S'lhor [solor]; 38) Manila; 39) Sharinov [Siam]; 40) Jabal'sdan [Japan??].[81]

Most of the emporia listed under numbers 25 to 40 are situated in Southeast Asia or "insular Asia" and, as Constant Jughayetsi's list indicates, were seen by Julfans as natural extensions of Julfan settlements in Mughal India.[82] Though Julfan merchants visited most of the places listed by Constant, not all of them had Julfan settlements.

The earliest reference to Armenian merchants in Southeast Asia predates the founding of New Julfa. Writing in the early 1510s, the Portuguese writer Tome Pires noted the involvement of "Christian Armenians" alongside other Asians in the monsoon trade of Malacca, which had just come under Portuguese dominance. He comments: "These Armenians come and take up their companies for their cargo in Gujarat, and from there they embark in March and sail direct for Malacca; and on their return journey they call at the Maldive Islands."[83]

As in Mughal India, the founding of New Julfa in 1605 stimulated a larger Armenian presence in Southeast Asia. Most of the Armenian settlements there were established by Julfan merchants as offshoots of their mercantile communities in India. Julfan presence in Malacca and Penang (present-day Malaysia) is dated in the first half of the eighteenth century, though a Julfan merchant named Khwaja

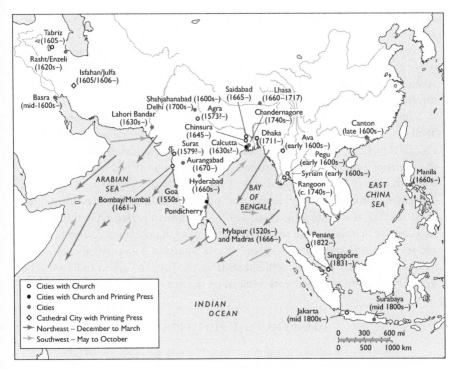

MAP 1. The Julfan Armenian trade network and settlements in the early modern Indian Ocean world.

Solima[n] is recorded as a resident in Macassar as early as 1654.[84] By the following century, a small Julfan community had taken root under Dutch colonial rule. In Penang, the community had its own church (built in 1822) and local constitution. In Java and Batavia in particular, the Julfans had their own school in the nineteenth century as well as a local community constitution. Julfan communities also existed in Surabaya, Macassar/Moluccas, and possibly Bali. In the same period, a Julfan community had sprung up in British-controlled Singapore, also with its own church (Saint Gregory's Church), built in 1834, and even a short-lived community newspaper.[85]

On the South China coast, Canton had attracted a small number of Julfan merchants soon after the Chinese began to welcome more foreign traders to their shores in the 1680s and 1690s. The Frenchman François Froger, who arrived in Canton on the ship L'Amphitrite in 1698, discovered Julfan merchants in the city already trading with Macao and Manila.[86] Julfans traded with Canton from India (mostly from Madras) and were involved with the tea trade. A 1783 census referred to by Hosea Balou Morse lists one Danish and one English resident in Canton and "about thirty Armenians."[87] One of these Armenians, Mateos ordi Ohanessi (known in European sources as Matheus Joannes), who died in Canton in 1794, was a naturalized Portuguese subject and appears to have emerged in the 1780s and 1790s as "a prominent player in both the Macao and Canton trade" and "one of the most prominent private merchants in China."[88] His estimated net worth was said to have been several times the annual budget of Macao. Portuguese Macao also had a small but thriving Julfan community in the eighteenth century.

Similarly, a small number of Julfans appear to have settled in Siam (present-day Thailand) as early as the 1670s. The area was known to Julfans as Sharinov (<P: Shah'r i Nau, "New City," or Shah'r i Nav, "City of Boats"—the name ascribed to the medieval city of Ayuthaya), where a sizable Iranian community had settled in the seventeenth century.[89] At the funeral of the French bishop de Bérythe in 1679 enough Armenians (probably mostly Julfans) were present in the Thai city to be mentioned by nationality as attending his obsequies.[90] A document preserved in the All Savior's Archive in Julfa/Isfahan records the death of a Julfan *commenda* agent trading and residing in Sharinov in the 1680s.[91] These Southeast Asian settlements served to link the network of Julfan settlements from the Persian Gulf to India with the most distant node of the network situated on the rim of the Pacific Ocean.

## MANILA (THE PHILIPPINES)

*There has been increasing evidence of voyages between the Indian Ocean ports and Manila financed chiefly by Armenian merchants in India. The whole subject of Armenian activities in India, especially in Bengal, needs more attention, preferably by a scholar with an Armenian background.[92]*

The paucity of archival evidence does not permit us at present to date the first settlement of Julfan merchants in Manila.[93] The available evidence, from both the English East India Company records and the Spanish documents in the Archivo de Indias in Seville (Spain), indicates that Julfan merchants were already conducting trade with the Philippines as early as the middle of the seventeenth century, that is only fifty years or so after the founding of New Julfa. Most Julfans trading in Manila seem to have done so by way of Surat and especially Madras, relying on the profitable maritime route from India to Manila.[94] The Spanish ban on English and French commerce with the Philippines, aimed at protecting Spanish merchants from their more powerful European rivals by making it officially illegal for ships flying the colors of those nations to trade in the Philippines, was a great boon not only for local Asian shipping (both Chinese and Mughal), but especially for Armenian merchants.[95] Taking advantage of this window of opportunity, Armenian merchants (predominantly if not exclusively from Julfa) began sailing their ships directly from their outposts in India to Manila. Most Armenian-owned (or -leased) ships flew their own "Armenian colors"—red, yellow, and red, with the Lamb of God in the middle yellow stripe.[96] Contemporary records testify that this flag was respected not only in the Philippines, but also in some Portuguese ports in the Indian Ocean, such as Cochin on the Malabar Coast of India.[97]

Julfan merchants seem to have been pioneers in the Indian Ocean maritime trade with the Philippines (known in English records as the "Manilha Trade"). Probably one of the first privately owned vessels to sail from India to Manila was that of the Julfan shipping tycoon Khwaja Minas of Surat, who sent his ship, the *Hopewell,* to the Spanish outpost on its maiden voyage in 1668.[98] By the late seventeenth century, a significant number of the vessels sailing from India to Manila were either Armenian-owned or sailed with Julfan Armenian captains. Some of the East India Company's vessels also flew "Armenian colors," thereby avoiding the Spanish ban on their commerce in the Philippines. Most operated in the maritime corridor between Madras and Manila. The "country trade," that is, port-to-port trade within the Indian Ocean, with the Philippines was a lucrative one for Julfan merchants operating out of India.[99]

The principal commodities circulating between India and Manila were silk (both Iranian and local Indian varieties) as well as Bengali textiles and Chinese goods purchased in Malacca and Canton, cinnamon from Ceylon purchased in Batavia for the Manila market, all of which Julfan merchants traded in Manila in exchange for Spanish silver from Acapulco.[100] So successful was the Julfan role in this "country trade" that by the last quarter of the seventeenth century, English private traders as well as East India Company officials were hiring Armenian captains (a practice referred to as using "dummies") as well as flying Armenian colors on their own vessels to gain access to the Manila market. The Spanish author José Montero y Vidal, writing in the nineteenth century, referred to the drawbacks of Spanish commercial policy and how the Spanish ban on trade with English and French merchants was so frequently circumvented by means of Armenian go-betweens:

> And the merchants of Manila, not being able to frequent the ports of India held by the English, the Dutch, [and] the Portuguese, when European commerce acquired its natural development in those said countries, other nations benefited from the grants of monopoly so foolishly conceded to the Chinese; *moreover, those among the English and French who were in the know regarding our absurd system began to appear in the port of Manila in ships flying flags of Asian nations and with goods coming from those places, carrying aboard them an Armenian or Moorish front man as the owner of the expedition, at times acting as though they were the real captains or supercargoes [of the vessels].* And thus it happened that the foreigners succeeded in carrying out their contracts in the business houses and even bargaining in the offices of the governor despite the presence of those who were charged with enforcing such strict laws.[101]

It should occasion no surprise, therefore, that Charles Lockyer, an English traveler and former servant to the East India Company, counseled his enterprising readers eager to learn about business opportunities in India to invest in Armeniansponsored shipping ventures to the Philippines: "Manila under Armenian colours is a profitable voyage."[102]

Though tolerated for many years by careless Spanish officials in Manila, this practice did not go unnoticed for long. Indeed, the Spanish crown seems to have introduced some draconian measures to crack down on this illicit trade, so much so that at least one Julfan merchant was prosecuted by the Real Audiencia of Manila (the highest legal body in the Spanish colony)[103] in the 1660s and 1680s. The records of these *autos* (or court minutes) against Julfan merchants are stored in the Archivo de Indias in Seville and have a great deal to reveal about this aspect of Julfan trade, which overlapped with the coexisting and rival network of the English East India Company in the Indian Ocean.[104]

Julfan merchants were not only maritime traders occasionally visiting Manila for the monsoonal trade. Some Julfans had also settled in the Spanish colony, thus setting up a communal infrastructure for their peripatetic compatriots who circulated between the ports of the Indian Ocean and Manila. Unfortunately, little light has been cast on the history and composition of this resident merchant community, since we possess few pertinent documents from the period. However, we know from the fragmentary evidence of travelers that has reached us that a Spanish decree of 1713 forced "all Moros, Armenians, Malabars, Chinese, and other enemies of the Holy Faith" to reside in Manila's Parián ghetto; subsequently, it seems that the Armenians moved out and settled in a residential area known as Santa Cruz, on the outskirts of Manila.[105] Their numbers must have been very small at the time (Inquisition depositions given by Julfans converting to Catholicism in the 1730s indicate that there were, not counting those already converted to Catholicism, around ten "schismatic" Julfan merchants residing in Manila at the time),[106] and they did not have a church of their own.

Despite the lure of New World silver, trading and especially residing in Manila posed a number of difficulties for Julfan merchants. First and foremost, there were the great distances to be overcome. Most Julfans traveling to the Spanish outpost would have to travel by way of Basra to either Surat or Madras and use the subcontinent as a way station to the Philippines. We have a number of remarkable itineraries from the first part of the eighteenth century left in the Inquisition office in Manila by Julfan merchants (most of whom were *commenda* agents trading and residing for long stretches of time in Manila) that shed important light on this question. Most arrived in India from Julfa at a young age and briefly resided in places like Madras, where they could rely on the local Julfan community, before boarding a Julfan Armenian ship to Manila. The case of the merchant Zafar di Xavier is an interesting one because it demonstrates the uses Julfan merchants traveling over enormous distances made of fellow Julfans with whom they resided while en route to faraway destinations. Zafar, it seems, had left Julfa at the tender age of sixteen in search of his father who had probably left home without leaving any information about his safety or whereabouts. By the time Zafar had caught up with his father in Madras and traveled with him to Manila he had decided, like many Julfans in Manila, to convert to Catholicism. During a brief visit to the Inquisition in 1734 to profess his faith, Zafar left an interesting record of his misadventures across Basra, Pondicherry, and Madras, and all the way to Manila. The Inquisition officer responsible for hearing Zafar's "confession" recorded the following response to the Inquisition's formulaic question as to "where he was born, who his parents were, what sect or religion he adhered to and in which provinces and places he has lived until the present moment and how long he has resided in each place and what sciences or arts he has studied":

He said that he was born in the neighborhood of Julfa of Isfahan, the court of Persia, and there he was raised and lived until he was a little over fifteen years of age and that his parents belonged to the sect of the same Armenian heresy, and that at the age of fifteen, he got married in the same neighborhood, to a damsel named Mamakhatun, daughter also of schismatics, and after completing his sixteenth year, he left Julfa for Basra, the port city of the Great Turk, in search of his father, Nazar Agamal, where he was for about one month. And not running into his father there, he left for Pondicherry, a port on the coast of Coromandel, where he resided for about eleven months, living at the house of one of his countrymen named Elias Isaac,[107] and from there he left, in search of his father, for the coast of Madras, where he lived for the said eleven months, and there [i.e., in Madras] he lived for only fifteen days, and from the said Madras he traveled, in the company of his father, to this city of Manila, where it has been seven months since he has arrived, and he is staying with his father. [He also said that] he has not studied any science or the arts but only reading and writing in the script of the Armenian language and that here in Manila he has started to learn the Christian doctrine in the Spanish language, and his design [in life] has been to apply himself to the vocation of trade.[108]

Zafar's case is broadly representative of the dozens of such itineraries left by Julfans at the Inquisition office in the Philippines. In most cases, the evidence suggests that the voyage to Manila was punctuated by brief layovers in Southeast Asian ports such as Batavia, Bantam, or Canton, where the traveling merchants would purchase goods to sell in Manila. The distances covered by these voyages were enormous, and some trips lasted for several years and up to a decade or two. In one case, at least, a *commenda* agent named Santiago di Barrachiel has left us a mind-boggling itinerary including his movements not only in the Indian Ocean but also across Russia to Amsterdam with a number of stopovers in northern Europe (Amsterdam, Anvers, etc.) and the Mediterranean (including stints in Venice, Livorno, and Malta) before resuming his travels by way of India and Southeast Asia to Manila, where he resided for several years.[109] For some Julfans, Manila was not the terminal point of their travels. The records indicate that several Julfan merchants used the Spanish colonial outpost as a point of departure to the New World. In response to the same ques-

tion posed earlier to Zafar, another Julfan merchant named Nazar di Aghamal provided the following impressive response in 1735:

> He said that he was born in the neighborhood of Julfa at the court of Isfahan, and he
> remained there until the age of seventeen and that his parents were Aghamal di Tsatur
> and Valide, raised in the sect of the Armenian heresy. And that at the age of seven-
> teen, he left Julfa at Isfahan for Moscow to conduct commerce, and from Moscow he
> went to Holland; from Holland to Moscow and from Moscow to Isfahan, where he
> resided for about three years, and from there he again departed for Moscow and from
> Moscow for Holland and from Holland to Koln [Colonia, i.e., in Germany] and from
> Koln to Venice and from Venice to Livorno and from Livorno to Smyrna [Csmirna],
> and from Smyrna he returned to Isfahan, where he resided for the second time for
> about three years, and from where he departed for the port of Madras, on the Coro-
> mandel coast, where he reached at the age of twenty-two, and from there he made a
> trip to Batavia and trips to this city of Manila, where at the age of twenty-six he at-
> tempted to go to Acapulco, and in fact he embarked on the ship of Santa [?], which
> was moored at the port straits. He has studied to read and write in the language of his
> country [i.e., in Julfan Armenian], that he has not undertaken more studies other than
> to read the Bible in Armenian a few times, and that his training and vocation for his
> entire life have been in commerce.[110]

Where Nazar failed, others succeeded. Thus a Julfan merchant named Gregorio
de Xavier successfully traveled to Acapulco in the 1730s on the Manila galleon and
spent about five months in that distant port before returning to Manila on the same
ship.[111] In another case, we have documentation from a Julfan named Don Pedro
di Zarate (Agha Petros di Sarhat?), possibly a member of the famous Catholic Armenian family known as the Scerimans/Shahrimanians,[112] who was a resident merchant in Mexico City in the 1720s and fortunately, for us at least, was hauled before
the Mexican Inquisition on charges of heresy.[113] Don Pedro had also traveled to New
Spain from Manila and had arrived in Acapulco sometime in 1722 before moving
to Mexico City to take up his residence there. He was still residing there until 1731,
when he was compelled to appear before the Inquisition for a second time. According to his deposition, he had arrived in Mexico with the objective of traveling to
Spain, Rome, and finally England, where he had a brother.[114] His trial proceedings
indicate that there were at least three other Armenians in Mexico, including a
Catholic missionary named Domingo Giraganian who was stationed at the Dominican mission in Yucatan. Yet a few others traveled further, such as the Julfan
Juan Bautista Jacome, who had arrived in Mexico from Cadiz in the 1690s and had
later settled in Peru.[115]

Religion was the second difficulty with trading in Manila that Julfans had to overcome. The Spanish authorities appear to have been tolerant enough to allow Julfan
merchants to settle there despite the fact that, in the eyes of the Vatican, the Armenian Gregorian Church, to which most Julfans nominally belonged, was regarded

as a heretical and schismatic entity. Conversion to Catholicism, however, brought with it many advantages, especially to merchants who desired to conduct trade in Manila for longer periods. It thus comes as no surprise that several dozen Julfans are recorded throughout the eighteenth century as having visited the Inquisition office in Manila to undergo the process of "secret conversion." Many of these *conversos* converted mainly for strategic and practical reasons, often reverting to their Armenian Gregorian faith upon returning to Julfa.[116] This is not to say that all Julfan converts to Catholicism were "trickster travelers." Some like Khwaja Petros di Woscan, the famous Julfan merchant of Madras who had also converted to Catholicism in Manila, appear to have been "sincere" converts.[117] On the whole, however, most Julfan merchants had a rational and practical attitude when it came to matters of identity, including religious identity, and this applied to Catholicism as well as Islam. In this respect, the Julfans were similar to Sephardic Jewish *conversos* or "crypto-Jews" in the Mediterranean.[118] It is in fact thanks to these conversions that we have a valuable trail of documentation about the activities of various Julfans in the Philippines.[119]

Numerically small though their presence in Manila may have been, the Julfans appear to have left a lasting impression on Spanish officials interested in reviving the trade of their realm. In this connection, it is interesting to note that as late as 1792, Dom Josef di Perreira Viana, a consultant to the board of directors or *junta* of the Real Compania de Filipinas, founded in 1785, recommended that the upstart company sign a treaty with the Julfan Armenians and invite them to officially settle in Manila.[120] In his report, entitled "The Method I Propose to Make Manila the [Principal] Emporium in the Gulf of China,"[121] submitted to the *junta,* Viana had rather glowing things to say about the reputation of the Julfan Armenian merchants:

> The Armenians, among whom are a number of Catholics, are the most capable and astute businessmen in all of Asia; they know the trading centers and deal with all the manufacturers both in the coastal areas as well as the interior of those countries. It is they who have taught the English the commerce of that part of the world, and they who have made with them [i.e., the English] on 22 June 1688 a treaty bringing their skills to their [i.e., English] establishments. However, the English having reneged on their promises, the Armenians now find themselves disappointed with this nation and feel oppressed by the impediments that have been imposed upon them. Experience demonstrates that whatever country where the Armenians have settled, they have not only enriched it with the great wealth they have brought with them, but have also made industrious through their skill and through their relations with that country.[122]

Imitating the earlier Julfan treaty with the English East India Company, Viana then proposed that the newly created Royal Philippine Company "invite the Armenians to the Philippine Islands and bring through them the manufactures of the Coromandel Coast and Bengal."[123] He argued that this could be achieved by signing a treaty with the Armenians containing the following cardinal points: (1) that the Armenians "enjoy the same privileges as the Spaniards"; (2) that they "be able to live in any ports of those islands and to have trading settlements"; (3) "that they be eligible to hold any office"; (4) "that they be exempt from paying more customs fees than the Spaniards"; and (5) that "they be allowed to navigate with full freedom to any of the ports of Asia."[124] For Viana, the settlement of the Armenians in the Philippines would result in "attracting all the manufactures and fruits of all of Asia by means of the extension they would give to the port-to-port trade [i.e., the "country trade"] in the Indian Ocean."[125] This to him could only benefit the Royal Philippine Company and the economy of Manila as the Armenians had done, in Viana's mind, for the English East India Company and its settlements in India. It is important to note here that while Viana's proposal was self-consciously modeled on the 1688 treaty between the Armenians and the English East India Company, the main points of which are reproduced in his document, Viana did not and probably could not offer the Armenians the freedom to build their own churches and tend to their religious needs by following their own church.[126] This was not an option for Viana probably because of the powerful influence the Inquisition still had on Spanish colonial life. That is why Viana went to great lengths and exaggerations persuading the company's *junta* that there were a great number of Armenians who followed the Catholic rite and were loyal to the Church of Rome.[127] What Viana did not realize was that Catholics represented a negligible minority among Julfan merchants and Armenians in general. He also failed to note that by the time he drafted his proposal in 1792, Julfa had collapsed as a nodal center of a global trade network, and Julfans, for the most part, had ceased being "the most capable and astute businessmen in all of Asia," as Viana had thought they were.

The surviving documentation does not permit us to say anything about how Viana's proposal was received by the *junta* of the Royal Philippine Company or what became of this interesting but ill-conceived plan once again to attract the Julfans to relocate the center of their commerce. At any rate, the evidence suggests that Julfan migration peaked for a short period following the opening of the port of Manila to foreigners in 1790 but declined sharply afterward;[128] a small number of Julfans continued visiting and trading in Manila in the early nineteenth century,[129] and then maintained a shadowy presence there until the early 1820s, when they "flocked out of Manila."[130] One factor in bringing the Julfan presence in Manila to an end was the cessation of silver shipments to the Philippines after the independence of Mexico and Peru.

The Armenian presence in the world of the Indian Ocean overlapped with the expansion of European maritime networks in the region. The Portuguese, followed in quick succession by the English, the Dutch, and the French, extended their network into the space where the Armenians had already settled. How did the Armenian network resemble or differ from the other European networks? The Julfans, as we have seen, had come to establish a far-flung network by the late seventeenth century, which, like those of their European counterparts, was also anchored in one nodal center (New Julfa for the Julfan Armenians, and Lisbon, London, Amsterdam, or Paris for the Europeans). Furthermore, both Julfan and European company networks functioned on the basis of a nodular structure overseas in which the nodes (community settlements for the Julfans, and the "factory" system of trade settlements for the European companies) were connected to each other as well as to the nodal center through various types of circulatory flows. However, while there are some similarities between the Julfan Armenian expansion into India and the Indian Ocean and the parallel European proliferation, crucial differences separate the two. Like other Asian trading networks, the Julfan Armenian engagement with the Indian Ocean was *not* accompanied and supported by a European-style armed and mobile state that did not shirk from resorting to violence to defend its state-chartered East India Companies and their monopolies of trade. The Julfans established trade settlements across vast stretches of the Indian Ocean, but they did not create a militarized trading-post empire with fortified trading settlements, as the Europeans did; also, unlike the European-chartered companies, the Julfans did not have a private army nor did their mercantile vessels routinely travel with armed cannon on board. "Rather than elbow their way in," the Julfans, like their Hadrami counterparts from Yemen, "comported themselves to local arrangements wherever they went. They settled and sojourned in towns big and small and entered into relations with locals that were more intimate, sticky, and prolonged than the Europeans could countenance."[131]

As we have seen, the Julfan presence in the world of the Indian Ocean and extending to the rim of the Pacific and beyond was indeed impressive and far-flung. This presence, however, was only one part of a much larger network. In the next chapter, we shall explore the expansion of the Julfan network from the Indian Ocean toward the Mediterranean and Europe in the west and the Russian Empire in the north.

4

# The Julfan Trade Network II

## The Mediterranean, Northwestern European, and Russian Networks

The extension of the Julfan network into the "West"—the Mediterranean, northwestern European, and Russian circuits—was one of its distinctive features and an important reason for its continuous growth and prosperity in the seventeenth and first half of the eighteenth century. Western expansion made the Julfan merchant community an important bridge in the early modern period for economic and cultural encounters between the two great zones of the world economy, the Mediterranean and the Indian Ocean, as well as the Eurasian landmass, which was a link between these zones. Julfan merchants who circulated and made a living in this network did not limit themselves to one or two of its settlements but often were residents in multiple states, empires, and regions simultaneously. Many Julfan merchants spoke half a dozen languages and felt as at home in the largely Islamicate world of the Indian Ocean as they did in the Christian world of Europe and the Mediterranean. One could argue that the Julfans were among the leading "trans-imperial subjects," borrowing Natalie Rothman's term for "men and women who straddled and brokered political, linguistic, and religious boundaries between the Venetian and Ottoman empires in the sixteenth and seventeenth centuries,"[1] or, in my own terminology, "transimperial cosmopolitans" of the early modern period, and one of the few mercantile communities whose network spanned the Mughal, Ottoman, and Safavid empires, Muscovite Russia, Qing China, and the rising seaborne empires of the British and the Dutch and the residual empire of the Portuguese Estado da India. Because of the vast nature of their network, Julfan Armenians were able to live in a cultural world whose ethos embodied "transimperial cosmopolitanism," a world that was to vanish for the most part after the erection of cultural, linguistic, and national boundaries beginning in the late eighteenth and nineteenth centuries.

This chapter explores the cosmopolitan world of Julfan merchants in the Mediterranean, western European, and Russian zones through its component parts . It begins with a discussion of Julfan settlements in the Levant, explores their links with other settlements in the Mediterranean and northwestern Europe, and concludes with a brief assessment of Julfan settlements across the Eurasian landmass in the Russian Empire.

## ALEPPO

At the beginning of the seventeenth century, an Armenian scribe from Poland named Simeon Lehatsi passed through Aleppo on his way to Jerusalem.[2] He noted the presence of two Armenian churches and a community boasting about three hundred households (or roughly 1,500 individuals) with many wealthy Armenian merchants.[3] The most prominent, according to him, were originally from Old Julfa.

Armenians began to settle in Aleppo in the second half of the sixteenth century. They were mostly from Marash and Zeytun in the nearby region of Cilicia.[4] Toward the end of the sixteenth century, another wave of Armenians, predominantly from the town of Old Julfa, arrived in Aleppo. Although the city's Armenian population was mixed, representing Armenians from both the Ottoman and the Safavid empires, the dominant group among the Armenian merchants of Aleppo were from (Old) Julfa. The latter were attracted to Aleppo principally for two reasons: first, the politically and militarily unstable situation of their town astride the Ottoman and Safavid frontiers, which drove them to seek safer havens elsewhere; and, second, Aleppo's rapid economic rise as one of the leading centers for European merchants in the Levant. As a result of treaties between the Ottomans and various European powers in the first half of the sixteenth century, Aleppo had become the most important entrepôt for Iranian raw silk exports to Europe during the sixteenth and part of the seventeenth century.[5] By the middle of the sixteenth century, the city's fame as a distribution center for Iranian silk and spices from the East had attracted Venetian, English, French, and Dutch merchants.[6]

The first mention of Julfan merchants at Aleppo dates from the last quarter of the fifteenth century, according to Artavazd Surmeyan.[7] "By the 1550s the local Armenian community counted in its ranks a large number of prominent merchants from Julfa, who as enterprising and wealthy magnates occupied an important position in Aleppo's international trade."[8] The Portuguese traveler Pedro Teixeira noted the Julfans' palatial residences, "fit to harbour princes," when he passed through the city during the 1590s.[9] The wealth of the resident Julfan merchants brought about many changes in Aleppo's Armenian community. As Bruce Masters notes, "The presence of these Iranian Armenian merchants in Aleppo triggered a cultural flourishing of the city's Armenian community as a whole. Supported by the silk merchants, new churches were constructed and illuminated manuscripts were commissioned."[10]

Even the seat of the Catholicosate of Cilicia with its catholicos Azaria (1581–1601), himself from Old Julfa and elected to the seat of the catholicosate with Julfan support, moved from Sis to Aleppo during this period, thus indicating the stature and importance of the Aleppine Armenian community and its Julfan merchants.[11]

The most notable Julfan merchant in Aleppo during the late sixteenth and early seventeenth century was Khwaja Petik (originally from Old Julfa), who, along with his brother Sanos, seems to have monopolized the silk trade in the city. Petik (diminutive for Petros) is said to have operated a vast commercial network extending to Amsterdam and India. In addition to being the richest merchant in Aleppo, Petik was also the customs director of all of Ottoman Syria, from Alexandretta to Tripoli, and the superintendent of all the khans, baths, and other institutions of Aleppo. He also had contacts with the sultan's palace in Constantinople.[12] He is said to have been the representative of Holland in Aleppo. Like many wealthy Julfans, Petik was an important patron of the Armenian community. He and his brother donated the funds for the construction of Aleppo's second Armenian church in 1616.[13] Simeon Lehatsi comments on Petik's legendary fame, noting in particular how he used to travel around the city with his personal retinue of forty guards, very much in the fashion of a local pasha.[14] From about 1590 to 1632, Venetian, French, English, Dutch, and Spanish merchants in Aleppo conducted their silk trade mostly through the business network of this rich Julfan.[15]

Julfans began losing their predominant role in Aleppo toward the end of the seventeenth century with the arrival of Armenian merchants from Akin and Arapkir in Anatolia, who gradually replaced them as the leading Armenian merchants of the place.[16] However, already by the second half of the seventeenth century, Aleppo's Julfan merchants had begun taking their silk to Izmir/Smyrna to sell, as taxes and customs duties were lower there.

IZMIR

Armenians settled in Izmir in three general waves: (1) in the eleventh to twelfth century, after the Seljuk conquest of the Bagradit kingdom; (2) in the period after 1380, following the collapse of the Kingdom of Cilician Armenia; and (3) in the aftermath of the Safavid-Ottoman war of 1604 when a segment of the eastern Armenian population that had not been forcibly relocated to Iran by Shah 'Abbas I had migrated and settled in Izmir.[17] When Simeon Lehatsi passed through Izmir in 1604, he noted the presence of a hundred Armenian households (about 500 to 600 individuals) and two churches.[18] In 1631, the French traveler Jean Baptiste Tavernier provided the figure of 8,000 Armenians residing in Izmir, constituting slightly less than 10 percent of the city's total population.[19] This suggests that either the number of Armenians must have dramatically expanded in the few decades after Lehatsi's visit or that Tavernier's figure, which has been uncritically accepted by a number of scholars, is exaggerated.[20] The celebrated French Orientalist Antoine Galland, visiting the port city in the 1670s, noted only 130 families of Armenians, a figure that seems to corroborate Lehatsi's earlier observation and cast doubt on Tavernier's exaggerated claim.[21]

Izmir "first emerged as an outlet for Iranian silk exports in the early seventeenth century."[22] In 1621 the French traveler Louis Deshayes, baron de Courmenin, arrived in Izmir from Constantinople on his way to Jerusalem and noted the connection between Iranian silk and Armenian merchants: "At present Izmir has a great traffick in wool, beeswax, cotton and silk, which the Armenians bring there instead of going to Aleppo. It is more advantageous for them to go there because they do not pay as many dues."[23]

What is noteworthy in Deshayes's testimony is not only the association between silk and Armenian merchants but also the Armenian merchants' preference of Izmir over Aleppo as a distribution center of their silk to European merchants. This shift from Aleppo to Izmir, as the quoted passage suggests, was made because the customs dues that Julfan merchants were required to pay on Iranian silk were lower in Izmir. Moreover, as V. H. P'ap'azyan's excellent study of trade routes and the road taxes merchants had to pay on them demonstrates, Izmir was preferred over Aleppo because the route from Tabriz to Izmir had only eleven separate stops where taxes were collected as opposed to seventeen on the Tabriz-Aleppo route. Thus the lower transport expenses on the road to Izmir made it the preferred route for Julfan merchants despite the fact that it was longer.[24]

When Julfan merchants first settled in Izmir in the first or second decade of the seventeenth century, they must have found a well-established Armenian community where they could easily adjust. The principal "pull" factors attracting them to Izmir were, in addition to the low custom fees on silk, the excellent port facilities of the city as well as its ideal geographic position near all the important ports of the Mediterranean where the Julfans conducted trade in the seventeenth and eighteenth centuries.[25] Iranian raw silk was the principal commodity of trade for Julfan merchants. This silk was transported overland by caravan to Izmir where it was initially sold to European buyers in the city. By the middle of the seventeenth century, Julfans had worked out an arrangement with the Dutch Republic, which maintained a "consul" in Izmir, to load their goods on Dutch vessels and take them to Venice, Livorno, Marseilles, and especially Amsterdam.[26] Some Armenian merchants also owned their own ships, as the names of several Armenian-owned ships mentioned in Dutch records testify.[27] Izmir's geographic position between the Mediterranean markets and settlements and the nodal center of Julfa/Isfahan made it a particularly important way station and regional center for Julfan merchants operating out of Venice. Most Julfan merchants traveled to Venice and beyond into Europe by way of Izmir or Istanbul to the Dalmatian coast (Ragusa or Dubrovnik as well as Split or Spalato further north), which was then under Venetian control, and finally to Venice. During his visit to Split or Spalato in the early 1610s, Lehatsi noted the presence of Armenian merchants, including those from Julfa.[28]

As in the case of several other settlements in which Julfan merchants resided in the seventeenth century, Izmir was not only a commercial base for the Armenians but also an important cultural center. Apart from having Armenian churches in the seventeenth century, the city also had an important printing press, founded in 1676. A number of seventeenth-century letters and contracts from Izmir stored in the All Savior's Monastery Archive in Julfa indicate that the Julfan community in Izmir kept in touch with the nodal center of its commercial network in Isfahan.[29]

## VENICE

*In the time of the dominion of Uzun Hassan, king of Iran and Armenia, the Armenians came to Venice, and it was from the year 1497 that they took back from the most Excellent Procurators of San Marco their house there in virtue of the testament of Zianni.*[30]

The "house" mentioned in this document from the Archivio di Stato of Venice was a hospice built for Armenian merchants in the middle of the thirteenth century by a Venetian nobleman named Marco Zianni, who was later elected doge.[31] Armenian merchants used the building, located in the parish of San Zulian, as a *fondaco* (from Arabic *funduq,* meaning "inn") from the thirteenth through the fifteenth century.[32] When their numbers increased in the last decades of the 1500s, especially after the arrival of merchants from Old Julfa, the Armenians appealed to the Venetian authorities to turn over their *fondaco* to destitute Armenians, because by that time the wealthy merchants had moved into rented apartments in various parts of the city, especially in the parish of Santa Maria Formosa, where there is still a street bearing the name Ruga Giuffa (Julfa Street). An altar and chapel were erected on the premises of the Armenian *fondaco* in 1434 (and renovated in 1496, 1510–1520, and finally 1689) to serve the spiritual needs of the growing community of merchants.[33] In 1688, a wealthy Julfan merchant named Khwaja Gregorio di Guerak Mirman (Guerak Mirmanian) appealed to the Venetian prelate to expand the chapel into a full-fledged church.[34] Permission was granted shortly afterward, and the church, known as Santa Croce degli Armeni (Surb Khatch, in Armenian) became an important institution and gathering place for Venice's Julfan community of merchants. A manuscript of gospels donated in 1608 to Venice's Santa Croce Church by an Armenian merchant named Khwaja Shirin, who had the manuscript sent to Venice from Anatolia by way of Aleppo, is evidence of the transregional ties that connected Julfans in the Levant to their important settlement in Venice.[35]

Of all the cities in Europe, Venice seems to have served as a bridgehead for Armenian merchants from very early on. Beginning in the middle of the twelfth century, as we have already noted, there was an Armenian hospice in Venice to shelter itinerant Armenian merchants visiting the city. The republic also carried on a very active trade with the medieval kingdom of Cilician Armenia (also known as "Little Armenia") on the shores of the Mediterranean. Venice was an important cultural center for the Armenians; the first Armenian book was published there in 1512, and numerous Armenian books were printed in the Serenissima during the late seventeenth and especially eighteenth century when a band of erudite Armenian Catholic priests known as the Mkhitarist Congregation were given the island of San Lazzaro in the Venetian lagoon (1717) and set to work on forming the modern Armenian literary canon, a process referred to as the Armenian "revival movement."[36]

The first recorded notice of Julfans in Venice, according to Ghevont Alishan, dates from 1572, when merchants from Old Julfa began to frequent Venice carrying bales of Iranian silk.[37] Venice was one of the most important markets of Iranian silk in the sixteenth and seventeenth centuries. In the 1590s, Armenian merchants formed the most numerous group after "Turkish" [i.e., Ottoman Muslim] merchants, according to Giorgio Vercellin's investigations in the Archivio di Stato di Venezia. Vercellin notes that at least twenty-four Armenian merchants were registered as permanent residents in Venice in the 1590s, while many others were probably coming and going. Vercellin's research does not indicate the provenance or regional identity of these merchants, but it would not be far-fetched to presume that many were originally from Old Julfa. This possibility is, in fact, suggested by the Julfan dialectal traits found in some of the signatures recorded by Vercellin in his transcription of some documents.[38] The number of Julfans in Venice increased dramatically after the foundation of New Julfa in part because of a 1614 decree passed by the Venetian senate providing tax exemption on the import of Iranian raw silk.[39] When Simeon Lehatsi spent two months in the city on his way to Rome in the early years of the 1600s, he noted a stone-built Armenian church (i.e., Santa Croce degli Armeni) along with a hospice for Armenians, as well as ten Armenian resident families belonging to the Armenian Gregorian Church and many others who were converts to Catholicism. He also noted the presence of "numerous merchants [bazirgan]."[40] According to Claudia Bonardi, a document in the Venetian archives dating from 1653 has the names of seventy-three Armenians residing in Venice, almost all of whom were from the suburb of Isfahan.[41] Half a century later, the Armenian community in Venice was still dominated by Julfans, some of whom, such as the city's most notable Armenian family, the Scerimans or Shahrimanians, were Catholics. Though the number of Armenians and Julfans continued to increase into the eighteenth century, we should keep in mind that the community always remained relatively small; a census report from 1750 on the Armenian community of the city contains a list of seventy Armenian merchants associated with the Santa Croce church and seventeen religious people, making a total of eighty-seven registered Armenians.[42] Many of the Julfans listed in these reports no doubt used the city of the doges as a base to conduct trade with Amsterdam in the north as well as Smyrna/Izmir, Marseilles, and especially Livorno to the west.[43]

## LIVORNO

The earliest evidence of Armenians residing in Livorno dates from the middle of the sixteenth century;[44] a group of about fifteen Armenian merchants settled there around the year 1553.[45] The first specific mention of a Julfan merchant in Livorno is from 1582, when a merchant named Khwaja Gregorio di Guerak Mirman, originally from Old Julfa, is believed to have resided there as the "agent of the shah of Iran."[46] If true, this would suggest that Gregorio di Guerak Mirman was an agent for Shah Mohammad Khodabanda (r. 1578–1587) and that some merchants from Old Julfa were being used as royal merchants by the Safavids even before the reign of Shah 'Abbas I (r. 1587–1629).

In 1591 and 1593, when Ferdinand I Grand Duke of Tuscany wrote his *Livornina*, or letter of invitation, to foreign merchants to settle in Pisa and the tax-free port of Livorno, among the communities he singled out were the Armenians.[47] The Armenian community of Livorno must have been very small at the turn of the seventeenth century. In 1600, according to one source, there were close to 200 Armenians there and about 110 businesses belonging presumably to Julfans.[48] This figure has been contested by Lucia Frattarelli Fischer, who rightly points out that though there were numerous itinerant Armenian merchants in Livorno at the turn of the century, the actual number of resident merchants was very minimal. Relying on archival documents from the Archivio di Stato of Florence, Fischer points out that in 1609 a ship sailing from Tunis to Livorno was carrying four Armenian merchants who were residents of Livorno.[49] Two years earlier, when a galleon belonging to the Grand Duke of Tuscany seized an English vessel near Livorno as a prize, ninety Turks (sixty men and thirty women), forty Indians (thirty-five Muslims and five Christians), seven Jews, thirty-five Englishmen, and thirty to forty Armenians were found on board; all of them were apparently trading out of Livorno already at such an early date.[50] According to Fischer, this indicates the first substantial influx of Easterners flocking to the markets of Livorno.[51] It was not until the 1630s that Julfans began to arrive in greater numbers. Favorable tax breaks, low customs duties on Iranian silk, and promises of religious tolerance (all outlined in Ferdinand's petition) were the principal "pull" factors attracting Julfan merchants.

The Julfan community must have reached its height in the 1650s. A *commenda* contract signed in Livorno in 1659 and preserved in the All Savior's Monastery Archive in New Julfa lists some fourteen merchants as witnesses to the agreement.[52] The majority of these signatories were Julfans. As we shall see below, one possible reason Livorno seems to have experienced a surge in the arrival and settlement of Julfan merchants during this period might be the stringent tax policies and protectionist measures aimed at pushing Julfans out of neighboring Marseilles in the 1640s and especially 1650s (see below).[53] Since Marseilles and Livorno were both favored by Julfans because of their strategic position and their proximity to the markets of Amsterdam in the north, the protectionist policies of Marseilles promoted Livorno as a leading Julfan commercial center in the Mediterranean.

By the 1660s, Livorno's merchant population seems to have increased substantially. A report sent to the Propaganda Fide by a Roman nuncio there in 1669 mentions that the city had some three hundred resident Armenian merchants, subjects of both the Safavids and the Ottomans (i.e., "Western" Armenians from Ottoman cities such as Izmir, Constantinople, Ani, Van, Akn and Angora/Ankara).[54] The reliability of this source has been criticized by Fischer and Francesca Trivellato, the latter providing a low figure of forty-seven Armenians residing in the city at the peak of their presence there.[55] The overwhelming majority of the Iranian-Armenian merchants were from New Julfa, though some were also from trading towns such as Agulis in the region of Goghtan in Nakhichevan. Several wealthy Armenian merchant families, such as the Chelebies, were originally from Bursa and Izmir and were very active members in the community.[56] While residing and operating out of Livorno, some of these merchants also circulated from one settlement in the Armenian trade network to another. For instance, when the French traveler Abbé Carré made a brief stop in Livorno in the 1660s on his second voyage to India, he remarked: "I was surprised to meet several Armenian, Persian, and Indian merchants whom I had known in the East during my first Travels."[57] Though Carré does not give any names, it is apparent from the context of his discussion that most likely he had met these Julfan Armenian merchants during his first visit to Surat a few years before his chance encounter with them in Livorno.

Like Venice, Amsterdam, and to a lesser extent Marseilles, Livorno also served the Armenians as a center for cultural production, and particularly for printing. The first book printed in the city was an Armenian psalter, printed in 1643 by a priest from Julfa named Hovannes, who was sent to Europe in 1639 by the archbishop/primate of Julfa, Khachatur of Caesarea, to perfect his knowledge of the European craft of printing before returning home to help in improving the Armenian printing press in New Julfa set up by Khachiatur around the same period.[58]

Livorno also had an important Armenian church from the early years of the eighteenth century. Before the establishment of that church, Armenians of the city frequented the city's Catholic churches, where a number of them were buried. While writing his history in the 1880s, Mesrop Vardapet Ughurlian noted that the Franciscan Church of Santa Maria had six tombstones belonging to Julfa merchants dating from the 1660s.[59] As we shall see later, the parallels with the Armenian merchant community of Cadiz are quite striking, with the difference that the larger presence of Armenians in Livorno and the city's relatively more tolerant policies allowed them to eventually erect a church of their own, unlike their counterparts in Cadiz, who settled for a small chapel in one of the city's Catholic churches, where they were allotted space to worship in their own fashion.

The initiative of establishing a church in Livorno to serve the needs of the local

Armenian community was taken by the community's leading merchants as early as the 1680s. In 1691, the Armenian community there drafted its first "national constitution" and appealed to Rome to have its own church where the liturgy would be in Armenian and in accordance with the Armenian Gregorian Church. After initial reluctance by the Vatican, which looked upon the Armenian Church as a heretical and schismatic entity and, therefore, was careful about granting permission for a church that would operate outside its spiritual jurisdiction, permission was finally granted in the early years of the 1700s, after the Armenians agreed to the Vatican's demands and accepted Roman Catholic supervision with the condition that *Roman liturgy would be performed in Armenian.*[60] The mediation efforts by the Grand Duke, who was eager to cultivate good relations with the city's Armenian merchants, played an important role in gaining Rome's permission. The Church of Saint Gregory the Illuminator finally opened its doors in 1714.[61]

Next only to Venice, the Livorno community was arguably the most vital Armenian trade settlement in the Mediterranean. It was an integral part of the vast Julfan-Armenian network because it connected the western (Mediterranean) end of the circuit to its eastern (Indian Ocean and Iranian) heartland. Though silk was the most prominent commodity circulating from the nodal center at Julfa to the markets in Europe, other commodities also circulated in this network, including Indian textiles and the skills of manufacturing calico printing.[62] In this connection, the trade in precious gems and diamonds, for which Livorno was a vital center in the seventeenth century, was an important aspect of Julfan commerce. The diamond trade was particularly important, as it integrated the two poles of the Julfan network: Surat and Livorno. A contract for diamonds and precious stones preserved in the archives of the Museo Correr in Venice gives us a good idea of the extent of this trade.[63] The document in question is a leather-bound book with sixteen folded pages containing what Julfans called a *tomar* (roll) that provides a succinct summary of detailed commercial transactions recorded by a *commenda* agent for his master in Julfa in a *roozlama,* or account ledger (Julfan dialect for the original Persian term, *ruznameh*).[64] This document provides a catalogue of a number of complex transactions between the *commenda* agent, one Agha di Matus of Tabriz,[65] and his "master" in Julfa, named Khwaja Minas.[66] According to the contract, Agha di Matus received a consignment of diamonds of various grades in Surat in 1673 and was ordered to take it to Izmir, Constantinople, and thence to "Frank'stan" (i.e., Europe and in particular the Mediterranean) where he was to sell his merchandise. Agha di Matus's *tomar* contains an inventory of his travels from Julfa to Izmir, Venice, and finally Livorno, where he must have settled in the 1680s, already a rich merchant. He appears again in the documents of the Propaganda Fide Archives in the Vatican: his name crops up in papers from the 1690s as a delegate chosen by the "Armenian Assembly" in Livorno to represent the community in Rome, where Matus had traveled and presented his credentials as the principal merchant financially bankrolling the city's proposed

Armenian church. Matus's case is an illustration of the great distances covered by Julfan merchants (from Julfa to Surat to Izmir, Venice, and finally Livorno). One can only assume that fellow Julfan merchants residing in the various settlements in the network assisted him in each stage of his journey. Matus's career also highlights the symbiotic relationship between Julfan merchants and the Armenian Church, which in the absence of a state played a vital role in maintaining the identity and smooth functioning of the Julfan trade network. Finally, his case demonstrates the formation of a merchant who began as a lowly factor or *commenda* agent and became wealthy and powerful. He was not only the leading figure in his community but was on close terms with the Grand Duke of Tuscany (Cosimo II), was granted full citizenship in Rome (1698), and received various titles from the Vatican, including Prince of the Order of the Cross and Count of the Laterans.[67]

## MARSEILLES

In July 1623, the consuls of Marseilles wrote a letter to the king complaining of the invasion of Armenians with their bales of silk and warning the king of the "grave and dangerous consequences" posed to the welfare and prosperity of his subjects by the arrival of Armenian merchants.[68] "There is no nation in the world," they wrote, "as greedy [as this]; although they have plenty of opportunity to sell these silks in great markets like Aleppo or Smyrna and other markets and make an honest profit, nevertheless to make even more money, they come running to the other end of the world [i.e., Marseilles]."[69] It appears that Julfan merchants selling silk to merchant companies from Marseilles, Lyon, and Tours (the two last cities were important hubs for France's silk industry) in Aleppo had traveled directly to Marseilles, and to Toulon a year before the complaints by the consuls of Marseille, to reclaim debts owed to them in the Levant.[70] As Edmund Herzig observes, "Armenian trade must already have been strongly established by this time for it to have been perceived as such a serious threat to local interests."[71] During the 1620s, the chamber of commerce in Marseilles passed a series of stringent protectionist measures aimed at banning Armenian silk merchants from trading in the city. Measures were also taken to prohibit the shipment of Armenian goods (especially silk) on French ships. These restrictions did not succeed in entirely excluding Armenian traders from Marseilles, because, in 1629, Louis XIII granted a letter patent allowing Iranians and Armenians to trade in France through the agency of Louis Frejus, a notable French merchant with business connections in the Levant, and an Armenian named Antoine Armenis, who had been a resident of Marseilles since 1612 and was naturalized as a French subject in 1625. Several Julfan merchants, such as "Alexandre, fils de Mussegen" (Alexandre di Mnatsakan or Musheghian?) and "Jouan" (Hovan?), are known to have used Marseilles as a springboard to make "business trips" to Paris and Fontainebleau as early as 1625, as notarial documents discovered by Olivier

Raveux in Paris indicate.[72] In 1635, Cardinal Richelieu allowed free trade to "Armenians, Julfans, and Persians," but protectionist measures were reintroduced following his death in 1642. After 1650, stricter measures were put in place to shut Julfans and other Armenians out of the French market. These included a draconian tax on foreign imported Iranian silk, passed in 1658.[73] The measures forced Julfans to abandon Marseilles in favor of the tax-free port of neighboring Livorno, where they were welcomed by Duke Ferdinand's policy of attracting foreign merchants.[74] Things changed under the ministry of Jean Baptiste Colbert (1619–1683), who adopted policies in the 1660s to once again make Marseilles attractive to Armenian merchants. By that time, the city's Armenian population, as in Livorno around the same period, consisted of Ottoman subjects as well as Iranian-Armenians from Julfa (referred to in the sources as "Choffelines"). Julfa merchants were the most prominent members of the tiny Armenian population of Marseilles. Some, like the merchant Safraz de Avedit (Shafraz di Avedik?), are known to have resided in Marseilles as well as Paris and London in the 1680s.[75] Others were like Harut'iwn (better known by his French name, Pascal), who, originally from Aleppo, first opened a coffee establishment in Marseilles and then moved in 1672 to Paris, where he opened the city's first café; he was followed by another Armenian café owner and resident of Paris, this time a Julfan Armenian named Grigor.[76]

The importance of Marseilles as a base for the Julfans in the Mediterranean can be gauged by the fact that in the early 1680s Julfan merchants in Isfahan and Surat (India) made overtures to the French East India Company to ship their merchandise on French vessels from the Persian Gulf and Surat directly to Marseilles—a proposal that failed due to disagreements between the parties.[77] In the last quarter of the seventeenth century, Julfans in Marseilles were favored by the anti-Ottoman policies of Paris and by close relations between Paris and Isfahan. As in other Mediterranean settlements, their numbers were fairly small, with only about twenty to twenty-five permanent Julfan residents living at the same time in the city between 1669 and 1695, and a total of thirty-eight Julfan merchants for the same period.[78] In addition to trading in silk, Julfans in Marseilles were engaged in the textile trade supplying the market in Marseilles with much needed fine South Asian textiles and calicoes, the bulk of which was transported by caravan routes to the Levant ports of Aleppo and especially Smyrna, and thence to Marseilles and other Mediterranean ports, such as Livorno and Genoa. According to Raveux, in 1687 the Julfans are said to have transported most of the 25,000 units of cotton goods across the overland routes to Marseilles, compared to the 33,000 units transported by the East India Company across the Cape route.[79] The Armenians already had a reputation for being "pivotal in the technological transfer of cotton printing from India to Persia and various parts of the Ottoman Empire."[80] After their settlement in Marseilles, they also played a crucial role in introducing the art of calico printing "in the Oriental manner" to the Mediterranean region.[81] It seems that some Julfans in Marseilles who had

arrived there as silk merchants in the 1660s "soon took advantage of investing in calico printing." For instance, a certain Arapie[t] d'Arachel and Dominique Ellia were
owners of a calico workshop in Marseilles from 1672 to the early 1680s, as was another Julfan, Paul de Serquis, as well as others.[82] In collaboration with Armenian artisans from Istanbul, Diyarbakir, and Izmir in the Ottoman Empire, the Julfans of
Marseilles set up local calico workshops "to produce items that suited the changing
tastes and expectations of local customers."[83] In 1720, the Julfans in Marseilles had
even succeeded in electing one of their own as the Iranian consul there.[84]

Marseilles was also an important center of Armenian printing in the 1660s, second only to Amsterdam. Armenian printers in Marseilles were financed largely by
the patronage of Julfan merchants. Some of the books printed in Marseilles reflected
the needs of their patrons, both in their contents and in their language or dialect.
Thus at least one book printed in the city was devoted to commercial arithmetic,
one was a manual comparing the different calendrical systems (Gregorian, Julian,
Greater Armenian, Azaria, and so on), and another a language manual for learning Italian. All these works were written not in the literary language of Classical Armenian (*grabar*), which was largely confined to a small clerical circle, but in the
Julfa dialect, the language of the merchants.[85]

## CADIZ

One of the least studied and least known of Julfa settlements on the fringes of the
Mediterranean world is that of Cadiz, Spain.[86] There is no conclusive evidence as
to when Armenian merchants first settled in this Spanish city at the gateway to the
Americas. Some nineteenth-century Spanish authors had initially placed the arrival
of the Armenians in Cadiz in the early years of the sixteenth century. Others, such
as Antonio Domingues Ortiz, claimed that this settlement must have taken place
a century later.[87] However, in his article "Los Armenios en Cádiz," the Spanish
scholar Hipólito Sancho de Sopranis, who has the most persuasive account to date,
puts the date somewhere in the early 1660s, when the Armenians first began to make
an appearance in the archives of the city. Sopranis's claims are borne out by the notarial records in the Archivo Histórico Provincial de Cádiz, where the earliest evidence of resident Armenians in Cadiz dates to 1664.

The composition of this tiny community was quite heterogeneous. Not all its
members were from Julfa, though a significant number, including the community's
wealthiest and most distinguished merchants, hailed from the famous suburb of
Isfahan. If the testaments and notarial records in the Cadiz archives are reliable
demographic indicators, then about 60 percent of the Armenian merchant population of this city consisted of Iranian-Armenians; less than 20 percent were from
cities or towns in the Ottoman Empire.[88] In the fifty-four extant wills of Armenian
merchants in the Cadiz archives, nine had registered their place of origin as Julfa

or Isfahan, whereas seven were registered as natives of Agulis and Dasht, and seven from the region of Vanant, all Armenian-inhabited places under Safavid dominion.

There is no conclusive evidence on the population numbers of the Armenian community of Cadiz during the seventeenth and early eighteenth centuries. Sopranis claims that earlier authors had exaggerated these numbers, arguing that the community boasted several hundred individuals.[89] In contrast to these authors, Sopranis maintains a minimalist position, placing the population figure somewhere above a dozen or so merchants. This view, however, has been challenged by Manuel Ravina Martin, who, based on his detailed work in the notarial documents in the Cadiz archives, claims that Sopranis's figures must be increased tenfold to arrive at a closer estimate of the actual numbers.[90] At any rate, the city's Armenian population must have consisted of mostly male merchants, the majority of whom were engaged in commerce on behalf of their masters residing elsewhere. Some were clearly itinerant *commenda* agents from Julfa who were passing through the city, such as the ill-fated Edigar son of Shekhik whose death in Cadiz became known in Julfa, compelling his *commenda* master (Hovhannes son of Ghara Melik) as well as his mother (Ghadum), wife (Manishak), and daughter (Tank Khatun) to appoint a power of attorney to travel to Cadiz to collect their dues.[91] There were, however, a few families recorded as being longtime residents of Cadiz, such as the wealthy Shakarian family from Julfa, led by David Shakarian[92] (known in the Spanish records under the name of David Zukar), whose family was in Cadiz from the 1660s until the 1720s. Some of these merchants were circulating between Cadiz, Livorno, Lisbon, Venice, Amsterdam, and even Tangier in North Africa,[93] but most seemed to have returned periodically to their base in Cadiz. In any case, there must have been a significant population core that resided in Cadiz for the Armenian community to have its own private chapel inside the city's Catholic Church of Santa Maria in the old district near the port.[94] In fact, the Armenians of Cadiz were great patrons and followers of the local religious confraternity known as the Brotherhood of Jesus the Nazarene, which was centered in the Church of Santa Maria, where the Armenians were granted their own chapel of worship. They were among the most generous patrons of this order, and at least one family among them, namely, the Shakarian/Zukar family of Julfa, headed by David Shakarian/Zukar, is listed as one of the founding members of this religious group. David Shakarian/Zukar not only paid handsome sums for the maintenance and growth of this order but also had special ceramic tiles, many of them with Armenian inscriptions, designed and imported from Amsterdam in the 1660s for the decoration of the church.[95] More interestingly, he was most likely also the founder of Amsterdam's first Armenian church, built in 1664.[96] These details about David Shakarian/Zukar demonstrate how Julfan merchants circulated from one settlement in the network to another, often serving as important actors in the community life of more than one settlement.

The Julfans' devotion to the Church of Santa Maria and their acts of public piety to the Brotherhood of Jesus of Nazarene seem to have saved the Armenian community from being exiled from Cadiz. Apparently, complaints against the Armenian merchants had begun to circulate in 1684, reminiscent of the inquisition against Jews and Muslims, albeit on a much smaller scale, and more particularly of the anti-Armenian protectionist policies in Marseilles only decades earlier that led to their banishment from the French port. These "popular grievances" found support among the councillors to the king and the chamber of commerce in Madrid,[97] and then "were brought to the attention of the monarch with a proposal to expel within six months, all the members of the nation who conducted commerce in the cities of the peninsula."[98] On February 26, 1684, notices were placed in various locales in Madrid frequented by merchants, and in Cadiz, announcing the royal edict:

> Ordered by the King our Lord that all Armenians who are found in our court [i.e., Madrid] and in any other cities, towns, and places of our kingdom must leave within six months of the publication of this proclamation, and that within the said six months they can freely sell all the merchandise that they possess.[99]

Taking advantage of their public generosity in the past and their continued patronage of the Church of Santa Maria, the Armenians appealed to the governor of Cadiz as well as to the local prelate, Don Antonio de Ibarra, who in turn petitioned the king, imploring him to exempt the Armenians of Cadiz from his proclamation on the grounds that they had been important to the public welfare of their host society. The order was rescinded in January of the following year.[100]

The Cadiz Armenian community seems to have dwindled and disappeared in the second quarter of the eighteenth century. At any rate, their presence in the archives also trails off after the 1720s, with only one notarial document dating from 1786.[101]

## AMSTERDAM

Amsterdam was in many ways an exceptional settlement for the Julfa merchants.[102] As we have seen, most Julfan settlements in Europe were positioned on the shores of the Mediterranean with relatively easy transport access to and from the nodal center of the trade network in New Julfa, Isfahan. Amsterdam and London, however, were on the westernmost edge of the Julfan network in what we have called the northwestern European circuit, far from the nodal center to which they were nonetheless connected.

Julfans were attracted to Amsterdam because of the "strength of Dutch capital" that made it "possible for [them] to receive prompt payment in cash and to place orders for their return cargos of cloth as soon as they arrived."[103] Moreover, the city had the advantage of being the seat of the Dutch East India Company (VOC) and was famous for hosting dissident minorities, such as French Huguenots and Sephardic Jews from Portugal. The first mention of Armenians in Amsterdam dates from the 1560s, when several Armenian jewel merchants are said to have visited the city.[104] It was not until the 1620s (around the same time as the arrival of Armenians in Marseilles), however, that Armenians from Izmir and Constantinople began to settle in Amsterdam.[105] By 1627, at least two Julfan merchants, Khwaja Sarhat (Godge Sarhatd) and Hovannes Zak'aria (Jan Sacharis), were permanently settled in Amsterdam.[106] As elsewhere, New Julfa's dramatic expansion in the seventeenth and eighteenth centuries led to the growth of Amsterdam's Armenian community, making it by far the most significant New Julfan outpost in western Europe. Like other Armenian communities in Europe at the time, the population of Amsterdam's Armenian community probably did not exceed a hundred members at its height.[107] By the 1690s, the most eminent members of Amsterdam's Armenian community were from New Julfa. Several Julfan families had set up business branches in the Dutch capital.[108] As was the case with many other Armenian trade settlements, it did not take very long for the Armenian community of Amsterdam to establish important community institutions designed to maintain its own identity and generate communal solidarity. The first Armenian church in Amsterdam was founded in 1663–1664.[109] A new church was erected in 1714 (and renovated in 1748). Interestingly, Julfan merchants endowed both churches. Moreover, a series of Armenian printing presses operated there from 1660 to 1718, supported by the financial patronage of Julfa merchants, thus making Amsterdam one of the leading centers of Armenian printing in the world and the city where the first Armenian Bible was printed in 1666.[110] Armenian printers in Amsterdam produced some of the most important works in modern Armenian literature, including the first printed edition of the classic work of the "father of Armenian historiography," Moses of Khoren (fl. between the sixth and eighth century). His *History of Armenia* was printed in 1695. In addition, Armenian printers published several important works that were of practical use for Armenian merchants, including a manual of trade entitled *A Treasure of Measures, Weights, Numbers, and Currencies Used throughout the World* (1699) as well as the first modern Armenian world atlas (1695), which was accompanied by a treatise on world geography and a universal atlas (1698). All were commissioned by Julfan merchants and published with the express intention of aiding fellow Armenian merchants in their global trading ventures.[111]

Geographically and in terms of trade routes used by Julfan merchants, Amsterdam was connected to the nodal center in New Julfa via the long overland route across the Baltic region to Moscow or Archangel and thence via Astrakhan to New Julfa. It was also an important peripheral node for the smaller Julfan community of London to the west.

## LONDON

There was no resident Armenian community in London until the late seventeenth century. Though Julfa merchants had visited London as early as 1645, it was only in

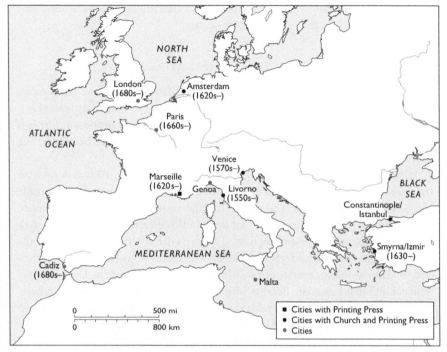

MAP 2. The Julfan Armenian trade network and settlements in the early modern Mediterranean/northwestern European world.

the 1680s and 1690s that London became home to some forty Armenian merchants, mostly from India and Julfa. At least one prominent Julfa family, the Ghalandarians (known in English records as the Calander family), had a resident representative in the city. Indeed it was a member of this family, Khwaja Panos Calendar, who signed the famous 1688 "Treaty of East India Company with the Armenian Nation."[112] We have also noted above that another Julfan, Shafraz di Avedik, lived in London in the 1680s. Avedik served as an agent for Marseilles' most prominent Julfan, Melchon de Nazar.[113] A handful of New Julfa Armenians resided in London in the first half of the eighteenth century; however, their numbers had declined to two or three individuals in the 1750s.[114] Whatever ties Julfa merchants had with the English capital were not institutional in nature, but based on individual initiative, with Armenian merchants from the community of Amsterdam periodically moving back and forth between the two commercial centers, using Amsterdam as a "regional node" in northwestern Europe. That the London Armenian community was a "satellite" community of the Dutch capital is indicated by half a dozen letters stored at the British Library relating to the Armenian community in London. Most are written by Armenians in Amsterdam.[115] The first Armenian church in England was consecrated in Manchester only in the late nineteenth century.[116]

## THE RUSSIAN NETWORK

The Levantine and Mediterranean nodes in the Julfan network were not the sole means of access to the markets located farther northwest in Amsterdam and London. Another important avenue of Julfan expansion toward Europe was through the overland trade route running north across the Russian Empire before turning southwest over the Baltic Sea into northern Europe.

Julfan merchants began exploring the possibility of using the Russian route to transport their silk to Europe in the middle of the seventeenth century. The chronic insecurity of Ottoman routes and the fact that the northern route was shorter made Russia attractive to the Julfans. The first steps in this direction were taken in 1659 when a prominent Julfan merchant named Zaccaria di Sarat, the eldest of five brothers belonging to Julfa's wealthy Sceriman/Shahrimanian family (see chapter 6), traveled to Moscow in the capacity of a royal merchant for the *itimad al dawle,* or chief minister, of Shah Suleiman, bearing with him a golden throne studded with hundreds of diamonds and innumerable precious stones as a gift from his family and the Julfan community for Czar Alexei Mikhaylovich. This generous gift, which later served as the throne for the coronation ceremonies of many czars, seems to have paid off, because in 1667, Julfa's most prominent merchant families signed a trade agreement (reaffirmed in 1673) with the Russian state obtaining a favor that had eluded the English and the Dutch: the right to transport their merchandise overland from Iran across Russia to northwestern Europe by way of the Russian port of Narva or Archangel, and to do so by paying low customs fees.[117] In 1692, a Julfan adventurer and "trickster traveler," known variously as Khwaja Phillip'os, Compte de Siry, Husayn Beg Talish, and finally Philip de Zagly, acting on behalf of other Julfans, signed two other agreements, one with the Dutchy of Kurland (present-day Latvia), allowing them access to the port of Libau, and another with the Kingdom of Sweden, receiving permission to use the region to gain access, across the Baltic Sea, to Germany and Holland.[118]

The opening of the Russian circuit to Julfan commerce paved the way for the founding of a series of settlements in the northern Russian zone. One of the most important of these was in Astrakhan, on the northern shores of the Caspian Sea and in close proximity to Iran. Astrakhan had a small Armenian community even before the official opening of the northern route. In 1616, eleven Armenian families were recorded as residing there.[119] Though the sources do not indicate the background of these Armenians, it would not be far-fetched to speculate that they were mostly Iranian and possibly merchants from the newly settled mercantile suburb of New Julfa. By 1630, the number of Armenians in Astrakhan was significant enough for the construction of a wooden church.[120] After the opening of the northern route, more Armenians flowed into the city. Passing through Astrakhan in 1703, the Dutch traveler Cornelius De Bruyn noted the presence of forty Armenian families in Astrakhan, or about two hundred to three hundred individuals. De Bruyn lodged with them on his way to Iran. He also noted the presence of an equal number of Indian merchants but was quick to point out that unlike the Armenians the Indians did not have their women with them.[121] According to the Russian census of 1747, the Armenian population had risen to 1,512 individuals, the majority of whom were Iranian Armenians and a significant number from New Julfa.[122] Less than thirty years later, their numbers had more than doubled to 3,500 individuals, according to the census of 1781, with a significant portion directly involved in commerce.[123]

As with the English settlements in India, the granting of special privileges, such as the low customs duties outlined in the 1667 and 1673 treaties, and most importantly the right to build their own churches, attracted Julfans to settle in Astrakhan. In 1706, after an edict issued by Peter the Great, the Armenian community in Astrakhan erected a new stone church. A second church followed in 1737, when the community's numbers grew, possibly from more migration from New Julfa.[124] Along with other mercantile communities, such as Indians (many of whom appear to have been Multanis) and Catholic Europeans, the Armenians of Astrakhan were allowed to have their own community court in 1744 and in 1763 were given the right to have a separate courthouse (rathaus).[125] The leaders of the community compiled a private legal code (known as the Code of Laws of the Armenians of Astrakhan; see chapter 6), the bulk of which was devoted to the customary commercial law practiced by Julfan merchants in Julfa and abroad in the network settlements, but which was not codified until its incorporation into the Astrakhan Code of Laws.

Other Armenian communities in Russia included Kazan, where an Armenian presence can be traced to the 1640s; St. Petersburg, where Armenian merchants, mostly from New Julfa, had settled in 1710 (only seven years after the city's foundation); and Moscow, again with an important New Julfan mercantile community and a church dating to the 1660s.[126] Some prominent Julfan families, such as the Lazarians (known as the Lazareffs in Russia, of Lazarian College fame), permanently migrated and settled in Moscow and St. Petersburg in the 1740s after the rapid decline in the social and economic conditions in Iran.[127] A number of Julfan mercantile families played a vital role in the Russian economy. Julfans, including Ignatius Shahrimanian (the son of Zaccaria di Sarat, who gave the diamond-studded throne to Czar Alexei), established Russia's first silk-manufacturing workshop in Moscow.[128]

In concluding this and the preceding chapter, we can agree with Edmund Herzig's views concerning the expansion and importance of the Julfan commercial network:

> The Julfans started up as a small community fortuitously located on the way to and from Persia's silk-growing regions to the Mediterranean. Within only a few decades they were able to turn this slender advantage into a virtual monopoly of the Iranian

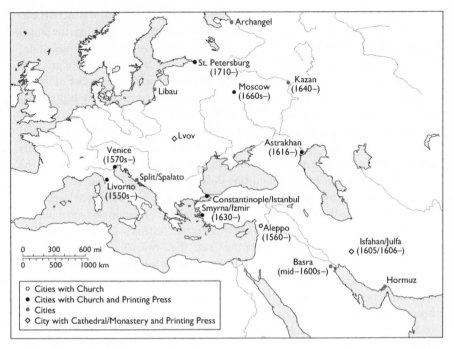

MAP 3. The Julfan Armenian trade network and settlements in the early modern Eurasian world.

silk export trade to Europe, and in a not much longer period of time to diversify and expand their activities from the Atlantic coast of Europe to the edge of the Pacific. The underlying economic dynamic for this expansion was the bullion price differential between Western Europe, the Middle East and India; this provided the commercial opportunity that Julfans seized with both hands.[129]

In addition to these observations, the overview of Armenian settlements in the Mediterranean and Indian Ocean worlds provided in this and the preceding chapter enables us to reach the following conclusions concerning the logic of circulation inherent in the Julfan commercial network as a whole. In the first place, the location of settlements was primarily determined by economic motives, such as the host society's geographic location along an important trade route with open access to other markets where Julfan merchants could profitably exchange their commodities. Transportation and communication access (through the courier network explored in the next chapter) to the nodal center of the trade network in New Julfa, Isfahan, must also have been an important factor in the establishment of some settlements. This would explain the predominant role of the settlements in the Mediterranean basin, which, as we have seen, were all located in important port towns with access to other settlements and markets nearer to the network's nodal center at New Julfa and, therefore, in locations that made it relatively easy for couriers to deliver news and information crucial for Julfan commercial success. In this scheme, the settlements in Tibet and Manila proved to be exceptions. In both cases, however, other factors, such as, most notably, access to Chinese gold and Mexican silver seem to have taken precedence.

Second, where there was a sufficient number of Julfan merchants and where the host society's polity was tolerant, Julfan merchants established their own churches as well as printing presses. This was the case with settlements in Venice, Livorno, and most notably Amsterdam, but not Cadiz and Marseilles. Such institutions could be crucial to the maintenance of the network's overall ethno-religious identity, which, as we shall see in chapter 7, was in turn important to the commercial success and integrity of the network as a whole. In this connection, it is important to remember that the Julfan commercial elite financially patronized Armenian churches and printing establishments set up in the settlements in the network. One could say that a great part of the capital surplus accumulated by Julfan merchants was pumped back into the network in the form of patronage and benevolence toward maintaining and supporting the cultural, educational, and religious work of the mostly clerical elite. In the Mediterranean and northwestern European circuits, Armenian churches and printing presses were not always directly linked to the nodal center in New Julfa; rather, since many of these settlements were initially settled by Armenian merchants who were not from Julfa, or had a significant non-Julfan Armenian population, their churches and printing establishments were linked to the Catholicosate at Etchmiatzin or Cilicia. Thus, as we shall see in the following chapters, while credit, merchants, and information circulated from one settlement to another in the Mediterranean circuit of the network and between it and the nodal center at New Julfa, this was not the case with priests, whose circulation was limited to the settlements in the Indian Ocean world, where most settlements were direct offshoots of New Julfa, populated by its great merchant families and their agents. Consequently, they were connected to and through that great suburb of Isfahan. However, the same cannot be said for all the colonies in the Mediterranean and northwestern Europe. In the latter case, other settlements of the Armenian "trade diaspora," such as those in the Crimea, Constantinople, and Izmir, acted as "subsidiary centers," as Fernand Braudel has called them, or as "regional centers," as I refer to them.[130] The next chapters will demonstrate how this immense network was glued together by the constant circulation of information, credit, merchants, and priests from the nodal center in New Julfa.

# 5

# "The salt in a merchant's letter"

## Business Correspondence and the Courier System

It is now widely acknowledged that "information was the most precious good" in the lives of early modern merchant communities.[1] Claude Markovits explains:

> It is the capacity of the merchants to maintain a constant flow of information within the network that ensures its success. This means two things: first, that "leaks" have to be avoided as much as possible to the outside world, secondly, that information must circulate smoothly within the network, both spatially and temporally, as it gets transmitted from one generation to another . . . , in the long run, the most successful merchant networks have been those most able to process information into a body of knowledge susceptible of continuous refinement. This body of knowledge, of a pragmatic nature, which is mostly about markets, is more or less congruent with what is often called the "secrets of the trade."[2]

Information flows were particularly important for Armenian merchants from New Julfa who by the eighteenth century had branched out from their small mercantile suburb on the outskirts of Isfahan across a global trading network stretching from Amsterdam and Cadiz in the West to Canton and Manila on the rim of the Pacific Ocean in the East. Information sharing was important not only for merchants in managing their daily commercial affairs, but also for maintaining the integrity of the Julfan network as a whole. Letter writing connected distant *commenda* agents to their masters in New Julfa and also unified the trade settlements on the periphery of the network to its nodal center in New Julfa.

Given that this was the case, the question arises, how was information circulated in the Julfan network? Did merchants use a courier system to deliver news to each other? What role did commercial correspondence play in Julfan society and the long-distance trade of its merchants?

This chapter will explore these questions through an examination of Julfan commercial correspondence from archives in London, Venice, and New Julfa, and will demonstrate that the Julfan trade network was built on and unified through a culture of long-distance commercial correspondence. Moreover, as a close examination of thousands of business letters reveals, Julfan merchants had a sophisticated system of circulating information. Following Rene Barendse, I call this system the "intelligence network."[3] Most of my discussion will focus on the presence of this network in the Indian Ocean and the Mediterranean, because the data almost exclusively pertain to these spheres of Julfan activity. First, I examine the culture of commercial correspondence in Julfan society by analyzing the style and content of Julfan business letters, illustrating the discussion with examples drawn from a broad sample of commercial correspondence. Then, I consider the uses of the courier network in Julfan society. Relying on data found in Julfan business letters, I provide statistical information on the average "speed" of the delivery of news between the Mediterranean settlements (especially Venice, Livorno, Izmir, and Aleppo), on the one hand, and those in the Indian Ocean, on the other, to the network's nodal center in New Julfa, Isfahan. Tables featuring data on mail delivery between these spheres of Julfan commerce are provided. These data are important in helping us to understand both the confines in which communication in the seventeenth and eighteenth centuries circulated and the way in which the circulation of information was able to overcome what Fernand Braudel famously called "distance: the first enemy."[4]

THE CULTURE OF COMMERCIAL
CORRESPONDENCE IN JULFAN SOCIETY

*. . . a Factor is created by Merchants Letters.*[5]

When the first Armenian newspaper, *Azdarar* (Intelligencer), was launched in Madras in the fall of 1794, it contained special features that struck its eighteenth-century readers as quite novel. In the first place, the new newspaper devoted a number of pages in its serialized issues to making commercial information publicly available for the benefit of Madras's Armenian merchant community. It included detailed timetables of commercial shipping traffic at the port of Madras, a price list of various commodities traded in the local markets, and brief "notices" by merchants advertising goods for sale, along with their prices. Each issue of *Azdarar* also included social and political news regarding the various Armenian communities in India, as well as a quick recap of world news (mostly concerning affairs in Europe) excerpted and translated from English-language newspapers in India and Europe. Many of these innovative features were creative adaptations from English-language newspapers that had just begun to appear in India, including the idea of presenting information pertinent to the business community in a public forum. Clearly, the aim of *Azdarar*'s editor, as he himself noted in his first "editorial," was to provide useful news to Madras's then fledgling Armenian community and especially to its business leaders.

In his *Structural Transformation of the Public Sphere*, Jurgen Habermas argues that the emergence of commercial newspapers in Europe in the late seventeenth century marked a radical break from medieval practices of business correspondence.[6] In place of the secretive and *private* conveyance of economic information, characteristic of medieval business correspondence, the modern newspaper and gazette, for Habermas, made possible the *public* dissemination of economic news, which Habermas identified as crucial for the development of modern capitalism.[7] More recently work in early modern economic history, especially by Francesca Trivellato, has pointed out that the importance Habermas and others ascribed to the influence of print technology in Europe in fueling the growth of modern capitalism has obscured the vital role of business correspondence in the lives of early modern merchants.[8] As Trivellato notes, many of the functions attributed to newspapers (such as intelligence gathering and reporting of business and other news) were long the preserve of business correspondence. She also points out that merchant correspondence in Europe continued to play a crucial role in the lives of merchant communities long after the rise of print technology and newspapers. Moreover, Trivellato demonstrates that business correspondence was far more efficient in conveying information to a large number of merchants than were most newspapers of the period. These conclusions are also applicable to the history of early modern Armenian, and specifically Julfan, merchants in the Indian Ocean and Mediterranean. In fact, one could argue that many features first appearing in *Azdarar* as novel innovations in Armenian history were actually continuations, albeit in the novel form of print technology, of practices inherent in Julfan business correspondence, which had flourished in the seventeenth century and continued to play a vital role in Julfan commercial life well into the eighteenth and nineteenth centuries. Business correspondence and the mode of circulating it across the vast spaces covered by Julfan merchants and their overseas settlements was such a fundamental aspect of Julfan economy and society that it is impossible to exaggerate its importance. Indeed, the long-distance network of trade settlements created by Julfan merchants in the seventeenth and eighteenth centuries was built on the dual bases of the culture of letter writing and the infrastructure of a courier service that enabled merchants to circulate and share their correspondence.

Before we look at the courier service and its uses in Julfan society, it is essential to examine the elements of business correspondence among Julfan merchants. An analysis of the stylistic and other properties of Julfan correspondence will demonstrate that such correspondence was to Julfan communities what print technology or "print capitalism" is to modern nations. Letter writing was the principal means of unifying the dispersed Julfan merchants and constituting them into an "imagined" merchant community.[9]

## Elements of Business Letter Writing

A typical Julfan business letter consisted of ordinary sheets of paper (normally purchased from a paper supplier in the letter's place of origin) ranging from a single sheet for a brief letter to several sheets of paper for more detailed correspondence. Some letters could be up to twenty pages in length when fully transcribed. Writers usually made every effort to fill all the available blank space on a page to convey their information, which meant that they often resorted to writing in the left margin. The sheets were then folded and sealed with red wax to produce the effect of an envelope (see fig. 1). A short instruction on delivering the mail to the addressee was written on the outside, most often only in Armenian. The name of the merchant to whom the letter was to be delivered and the merchant's presumed place of residence followed. Since most Julfan merchants were constantly on the move and changed their place of residence frequently according to the demands of the market, it is not uncommon to find two or three place-names written on the "envelope." This was mostly the case with letters written in Julfa in the 1740s and addressed to merchants in India, where the addressee's place of residence is given as "Basra, Madras, or Pondicherry or wherever he [i.e., the addressee] may be." That most letters have the addressee's information only in Armenian suggests that the couriers to whom they were entrusted were mostly fellow Armenians/Julfans (either merchants themselves or often family members of merchants, or professional couriers who worked within the network and were thus able to read Armenian). However, this was not always the case, for on some letters the addressee's entry is also written in languages other than Armenian (see fig. 2). Thus letters sent to the Sceriman family in Venice and Livorno are addressed in Italian, often giving the Italianized version of the addressee's name (for instance, "Signor Pietro di Sceriman," as opposed to Paron Petros Shahrimanian; see fig. 3).[10] Similarly, letters to Madras or Calcutta use English and seldom French.[11] Surprisingly, one does not come across many instances of Persian (the official language of not only Safavid Iran but also Mughal India) or Arabic on Julfan merchant letters, which suggests that most couriers used by Julfan merchants could understand instructions written in Armenian script.[12] The following, from a letter from an Armenian priest in Tokat (Ottoman Empire) to an Armenian merchant in China, is an example of the typical content of an "envelope" (fig. 4):

Deliver this letter to the hands of Padre Savera [i.e., Padre Severini][13] in the good city of Canton in China, so that he may safely deliver it to Khwaja Shükür Agha of Bursa, whatever city he may be in. [Padre Severini] must absolutely deliver this letter to him and receive his recompense from the Lord. Amen.
In the year of the Lord, March 12, 1747
In Tokhat[14]

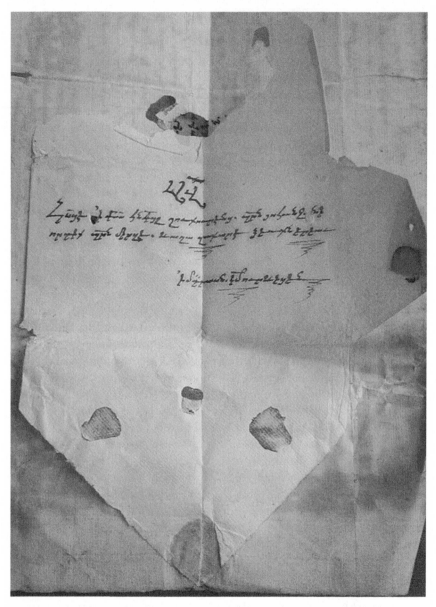

FIGURE 1. Envelope; HCA 32/1833, PRO, letter no. 195. Courtesy of the National Archives.

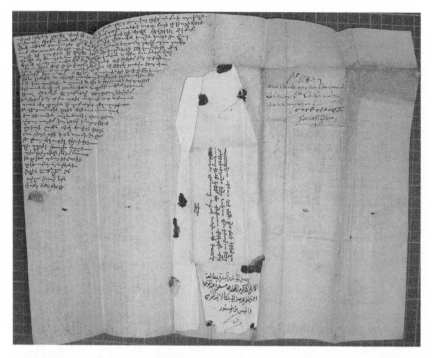

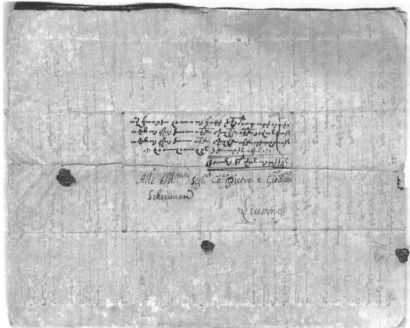

FIGURE 2.*(top)* Envelope with part of "addressee entry" in Arabic; HCA 30/682, PRO, letter no. 1180. Courtesy of the National Archives.

FIGURE 3. *(bottom)* Envelope addressed to Signior Conte Pietro e Gio. Battista Scheriman; Documenti Armeni Mercantile, ASV, busta 2. Courtesy of the Archivio di Stato di Venezia.

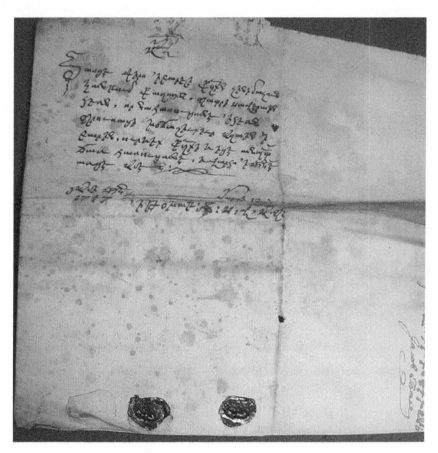

FIGURE 4. Envelope for letter to Canton, 1747; HCA 30/682, PRO, letter no. 1172. Courtesy of the National Archives.

In general, most correspondents maintained high levels of penmanship, a skill most likely acquired in a commercial school operating in Julfa in the 1680s.[15] In addition to a solid reputation and competence in mathematics and commercial accounting, literacy and good penmanship were also attributes merchants sought in a factor. Nonetheless, occasional letters exhibit rather poor levels of penmanship, although fortunately for the historian these are rare exceptions. The language of Julfan correspondence is the defunct, peculiar dialect of Julfan Armenian that flourished between the seventeenth and nineteenth centuries throughout the commercial settlements where Julfans resided, especially in India and the Far East.[16] This dialect is so distinct from other dialects of Armenian and from modern standard Armenian that it was and still is nearly incomprehensible to most Armenians. It

FIGURE 5. Sceriman family firm letter, 1693; Sceriman Family Papers, Don Mazza, busta 1. Courtesy of the Don Mazza Archives.

was, therefore, an ideal medium for confidential communication in an age when information sharing was regarded as the lifeline of merchant communities, and when a merchant could never be certain that his letters would not be intercepted and read by rivals in commerce or politics. Julfan letters, like most writing before the nineteenth century, do not display standard punctuation or spelling and contain no paragraph breaks except those indicated by the word *dardzeal* (again). Some letters also had important bills of exchange or notarized powers of attorney enclosed in them; in one case at least, we have a letter that had a lock of a woman's hair ensconced inside the envelope and probably used in place of a seal or signature as an identification mechanism by the author, who was illiterate and did not own her own seal (fig. 5).[17]

Most Julfan business letters follow a certain formulaic structure and have stylistic elements in common. There are relatively few known samples of business correspondence from other Asian communities dating from the same period, and these samples suggest that, despite certain cultural, religious, and script differences, most "mercantile groups of eighteenth-century Islamic Eurasia, no matter how they are defined, approached correspondence in a similar fashion."[18] Analogous epistolary conventions in Julfan mercantile correspondence written in Armenian (as opposed to Arabic) script, and in Arabic script correspondence written by Iranian, Gujarati, and other merchants in Islamic Eurasia, include the custom of beginning a letter by invoking God's presence, incorporating a long preamble with an ornate introduction, and concluding with a self-deprecating phrase.[19] These shared epistolary practices should not come as a surprise, given the larger Persianate and or Islamicate conventions, including a literary, commercial, and legal culture shared between Christian Armenians writing in their own script and Muslim and possibly Hindu merchants writing in Arabic script.[20] Julfan business letters and other commercial documents almost invariably begin by invoking the presence of God, using the seventh letter of the Armenian alphabet "Է"[21] placed at the top of the letter much as Arabic script letters written by other Asian merchants begin by using the letter *alif* or the word *huwa* to invoke the name of God.[22] Most letters then follow with one of two formulaic introductory phrases. The most common of these is the following: "Arz b[a]nd[a]yki h[a]sts'ē veroy greal [sahap]anun ghulughn i barin. T[ē]r a[stua]tsn s[a]hapanun herk[a]r umpr ivelum dōvl[a]t misht bari achoghum pargevi minchi khorhin tserut'iwn amēn." (Let this be submitted or petitioned to the above-mentioned masters. May the Lord God grant [my] masters long lives and more wealth and continuous good success until [their] ripe old age.) The other formula is "I kaminay[23] kamtar[24] tsarayēt aṙz[25] lini veṙōy greal paronin or . . ."[26] (From your small and menial servant, let it be submitted to the above-mentioned Sir, that . . . ) Common courtesy and expressions of obeisance and subordination are the usual fare in Julfan letters, especially when the writer happens to be a mere factor to a rich and powerful *khwaja* residing in his comfortable abode in Julfa/Isfahan. Self-deprecating phrases, such as *kamin kamptor* (menial servant) and *odits hogh yev mokhir* (the dust and ashes of your feet), roughly similar to the terms *aḥkar* (contemptible) and *bandah* (servant), which appear in Arabic script letters from the same period,[27] are also used between individuals who appear to be social and economic equals.[28] After "petitioning" the addressee, the correspondent almost always asks about the recipient's health and well-being, often expressing his prayers to God to grant the recipient a thousand years for each year in his life.

Subsequent to the opening wishes of prolonged good health and fortune contained in a letter's long preamble, the writer usually adopts the following segue to the task at hand: "ew etē duk ĕzmer meghavorats'ḥs harts'aneloy arzhan aṙnuk paṙk a[stutso]y saghemk."[29] (And if you were to deem it appropriate to ask about the well-being of us sinners, glory be to God, for we are healthy.) Another phrase used quite frequently is the following: "ew ayl erkris afaln[30] khatir berĕk'..." (And if it pleases you [to know about] the condition of this country...) These phrases allow the writer to make a smooth transition to the narration of his news.

A typical business letter from family members in India or Italy to their brothers in New Julfa (or vice versa) contains news about the family's well-being. Sometimes a letter begins with a long preamble preparing the recipient for some tragic news about the death or murder of a relative. Even in the midst of tragedy, however, the writer never shirks from addressing the business at hand, namely, reporting information deemed important for commerce. Consider the case of the merchant Harutiun di Emniaz, a member of one of Julfa's wealthiest merchant families, the *khwaja* Minasians. Harutiun's father, Khwaja Emniaz Minasian, was one of two Armenians, along with two merchants each from the Jewish, Zoroastrian, and Hindu communities, burned alive at the stake by Nadir Shah on January 14, 1747, in Isfahan's central square (Meydan-i Shah) before a large crowd of spectators. The foreign missionaries who witnessed this horrific event were unanimous in attributing the final collapse of Julfa as a mercantile center and the mass exodus of its leading Armenian families to Russia, the Mediterranean, and most notably to India to this event. Harutiun di Emniaz probably witnessed his father's auto-da-fé;[31] he was clearly so traumatized by the event that he fled from his hometown to Basra. In a postscript to a letter dated 16 November 1747 (1 Hamira 132), Harutiun di Emniaz wrote to his correspondents in Bengal, alluding to the murder of his father:

> You will have surely heard about the incurable grief of this inconsolable servant [i.e., the writer of the letter]. It remains to be added that during these [last] six months, having been bereft of hope in every possible way, I had withdrawn from everything including commerce, until the compassionate God took revenge upon that most evil, pagan, and lawless Nadir Shah for the just blood of my deceased father, that Salih Khan, the officer of the shah's permanent corps of bodyguards, entered his tent at night and killed the shah like a dog. They have nominated the son of Nadir's brother, Ali Quli Khan, as the king and put to the sword all the grandsons of that pharaoh [i.e., Nadir],

about thirty-five souls in all, and extirpated his name from this world. I swear upon God that you won't believe me if I tell you that during these last eight or nine months I have not known whether I am alive or dead. For me it is the end of this world on account of the passing away of my father, who was my pride in Isfahan as well as the ruin of our families there.[32]

After apologizing for his failure to send regular correspondence to India on account of his grief, he quickly regains his composure and, despite the gravity of the situation, goes on to narrate a very lengthy letter in which he addresses, among other things, the market situation in Basra and other business news. Lest one think that this letter is an exception, it should be noted that most of the Julfa correspondence dating from the late 1740s, and especially from 1745–1747, during Nadir Shah's brutal policies against the population of Julfa, are filled with tragic news. The wretched tenor of these letters, however, did not prevent their authors from switching from lamentation to business reportage. All this calls to mind Tadeus Krusinski's pithy, stereotyping remark "The *Armenians* of *Zulfa* are traders, and have nothing in their heads but Trade."[33]

### Conveying Political or Social News

Julfan commercial correspondence conveyed three categories of news or information also found in European business letters. The first category was political or social news. Julfan business letters often included interesting bits of political or social news, particularly about Julfa itself, that had a direct bearing on business. Julfa's welfare as a nodal center was crucial for Julfa merchants trading in India and Italy. Thus it is no surprise that letters mailed from Julfa to India in the late 1740s, and especially in 1747 (the bleakest year in Julfa's history), contain many pages of detailed information on the ravages Julfa endured as a result of Nadir Shah's extortionist policies. As already noted above, Nadir Shah's assassination in July 1747 and the subsequent ascent to the throne of Ali Quli Khan, who adopted the name Adil Shah, were conveyed in Harutiun di Emniaz's letter. Almost all the correspondents in this period were euphoric about Nadir's assassination and Adil Shah's rise to power. Many Julfans believed that Adil Shah would usher in a period of security and economic renewal because of his pledge not to collect taxes from Julfan merchants for several years.[34] Political and military news was also reported at length when it posed a direct risk to trade routes. Thus at the height of the War of Austrian Succession (1740–1748), when Anglo-French hostilities spilled into the waters of the Indian Ocean, and numerous Asian (including Armenian) ships were seized as "wartime prizes" on the pretext that they belonged to "the enemy," we find the factors of the Khwaja Minasian family firm telling their correspondents in Julfa how they learned of the presence of English men-of-war on the seas. An illustrative case is Khwaja Minas di Elias's letter from Calcutta in 1745 to his associates in Basra in which he explains how, through some Armenian passengers on a ship that had lately arrived in Calcutta by way of Mahé on the southwestern coast of India, he "received the News and Intelligence that the English men of War are in those Seas."[35] Likewise, a letter sent by a Julfan merchant from the French settlement of Chandernagor to a Julfan merchant in Calcutta tells of the French occupation of Madras by La Bourdonnais on September 6, 1746;[36] similar news regarding the Afghan occupation of Isfahan in 1722[37] and the impending battle of Plassey in India in 1757[38] are also found in Julfan correspondence. At times, the news was purely personal, as when a general company letter of the Minasian firm in Julfa informed its junior member, Minas di Elias, who was tending company affairs in Bengal that "[On the] 26 of Nadar [September 12] the Lord has been pleased to bless you Mr. Minas, for your wife was brought to bed on that Day of a Daughter." The letter then wishes that all the members of the Minasian family firm away on business in India "may come home and have each a son." It also comforts the new father by telling him not to worry, for the wife of a rival merchant had had a daughter.[39]

The second category of information conveyed by Julfan business letters relates to the merchants themselves. In a society where long-distance trade was carried out almost exclusively through agents, who were given large sums of capital to trade overseas on behalf of their masters at home, and where formal institutions such as courts were ineffective at enforcing contracts, trust and reputation were critical. To avoid being cheated by their agents, merchants therefore "conditioned future employment on past conduct."[40] Commercial correspondence played a crucial role in conveying information about the reputation and trustworthiness of fellow merchants and potential agents. As we shall see in chapter 7, merchants, in turn, generally conducted themselves with remarkable probity because they knew that acquiring a bad reputation was disastrous for their future, as they, and their relatives, would be shunned by members of the Julfan "coalition."[41]

But all other news paled in comparison with news about commerce—the third category of information conveyed by Julfan business correspondence. These were after all merchants' letters, and merchants who sent letters to each other in the seventeenth and eighteenth centuries wrote with the express intention of sharing commercial news. Most prominent in such news were lists of current prices for various commodities covered in the correspondents' business transactions. Sometimes this information was presented in the form of tables. European business letters, especially those of Italian merchants, contained information on weights and currencies in lands where the corresponding factor was based.[42] But this type of information does not seem to have been very important in Julfan business letters, most likely because Julfans already had access to special trade manuals (in both manuscript and printed form) compiled for the use of "merchants belonging to the Armenian nation" and providing detailed information on trade routes, weights, measures, and currencies used in many parts of the world.[43] We know, for instance, that the most important trade manual of this type, the trading "Compendium" of Constant of Julfa, written in manuscript form in the 1680s, was not only used as a textbook to train young merchant apprentices attending a special trade school in Julfa, but was also carried by merchants to places such as Surat and Izmir, presumably during their business trips there at the behest of their masters in Julfa.[44] But fresh information, the kind not available in Constant's manual, such as current exchange rates between European currencies like the silver *zolota* and Persian *toman* and their Mughal counterparts, customs duties, and road protection fares, was frequently communicated.

The communication of accurate and up-to-date price lists of various commodities helped Julfan merchants manipulate the market and use the "asymmetric information" at their disposal to compete with merchants belonging to rival networks. Consider the following excerpt from a long letter posted from Basra to India in the 1740s, in which the writer gives a detailed breakdown of the "prices of goods that have been sold by the English" and adds the following note:

> And at present the people offer higher prices to the Goods that those of our Nation have in this place and they will not sell, and we do really think together with the People of our Nation that we shall be able to sell our Goods at an Extraordinary [sic] good price. And we have not received any Advice from you about the Number of Goods that are on Board of the said ships, Notice has been given to us that on Board of them there is an account of the Europeans on freight Four hundred and fifty bales of Goods; And this is the reason why the merchants here refused to sell any Goods then. And for the future we must beg of you to be pleased to advise us in a most distinct manner, when any ship shall sail from that Place to this of the number of Goods and Fruits that she brings, for as often one Ship arrives after the other *if we know what they bring then we could take our measures in and about selling of what we have.*[45]

The importance of receiving accurate information or "intelligence" regarding market conditions in distant places cannot be underestimated. Such information, conveyed in business correspondence, alerted a merchant about the potential dangers or benefits of selling his merchandise in a particular market. An illustrative example of sensitive market information relayed between India and Julfa is contained in a company letter sent to India by Khwaja Emniaz Minasian on May 24, 1745 (not long before he was burned alive at the stake on the orders of Nadir Shah). In the letter he informs his junior associates in Basra and Calcutta that the pearls the company has purchased at a considerable value of seven hundred *tomans* cannot be sold in Surat (an important venue for the gem trade), as his associates had presumably expected, because of the intelligence he had received from India that "all the Merchants and Dealers in such sorts of Goods have disappeared from that place."[46]

Correspondents also wanted to be kept fully abreast of all the business transactions carried out by their overseas factors. The most senior members of a family firm in Julfa, for instance, needed to be fully informed of their firm's investments in different parts of the world in order to keep their account books up-to-date and to evaluate their commercial solvency. This function of business correspondence is revealed in the following exchange between a member of the Sceriman/Shahrimanian family who was based at the family's traditional headquarters in Julfa and the family's junior members who were newly resettled in Livorno and Venice. In his letter of 1711, one of the Scerimans in Julfa informs his cousin Paron Petros in Livorno that though he is delighted to hear about his cousin's personal well-being, he is most interested in news concerning the family's investments in Italy. It seems that Paron Petros had failed to fulfill his responsibility to convey accurate details regarding the family's business affairs:

> Paron Petros, your letter from Livorno dated Atam 22 [May 11] reached us on Hamira 8 [November 23], and we became acquainted with your situation. [However,] your letter was without flavor or salt [*bi namak*<P: literally, "without salt"] because it contained no news about purchases and expenditures. *The salt in a merchant's letter is [the news about] purchases and expenditures.* When you send us your next letter, be sure to write about the state of purchases and expenditures both in Livorno and in Venice, so we too can be more satisfied.[47]

The evidence from Julfan merchant correspondence suggests that commercial intelligence in the form of detailed updates on market conditions in faraway centers was one of the most significant functions of letter writing, as it also was in the case of Venetian and Genoese merchants in the sixteenth century.[48] In light of this evidence, we can further question the controversial, and by now largely discredited, view of Asian trade as a "peddler economy." According to this view, first advanced by Jacob Cornelius van Leur in the 1930s but popularized by Niels Steensgaard in the early 1970s, the Asian peddler did not possess the "rationality" introduced into the trading world of the Indian Ocean by the European joint-stock companies in the course of the seventeenth century. Steensgaard suggests that this was in part the result of "imperfect communication" about the volatility of distant markets that remained "non-transparent" to the peddler.[49] K. N. Chaudhuri's empirically grounded work on the English East India Company suggests that "the effective functioning of the Company's trading system depended critically on the proper functioning of the communication structure."[50] According to Chaudhuri, information sent in packets to and from the company's court of directors in London and its employees in India enabled its directors to make rational decisions and minimize risks: "[The Company's] information system was an aid to management, an indispensable condition of decision-making. It was also an instrument of power and authority. The hierarchy of information channels was just as important to the process of control as the formal structure of management responsibilities."[51] In short, as Chaudhuri points out, the company's bureaucratic and administrative apparatus at its headquarters in London, which received, catalogued, and summarized letters from agents in India, enabled the directors of the company to use letters and the commercial intelligence they contained as rational "guides to policy."[52] Philip Lawson and Willem Kuiters have also written in the same vein regarding the role of correspondence in the decision-making process of the English East India Company.[53] The Dutch East India Company, or VOC, had a similar bureaucratic system of monitoring correspondence between the company headquarters, mostly situated in Amsterdam, and its factories or trading outposts in the Indian Ocean.[54] Other joint-stock companies of the period, such as the Royal African Company and the Hudson's Bay Company, following the model of the English East India Company, had their own "Committees for Correspondence," which efficiently coordinated vital correspondence with factors overseas.[55]

To be sure, the Julfan Armenian merchants, like other Asian mercantile communities, did not operate on the basis of joint-stock companies, and their firms do not appear to have had the complex administrative structures of the English East India Company, with ten separate subcommittees, including a "committee of correspondence," each tasked with monitoring a specific aspect of their corporation's interest.[56] Rather, as we shall see in chapter 6, the Julfans relied on the patriarchal structure of the extended family as the basis of their family firms, each with its own director (usually the eldest male patriarch of the family), junior members of the family, and numerous *commenda* agents and other firm employees dispersed in all the important markets of the Indian Ocean and the Mediterranean. But this did not mean that Julfan trading practices were any less "rational" than those of the European companies or that markets were any less "transparent" to them because they lacked "comprehensive coordinated organizations" to help them operate in long-distance markets, as Steensgaard suggests.[57] In fact, the business correspondence from several Julfan family firms exhibits certain similarities to the methods European companies used to manage information. Such similarities included the coordinated and centralized system of remitting mail from the director of the family firm and senior family members usually headquartered in New Julfa to junior members living in various parts of India. Some Julfan family firms remitted two types of business correspondence: the first was in the form of circulars sent by the director of the firm to important junior members (usually younger brothers or cousins); the second was directed individually to *commenda* agents.[58] In either case, business intelligence on market conditions was a vital part of the news shared between firm members and the director of the firm in Julfa, and arguably one of the factors contributing to Julfan success in long-distance Indian Ocean trade. As Georges Roques, an official in the French East India Company working in India in the 1670s, notes in his trade manual, the enterprising Armenians he encountered "did not ignore the price of any merchandise, either from Europe or Asia or any other place, because they had correspondents everywhere who informed them about current prices on the spot. Therefore, they cannot be cheated in their purchases."[59]

A final aspect of Julfan business correspondence needs to be discussed before

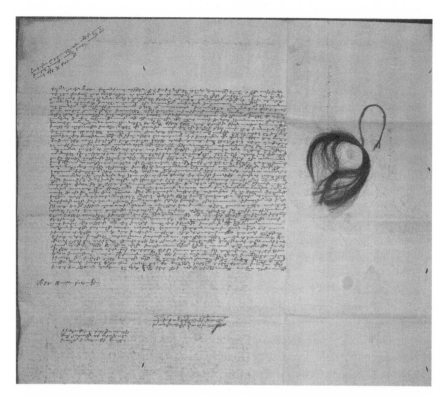

FIGURE 6. Letter with lock of hair, written by Anna Khatun, wife of Davit Sultan Sha-hamirian, 1747; HCA 30/682, PRO, letter no. 1534. Courtesy of the National Archives.

we consider the "courier system" that enabled merchants to send and receive let-ters across vast distances. We know from the personal papers of a few merchants that have been preserved in various archives that Julfan merchants were extremely diligent in their business correspondence. Like other merchants in Islamicate Eur-asia as well as in Europe, many Julfan merchants in fact kept special "letter books" or ledgers where they scribbled the originals of their letters and only then made copies of them to send to their correspondents.[60] One such letter book, bound in leather and containing neatly numbered pages, belonged to Khwaja Minas di Elias and is currently stored in the Public Records Office; another, stored in the Archivio di Stato di Venezia, belonged to Hakob di Murat Shahrimanian.[61] The voluminous correspondence of Amirbek di Vardan, from 1694–1704, has also been preserved in multiple notebooks in the Venetian archives.[62]

Julfan merchants also meticulously classified the correspondence they received in separate folders according to the correspondents' names and the dates covered by the letters. Yeghia Karnetsi, a merchant with close ties to Julfa, for example, seems to have exchanged tens of thousands of letters between the years 1715 and 1722. His personal papers were confiscated from him by Russian authorities in 1724 and are now stored in a Moscow archive. They contain no less than twenty-three special folders of thousands of letters he received from diverse correspondents.[63]

According to Trivellato, European merchants preserved copies of their correspondence because, among other things, by the late medieval period such correspondence was considered valid evidence in court.[64] This might also have been the case with Julfa merchants and might account for the presence of thousands of letters, alongside contracts and other legal documents, in the All Savior's Monastery Archive in Julfa; we cannot be certain of this, however, since so little is known about Julfan legal history. Certainly the hundreds, if not thousands, of letters exchanged between the Armenian merchant Hierapet di Martin (Hayrapet ordi Martirosi) and his factors in Italy, Amirbek di Vardan and Martiros di Sargis, were stored in the Archivio di Stato di Venezia because they were presented as evidence in various lawsuits.[65] But Julfans also preserved copies of mail (both sent and received) for the purpose of retroactively adjusting their account books based on the detailed price lists and records of purchased and sold commodities, as well as other market-oriented information contained in commercial correspondence. This practice was also common among Venetian merchants trading between Venice, Alexandria, and Aleppo during the sixteenth century, as Fredric Lane's work on the Barbarigo family firm demonstrates.[66] That business letters were preserved and stored with a view to later use is evidenced by the notes inscribed on the verso side of the correspondence received by the Sceriman family in Venice and Livorno. In addition to notes recording the reception and date of dispatch of a letter, each letter received by the Sceriman family also contains a summary of its contents for easy reference later. This custom of preserving correspondence for future reference is one of the reasons the Sceriman correspondence from the late seventeenth to the mid-eighteenth century seems to have survived relatively intact in the Archivio di Stato di Venezia, as well as in a private archive in Verona. It also appears that the Scerimans in Venice deposited their business letters in individually numbered bags, presumably for easy access later. Thus, on the verso side of a letter from Isfahan, we read the following note in Italian: *Dal Sachetto No. dieci.* (From bag number ten).[67]

## MONSOONS, THE COURIER NETWORK, AND JULFA MERCHANTS IN THE INDIAN OCEAN

Julfan commercial correspondence in the Indian Ocean was delivered from one Armenian settlement in India to another and eventually to the nodal center of the network in New Julfa itself through an elaborate courier system that provided Julfans with an "intelligence network" spanning their commercial settlements (see table 1).[68] Sometimes letters were delivered by professional couriers (known in Persian,

Turkish, and Arabic as *chapars,*[69] *shatirs,*[70] or most commonly *qasids*), but more frequently they were carried by traveling merchants. Most mail from India to Julfa traveled on European company vessels (usually those of the English, French, and Dutch East India Companies) and ships freighted or owned by Armenian merchants. Armenian merchants also used Mughal-owned ships, such as those in the formidable commercial fleet belonging to the famous Surat-based maritime merchant family known as the Chalabies.[71] When professional couriers were not used, mail would be handed over (*taslim*) to an Armenian merchant traveling to Isfahan or the Persian Gulf.

Mail traveling from Bengal to New Julfa would follow one of two routes. The most traveled was the maritime route, which relied on ships embarking at the port of Hugli or the busier harbor of Calcutta. From there mail was likely to travel in stages down the eastern coast of India making calls at Madras and Surat from where it would be shipped to the Persian Gulf port of Basra. In Basra, it would be transferred to Armenian merchants traveling overland to Isfahan. Sometimes, professional couriers working for Julfan family firms would be waiting at busy ports such as Basra to deliver important mail to their masters in Julfa.[72] In some cases, mail would be unloaded at the port of Bandar Rig in the Persian Gulf, where it would be handed over to couriers to be delivered overland north to Julfa. Reading the bundles of letters among the *Santa Catharina* documents at the PRO, one gets the impression that many Julfan merchants were feverishly writing their letters at one of the Persian Gulf emporia, getting prepared to hand their dispatches to the next arriving ship. The evidence suggests that correspondents stationed in those ports had a remarkably detailed knowledge of the schedule of arriving and departing ships. They often relied on hearsay from other merchants that, for instance, such and such a ship was scheduled to depart from Surat two days after their own ship. Using this kind of information, the correspondents could calculate that the next ship would arrive in a few days' time. Often, a correspondent mentions that the ship arrived while he was still writing his letter and notes that so-and-so (usually a prominent Julfan merchant in Madras) has sent a letter by this or that ship and the letter has been dispatched to Isfahan by special courier. We are dealing here with a very sophisticated network, a complex system of receiving and remitting information. One reason Julfan merchants paid attention to the schedule of ships arriving in the Persian Gulf from India was because they were conscious of the fact that the next incoming ship might bring with it important mail, including contracts and letters of credit, not to mention goods. It is not unusual to find in one letter references to several ships (mostly English, but also French and Mughal ships, as was the case of "Chalaby's ships," plying the busy waterway between Basra, Gombroon [i.e., Bandar 'Abbas], and Surat). Khoja Emniaz, in his long company letter of 24 May 1745, informs his business associates in India: "We have also received Advice that an English ship called the Tenny [read: the Fenny] has sailed from thence for Gomeron [read: Gombroon, i.e., Bandar 'Abbas], by which we expect likewise to receive some letters and the contracts that have been on Bottomree upon her;[73] it is probable that this ship will sail also for your place, but we have not received any advice thereupon."[74]

Mail was also sent through a messenger (*pattamar*[75] or *dak*,[76] to use terms in currency in Mughal India) on an overland route from Bengal across the Indo-Gangetic Plain to Surat and from there by ship to the Persian Gulf. Julfan merchants' reliance on this service is attested in a letter sent from Surat to Calcutta by Tsadur di Elias to his brother Minas di Elias, in which the writer states that he is dispatching his letter through an "express courier" named Mr. Mainchim, who seems to have been a *dak* or *pattamar* of Indian (most likely Hindu) origin. The letter reached its destination in forty-seven days.[77] This combination of overland and maritime transportation could shave off a few weeks of travel time.

Generally speaking, Julfan merchants in the Indian Ocean relied on a peculiar logic of information relays to circulate news and mail between their home base in Julfa and various parts of India. The picture that emerges from the available corpus of letters is the following: merchants stationed in Surat, who were closer on the communication circuit to the nodal center of Julfa, relayed sensitive news about the socioeconomic situation in Julfa to their associates in Bengal or elsewhere in India. Information about the home base was remitted in stages, with those residing in settlements closest to the center passing information to others on the margins of the network. This seems to be the system of information flows that glued the nodal center of the Julfan trade network at Julfa/Isfahan to its satellite communities in the Indian Ocean. Unfortunately, there is no evidence of surviving correspondence from Julfans in Manila or Tibet, so we can only conjecture that whatever communication there was between these outposts in the larger world of the Indian Ocean and their center at Julfa must have obeyed the same logic of information relays that applied to the settlements in India, with the difference that the distances were far greater and the time it took to remit information far longer than that for most settlements in India.[78]

The mail service between India and Julfa was predicated on many contingent factors, the most important of which was the monsoon system (known in Julfa dialect as *mowsum,* from the Arabic *mawsim*,[79] or trading season, from which the Indian and English *monsoon* also derives), which dominated the lives of everyone living along the shores of the Great Ocean. There were two general monsoon seasons in the Indian Ocean.[80] The first, or the northeast, monsoon extended from October to March, marking the beginning of the season for the departure of ships from India to the Persian Gulf. Ships wishing to travel to the Persian Gulf had usually to depart India in January in order to catch the winds blowing west. Failure to do so, and thus missing the monsoon, meant a delay of up to one year. The other monsoon season lasted from April to September, with easterly winds blowing from the African coast toward the western shores of India. This meant that ships heading from the Persian Gulf (or the Red Sea) to India had to depart early in the summer to make landfall in India by late autumn.[81] The voyage in either direction usually lasted from four to six months. This peculiar ecostructure of the Indian Ocean "imposed limits upon man's achievement,"[82] to borrow Fernand Braudel's famous expression. As Chaudhuri, Michael Pearson,[83] and others have demonstrated, it is virtually impossible to understand commercial and social life in the Indian Ocean without first taking into account the impositions of the ocean's geography and ecology. This was particularly the case for communities of merchants like the Julfa Armenians whose settlements in India and beyond needed to be constantly replenished with the regular circulation of merchants, credit, priests, and above all information from their nodal center in Julfa. The circulation of all these men and things was dependent on the monsoon system. This was especially the case with the delivery of commercial correspondence.

There are no available printed data on the speed with which mail traveled between India and Julfa; however, it is possible to calculate the time it took for letters to travel from Julfa to Bengal, because, as noted above, merchants receiving important correspondence (whether in Madras or Venice) had the habit of recording the date a letter reached their hands.[84] An examination of many such letters from the All Savior's Monastery Archive, as well as from archives in Venice, Verona, Florence, and London, suggests that the average time of courier delivery between Isfahan and Calcutta in the mid-eighteenth century ranged from three months (the fastest speed found in the documents in our collection) to seven months (the slowest delivery) for urgent business letters; up to two weeks between Chinsura and Calcutta; and only one day between Chandernagor and Calcutta. As noted above, we have one recorded case of a letter sent from Surat to Calcutta that reached its destination in forty-seven days. This letter was sent not by ship but by an Indian *dak* or *pattamar* probably across the great Indo-Gangetic Plain. In 1747 mail from Basra to Isfahan was delivered by overland courier in sixteen days, from Bushire to Isfahan in two months. These are the times for business letters that contained vital information for the conduct of trade. Since time was of the essence in sharing information, we would expect to discover that business letters were delivered with the greatest speed. This was not the case with letters sent by the clergy. Thus we discover from a letter sent from Chinsura to Julfa in 1727 by an Armenian priest that a letter of blessing from the primate in Julfa for the Armenian Church of Chinsura (Bengal) was dated 18 June 1725 and arrived in Chinsura on 23 September of the following year by way of the senior priest in Madras, who must have received the letter first. This means that it took about one year and three months to reach its destination in Bengal.[85]

Needless to say, the mail system in the eighteenth-century Indian Ocean was very slow and inefficient by modern standards. Mail often got lost; ships fell prey to pirates, were lost at sea, or were captured as prizes during one of the many wars in

TABLE 1  Mail delivery between Julfa and the Indian Ocean region

| Sender(s) | Recipient(s) | Origin | Destination | Date sent[a] | Date received | Travel time | Transportation mode |
|---|---|---|---|---|---|---|---|
| Mr. Gregory[b] | Minas di Elias | Surat | Calcutta | 1 Tira (17 Sept.) | 10 Tamaw (26 Oct.) | 39 days | Unknown |
| Mr. Tsatur[c] | Minas di Elias | Surat | Calcutta | 27 Tira (13 Oct.) | 15 Aram (30 Dec.) | 78 days | Unknown |
| Mr. Tsatur[d] | Minas di Elias | Surat | Calcutta | 27 Tira (13 Oct.) | 16 Hamira (1 Dec.) | 49 days | Dak |
| Emniaz, Gregory, Aghamal (Hagamal)[e] | Mr. Tsatur, Minas di Elias, Paolo | Isfahan | Calcutta | 21 Tira (7 Oct.) | 26 Hamira (11 Dec.) | 67 days | Unknown |
| Emniaz, Gregory, Aghamal (Hagamal)[f] | Mfinas, Meliknas, Seth, and Johanes | Isfahan | Calcutta | 5 Shabat (24 May) | 29 Tira (15 Oct.) | 144 days | Unknown |
| Emniaz, Gregory, Aghamal (Hagamal)[g] | Minas, Meliknas, Seth, and Johanes | Isfahan | Calcutta | 17 Shabat (5 July) | 10 Tira (26 Sept.) | 83 days | Unknown |
| Emniaz, Gregory, Aghamal (Hagamal)[h] | Minas, Meliknas, Seth, and Johanes | Isfahan | Calcutta | 17 Shabat (5 July) | 11 Ovtan (25 Jan.) | 210 days | Unknown |
| Emniaz, Gregory, Aghamal (Hagamal)[i] | Aratun Lukas, Simon, Abdalmessy, Tarkhan, Johannes | Isfahan | Basra | 5 Shabat (24 May) | 21 Shabat (9 June) | 16 days | Unknown |
| Emniaz, Gregory, Aghamal (Hagamal)[j] | Aratun Simon, Meliknas, Minas, Mickertun, Khachick | Isfahan | Calcutta | 10 Nadar (27 Aug.) | 26 Hamira (11 Dec.) | 106 days | Unknown |
| Aghamal (Hagamal), Gregory, Shafras[k] | Minas di Elias | Isfahan | Calcutta | 11 Nadar (28 Aug.) | 19 Thamaw (4 Nov.) | 69 days | Unknown |
| Aghamal (Hagamal) di Shafras[l] | Minas di Elias | Isfahan | Busher | 30 Nirhan (15 March) | 27 Atam (16 May) | 62 days | Unknown |
| Aghamal (Hagamal) di Shafras[m] | Minas di Elias | Isfahan | Calcutta | 5 Shabat (24 May) | 10 Tira (26 Sept.) | 145 days | Unknown |
| Gregory son of Seth[n] | Minas di Elias | Isfahan | Calcutta | 4 Shabat (23 May) | 10 Tira (26 Sept.) | 146 days | Unknown |
| Gregory son of Seth[o] | Minas di Elias | Isfahan | Calcutta | 30 Thamaw (15 Nov.) | 11 Ovtan (25 Jan.) | 70 days | Unknown |
| Gregory son of Seth[p] | Minas di Elias | Isfahan | Calcutta | 28 Nadar (14 Sept.) | 11 Ovtan (25 Jan.) | 131 days | Unknown |
| Gregory son of Seth[q] | Minas di Elias | Isfahan | Calcutta | 30 Atam (19 May) | 10 Tira (26 Sept.) | 150 days | Unknown |

| | | | | | | | |
|---|---|---|---|---|---|---|---|
| Gregory son of Seth, Petrus son of Gregory Minas di Elias, | Gregory son of Shafras | Basra | Calcutta | 22 Nadar (8 Sept.) | 10 Tira (26 Sept.) | 18 days | Unknown |
| Gregory son of Seth, Petrus son of Gregory[r] | Minas di Elias, Gregory son of Shafras | Isfahan | Basra | 2 Shabat (21 May) | 10 Nadar (27 Aug.) | 98 days | Unknown |
| Petros son of Gregory[s] | Minas di Elias | Basra | Calcutta | 25 Shabat (13 June) | 10 Nadar (27 Aug.) | 75 days | Unknown |
| Petros son of Gregory[t] | Minas di Elias | Isfahan | Calcutta | 22 Nadar (8 Sept.) | 10 Tira (26 Sept.) | 18 days | Unknown |
| Gregory son of Shafras[u] | Minas di Elias | Saidabad (Bengal) | Basra | 30 Shabat (18 June) | 30 Tira (16 Oct.) | 120 days | English ship |
| Paron Sarkis[v] | Astuatsatur di Petros | Basra | Calcutta | 22 Aram 131 (6 Jan. 1746) | 15 Nakha 132 (4 July 1747) | 1 year and 180 days | Unknown, mostly likely via port of Calcutta |
| Simeon, Abdalmassey, Khachatur | Minas di Elias, Johanes, √ Minas, Tarhan, Johaneses, Hachick | Basra | Calcutta | 27 Nadar (13 Sept.) | 13 Tira (29 Sept.) | 16 days | English ship |
| Poghos di Khachik Topchents[x] | Minas di Elias | Madras | Calcutta | 14 Tira 130 (30 Sept. 1745) | 22 Dama 130 (7 Nov. 1745) | 38 days | Unknown |
| Grigor di Safras[y] | Minas di Elias | Madras | Calcutta | 24 Nadar 130 (10 Sept. 1745)(5 Oct. 1745) | 19 Tira 130 (5 Oct. 1745) | 25 days | Unknown |
| Hovakim di Manuel[z] | Minas di Elias | Chandernagor | Calcutta | 22 Ghamar 130 (9 Aug. 1745) | 23 Ghamar 130 (10 Aug. 1745) | 1 day | Unknown |
| Hovakim di Manuel[aa] | Minas di Elias | Chandernagor | Calcutta | 26 Nadar 130 (12 Sept. 1745) | 27 Nadar 130 (13 Sept. 1745) | 1 day | Unknown |
| Gevork Vardapet[bb] | Minas di Elias | Chinsura | Calcutta | 28 Tira 129 (14 Oct. 1744) | 1 Dama 129 (17 Oct. 1744) | 3 days | Unknown |
| Sarkis[cc] | Minas di Elias | Surat | Calcutta | 19 Shems 131 (8 April 1746) | 30 Adam 131 (19 May 1746) | 41 days | Unknown |
| David Ghoslumian[dd] | Minas di Elias | Dhaka | Calcutta | 2 Tira 130 (18 Sept. 1745) | 9 Tira 130 (25 Sept. 1745) | 7 days | Post |

a The dates used in these letters are, for the most part, drawn from the peculiar calendar used almost exclusively by Julfan merchants. Known as the calendar of Azaria or the small calendar, this calendrical system was invented by Catholicos Azaria (himself from Old Julfa) in the sixteenth century and was formally instituted in 1616 to replace the traditional Armenian calendar (known as the greater Armenian calendar), which started in A.D. 552 To convert Azaria dates, one adds 1615 to the Azaria year for all dates after 21 March (the beginning of the year) and 1616 to dates before 21 March. Thus Azaria year 75 (after 21 March) would correspond to 1690 (1615+75). It should be noted that Julfan merchants and especially priests often employed both the greater Armenian calendar and that of Azaria. A typical Julfan document might give the date as 1143 in the greater Armenian calendar and 79 according to the Azaria calendar, both of which would correspond to the

Gregorian date 1694. The Azaria calendar also had a unique nomenclature for months (thirteen months in all including a month of five days called Haveleats). In converting Azaria dates to Gregorian, I have relied on the conversion tables found in Abrahamyan 1972, 118–120. Abrahamyan's book also has an insightful discussion (115–120) on the origins of the Azaria calendar and its use until the mid-nineteenth century among Julfans both in Julfa and in its overseas settlements, especially in India and Indonesia.

b *Santa Catharina* logbook of Spanish and English translations, HCA 42/026, PRO, letter no. 9, folio 23.

c Ibid., letter no. 58, folio 201.

d Ibid., letter no. 57.

e Ibid., letter no. 16.

f Ibid., letter no. 17.

g Ibid., letter no. 18.

h Ibid., letter no. 19.

i Ibid., letter no. 20.

j Ibid., letter no. 23.

k Ibid., letter no. 27.

l Ibid., letter no. 28.

m Ibid., letter no. 29.

n Ibid., letter no. 32.

o Ibid., letter no. 33.

p Ibid.

q Ibid., letter no. 34.

r Ibid., letter no. 35. It took fifteen days for commercial mail to travel between Basra and Isfahan. Letters by priests took longer to travel the distance.

s *Santa Catharina* logbook, English translations and court papers, HCA 42/026, PRO, letter no. 35.

t Ibid., letter no. 43.

u Ibid., letter no. 47

v Information culled from HCA 30/682, PRO, letter no. 1436: Astuatsatur di Petros to Paron Sarkis, 30 Dama 132 (15 November 1747).

w Ibid., letter no. 52.

x HCA 32/1832, PRO, letter no. 441.

y Ibid.

z HCA 30/682, PRO, letter no. 1015.

aa Ibid., letter no. 1020.

bb Ibid., letter no. 920.

cc Ibid., letter no. 1149.

dd Ibid., letter no. 841.

the Indian Ocean fought by European powers; from time to time, messengers also were robbed en route.[86] This is why if a letter was important enough, as was often the case, the writer made sure to send as many as four or five copies via different couriers. The practice of sending several copies of the same letter to increase the chances of it being received by the recipient was also common in the European East India Companies and other Asian communities.[87]

A common complaint in Julfan correspondence between Persia and India was the failure of one of the parties to send news to his family in either Julfa or India. Thus, in a letter written from Pegu (Burma) by a Julfan merchant to a family member in 1676, the writer bitterly complains: "You have been gone now for sixteen years, and what do you have to say? Is there no pity in your heart? Your father passed away a year ago from the pain of longing to see your face, your mother's eyes have gone blind from crying, and your wife has withered away."[88] He ends his melancholic letter by chiding his brother for not responding to a single one of his letters. Similar complaints appear in another letter, posted from Tokhat (a town in the eastern provinces of the Ottoman Empire) and addressed to an Armenian merchant residing in Canton (China): "My dear one, it has been five letters, including this one, that I have written and sent by way of sea and land, and I have not received a single response to any of my letters. I don't know whether they have arrived, and you have ignored them, or if they haven't arrived. Only you know that."[89] Certainly, these were rare cases, since most family members or friends managed to keep in touch with each other at least once every two years and often more regularly even when they traveled fast and far. In the case of merchants, the turnaround rate between letters was much faster. Nonetheless, frequent complaints about delays in receiving mail are found in most of the correspondence that has reached us, thus indicating the difficulties of communicating across the Indian Ocean in the seventeenth and eighteenth centuries.

Despite these drawbacks, the commercial mail system was indispensable for Julfan society. In fact, almost every aspect of Julfan life was dependent on the functioning of the courier network. Merchants needed it to circulate vital information from their headquarters in Julfa to their agents and business associates in India. Often, their ability to expedite information in a timely fashion meant the difference between making a favorable investment in a volatile market and being stuck with merchandise when the market was down. *Commenda* agents in faraway India needed to receive orders (*barovagir*[90] or, more specifically, *ordnagir*: from the Italian *ordine* for "order" and the Armenian *gir* for "letter"[91]) and advice on what to do with their consignment of goods from masters back in Julfa; when they needed to make money transfers, they had to do so by mailing their letters of credit. Families needed to hear from their members residing overseas from time to time. Most importantly, merchants residing in India needed to be apprised of the latest developments and news (including political news) concerning the welfare of their mother community in Julfa; in this connection, it is interesting to note that almost every business letter sent to India in the mid-eighteenth century begins with a rapid summary of the political and social news in Julfa that transpired during the last monsoon season.

As we have already noted, however, merchants were not the only ones to depend on the intelligence network connecting the communities in India and the East with the nodal center in Julfa. The church also depended on this system to send information to its diocesan sees in India. General encyclicals, pontifical bulls from Etchmiatzin, letters of blessing, alms donations, payment of church taxes, correspondence between priests overseeing a parish in India and the primate in New Julfa, and, in rare cases, letters of excommunication all circulated between the diocesan center of the All Savior's Monastery in Julfa and its daughter churches in India and farther east by means of the same courier system.[92] The ability of this system to circulate information from one end of the Julfan network to another was thus just as crucial for merchants as it was for the clergy, one of whose functions was to maintain the integrity of the commercial network by ensuring that its members stayed firm in their ethno-religious identity and, therefore, also continued making generous donations to the church.

## THE OVERLAND COURIER SYSTEM
## FROM JULFA TO THE MEDITERRANEAN

Unlike mail in the Indian Ocean zone, mail from Julfa to various settlements in the Mediterranean was not subject to the constraints of nature such as those of the monsoon seasons. It was also not predominantly dependent on maritime routes, but on a combination of overland and maritime transport. The bulk of our data on the Julfa-Mediterranean mail service comes from letters stored in the Archivio di Stato di Venezia, the Alishan archives in San Lazzaro, and a private archive in Verona, all of which contain the correspondence of one Julfan family: the Sceriman/Shahrimanian family of Catholic Armenians, many of whom had fled Iran and permanently settled in Venice and Livorno in 1698. Since the members of this family were simultaneously based in Julfa, Livorno, Venice, and various cities in India, their correspondence contains important data on the delivery of mail between all these places.

Most of the business and family letters the Scerimans received in Venice were sent from Julfa along three general directions. Mail traveled by way of overland caravan routes to Tabriz or Hamadan in the northwest, whence it would be sent to Aleppo, and from there by ship (from the port of Iskenderun/Alexandretta) to Venice or Livorno.[93] It could also be sent south to Basra and transported from there by caravan to Aleppo. Mail could also be sent to Tokhat (farther northwest in the Ottoman Empire), whence it would travel to Izmir or to Istanbul, where it would be placed on a ship heading to Venice or Livorno. At times, up to three copies of a letter were made, the first sent to Basra and then Aleppo, the second to Izmir, and the last to Istanbul, as we learn from a Sceriman letter sent to Venice in 1725: "We sent three letters last year. One was to Basra to Paron Martiros, and two copies of another letter we gave to Hakobjan, a coworker of the Tsarakatar family, in the entourage of the Ottoman embassy to Iran,[94] who was going to Basra, so that one [letter] would be sent from Tokhat to Izmir or Aleppo, the other by way of Istanbul. We hope to God that they have reached our masters."[95]

Usually such mail was entrusted to a private *shatir* or *qasid* (messenger/runner) belonging to a Julfan business firm. Once the letter was received by a Sceriman associate in Izmir, Aleppo, or Istanbul, it was shipped either directly to Venice to be remitted to Livorno, or directly to Livorno whence it was relayed to Venice by a courier. The journey from Julfa to Venice could last anywhere from five to thirteen months (see table 2). The overland journey from Isfahan to Izmir could last as little as three months. From Izmir to Venice, there is evidence from a letter mailed to a Julfan merchant in Venice by his correspondents in Izmir that a letter from Venice was received in Izmir in forty-three days.[96] This must have been rather fast, for there is another instance where a ship sailing from Izmir took two months and six days to reach Venice—that is, sixty-six days.[97]

It appears that most Armenian merchants in Izmir who had associates in Venice sent their mail to Venice via Livorno. The evidence does not indicate whether this was because their associates in Venice also had merchants working for them in Livorno or because there were more ships sailing from Izmir for Livorno than to Venice, and therefore it made sense for merchants to mail their parcels to Livorno and have them delivered from there to Venice by a special courier. Data gathered from the correspondence of the Venice-based merchant Hierapet di Martin, who had an agent named Amirbek di Vardan conducting business for him in Naples, Florence, and Livorno, suggest that the Livorno-Venice leg could take as little as six days in the 1690s. All things considered, there was very little if any difference between Aleppo, Izmir, or Istanbul as transit venues on the overland courier network to Venice or Livorno. Each of these transit stations produced more or less the same delivery time for mail from Julfa to Venice and Livorno, namely, five to thirteen months (quite a considerable variation in time). Given this parity in delivery time, the choice between these three locations must have depended on other factors, such as the availability of a courier heading in that direction, the safety of the routes in question, or, more likely, the shipping schedules in those ports.

Though professional couriers or runners working for the family firm of a friend or even for the Capuchin monks in Aleppo were known to have delivered mail for the Sceriman family, this was not always the case.[98] In some instances, mail was carried by family members who happened to be heading in the desired direction. Thus, in 1725, members of the Sceriman family residing in Julfa/Isfahan sent some

TABLE 2  Mail delivery between Julfa, the Mediterranean, Russia, and northwestern Europe

| Sender(s) | Recipient(s) | Origin | Destination |
|---|---|---|---|
| Shahriman brothers Nazar, Sarhat, Simon, Astuatsatur[a] | Family members Mr. Petros, Mr. Johanes | Isfahan | Livorno |
|  |  |  | Venice |
| Shahriman brothers Nazar, Sarhat, Simon, Astuatsatur | Family members Mr. Petros, Mr. Johanes | Isfahan | Venice |
| Shahriman brothers Sarhat, Astuatsatur, Simon, Bartolomeus, Jacob | Mr. Ohannes, Mr. Petros | Isfahan | Venice |
| Shahriman brothers Sarhat, Astuatsatur, Simon, Tadeos, Bartolomeus, Jacob | Mr. Ohannes, Mr. Petros | Isfahan | Venice |
| Shahriman brothers Sarhat, Astuatsatur, Simon, Tadeos, Bartolomeus, Jacob | Mr. Ohannes, Mr. Petros | Isfahan | Venice |
| Shahriman brothers Sarhat, Astuatsatur, Shahriman, Tadeos Bartolomeus, Jacob | Mr. Ohannes, Mr. Petros | Isfahan | Izmir |
|  |  |  | Venice |
| Shahriman brothers Sarhad, Astuatsatur, Shahriman, Tadeos Bartolomeus, Jacob | Mr. Ohannes, Mr. Petros | Isfahan | Venice |
| Shahriman brothers Sarhat, Astuatsatur, Shahriman, Tadeos Bartolomeus, Jacob | Mr. Ohannes, Mr. Petros, Hakob | Isfahan | Livorno |
| Shahriman brothers Sarhat, Astuatsatur, Shahriman, Murat, Tadeos Bartolomeus, Jacob | Mr. Ohannes, Mr. Petros | Isfahan | Venice |
| Shahriman brothers Sarhat, Astuatsatur, Shahriman, Murat, Tadeos Bartolomeus, Jacob | Mr. Ohannes, Mr. Petros | Isfahan | Venice |
| Mr. Manuel, Astuatsatur, Mukel, Hakobjan, Harutiun, Petros, Joseph, Murat | Mr. Stepan, Velijan, Sarhat | Isfahan | Venice |

| Date sent | Date received | Travel time | Transportation mode |
|---|---|---|---|
| 7 Aram 98 | June 12 (13 Shabat?) 98 (1 June) in Livorno | 5 months, 10 days 8 days from Livorno to Venice | Unknown |
| | 20 June 98 in Venice (22 Dec. 1713) | 5 months, 18 days from Isfahan to Venice via Livorno | |
| 10 Ghamar 96 (28 July 1711) | 25 Ovdan 96 (8 Feb. 1712) | 7 months, 5 days | Via Istanbul |
| 22 Nakha 96 (10 July 1711) | 2 Nirhan 96 (15 Feb. 1712) Feb.? 1712 | 6 months, 25 days | Unknown |
| 28 Nakha 96 (16 July 1711) | 10 Aram 96 (25 Dec. 1711) | 5 months, 9 days | Via Istanbul |
| 23 Hamira 97 (8 Dec. 1713) | 14? July 14? Nakha 98 (2 July 1714) | 6 months, 24 days | Unknown |
| 14 Shams 97 (3 April 1713) | 16 Nakha 97 (4 July 1713) 10 Sept. 97 reached Venice, 1712 | 3 months 5 months, 7 days to Venice 2 months, 6 days from Izmir to Venice by ship | Arrived in Izmir "brought by the *shatir* of Paron Maler" Arrived in Venice on the ship *Madonna del [Rey?]* |
| 1 Shabat (?) 98 (20 May 1713) | 22 Dec. 26? Hamira 98 (11 Dec. 1713) | 6 months, 20 days | Arrived via Livorno |
| 15 Nakha 99 (1714) | 4 Hamira 99 (30 Nov. 1714) | 4 months, 27 days | Unknown |
| 6 Atam (25 April) | 2 Nov. 96 6? Dama 1711 (22 Oct. 1711) | 5 months, 27 days | Reached Venice via Aleppo |
| 13 Nirhan 95 (26 Feb. 1711) | 24 July 25? Nakha 1712 (13 July 1711) | 4 months, 17 days | Via Gregory di (?) |
| 18 Ghamar (5 Aug.) | 23 Aram (Jan. 7) | 5 months, 2 days | Unknown |

TABLE 2 *(continued)*

| Sender(s) | Recipient(s) | Origin | Destination |
|---|---|---|---|
| Mr. Nazar, Astuatsatur, Shahriman, Hakob, Bartolomeus, Tadeos | Mr. Ohannes, Mr. Petros | Isfahan | Livorno Venice |
| Shahriman brothers Sarhat, Astuatsatur, Shahriman, Jacob | Mr. Ohannes, Mr. Petros | Isfahan | Venice |
| Mr. Nazar, Astuatsatur, Shahriman, Hakob, Bartolomeus Tadeos | Mr. Ohannes, Mr. Petros | Isfahan | Livorno |
| Mr. Nazar, Astuatsatur, Shahriman Hakob, Bartolomeus, Tadeos | Mr. Ohannes, Mr. Petros | Isfahan | Venice |
| Mr. Nazar, Astuatsatur, Shahriman, Hakob, Murat, Bartolomeus, Tadeos | Mr. Ohannes, Mr. Petros | Isfahan | Venice |
| 4 Mr. Nazar, Astuatsatur, Shahriman, Hakob, Murat, Bartolomeus, Tadeos | Mr. Ohannes, Mr. Petros | Isfahan | Venice |
| Mr. Nazar, Astuatsatur, Shahriman, Hakob, Murat, Bartolomeus, Tadeos | Mr. Ohannes, Mr. Petros | Isfahan | Venice |
| Parons Markar, Manuel, Astuadsatur, Mukel, Hakobjan, Haroutyun, Leon, Petros, Housep, Manuel, Grigor, Murat, Shariman, Petros, and Servant Hakob | Gaspar, Stepan, Velijan, Sarhat | Isfahan | Venice |
| Parons Stepan and Barsegh[c] | Parons Nazar, Shariman, Poghos, Khachatur, Housep, Safar, Vatan, Petros, Hovakim, Grigor, and others | Isfahan | Livorno |
| Serafin (Serapion) di Murat and Paron Ohan[d] | Oscan di Nubar | Venice | Izmir |
| Paron Barsegh[e] | Sceriman brothers Mr. Nazar, Astuatsatur, Shahriman, Hakob, Murat, Bartolomeus Tadeos | Izmir | Isfahan |
| Sceriman brothers Mr. Nazar, Astuatsatur, Shahriman, Hakob, Murat, Bartolomeus Tadeos | Parons Stepan and Barsegh | Venice | Isfahan |
| Paron Petros | Mr. Nazar, Astuatsatur, Shahriman, Hakob, Murat, Bartolomeus Tadeos | Livorno | Isfahan |
| Paron Petros[f] | Sceriman brothers Mr. Nazar, Astuatsatur, Shahriman, Hakob, Murat, Bartolomeus Tadeos | Livorno | Isfahan |

| Date sent | Date received | Travel time | Transportation mode |
|---|---|---|---|
| 13 Hamira 96 (28 Nov.) | 15 June (16? Shabat) 97 (4 June 1712) | 6 months, 6 days | Unknown |
| 15 Atam 98 (4 May 1713) | 26 Oct. 1713 (29 Tira 98) (15 Oct. 1713) | 5 months, 19 days | Via Aleppo |
| 22 Nadar 98 (19 July 1714) | 30 July 1 Ghamar 1714 (14 Sept. 1713) | 10 months, 25 days | Unknown |
| 15 Ghamar 98 (2 Aug. 1713) | 2 June (4? Shabat) 1714 (23 May 1714) | 9 months, 21 days | Via Izmir |
| 4 Tira 98 (20 Sept. 1713) | 4 May 1714 (23 April 1714)[b] | 6 months, 28 days | Unknown |
| 7 Aram 98 (22 Dec. 1713) | 4 June (4? Shabat) 1714 (23 May 1714) | 5 months, 1 day | Unknown |
| 1 Aram 98 (16 Dec. 1713) | 20 Nov. (20? Dama) 1714 (5 Nov.) | 9 months, 19 days | Unknown |
| 18 Ghamar 85 (1700) | 23 Ayram (23 Aram) 85 (1700) | | Unknown |
| 30 Nakha 82 (1687) | 4 Shams 83 (1688) | | Unknown |
| 5 Oct. 1720 | 18 Nov. 1720 | 43 days | By the ship *Madonna Marina* |
| 30 Hamira 97 (1712) | 4 Haveleats 97 (1712) | | Unknown |
| 15 Shabat 80 (1695) | | | Unknown |
| 22 Atam 96 (1711) | 9 Hamira 96 (1711) | | Unknown |
| 22 Ghamar 97 (1712) | 4 Haveleats | | Unknown |

TABLE 2 *(continued)*

| Sender(s) | Recipient(s) | Origin | Destination |
| --- | --- | --- | --- |
| Mateo di Minas[g] | Daniele di Israel | Izmir | Livorno |
| Amirbek di Vardan[h] | Hierapet di Martin | Naples | Venice |
| Amirbek di Vardan | Herapet di Martin | Naples | Venice |
| Amirbek di Vardan | Herapet di Martin | ?Naples | Venice |
| Amirbek di Vardan | Herapet di Martin | Naples | Venice |
| Amirbek di Vardan | Herapet di Martin | Livorno | Venice |
| Amirbek di Vardan | Herapet di Martin | Livorno | Venice |
| Amirbek di Vardan | Herapet di Martin | Livorno | Venice |
| Martiros di Sargis | Herapet di Martin | Livorno | Venice |
| Amirbek di Vardan | Herapet di Martin | Naples | Venice |
| Amirbek di Vardan | Herapet di Martin | Naples | Venice |
| Martiros di Sargis | Herapet di Martin | Livorno | Venice |
| Amirbek di Vardan | Herapet di Martin | Florence | Venice |
| Ter Astuatsatsur[i] | Dateo di Nazar Sceriman/ Shahrimanian | Moscow | Venice |
| Petros di Ibrahim[j] | Dateo di Nazar Sceriman/ Shahrimanian | Istanbul | Venice |
| Petros di Ibrahim (Saidian)[k] | Dateo di Nazar Sceriman/ Shahrimanian, Agha Nazar Sceriman/ Shahrimanian | Baghdad | Venice |
| Stepan di Sceriman/ Shahrimanian[l] | Hakop di Scheriman/ Shahrimanian | Venice | Amsterdam |
| Harutiun di Petros[m] | Dateo di Nazar Sceriman/ Shahrimanian | Amsterdam | Venice |

[a] All Sheriman correspondence, unless otherwise noted, is from Documenti Armeni Mercantile, ASV, busta 2. The letters this box are not classified in any particular fashion but can be identified by their dates.

[b] Adjusted to the Julian calendar by subtracting 11 days. The date provided in the letter is Gregorian with no correspondi Azaria date. Thus the arrival date has been adjusted here to make it consistent with the rest of the dates in this table.

[c] It should be noted that this letter was sent to Livorno and Venice before the Sceriman family's official resettlement in Venice, which according to most authorities took place in 1698. Note also that the handwriting in this letter is rather poo and the page containing the information about when the letter was received is partially torn, revealing only the date wher the letter arrived in Livorno.

[d] Uscan di Nubar in Izmir to Serafin (Serapion) di Murat in Venice, 1 December 1720, Avogaria di Comun, ASV. The delivery time for the letter from Venice to Izmir is mentioned by the author: Արզ եւ մալում լ[ի]նի երք[ն]ոս դունլունն *[si*e որ իմանաս մադրնայ մարինա նավումս քոյ հր[ա]մ[ա]նոցն գրած շավադրութւամեն եկաւ 43 օրում մեզ հասաւ նոյեն/պր[ն] 18 ին գարթագիք ամեն ահվալն իմագիք. (Let it be submitted and known to my brother that the letter you had written reached us in 43 days on November 18 by the ship *Madonna Marina*. We read it and became apprised of all your news.)

[e] Documenti Armeni Mercantile, ASV, busta 2, "Sceriman Family Letters." Paron Barsegh was an agent or factor for the Sceriman family based in Izmir. The data concerning the delivery time of his letter is extracted from a letter sent from Isfahan/Julfa to Venice on 14 Shams 97 (3 April 1712). It seems that Barsegh had also forwarded family correspondence

| Date sent | Date received | Travel time | Transportation mode |
|---|---|---|---|
| 5 July 1665 | 9 Nov. 1665 | 4 months, 4 days | By the ship *Europa* |
| 8 Jan. | 28 Jan. | 20 days | Overland courier? |
| 15 Feb. 1149 (1700) | 24 Feb.1149 (1700) | 9 days | Unknown |
| 20 Dec. 1139 (1690) | 27 Dec. 1139 (1690) | 7 days | Overland courier |
| 31 Jan. 1142(1693) | 10 Feb. 1142 (1693) | 11 days | Overland courier |
| 12 April 1144 (1695) | 18 April 1144(1695) | 6 days | Overland courier |
| 5 Feb. 1141 (1692) | 13 Feb. 1141 (1692) | 12 days | Overland courier |
| 28 Dec. 1143 (1694) | 6 Jan. 1143 (1694) | 9 days | |
| 3 May 1144 (1695) | 9 May 1144 (1695) | 6 days | Overland courier |
| 9 Jan. 1154 (1705) | 30 Feb. 1154 (1705) | 9 days | Overland courier |
| 4 Oct. 1147 (1699) | 13 Oct. 1147 (1699) | 9 days | Overland courier |
| 30 Nov. 1141 (1692) | 9 Dec. 1141(1692) | 9 days | Overland courier |
| 20 May 1140 (1691) | 26 May 1140 (1691) | 6 days | Overland courier |
| 11 July 1755 | 10 Jan. 1756 | 6 months | Unknown |
| 31 Aug. 1757 | 12 Nov. 1757 | 42 days | Via Mkhitarist monk visiting Istanbul |
| 10 March 1760 | 1 July 1760 | 50 days | Unknown |
| 14 Nov. 1732 | 13 Dec. 1732 | 29 days | Unknown |
| 7 Nov. 1753 | 23 Nov. 1753 | 16 days | Unknown |

from Venice to Isfahan along with his letter. This suggests that the Sceriman family was using its factors in Izmir and Istanbul and most likely in Aleppo to remit its letters to the home base in Isfahan.

[f] Data extracted from a letter from Isfahan dated 14 Shams 97 (3 April 1712) inDocumenti Armeni Mercantile, ASV, busta 2, "Sceriman Family Letters." This letter was most likely sent from Livorno to the family agent Paron Barsegh in Izmir and relayed to Isfahan along with Barsegh's letter of 30 Hamira 97 (18 November 1713) (see three rows above).

[g] Avogaria di Comun, ASV, busta 286 (C12).

[h] Avogaria di Comun, ASV, busta 17, "Di Martino Hierapit—Lettere in Armeno." All of the following letters to Hierapet di Martin are from the same folder.

[i] Sceriman documents, Don Mazza Archives, Verona, busta 1.

[j] Ibid.

[k] Ibid., busta 2.

[l] Avogaria di Comun, ASV, busta 17, "Letter book of Hakop di Murat."

[m] Sceriman documents, Don Mazza, busta 3.

letters to their relatives in Venice and Livorno by way of one of their brothers, Manuel Sceriman, who was appointed as the secretary to the embassy of Shah Ashraf to Istanbul. Manuel took the letters with him to the Ottoman capital whence he most likely had them mailed to Venice by ship: "They also sent an ambassador from here to Hamadan so he may proceed from there to Istanbul. They ordered Paron Manuel to go with the ambassador. He went, and we gave our letters to him."[99] Similarly, we learn from another letter that in 1711, when Parons Sarhat and Manuel returned to Julfa/Isfahan from Italy, they brought several letters with them.[100]

As we have seen, the Julfan "courier system" played an important role in circulating information through the medium of commercial correspondence in the Indian Ocean and the Mediterranean Sea, where Julfan commercial settlements were clustered. These two zones were each governed by a different "circulatory regime" with distinct laws and patterns. In the Indian Ocean zone, monsoons and ship travel determined how information was circulated, whereas the Mediterranean zone was governed by the exigencies of caravan transport across West Asia. In both zones, however, the intelligence networks and their underlying structure of courier communication fulfilled the same vital function: to connect the scattered communities of merchants to the nodal center of the network in Julfa. Some questions, however, still remain. What kinds of links existed between the two extreme poles of the Julfan commercial network? Was the intelligence network able to bridge the distance between India and the Mediterranean? Did merchants residing and trading in the Mediterranean world maintain an active and open channel of communication and information sharing with their associates in India? Did commercial correspondence travel between India and Europe?

The Sceriman family business letters provide a good illustration of information sharing between these two poles of the Julfan commercial network. In fact, the Sceriman correspondence gives the impression that the "intelligence network" of this family was essentially similar to that used by Julfans operating almost exclusively between India and Isfahan, with the significant difference that the distances the family network covered were far greater and the range of issues therein more diverse. A typical business letter received by the Scerimans in Venice contains data regarding business transactions with Amsterdam, Krakow, Moscow, Cadiz, Istanbul, Izmir, and Basra, but more importantly with India (all the typical places: Madras/"Chinipatan," Surat, Calcutta, Hugli, i.e., Chinsura/Chichra, Patna), the Arabian Peninsula (Jedda), and Southeast Asia (Macao, Burma, and Malaysia).[101] The Sceriman had agents or family members in the principal emporia of these regions. There is even evidence that the family was possibly engaged in trade with Portuguese Brazil in the late seventeenth and early eighteenth centuries.[102] In general, the Sceriman agents in India (a certain Paron Abraham based in Surat and elsewhere, and Paron Khachik in Bengal) would regularly remit information to Julfa relying on the mail service in the Indian Ocean, and the members of the Sceriman family based in Julfa would then forward all the relevant information by mail to Izmir where their agent, a certain Paron Serapion (known as "Signor Serafin" in the Venetian archives) or someone else, would in turn forward the information to Venice or Livorno.[103] In this fashion, the Scerimans were able to share complex and sensitive information about the markets in Mughal India coming from well-placed and reliable agents in the field halfway around the world with family members in Italy, where the firm's business headquarters seem to have been gradually relocated at the beginning of the eighteenth century. Needless to say, Venice and Livorno were safer and more stable places for the Scerimans to operate their family firm's business than Isfahan in the turbulent period following the Afghan invasion of Iran and the ensuing collapse of the Safavid dynasty in 1722. Based on the information available to us from the Indian Ocean zone of the mail service, we can arrive at a rough calculation of how long it took the Scerimans to convey information and intelligence from one end of their network in India to the other in Venice. Assuming that it took about three months to send mail from India to Isfahan (the fastest time) during the monsoon season and about four months to relay it via Izmir, Aleppo, or Istanbul to Livorno or Venice (again the fastest time), we can conclude that the entire voyage could be undertaken in a record time of seven months. To get some perspective on these figures, let us consider that it took the East India Company about eight to ten months to send their dispatches overland to Surat, and six months via the Cape route.[104] Needless to say, the drawback of relying on the Cape route was that ships could sail to and from India only during a one-month period each year, due to the monsoon regime in the Indian Ocean; missing this period thus meant that letters would be stranded for an entire year. Thus sending mail to India via the Cape route and receiving a response to it would usually take two years or longer during the age of sail and monsoon travel; only with the coming of steamships and, later, telegraphs in the 1850s would there be a significant reduction of time for communication between Europe and India.[105] Given their well-honed "intelligence network," the Sceriman family in Venice and Isfahan were thus well placed to make important business decisions based on relatively "fresh" market information from India. One of the ways the Scerimans turned information to their advantage was the network of informants they maintained in Amsterdam, Moscow, Izmir, Istanbul, Isfahan, Surat, Madras, Bengal, and most likely also in Canton/Macao (China).


Commercial correspondence and courier networks were an integral part of Julfan economy and society in the early modern period. As this chapter has demonstrated, they were the principal means through which Julfans circulated information throughout their far-flung network. Business correspondence was a vital aspect of Julfan long-distance trade because it helped merchants share sensitive market-related information and intelligence with their business partners and agents in faraway places. Thus the Julfans had a crucial edge over their business rivals. In this connection, Rene Barendse comments on the importance of sharing information in the long-term success of merchant communities in the Indian Ocean and Eurasia: "This was also a major reason why the trade of the Armenians, disposing of a network of informers from Amsterdam to Moscow and from Istanbul or Irkutsk to Cochin, Calcutta or Gondar (in Abyssinia), thrived."[106]

Commercial correspondence was also important because it helped maintain high levels of trust and, therefore, cooperation between Julfan merchants, who often resided far from each other and, consequently, could not personally monitor each other's actions. As we shall see in chapter 7, letter writing was a crucial method of sharing news about a merchant's reputation and trustworthiness, which in turn discouraged merchants from defrauding their fellow Julfans. Finally and perhaps most importantly, letter writing acted as a conduit for information (strictly business as well as personal or social) that connected Julfans residing in distant trade settlements in the Mediterranean and Indian Ocean worlds with others in neighboring settlements or in "regional centers" (e.g., as Smyrna was to Venice, Marseilles, or Amsterdam in the Mediterranean, or Madras to Calcutta, Pegu, Batavia, or Manila in the Indian Ocean) and finally to the central node of the network in Julfa. In circulating information throughout the network, commercial correspondence and the courier network that handled Julfan mail thus preserved the ethno-religious integrity of the network as a whole and allowed its members to maintain their identity as participants in the same "coalition" of merchants who shared New Julfa as their central node and ultimately as their common "homeland."

6

## The Circulation of Men and Credit

### *The* Commenda *and the Family Firm*

*With blind eyes, they do not heed the Holy Gospels, and they abandon their wives, sons, daughters, in a state of forlornness, in need and afflicted, and they scatter themselves throughout the world like locusts or like snow until the depths of the Indies, to Ethiopia and Egypt and throughout all the lands of Europe [ashkhars Frankats‘] and in Constantinople and throughout the Balkans and the region of Scandinavia [yerkirn gutats‘vots‘] and in Poland, Russia, and Muscovy as well as throughout Hyrcania and Central Asia [?vrkana], the lands of the Turks and Kurds as well as that of the Chaldeans and throughout Persia and the East until China [Chinumachin] in Ton [?] and Tonquin and in England and throughout all the lands of the Tatars and the Abkhaz until the limits of the unknown world, scattered like dust on account of the vice of greed and in order to heap more wealth.*[1]

This description of the peripatetic lifestyle of Julfan merchants is from a seventeenth-century Armenian chronicle written by a priest named Grigor of Daranagh. Unusual for a chronicler of his times, Grigor was not favorably inclined toward Julfans and, in the course of his chronicle, categorically condemns their greed and their "worship of Mammon" as opposed to God, which in his view led them to wander and circulate for long years throughout the world (including the New World, as this passage intimates) at the expense of abandoning their families in Julfa for many years. The objects of Grigor's contempt, it should be noted, are not the wealthy Julfan merchants known as *khwajas,* but the countless junior traders known as factors or *commenda* agents, who traveled for their wealthy *khwaja* patrons in order to make a living and with the dream of striking it rich one day.

This chapter explores the role of the *commenda* contract in Julfan trade during the seventeenth and eighteenth centuries by situating the *commenda* within the context of the "family firm," the basic organizational unit of Julfan commerce. I argue that in the Julfan context, as in the context of medieval European and Near Eastern trade, the *commenda* provided the ideal means for the circulation of merchants, goods, and credit across vast distances. Of all commercial institutions, the *commenda* was, in fact, the single most important cause of the dramatic expansion of Julfan commerce in the seventeenth and eighteenth centuries.

The first section of this chapter discusses the uses of the *commenda* in Mediterranean trade and provides a brief history of its possible origins in the Islamicate world in which the Julfans lived. The second section explores various aspects of the *commenda* contract among Julfans through a detailed examination of the treatment of the *commenda* in Julfan commercial law. In addition to highlighting the legal status of the *commenda* among Julfan merchants, the chapter emphasizes the *commenda*'s role in facilitating the circulation of men (merchants and *commenda* agents), goods (European bullion, Iranian raw silk, Indian diamonds, gems, cloth, and other commodities), and capital (credit) throughout the Julfan network in the Indian Ocean and Mediterranean zones. The third section examines the making of *commenda* agents by briefly looking at the educational activities of a trading school in Julfa. In the fourth section I examine several travel itineraries of Julfan *commenda* agents in the far reaches of the Indian Ocean. The fifth section looks at the role of the patriarchal family in Julfan society and commerce and discusses how Julfans easily accommodated the *commenda* into the patriarchal structure of the family firm in Julfa.

The discussion of these issues is based almost entirely on archival documents, such as actual surviving *commenda* contracts and business and family correspondence. In addition, I rely heavily on the codification of Julfan commercial law found in the *Datastanagirk' Astrakhani Hayots'*, a code of laws written and used by the Armenian community of Astrakhan in the 1760s, in which the *commenda* and the rules governing its use receive the lion's share of the legal discussion pertaining to commercial law.

## THE HISTORY OF THE *COMMENDA*
### AND ITS VARIETIES

In its simplest form, the *commenda* is a type of commercial contract that involves at least two parties: a merchant with ready capital, credit, or merchandise and an agent or factor with the required business skills, a good reputation, and a willingness to travel great distances to put his master's capital to work and sell the merchandise entrusted to him (see fig. 7). Profits accruing from *commenda* transactions are divided in accordance with the terms specified in the particular contract. In most cases, the principal merchant, known as the *stans* in Genoese sources, who provides the capital receives about three-fourths of the profit, while the agent, known as the *tractator* or *porocertans*,[2] who provides the labor, keeps the remaining one-fourth. One of the most innovative features of the *commenda* was the stipulation that any "loss resulting from the exigencies of travel or from an unsuccessful business venture is borne exclusively by the investor(s); the agent is in no way liable for a loss of this nature, losing only his expended time and effort."[3]

Scholars have already established the pivotal role of the *commenda* in the history of commercial capitalism. Many, in fact, trace the institutional "origins" of capitalism to the emergence and dissemination of this contract in the medieval Mediterranean markets.[4] As a clever means for "combining financial and human resources for the purposes of trade,"[5] the *commenda* was the dominant institutional form of conducting long-distance trade from the medieval period, when its use became widespread in the Mediterranean, until the early seventeenth century, when it, along with other forms of partnerships, was gradually replaced by the rise of joint-stock companies in Europe, such as the English and Dutch East India Companies, themselves the forerunners of the modern multinational firm.[6]

The *commenda* as we know it today was known by different names in different places. In Venice, where the earliest surviving *commenda* dates from the second half of the eleventh century, it was known as an *accomendatio* or *collegantia*.[7] However, it was most commonly known in other Mediterranean ports as far as Barcelona as a *commenda*. The unilateral *commenda* was the most basic form of this contract, according to which the sedentary investor (sometimes erroneously described as the "sleeping partner") advanced the capital and merchandise, while the agent was expected to provide only his labor. For most Mediterranean unilateral *commendas*, the sedentary or principal investor received 75 percent of the profit, while the agent kept only the remaining portion. It is this unilateral form that made the *commenda* an ideal instrument for capitalist expansion. It is not difficult to understand why this arrangement would be particularly suitable for societies where capital was not evenly shared and where an individual with no capital of his own initially could eventually become a "capitalist" in his own right.

In the bilateral form of the *commenda*, known as a *societas maris* in Genoa,[8] the agent also invests capital of his own in the joint venture, which amounts usually to one-third of the total investment. In this case, the profits are divided according to the relative investments. In most bilateral *commendas*, both parties shared the profit equally. Many legal aspects of the Mediterranean *commenda* continue to be heatedly debated by historians, but, as Robert Lopez and Irving Raymond have pointed out, no single aspect has caused as much controversy as the historical "origins" of this contract.[9]

Many economic historians of Europe saw the *commenda* as a product of Greco-Roman law, thus giving this important economic institution a purely European pedigree. In the 1960s, Abraham Udovitch began to propose an alternative history of the *commenda*'s possible origins.[10] Udovitch argued that though antecedents to the Mediterranean *commenda* could be sought in Byzantium, Islam, Jewish law, and even as far back as Mesopotamia, the best candidate for the original source was Islam. According to Udovitch, the closest contract to the *commenda* that historically predated it was the Islamic partnership known as the *qirad* (according to the Maliki school of Islamic law) or the *mudaraba* (as defined by the Hanafi school). Like the Mediterranean *commenda,* the *qirad/mudaraba* of Islam was a partnership arrangement between a sedentary merchant and a traveling agent. Profit sharing was also similar to that in the *commenda,* as was, most importantly, the clause that limited the liability of the agent in case the venture failed. One of the few differences between the Mediterranean and Islamic versions of this contract was that the Islamic *qirad/mudaraba* was used for both overland and maritime long-distance trade and was open-ended in the sense that it could last for many years, as opposed to the European *commenda,* which was limited to maritime ventures that lasted the duration of a single voyage.

Udovitch points out that while the earliest appearance of the *commenda* on the shores of the Mediterranean dates from the late eleventh century, the *mudaraba* was known in the Arabian Peninsula possibly before the dawn of Islam. After all, the Prophet Muhammad was a *commenda* agent for his first wife, Khadija.[11] Udovitch is careful to note that there is no conclusive proof that the *qirad* or *mudaraba* was borrowed by Mediterranean traders; he suggests, however, that the evidence overwhelmingly points toward the Islamic origins of this European contract, and indicates that European traders might have adopted this Islamic practice (along with many others) through their regular interactions in the Muslim port cities of the Mediterranean.[12]

## THE *ENKERAGIR* OR *MUZARBA*:
## THE USAGES OF THE JULFAN *COMMENDA*

The centrality of a partnership arrangement among the Julfans resembling the *commenda* is seen in the Astrakhan Code of Laws (see fig. 8).[13] In Chapter 14 of this code, entitled "Concerning the Laws of Commerce," the authors divide commercial activity into four related fields, all of which have some form of partnership in common. The first of these is described in terms that are uncannily similar to the *commenda.* Accordingly, commerce is said to occur "when one person extends money to someone else for the latter to put it to work, and return the [initial] capital along with two-thirds of the profits to him [the investor], and have one-third go to the laborer, or otherwise as shall have been agreed upon among themselves. For such individuals, in the vernacular language, the one who extends the money is called *agha,* and he who receives it, *enker.*"[14] The *agha* in this passage is later also described as *ter* (Armenian for "master" or "lord") and is referred to by the Persian honorific as *khwaja* when it is used as part of a merchant's name, leaving no room for doubt as to which party was the more powerful one. Both terms used in this passage clearly have their counterparts in the Mediterranean *commenda*: the *agha* or *ter* corresponds to the Mediterranean *stans,* while *enker* (from the Armenian word for "associate") is the Armenian designation for the *tractator* or *commenda* agent. The authors of the Astrakhan Code go on to devote fifty-eight articles or almost a third of the chapter dealing with commercial organization to the *commenda* contract described as *enkeragir*.[15]

The first scholar to note the parallels between the Julfan and Mediterranean *commenda*s and to study them systematically was Shushanik Khachikian. In her chapter devoted to the *commenda,* Khachikian notes the similarities between the Julfan Armenian *commenda* and its medieval counterpart in Venice.[16] Based on these similarities, Khachikian suggests that the Armenians probably borrowed their *commenda* from the Venetians, with whom they had close commercial contacts during the twelfth century, when the maritime kingdom of Cilician Armenia was one of Venice's most important trading partners in the Mediterranean.[17]

A few years after the publication of Khachikian's groundbreaking study, Edmund Herzig questioned her hypothesis concerning the genealogy of the Julfan *commenda*.[18] While accepting the remarkable similarities between Julfan and Venetian *commenda*s, Herzig pointed out that there are even more striking parallels between the Julfan Armenian *commenda* and the Islamic version of this contract. Following the work of Udovitch, Herzig noted that the Mediterranean *commenda* itself was most likely of Islamic origin.[19] Though no definitive proof exists for the Islamic "origins" of either the Mediterranean *commenda* or its Julfan counterpart, there are compelling reasons, at least, to allow for the possibility that the Julfan Armenian *commenda* originated from the Islamic *mudaraba* or one of its other variants. First, Julfans lived in an Islamicate world not only geographically, but, their religious differences notwithstanding, also culturally. As in other areas of cultural identity, where cross-cultural borrowings from the Islamicate world are greater than Armenian nationalist writers would have us believe, there would seem little reason to rule out similar borrowings in commercial practice, especially since commercial life is among the leading conduits for cross-cultural encounters and borrowings. Armenians could have borrowed the *commenda* from the Islamic *mudaraba* from a number of places, including perhaps directly from the Arabs, when parts of "historic Armenia" were under the Umayyad dynasty, starting in the mid-seventh century, and remained so until the Abbasid period, in the mid-ninth century.[20] Unfortunately, the surviving codes of law used by the Armenians, including the twelfth-century lawbook of Mkhitar Kosh, do not shed light on this matter, and neither do other Armenian sources from the medieval period. It could also be the case that such borrowing, if it did occur, took place much later in time and was the direct result of Iranian influence.[21]

Structural and terminological similarities between the Julfan and Islamic *commenda*s might shed further light on this matter. Terminologically, Julfan usage has several designations for the *commenda,* including, as we have seen, the widespread *enkeragir,* which would seem to indicate affinities to the Byzantine *societas*

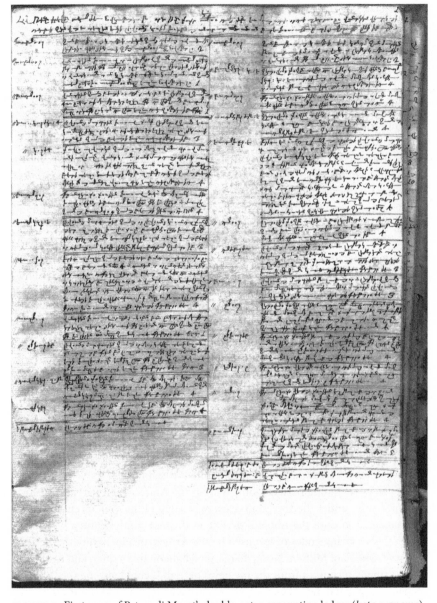

FIGURE 7. First page of Petros di Murat's double-entry accounting ledger (*kata ruznama*) containing his transactions in Genoa and Livorno, 9 November 1715; "Journal of Petros di Murat, 1714–1723," Documenti Armeni Mercantile, ASV, busta 1. Courtesy of the Archivio di Stato di Venezia.

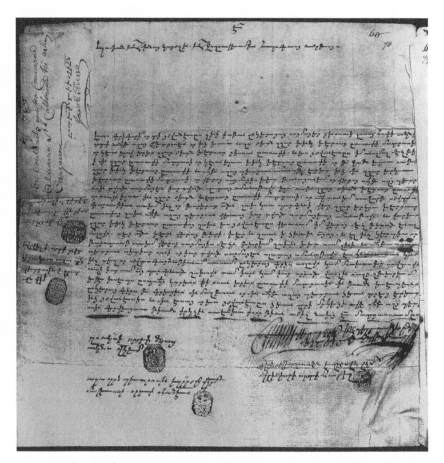

FIGURE 8. *Commenda* contract, Chinipatan/Madras, 1741; Lansdowne MS 1047, BL, folio 78. Courtesy of the British Library.

(association, partnership), the Genoese *societas maris,* or the Venetian *collegantia* (colleagueship), or the less common but nonetheless important designation *muzarbay,* which would indicate an Islamicate etymology from the Persian pronunciation of the Arabic *mudaraba.* Given the current state of our knowledge of Julfan economic history, we can only speculate on possible origins and should resist the temptation to make definitive statements regarding the matter.[22] Clearly, more work needs to be done not only in Julfan economic history but also in the history of medieval Armenian commercial law before we can reach a more definitive conclusion.[23] The surviving Julfan documents from the early modern period do not appear to address the prehistory of the Julfan *commenda.*

One area where the documentary record is sufficiently rich concerns the legal dimension to the Julfan *commenda* and the elaborate codes of conduct associated with it. As in the medieval Mediterranean or the Islamicate societies in the Near East and the Indian Ocean, keeping accurate accounts was one of the most important responsibilities of the *commenda* agent toward his master, a fact that, as Max Weber noted long ago, most likely played a significant role in the development of sophisticated accounting methods, including double-entry accounting.[24] Article 11 of Chapter 14 of the Astrakhan Code of Laws indicates that maintaining an accurate account ledger, known in the Julfa dialect as a *kata ruznama* (see fig. 9),[25] is among the chief obligations of a *commenda* agent to his master:

> Every *commenda* agent is obliged to record each one of his transactions one after another in a lawful account book to the best of his abilities. And upon hearing of such lawful account books, let no one consider that it is something that is not possible to keep, saying that not everyone knows how to write a lawful account book, or as they say in the vernacular language, who is capable of writing a *kata ruznama*? For such people it can be said, would that everyone knew how to write a *kata ruznama,* but also be acquainted with all the philosophical arts, because knowledge is not something contemptible but is singularly commendable. But our problem is not about the writing of the *kata ruznama;* it is the following: [*commenda* agents] should write truthfully as much about all their transactions as they are cognizant of, without putting aside any time. For, is not an account that is written truthfully but is vulgar and lacking in eloquence more honorable and commendable than a *kata ruznama* that is written dishonestly but might possess a profound composition and civility? If it so happens that one is not capable of writing [i.e., is illiterate], he may request someone else to write for him. And if a *commenda* agent does not show his account book to his master, he shall be imprisoned and fed only bread and water and periodically whipped for up to one year. And if he is brought into line and reveals his accounts and book of transactions, then it is good. If he does not reveal [his account book] upon the conclusion of the year, the master shall terminate the accounts of his *commenda* partnership in the following fashion. If the transactions have borne profits, they shall settle their accounts in accordance with their *commenda* contract. But if the money from the [initial] capital investment is missing, the *commenda* agent is obliged to pay his master the missing portion.[26]

The Astrakhan Code makes it abundantly clear that relations between an agent and a master were anything but equal. This inequality is manifest in the ratio of the profits that each party received. Most Julfan unilateral *commendas,* as Shushanik Khachikian observed, allotted anywhere from 25 to 33.33 percent of the total profits to the *commenda* agent who did all the work, while the "master" who invested the capital received the remaining share.[27] According to Khachikian, the discrepancy between these figures can be accounted for by the experience of the agent. The more experienced a *commenda* agent was the greater his share of the profits. Experience

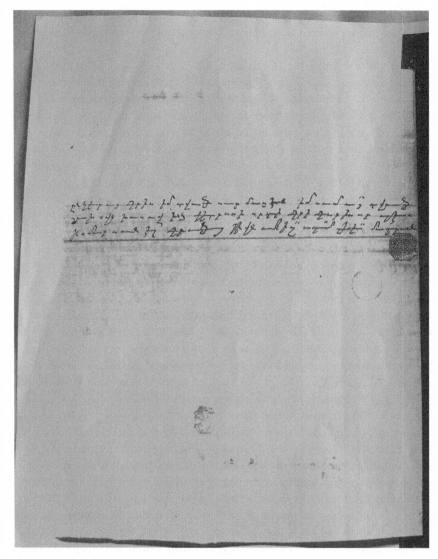

FIGURE 9. *Ghatilayagir*/letter of severance, Madras, 1741; Lansdowne MS 1047, BL, folio 79. Courtesy of the British Library.

on the job meant that an agent could be trusted to make investments while overseas as he saw fit, without the master's constant supervision in the form of letters of instruction sent from Julfa.

Alongside the simple unilateral *commenda,* Julfans also employed its bilateral version, known to them as the *yerkkoghmani enkeragir.* As in the Mediterranean version, the *yerkkoghmani enkeragir* implied at least two separate parties to the contract consisting of the principal investor(s) or *agha*(s) and the agent (*enker*), who also invested his own share (known in Julfa usage as the *enalmal*<A/P, *'ayn al-mal,* "capital, principal, stock-in-trade") in the joint venture. In the Julfan bilateral *commenda,* the profit ratio for the agent would usually be greater than the normal 25–33.33 percent stipulated in the unilateral *commenda* and could be as high as 50 percent.

While in some cases agents were given considerable leeway to invest their master's money as they saw fit, the norm seems to have been for the masters to exercise a direct say in the management of their funds (hence the inappropriateness of the term "sleeping partner"). Exactly how they determined when to exercise control over their agents and when to allow them discretionary powers in investing the funds entrusted to them are not codified in any account. It seems safe to assume that direct intervention by a master or *khwaja* residing in New Julfa in the management of capital given to one of his agents operating in a distant market in the Indian Ocean or the Mediterranean was probably based on the experience of the agent and his reputation as a shrewd custodian of his master's investment. Those agents who were not seasoned in trade, however, would receive regular advice or instructions from Julfa in the form of letters of instruction known in Julfa dialect as *ordnagir* (a compound word possibly based on the Italian *ordine,* or "instruction/ order," and the Armenian suffix *-gir,* or "letter").[28] These *ordnagirs* were sent to agents through the courier system examined in chapter 5 and represented important instruments through which *khwajas* or sedentary capitalists residing in New Julfa could exercise leverage over the behavior of their agents. Article 10 of the Astrakhan Code of Laws introduces the *ordnagir* and leaves no room for doubt about the binding nature of its instructions: "If one appoints an agent to himself and gives him a letter of instruction which in the vernacular is called an *ordnagir* it is necessary for the agent to follow the instructions of his master and not to do anything that goes against them."[29] If an agent disobeys instructions and loss results from his actions, then only the agent and not the master is liable for such loss. The *ordnagir* was invested with such binding power that the agent was expected to follow it even if his master wrote to him and ordered him to return home immediately and terminate his contract.[30] Most *commenda* contracts have the following special clause making the binding nature of the *ordnagir* explicit: "If [the master] demands his capital investment [*sarmayea*<P: *sarmaya,* "capital"] at whatever time [*vaght*<P: *vaqt,* "time"] or whatever place, I shall return his capital as well as the profit granted by God to him or to his representative [vakil <P: *vakil,* "agent or ap-

pointed representative"] without any excuse [*bi uz'r*<P: *bi ozr,* "without pretense or excuse"]."[31]

The patriarchal nature of the master's power over the lives of his agents is evident not only in the term *ter* or "master" but also in one of the few responsibilities that Julfan commercial law assigned to him, namely, to tend to the needs of his agent's family while the latter was away on his errands. Article 13 states that if a *commenda* agent entrusts the care of his wife and sons to his master upon traveling elsewhere, the master is obliged to provide sufficient and adequate money to meet their needs, and he may demand the money he has given with a lawful interest rate from his *commenda* agent at the time of concluding their accounts.[32] As we shall see in chapter 9, the Multani merchants from northwestern India had a similar practice, and in both cases it is not unreasonable to conclude that the practice amounted to a form of hostage taking whereby wealthy masters could hold the family members of their agents as collateral for their agents' honest conduct while away on their travels. Patriarchal obedience and even subjugation are also written into Julfan law when it comes to the protocols that the agent has to follow upon returning home from his far-flung voyages in the service of his master.

These protocols are addressed in Article 15 as follows:

> When a *commenda* agent returns to his master from another country or city, upon arriving in the city [where his master resides] he is obliged to take to his master's house not only his goods along with all his account books and other papers, but also all his belongings including his furniture regardless of their worth. And if a *commenda* agent goes against what is written here and does not take his goods, account books, and papers along with all his furniture to his master's house, such a *commenda* agent shall be treated, in matters of punishment and fines, as a common thief, without any compassion.[33]

One of the most crucial passages in the Astrakhan Code of Laws concerns the method of concluding a *commenda* contract. Article 16 states:

> When the *commenda* agent returns to his master, the master must become acquainted with his accounts and without delay. If he [the master] finds his factor to be correct in his work, he must conclude his [affairs with the agent with care]. And they shall write a brief selection of all the accounts of the factor, which in the vernacular language is called a *tomar,* and they should give [this *tomar*] to each other along with the *commenda* contract. Moreover, they must write on the *commenda* contract in the following fashion: The account of this *commenda* contract of the said partnership of such and such a year and month has been concluded, as it is also written in the *tomar,* and each of us has received his right due; henceforth if we make any claims on each other concerning [this, our *commenda* contract], it shall be [considered] invalid [*anhastat*]. And under this writing the factor shall sign one [copy], the master the other, and they shall give each other [their copies]. And if the copy of the *commenda* contract is missing, the master shall sign one copy of the *tomar* and give it to the factor.[34]

The *tomar* referred to in this passage is simply the shortened version of the double-entry accounting ledger (*kata ruznama*) that the agent was obliged to update routinely during his travels overseas. In other words, the *tomar* contains an accurate summary of the most essential transactions carried out by the agent. Most *tomars* were written on rolls of paper (the word *tomar* being a borrowing from the Greek word for "roll"), some of which can be up to four or five yards long when unfolded. *Tomars* are exceedingly important for economic historians working on Julfan trade for two reasons. First, they contain an accurate reflection of the transactions undertaken by *commenda* agents and provide precious information on the prices of commodities as well as the rate of profit earned by agents in the service of wealthy masters in Julfa. Second, while very few accounting ledgers have survived from the seventeenth and eighteenth centuries, probably because parties to a transaction were legally required to maintain only one copy of such ledgers, as opposed to two copies of *tomars*, a great number of *tomars* have been preserved in various archival collections in Europe and especially in Julfa. Given their nature as summary documents, *tomars* also contain valuable information on the nature of the initial *commenda* contract signed between master and agent (see figs. 11 and 12).

A typical *tomar* begins with a summary of the terms of the *commenda* contract that set in motion the long list of transactions carefully reproduced in the *tomar*.[35] This is followed by an itemized list of the commodities handled by the *commenda* agent, arranged in terms of double-entry accounting, listing debits and credits (see above, figs. 11 and 12). A significant aspect of the *tomar* is the division of the *commenda* agent's transactions in geographic terms. Thus a *tomar* stored in a Venetian archive concerning the commercial affairs of a *commenda* agent trading in diamonds and gems has individual sections devoted to his activities in Isfahan (where his journeys began), Surat (an important market for Indian diamonds and other precious stones), Izmir (a way station en route to the European ports of the Mediterranean), and Venice and Livorno (both important centers for the diamond trade in Europe).[36]

With the successful completion of a *commenda* contract and drafting of the *tomar*, the master and agent drafted another document referred to as *ghatilayagir*, or letter of release, in which the master reaffirmed that he had received his share of the profit along with the initial capital per the terms of the original contract. Thus a contract between a Julfan *commenda* agent named Hovannes son of Grum and Grigor son of the deceased Petros was successfully sealed in Madras in 1741 with the following words: "I Grigor son of Petros have received the profit granted by God upon the initial capital I had advanced toward this *commenda* contract, as is also written in the *tomar*, in the year 126 [1741], fifteenth day of Adam [April 4] in Madras" (fig. 9).[37] The evidence suggests that the *ghatilayagir* was akin to a certificate of manumission. According to a court case between a Julfan *commenda* agent and his masters, brought before the Mayor's Court of Madras in 1734, it was "the custom of the Armenians" to "disable [a *commenda* agent] from entering into trade,

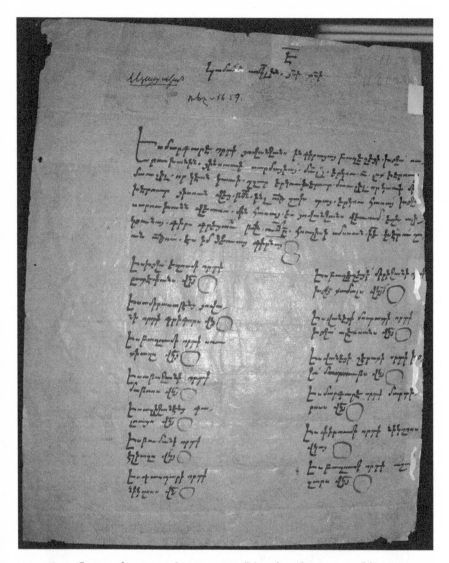

FIGURE 10. *Commenda* contract, Livorno, 1659; "Namak—Aligorna, 1659" [Letter—Livorno, 1659], ASMA, folder 6. Courtesy of the All Savior's Monastery Archive.

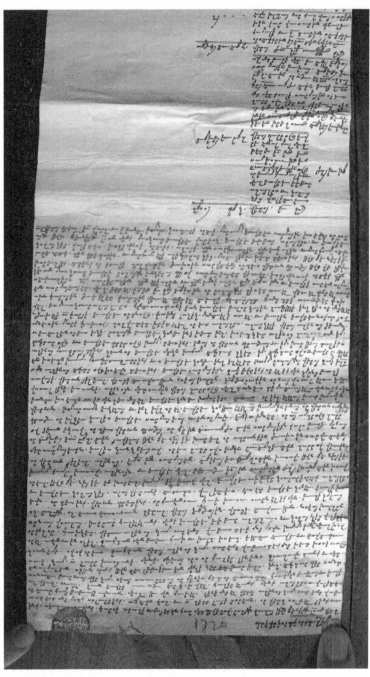

FIGURE 11. *Tomar*, concluding summary of Yeavre di Gospar, Surat, 1710; "Hashvetghteri kapots'ner," "Hashvetghter anhatakan, 1703–1729" [Individual accounting papers, 1703–1729], ASMA, box no. 35/2. Courtesy of the All Savior's Monastery Archive.

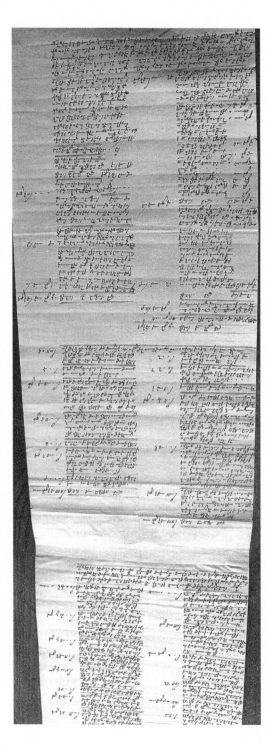

FIGURE 12. *Tomar,* Yeavre di Gospar, Surat, 1710; "Hashvetghter anhatakan, 1703–1729" [Individual accounting papers, 1703–1729], ASMA, box no. 35/2. Courtesy of the All Savior's Monastery Archive.

either by himself or in conjunction with any other person, until he shall have settled his accounts with his first employers and obtained a general release and discharge from them."[38] As we shall see in chapter 9, this clause in Julfan commercial
law, which helped reduce cases of malfeasance and cheating by agents traveling
abroad, made the *commenda* contract highly appealing to Julfan merchants but came
with a heavy cost.

## THE MAKING OF *COMMENDA* AGENTS

The surviving mass of archival documents and the Astrakhan Code of Laws go a long
way in clarifying how *commenda* contracts were drafted, what legal ramifications they
had, and how they were eventually concluded. They do not, however, shed light on
how young Julfan men were trained as *commenda* agents. The making of *commenda*
agents is a topic that has yet to receive sufficient treatment by scholars of Julfan trade.[39]
This lack of attention is in part the result of a lack of pertinent documentation.

Most Julfan *commenda* agents began their careers as agents through informal
training under the tutelage of senior male members of their families. A good example of this is the case of Zak'aria of Agulis, an Armenian merchant from the town
of Agulis (in present-day Azerbaijan) who entered the world of trade in 1647 as an
apprentice to his older and more experienced cousin Nikoghos.[40] The pattern of
tutelage by older male members of an extended family exemplified in Zak'aria's case
seems also to have been a common avenue into the world of trade for many young
Julfans, as it was for most Asian merchants. However, what makes the Julfan case
distinct among other Asian communities was the centralized and institutionalized
nature of training individuals in the arts of commerce. In this respect, the most important institutionalized avenue to commerce was a special trade school for the
training of young merchants. This institution, which functioned as a kind of fore-
runner to modern MBA programs, was most likely located in the compound of the
All Savior's Monastery in Julfa and was managed by a schoolmaster named Constant. Scholars have been skeptical about the existence of such a school ever since
it was revealed in 1880 in the second volume of Harut'iwn Ter Hovhaniants's monumental *History of New Julfa* and was later picked up in Levon Khachikian's works.[41]
While Ter Hovhaniants mentions this school and asserts that it had 250 students,
he does not provide archival references to substantiate his claims.[42] Other scholars
have simply taken his assertion at face value. My own efforts to track down documentation on this school in the Julfa archives while on a visit to Isfahan in January
of 2005 were also fruitless. Luckily, however, one of the textbooks used by Constant
to educate the sons of merchants has survived in several redactions, one of which,
stored in the Bodleian collection at Oxford University, dates from the late seventeenth century and explicitly refers to Constant's trade school, stating that it had
"three hundred students" in the mid-1680s.[43]

Entitled *Compendium concerning Commercial Advice to the Adolescent and to Young Merchants,* Constant's trade manual gives us a good idea of what the formal education of a Julfan merchant entailed in the seventeenth century. The work is divided into several sections beginning with an introductory discussion in the format of question and answer on the meaning and use of commerce in society and containing tenets or maxims about honest behavior and about being cautious in trusting strangers. Next comes a long discussion of trade routes stretching from New Julfa all the way to Manila in the East and to Cadiz and Amsterdam in the West and the East African Coast as far south as the Mwene mutapa kingdom or present-day Zimbabwe. All the names of important markets are provided, along with detailed information about the currencies and weights used in each place and practical means of converting these units into more common ones familiar to Julfans. The dominant commodities of each market are also listed, as are their current prices, and advice is proffered on the goods in which to invest and those to avoid.

It becomes clear from even a cursory glance at this valuable trade manual that while geography (in the form of trade routes), some ethnographic history (in the form of general commentary on each regional state), and, more importantly, the listing of commodities, exchange rates between various currencies, and weights played a vital role in the curriculum for a business education, none were perhaps as important as a solid education in arithmetic and accounting. The bulk of Constant's trade manual is devoted to solving very complex mathematical problems and to maintaining orderly accounts in one's *kata ruznama,* or daily financial ledger, the keeping of which was mandatory for every *commenda* agent. The few copies of the manual that have survived bear colophons or biographical notes scribbled on the opening and closing pages, all of which indicate that their owners were Julfan merchants and most probably *commenda* agents who had taken the manual with them on their trips to the marketplaces of India or the Levant.[44]

Copies of Constant's work must have been hard to come by especially for men who were not enrolled in his classes. To overcome this shortage, Armenian printers in Amsterdam published a condensed version of this lengthy treatise in a slightly altered form in 1699.[45] The fact that the expenses for publishing such a work and making it more widely available were paid for by a Julfan merchant with business connections in Amsterdam indicates both the continued importance ascribed to this do-it-yourself manual for enterprising *commenda* agents and the possibility that manuscript copies of the original text had become rare by the closing years of the seventeenth century.[46]

In addition to attending Constant's trade school in Julfa or studying his trade manual, it appears that, in the 1680s, young Julfans interested in becoming *commenda* agents also received training from Jesuit missionaries in Isfahan in foreign languages, such as French, Portuguese, and Italian, and in geography and arithmetic.[47] As early as the 1660s, Jean Baptiste Tavernier reports that some Julfan families were sending their sons to Capuchin missionaries in Julfa to study French in the hopes of "establishing a Trade with *France.* "[48] The importance assigned to learning foreign languages as part of a *commenda* agent's education is revealed in John Fryer's observation while visiting Isfahan in 1677 that the Julfans "were addicted to learn[ing] languages."[49] As Olivier Raveux's important work has suggested, Julfan merchants trading in the Mediterranean ports studied lingua franca and French through Italian, for which there were several printed grammars in the Julfa dialect during the seventeenth century.[50]

### THE *COMMENDA* AGENT ABROAD

Because the *commenda* was a contract between a sedentary merchant who possessed capital for commercial transactions and an agent with the labor power and willingness to travel overseas to put his master's capital to work, it acted as the central institutional mechanism that made the circulation of men and capital in the Julfan network not only possible but also a necessary feature of Julfan commerce. In general, the wealthy *aghas* or *khwajas* rarely circulated in the Julfan global network; *commenda* agents did most of the circulation and travel.[51] In his well-known seventeenth-century travelogue, the English traveler John Fryer describes the Julfan *commenda* agents while discussing the long-distance trade in Iran during the third quarter of the seventeenth century:

> On which account it is, the Armenians being skill'd in all the Intricacies and subtlities of Trade at home, and traveling with these into the remotest kingdoms, become by their own Industry, and by being Factors of their own kindreds Honesty, the Wealthiest Men, being expert of at bargains wherever they come, evading thereby brokeridge, and studying all the Arts of Thrift, will Travel for Fifty shillings, where we cannot for Fifty Thomands; setting out with a stock of Hard Eggs and a Metarrah of Wine, which will last them from Spahaun to the Port, riding on a mean Beast, which they sell or ship off for Advance, their only expence being Horse-Meat; traveling with no Attendance, their Matrass serving at once for Horse-cloth and them to lye on; they are kind of Privateers in Trade, no Purchase, no Pay; *they enter the Theater of Commerce by means of some Benefactor, whose Money they adventure upon, and on Return, a Quarter Part of the Gain is their own: From such Beginnings do they Raise sometimes great Fortunes for themselves and Masters.*[52]

The image of the thrifty Julfan *commenda* agents, often portrayed in European sources, as in Grigor of Daranagh's *Chronicle* with which this chapter began, as greedy and monopolizing engrossers,[53] can also be found in the following well-known description of them in Jean Baptiste Tavernier's collection of travels through Persia, in which the extreme frugality of Julfan *commenda* agents is singled out for attention:

And indeed the *Armenians* are so much the more fit for Trading, because they are a people very Sparing, and very Sober, though whether it be their virtue or their avarice I know not. For when they are going a long Journey, they only make provision of Brisket, Smoak't *Buffalo's* flesh, Onions, bak't Butter, Flowr, Wine, and dry Fruits. They never buy fresh Victuals, but when they meet with Lambs or Kids very cheap in the Mountainous Countries; nor is there one of them that does not carry his own Angle to fish withal, when they come to any Ponds or Rivers. All these provisions cost them little the Carriage. And when they come to any Town where they are to stay, they club five or six together and lye in an empty Chamber which they furnish themselves; every one carrying his Matress his coverlet and his Kitchin-Instruments, which is a great piece of Thrift. When they travel in Christendome, they carry along with them Saffron, Pepper, Nutmegs, and other Spices; which they exchange in the Country-Towns for Bread, Wine, Butter, Cheese, Milk-Meats and other Provisions which they buy of the poor Women. When they return out of Christendom, they bring along with them all sorts of Mercery-ware, and Pedlery-ware of *Norenberg,* and *Venice;* as little Looking-glasses, trifles of Tin enamel'd, false Pearls, and other things of that nature; which pays for the Victuals they call for among the Country-people.[54]

Elsewhere in his account of Julfa, Fryer makes it clear that the "Masters," or the rich Julfan merchants known as *khwajas,* usually stayed at home, leaving the hard work and the traveling to their factors, whom he compares to a swarm of bees. Referring to these wealthy *khwajas,* Fryer writes: "For whilst they sit lazily at Home, their Factors abroad in all parts of the Earth return to their hives laden with Honey; to which Exercise, after they themselves have been brought up, they train their Children under the safe Conduct of Experienced Tutors, who instruct them first to Labour for a Livelihood, before they are permitted to Expend."[55]

To get a good idea of how tireless some *commenda* agents were in their efforts to travel great distances in order to find lucrative markets, we have to look at evidence from the easternmost settlement on the outer edges of the Julfan trade network. Situated on the periphery of the Indian Ocean and serving as a gateway to Mexico or New Spain in the New World, the Spanish colonial city of Manila had attracted a number of Julfan merchants probably as early as the 1680s. By the 1730s, the city had become an important port of destination for Julfan *commenda* agents, who arrived from Isfahan using Julfan nodes or settlements in India and Southeast Asia as routing stations. Once in Manila, many felt compelled to convert officially to Catholicism to improve their trading prospects and reside in Manila without harassment. To do this, they visited the local Inquisition office, where they were interrogated at length about their biographical information, including information on where they had traveled and how long they had resided in each place before their arrival in Manila. Because of the detailed scrutiny to which Inquisition examiners subjected potential converts, the Manila Inquisition records contain a rich trove of documentation on the complex itineraries of Julfan *commenda* agents that has escaped the notice of previous scholars of Julfan history. The most remarkable of these records concerns a Julfan *commenda* agent whose name appears in its Latinized version as Santiago Barrachiel (or Ter Ohannes ordi Barakiali, as he was known to other Julfans).[56] Upon visiting the Inquisition office in Manila in 1735 to make a secret conversion to Catholicism, Santiago was given the same questionnaire as other Julfans who also visited the Inquisition office to make a "spontaneous reconciliation" to the Church of Rome. Among the questions Santiago was posed by his Inquisition interrogator was the following: "What places have you visited until the present moment and how long have you lived in each place and what have you studied?"[57] Santiago's response to this query is truly remarkable because of the global scale of his travels. For this reason alone it is worth reproducing in full:

He said that at the age of thirteen, he left Julfa by land for Khanbao [?illegible], and at the same Persian city he remained for five months, and from there in a Russian ship [en un navio de Moscobita] he crossed to Astrakhan, the port of Moscovi, where he resided for three months, and by river he took passage crossing the kingdom of Muscovi to the city of Sanatoc [?], where he stayed for three months. From there he went to the capital of Moscow and resided there for eight months, whence he went to St. Petersburg, also in that kingdom, where he remained for two months; he took passage on a Russian ship to Libau, the port of the kingdom of Sweden, and lived there for about four months. And from there he traveled by land to Rebla [Reval? Now Tallin in Estonia, then in Swedish control?] in the same kingdom of Sweden, where he resided about six months. And from there he traveled to the Republic of Lubec in a [?] ship and remained there for [?] months, whence by land he traveled to Amsterdam in Holland and remained there for two months. From there he took passage on a [?] ship to Archangel, the port of Moscovy, and resided there for about three months, whence he traveled by land to the capital of Moscow and resided there for about seven months. He left there by land and traveled to the port of Astrakhan, where he resided for about two months. From there he returned to Xanbali [Enzeli?], a Persian city, and remained there for [? unclear] months, whence he returned to his homeland [*patria*] of Julfa and remained there for about eight days. From [? illegible] in a Moorish ship he took passage to the port of Surat in the lands of Mughal India [Gran Mogor] and stayed there for two months and took a Moorish ship and headed to the kingdom of Bengal, where he was for about five months. From there he traveled to Tranquebar [Trancambar ], a port and Danish factory on the Coromandel, and resided there for five months, and by a Danish ship he crossed over to diverse places on the Coromandel coast and that of Malabar for a period of about four months until he arrived in Ormuz, the port of Persia, and from there he entered Isfahan, where he remained for a year and a half. During this period he got married in Julfa with Isabel of the Armenian nation and schismatic faith. And from there he traveled to the city of Tabriz within the same kingdom and lived there for about two months and traveled from there by land to the city of Yerevan [Araban] on the Turkish frontier and the place where the Catholicos [Catholicon], as they call the patriarch of Armenia, is found, and he stayed there for about two months. And from there by land he traveled to Arzadam [? Arzrum/Arzingan] in the kingdom of Turkey, where he resided for about one month and a half, and traveled from there to C . . . [illegible broken word in inner margin: Constantinople?], where he lived for a month and a half before going to the port of Smyrna [i.e., Esmirna], where he stopped for about two months, and from there he traveled to Malta on an English ship and stayed there for about [?] weeks and traveled from there to Livorno; here he was for about one month before crossing from there to Florence and Venice, where he resided for one year. From Venice he went to Germany [Alemania] at Abstendan [?], where he lived for about eleven months, and from there he traveled to the city of Antwerp [Amberes], where he lived for one month, whence he returned by Brussels [Brusela] to Amsterdam, where he lived for about twenty days, and from there he took passage on a Dutch ship to the Russian port of Archangel and lived there for three months and entered the capital city of Moscow from there and lived in that city for about seven months. From there he traveled to the city of Kazan [Casanca?] in the same kingdom and lived there for two months and embarked for the port of Astrakhan and lived there for two months before taking passage on a Muscovite ship to Shamakhi? [Xambahi?], a Persian city, where he lived for two months; from there he returned to Isfahan and lived there for four months, and from there he traveled to the port of Surat in an English ship and stayed there for four years. He took passage on an Armenian ship and traveled to Madras and lived there for two months. And from there he traveled to Pondicherry [Policheri ?], where he was for two weeks before taking a French ship to this city of Manila, where he lived for four months and with the same ship returned to Pondicherry and thence to Madras, where he resided for four months before returning to this city of Manila on an Armenian ship, where he lived for five years, and from here he traveled on a Spanish ship to Batavia, where he lived for two months before returning on the same ship to Manila, where he lived for seven months, and from here he made a voyage on a Spanish ship to Batavia and stayed there for about a month and a half before returning to Manila on the same ship to live for about a year and a half. From here he traveled to Madras on an Armenian ship and lived there for four months and returned to this city on the same Armenian ship, where he has been living for about eighteen months until the present moment. And [he said] he hasn't studied any other art but reading and accounting in the language of his homeland and speaks Dutch and a little Italian and reads and writes in Spanish. He has also studied the art of commercial bookkeeping in Spanish here in Manila.[58]

Santiago was by all means not the only Julfan globe-trotter to visit the Inquisition. Many others left similar accounts, though none rivaled his in terms of covering the Indian Ocean, Mediterranean, northwest European, and Eurasian circuits of the Julfan network. Some *commenda* agents gave more detailed *testimonios* about their travels in the Indian Ocean and Mediterranean circuits of the Julfan network, bypassing the Russian zone altogether. Thus, a year prior to Santiago's visit to Inquisition, another Julfan agent named Gregorio di Zaccarias left the following account of his travels in response to the same question posed to Santiago:

He said that he was born in the neighborhood of Isfahan [the capital of Persia] and his parents were Zacharias and Maria, belonging to the same sect as the schismatic Armenians, in which he also believed. And he remained [in Julfa] *until he was fifteen years of age, at which time, having learned how to read write and do accounting in the language of this neighborhood and the kingdom of Persia,* he left [Julfa] and made a voyage to Madras, where he resided for three months, and from there he traveled to the kingdom of Bengal [Regno de Vengala] in a [Armenian? word is broken] ship and stayed there for two years and six months. And from there he returned on an English ship to Madras, where he lived for nine months. Boarding an English ship he traveled [first] to the port of Macao and from there to Batavia, where he resided for six months before returning in an English ship to Madras, where he stayed for one year and four months before traveling on an English ship to the port of [? broken], the Dutch factory, where he resided for eleven months. From there he crossed to Batavia on an English ship and lived there for five months before traveling on an English ship to Tenesserim in the kingdom of Siam, where he lived for five months. He traveled from there on an English ship to Madras, where he stayed about twenty months, and from there on a Portuguese ship he traveled to Macao, where he lived for eighteen months, and traveled to Batavia on a Portuguese ship, lived there for [?] months, and returned to Macao, where he stayed for seven months and from there traveled to Madras on a Portuguese ship to stay there for about two months. He returned from there to Macao on a Portuguese ship and resided there for six months, and from there on a Portuguese ship he crossed over to Batavia and stayed there for one [month or year? word broken] and returned from there to Madras on a Portuguese ship and resided there for two months. From there, he traveled to Cochinchina on a Portuguese ship and resided there for four months at the port city of Puntramas [?illegible]. And from there on a Portuguese ship he traveled to Macao and stayed there for nine months and traveled from there on a Portuguese ship to Madras, where he stayed for three months. He traveled from there on a Portuguese ship to Macao and resided there for seven months and arrived in this city of Manila on a Portuguese ship and resided here for nine months before traveling to Batavia, where he lived for two months before returning to Manila on the same ship, where he has resided for nine months until the present moment. He has made all these voyages with the goal of earning a living in trade and commerce.[59]

In at least one case, we have a Julfan, Constantino di Lazzaro, who followed an itinerary similar to Gregorio di Zaccarias and other Julfans, except that at one point, when Constantino reached Batavia, he suddenly decided to travel on a Dutch ship all the way to Amsterdam and return to Batavia on the same vessel before heading to Manila.[60] We also have a few cases of Julfan *commenda* agents who were not satisfied with reaching Manila and pressed on to Acapulco in New Spain, traveling on one of the Manila galleons and residing for brief periods in the New World before returning to New Julfa by way of Manila and India.[61]

Most *testimonios* given by Julfan *commenda* agents in Manila indicate that these enterprising men received a basic education in "reading and accounting" in the Julfa dialect at a remarkably young age (thirteen for Santiago and fifteen for Constan-

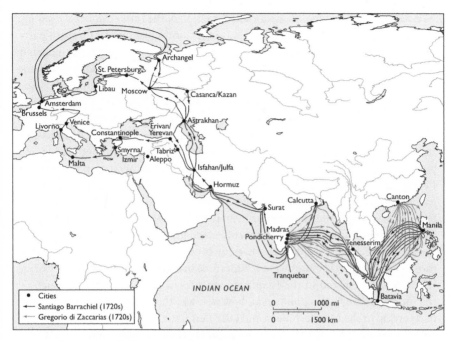

MAP 4. Itineraries of Julfan *commenda* agents.

tino) after which they left their homes in search of profitable investments overseas. The young age of these agents indicates that they were already considered adults before they left home on their travels. Indeed, this is supported by a testimony at a notary public in Amsterdam given in the second half of the seventeenth century, according to which "among the Armenians [of Julfa] one is considered to be able to conduct business if he has only the age of 15 or 16 . . . [after which] all his acts are considered as being valid like those of a mature person."[62] By the time some of these men had reached Manila and had decided to convert to Catholicism, they had already been away from their families for at least a decade. Some, like Santiago, worked in a brief visit home in the course of their long travels for the purpose of marrying a bride from their home community. Others probably married local women in the marketplaces they visited, thus "creolizing" as they traveled, as Georges Roques suggests in his manual of trade in India.[63] Most of the Julfans who crop up in the Inquisition records in Manila were clearly seasoned agents in the employ of wealthy *aghas* or *khwajas* residing in Julfa. Though the Inquisition records do not provide us with the names of the masters for whom these forlorn agents toiled, we can be certain that their employers were wealthy Julfan family firms with their headquarters in the nodal center in New Julfa.

As a number of economic historians have noted, the *commenda* as a legal institution in medieval European trade was only one among several forms of partnership that facilitated the combination of credit and labor. Other forms included "commission agency," in which one merchant, usually residing abroad, would work for another for a set fee or commission for a limited number of transactions, instead of a preset percentage for an undefined number of commercial ventures with an open-ended contract that could last anywhere from a few years to several decades, as in the *commenda*. As Edmund Herzig's work demonstrates, commission agencies were also present in Julfan commerce, though they did not play as important a role as *commendas*.[64] Another early form of partnership in the trade of the medieval Mediterranean was what was known as the *fraterna,* or the later *compagnia*.[65] As their etymologies indicate, both were means of uniting family members or kin into a partnership arrangement in which capital investments and profits were shared by brothers in the *fraterna* or extended family in the *compagnia* (from *cumpanis,* meaning "people who share or break bread together").[66] Both these forms of family partnerships were Mediterranean counterparts to the family firm, which was widespread in the Islamicate societies of Eurasia, including much of the Indian Ocean.[67] The *commenda,* however, was the more widespread form of partnership in the Mediterranean and lasted until the late medieval period, when it was superseded by commission agencies and later by the more economically efficient form of the joint-stock company, which formed the organizational basis for the European expansion and conquest of the Indian Ocean.[68] One reason the *commenda* was so widespread was its legal and organizational versatility; it could unite an individual sedentary capitalist with an agent or agents, or a great number of such capitalists with agent(s). The latter possibility was the case when *fraternas* or *compagnias* hired agents to conduct their affairs in distant places. In such cases, the *commenda* became a practical means of expanding the family firm beyond the limits imposed by kinship. This affinity between the *commenda* and the family firm was also the basis for the dramatic expansion of Julfan trade in the seventeenth and eighteenth centuries.

## CLAN AND KINSHIP IN MERCANTILE NETWORKS

*In most societies, at most times, it has been the great family which by its wealth, power, prestige, and presumption of permanence has been the outstanding institution for private economic enterprise.*[69]

Most scholars are now in agreement that the extended family played a crucial role in European trade from at least the early medieval period to the sixteenth century, when it began to give way to a bureaucratic and sophisticated form of organization known as the joint-stock company. The role of the family was even more entrenched in the Indian Subcontinent, where it continued to serve as an important means of capitalist enterprise long after the intrusion of European chartered, joint-stock companies transformed the face of Asian trade.[70]

All the available documentation indicates that Julfan Armenians also organized their commercial affairs around the patriarchal structure of the family and its traditional role in Julfan life. In doing so, they were conforming to a practice that was widespread both in the Islamicate societies of Eurasia, where Julfans were for the most part based, and in the early modern Mediterranean societies, with whom they were in frequent contact. Despite the abundance of evidence regarding the central role of the extended family in Julfan trade, some Soviet Armenian scholars in the 1940s and 1950s began popularizing a revisionist view that the Julfans actually had a unified trading company along the lines of the European joint-stock-trading companies of the period. Such a view was encouraged by a misinterpretation of vital aspects of an agreement between Julfan merchants and Czar Alexevich of Russia in 1667–1673. (See chapter 4 for a discussion of this agreement.) According to the Russian translation of this treaty, which was made at the time by a court-appointed translator and subsequently deposited in the Russian archives and published in Yerevan in 1953 in a collection of archival documents concerning Russian-Armenian relations, the agreement was signed by the "representatives of the Armenian Trading Company" and the Russian monarch.[71] On this basis, Soviet Armenian scholars, such as Leo (Arakel Babakhanian) and later Ashot Hovhannisyan, [72] began to propagate the view that the Julfans had moved beyond the traditional confines of the family firm and managed themselves around an organizationally more sophisticated structure of a unified "Julfa Trading Company" whose board of directors were empowered to sign important treaties with foreign states and to coordinate the commercial affairs of their community. This view, however, was based in large part on a mistranslation of the 1673 agreement, the original of which was written in the Julfa dialect. According to the Julfa dialect version of this treaty, the signatories of the agreement between the Russian czar and the Armenian merchants were "representatives of the Armenian trading companies [*kupanek*]."[73] In other words, the Julfans who had signed this important agreement with the Russian court were described in the treaty as agents for Julfa's leading family firms with the backing of the township's Assembly of Merchants (see chapter 7 on the Assembly of Merchants). The key distinction between the Russian translation and the original text in the Julfa dialect revolves around the word *kupanek,* in which the final suffix *-k* represents the Classical Armenian marker for the plural form, which the Russian translator at the court had mistranslated in its singular form. In 1980 and 1988, Shushanik Khachikian definitively debunked the myth of the Julfa Trading Company.[74] In her painstaking analysis of the famous 1673 agreement, Khachikian pointed out that the signatories of the treaty were *not* members of the fictitious trading company but rather representatives of the administrative body in Julfa known as the Assembly of Merchants whose members consisted of the township's twenty district heads (who were themselves representatives of Julfa's wealthiest families, each with its own family firm) as well as the *kalantar*, or mayor, of the Julfans (see chapter 7 for an extensive discussion). Khachikian also pointed out that the views regarding a unified Julfan Trading Company stemmed from the mistranslation of the plural form of "companies" (*kupanek*) into a singular "company."

Despite these definitive findings, Ina Baghdiantz McCabe has attempted to rekindle the idea of a Julfan Trading Company in *The Shah's Silk for Europe's Silver*. In chapter 8 of this work, Baghdiantz McCabe takes issue with Khachikian's interpretation of the 1673 agreement. As she puts it, "There is a problem in Šušanik Xachikyan's assertion that there was not a large commercial company on the European model in New Julfa: her identification of the signatories of the treaty as the administrators of New Julfa does not negate the possibility of the existence of a company. In fact the opposite is easily argued."[75] Although she spends a great deal of time in chapter 7 of her work discussing the role of the family in Julfan society and giving it the importance it deserves in Julfan life, Baghdiantz McCabe still contends that the "municipal council of New Julfa and the directors of the Armenian Commercial Association are one and the same."[76] In other words, for Baghdiantz McCabe, the Assembly of Merchants, whose members were the real signatories of the Russian-Julfan agreements, was in fact nothing other than a kind of "Court of Directors" of what she describes as the "Trading Association [read: Company] of New Julfa." This attempt to incorporate a unified trading company into the family firm structure of Julfan trade is not supported by a single document known to have survived, as Baghdiantz McCabe herself states: "There is no mention of a large Armenian Company in any of the European travel accounts, nor, seemingly, elsewhere."[77] However, she continues to assert throughout her book and in subsequent publications:[78] "the fact remains that they [i.e., the Julfans] did have an organized company."[79] At one point she even claims that the "Armenian Company was a government, though one subject to the Persian court."[80]

The evidence, both Julfan and European, however, points to a picture very different from the one proposed by Baghdiantz McCabe and much closer to that suggested by Khachikian. If the Julfans lacked a centralized trading company, how then did they organize their trade? A pamphlet published in London at the conclusion of a lengthy trial at the High Court of Admiralty involving some Julfan merchants describes the organizational basis of Julfan trade in the following terms:

> It further appears by these papers, that the custom among these People is to keep a Capital in their Families to trade with, and that the Chiefs of the Family, in the Nature of a patriarchal Government, manage the Affairs and Trade of the Family at Home, at Julpha, and send the younger Branches to different parts to trade, with such and such Sums as they advance to them, out of, and on Account of, the general Capital of

the Family: Beside which Sums, each Person has a Stock to trade with, on his own Separate Account.[81]

As the above passage suggests, the key to understanding the organizational basis of Julfan Armenian trade lies not in the so-called Trading Company of New Julfa but in the patriarchal institution of the family. Unfortunately, sociological research on the social and economic role of the Armenian patriarchal family in the early modern period is practically nonexistent. Julfan documents preserved in various archives are also remarkably silent when it comes to information about how the patriarchal family actually functioned in Julfan society. What we have to rely upon are a handful of observations made by European travelers and sections of the Astrakhan Code of Laws that cover inheritance law. Other information must be gathered and carefully pieced together from contracts and business correspondence of particular Julfan families.[82]

Our earliest glimpse into the social structure of the traditional Armenian family in the early modern period comes from the pen of the English traveler John Cartwright, who traveled through Old Julfa in the closing years of the sixteenth century:

> Their families are very great; for, both Sonnes, Nephewes and Nieces doe dwell under one roofe, having all their substance in common: and when the father dyeth, the eldest Sonne doth governe the rest, all submitting themselves under his regiment. But when the eldest Sonne dyeth, the government doth not passe to his sonnes, but to the eldest brother. And if it chance to fall out, that all the brethren doe die, then the government doth belong to the eldest Sonne of the eldest Brother, and so from one to the another.[83]

Needless to say, the rigidly patriarchal nature of the family described in these lines was not unique to Julfans, as many Mediterranean and Indian Ocean communities during this period also shared this trait. Like its counterparts in the Mediterranean and Indian Ocean, the Julfan patriarchal household tended to have a far larger number of members than the modern nuclear family. Some families had several dozen members, as the Julfan family known as the Kars'nmankants (from the Armenian compound for forty children) indicates. Jean Chardin suggests that some Julfan households had as many as five hundred extended members, a fact that sometimes allowed them to survive as a corporate entity for several centuries.[84]

What was perhaps more unique to the Julfan Armenian patriarchal tradition was that it did not seem to pay much attention to the law of primogenitor, as patriarchal succession does not appear to have devolved automatically from the father to his oldest son but to the oldest surviving male member of the extended family, such as the deceased father's brother or one of his sons. This is evident in two related aspects of Julfan commercial life. First, the eldest male was expected to be in charge of the entire household and even have authority over the families of his younger brothers or nephews. Most Julfan families lived in one great house in which the brothers with their families would share the same roof ruled by the eldest male member of the extended family. Thus, after the death of the patriarch of the *khwaja* Minasian family in Julfa in 1702, the five surviving sons continued to live under the same roof for quite some time and were under the authority of the eldest brother. Second, the rule of male seniority also applied to the running of the family business, where the eldest surviving male after the death of the patriarch would be in charge of managing or directing the collective affairs of the firm. Younger brothers were expected to defer to their senior siblings.[85]

Julfans organized their businesses primarily by combining the archaic structure of the patriarchal family outlined above with sophisticated techniques of capital investment in overseas markets, credit-sharing mechanisms, complex accounting, and information monitoring. It is important to point out that *pace* Baghdiantz McCabe and others who continue to adhere to the unified "Julfan Trading Company" thesis, Julfan merchants did not have a modern joint-stock principle as the basis of their trade. Thus, unlike the anonymous nature of the modern multinational joint-stock firm, whose origins go back to the East India Companies of the seventeenth century, Julfan family firms were not able to raise their capital base from as wide a pool of investors as the English East India Company and its Dutch counterpart, the Vereenigde Oost-Indische Compagnie (VOC), many of whose shareholders were unrelated to one another and often did not even know each other. Moreover, unlike the European East India Companies, whose large volume and high frequency of long-distance transactions required them to develop a sophisticated bureaucracy of management resulting in the employment of several hundred salaried employees to look after every aspect of the firm's overseas trade, the typical Julfan family firm did not feature a separation of ownership and management, which was a hallmark of the modern firm.[86]

As we shall see in the course of the brief discussion of the administrative structure of Julfa in chapter 7, each of Julfa's twenty districts had its own representative official called the *kadkhuda,* or district head, who was in charge of the internal administration of his district. The *kadkhuda* was chosen from the wealthiest family residing in each district, and, in addition to representing his district, he played an important role in the township's two major autonomous administrative bodies: the Assembly of Merchants and the more general Municipal Assembly. Now, some of these twenty families from whose ranks New Julfa's district heads were appointed were in all likelihood also among the wealthiest families in Old Julfa, and some may even have had the genuine roots they claimed in the former landed aristocracy of classical Armenia, before they were forcibly relocated to Isfahan in 1605.[87] It would not be an exaggeration to say that together these twenty or so elite families ran the economy of Julfa. What is important for our discussion here is to note that the sons of these families used their inheritance money as capital for investments overseas by organizing their business ventures around the preexisting structure of the patriarchal household. Below, I will briefly look at two of Julfa's wealthiest families and use their life histories to demonstrate how the Julfan family firm functioned and how it incorporated the institution of the *commenda* into its activities. The incorporation of the *commenda* into the operation of family firms allowed them to expand the spheres of their economic activities far beyond the confines of kinship. Family firms, as we shall see, consisted of more than family members or blood relatives; most Julfan family firms also hired numerous employees, including low-level servants and couriers as well as trusted *commenda* agents, many of whom were *not* blood relatives.

## THE SCERIMAN/SHAHRIMAN/ SHAHRIMANIAN FAMILY FIRM

*The Sirs Scerimans/Shahrimanians, the name to which our most vivid gratitude will forever render us infinitely more respectable, are today the only noblemen among those of the Armenian nation, a glorious title that the kings of Persia have given them along with the privilege of having their own private church where the Divine service is held in the Catholic fashion, albeit in the Armenian language, and which is served by two bishops and three Armenian priests united to the Roman Church, maintained by the generosity of these sirs. The kings of Persia have granted them all these favors as reward for the services they have rendered to the State. They were five brothers, all united in the same business, having large and flourishing families, factors, and correspondents in all the major cities of Europe and Asia; and God having given them so much blessing to their affairs, which made them, without exception, the richest and most powerful of the nation; distinguished by their piety and their zeal for the propagation of the faith even more so than by their nobility and their wealth, they took pride in being the declared protectors of the missionaries and above all the Jesuits in Julfa, where they built for them the beautiful church that I mentioned earlier, and in their love for religion and in their attachment to the company [of Jesus]. So many services rendered by these pious and illustrious sirs have actually prompted [Pope] Clement XI to promote one of their children, Monsignor Basilio Sceriman, to the illustrious post of Prelate of the Roman Church and to entrust him with the governorship of the most considerable cities of the Ecclesiastical State. A blessed augury of an even higher eminence is that there are grounds to believe that the Sovereign Pontifs would crown this enlightened and virtuous Prelate for his personal merits.*[88]

The Sceriman/Shahrimanian family was the most influential and wealthiest family of Roman Catholic Armenians in Julfa (see figs. 13 and 14).[89] Like most Julfan families, the Shahrimanians were originally from Old Julfa. The great patriarch of the family, Agha Murat, was among those deported from Old Julfa by Shah 'Abbas I during the first years of the seventeenth century.[90] We know nothing about Murat's life in Old Julfa or about his career in Julfa after his resettlement there in 1605. Of his two grandsons, Nazar and Shahriman, the first does not seem to have had any offspring, so the family continued through Shahriman's line and bore his name.[91] Shahriman's son Sarhat was responsible for expanding the family's wealth and influence in the mid-seventeenth century. The evidence suggests that unlike most Armenian merchants from Julfa, the Shahrimanians were from very early on primarily diamond and gem merchants. Sarhat's eldest son, Zaccaria, was a royal merchant for Shah Suleyman (Shah Safi II, 1666–1694) and for the chief minister (*i'timad al dawla*) of Iran.[92] It was Zaccaria who presented numerous gifts to the Russian court, including a golden throne decorated with thousands of diamonds and precious stones in 1659.[93] This generous gesture paved the way to Czar Alexei's granting of special privileges to Julfan merchants to use the Russian route to export silk to Europe (see chapter 4). At the same time, the Shahrimanian family began exploring other avenues for expansion.

Already in 1613, the family owned a house in Venice, which served as a temporary residence for use by their agents and family members who had business to attend to in the Mediterranean and elsewhere in Europe.[94] Italy had become a favorite business destination for various senior members of the Shahrimanian family from very early on. In the 1650s and 1660s, Gaspar Shahriman, the fourth son of Khwaja Sarhat, was spending long periods in Venice, Livorno, and Rome. In the 1690s, Nazar and Shahriman, the sons of Murat di Sceriman, another son of Sarhat, had invested close to 720,000 ducats in interest-bearing accounts in various Venetian banks and offered other substantial loans to the republic to help finance its wars against the Ottomans.[95] The family's orientation toward the Italian city-states was reflected not only in their financial concerns. It had a cultural component as well.

In 1646, Khwaja Sarhat is said to have converted to Catholicism.[96] Several decades later, in 1684, eleven members of the family formally abjured loyalty to the Armenian Church and embraced Catholicism in Julfa in the presence of a Carmelite missionary.[97] From then on, they became the pillars of Catholicism in Julfa and great supporters of the Vatican. As a result of their generous financial support, they were granted numerous privileges by a grateful Rome. As in Russia, numerous favors for the Vatican, starting in the 1680s while the family was still in Julfa, resulted in a papal bull of 1696, granting the family trading privileges in Rome, Ancona, and Civitavecchia, as well as full citizenship in Rome.[98] The Shahrimanian family's patronage of the Vatican was also crucial in gaining them an audience with Emperor Leopold in the late 1690s.[99] In 1699, the recommendation of the papacy and similar favors by the family to the Austro-Hungarian Empire resulted in the granting of the titles of counts in Hungary by Emperor Leopold II.[100] Similarly, when the Shahrimanians loaned Venice 720,000 ducats (an astronomical sum probably worth several billion U.S. dollars) to help finance its wars against the Ottomans in the early 1690s, the family was accorded numerous privileges by the Venetian senate. Incidentally, the family settled in Venice in 1698, shortly after extending these loans. Two years earlier, in 1696, they had been enrolled "in the citizenship of Rome, and granted

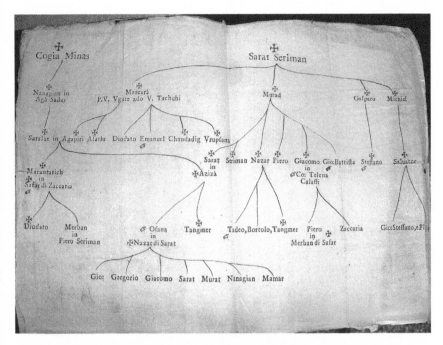

FIGURE 13. Sceriman family tree *stampa*; *Resultato del processo per la verificazione dei requisiti alla N.V. nella famiglia de Co. Co: Fr[ate]lli Sceriman,* ABMC, MS Cod. Cigogna 3428/9. Courtesy of the Archivio della Biblioteca di Museo Correr.

the freedom of Civitavecchia and Ancona: two ports through which Pope Innocent XII was hoping to improve the commerce of the Papal States."[101] They were also made members of the nobility in a string of Italian city-states, including Orvieto (1736), Spoleto (1740), Viterbo (1749), Perugia (1749), and Macerata (1751).[102]

Privileges abroad came at a heavy price at home and alienated the Shahrimanians from the Armenian Church hierarchy in Julfa. In 1694, when tensions between Catholic missionaries in Julfa and the Armenian Church came to a head, the Shahrimanians bore the brunt of anti-Catholic fervor in Isfahan, which was fueled under increasing pressure by Shah Sultan Hussein.[103] As life in Julfa became increasingly difficult for the Shahrimanians, the family banked on its financial and cultural investments in Italy. In 1698, Khwaja Gaspar, the son of Khwaja Sarhat, migrated and settled in Venice, bringing his family with him. He was joined shortly afterward by his older brother Khwaja Marcara and his family.[104] Perhaps in light of the deteriorating situation in Iran and with a strategic view to secure a hospitable haven in the future, Marcara had earlier made a personal loan to the Venetian republic of 200,000 ducats,[105] to help in their war with the Ottomans.[106]

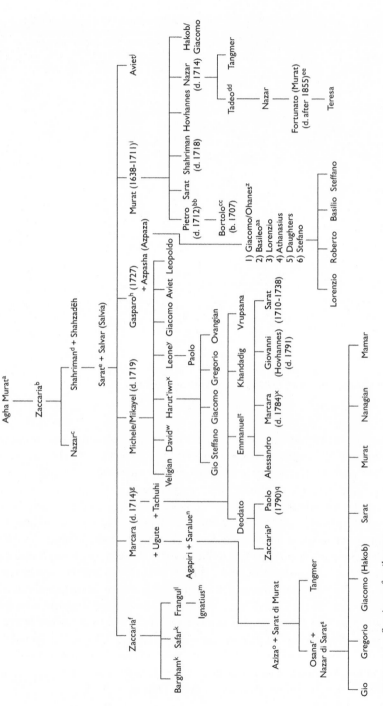

FIGURE 14. Sceriman family tree.

a. Almost nothing is known about the origins of the Sceriman/Shahrimanian family. We know from Ter Hovhaniants (1880, 1: 110–128) that the family was originally from Old Julfa and was among those deported from there in 1604 and later resettled in Isfahan/New Julfa by 'Abbas I. None of the known sources shed any light on the family's history before the deportation of 1604, but Armenian sources from the post-deportation period claim a noble status for the family and indicate that they belonged to an ancient clan of nobles (*nakharark*') with possible roots in the historic Armenian city of Ani. The family's branches settled in Italy in the eighteenth century and, applying for induction into the Venetian patriciate, went so far as to claim ("invent"?) for themselves European or French origins as well as noble status in ancient Armenia. Monsignor Basilio Sceriman in his "Libro di memorie," of which only an abridged version has come down to us, claims that the family descended from French Crusaders who had settled in Armenia after the Crusades ("Libro di memorie di Monsignor Basilio Sceriman," Avogaria di Comun 348, Processi di Nobiltà—Sceriman, ASV, n.p.). According to Ter Hovhaniants (1880, 1: 110), the earliest known patriarch of the family was Agha Murat, who was born in Old Julfa and presumably passed away in New Julfa, though his dates of birth and death are not mentioned in any known source.

b. Zaccaria was the first member of the family to have been born in New Julfa, but his dates of birth and death are not mentioned in any known source. According to Monsignor Basilio Sceriman, "Communque la [?] Giulfa nuova e stata la nostra comun Patria, dove sono nati in primo, per qualchesia a mia notizia, il nostro Tirzavolo nome Zaccaria, da questo nacque il Bisavolo Sceriman, che ha dato il cognome alla casa, e da cui nacque Sarhad nostro avo qual nome significa in Persiano Contermine" ("Libro di memorie, Avogaria di Comun 348, Processi di Nobiltà—Sceriman, ASV, n.p.). (In any case, New Julfa was our common homeland where, first, was born our great-great-grandfather Zaccaria, from whom was born our great-grandfather Sceriman, who gave the family name to the family, and from him was born our grandfather Sarhad, which name in Persian signifies boundary or limit.) Note that Monsignor Basilio does not mention Agha Murat as the great patriarch. Ter Hovhaniants appears to be confused when he asserts that Zaccaria was the son of Shahriman and brother of Sarat (1880, 1: 110; 1980, 124).

c. Nazar does not appear to have produced any descendants. The family bore his brother's name.

d. Shahriman son of Zaccaria is mentioned in a colophon to an Armenian psalter published in Amsterdam in 1661–1662 as the principal benefactor of that work. This reference to him is among the first known references to the family in the surviving documentation. It also suggests that he was alive as late as 1661–1662, and provides the names of his descendants up to the generation of his grandchildren. It is also the only known source to provide the name of his wife, Shahzadēh. See Voskanyan et al. 1988, 40a.

e. Sarat is also referred to in Fortunato Seriman's family tree as "Giacomo" (Fortunato Seriman, *Brevie memorie sulla famiglia Seriman*, MS Cod. Cigogna 3403 [1855], ABMC, last folio). His wife's name, as in the case of the names of most of his progeny who settled in Italy, is Italianized as "Salvia" or "Silvia." Armenian-language colophonic material from the seventeenth and eighteenth centuries refers to her as "Salvar." See Voskanyan et al. 1988, 40a, 100a; and Ērzrumetsʻi 1713, 309.

f. Zaccaria was Sarat's first born and eldest of six brothers. His branch of the family is missing from most of the family trees compiled in Italy with the exception of that found in Fortunato Seriman's *Brevie memorie sulla famiglia Seriman* (Ms. Cod. Cigogna 3403 [1855], ABMC). As eldest brother, Zaccaria was clearly the representative of the family during its period of commercial ascendance in the 1660s in New Julfa. His name is strangely missing from the list of signatories to the agreements signed between the Julfans and the Russian state in 1667 and 1673 (Khachikian 1988, 27–28). He was also the person who donated a diamond-studded throne to Czar Alexeivich in 1659 (see chapters 4 and 6). He appears to have been alive in 1673 and as late as 1684, as his name and signature are affixed to the letter of confession sent by the family in New Julfa to the Vatican; see "Sceriman Family Letter of Confession and Loyalty to the Catholic Church," Fondo SOCG, vol. 495, PROP FIDE, folios 241b–262a (folios 247 and 249). His branch of the family settled in Russia.

g. Data for dates of death in this family tree have been taken from printed (*stampa*) family trees in Avogaria di Comun 348, Processi di Nobiltà—Sceriman, ASV, as well as from similar family trees in Sceriman Family Papers, buste 1 and 3, Don Mazza.

h. Gasparo di Sarat passed away in Venice in 1727. The last codicil of his will and testament was written on 15 January 1726 and is found in Avogaria di Comun 348, Processi di Nobiltà—Sceriman, ASV, n.p.

i. An Italian translation of a segment of Murat's will, dated 28 July 1709, is found in "Procuratia Eccelentiss[ima] di Citra, e Chiesa di Santa Croce degl' Armeni" (*stampa* booklet), 36, Procuratori di San Marco, ASV, busta 180 (Santa Croce).

j. Aviet was the youngest of Sarat's sons but did not have any offspring. Monsignor Basilio writes: "Il Zio Avied, o Nunziato, benche l'ultimo nato e figlio di Padre vecchio premori avanti li suoi fra[tel]li senza lasciar figli . . ." ("Libro di memorie," ASV, n.p.). (Uncle Avied or nunziato, though the last-born son of the old father [i.e., Sarat] passed away before his brothers without leaving any sons.)

k. Bargham is mentioned as the son of Zaccaria di Sarat in "Sceriman Family Letter of Confession and Loyalty to the Catholic Church," Fondo SOCG, vol. 495, PROP FIDE, folios 241b–262a (folios 247 and 249).

l. Frangul is one of the writers of a letter sent by the family in New Julfa to relatives in Venice on 2 Adam 78 (21 April 1693). See Sceriman Family Papers, Don Mazza, busta 3.

m. Ignatius was residing in Moscow in the 1730s. See the letter to Paron Ignatius and Paron Zaccaria in Moscow, written and sent from St. Petersburg, 28 August 1732. Ignatius was the grandson of Zaccaria di Sarat, who had opened a silk factory in Moscow in 1717, according to Shushanik Khachikian (1988, 74–75), but is said to have relocated to St. Petersburg after selling the factory to one of the Lazarians. See also the letter sent from Amsterdam to Paron Ignatius and Zaccaria in Moscow, dated 7 November 1732 ("Letter book of Hakob di Murat," Avogaria di Comun, ASV, busta 17). Ignatius is also mentioned in a legal document (Avogaria di Comun, ASV, busta 198) written on 25 July 1732 in Moscow by Hakob di Murat: Ձոռորեհն զորս այս է դո իմ մոբազդ որդի յակոբոս ըսերջ ստեֆ որոդ փսանոսն ճսանութ հոգե Ֆրասուղոբ որոդ սերջանու որդի սե[ս]ս[ս]ն հջսասղսոսես փսես սյ[ս]ս[ս]ն հջսասղսոսես [սսե] ճսսճսսխսսե. (The force of this document is that I, Hakob son of Murat, had an agent, Panos the son of Seth, who had an account with Paron Ignatius son of the deceased Frangul while [Panos son of Seth] was [still] alive. . . . ). Ignatius's father, Frangul, was also known by the name of Franz (Khachikian 1988, 74–75). Khachikian's hypothesis that Franz was most likely the Europeanized name for Nazar son of Murat di Sarat Shahrimanian seems incorrect, as does her suggestion (based on Ter Hovhaniants's work [1880, 1: 110]) that Ignatius's grandfather Zaccaria di Sarat Shahrimanian was Sarat's brother instead of Sarat's eldest son (Khachikian, 74–75 n. 114).

n. Agapiri's wife Saralue appears to have been a descendant of the Khwaja Minasian family. See the *stampa* family tree for the Sceriman family (fig. 13).

o. As the granddaughter of Khwaja Marcara, Aziza was a beneficiary of her grandfather's investments on her behalf. According to Shahriman family accounts listed in a journal by Hakob di Murad Shahriman or Gianbattista Sceriman (Documenti Armeni Mercantile, ASV, busta 1), Khwaja Marcara had invested 14,000 ducats on behalf of Aziza and deposited the money with one of the Scerimans in Italy to be employed in a profitable venture. (According to the Dutch account of the Afghan occupation of Isfahan translated and compiled by Willem Floor [1998, 117], the Afghan leader Mahmud apparently had appointed Khwaja Marcara as Julfa's *kalantar* on 22 April 1722. This appears to be an error, however, since most Sceriman family trees in the Italian archives (e.g., Avogaria di Comun 348, Processi di Nobiltà—Sceriman, ASV; and Sceriman Family Papers, Don Mazza, buste 1 and 2) confirm that Marcara had passed away in 1714.) Aziza was married to her cousin Nazar di Murat, a practice that was not condoned by the Armenian Church. The family converted to Catholicism in 1684, primarily, it seems, to be allowed the right to marry second and third cousins: այսու թսսսդ սսո սսս սսխս սս[սս] սսսսդ ձսո[սս]սս ե սսս սսսսբտսս[սս] շստսհեշտսդ սսեզ եւ սսսսսսող հրասմանի սասլս ամունալսալիս աուեղ աուհներին... ("Sceriman Family Letter of Confession and Loyalty to the Catholic Church," Fondo SOCG, vol. 495, PROP FIDE, folio 247). (With this letter which we are writing to the Sacred Congregation, in gratitude for the permission granted to us to marry cousins in the second and third degrees . . . ) For the Armenian church's ban on marrying kin up to the fourth degree or generation, see Berberian 2010 and the twelfth-century code of laws by Mkhitar Gosh (Gosh 2000, 255–258), where the ban is discussed. It is plausible that the Shahrimanians' decision to ask permission to marry cousins could have been motivated by a ban on Catholic-Gregorian marriages passed by the Armenian church in Julfa in 1680/81, which could have restricted the choices open to the family, since there appear to have been only twenty other Catholic families in Julfa. The hypothesis about the family's marriage preferences is my own and is not supported by evidence.

p. Zaccaria son of Deodato son of Marcara Sceriman was a celebrated writer, man of letters, and satirist in Venice in the 1760s. His mother was a Venetian noblewoman. See White 1961 for a detailed study.

q. Conte Paulo was a general in the Austro-Hungarian army during Empress Theresa's reign. He served in Bohemia, Dalmatia, then lived in Vienna, Trieste, and finally in Fiume and Gorizia, where he settled with his family; he died at the age of 69 in 1790. See Ughurlian 1891, 208.

r. Osana/Ovsana's papers are preserved in Documenti Armeni Mercantile, ASV, busta 198. See in particular the notarized document signed and sealed in Julfa, Isfahan by the Municipal Assembly of Julfa bearing the seals and signatures of Kalantar Hovannes di Papum and Vardapet Astuatsatur, along with those of a number of eminent merchants and *kadkhudas*. The document is dated 5 Tira 119 (21 September 1734). Osana/Ovsana, like a few other members of her family, appears to have married a cousin.

s. See the notarized copy of the will of Nazar di Sarhat Shahrimanian naming his wife Ovsana heir to his property (Avogaria di Comun, ASV, busta 198). The will was dated and sealed in New Julfa on 10 Nirhan 121 (23 February 1736).

t. Emmanuel served in the Iranian ambassadorial delegation sent to Istanbul during the reign of the Afghan ruler Ashraf in 1725. See chapters 5 and 8.

u. Marcara son of Emmanuel was a resident in Livorno and Madras during the eighteenth century. A man of great learning and an ardent supporter of Armenian printed books, he translated a number of works from English, Spanish, and Italian into Classical Armenian and had them published by Armenian Catholic monks established in Trieste. His published oeuvre includes *Patmuťiwn Metsin Gengizkhani arajin kayser nakhni mghulats' ev t'at'arats'; bazhaneal i chors girs* [A history of the Great Genghis Khan, the first emperor of the former Mongols and Tatars, comprising four letters] (Trieste, 1788). This work was a translation of Petis de la Croix's *Histoire du Grand Genghizcan*, originally published in 1710 in Paris. In this work Marcara describes himself as the most widely traveled and learned person among the Armenians: "And I circulated for forty years in the East Indies, among numerous pagan nations belonging to a variety of sects, including Muslim nations [*Mahmetakan azgats'*], and I can say this without a doubt, that during those forty years I did not meet a single person from our nation [i.e., among Armenians] who had circulated in exile [*pandkhtut'eants'*] on land and sea as I had" (9).

v. Sarat di Emmanuel was only twenty-eight years old when he died in Calcutta in 1738. He was buried in the Roman Catholic church in Calcutta. For his tombstone inscription in Armenian and Latin, see Seth (1922–1923, 303 n. 1).

w. David Sceriman, a rich coral and diamond merchant and resident in Livorno, died in Livorno in July 1757. He was without offspring and left his wealth to his relatives Gregorio, Michiele junior, and Zaccaria, who had arrived from New Julfa. See Sanacore 1988, 142.

x. Harut'iwn, also known as Arutun or Salvatore in Italian sources, was burned alive at the stake in Isfahan on January 14, 1747, by the order of Nadir Shah. See the discussion in chapter 8 and in Aslanian 2006c.

y. Leo or Leone is the same person referred to by Carmelite missionaries as "Count Leo Shariman." He is said to have "died of a broken heart [heart attack?] and freight" after his brother Harut'iwn [Arutun/Salvatore] was burned alive by Nadir Shah. See Chick 1939, 1: 654. His other brother, Count Peter Leopold Shah-riman, was also singled out by Nadir Shah for burning but managed to escape by hiding in the Carmelite mission.

z. Giacomo or Ohanes was Gasparo Sceriman's first-born son. In a family *stampa* booklet bearing translations into Italian of important Julfa dialect documents, we come across a legal paper written by Gasparo Sceriman on 10 April 1707 in Venice stating that according to the annual accounting of the family's net worth done on 1 April 1707 the family of Gasparo was worth 401,000 ducats. Gasparo then divides his wealth into four sections, of which one section was the inalienable property of his first-born son, Giacomo or Ohanes, and would belong to him without any claims on it being made by his other brothers; and three-fourths the property of Gasparo. Gasparo states clearly that he has other sons — Signor Steffano, Don Basilio [the monsignor], and Lorenzo—and a daughter named Maria who was in Isfahan. It seems that around 1713 Giacomo was residing in Amsterdam for long periods and corresponding with his father in Venice. There are references in these letters suggesting that Giacomo did not get along with his other brothers, especially Steffano. Also interesting is Gasparo's insistence that Giacomo return to Venice from Amsterdam and marry. Mention is also made of arranging a marriage with the youngest daughter of the Malatesta family. See documents in *stampa* booklet no. 22, "Commissaria et Eredita del Co. Giacomo Sarat Scerimann [*sic*], testator 1745," 8–11, Sceriman Family Papers, ASP, busta 28.

aa. Basilio Sceriman was educated at the Vatican from a very young age and went on to become a monsignor and governor of several Italian cities under Rome's influence, including Perugia. He is reported to have written in the 1740s a lengthy account of the family's history known as the "Libro di memorie," a drastically abridged version of which has come down to us in the form preserved in the family's legal petition during its unsuccessful bid to be enrolled into the Venetian patriciate.

bb. Sarat and Nazar Sceriman, sons of Khwaja Murat, were responsible for making large loans to the Venetian senate in the 1690s and similar loans to the Austro-Hungarian Empire in 1698 as a result of which the family became ennobled as counts and countesses by the Austro-Hungarian emperor Leopold II. See the discussion in chapter 7.

cc. Bortolo is referred to as the son of Pietro di Murat Sceriman/Shahriman in a letter dated 25 September 1734 in Izmir from a certain Babajan di Avedik and stored in the Public Records Office at Staffordshire. See "Letter of Babajan di Avedik," Staffordshire Records Office, Anson Papers, D615/PA/2. (The letter is included in a bundle of correspondence with John Dick, Thomas Anson's agent in Livorno.) I am grateful to Andrew Baker for bringing this letter to my attention and giving me an opportunity to translate it for him. For background and translation of this letter, see Baker's weblog, http://www.heardmusic.co.uk/page.asp?pid=83 (accessed 21 July 2010).

dd. Tadeo/Tadeos di Nazar Sceriman settled in Venice in the 1740s. Most of the surviving family papers in archival collections across northern Italy belong to his branch of the family. The important collection of family papers stored in the private collection of the Don Mazza archives in Verona is entirely from Tadeo's own collection.

ee. Fortunato Seriman appears to have been the last surviving male family member. In the nineteenth century he was active in Venetian politics during the period of the Austrian occupation of the city and wrote a very important brief account of the family's history that is preserved in the Museo Correr archives in Venice. He died sometime after 1855. Some of his papers are stored in the Don Mazza Archives, buste 3 and 4.

As a family firm, the Shahrimanians followed the principle of the eldest male being the director of the company's business and having patriarchal and managerial authority over his siblings and their families. In the 1660s, the most senior member of the Shahrimanian firm appears to have been Sarhat's son Marcara, whose signature is affixed to the 1667 trade agreement between Julfan merchants and the Russian court, thus suggesting that he was also the *kadkhuda,* or district head, of the neighborhood in Julfa (named after the family) where the family resided.[107] After the relocation of a large segment of the Shahrimanian family to Venice and Livorno, the firm's headquarters also seem to have moved with them, though we cannot know for certain how the firm's organization was affected as a result of this move. It could be that the branch in Venice and Livorno was subservient to the one in Julfa, where all the important decisions regarding the business of the family were made and the account books regularly updated. It could also be that the headquarters of the Shahrimanian firm shifted to Venice in 1698 and relied on the Julfa branch as a regional office in West Asia until the firm was somehow dissolved in the late eighteenth century. The third possibility, raised by Claudia Bonardi, is that the firm broke apart into separate and independent branches in 1717.[108] The available documents do not shed much light on this issue, and more work needs to be done on the family papers stored in Venice, Padua, and Verona to arrive at a more definitive conclusion. The second hypothesis—namely, that Venice or Livorno acted as the headquarters of the firm—is supported by the fact that the most senior members of the Shahrimanian family (i.e., the brothers Marcara, Murat, and Gasparo) had permanently immigrated to Italy in the 1690s and considered Italy as their new home. In any case, the surviving family and business letters stored in the Archivio di Stato di Venezia, in the Alishan archives in San Lazzaro, and the Don Mazza archives in Verona indicate that a lively correspondence was maintained between the Venice/Livorno and Julfa branches of the family. If we allow for Bonardi's undocumented assertion that the firm was "liquidated" in 1717, resulting in several independent branches defined by regional location, and managed by brothers who had grown apart from each other due to their different lifestyles in their respective host societies, then we must allow for the possibility that these independent family units still cooperated with one another after the dissolution of the original family firm. That this is a possibility is demonstrated by the letter book of Hakob di Murat (Jacobo or Giacomo di Murat Sceriman), which contains business correspondence in the Julfa dialect with family members dispersed in many directions from 1731 to 1734.[109]

Like other Julfan family firms, the Shahrimanian family firm did not employ only immediate family members but recruited its *commenda* agents and servants from the Julfan community at large. Whether these agents were recruited because they were Catholics like the Shahrimanians is an interesting question but one that the sources do not shed light on; we do know that in one case at least one of the family's agents (a certain Grigor son of Kaluts/Galuts) also had a father (Kaluts/Galuts son of Astuatsapov) who was a Shahriman agent, thus suggesting that some agents were specifically recruited from well-tested and trusted families.[110] A similar tendency of hiring *commenda* agents from the same trusted families can also be seen in the case of the Khwaja Minasian family, who hired at least two agents of the same family, the brothers Agha di Matos of Venice/Livorno and Melkum di Matos.[111] The evidence indicates that the overwhelming majority of the Shahrimanian *commenda* agents were members of the Julfan coalition; only a few were originally from the Armenian town of Agulis, and possibly one was a Hindu agent named Chanderbahan who seems to have handled the firm's "corrals for diamonds" business in Goa, India. The evidence does not indicate whether this Hindu agent was employed under a *commenda* contract or, more likely, worked for the family in another capacity, as a commission agent, for instance.[112] A 1699 report sent to the Propaganda Fide in Rome indicates that in Isfahan alone, the Shahrimanians had "50 domestics and 100 employees in their merchants' business."[113] In other words, their family firm branch in Julfa employed fifty servants (probably couriers and other low-level laborers) and up to a hundred agents who were dispatched in all directions under *commenda* contracts, with the purpose of putting the family's capital to work. Besides Venice and Livorno, these factors worked in Mughal India (mostly in Surat, Goa, Hugli, and Madras), the Ottoman Empire (in Izmir, Istanbul, and Aleppo, among other places),[114] Iran, Russia (Astrakhan, Moscow, and St. Petersburg), Holland (Amsterdam where the family polished and sold its diamonds from India), Spain (Cadiz), and the Austro-Hungarian Empire (Vienna). In addition, the older males of the family periodically dispatched their younger brothers to various parts of the Julfan network where the family saw the need to maintain permanent representatives drawn from their ranks. Thus Sarhat Shahriman the son of Emanuel was based in Calcutta during the first half of the eighteenth century, while Marcara Shahriman, a descendant of the Shahriman line in Livorno, shuttled back and forth between Livorno and Madras before dying in Livorno in the 1780s.[115] Another family member, Ignatius Shahrimanian, was stationed in Moscow and St. Petersburg in the first two decades of the eighteenth century. In 1717, Ignatius opened Russia's first silk-manufacturing workshop in Moscow.[116] In the 1670s, the family had factors and cousins stationed in Pegu (Burma).[117] Fifty years later, Hovhannes son of Zaccaria Shahriman was residing in Dutch-controlled Malacca.[118]

The picture of the family that emerges from these details is one of a shrewd and strategizing band of brothers and male cousins who seem always to have not only the future of their family's commercial interests in mind but also its survival and staying power in new lands, and they made these new lands their home while still being bound in one way or another, whether through trade, language, personal relationships, food, or otherwise, to their original home in Iran.

## THE KHWAJA MINASIAN FAMILY FIRM

Along with the Shahrimanians and contemporaneously, the Khwaja Minasians were among the leading merchant families of New Julfa. The patriarch of the family was one Khwaja Minas, son of Panos. The available evidence regarding this merchant paints a picture of an extremely affluent transimperial businessman with contacts in Mughal India, his native Isfahan, and Russia. Very little is known of Khwaja Minas's early commercial activities. It is likely that he became a wealthy *khwaja* or *agha* in the same manner as some of his fellow Julfan merchants, that is, by working as a *commenda* agent for another wealthy merchant. That this might well be the case is suggested by the "Book of Memoirs" of Monsignor Basilio Sceriman, written in Italy in 1733, in which the author notes that "a certain Minas, who was Mister Sarat's factor [i.e., *commenda* agent], in the course of time had come to possess almost one million Venetian ducats [in wealth] and was the richest [merchant] of almost all the Julfans."[119] The same source mentions that Sarat Sceriman had married off one of his offspring to the eldest daughter of this Minas, who was apparently trading on behalf of his master in India, in the mid-seventeenth century.[120] In any case, in the 1660s, Khwaja Minas seems to have settled in Surat, where he conducted business with local merchants as well as the Portuguese and the English.[121] An English East India Company document from 1662 refers to one of Minas's ships, the *St. Michael,* giving passage to two company officials traveling to Mocha.[122] Other documents from the Surat dispatch books indicate that Minas owned a fleet of merchant vessels, which plied the waters of the South China Sea (Siam and Timor) and traded as far away as Manila.[123] In 1669, Khwaja Minas "ranked as one of the wealthiest merchants of Surat."[124] An "able and well-reputed Armenian merchant," Minas is already mentioned in 1665 as the "President of the Armenians" of Surat.[125] In 1676, he seems to have settled in Bombay, following the invitation of the English.[126] An indication of his stature back home in Julfa can be surmised from his presence as one of twenty-three signatories to a letter sent by the Assembly of Merchants to the Russian czar in March 1671.[127] In his last will and testament (fig. 15), written in Julfa in 1700 shortly before his death, Khwaja Minas left his fortune to his four sons.[128]

Like many wealthy Julfan families, the Minasians seem to have weathered the political and economic storms caused by the collapse of the Safavid dynasty in 1722 and the sacking of Isfahan by Afghan troops. The real blow to their fortunes came with the usurpation of the Safavid mantle by the Afshar tribal leader Tahmas Kuli Khan (who adopted the name Nadir Shah upon assuming the Iranian throne in 1737). The political and economic instability resulting from Nadir's despotic and extortionist policies had a direct impact on the Minasians. In a well-known incident, Nadir had two Armenians, four Jews, and two Indians burned alive at the stake in Isfahan's Central Square (Meydan-i Shah) in 1747 over an incident involving the

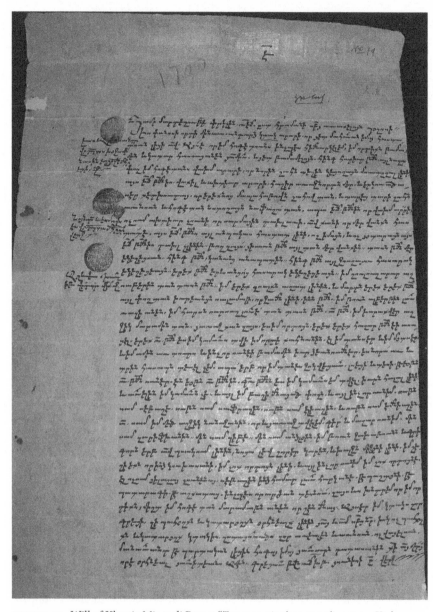

FIGURE 15. Will of Khwaja Minas di Panos; "Zanazan niwt'erov grut'iwnner—Ktakner Nor Jugha," ASMA, folder 28/13. Courtesy of the All Savior's Monastery Archive.

purchase of a valuable horse cloth. (See chapter 8 for details and references.) The object was studded with precious jewels, exciting Nadir's rapacity and moving him to torture its owners in order to extort money from their families. Nadir's Armenian victims were wealthy sexagenarian merchants: Khwaja Emniaz, the last surviving son of Khwaja Minas di Panos and the most senior member of the Minasian family firm, and Harut'iwn (Aratoon) Shahrimanian, a scion of the Shahrimanian family, who, unlike his brothers and sons residing in Venice, Livorno, and Madras, had decided to stay behind in Julfa. This incident caused the mass exodus of Julfa's leading families. Some of these families, including the Minasians, fled by caravan to the Ottoman-held cities of Baghdad and Basra as well as to the Persian Gulf port of Bandar Rig, which they used as a springboard to India.

From Basra, the remnants of the Minasian family migrated to Surat, where the patriarch of the family appears to have resided in the seventeenth century, and thence to the rich commercial centers of Bengal, such as Saidabad (the Armenian suburb of the provincial capital of Murshidabad), Hugli, Calcutta, and as far south as Madras. Khwaja Minas di Elias, the grandson of the patriarch and an important member of the Minasian family firm in the 1740s, was a resident of Murshidabad and Calcutta in the 1750s; his descendants were still living in Chinsura and Calcutta in the middle of the nineteenth century.[129] There were also Minasians residing as far away as Tiflis/Tbilisi (in the Russian Empire) in the first half of the nineteenth century and the Dutch East Indies (present-day Indonesia and Malaysia/Penang).[130]

Though they were scattered in India and Iran, the Minasians arranged their business affairs by working together as a family firm. After the death of the patriarch, his eldest sons, beginning with Seth Agha and followed by Elias, were in charge of both the Minasian family and the family firm (see fig. 16). By the early 1740s, Khwaja Minas di Panos's only surviving son, Khwaja Emniaz di Minas, was the firm's director. Upon his murder in 1747, authority was passed not to one of his sons but to Aghamal, the son of his brother Shafraz, who was the eldest male in the family. While the oldest males took charge of the family firm, younger cousins worked for the firm as business associates. Some younger members were entrusted with small sums of the family's capital to trade overseas, often under *commenda* arrangements, for their older siblings. Thus Minas di Elias was sent to India in 1744 to invest a sizable part of the family's capital in a business venture that ultimately fell victim to the British navy.[131] Much earlier, when Minas di Elias was in his early twenties, he was sent to Manila on a smaller mission.[132] In principle, the brothers invested their family firm's capital in their business ventures, but outside investors also made joint ventures, adding their own capital to a growing pool of investments.

It seems that the principal difference between the Minasian and Shahrimanian family firms was in the geographic scope of their operations and in their organizational structure. The Shahrimanian family was the larger of the two; it had more

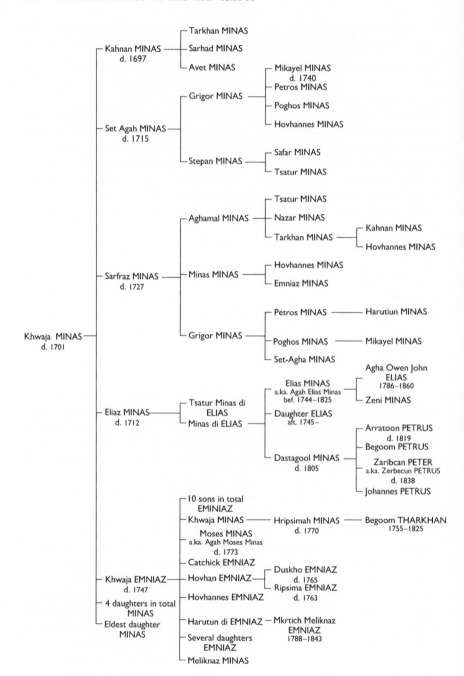

FIGURE 16. Minasian family tree.

members, especially sons, who were able to take important positions as junior members of the firm and act as direct representatives of their family's interests in diverse places. The structure of the Shahrimanian family firm also differed significantly from that of the Minasian family firm. The Minasians were headquartered in Julfa from the beginning of their firm in the 1660s. They seemed to have survived several upheavals in Julfa, including the Afghan invasion of 1722, and continued to maintain a strictly centralized operation in the Armenian suburb. The senior heads of the firm were always in the nodal center of the network, where they had close ties with the township's Assembly of Merchants and were thus able to resolve disputes with their employees. The Minasian head office remained in Julfa until 1747, when the senior members of the family were forced to abandon their homes after Nadir Shah's extortionist policies drove many of Julfa's most wealthy members into exile. After their dispersal from Julfa to India, the Minasian firm seems to have financially collapsed, for we do not have any evidence of their activities, indicating that they were not able to survive the losses they endured in 1747. The few Minasians who were able to resettle in India do not seem to have been financially influential.

The Shahrimanians, on the other hand, do not appear to have been able to maintain their firm's headquarters firmly in place in Julfa for very long. As Catholic Armenians, they would be subject to too many risks in Julfa. As we have seen, three of the most important branches of the family, that of Markar, Gaspar, and Murat, permanently resettled in Italy in the 1690s. Nevertheless, the family maintained a continued presence in its ancestral suburb, where other branches continued to reside. Thus, from the 1690s, the firm's headquarters appear to have shifted along with some members of the family to Venice and Livorno, whence the Shahrimanians continued to operate for roughly another century, until late in the 1700s, when their business fortunes declined. The evidence suggests that in the first half of the eighteenth century, when the Shahrimanian firm was still experiencing a rise in its financial fortune, the office in Venice (and to a lesser extent, Livorno) frequently communicated with the branch in Julfa to coordinate its overall activities. It seems sensible to speculate that the Julfa branch, despite appearing to be subordinate to the office in Venice, was integral to the smooth functioning of the firm and was, therefore, maintained as long as possible for at least two reasons. First, the firm's traditional capital-generating markets were in India and Southeast Asia, which meant that having a regional office in Julfa was important in coordinating the affairs of the firm's *commenda* agents. The Julfa office, in other words, was strategically useful in linking the Mediterranean sphere of the family's activities with the diamond and gem markets in the Indian Ocean. Second, despite their Catholicism and eagerness to integrate, assimilate, and succeed in their host society in Venice, the Shahrimanians were still Julfan Armenians. Their trade was also confined to and shaped by the Julfan "coalition." For instance, there is no evidence that the Scerimans ever hired more than a handful of noncoalition members to work for their firm; almost all of the Shahrimanian factors we know of were Julfan Armenians. This meant that the Julfa office could more effectively monitor and sanction the behavior of the firm's *commenda* agents and other dependents. In all probability, the Shahrimanian members in Julfa could and did make use of the township's Assembly of Merchants. In cases involving legal disputes, no petition of this sort to the assembly seems to have survived in the archives; however, there are dozens of other legal papers indicating that members of the Shahrimanian family, despite their Catholicism, made liberal use of Julfa's Municipal Assembly to ratify important documents, including those related to business contracts and powers of attorney.[133]

Despite these differences, however, both family firms were organized around the patriarchal unit of the family, and, more importantly, both made liberal use of *commenda* agents from outside their immediate families as the bulk of their employees.

The *commenda* contract was arguably the most significant legal instrument for Julfan long-distance trade. It was significant because it enabled wealthy merchants with capital to become even wealthier, while at the same time allowing young Julfans with little or no capital of their own to enter the world of trade and eventually become well-to-do merchants themselves. The legal responsibilities assigned to the parties as well as the highly unequal ratios of profit and the patriarchal rituals involving the unconditional obedience of agent to "master" seem harsh and exploitative by modern standards, but they were ideally suited to life in the early modern period, when capital was in short supply and men's lives were not held in as high esteem as they generally are today. The *commenda* was not only suitable for young men with no capital of their own; it was also eminently suitable for the expansion of the organizational building blocks of Julfan trade, namely, the family firms. As a result of the *commenda*, Julfan merchants were able to broaden their firms beyond the limits imposed by kinship ties and thus hire a broad variety of employees from within the Julfan network, based on the quality of their skills and their success in the field. Moreover, as an economic institution, the Julfan *commenda* was equipped with built-in features that significantly reduced acts of opportunism and malfeasance by agents, who were entrusted with large sums of capital with which to trade while away from their masters at home in Julfa. These mechanisms for policing long-distance trust relations between *khwajas* in Julfa and their agents overseas included (1) the stipulation in Julfan commercial law that "masters" were obliged to look after the needs of their agents' families while the agents were traveling abroad, which amounted to keeping agents' family members in Julfa essentially as "hostages" or collateral against the money that was entrusted to the agents; (2) making the improper keeping of accounts by agents punishable by flogging or bastinadoing; and (3) making it legally difficult, if not impossible, for agents to continue working inside the network without getting a letter of severance (*ghatilayagir*) from their original masters. Of course, for the *commenda* to function properly as a mechanism for regulating long-distance trust, it helped for the agents to be from Julfa. Thus it is clear that the *commenda* was the principal engine of Julfan expansion, and the surviving contracts and other evidence indicate that all agents working for Julfan masters had family relations in Julfa.

The *commenda,* however, had a dark side that scholars have neglected to study. In the short term the *commenda* was ideal for enforcing "trust" between agents and principals, but it limited the Julfan network's ability to expand to new markets in the long term. The next chapter will look at the role of "trust" in Julfan trade from a broader perspective.

# 7

# Trust, Social Capital, and Networks

## Informal and Semiformal Institutions at Work

*Trust consists of placing valued outcomes at risk to others' malfeasance, mistakes, or failures. Trust relationships include those in which people regularly take such risks. Although some trust relationships remain purely dyadic, for the most part they operate within a network of similar relationships. Trust networks, then, consist of* ramified interpersonal connections, consisting mainly of strong ties, within which people set valued, consequential, long-term resources and enterprises at risk to the malfeasance, mistakes, or failures of others.[1]

*A group within which there is extensive trustworthiness and extensive trust is able to accomplish much more than a comparable group without that trustworthiness and trust.*[2]

Trust was an essential component of early modern long-distance trade, as such trade depended upon a modicum of mutual confidence and expectation that neither party would be defrauded by the other in a potentially profitable venture. Trust emerges as an issue because economic transactions in early modern long-distance trade were rarely based on "simultaneous exchange."[3] Rather, the *quid* was separated from the *quo* over time and space in such transactions, to paraphrase Avner Greif.[4] Risk and potential malfeasance arise because of this separation.[5] For instance, as we have seen, an eighteenth-century Armenian merchant from Julfa who wanted to sell his merchandise or invest his capital in purchasing goods in a market situated at a great distance from his base usually did not travel with his goods or capital to that distant market himself. Instead, he delegated a *commenda* agent or factor to carry out this task on his behalf. In such a situation, the stationary merchant needed to have some level of trust that his agent would not disappear with his capital once he had left his sight. After all, what would prevent a factor from absconding with his master's money once he had traveled from Isfahan to India or Italy and was out of reach? Given the potential risks inherent in such a venture, why would a merchant in Julfa wanting to do business in India or the Mediterranean entrust large sums of capital and consign goods to a factor, knowing that the factor might cheat him? Trust was also vital for merchants who needed to appoint representatives and give them powers of attorney to carry out important services, often in distant places where the merchants themselves could not be present. It was equally important in cases where large sums of money were loaned on credit to be repaid at some specified time or place in the future. For these and other similar transactions to take place, some level of trust between the interested parties was necessary. If such trust existed, the parties to a transaction would cooperate more effectively. Thus trust was essential in generating an atmosphere of cooperation and collective action among merchants conducting long-distance trade. But how was trust itself generated?

Most scholars of early modern merchant communities have either altogether ignored the role of trust as an important factor in the lives of early modern long-distance merchants or, when they have realized its importance, have merely posited trust as a given attribute of such communities, *not as a factor requiring historical explanation or analysis.* As Francesca Trivellato has noted, the tendency of some scholars to take trust for granted is a legacy of the school of "trade diaspora" scholarship, whose followers have worked under the influence of Philip Curtin and Abner Cohen.[6] Trivellato suggests that such scholars have treated merchant communities under the label of "trade diasporas" as "communities of mercantile trust" (to use Chris Bayly's term), thus giving the false impression that trust is a natural byproduct of "closely knit communities."[7] Even scholars who do not use the term "trade diaspora" but stick to the less problematic label of "merchant community" have invoked trust as a "self evident attribute of a merchant community."[8] For instance, Frédéric Mauro, in an otherwise excellent account of Julfan merchants, remarks: "One of the reasons for the success of the Armenians was the atmosphere that prevailed at the heart of this merchant community: a great sense of solidarity based on kinship ties or marriage and on contractual relations, especially relations of trust."[9] Mauro, however, does not explain what these "relations of trust" are, implying instead that they somehow arise from "kinship ties or marriage." Another scholar, Vahe Baladouni, also attempting to answer a question first posed by Fernand Braudel— namely, what constituted "the key to [the Armenians'] fabulous success,"[10] in comparison to the more advanced organizational form embodied by the European joint-stock companies—posits "the ethos of trust" as his response.[11] However, he fails to provide a sustained discussion of how this ethos was created and what characterized its functioning in Julfan society. Similarly, Sushil Chaudhury, one of the latest in a long line of scholars puzzled by the success of Julfan merchants, offers the following account for their success: "In all probability, the Armenians succeeded because they were able to create networks of trust, shared information and mutual support *based on the fact that they were a distinctive ethnic and religious minority.*"[12] Chaudhury then goes on to assert that the "ethos of trust" among Julfan Armenians stemmed from their business arrangements, which were based on "family kin-ship and trusted fellow-countrymen." The problem with this line of reasoning is that it conflates the notion of "a distinctive ethnic and religious [minority] com-munity" with trust. It also leads to the absurd conclusion that Armenians trusted one another simply because they were Armenians. In other words, for Chaudhury and others, kinship or ethno-religious ties appear to serve as self-evident explana-tions for trust. This inability to explain trust in a historical and rigorously analyti-cal manner seems to account for the strange absence of the topic in a recently com-piled collection of essays devoted to the "diaspora entrepreneurial networks," in which one would have expected the discussion of trust to occupy an important place.[13]

This chapter seeks to provide a historical explanation for the role of trust and cooperation in the Julfan trade network of the seventeenth and eighteenth centuries. Unlike other discussions of trust, it approaches the topic not through an examina-tion of the now burgeoning and "abstract" literature on the varieties of trust and their different meanings,[14] but through an exploration of trust in the context of what political scientists and economic sociologists term "social capital theory." By re-moving trust and cooperation from the field of abstract philosophical discussions and embedding them within the concrete context of social networks, their "norms" for proper conduct, and the sanctions used to enforce these norms, the literature on social capital has proved a fruitful tool for the analysis of a host of problems, ranging from third world underdevelopment to societies and economies under-going post-Soviet transition. Surprisingly, however, it has had little influence on scholars working on early modern merchant communities.[15] One of the aims of this chapter is to import the concept of "social capital" from the literature of sociology, economic sociology, and political science into the study of early modern merchant communities. In doing so, this chapter seeks to shed light not only on the "elusive notion of trust" in the context of Julfan trade in the seventeenth and eighteenth cen-turies,[16] but also to suggest new ways of exploring trust and cooperation in early modern merchant communities in general. The chapter argues that the Julfan net-work and the community of merchants it supported was characterized by high levels of social capital and that this social capital, inherent in the network's peculiar social structure, was the key factor that enabled Julfan merchants to generate and maintain trust, trustworthiness, and uniform norms necessary for cooperation and collective action. My treatment of Julfan "trust relations" focuses mostly on intra-Julfan relations and addresses the question of how Julfans managed trust in the con-text of long-distance trade involving the *commenda* form of partnership examined in detail in chapter 6. Unlike the important work of Trivellato on Sephardic mer-chants,[17] I do not examine cross-cultural trust relations between Julfans and out-siders, for two reasons: (1) the evidence at our disposal suggests that the highest levels of trust in Julfan long-distance trade involved *commenda* partnerships, and most if not all such partnerships were between members of the Julfan community and did not involve outsiders; and (2) in cases involving money lending between Julfans and Indian *sarrafs* in Isfahan, where trust would have been a vital concern,[18] the evidence at hand does not allow us to discuss the matter extensively. This important element of Julfan trade remains to be examined sometime in the future.

## TRUST AND SOCIAL CAPITAL

Most of the literature on trust during the last two decades of the twentieth century has focused on what trust means rather than how it functions in society. This preoccupation with semantic concerns, and the rather abstract level of discussion it has produced, are to a great extent a result of the inherent ambiguity in the term itself. Standard dictionary definitions usually list a spectrum of meanings for the word *trust* (including "confidence," "reliance," "faith," and "dependence"),[19] not all of which are consistent with one another.

For the purposes of our discussion here, Diego Gambetta's and Partha Dasgupta's definitions can serve as points of departure. For both scholars, trust is essentially a matter connected with expectations and risk. According to Gambetta, "Trust . . . is a particular level of subjective probability with which an agent assesses that another agent or group of agents will perform a particular action, both *before* he can monitor such action (or independent of his capacity ever to be able to monitor it) *and* in a context in which it affects *his own* action."[20] Thus, concludes Gambetta, "when we say we trust someone or that someone is trustworthy, we implicitly mean that the *probability* that he will perform an action that is beneficial or at least not detrimental to us is high enough for us to consider engaging in some form of cooperation with him."[21] Dasgupta also develops his theory of trust around the key notion of expectation but argues that one's expectations of another's course of action are based on the other person's reputation. Such "reputation" is the opinion that others have formed about the person based on their observations of his past behavior.[22]

One of the most compelling attempts to incorporate theoretically the effect of reputation in relations of trust has come from sociologists working in the field of social capital theory. Although precursors to the concept of "social capital" can be traced back to the works of Adam Smith, David Hume, and Alexis de Tocqueville, it was not until the 1980s and 1990s that the concept entered the mainstream social sciences and became a buzzword for economists, political scientists, sociologists, and even policy makers at the World Bank and the United Nations.[23] The intellectual father of the concept is generally recognized to be the influential French sociologist Pierre Bourdieu, who first discussed the term in its modern sense while criticizing conventional economic thought for narrowly focusing on only one form of capital in social relations—that is, capital as envisaged in neoclassical economic theory[24]—at the expense of other varieties of capital, among which he listed social capital. Other thinkers who developed and popularized the concept, particularly in North America, were James Coleman, who wrote a pathbreaking essay on the concept in 1988, and political scientist Robert Putnam, who perhaps more than any thinker took the concept to new heights in his numerous works on civic culture.[25]

But what exactly is social capital, and how is it generated? Putnam defines it as "features of social organizations such as networks, norms and social trust that facilitate coordination and cooperation for mutual benefit."[26] Similarly, the World Bank describes social capital as "the norms and social relations embedded in social structures that enable people to coordinate action to achieve desired goals."[27] Both definitions stress the importance of social networks, norms, and trust in generating efficient collective action.

In keeping with the definitions above, for purposes of this chapter I shall define social capital as the value generated when individuals join together and invest resources in the formation of ongoing and structured relationships with each other (known as a "social network") that generate collective and individual benefits.[28] These benefits are diverse, but they all have one thing in common. They help the social network of individuals to achieve their common goals, whether these goals are collective action in pursuit of political objectives, as in the case of interest groups, social movements, or civil society in democratic regimes, or economic objectives and maintenance of a network's social/communal cohesion, as in the case of the trade networks of merchant communities in the early modern period. Fostering trust and trustworthiness is one important way, albeit not the only one, in which social capital helps promote collective action toward a common goal.

Theorists of social capital argue that collective action in the sense outlined above results from the creation of four related components of social capital: (1) a social network; (2) a set of norms, either formal, as in codified and written laws, or informal, as in tacit and habitual norms of conduct internalized by individuals and groups, in the form of what Bourdieu refers to as *habitus*,[29] by which members of a social network are expected to abide; (3) information flows within the social network that disseminate knowledge about the norms and ensure that people are loyal to them by sanctioning those who break a given network's norms or rewarding those who uphold them; and finally, (4) trust and trustworthiness between network members, created as a result of the preceding three aspects of social capital. All four of these attributes of social capital are important, because they enable individual members of a social network (and the social network as a whole) to achieve goals and objectives (economic objectives in the case of merchant communities) in a collective and coordinated manner. In the case of early modern merchant communities, one of the principal benefits of social capital is to reduce what economic historians call "transaction costs," that is, "the costs of measuring and defining the attributes of the goods and services being exchanged *and the costs of enforcing agreements with respect to contracts that are made.*"[30] Transaction costs and production costs together make up the total costs of economic activity and determine whether such activity takes place. In this connection, lack of trustworthiness, malfeasance, and resulting expensive litigation in courts can significantly increase transaction costs, thereby making economic activity less profitable. Social capital is thus an important aspect of a network's organization, because, among other things, it helps trim transaction costs and generate more effective collective action.

The next logical question then is, what are the conditions for the creation of social capital? Do all networks automatically create social capital? According to Coleman, the presence of two factors is said to help generate social capital. The first is for a social network to be characterized by "closure."[31] By this, Coleman means that a network must have clearly defined borders and set rules limiting membership in the network to certain individuals who share common values and beliefs. "Closure" of a network is an important precondition for social capital because it helps maintain a clearly defined, though not necessarily codified or written-down, set of norms to which members of the closed network are expected to remain faithful. When network membership is clearly defined, "members can be easily monitored, norm violating behaviour effectively punished and norm-compliant behaviour collectively rewarded."[32] Closure helps maintain strict adherence to shared norms of behavior because it enables what some economists call "reputation effects."[33] It does so because in networks where most individuals are connected to each other either directly or through friends, people prize their reputations and do their utmost to keep them clean. Information flows are vital to the maintenance of social norms because they spread news. Monitoring individuals' reputations is easier, and information normally flows more effectively and at less expense when networks are defined by closure.

The second condition for the emergence of social capital is what Coleman, following Max Gluckman, calls "multiplex" relationships. By "multiplexity," Coleman means a network's ability to connect its members to each other through more than one role, position, or context.[34] Thus a network can be characterized as being multiplex or "dense," to use Mark Granovetter's term, if the individuals that comprise it are socially related to each other not only through business ties but also through membership in the same church, social club, or school system. The "denseness of ties" is important because it establishes memberships that are *crosscutting*. In general, "the denser the network of trading relationships, the greater the value of reputation, and so—for purely self-interested reasons—the greater is the degree of trust."[35] Like closure, multiplex ties are crucial for developing social capital because the resulting "multi-stranded" ties between individuals in a network "endow members with multiple means of getting information about, punishing deviancies in and urging collective action on one another."[36]

When theorists of social capital discuss the concept, they often refer to the community of diamond merchants in New York City, whose network embodies many of the attributes of social capital outlined above. Thus a brief discussion of this community may help us arrive at a better understanding of social capital. Social capital theorists single out trust and trustworthiness as defining hallmarks of the community of New York diamond merchants.[37] They point out, for instance, that it is customary for these diamond merchants to entrust bags of priceless gems to fellow merchants for casual inspection at their own leisure. Contracts and paperwork are not required in such transactions because cases of malfeasance are almost nonexistent in the community. Indeed, trust and trustworthiness are said to be so high that merchants seal multimillion-dollar deals often with a "hand shake accompanied with the words *mazel u' broche*" (Hebrew for "luck" and "benediction").[38] These are considered sufficient for binding complex deals and do not incur high transaction costs, thus giving these merchants a competitive edge over others. Social capital theorists also refer to the diamond industry to illustrate their theory because of another feature of economic organization that seems unique to this industry. As Lisa Bernstein points out in a landmark study, diamond merchants do not resort to the public legal system to resolve problems arising from disputes among members. Instead, they resolve disputes through a private-order arbitration board that pronounces its binding decisions on the disputing parties without resorting to costly and often inefficient court appeals.[39]

What accounts for the high levels of trust and cooperation among these merchants? About 95 percent of the diamond industry in New York City is controlled by ultra-Orthodox Jews who are members of a social network exemplifying the kind of "closure" noted by Coleman and others as essential for social capital.[40] The social network is closed because the number of merchants in the network is relatively small (about a thousand active members who are overwhelmingly ultra-Orthodox Jews residing in the same community neighborhoods in Brooklyn). This "closure" enables the network to impose uniform norms of conduct that are binding on all members and creates an effective means of monitoring and enforcing these norms. In general, members are motivated by their self-interest not to cheat their fellow members because of fear of jeopardizing their reputations and incurring sanctions from other members. Cheating, and thus breaking the network's norms of conduct, are punishable by collective ostracism in the form of being permanently banished from the network, therefore making it very difficult, if not impossible, for dishonest merchants to conduct their trade. In addition to informal punishments in the form of sanctions imposed by members of the social network on individuals who break the norms of conduct shared by the network as a whole, punishment in the New York diamond industry is also meted out by the Diamond Dealers Club (DDC), which has its own private board of arbitrators who review cases of irregularities among DDC members. As Bernstein notes, the decisions of the DDC arbitration board are binding on its members and must be observed within ten working days. In the event that they are not fulfilled by the guilty party, the board's verdict along with a picture of the noncomplying member are "posted in a conspicuous place in the Club rooms [and this] information is communicated to all bourses in the world federation."[41] The World Federation of Diamond Dealers, of which the New York branch is a member, compels its member bourses to enforce judgments made by another bourse. Given the fact that most diamond dealers frequently transact business in foreign bourses, "this reciprocity of enforcement greatly increases the penalty for failing to voluntarily comply with an arbitration judgment."[42] The DDC also has the power of suspending or expelling a member for failing to pay a judgment or for breaching the code of conduct among its merchants. Conversely, honest members in the diamond industry are rewarded for their probity with the improvement of their reputation in the network and thus receive future gains in the form of more business dealings with other members. The reputation mechanism employed in the diamond industry is based on the principle that individual behavior is motivated by the pursuit of rational self-interest. Thus any future benefits that accrue from consistently honest behavior far outweigh any short-term benefits from cheating. The closure of the network of diamond merchants in New York is crucial in maintaining high levels of trust and trustworthiness among its members, because most members know of each other and can thus assess their expectations of others' behavior by monitoring their reputations before trusting them in business dealings. Closure also helps generate trust and cooperation, because it implies that members of the network share the same norms of conduct and have a rational stake in ensuring that all others maintain these norms.

The multiplex nature of social ties within the diamond traders' network also helps foster high levels of trust and cooperation among its members. As Coleman noted in his pioneering essay on social capital, the overwhelming majority of Orthodox Jews involved in New York City's diamond trade live in the same cluster of neighborhoods in Brooklyn.[43] They attend the same synagogues, send their children to the same schools, belong to the same social clubs, and are related to each other through marriage. In other words, these merchants have *crosscutting* relationships; they are not related to each other solely as merchants working on 47th Street, but as members who share a variety of ties (synagogues, schools, social clubs, and families). These multiplex ties or the density of the social network facilitates the efficient flow of information among members, which can either improve a merchant's reputation or kill it. Few people dare to cheat, because if an incident of cheating occurs, news spreads rapidly and members of the network exercise collective sanctions on the guilty party, thus making it impossible for the guilty to continue doing future business. What is more, the guilty party is also ostracized from the network's other spheres and endangers his family's continued welfare in the community, including diminishing if not ending his children's chances of marrying into the community.[44]

As we shall see below, the Julfan trade network of the seventeenth and eighteenth centuries exhibits many of the social capital traits present in the diamond merchants network briefly touched upon above. Before I turn to an examination of the network of Julfan merchants using the analytical framework of social capital theory, it is first necessary to discuss briefly the nature of the Julfan network's social norms. These norms consisted of codes of proper conduct for merchants and were embodied in the principles of Julfan commercial law.

## A CODE OF CONDUCT FOR JULFAN MERCHANTS

Very little is known about the origins and development of Julfan commercial law. We know that Julfan merchants had their own body of commercial law at least by the seventeenth century. This law was not codified in writing and was most likely customary in nature. The most direct evidence we have of its existence and its statutes comes from the *Datastanagirk Astrakhani Hayots,* a code of laws used by the Armenian community in Astrakhan, Russia. This code was written down for use by the Armenian community court (*rathaus*) of the Russian city in the 1760s, after the community was granted wide administrative and legal autonomy by Russian officials.[45] In the 1760s, members of the Armenian *rathaus* of Astrakhan felt compelled to codify laws with which to administer the internal affairs of their community. The greater part of these laws is devoted to commercial affairs. In compiling them, the authors of this interesting work make it abundantly clear that they relied on the commercial law of Julfan merchants, which perhaps is not surprising given the fact that Julfans made up a significant portion of the Armenian community of Astrakhan:[46]

> Those customs and laws of commerce that we have written down in this manuscript are especially found among the Armenians who are under the rule of the Persians, and not among those Armenians who are under the dominion of the Turks. And the reason for this is that, by residing in every Turkish and Persian province, the Armenians follow their civil laws, values, and conditions. And everyone already knows that Turkish merchants conduct their commerce quite artlessly and without laws and codes. And [those of] our nation who dwell in the lands of the Turks, following their manners and conditions, are artless and bereft of rules and canons, whereas those who live in the lands of the Persians have commercial rules and canons, which we have followed.[47]

The authors also make it clear that, though the Julfa Armenians had wide administrative autonomy to conduct themselves in accordance with their own laws, except in cases of "capital punishment," "they did not conduct themselves in accordance with codified laws."[48] The authors explain that this was because the Julfa Armenians followed the customs of the Iranians, who also did not keep law books but practiced law by custom or "by word."[49]

These passages indicate that Julfan commercial law was largely based on the prevailing laws of Safavid Iran. The reliance of Christian Armenian merchants on Safavid *sharia* law in commercial matters should come as no surprise. After all, Julfan merchants had been living under Iranian and Muslim influence long before they were resettled in Iran. They were, in a sense, ideal typical bearers of a culture that Marshal Hodgson famously described as "Islamicate," that is, possessing cultural markers and practices that referred "not directly to the religion, Islam, itself, but to the social and cultural complex historically associated with Islam and the Muslims, both among Muslims themselves and even found among non-Muslims."[50] Islamicate elements of Julfan culture include their sartorial customs (their dress code, including the use of turbans, was remarkably similar to those of fellow Muslims throughout Islamicate Eurasia, even if there were particular sartorial variations that set the Julfans apart), architecture (in their exterior use of domes and arches at least, the All Savior's Monastery and other church complexes in Julfa architecturally resemble mosques), dialect (the Julfa dialect had a significant vocabulary base of loanwords from Arabic, Persian, Turkish, and Hindustani, among other languages), culinary practices, and especially commercial law. In this context, it should be noted that most Julfan legal and mercantile terminology was directly borrowed from Islamic law. The overlap of Julfan and Persian and Islamic commercial terminology is evidenced by the following key commercial terms: *muzarba* (Julfa dialect for *commenda,* deriving from the Arabic *mudaraba*), *vekil* ("representative," used in connection with powers of attorney and derived from Arabic/Persian *wakil/vakil*), *ruzlama* (Julfa dialect for "accounting ledger," derived from Persian *ruzname), sanad* (Arabic loanword in Persian and Turkish meaning "bill"), *barat* (Julfa dialect for "certificate" derived from Persian/Turkish *berat), amanat* (Persian for "consignment of goods entrusted to an agent"), *enalmal* (the money or credit an agent added to a *commenda* contract, from the Persian/Arabic *'ayn al mal* ). Edmund Herzig has also demonstrated how Julfan Armenians were operating in an Islamic commercial *ecumene* that stretched from the shores of the Mediterranean to Mughal India and farther east into the eastern recesses of the Indian Ocean, where many precepts of Islamic commercial law were widely known and shared by peoples of diverse backgrounds.[51] The passage from the Astrakhan Code of Laws quoted above also indicates that Julfans, like Muslim Iranians, had not codified their commercial law but nonetheless practiced its principles in their commercial affairs.

Whatever the ultimate origins of Julfan commercial law, we can be certain that most of the legal precepts codified in the Astrakhan Code of Laws were also practiced in Julfa in the seventeenth and eighteenth centuries. We know this because the archival documents (contracts, legal petitions, bills of exchange, and so on) demonstrate a homology between seventeenth- and eighteenth-century practices and the legal precepts codified in the Astrakhan Code of Laws. Thus, according to the section in the Astrakhan Code of Laws discussing the rules for drafting and concluding *commenda* contracts, we are told that in such a contract the party (described as the *agha/ter,* or master) that forwards the capital or goods to the agent gets to keep anywhere from 70 to 80 percent of the profits accrued from the venture, while the remaining profits go to the agent (known as the *enker,* or associate). That this arrangement was part of Julfan commercial law in the seventeenth and eighteenth centuries is evident in the *commenda* contracts that have reached us through the archives (see chapter 6 for a full discussion). Similarly, the Astrakhan Code of Laws tells us that a *commenda* agent was legally bound to follow the advice or orders that his master sent him in a "letter of advice" called the *ordnagir,*[52] and, furthermore, that he was obliged to submit a detailed account book of all his transactions to his master soon after returning to Julfa. "Every *commenda* agent [*enker*] is bound to enter each transaction in a lawful account book, truthfully and in time," states article 11 of chapter 14 (devoted mostly to *commenda* law) of the Astrakhan Code of Laws. "And if a *commenda* agent fails to show the accounting book to his master, he will be jailed, barely fed on bread and water alone, and periodically whipped for a period of up to one year."[53] As we shall see below, Julfan officials did not have a jail at their disposal, nor, it seems, could they administer corporal punishment by themselves. However, it is likely that those who broke Julfan commercial law were considered criminals, and if their crimes were serious enough, they were punished by Safavid officials (most likely by the *darugha* who was responsible for policing Julfa in collaboration with Julfan officials). That Julfans in the seventeenth century regarded it as a serious crime for a wayward *commenda* agent to return home and *not* render an exact account of his business transactions to his master is attested by Jean Baptiste Tavernier, the famous French traveler who spent many years residing in Isfahan and knew the Julfan Armenians intimately. In his travel narrative, Tavernier alludes to the seriousness of this crime in the following passage, in which he discusses the long travels and hard work of Julfan agents: "If they do not thrive, they never return, as being a place where they must give an exact Account, or else suffer the quick and severe Justice of Drubbing, which never fails those factors that are ill husbands for their Masters."[54]

The above examples provide evidence that many of the legal precepts outlined in the Astrakhan Code of Laws formed the basis upon which, as we shall see below, a private order legal system known as the Assembly of Merchants adjudicated commercial disputes between members of the Julfan network. Moreover, Julfan merchants relied upon these legal precepts and treated them as the bases for their code of conduct in their relations with one another.

## COALITIONS, REPUTATION, AND TRUST

We have seen above how trust and social capital arise from "social networks" characterized by "closure" and "multiplex" relations. The network of New Julfa merchants embodied both characteristics. To understand the "closure" aspect of the Julfan network, we must examine the network of relations among Julfan merchants in terms of what Greif, in the context of Maghribi Jewish merchants of the twelfth century, refers to as a "coalition."[55] Greif's coalition is a kind of private club with restrictive membership requirements and mandatory rules of conduct for all members. Restrictive membership rules insure that the network is closed and bounded, meaning that not everyone can be a member of a coalition. To become a coalition member, one has to meet specific membership requirements. In the case of Julfan merchants, this meant that one had to be a merchant, either a wealthy *khwaja* who employed his capital abroad through a trusted agent or an agent who had the required training, expertise, and reputation as a trustworthy custodian of a *khwaja*'s capital. The second membership requirement was more social and culturally discriminatory in nature: a member had to be a bona fide member of Julfan society, that is, Armenian-born with lineage in New Julfa and possibly even ancestry in Old Julfa itself. Being an Armenian merchant did not automatically entitle one to membership in the Julfan coalition. Evidence of this bounded or exclusionary nature of the coalition's identity can be seen in the Julfan documents that have survived. The evidence suggests that Julfan merchants overwhelmingly cooperated more frequently with fellow Julfans than with Armenians from other regions. References in Julfan correspondence and contracts to "one of our own," "our people" (*mer jumiat*), and "our nation of Julfa" are all indications that the sense of community invoked is place- and culture-specific. They refer to individuals with firm family ties to Julfa. It bears remembering here that Julfan Armenians were, to use Jonathan Israel's description of Sephardic Jews, a "diaspora within a diaspora."[56] They were distinguished from other Armenians by their shared history and collective trauma of mass exile from Old Julfa, their unique dialect of Armenian (not spoken or easily understood by other Armenians), their own peculiar calendar, and, above all, their shared experience of being citizens of the trading colony of New Julfa. Moreover, as citizens of the Isfahani suburb, members of the Julfan coalition overwhelmingly belonged to the same Armenian Gregorian church, with its diocesan headquarters in Julfa; Catholic Julfan merchants, some of whom appear to have hired Julfan agents who were Gregorians or who worked themselves as agents for non-Catholic Julfans, were a statistically insignificant minority of the Julfan population, constituting about 300 persons in Julfa in the second half of the seventeenth century out of a population of around 30,000.[57] Commenting on the peculiar nature of the Sephardic Jewish community in the early modern period, Isaac de Pinto observed: "They are very particular and do not mingle . . . with the Jews of other nations."[58] What de Pinto says about the Sephardic Jews is also true of the Julfan Armenians. In both cases, the evidence suggests that these communities distinguished themselves from other communities of the larger "diaspora" on the basis of their cultural, social, and, above all, economic traits. As far as the Julfans are concerned, the closed nature of their coalition made them aloof from other communities, including those of other Armenians. This does not mean, however, that members of the Julfan coalition did not have *any* commercial interactions with "outsiders." Julfans residing in overseas settlements for long periods did, in some specific cases, engage in economic relations with individuals who would otherwise not be considered coalition members. For instance, Julfans in Venice had ongoing relations with Armenian merchants originally from Agulis, a town near Old Julfa, while those who had settled in Marseilles for long periods had credit relations with local Frenchmen, Maronites, Turks, and Armenians from the Ottoman Empire. These cases, however, are the exceptions and not the norm, and none of them involve long-distance partnerships based on the *commenda* contract. In the case of Marseilles, Julfan interaction with others, and notably with Armenians from the Ottoman Empire, as we saw in chapter 4, involved local partnerships in setting up calico workshops and a coffeehouse. Similar partnerships between Julfans and Ottoman Armenians existed in Tuscany in the eighteenth century in coral manufacturing.[59] These examples— and all we can find in India—raise the question of the involvement of the Julfans in production activities that served their trade, and only highlight distinctions between long-distance and local trade and between business with contracts and direct exchanges. In Julfa or Isfahan, Julfans also had prolonged credit relations with Indian moneylenders (see chapter 9). In all these cases, the mechanisms used to create and secure relations of trust need to be further investigated but lie outside the scope of the present study. The few scattered cases of Julfan commercial interaction with "outsiders" mentioned above do not appear to have been significant enough to alter the overall bounded nature of the Julfan coalition characterized by what social capital theorists would call "closure."

As we shall see later, the closure element of the Julfan network helped facilitate the flow of information between its members and made it easier for members to monitor and sanction individuals who were caught breaking the network's norms or to reward those who upheld them. Coalition members would be able to distinguish opportunistic members or "cheaters" from honest, reliable ones on the basis of their understanding of Julfan commercial law and its norms of proper business behavior. Those coalition members who did not follow Julfan commercial law (i.e., who did not "play by the rules of the game") were regarded as cheaters. Trust and cooperation were thus firmly based on the tacit understanding among coalition members that members who cheated had reduced chances of profiting from future transactions with other members, because breaking the network's norms and cheating made others cautious about engaging in relations with them. Being caught cheating would severely compromise one's reputation as a trustworthy merchant and would probably raise the "opportunity cost" and reduce future transactions for the opportunistic party.[60] A bad reputation meant loss of trust. In some cases, it also meant loss of coalition membership, which was tantamount to losing all trading privileges. This brings us to the vital question of how coalition members were informed of other coalition members' reputations.

It should be noted that, however small, the Julfan coalition was never a "face-to-face" type of community. Throughout the seventeenth and eighteenth centuries, the population of New Julfa ranged from 10,000 to 30,000 people, and even assuming that only a tiny portion of the Julfan community was engaged in some form of trade, this would still bring the potential membership of the trade coalition to around 1,000 individuals.[61] It would be highly unlikely (if not impossible) for all coalition members to know each other on a personal basis. Given the anonymous or "imagined" nature of their community, coalition members would thus have to base their reputation mechanism on the effective and affordable circulation of information inside their network. As we saw in chapter 5, this circulation of information was predicated on the existence of a courier or information network, which circulated business correspondence and commercial intelligence among coalition members. Suffice it to say here that one of the functions of the courier or information network was to circulate information about the business activities and reputations of fellow coalition members.

Because long-distance trade was carried out almost exclusively through agents who were given large sums of capital to trade overseas on behalf of their masters at home, and formal institutions such as international courts were either nonexistent or ineffective at enforcing contracts, these overseas agents could, in theory, have embezzled the money entrusted to them. Thus trust and reputation were crucial factors in organizing long-distance trade. The costly and time-consuming nature of "suits at law" to resolve commercial conflicts was a major concern for merchants, as Khwaja Minas di Elias notes in one of his letters to members of the Minasian family firm in the 1740s.[62] To avoid going to court or being cheated by agents or other business associates, merchants therefore "conditioned future employment on past conduct."[63] If an agent or business associate had a checkered past and was known to be dishonest, he would lose future prospects of being hired or trusted by other merchants in the coalition. Consider Minas di Elias's letter to junior members of the family firm and *commenda* agents concerning the need to avoid doing business in the future with a group of other merchants associated with a certain merchant named Agazar, whose previous dealings with the Minasian family had apparently been irregular. In his letter, Minas di Elias reproaches one of his correspondents for doing business with Agazar and informs him that the latter and his associates had behaved in a less than honorable way with the Minasian family firm. He then urges his correspondents to shun business with Agazar and associates in the future, "for last year I did not know so much of these people as I do at present, and it is better for us to deal with them as little as we can."[64]

How were Julfan merchants able to judge whether an agent had a good reputation and was therefore trustworthy? Commercial correspondence played a signifi-

cant role in circulating information about merchants' reputations. Such information (mostly based on community hearsay, gossip, and "talk") enabled merchant-
correspondents to ascertain whether a particular agent was worthy of their trust
and therefore whether they should conduct business with him. In his impressive
account of the Portuguese trans-Atlantic diaspora of the sixteenth and seventeenth
centuries, Daviken Studnicki-Gizbert has demonstrated that this far-flung community of merchants also relied on commercial correspondence to spread information and gossip on merchants' reputations and honor in an attempt to establish
trust and trustworthiness in their community. He states: "A good reputation was a
merchant's most precious asset. . . . It established his standing within the community, helped him secure long-standing commercial relations, and provided a collective confirmation of his self-worth."[65] Studnicki-Gizbert notes that reputations
"were continually being fashioned and refashioned" through the spread of news and
gossip in "page after page of correspondence that circulated throughout the wider
Atlantic network of houses," which he likens to a "neighborhood abuzz with gossip."[66] Similarly, Søren Mentz, in his analysis of the private trade of English East India Company officials, notes that the "gentlemanly capitalism" of these traders was
predicated on "personal integrity, a good reputation, good manners and keeping
one's word."[67] At stake for the commercial success of Portuguese merchants in the
Atlantic, English private merchants in the Indian Ocean, and Julfan Armenians in
both the Indian Ocean and the Mediterranean were the reputations and trustworthiness of merchants—intangible attributes that were nonetheless powerful factors
in long-distance trade.

In this regard, it is interesting to note that the Julfa dialect does not have a specific
term for "reputation." The word that most closely approximates *reputation* and seems
to be used as a synonym for it is *akhtibar,* a loanword from the Persian *i'tibar,* meaning "honor, reverence, veneration, respect; credit, authority, credibility; weight, importance."[68] Other words used by Julfans to indicate reputation revolve around the
concept of honor,[69] such as the Classical Armenian *pativ* or the Persian *namus*
(defined as "reputation, fame, renown, esteem, honor") and the more common version of the latter: *binamus* (without honor, dishonorable).[70] To say that someone
was *binamus* meant that he was not worthy of association, especially in commercial affairs. Someone with *akhtibar,* on the other hand, was a person who had a good
reputation for honesty and probity in business and, therefore, could be trusted to
carry out an agreement or contract.

That reputation was deeply connected to the circulation of information and news
in Julfan commercial history is evident not only conceptually but also semantically.
The modern Armenian word for "reputation," *hambav,* is a Classical Armenian word
that did not acquire its current near-exclusive meaning of "reputation" until late
in the nineteenth century, when the modern Armenian lexicon was standardized.
In the eighteenth century, *hambav* meant a combination of things, ranging from

"news," "information," "rumor," and "gossip" to "tidings."[71] Some letters in the Julfa dialect also indicate that *hambav* meant "reputation" as early as in the eighteenth century.[72] Indeed, the confluence of reputation and gossip in one word, *hambav,* is not confined only to Armenian but also exists in other languages. In Latin, for instance, the word for "reputation" during the medieval period and up to the sixteenth century, *fama,* was intimately related to what today would be identified as gossip, rumor, and hearsay/information. *Fama,* as a number of scholars have noted, had a broad semantic range: "It meant public opinion, idle talk, rumor, reputation as well as fame . . . and while *fama* denoted information or news, at the same time it meant the image formed of a person by that information."[73] *Fama* was one of the principal means by which people's reputations were made or broken before the modern era. *Fama* was an important genre of sharing information. For the Julfans, too, *fama/hambav/akhtibar* played a vital role in commercial life. Indeed, it seems to have been a central genre of information sharing in Julfan correspondence and business letters. Merchants were very careful about recording hearsay about other merchants' conduct and, in doing so, transmitting information about other people's reputations. For instance, in a letter written by a Julfan merchant in Basra to his correspondent in Pondicherry, we read the following: "It suffices to say that I always hear of your lordship's welfare [*S'lamat*] from the letters of others [*aylots' grerots'en*] or they say it to Hovanjan and later it becomes known in Isfahan. May God grant that I always hear and see your lordship's good reputation [*bari ambavn*]."[74] Similarly, the rapid and wide circulation of information on merchants' reputations can be seen in the following excerpt from a letter by an Armenian priest in Jerusalem to a wealthy Julfan merchant in Livorno dating from the second half of the seventeenth century. Writing to the Livorno-based merchant Agha di Matus, a priest named Mesrob Vardapet remarks: "And though I have not seen your eminence's face, I know you by name, since your name shines brightly like a torch among the Armenian nation, and your good reputation [*bari hambavd*] and greatness are spread everywhere."[75]

Julfans excelled in circulating *fama/hambav,* which acquired a legal status when it was conveyed through petitions and correspondence through the Assembly of Merchants. The "closed" nature of the Julfan coalition or network promoted the circulation of information, including *fama/hambav,* across vast distances and to the vast majority of network members. The network's multiplex nature also had a significant effect on the flow of information and the maintenance of norms through sanctions. Multiplexity in a network is produced by the existence of what we may call "structural connectivity nodes," which connect individuals with memberships in different fields of activity to one another through a shared structural connectivity node. For the Julfan network, multiplexity was produced through two centralized structural connectivity nodes: the Armenian Church, to which most merchants in the coalition belonged, and the legal/administrative body in Julfa known as the

Assembly of Merchants, which had branches throughout the broad spectrum of trade settlements comprising the Julfan trade network (see below). Connectivity nodes play a vital role not only in connecting individuals with different role relations, but also in receiving and disseminating information. As we shall see below in our analysis of the Assembly of Merchants, its function in the Julfan network can be compared to that of a "bandwidth" in a transistor radio: it can receive signals from multiple places and in turn disseminate them in different directions.[76] Before we turn to the Assembly of Merchants, let us first examine the church's role in creating Julfan multiplexity.

By the late seventeenth century, as Julfan merchants branched out into the Indian Ocean, the Armenian Church centered in New Julfa also expanded through its elaborate network of diocesan sees in the communities where Julfan merchants had settled, especially in India. Eventually, the trade network and its merchants came to overlap and absorb the parallel network of the Armenian Church. This overlap of church and merchant networks gave the Julfan network its distinctive multiplex structure, which helped generate social capital, thus allowing the members of the network to achieve high degrees of solidarity and carry out coordinated collective action as a merchant community. The presence of the church, with which most Julfan merchants had ongoing relations, both as faithful and pious members of a flock and more importantly as generous benefactors, meant that members of the Julfan network were connected to each other not only through their roles as merchants but also through their church membership; some Julfan mercantile families also had members who were clerics in the church.[77] Thus their channels of information became more diversified, so that instead of receiving news about fellow merchants' activities in India through business correspondence alone they would also have access to the grapevine controlled by the church itself. Most letters sent from Julfan parish priests in India to their ecclesiastical headquarters at the All Savior's Monastery in Julfa contain a significant volume of information on the activities of various merchants in the East who were connected to the church through their role as patrons and believers. Some of this information concerned the reputations of merchants. The All Savior's Monastery in Julfa received regular letters from its missions and in turn spread vital information (most likely through hearsay and personal communication within the small community in Julfa) concerning various merchants in distant settlements to the merchant families in Julfa, who subsequently included such hearsay in their correspondence with fellow merchants and business agents in other settlements. This increased the likelihood that if an individual member of the network broke the network's norms, news of his behavior would reach Julfa and from there would spread to other places.[78] As a result of these multistranded ties, facilitated in large measure by the church's own network of informants, members of the Julfan network were better equipped to monitor merchants' behavior and impose sanctions on violators of their common norms. Fear of sanctions and of acquiring a bad reputation or becoming known as someone with no *akhtibar* or characterized as *binamus* motivated members of the Julfan network to remain honest in their behavior, which in turn fostered trust and trustworthiness among network members, thereby, increasing cooperation within the network.

The importance of reputation, or *akhtibar*, in Julfan life is revealed in the following passage from a trade manual used as a textbook for training young Julfan merchants in the 1680s:

> Do not give money or a consignment [of goods] to an inexperienced man. *Even if you know for certain that he is a man of good reputation [akhtibar], ascertain the truth by interrogating or questioning several people.* Only then give him money or credit with a bill [*tamasuk*] and with witnesses. But [make sure] to write down all your transactions several times. Do not leave for tomorrow what should be done today.[79]

As the above passage suggests, reputation, or what other people said about a man and his trustworthiness, was a very important asset for Julfan merchants. It was a precondition of earning trust and receiving "money or a consignment of goods" with which to trade. As we saw in chapter 6, this was particularly the case for *commenda* agents, who, in addition to possessing excellent skills in accounting and trade, needed to have impeccable reputations to earn the trust of their masters, at least initially, before being hired. Having a bad reputation or even being closely associated with individuals known to be disreputable could jeopardize one's chances of success in the world of trade. Thus in one documented case a *commenda* agent named Zak'aria of Agulis (a mercantile town in northern Iran) was refused a potentially lucrative partnership contract because of the tarnished reputation of his brother, who had once lost money entrusted to him because he was drunk.[80]

Given the centrality of reputation in Julfan society, merchants in turn generally conducted themselves with remarkable probity because they knew that acquiring a bad reputation was disastrous for their future, as they and their relatives would be sanctioned by members of the Julfan coalition. As Greif's studies of Maghribi Jewish merchants have demonstrated, maintaining honesty and, therefore, remaining faithful to the network norms of pre-modern merchants had more to do with rationality than any religious fear or generalized morality.[81] In other words, merchants were motivated to conduct themselves with honesty in relation to fellow merchants of the same network not necessarily because they were inherently moral individuals driven to honesty through religious fear (though this was certainly a possibility) but principally because honesty and respect for a given network's norms were in their rational self-interest as profit-maximizing individuals. For most merchants, the long-term benefits of being honest far outweighed any short-term gains from cheating. It appears that what merchants feared most was having their names "blotted out" of the list of honest and reliable men. That is, they feared being what we might call "blacklisted." As a Julfa merchant writing to his brother in

India observed, "I would rather chuse to dye, than for them to [blot my] name out of the List."[82] The same writer reminds his brother that having one's name "blotted out" of the list in Julfa was "the same as if you was a dead man." Perhaps this explains why cases of cheating and dishonesty are rarely mentioned in Julfan correspondence. Reputation was everything in the seventeenth- and eighteenth-century world of Julfans, because news traveled fast and far. In his illuminating study of English private trade Mentz makes a similar observation, when he writes that if "a merchant was exposed as a fraud, it would immediately affect his reputation, as this kind of information would spread fast." The upshot would be that "nobody would trust a dishonest person in commercial transactions and the perpetrator was shunned, thereby ending his career."[83] Mentz's observations indicate that Julfans' use of reputation to regulate their relations with others was not unique to any group (including gentlemanly English merchants) but part of a larger, shared Eurasian mercantile *ecumene*.

Because the social network or coalition within which most Julfan merchants operated was closed and was characterized by multiplex relations in which individuals were connected to each other through crosscutting ties, the likelihood of the circulation of rumors and information regarding dishonest behavior was very high. If such rumors regarding the dishonesty of a given merchant spread throughout the network, the merchant in question would be forced to repair his damaged reputation in order not to risk being permanently banned from the network as a whole. In this regard, no "reputation-regulating mechanism" was better suited to Julfan merchants than frequent business correspondence. As Trivellato has perspicaciously noted, "merchant letters remained uniquely valuable for circulating information about the aptitude and trustworthiness of distant agents."[84]

Given our discussion above, we can conclude that the ability of members of the Julfan coalition to trust fellow coalition members—that is to say, to have rational expectations that the actions of other coalition members would not be harmful to their own self-interest—was predicated upon their ability to base their decision to cooperate with other coalition merchants on the record of their past performance, or, simply put, on their "reputation." By supplying information on merchants' reputations and by motivating coalition members to boycott cheaters among them, the informal reputation-based mechanism of Julfan merchants was an effective way of generating an atmosphere of honesty, trust, and cooperation. The key to the smooth functioning of this informal institution was the credible threat of punishment for individuals who would otherwise be prone to embezzle their associates' money. But was this informal method of policing merchants' behavior sufficient to create trust and trustworthiness among Julfans? Was the circulation of information in business correspondence effective in providing a signal to coalition members to avoid dealing with a merchant of questionable reputation? A few cases of cheating that I have come across in Julfan documents dealing with the India trade have led me to question how effective information sharing about reputation really was. As we have seen, there were probably close to a thousand active members in the Julfan coalition at any given time, thus making it difficult to share information with everyone about every merchant. Letter writing was certainly an effective means of sharing information, but it did not create full transparency.

The ultimate weakness of the reputation-based informal model of trust, associated with the work of Avner Greif, is its inability to be exhaustive. For there to be higher levels of trust and by extension cooperation between coalition members, a centralized merchant juridical institution with some formal attributes is necessary. The latter would not only demonstrate a credible threat of retaliation in case of malfeasance but would also be endowed with the institutional means of rendering financial restitution to parties suffering from embezzlement. Such a juridical institution did exist in the coalition's nodal center in Julfa. To understand its nature, its mode of operation, and its vital role in creating institutional trust among merchants, we need to look at the autonomous administrative structure of New Julfa as an Armenian trading colony.

## NEW JULFA'S ADMINISTRATIVE AUTONOMY

Soon after its foundation in 1605, the Armenian community in New Julfa was granted administrative and legal autonomy under Safavid rule. This autonomy was personified in the office of the *kalantar* of the trading colony. *Kalantar* is a Safavid administrative term that can be traced to post-Il-Khanid times and was used to designate an urban official who served as an intermediary between the government and the population.[85] The *kalantar*'s responsibilities included collecting taxes, acting as a judge in local affairs, and maintaining public order.[86] Though this office existed throughout Safavid Iran, its place in Julfan life was unique. In the Julfan case, the *kalantar* was always chosen from the local Armenian community, and his appointment seems to have resulted from a combination of royal favor, popular election, and a strong hereditary tendency associated with wealth and family prestige. The first *kalantar* of new Julfa was Khwaja Safar (1605–1618), who was appointed by Shah 'Abbas I in recognition of the post of community leader, or *"melik,"* of Old Julfa held by his father, Khwaja Khachik, who gave the shah a memorable reception in 1603.[87] The next three *kalantars* also came from the same family. Khwaja Nazar (1618–1636), the most famous of Julfa's *kalantars,* was Safar's brother and was succeeded by his son Khwaja Safraz (1636–1656). The last *kalantar* who hailed from this family was Safraz's brother Khwaja Haikaz (1656–1660), who, like his predecessors, died in office.[88] During this time, the policy of royal appointment of the *kalantar* from the same wealthy family seems to have been the norm. After Haikaz's death, a number of *kalantars* came and went in rapid succession.[89] It appears that beginning at this time, the office was filled through popular election followed by royal ratification. A document from 1751, preserved in the Julfa archives, clearly indicates that the new incumbent to the office of the *kalantar,* Hovhannes son of Babum, was popularly elected by the entire community of Julfa.[90] The document also suggests that after the community had elected its official, a petition was sent to the ruling sovereign, Karim Khan Zand, asking for royal ratification and investiture. The rapid turnover rate and political jockeying in support of different candidates associated with this prestigious office suggest that the same process was most likely also in place at least beginning in the last quarter of the seventeenth century. Seventeenth-century European travel accounts, such as those of Chardin and Tavernier, compare the office of the *kalantar* to that of a mayor or provost of merchants in Europe. Some accounts also describe the holder of the office as a kind of "governor" or even a "prince"[91] or "lord."[92] Julfans also used the term *ishkhan* ("prince," in Armenian) to refer to him; the term *kalantar* appears to have become more widespread in Julfan usage only in the second half of the seventeenth century. Tavernier, writing at a time when royal appointment seems to have been the main way of filling this office, comments: "The king names whom he pleases among the Armenians to be their Chief; whom they call *kelonter [sic],* who judges all their differences, and taxes them to make up the Sum which they are to pay to the King every year."[93] The *kalantar* was the most important official in the administration of New Julfa. Vladimir Minorsky, commenting on *Tadhkirat al-Muluk,* the famous Safavid manual of administration, notes: "The Kalantar appointed the kadkhudas, contributed to the repartition of taxes among guilds, formulated the desiderata of the latter, protected the ra'iyyat (peasants, or lower classes etc.)."[94]

In the context of New Julfa, the Persian term *kadkhuda* referred to individuals who were representatives and heads of the township's twenty districts or neighborhoods, which were formed around the ten perpendicular streets running north to south that cut across the township's central thoroughfare, known as Nazar Khiavan or Nazar Avenue, named after Julfa's famous *kalantar.*[95] According to Shushanik Khachikian, these streets became the administrative boundaries of Julfa's twenty districts (ten each for the northern and southern segments of Nazar Avenue), which were known by the Armenian term *tasnak,* meaning "one-tenth."[96] Each of these districts was named after the most prominent family residing there. Hence *Mirmanents tasnak* was where the wealthy Mirman family resided. According to Khachikian, each of these districts was also invested with administrative autonomy and was represented by the most senior merchant belonging to the wealthiest family of the district. Although Khachikian and, following her, Ina Baghdiantz McCabe refer to these representatives by their Armenian title *tasnakavak* (district elder), their official nomenclature in Persian was *kadkhuda,* a word signifying "district head or judge."[97]

The *kadkhudas* were not only in charge of administering their respective districts, but, more importantly, they were members of a special administrative body tasked with running day-to-day affairs in Julfa. As Khachikian has pointed out, Julfa's twenty *kadkhudas* were members of the suburb's key administrative body, known as the *Vacharakanats zhoghov,* or the Assembly of Merchants,[98] which, in addition to the *kadkhudas,* included the *kalantar.*[99] The existence of this special administrative and legal body has been known since Harut'iwn Ter Hovhaniants's two-volume work on the history of Julfa was published in 1880.[100] Building on the latter work, Levon Khachikian elaborated on this body in his classic 1966 essay.[101] Shushanik Khachikian, in turn, devoted a number of illuminating pages in her work to further clarifying the workings of this body. Baghdiantz McCabe's discussion is essentially a repetition of Khachikian's findings. Edmund Herzig, in an excellent contribution on Julfan commercial law, raises doubts about the existence of this assembly as a formal institution.[102] Herzig's skepticism here is certainly understandable. As he correctly points out, all discussions of this legal/administrative body are derivative of Ter Hovaniants's work and rely on it for documentary evidence. In the absence of further research in the Julfa archives, Herzig concludes, we cannot be certain that this institution actually existed and arbitrated legal and other affairs. Herzig also notes that "preliminary researches in the Julfa Cathedral Archive . . . have not turned up any surviving examples of the kinds of document cited by Ter Hovhaniants"; he is skeptical about whether the petitions to this body (referred to in Ter Hovaniants's work but not consulted by other scholars with the exception of the present writer)[103] have indeed survived, because the only catalogue for the Julfa archives does not list such documents separately.[104] As we shall see, the Julfa archives contains many documents of this sort, many of which are specifically addressed to the *kadkhudas* and the *kalantar* of Julfa, and some do in fact contain verdicts handed down by this institution. Given the surfeit of archival evidence concerning this institution, we cannot but be certain that this institution actually existed and played a vital role in the administration of Julfa. This evidence corroborates the contemporary observations about this body by the Dutch traveler Cornelius De Bruyn, who visited Julfa in the second half of the seventeenth century and remarked regarding the administration of justice in the suburb: "They [the Julfans] have their own *kalantar* or burgo-master, and their *Betgoedaes* [read: *kadkhudas*] or chiefs of districts, who are judges to decide in all common cases, but those of importance are reserved for the King or the council of state, and afterward put into execution by the burgo-master and chiefs of districts."[105]

However, what we cannot be certain about at this early stage of our knowledge is whether this body conducted its affairs in a structured and formalized manner or operated informally according to the tasks at hand. In other words, while we know with great certainty that the assembly consisted of the *kalantar* and the *kadkhudas* of New Julfa, we do not know whether all twenty *kadkhudas* met to deliberate on each case referred to the assembly. Examination of seals and signatures found on the petitions to this body suggest that the *kalantar*'s signature and seal (placed on the top right margin) were always present on the petitions, accompanied at the bottom by seals and signatures of some of Julfa's leading merchants. In a few cases, however, a petition examined by the assembly has all twenty seals of Julfa's *kadkhudas*. A comparison of several petitions dating from the same period (1727 and 1731) reveals that around ten names and seals were consistently present across different petitions, thus suggesting that not all twenty representatives of the *kadkhudas* needed to be present to ratify a decision of this body.[106] This seems to make sense, since some of the township's *kadkhuda* families would be expected to be away from Julfa on some occasions. The evidence suggests that a minimum of ten to fifteen seals and sometimes more were required officially to ratify a legal decision endorsed by this body. We also do not know how often this body convened or whether it convened at a specific place (there is no mention of a special building for such a court)[107] at specific times or whether its meetings were decided on an ad hoc basis depending on the matter that needed to be addressed. Herzig points out that if such a body did in fact exist, its work was not as structured as Khachikian and, following her, Baghdiantz McCabe suggest. Rather, Herzig argues that it must have been an "informal" institution.[108] One argument in favor of this view is that the assembly, as we have already noted above, did not have a codified body of rules but rather administered law by word, as was the custom in Safavid Iran. It is too early at this stage of our limited knowledge of the administrative protocols of Julfan society to arrive at definitive conclusions on the particularities concerning the assembly's mode of operation. Much more research needs to be carried out on the documents connected to the assembly, and we need to know more about Safavid administrative and legal history than is available in the *Tadhkirat al-Muluk* (the manual of Safavid administration) or other similar sources before we can make sound judgments on the assembly's modus operandi.[109] The evidence suggests that the assembly's mode of operation was characterized both by informality (lack of written or codified rules or laws as well as ad hoc meetings) and by some elements of formality (such as being tied to and legitimated by the Safavid state and being legally authorized to impose punishments and to sanction offenders of Julfan commercial law). Given the state of our knowledge, it seems safe to conclude provisionally that the assembly as an institution occupied a gray zone between "formal" and "informal."

## THE ASSEMBLY OF MERCHANTS AT WORK

An examination of the petitions stored in the Julfa archives indicates that there were at least two classes of petitions. The first class dealt with strictly commercial matters, such as those arising from certain irregularities in the conduct of commerce both in the suburb and especially in Julfa's overseas colonies. Most of the petitions belonging to this category involve disputes between parties to a *commenda* contract. Such petitions are formulaically addressed to the "*Sahap K'alantarin, Kheran-*

*dish kadkhutek'onts', yev barebashd vacharakanats'"* (To the Master Kalantar, the benevolent district heads, and pious merchants).[110] These are the petitions addressed to the Assembly of Merchants proper.

A petition of such a nature begins with a summary of the dispute in question (which usually involves a *commenda* agent who has not abided by the customary laws concerning commerce, such as remaining overseas despite orders to return home or absconding with his master's share of the profit, a crime warranting a draconian punishment) and concludes by beseeching the honorable body to hand down its swift judgment. A number of such petitions preserved in the archives of All Savior's Monastery also contain the body's decision, usually handed down within a few months of the petition. These judgments are recorded on the original petition, in the following manner. The *kalantar* governing at the time records the body's decision on the left margin (horizontal inscription) followed by about twenty seals and signatures affirming the *kalantar*'s will at the foot of the document. An analysis of the several petitions that have the assembly's verdict affixed to them suggests that this body consisted of about twenty to twenty-five individuals, comprising at least ten or fifteen of the twenty *kadkhudas,* or district heads, representing the twenty *tasnaks,* or districts, of the suburb, headed by the *kalantar.* It is noteworthy that church officials are absent from the commercial petitions that have reached us through the archives.[111] Only merchants seem to have been involved in deliberating on secular issues. The *kalantar*'s verdict also appears to have been recorded in accordance with a formulaic convention. It usually begins with the following line: "*Kalantar Ohaness Jumiatov ēspes tastegh tesing or tujari dasturn ēs ay vor nerkoy grets'i piti amal goy.*"[112] ([I] Kalantar Ohaness along with the community of merchants saw it fit that the following is the verdict of the merchants, which I have written below and which must be implemented.)

A second group of petitions relates to legal documents that needed official ratification and legal endorsement. Such documents included powers of attorney, wills and testaments, and legal papers concerning property deeds involving various individuals or institutions. One of the most distinctive features of such documents is their mode of addressing the assembly. Unlike the strictly commercial documents mentioned above, documents belonging to this class are addressed both to the reigning *kalantar* and the archbishop/primate of the time. In other words, they appealed simultaneously to the spiritual and to the secular authorities of Julfa. This is manifested in the opening lines of the petition, in which the petitioner declares that at such and such a time he or she appeared before the court (*atean*) and "made a confession of an oath before the spiritual and secular fathers of the community." Apart from the *kalantar and* the senior religious authorities, the *kadkhudas* are also addressed. The *kadkhudas* are referred to invariably as "our strong fortresses of the Armenian community." The petitioner then presents his or her case and ends the petition by stating that he/she is prepared to make an appearance before the hon-

orable body to answer any questions in person. The petition also ends with a formulaic line in which the petitioner affirms that he/she has made an oath or pronounced the legal formula (*segha<sigheh* P: "legal formula or oath") regarding the
truth of what he/she has sworn in Arabic, Persian, and in accordance with the Lord's
Prayer of the Armenian Church. It is unclear why such an oath had to be made in
Arabic and Persian (presumably invoking the *shari'a*) in addition to Armenian. It
could be that the invocation of the Qur'an in Arabic was a move to ensure the ad-
missibility of the oath in a *shari'a* court. We can only conjecture at this point, until
more research is conducted in Safavid legal and social history. However, it is telling
that those petitions involving clergy of the Armenian Church do not contain the
line about an oath in Arabic and Persian.[113]

This second class of petitions, concerned with issues relating to legal ratification
and addressed to the *kalantar* and *kadkhudas* in addition to the spiritual hierarchy of
the suburb, suggests that there were two closely related but distinct administrative/
judicial bodies in Julfa. Scholars such as Levon Khachikian and Shushanik Khachikian and, following their lead, Baghdiantz McCabe, who have sought to address
the administrative aspect of Julfan life, have discussed only the Assembly of Merchants, thus giving the impression that this was the only administrative body
present in Julfa. Our examination of the petitions stored in the Julfa archives reveals, for the first time, the existence of two separate but interconnected bodies. The
first set of petitions (smaller in number) is clearly addressed to the Assembly of
Merchants, a body that did *not* include members of the church. The second set,
however, indicates that a larger municipal body was also in existence and seems
to have had essentially the same membership as the Assembly of Merchants but, in
addition to the *kalantar* and *kadkhudas,* included members of the church hierarchy. This body seems to have taken charge of more administrative tasks in Julfa than
the more specialized Assembly of Merchants if the sheer number of surviving petitions addressed to it is any indication. The principal distinction between the two
related bodies appears to be that the Municipal Assembly did not hear merchant
disputes and did not deliberate on commercial matters but mainly limited itself to
ratifying important documents.

A significant number of such documents are powers of attorney and, more importantly, transfer of title deeds (including quite a few by women). Ratification of
such documents by the municipal body was not only deemed important (perhaps
even mandatory) for conducting affairs in Julfa; the evidence suggests that merchants traveling to or residing in Julfa's overseas settlements also followed the practice of ratifying legal papers through the Municipal Assembly in Julfa. In this connection, numerous powers of attorney stored in the Archivio di Stato in Venice have
the seals and ratification of the same municipal body in Julfa. Perhaps even more
interesting is the fact that almost all such papers preserved in Venice belong to the
famous Sceriman family of Armenian Catholics. This indicates that, despite the in-

tense religious and confessional factionalism in Julfa, Catholic Julfans such as the Scerimans also resorted to the Municipal Assembly to have their legal papers ratified and thus respected by members of the *jumiat* (i.e., community of Julfan merchants) in places such as Venice.[114] The assembly's ratification also seems to have carried quite a bit of clout before the legal institutions of foreign states where Julfans were involved in trade. In this connection, it is worth remembering the case of Marcara Avachintz, one of the regional directors of the French East India Company, who was originally from Julfa. Avachintz was involved in a legal action against the company in Paris in which the French court had tried to undermine his case and have it thrown out of the courts on the grounds that he was not a nobleman but a mere commoner.[115] One of his sons traveled all the way to Iran and appealed to the Municipal Assembly of Julfa to send a ratified certificate, bearing the seals of the *kalantar,* the senior clergy, and the some twenty *kadkhudas,* testifying to Avachintz's noble origins.[116] The French court recognized the validity of this certificate.

Institutions similar to the Municipal Assembly of Julfa most likely also existed in other Armenian communities in Safavid Iran. We know from several archival documents that the towns of Agulis and Dasht in northern Iran, which had a high concentration of Armenian merchants with global connections, also had such a body. In this connection, an Armenian power of attorney dating from the closing years of the seventeenth century, discovered by the present author in the archives of Cadiz (Spain), contains the signature and seal of the local *kalantar* followed by those of the *kadkhudas* of Agulis (a small town in northern Iran—now in the Azerbaijani enclave of Nakhichevan—inhabited predominantly by Armenian merchants in the seventeenth and eighteenth centuries).[117] This power of attorney was written in Agulis in 1699 and sent to Europe, where it arrived the following year in Cadiz and was presented before the local court and a notary public along with its Spanish translation. Like the case of Marcara Avachintz in Paris, this power of attorney was also accepted by a European court, testifying again that documents ratified by merchant-dominated Armenian municipal bodies in Iran (whether in Julfa or Agulis) were normally invested with legitimacy in the eyes of some European courts.

## PORTABLE COURTS OF MERCHANTS

According to Levon Khachikian, many of Julfa's overseas commercial settlements where sufficient number of Julfans resided also had their own version of the Assembly of Merchants. Based on his scrupulous analysis of the travel ledger maintained by a Julfan *commenda* agent, Hovhannes Ter Davtian, who conducted commerce in India, Nepal, and Tibet in the years 1682–1693, Khachikian points out that even in remote places such as Lhasa (the Tibetan capital) or Patna, whenever disputes among Julfan merchants arose, the conflicting parties appealed to the local Julfan community of merchants (*jumiat*) to resolve their differences. In the ab-

sence of a sufficient number of Julfan merchants, the *jumiat* invited foreign merchants to sit on the board.[118] Thus in Lhasa, Kashmiris were invited to deliberate
on the local assembly board. Similar procedures were followed in other Armenian
settlements in India, as well as in Europe. As to how informal these "portable courts"
were can be seen from a notarial document in the Dutch archives that describes
how a dispute between some Julfa merchants and an Armenian printer in Amsterdam was resolved in 1695 at the home of a prominent Julfan merchant named Char-
riman di Murat (Sceriman di Murat or Shahriman ordi Murati).[119] A dispute in Marseilles between a Julfan and another Armenian merchant from Shorot (in the
Ottoman Empire) was similarly resolved by Melchon de Nazar, "consul de la nation
arménienne," in 1682.[120] Another document in the Julfa dialect preserved in the
Archivio di Stato di Venezia and also dating from the 1690s similarly indicates that
a dispute among some of Venice's Julfan merchants was resolved through the con-
vening of the local *jumiat*. In this case the disputing parties, Marut di Miaysar and
Yavre di Hovaness, appealed through a notary to four Julfan merchants residing
in Venice to go over their commercial papers and reach a consensus regarding
their dispute.[121] That the four Venice-based Julfa merchants adjudicating this dispute viewed themselves as community judges for Venice's Julfan merchant community is evident in their description of themselves as *giudizzi arbitri*" (written in
Armenian characters), or arbitrating judges. In this case as well, it seems that the
disputing parties met with the four arbitrating judges at the home of a prominent
Julfan merchant (most likely Gaspar di Sceriman or Shahriman) residing in Venice.

These portable courts provided members of the Julfan coalition residing or trading in Julfa's overseas settlements with a relatively cheap and effective means of resolving disputes and thus enabled them to adjudicate community disputes in accordance with Julfan commercial law, thereby doing away with the unnecessarily
long, costly, and, in some cases, unreliable use of foreign courts. (For instance, in
the case of the Julfan merchant Hovhannes Ter Davtian, who had traveled to Lhasa,
the decision to appeal to Tibetan adjudicators in a dispute with a fellow Julfan merchant resulted in the casting of dice—the local custom in Lhasa—at which Hovhannes lost.)[122] Thus if a Julfan merchant in Madras was not paid his loan by a fellow Julfan merchant to whom he had advanced credit, he would first and foremost
appeal to the Julfan *jumiat* (or community of merchants) in Madras and present
his case for their arbitrage. If the portable court of the *jumiat* ruled in favor of the
plaintiff, the members of the portable court would try to have the defendant pay
his loan along with the accumulated interest, or, if the defendant had already left
town or otherwise refused to pay his debt, the portable court would then draft a
special notarized document called a *manzara* in Julfan dialect (<P *mahzar*: any document attested by witnesses, attestation, testimony)[123] and send this document along
with supporting evidence (for instance, the plaintiff's petition to the *jumiat's*
portable court as well as original correspondence between the plaintiff and defen-

dant, all sealed and attested by the *jumiat*'s members) to the Assembly of Merchants in Julfa.[124] The assembly would then review the case and, if they too ruled on the plaintiff's behalf, they would pressure the defendant (if the latter happened to be in Julfa at the time) or his family members, including relatives, to restitute the owed money along with the interest. This relationship between the portable courts in the settlements and the Assembly of Merchants in Julfa is what I shall refer to as the "AMPC complex." The AMPC (Assembly of Merchants and Portable Courts) complex was the single most important institutional feature in Julfan society when it came to monitoring and sanctioning opportunistic behavior, be it in Julfa itself or in its settlements in India or the Mediterranean. The dozens of *manzaras* and other notarized documents sent to the Assembly of Merchants from portable courts in Julfan settlements in such places as Paris, Livorno, Venice, Madras, and Hyderabad indicate that the link between the Assembly of Merchants in Julfa and its offshoot courts in the settlements was an active and important one. The documents indicate that the assembly was the ultimate court of appeal for intra-Julfan disputes that could not be resolved in situ overseas. They also indicate that the assembly imposed effective sanctions on merchants who were deemed to have broken the coalition's norms. However, just how the assembly imposed such sanctions is not clearly indicated in the surviving documents. We know that often the assembly compelled the guilty party's family or relatives to right a wrong and probably also used boycotting and "shaming" as a tactic to bring the guilty party in line.[125] "Drubbing," flogging, or bastinadoing *commenda* agents who had defrauded their masters is known to have existed, as the Astrakhan Code of Laws and Tavernier's testimony suggest. However, the assembly does not seem to have had the authority to administer corporal punishment to guilty individuals in Julfa; as far as we know, there does not seem to have been a jail in Julfa under the authority of Julfan Armenian officials. Since cases involving corporal punishment in Julfa were usually referred to the *darugha* or to the Safavid *Orfi* courts (i.e., secular, non-*shari'a* courts),[126] it is quite possible that in extreme cases the assembly referred some cases involving egregious instances of malfeasance to the Safavid court system. Further research into Safavid legal history is needed before we can begin to speculate about how the assembly actually administered punishment to dishonest merchants and how it compelled them to restitute the wronged party in a dispute.

It seems that in addition to its juridical and arbitration activities, the Assembly of Merchants in Julfa was what one could call a centralized "information clearinghouse." As we have noted above, coalition members working in Julfa's overseas settlements would often send information in the form of notarized contracts (*manzaras*), powers of attorneys, petitions, and correspondence between litigants to the assembly. Once this information reached Julfa, news in the form of "gossip" about various merchants overseas and their business activities, including their reputations, would then be leaked to members of Julfa's resident merchant families, either through the *kalantar* or through one of the *kadkhuda* members of the assembly, and disseminated by members of Julfa's merchant families through business correspondence to their agents or associates overseas. An example of how this happened is found in a 1746 letter by a Julfan merchant named Raffael di Hagalar in Julfa to his associate Khwaja Minas di Elias in Calcutta. In his letter, Raffael refers to a Julfan merchant in Madras named Sultanum who had been having problems paying debts to creditors back in Julfa. "I do observe," writes Raffael in his business letter, "that Mr. Sultanum has not paid the Bill of Exchange. I know this because the same has been sent back. And though Mr. Hagamal is [of the] opinion that the money is as safe as if the same was in the Bank, for my part I look on the said Money as wholly lost."[127] The bill of exchange that had been "sent back," alluded to in Raffael's letter, was probably a *manzara* or notarized document accompanied by the original bill of exchange sent by the *jumiat's* portable court in Madras to the Assembly of Merchants in Julfa. What is interesting to note here is that Raffael had probably heard about Sultanum's "bounced check" through the members of the assembly and was conveying this hearsay along with other gossip about Sultanum's ordeals in India and Julfa to his associate in Calcutta in order to alert him to Sultanum's declining reputation. This and other evidence suggests that, along with the church hierarchy at All Savior's Monastery in Julfa, the Assembly of Merchants was another connectivity node that imbued the Julfan network with the kind of multiplex structure that made information flow faster and more extensively throughout the network. In this respect, the assembly's role in the flow of information throughout the network can be compared to a "bandwidth" in a transistor radio: it had multiple frequencies of receiving signals from different parts and broadcasting information to coalition members who were not necessarily directly connected to the source of the information and would probably not have heard it had it not been for the "connectivity node" of the assembly. The link between the Assembly of Merchants and the portable courts in the settlements (i.e., the assembly's participation in the AMPC complex) enabled the assembly to accumulate information in the form of legal petitions, notarized papers, or just correspondence containing business gossip or *fama*. One example of this commercial hearsay is found in an interesting document written by the Assembly of Merchants dated 22 March 1680 and signed and sealed by the *kalantar* and more than twenty prominent Julfan merchants in Julfa, Isfahan.[128] This document contains instructions by the assembly to members of the Julfan merchant community, the *jumiat*, in Surat concerning what to do with the effects of a deceased Julfan merchant named Zachariah son of Edigar who had passed away in Sharinov (Siam) the previous year.[129] The immediate impetus for drafting the document (the first of its kind discovered thus far) seems to have been a conflict between another Julfan, named Mirzajan di Margar, who had taken possession of the deceased merchant's goods and traveled with them to Surat, and a representative of a wealthy Julfan merchant named Khwaja Minas di Panos for whom the deceased was a *com-*

*menda* agent in Siam. According to the document, Khwaja Minas's agent had traveled to Siam with a full power of attorney to settle the deceased's accounts with his master, Khwaja Minas, and, after settling the accounts between master and agent, to receive the share belonging to Khwaja Minas and to return the same to its owner in Julfa. The conflict had emerged when Mirzajan (who had taken possession of the deceased merchant's goods in Sharinov) had refused to cooperate and insisted on shipping the deceased's goods to Surat in order to distribute them to heirs residing there. It seems that the community court in Surat had sent a *manzara* and accompanying documents to the assembly to adjudicate the dispute, thus prompting the assembly to send its instructions or verdict (*dastur*) to Surat, though we cannot be certain of this, since the original petition to the assembly does not seem to have been preserved. In any case, it is safe to assume that the assembly was asked to put a stop to this and to ensure that Khwaja Minas received his due share before the deceased's goods were disbursed to relatives.[130] We do not have enough contextual documentation regarding this case to be able to tell with certainty how the assembly's decisions were put into effect, but we can be sure that news of the passing away of the Julfan *commenda* agent in Siam and the subsequent lack of cooperation by Mirzajan must have spread, via the instuctions sent by the assembly to the *jumiat* in Surat, to other coalition members and especially to those who were operating in India and the East and might not have had direct business ties with the deceased merchant.

But portable courts or *jumiats* in the Julfan settlements not only shared information about merchants' reputation or behavior with the Assembly of Merchants at the nodal center in Julfa; they also circulated information to other portable courts in neighboring settlements in the network, as a case involving the *jumiats* in Venice and Livorno illustrates. In a document preserved in the state archives of Florence, we learn that Julfan merchants residing in Livorno had appealed to their counterparts in Venice for a "background check" on a merchant from Julfa, Poghos di Arakel, who was apparently newly arrived in Livorno via Izmir carrying silk from Iran. Though it is difficult to piece together the details of this case based on one seemingly isolated document, it seems that some Julfans in Livorno had reason to be suspicious of the newcomer and wanted more information on him, including whose *commenda* agent he was and where he had purchased his silk. In response to their query, the *jumiat* of Venice sent a notarized document (*manzara/mahzar*) to Livorno dated October 23, 1152 (1703), and written in Venice, containing three sworn statements from Julfan merchants in Venice who had earlier been in Izmir testifying that they knew Poghos di Arakel from Julfa, were aware that he purchased his silk in Gilan, and had seen him earlier in Izmir.[131] As this example suggests, *jumiat* or portable courts in the network's overseas settlements did not always transmit information back to the center but could also directly communicate with one another, especially when they were in close vicinity to each other, as were Venice and Livorno.

Our evidence regarding the *jumiat* courts, most of which is stored in the archives in Julfa, tends to highlight the flow of information between *jumiat* courts in the settlements and the Assembly of Merchants in Julfa. It is likely that other *jumiat* courts also shared information directly with similar courts in neighboring settlements, but the sources at our disposal are biased in favor of information links between *jumiat* courts and the Assembly of Merchants.

Another case of pertinent commercial information reaching the assembly from an overseas *jumiat* court comes from Chinapatan (Madras) in the mid-1690s. In this case, a Julfan merchant named Vatan was defrauded by one of his agents, named Mattos di Panos, who had taken loans in Madras and Bengal in his master's name and fled town without paying his debts.[132] After many futile attempts to contact his opportunistic agent and plead with him to restitute the huge debts he had left to his master, Vatan was forced to appeal to the *jumiat*'s portable court in Madras. The portable court had then notarized one of the long letters sent by Vatan to his agent (Mattos), along with two petitions written by Vatan regarding the fraudulent activities of Mattos, and sent them as *manzaras* to the Assembly of Merchants asking the assembly to have the fraudulent agent arrested if he happened to be in Julfa or to disseminate news about his behavior and compel him to return to Julfa to restitute his debt to representatives Vatan had dispatched to Julfa to receive his money.

As both examples illustrate, wronged parties called upon the Assembly of Merchants to intervene legally and punish coalition members who were regarded as having broken the norms of the network. Both cases also illustrate that, in addition to passing its judgments on guilty parties and restituting money owed to honest merchants, the assembly also stored a vast quantity of information received from its portable courts in the overseas settlements, information that might not have been available to individual coalition merchants with their own more limited network of relations. The assembly then pumped this vital information back into the network by making "leaks" to Julfan merchants in Julfa who in turn circulated the information to their agents and business correspondents in faraway places. As a result of its multiplex role as a kind of bandwidth for information gathering, the Assembly of Merchants as an integral part of the AMPC complex was thus able to supplement the flow of information in Julfan business correspondence and more effectively broadcast vital information to coalition members that might escape the notice of individual merchants and their networks of business correspondents. Without the multiplex grapevine of the assembly, the reputation-related information available to ordinary members of the coalition would be limited to information provided by business partners or *commenda* agents and thus would not be thorough enough to cover most cases of opportunism.

The evidence also suggests that the assembly was a coordinating agency for affairs taking place far away from the center. Thus one document preserved in the Julfa archives is a power of attorney sent to the Assembly of Merchants by coalition members in India who requested that the assembly welcome their representative sent from India and assist him in obtaining the original copy of a *commenda* contract that they had entrusted to one of the priests in Julfa and bring it back to the merchants in India. It seems in this and a few other cases that the assembly played the role of legal mediator. In another case, a Julfan merchant named Hakob son of Ter Petros sent a petition to the assembly from Paris in 1682 concerning a dispute he had had with another coalition member, Martiros di Marcar Avakshintz (Marcara Avachintz), then in Paris.[133] The notarized petition asked the assembly to investigate the matter and to send back to Paris a notarized paper regarding the results of their investigation.

To sum up, the combined work of the portable courts in the settlements and the Assembly of Merchants in Julfa (i.e., the AMPC complex) served to resolve most merchant disputes among members of the Julfan coalition during the seventeenth and eighteenth centuries. In sanctioning errant merchant behavior and circulating information about such behavior, the AMPC complex created favorable conditions for most Julfan merchants to trust their fellow coalition members and engage in mutually beneficial transactions. This allowed Julfan merchants trading or residing in overseas settlements for the most part to avoid relying on foreign courts to adjudicate their disputes, with results that were sometimes less than satisfying. We have already mentioned the case of the merchant Hovhannes whose dispute in Tibet was resolved by the throw of a dice.[134] In other cases, Julfans appealed to local tribunals in addition to making use of their own institutions. In Madras, for instance, such appeals seem more the norm than the exception, especially in the second half of the eighteenth century, for the local Armenian community was well integrated into the English settlement and made liberal use of the Mayor's Court of Fort St. George (Madras).[135] This is borne out by the numerous cases of disputes involving Armenian merchants recorded in the pages of the *Mayor's Court Proceedings*.[136] The proceedings of this court indicate that it relied on the customary law of the litigating parties in adjudicating their disputes. The court is also known to have consulted with local Julfans regarding Julfan commercial law for intra-Julfan disputes.[137] In Venice, too, appeals were made to the Senate and the *Cinque Savi,* a panel of judges that handed down verdicts on commercial and civil disputes and legal infringements.[138]

## TRUST IN GOSSIP BUT BASTINADO WHEN NEEDED

In addition to relying on social capital and reputational mechanisms, Julfans relied on a more direct and coercive method of policing trust within their network. This was especially the case when it came to the most trust-sensitive aspect of their long-distance trade, namely, their reliance on the *commenda* form of partnership. As we have seen in chapter 6, the *commenda,* in addition to the family firm, was the basic organizational unit and structuring principle of Julfan long-distance trade. The overwhelming bulk of the capital invested by Julfan merchants in long-distance trade was tied up in *commenda* ventures overseas. We have also seen that nearly all the *commenda* agents engaged in Julfan trade and known to us through surviving contracts were from Julfa or had strong family ties with the suburb. What can this tell us about how Julfans policed trust relations?

One of the reasons Julfans appear to have hired only fellow Julfans as *commenda* agents was because the *commenda* partnership as understood by Julfan commercial law had built-in checks against malfeasance that reinforced Julfans' reliance on reputational mechanisms and yielded high returns as far as the problem of trust was concerned. Such checks included the provision that the agent keep a detailed accounting ledger of his past transactions and submit it to his master upon returning home to Julfa. If the accounts turned out to be inaccurate or fraudulent, the agent could be legally imprisoned for up to one year and periodically flogged or bastinadoed until he restituted his master. The prospect of this form of coercion would provide a sufficient incentive for agents to be honest. Moreover, agents were also expected to leave the welfare of their families in Julfa in the care of their masters upon leaving the township on their overseas trips on behalf of their masters. Though the article of the Astrakhan Code of Laws that discusses this provision of the law presents it as a responsibility expected from the master of a *commenda* contract, it is not difficult to see this as another form of coercing agents into being honest with the large sums of money entrusted to them while away from home. Multani merchants from the northwest region of India used a similar provision to control the behavior of their agents abroad.[139] In both cases, families were essentially used as hostages or collateral in exchange for the proper behavior of agents. Also in both cases, the fact that the agents were all from the same home base (Julfa or Multan City) helped in policing the behavior of agents and thus reduced the risk of opportunism. In the worst case scenario, if a Julfan agent had absconded with money overseas, his family back in Julfa could lose its reputation and honor and be held accountable. Lastly, another provision in the law also helped minimize cases of opportunism. As we have seen in chapter 6, in order for a *commenda* agent to engage in future trade with fellow Julfans either as an agent for others or as a capitalist master hiring his own agents, he had first to conclude his contract with his initial employer and receive from him a *tomar* document followed by a *ghatilayagir,* or letter of severance/quittance. Without this letter of severance, an agent would have a hard time practicing trade. We know about this from a very important case in the Madras Mayor's Court proceedings from 1735 involving an Armenian factor or *commenda* agent who wanted to enter into an agency with another merchant but could not do so before acquiring a *ghatilayagir* (severance) from his previous masters according to Julfan law or custom. Sinnappah Arasaratnam, who first examined this case, explains: "An Armenian factor, employed by his principals, could not enter into trade by himself or in partnership with others unless he had settled accounts with his former employers and secured a general release and discharge from them."[140] In this case, when the agent's Julfan masters in Madras refused to terminate his contract, the court appointed a team of Julfan merchants and priests in Madras to look into the papers of this factor to determine if he had conducted himself honorably, and decided to release him.

In order for these built-in checks to curb possible opportunism or malfeasance of *commenda* agents traveling with large sums of credit abroad, all agents had to be recruited from the nodal center of the network in Julfa and have family relations there who could be held as bond in return for the trust invested in the agents; moreover, it would be easier to do detailed "background checks" on the reputations of potential *commenda* agents before hiring them if these agents were originally from Julfa. These were the principal reasons that Julfans almost always hired agents from their community. Hiring outsiders from other communities (whether non-Julfan Armenians or, say, Indians or Italians) would have seemed a very risky proposition to Julfans, given the short-term advantages that came with hiring agents from Julfa. Of course, it may be the case that Julfans made much more use of short-term "commission agency" contracts with "outsiders" than I have given them credit for in chapters 6 and 9; at this early stage of our knowledge of Julfan economic history, it appears that few if any commission agency partnerships with outsiders are known to exist. Future research into notarial archives in Europe might turn up evidence that may challenge the findings of this book, but it is unlikely that such evidence will lead to a reversal of the "closed" and essentially insular structure of the Julfan coalition that I have described here. As we shall see in chapter 9, the Julfan system of recruiting agents from inside the coalition had a cost: it prevented the Julfans from truly engaging in "cross-cultural trade." By making their trading habits insular, at least as far as their partnership arrangements were concerned, the Julfans' hiring of only Julfan agents can be considered one of the structural flaws of their system of trade, as it created long-term structural obstacles to the Julfans' diversification and expansion into new markets.

In sum, the evidence indicates that Julfans restricted the hiring of agents to their coalition for two reasons. First, as discussed above, the *commenda* came equipped with built-in mechanisms that enabled Julfans to monitor, and if need be to coerce, their agents and ensure that they did not engage in malfeasance. This coercive approach to ensuring trust, which one may call the "bastinado effect," could not be applied to outsiders who did not reside in Julfa. Second, the reputation-based informal institution and the legally based semiformal institution, which I have called the "AMPC complex," also could not provide adequate mechanisms for monitoring trust outside the coalition. The same factors also account for why powers of attorney and executors of wills were also almost always recruited from the Julfan coalition. In all three cases, the evidence overwhelmingly supports the view that Julfans transacted almost exclusively with fellow coalition members in interactions characterized by high levels of trust. The handful of cases in which foreigners acted as executors for Julfan wills are the exception and not the rule and, for the most part, can be accounted for by the fact that there were few Julfans in the places where the wills in question were drafted.[141]

The arguments presented above about social capital and trust in general and about their role in Julfan commerce in particular allow us to arrive at the following conclusions. First, it seems that for trust to exist as "social capital," a social network ought to have two overriding properties. As Coleman's work suggests, it helps if the network is "closed" to outsiders and if the web of social relations among its members is characterized by multiplex or multistranded ties. The argument for "closure" (Coleman) or "denseness" (Granovetter) appears to fit very well with Greif's notion of "coalition," which I have imported, with some qualifications, into my analysis of Julfan society. A closed and multiplex network or a coalition with strict membership rules allows for, among other things, easier and cheaper social monitoring, based on better information flows, better enforcement of social norms, and more effective application of sanctions for offenders and of rewards for those who comply with the norms. This does not mean that networks, such as the Julfan one, that share these properties are free from internal conflict and tension, that they eliminate all cases of opportunism, or that they are "monolithic" entities whose members always act with a common will.[142] It just means that such networks tend to go a long way in reducing and controlling acts of opportunism and malfeasance committed by their members. Closure and multiplex ties are crucial for communities of long-distance trade, because they tend to increase group cooperation and solidarity, reduce transaction costs by minimizing opportunistic behavior, and may give such networks an edge over others that do not enjoy these same advantages. One excellent example of this kind of "closed" and multiplex network is the ultra-Orthodox Jewish community of diamond merchants based in Brooklyn, where the merchants and their families attend the same synagogues and schools and control over 95 percent of New York's bustling diamond trade, which is located mostly on 47th Street. Observers of this industry have noted the casual confidence with which Jewish merchants deposit bags of diamonds worth several hundred thousand dollars with each other for examination later. Despite the great temptation for opportunistic behavior in these transactions, there are relatively few cases of cheating, because of the closed and multiplex nature of the network that allows Jewish diamond merchants in New York to closely monitor each other's behavior. Our analysis above suggests that Julfan Armenian merchants in the seventeenth and eighteenth centuries operated like their Jewish counterparts in New York City today, except that the Julfan network was much larger in scale and not circumscribed to a few neighborhoods in Brooklyn and a tiny district in midtown Manhattan.

Second, keeping the Julfan coalition or social network closed and numerically small was a built-in and rational feature of the organizational basis of Julfan trade. In other words, an argument can be made that maintaining Julfan identity was not driven primarily by cultural or religious concerns or influences as much of the Armenian-language, nationalist-inspired literature on Julfa would have us believe; on the contrary, it was motivated by the rational economic needs of their network. The network analysis inspired by social capital theory indicates that large networks with porous boundaries decrease trust and trustworthiness and increase transaction costs for network members. This provides a rational incentive for network members to keep their network a manageable size and ensure that its boundaries remain "closed" through persistent policing and monitoring. In other words, for the average Julfan merchant, maintaining his communal affiliation and thereby perpetuating the social identity of the network was a rationally motivated choice.[143] In chapter 9, we shall explore the negative impact of a closed network on its members' ability to expand and diversify into new markets.

8

## The Center Cannot Hold

*The Decline and Collapse of the Julfan Trade Network*

*All networks, even the most solid, sooner or later encountered difficulty or mis-
fortune. And any failing at the center of the network sent out ripples that affected all its outposts, perhaps most of all those on its periphery.*[1]

In his characteristically astute fashion Fernand Braudel remarks that trade networks collapse because of "failings" and attendant complications that occur at their
center but have devastating ramifications beyond the core. Braudel's account of
how trade networks collapse may not apply to all trade networks. For instance,
networks that have multiple centers, such as the Sephardic one in the Mediterranean and the Atlantic worlds, may not be susceptible to the kind of collapse envisaged by the great French historian and may be flexible enough to recover from
severe "shocks" to one of their centers by shifting their weight to another location.[2]
However, networks with a single nodal center regulating commercial life in other
nodes throughout a vast network dependent on the center, as was the case with
the Julfan network, are vulnerable to catastrophic collapse if the nodal center is
damaged beyond repair.

This chapter discusses the decline and collapse of the Julfan trade network in
the eighteenth century. It argues that in the case of the New Julfan network the most
severe "failing" of the network's center occurred in 1746–1747, when Nadir Shah
imposed more than 90,000 *tumans*—an astronomical figure—in taxes on the New
Julfans and allowed his soldiers to systematically loot the suburb. The first section
of the chapter explores how Julfa's decline and collapse have been treated in the historiography of the township and its trade network and rejects the hypothesis advanced by some scholars that Julfa declined and collapsed as a result of the reli-
giously intolerant policies of the Safavid shahs in the late seventeenth century or as
a consequence of the fall of the Safavid dynasty on the heels of the Afghan invasion
and conquest of Isfahan in 1722. The second section focuses on the crucial last year
of Nadir Shah's reign and examines the disastrous consequences of his policies on

the collapse of Julfa as a nodal center. Drawing from hitherto unexplored firsthand accounts of the social and economic situation in Julfa and Isfahan in 1747, this section casts new light on the history of Julfa and Isfahan, offering information not included in standard histories of Nadir Shah's reign.

## THREE VIEWS OF THE JULFAN COLLAPSE

According to some scholars of Julfan history, Julfa's decline began in the waning years of the seventeenth century when Safavid Iran increasingly became a rigid Shi'a state, intolerant of its religious minorities. Harut'iwn Ter Hovhaniants and, following him, Vazken Ghougassian point out that as a result of this atmosphere of intolerance the Safavid state actively encouraged the Julfan Armenians' conversion to Islam and weakened the township's administrative autonomy.[3] While these measures posed serious threats to Julfa's economic welfare and caused the departure of several wealthy Julfan families from Iran, Ghougassian argues that they did not spell Julfa's collapse. Julfa's final collapse, according to him, came in 1722, when the Afghans occupied Isfahan, and brought the Safavid dynasty to an end. Ghougassian explains: "The Afghan occupation of Isfahan, which lasted for seven years, until 1729, brought about the final downfall of the Armenian community of New Julfa. During this period, the economy was in total shambles and the physical security of the people was at stake. Many Armenians, being robbed of their wealth and persecuted, were abandoning their homes in a panic and fleeing to Iraq, India and Russia."[4]

A different interpretation of Julfa's collapse is found in the work of Ina Baghdiantz McCabe, who rejects Ghougassian's conclusions and argues in favor of an earlier dating for Julfa's decline. According to Baghdiantz McCabe, "The decline of New Julfa actually begins much earlier, under Shah 'Abbas II (1642–66), for there was a turning point in Iran's religious policies and strides toward homogenization that targeted minorities."[5] Baghdiantz McCabe then argues that the causes for Julfa's decline should be sought not only in changing religious policies but in the "total change in [the Julfans'] political role within Iran,"[6] which began when their role as "financiers of the khassa ceased" in the 1640s.[7]

Both interpretations are problematic. While it is true that the Afghans imposed a tax of 70,000 *tumans* on the Julfans in 1722,[8] in exchange for sparing the township from the devastation suffered by Isfahan, and that their invasion had deleterious consequences for Julfa's economic welfare, as Ghougassian claims, it is inaccurate to describe this period as ushering in the "final downfall" of Julfa. We know, for instance, that many well-to-do Julfan families managed to survive the Afghans, and the township continued to prosper for several decades after the Afghans took power. The earlier dating for the decline offered by Baghdiantz McCabe is equally untenable for the same reason: Julfan trade continued to expand in the first half of the eighteenth century, notwithstanding the Julfan fall in status that is supposed to have occurred in the 1640s and 1650s. Moreover, the evidence suggests that far from being hurt by the change of status, as Baghdiantz McCabe claims, the Julfan trade network, one could argue, actually reached its climax in the second half of the seventeenth century, thus well after the period she identifies as being a "turning" point in their decline. In fact, Baghdiantz McCabe's dates for the decline of New Julfa do not tally with her own account of Julfan prosperity in the second half of the seventeenth century, if not later. The 1640s periodization is so early in Julfan history that it hardly leaves room for the rise of New Julfan trade.

Edmund Herzig's assessment of Julfa's decline is on the whole carefully reasoned and nuanced. After noting that several prominent European observers, including Raphael du Mans and Jean Chardin, had observed symptoms of economic decline in Julfa by the second half of the seventeenth century, Herzig notes: "On balance, there is little evidence that Julfa's economic basis was seriously undermined until the turn of the eighteenth century at the earliest."[9] Julfa still won the admiration of travelers for "its wealth and thriving population."[10] Herzig also concedes Ter Hovhaniants's assessment that the reign of Shah Sultan Hussain marks the beginning of Julfa's decline, "as extortion by officials and litigation by Armenian converts to Islam began seriously to threaten the wealth of the major merchants, leading to the start of large scale emigration."[11]

Reports by European travelers and missionaries written during the Afghan period, however, all testify that the township continued to thrive during this period. The churches were still functioning as they had in earlier times, and Julfans seem to have worked out a modus vivendi with their Afghan overlords, so much so that some were integrated into high ruling circles because of the services they were able to provide the Afghan rulers. Such, for instance, was the case with Emmanuel Shahrimanian, who acted as the chief secretary to Shah Ashraf's embassy to Istanbul in 1725. Whatever the hardships of Afghan rule, Herzig claims, they were to pale in comparison to the suffering the Julfans endured under the reign of Nadir Shah (1737–1747).

To substantiate his claims, Herzig focuses on the heavy taxes imposed on the Julfans by Nadir. Herzig points out, for instance, that during Nadir's first visit to Isfahan in 1745, the Julfans were forced to pay a tax of 60,500 *tumans,* of which the township's ten leading families paid 23,500 *tumans.* On his second visit in the winter of 1746–1747, the shah levied an additional 30,000 *tumans.*[12] The cumulative effect of such taxes, the attendant insecurity of trade routes going to and from Isfahan/Julfa, and the rampant extortions suffered by Julfan merchants at the hands of corrupt officials all contributed to the mass exodus of Julfa's leading families, many of whom fled with whatever wealth they could manage to take to India, Russia, or the Mediterranean. Herzig sums up the disastrous consequences of this period on Julfa's welfare as follows:

Julfa's demise as a major commercial centre came not in the 1720s with the political collapse of the Safavid state, but in the years after 1745, when Nadir Shah's ruinous taxation and tyranny devastated the economy and society in much of Iran. While the level of taxation was high throughout Nadir's reign, it was the two periods of his residence in Isfahan (December to January 1745/6 and the same period the following year) that caused most damage to the Armenian suburb along with the rest of Isfahan.[13]

## AUTO-DA-FÉ IN ISFAHAN

In addition to the strains of paying heavy taxes, another source of concern for Julfan merchants was the climate of extreme insecurity fostered by Nadir's arbitrary rule. The private merchant correspondence that has survived from the period indicates that this aspect of Nadir's reign was particularly troubling to the merchants.[14] As early as 1745, we come across numerous references in Julfan business letters alluding to Nadir's arbitrary decisions ordering prominent Julfan merchants (usually in their sixties) to "repair to the army," that is, to report to the shah at one of his army camps. Thus, in a company letter written in 1745, Khwaja Emniaz Minasian, one of the pillars of the Julfan merchant community in Isfahan and a merchant who will resurface later in our narrative, informs his correspondents in India:

> On the ninth day of Woftan [read Ovdan, i.e., January 9, 1745], I as well as the Calendar [*kalantar*] and many other Gentlemen were obliged and ordered to go and repair to the army, and there the said Calendar or Governor of Julpha was fined and obliged to pay the sum of Two thousand Seven hundred and Seventy Tomanes, whom [*sic*] they delivered into the Hands and Power of Ashuljan [Ashur Khan?] the Governor of Hispahan thus to bring him to the said Hispahan and there to pay the said sum; and on the Thirteenth of Atham [i.e., May 2] I did arrive at my House in Company of the said Ashuljan, and did my utmost to assist the said Calendar to make up the said Sum of money, he having not so much Cash with him at that time, tho' the nation seems to be backwards in assisting him: I am at a loss to let you know how this affair will end; *The King has also deprived the Calendar of his Post and has appointed another Person in his Room;*[15] the King has done the same with several other Persons, which Causes great Confusions. And you will know the particulars of the whole by the Caravan that set out from hence on the first day of Shephot [read: *sh'bat*; i.e., May 20].[16]

Emniaz concludes his long letter with the intimation that he had just had a very close call and considers himself a lucky man: "It was a particular favour of God that I came off as I did, for three of the Gentlemen that went to it were kept there."[17] As we shall soon see, however, he was not that lucky.

Other letters from the period indicate that Khwaja Emniaz was not alone in his strange experiences. Around the same time as the incident recounted above, Emniaz's nephew Aghamal di Shafraz Minasian, the second most senior member of the Minasian family firm, was also called to "repair to the army," that is, to make an appearance before the shah at his military camp. Again, in a letter written in 1745, another member of the Minasian family informs his brother Astvatsatur in India that "there is no traffic in trade [*yelumut*] in our country and day by day [the economy is in ruins]."[18] He also writes about the king's greed and his desire to find a means of extorting more money from the Julfans. In this connection, he states that the king sent his officials to Julfa to investigate and find the truth [*Hagheghat*<A/P: *haqiqat*, truth, reality] about Julfa's wealth. When the king's officials arrived, three leading members of the Armenian merchant community, including Paron Ohanjan of the Shahriman family, Aghamal of the Minasian family, and Avet of the Khaldarents family, were called to see the king at his *qalat*, or army encampment, where Nadir was temporarily stationed.[19] But things were only to get worse for the Julfans, especially during Nadir's historic second visit to Isfahan.

Nadir passed through Isfahan in December of 1746 on his way to suppressing an uprising in Mashad. He spent forty-five days in the city, during which "all the injustices and cruelties that could be imagined were committed on his orders."[20] His army was spread out in the city and in the neighboring countryside. According to Père Bazin, a Jesuit who served as Nadir's chief physician from 1740 to 1747 and was, therefore, in a privileged position to witness events from close quarters, one could see soldiers running in the streets and roads of Isfahan, mercilessly bastinadoing people and looting homes in their quest to extort money.[21] The city was in a heightened state of confusion and fear. Nadir's excesses seem to have reached a crescendo during this period, so much so that the English traveler Jonas Hanway attests that during his brief stay in the city, the shah "committed barbarities beyond any of the former years of his reign."[22]

Accompanying Nadir in the winter of 1746/47, Bazin likened Isfahan to a city conquered by an assault and abandoned to the fury of the conquering soldiers. According to Bazin's testimony, every day upon leaving the palace he would come across twenty-five or thirty corpses strewn on the streets, all strangled upon Nadir's orders or having been beaten by his soldiers.[23] After describing the chaos and violence in Isfahan during Nadir's short respite there, Bazin provides the following account of an event that would seal Julfa's fate:

> Before his departure, [Nadir] wanted to make an exact stocktaking of all the precious furniture of his palace. A carpet that served to ornament the royal throne had disappeared for about three years. The suspicion fell upon the keeper of the king's jewels. The accused denied having thieved the object, but after a hardy beating with a bastinado, he declared that his predecessor had sold the carpet. And to whom? asked Thamas [i.e., Nadir]. Who would be so daring as to purchase the furniture of my palace? The accused pleaded for some time to look into the matter; he returned a few days later and denounced as the buyers eight merchants, of which two were Indians,

two Armenians, and four Jews. They were all arrested, and after some interrogations they each suffered the loss of one eye. Then all eight of them were tied by their necks to the same chain. The following day, a great fire was lit by the orders of Thamas, where the eight accused were thrown in together and enchained as they were. All the spectators and executioners themselves were aghast at this barbaric execution. This was the first act of its nature that [Thamas] had ordered. And despite all the searches and torments that were employed, the author of this theft remained unknown.[24]

The Carmelite missionaries who were stationed in Julfa and had close ties with the township's Armenian merchants also witnessed this event and wrote a more graphic description of it in their letters home. A report written in February of 1747 describes the incident as follows:

Ever keener to seek pretexts to have money the tyrant one day had summoned to him his chief "keeper of the harness" and reproached him for having thieved a certain horse cloth worked in gold and pearls. The "keeper of the harness" replied or protested that he knew nothing about any such thing: he had three committed to his charge, and he could account for three, as could be clearly seen from the daftar or book of accounts. Without saying more the Tyrant had both his eyes at once put out: then, after a few hours, having had the man again led before him, he threatened to make him die a painful death, unless he at once declared to whom he had sold that horse cloth. The luckless servant, fearing to lose his life, gave the names of four Hebrews, four Zoroastrians, and four Armenians—who were the two brothers Aratun and Peter Shariman, Aqa Nazar and Khwajeh Minas, the first three Catholics and the fourth a schismatic. Immediately diligent search was made for all but for all the zeal used they were never able to find Mr. Peter, for the reason given above that he had hidden himself some days before, nor Aqa Nazar, and two of the four Zoroastrians accused for the like reason that they had escaped or fled.

On 13.1.1747, therefore the others were led into the presence of the Tyrant, viz Mr. Aratun and Mr. Minas, the Armenians, two Zoroastrians and four Jews: and the same day without further inquiry he had one eye of each of them put out, their houses searched, their property confiscated. . . . So he had the poor sufferers again led before him, and without consenting to listen to reasoning or prayers, he gave orders that all of them should be burnt alive in the great square [Maidan i shah] of the city: and because "*jussio Regis urgebat*" (see the book of Daniel, 3–21) that same day, which was 14.1.1747, at the same hour, about four in the afternoon, there was soon lighted a great fire in the Meidan i shah. In it the first to be thrown were the unfortunate Mr. Aratun Shariman and Mr. Minas, bound together by a chain: then the two Zoroastrians, and lastly two by two, the four Jews, all of them "*cum braciis suis et tiaras et calceamentis et vestibus.*"

Mr. Minas died almost at once, because before he was thrown into the flames he had lost consciousness in a swoon; but Mr. Aratun lingered more than an hour in the flames, crying out for mercy and pardon for his sins till he expired. The night after, the relatives searched for their bones and, when recognized, those of Mr. Aratun were interred by the Catholics in the sepulchre of his ancestors, and those of Mr. Minas by the heretics in the Cemetery of the Armenians. Both were sexagenarians and former heads of Julfa.[25]

The Kwhaja Aratun [Harut'iwn] mentioned in this report was a scion of New Julfa's wealthiest Catholic Armenian family, the Shahrimanians, described in chapter 6. Unlike his brothers and sons, who had left Julfa years before and resettled in Venice, Livorno, and Madras, Aratun had decided to stay behind. The Khwaja Minas mentioned in the letter is actually the luckless Khwaja Emniaz, the youngest son of Khwaja Minas di Panos and the most senior member and director of the Khwaja Minasian family firm, also described in the chapter 6.[26]

These two merchants represented two of the wealthiest and most influential families still residing in Julfa in the 1740s. The Carmelite missionaries who witnessed this grizly spectacle noted the horror it struck into the hearts of its spectators and observed in particular how it "ended by throwing into consternation the whole Armenian community, already terrified by the fear of being all put to the sword in accordance with the threats of the barbarian Shah."[27] They also note that Nadir had already warned the community leaders in Julfa during his first visit in Isfahan in 1745 that he had intentions of massacring the entire community, a threat he repeated to the *kalantar* when the latter, following the usual Safavid protocol, went to wish him "a safe journey" on January 21, 1747, when the shah hastily departed with his army.[28] The missionary reports of the period indicate that Nadir's anger with the Armenians was partly explained by the behavior of the Catholicos Ghazar Chahgetsi, the spiritual head of the Armenians residing in Ejmiatsin under Iranian rule, who had earlier taken refuge in Ottoman territory after being unable to pay an exorbitant tax imposed on the church by Nadir.[29]

Julfa's tribulations did not end with Nadir's speedy departure from Isfahan, however. It appears from private correspondence of the period that prior to his departure Nadir had dispatched the governor of Isfahan to Julfa. The governor had turned out to be even more rapacious than Nadir and had used his post to extort money from the residents of both Isfahan and Julfa. He does not appear to be mentioned in any histories of Isfahan during this period, but his deeds during this turbulent and little-studied period are recorded in family and business letters written by Julfans. His name is not given, but he was most likely the same "Ashul Khan" mentioned in earlier correspondence.[30] We know of his deeds thanks to a letter by an Armenian priest named Vardapet Gevorg, written in September of 1747 in Julfa and addressed to a Julfan *commenda* agent in Madras named Paron Mirza di Ovanjan Shicur. After discussing the auto-da-fé incident in Isfahan, Vardapet Gevorg notes:

> Some few months after[,] the King sent to this place a Governor who if possible was worse than the king himself, and he directly laid an Imposition of five hundred Tomanes upon the Inhabitants of Julpha, in consequence of which the principal persons of the place applyyd to the said governor representing to him the impossibility

and difficulty there was to raise the said sum of money, in consideration of the most heavy Taxes that had been lay'd before upon them, but the said governor instead of moderating his demand sent one hundred and fifty soldiers to Julpha, at the sight of which the tradesmen with the lower sort of people rose in a tumultuous manner and were going to oppose the soldiers chusing to die than to be thus so ill treated; and it was thought proper for the principal inhabitants of the nation to go amongst them to desire and prevail with them to be quiet and pacified; an excommunication was also intimated to force them to be easy and to let the whole to the almighty Providence praying to him to free them from such things. The Principal Inhabitants foreseeing the fatal consequences that might proceed from the governors proceedings and con-tumacy and resolution of the people, came at last to resolve themselves to pay amongst themselves the said sum of money, thus to save so many souls and lives that might otherwise been lost; they went to the governor and represented to him that it was im-possible for them to pay the said sum in Cash, and that they would give him the value thereof in Goods, who answered to them that if they would but Pay him what he De-manded, he was willing to take it in any thing, for by his behaviour it seemed as if he would not Stay long in the Place.[31]

Gevorg then recounts how the governor fled Isfahan after learning of Nadir's assassination:

Soon after this happened, the Governor heard that the King was Killed upon which he went away to make his Escape and for fear of the people, which being known by the lower sort of people at Hispahan as well as Julpha they marched after him, over-took him in the Road, and after having killed him, they brought with them his Body to the city of Hispahan in Triumph, saying in a loud voice, there you see the punish-ment that is given to the person who over Tyranized the Good people of the Coun-try; and you must know that this tyrant has caused and done more Cruelties by a vast deal upon the people of Hispahan than upon our people at Julpha.[32]

New Julfa never recovered as a nodal center of a vast network from the blows it received under Nadir Shah's predatory policies. Nadir's assassination in June of 1747, and the enthronement of Ali Qoli Khan as the next ruler under the name of Adel Shah, brought temporary relief and a sense of optimism to Julfans who had remained in their suburb.[33] But these hopes proved to be short-lived, as five different shahs came and went in the two years following the tyrant's assassination, reflecting the period of extreme political and social uncertainty in Iran.[34] In 1750, the township was given as a gift to Kerim Khan Zand, a regional warlord who later came to rule Iran. Yet even his benevolent treatment of Julfa did not suffice to rescue the town-ship from what proved to be an irreversible collapse. In the aftermath of Julfa's ruin, many of the township's wealthy families had already fled from their homes, taking whatever capital they still possessed and settling in the network's peripheral settle-ments, especially in India, where they continued trading during the second half of the eighteenth century.

To understand "how sudden and complete" Julfa's collapse was, we only need to look at the township's ability to muster enough resources to pay taxes during the first half of the eighteenth century. About a decade after Nadir's fateful second visit to Isfahan, tax collectors for Hasan Khan were unable to raise 8,000 *tumans* in Julfa, whereas the Afghans had collected 70,000 *tumans* in 1722, and Nadir Shah 60,000 *tumans* in the winter of 1745/6 and an additional 30,000 *tumans* only a year later.[35]

In 1769, a Catholic missionary in Julfa wrote: "Here the townfolk are poor and wretched both in numbers and in worldly goods."[36] A census taken in Julfa in the following year refers to a population of just 1,667, down from about 20,000 in the first half of the eighteenth century.[37] Herzig best sums up the consequences that Julfa's dramatic collapse in the late 1740s would have in the second half of the century: "As a result of emigration and the forced sale of property to meet tax demands Julfa's exclusively Armenian character was lost, and in the later eighteenth century a considerable part of the population was Muslim."[38]

The ruin of Julfa was apparent to everyone who had lived through Nadir's whirlwind visit to Isfahan in the early days of 1747. A priest in Julfa writing to a correspondent in Madras later the same year remarks: "Both Julfa and Isfahan have been reduced; they are not the same places that you once knew."[39] A Dominican missionary in Julfa, Padri Raymond, writing to Tadeo Sceriman in Venice in 1750, pleads with him to come to terms with the fact that "Julfa does not exist anymore; it has been destroyed and is being destroyed day by day. Only three well-to-do families have remained: (1) the family of Emniaz [i.e., the Khwaja Minasians]; (2) Sev Tsatur's family; and (3) Yohannes di Gaspar's family."[40] A document from 1751, written only a few years after the devastating events that accompanied Nadir's visit, records that "on account of the evil happenings during the past few years, numerous rich merchants [*dolvatavork'*] were subjected to trouble [on account of being compelled to make] large payments, as a result of which many fled and went away, leaving this town empty."[41] Two years later, several members of the once prosperous Khwaja Minasian family who had fled Julfa and taken refuge in Basra wrote the following in a letter to their mother still residing in Julfa and apparently beseeching her sons to return home:

> With what heart and what hope could we return to that country, where every year and every month there is a new king—it must be obvious to all of you that that country does us no good. What became of the Khaldarians—the Shahrimanians, Salenjians, Sakhatunians, Petghians, Jamalians, Gerakians, Karasmankians, Khoja Poghosians, Khoja Safrazians, Franksisians, Agha Tavutianas, Khoja Nigoghosians, Chik Mukelians, Agha Papians, Parsadanians, Meds Shahenians, and all the other families? Honorable Mother you may well know that none of them has remained. We are not going to be their [Persians'] servants. During the time of Kings, under stable conditions and amid a large population they [the said families] perished. Therefore beloved

mother, how are we, four or five families, going to live in that country at a time of con-fusion and instability.[42]

Finally, another Sceriman/Shahrimanian family correspondent in Moscow in-forms Tadeo Sceriman in Venice in 1755 that, according to the news he has received from Iran, "our country [Julfa] is in a pitiful condition, that there is no hope to be expected from it and that out of the four remaining [wealthy] families only the fam-ily of Hovhanjan has survived; and God also save them [from that country]."[43]

## NODES, NODAL CENTERS,
## PERIPHERAL NODES, AND NETWORKS

The question arises as to whether the events described above as having caused the collapse of Julfa's economy actually also led to the collapse of the entire network, as Braudel's comments quoted at the beginning of this chapter would seem to suggest. If they did, then how is the collapse of the entire network to be explained? These questions are related to one of the central arguments of this book, namely, that the Julfan merchant community is best understood not as a "trade diaspora," as con-ventional wisdom would have it, but as a sociological variety of what I have termed a "circulation society," that is, a society defined by its circular relationship to a "nodal center" that shapes and gives life to its network of dispersed settlements or colonies through the circulation of men, capital, information, priests, and women. As I sought to clarify in chapter 1, it is the concept of circulation that infuses dynamism into our understanding of early modern merchant communities and their networks and sheds light on how these communities were able to generate and maintain distinct identities in both economic and cultural terms.

However, in advocating a model of a merchant community that is dependent on a strong nodal center, as the Julfan one clearly was, do we not run the risk of giv-ing too much agency to the center and making the periphery a passive recipient of stimuli emanating from the core? Certainly, the evidence suggests that the Julfan network was quite flexible and characterized by ties that were multifarious, rather than a simple model of circulation in which everything has its source in the center. Even a cursory glance at Julfan settlements scattered along the network seems to suggest that "regional centers" such as Madras in the Indian Ocean or Venice and Smyrna in the Mediterranean or Amsterdam in northwestern Europe possessed their own agency and were not passive recipients of decisions made in the nodal center. To what extent Julfa's regional centers were independent of the center at Julfa and thus, in theory, not only able to survive any catastrophic failures occurring there but also to become alternative nodal centers of a regenerated network is an im-portant question but one that is exceedingly difficult to answer at this early stage of our knowledge of Julfan economic history.[44] One way of tackling this question would be to determine, through rigorous data collection from the archives, roughly what proportion of the capital circulating in the network as a whole emanated from, and was "pumped" into the network from, Julfa. In this respect, we can be fairly certain that during much of the seventeenth century, when Julfa's social and economic security was safeguarded by a strong Safavid state, many if not all of the roughly thirty prominent Julfan families alluded to in Ter Hovhaniants's study were headquartered in Julfa. This would indicate that both capital and information, the two vital "objects" that circulated through the Julfan network via the mechanism of the family firm, had their origin and impulse in the nodal center of Julfa. But data on how many of these families continued to be headquartered in Julfa until the 1740s are scant at best. Preliminary research indicates that some of the elite families had left Julfa as early as the 1690s and the early years of the eighteenth century, although a significant number appear to have remained there until they were forced into exile in the 1740s, when Julfa was already collapsing under ruinous taxation. If we accept this as a reasonable hypothesis, then we can say that the destruction of Julfa by Nadir Shah would have disastrous consequences for the network as a whole and would lead to a severe decline in trading prospects even for those Julfan merchants who had managed to flee Julfa before 1747 with some capital.

In addition to circulating *commenda* agents, information, and capital, Julfa also circulated priests throughout its network. There can be little room for doubt regarding Julfa's preeminent role as a nodal center for the spiritual life of the network. After all, by the last quarter of the seventeenth century, when the Julfan network experienced a dramatic expansion of settlements, especially in the Indian Ocean, New Julfa had become its own diocese with broad administrative autonomy from the Catholicosate in Ejmiatsin and had its own network of churches in India and Southeast Asia in general that were directly controlled by the All Savior's Monastery in Julfa. The priests serving the spiritual and cultural needs of Julfan communities in the East were almost entirely sent from Julfa and played a vital role in maintaining Julfan identity in the network settlements. Moreover, there can be little doubt that Julfa also served as a legal and administrative nodal center for a vast network. As we saw in chapter 7, the suburb's Assembly of Merchants and its auxiliary Municipal Assembly were key institutions for resolving legal disputes, generating and maintaining "social capital" and trust, and ratifying important documents, such as powers of attorney and title deeds. In light of this information, it would be difficult not to see the fatal consequences for the rest of the network of the irreversible damage inflicted on the nodal center.

"Failings" of or shocks administered to the center of a network are not the only factors contributing to the decline and collapse of mercantile networks, as Braudel seems to suggest. Ashin Das Gupta's work on Surat indicates that events taking place on a macro level and beyond the nodal center can also have negative ramifications for a network's overall success.[45] In the Julfan case, the most important sources of such disturbances beyond the center were to be found in the Indian Ocean circuit of the network and were connected to the near-simultaneous decline and collapse of the Muslim empires of Safavid Iran and Mughal India, which had long supported the prosperity of the Julfan network.[46] Both of these empires were "hollow[ed] out" and then collapsed in the first half of the eighteenth century,[47] beginning with the sudden unraveling of the Safavids under an Afghan "tribal breakout" that led to the conquest of Isfahan and toppling of the Safavid dynasty in 1722, followed by the slower breakup of the Mughals in the period after Aurangzeb's death in 1707, which culminated in the capture of Delhi by Nadir Shah in 1739 and the Afghan and Maratha attacks of the late 1740s and 1750s.

In his assessment of how networks decline and collapse, Braudel adds the following thoughts to the quotation that began this chapter:

> However an active network once frustrated always has a tendency to compensate for its losses. Driven out of one region, it may press its capital and the advantages it offers upon another. This seems at any rate to have been the rule whenever a really vigorous and accumulative capitalism was concerned.[48]

That this scenario could in fact occur is demonstrated by the Multani Indian network, which we will briefly analyze in chapter 9. The Multanis, whose network was remarkably similar to that of the Julfans in that both were monocentric networks dominated by strong nodal centers, also suffered a decline followed by collapse when their center at Multan City was destroyed in the early years of the nineteenth century. Unlike the Julfans, however, the Multanis appear to have made a comeback by shifting their base to neighboring Shikarpur, in a way that seems to fit Braudel's sagacious analysis. The Julfans did not recover as a new network with an alternative center. Certainly, the best candidate for such an alternative center in the post-1747 period probably would have been in India and most likely in Madras or Calcutta, where many Julfans relocated both before and especially after the collapse of Julfa. Instead of returning as a new, Madras-based network, the Julfans in Madras appear to have opted for a far more ambitious project by planning to shift their base from India to a new, "imagined" center in the "homeland" of "historic Armenia." This shift was in part due to the fact that their prospects for a commercial comeback in India were severely hampered by the imperializing network of the European East India Companies and especially that of the English East India Company and its state-chartered monopoly in trade. As I have argued elsewhere, faced with decreasing prospects of trade in India, some Julfans in Madras began to "reimagine" and reinvent themselves not only as Julfans, but as members of the larger Armenian "nation."[49] This shift "from coalition to nation," as I call it, can be seen in the remarkable series of publications published in Madras in the 1770s and 1780s by a small group of Julfan merchants and neo-intellectuals, including Shahamir Sha-hamirian, in which republican ideas are formulated in a constitutional treatise for a future republic of Armenia that would not exist on a map for another 140 years or so. Thus, instead of reinventing a new mercantile network (as the Multanis appear to have done) with a new nodal center in India, the Julfans there advocated creating an Armenian national state where they hoped to relocate both themselves and their capital.

But even if the Julfans had not experienced a catastrophic blow to their center in 1747 or faced pressures from the European East India Companies, or had been successful at transplanting their nodal center to India, there are other indications that their network would probably not have endured much longer. As we shall discover in the next chapter, through a comparison of the Julfan network and two other networks, the Julfan network had a structural flaw that would have limited its long-term success, preventing its further expansion and diversification.

9

# Conclusion

## Comparative Thoughts on Julfan Armenians, Multani Indians, and Sephardic Jews

*In an era of when contracts could be hard to enforce, especially across political boundaries, it helped to deal with people who came from the same place you did. . . . In case a trading partner was tempted to cheat you, it helped that their relatives and yours lived near each other. If worse came to worst, there were people you could take your anger out on.*[1]

Most scholarship on "trade diasporas," or long-distance mercantile communities and their networks, has tended to be insular and narrowly focused on a single community of merchants. Little work has been done to conceptualize mercantile communities in a comparative context. As Jonathan Israel puts it, "The role of different diasporas in long-distance trade . . . [has] only rather rarely been systematically compared."[2]

This chapter offers a comparative excursus into Julfan Armenian, Multani Indian, and Sephardic Jewish trade networks and trading practices. The comparison is warranted because the three trade networks were arguably the leading long-distance mercantile communities of the early modern period and hence, either together or separately, can be taken to embody some of the more important traits of other early modern long-distance communities. Moreover, comparing the Julfan network with the Sephardic and Multani networks will be helpful in highlighting the peculiarities of each mercantile community and, for our purposes, will help us articulate more clearly some of the idiosyncrasies of the Julfan trade network and its merchants identified thus far. The chapter will examine the following: (1) how each network emerged, expanded, and eventually declined; (2) how each network was structured in relation to a single "nodal center" of circulation, as in the case of the Julfans and Multanis, or to multiple centers, as in the case of the Sephardim; and, most importantly, (3) how each network used different types of commercial contracts for partnerships to organize long-distance trade. The chapter will conclude by exploring the idea that the choice of a particular type of commercial contract over another could have serious ramifications for a given network's ability to expand into new markets and to police "trust relations" in long-distance trade. It will also explore the possible correlation between a network's structural properties (i.e., monocentric versus polycentric) and its tendency to privilege one form of partnership over another.

## THE JULFAN ARMENIANS

As we saw in chapter 2, the Julfan network had its origins in the mercantile town of Old Julfa on the Safavid-Ottoman frontier. Merchants from this town had become internationally renowned purveyors of Iranian silk in the second half of the sixteenth century largely due to a "global conjuncture" of several otherwise unrelated historical developments, including the inflow of New World silver into the Mediterranean, which increased the purchasing power of European merchants from the Mediterranean; the transformation of Iranian silk into the second most important global commodity after pepper (at least as far as the Levant trade was concerned); and the proximity of Old Julfa to the silk-producing regions of northern Iran. Their pivotal role in the silk trade enabled the merchants of Old Julfa to create a trade network that had already stretched to Mediterranean ports such as Venice and probably extended to South Asia in the closing decades of the sixteenth century.

The Safavid ruler Shah 'Abbas I decided to relocate the Julfans to the outskirts of his new capital of Isfahan in 1604–1605 during the Ottoman-Safavid wars, when much of the region's population was also forcibly displaced and resettled in different parts of Iran. Within a short period after their deportation and resettlement on the outskirts of the Safavid imperial capital, the Julfan merchants had come to preside over one of the greatest trade networks of the early modern period, with trade settlements or nodes spanning several empires, including the three most significant Muslim empires of Eurasia—the Ottoman, the Safavid, and the Mughal empires—as well as Muscovite Russia, Qing China, and all the major European seaborne empires, including the British, Dutch, French, Portuguese, and Spanish. Beneficiaries of and contributors to the Safavid state monopoly of the silk trade under 'Abbas I and of Iranian silk's increasingly important place in the global economy, the Julfans were able to branch out and establish a trade network with four interconnected circuits around New Julfa as a nodal center. Arguably the most important of these circuits was the Indian Ocean, to which the Julfans had access once Hormuz at the mouth of the Persian Gulf came under Safavid control in 1622 following the ousting of the Portuguese garrison there. This move allowed Julfan expansion into the maritime space of the Indian Ocean and the establishment of settlements across all the major trading centers of Mughal India and beyond to Southeast Asia, Canton, and Manila. A second circuit, established in the last quarter of the seventeenth century, spanned Muscovite Russia with settlements in Astrakhan, Moscow, and St. Petersburg. This circuit, in turn, served as a springboard to settlements across the Baltic region and south to Amsterdam and London, thus connecting it to a third, smaller circuit around northwestern Europe. Finally, a fourth circuit in the Mediterranean basin, fully formed by the second half of the seventeenth century, stretched west from Julfa across Ottoman territories to Aleppo/ Iskandarun, Smyrna, Venice, Livorno, Marseilles, and Cadiz on the Atlantic rim and was linked to the circuit in northwestern Europe by the end of the century. These overlapping circuits of the Julfan multinodal network were connected to each other through their convergence in the Isfahan suburb of New Julfa, the nodal center of the larger network, which kept the network's nodes or settlements glued to each other through the continuous circulation of merchants/credit, information in the form of commercial correspondence, some women albeit in small numbers, and priests at least with regard to the settlements in the Indian Ocean, which fell under the jurisdiction of the Armenian diocese centered also in the suburb and with its own religious network of parish churches in the East. Though all the nodes in the network were connected to and subordinate to the nodal center in Julfa, they were not equally subordinate; some nodes clearly played a more important role in the overall functioning of the greater network. This was the case with Madras in the Indian Ocean, Smyrna and Venice in the Mediterranean, and Amsterdam in northwestern Europe, each of which was a regional center to other satellite nodes that were connected to them. I refer to such settlements as "regional centers" to indicate their relative autonomy in structuring the subsidiary nodes that were dependent on them as regional centers.

As chapter 7 has illustrated, one of the most important engines of Julfan expansion into these circuits was a partnership contract known as the *commenda* or the *enkeragir.* Most likely derived from the Islamic prototype known as the *mudaraba* or *qirad,* the Julfan *commenda* was a partnership between a sedentary "capitalist" known as the *ter* or *agha,* usually residing in Julfa, and a younger agent known as the *enker.* The former would provide the capital or necessary consignment of goods (*amanat*), and the latter would supply his labor by traveling on his master's behalf to distant markets and putting the entrusted capital to use by investing it on behalf of the partnership. The *commenda* was usually open-ended and could last from a few years to several decades. Profits resulting from the joint venture would be divided between the master and the traveling agent in accordance with the agreed-upon ratio, usually with 30 percent going to the agent and the rest to the master. The Julfans, as we have seen, had integrated this form of partnership into the basic organizational unit of their trade, namely, the patriarchal family firm in which sons and male cousins were under the supervision of the most senior male member of the extended family and usually lived under the same roof. A Julfan family firm thus had a senior "director" residing in Julfa and a number of junior members of the firm consisting of sons, brothers, and cousins operating in various parts of the Julfan network where the firm had branch offices. In addition to these inner family members, however, Julfan family firms had anywhere from twenty to a hundred *commenda* agents, who were not family members, circulating across the network.

All surviving references to *commenda* agents in Julfan correspondence and all *commenda* contracts known to us indicate that Julfans recruited their agents only from within their "coalition," and none of the available evidence suggests that outsiders ever served Julfans as *commenda* agents. In chapter 6, I argued that hiring agents from inside the community was motivated by the merchants' need to monitor and police "trust relations" in their long-distance trade. Ultimately, Julfans hired only fellow Julfan *commenda* agents because they could control the behavior of their agents overseas by having access to the agents' families back in Julfa. According to Julfan commercial law, a *commenda* agent would normally leave his family in the care of his master while away on his overseas travels. The master was required to look after the needs of the agent's family and subtract the money spent on the family's upkeep from the agent's share of the profits when the latter returned home and gave a proper accounting of his transactions. Agents would normally leave behind family members as "hostages" or collateral in Julfa while they roamed throughout the network, providing Julfan merchants with a built-in mechanism for reducing cases of opportunism or malfeasance. If an agent cheated while away, he knew that his family back home in Julfa would ultimately pay the price. Another built-in feature of the Julfan *commenda* that provided incentives for the Julfans to hire agents from Julfa as opposed to non-Julfan outsiders (Armenians included) was the legal stipulation that *commenda* agents could not engage in agency relations with other Julfans or become "capitalists" themselves by hiring their own agents until they acquired a letter of quittance (*ghatilayagir*) from their original masters testifying that they had lawfully concluded their partnership. This could also function as a check against malfeasance.

In addition to these built-in control mechanisms, Julfans employed a reputational mechanism inside their network to circulate information about the behavior of other Julfans in the network efficiently and thoroughly in the form of gossip and rumor. As we have seen in chapter 7, such gossip occupied an important place in business correspondence that ultimately found its way to Julfa and reached a great number of merchants across the network. Even the priests in the church's own religious network usually included items that we would today regard as gossip or hearsay about fellow Julfans. Such gossip either made or broke the reputation of Julfan merchants, including *commenda* agents. A good reputation, or *hambav* (the Julfan term for both "gossip" and "reputation"), meant that the person bestowed with it could count on the trust and future cooperation of other merchants in the network. Conversely, a broken reputation usually meant some form of banishment from the network and sent signals to other Julfans far and wide not to engage in future relations with the stigmatized person and sometimes also his family members. On the whole, reputational mechanisms functioned quite well for the Julfans and kept cases of opportunism by other Julfans and especially by *commenda* agents to a minimum.

Lastly, in addition to relying on the power of gossip to police the behavior of the network's members and particularly the *commenda* agents, the Julfans had access to what I referred to as the "bastinado effect." This mechanism consisted of the ability to enforce contracts with agents through the meting out of violence or the credible threat of such violence. The evidence suggests that a mercantile court known as the Assembly of Merchants existed in the nodal center of the network at Julfa and was empowered by the Safavid state to adjudicate disputes among Julfan merchants and to enforce Julfan commercial law. In the statutes of Julfan commercial law concerning the rules for *commenda* agency was a clause stating that if an agent's account ledgers were deemed to be incorrect the agent could be imprisoned for up to one year and periodically flogged or bastinadoed. A centralized court institution located in the nodal center of the network and empowered to adjudicate intra-Julfan disputes but with no jurisdiction over non-Julfans also made the hiring of *commenda* agents from inside the Julfan coalition a necessity for Julfans.

Thus the Julfans had good reasons for privileging the *commenda* contract over other forms of partnership, such as commission agencies, in effect making the *commenda* the principal means of their commercial expansion. As we shall see below, however, while the *commenda* had the short-term advantage of curbing malfeasance by agents, it also made Julfan trade insular and thus limited the ability of the network to expand or diversify into new markets. Since the entire population in Julfa probably never exceeded 30,000 individuals (a demographic peak reached in the late 1690s), and since such a small community and its business school could generate only a limited number of trained agents ready to be employed in long-distance trade, it follows that in the long run the Julfan network would probably have encountered a demographic limit to network expansion/diversification. We can only speculate about this, however, since the network, as we have seen, declined and collapsed for reasons that had little to do with economic factors. The political situation in mid-eighteenth-century Iran affected the welfare of the nodal center of Julfa and had devastating ramifications for the prosperity of the rest of the network beyond the center.

Julfa's decline can be traced to the decline of the Safavid Empire itself. It began in the early years of the eighteenth century, when increasing taxation and a climate of religious intolerance under Shah Sultan Husayn (1693–1722) forced a gradual flight of some of Julfa's wealthiest families. The Safavid dynasty's collapse in the aftermath of the Afghan invasion, the conquest of Isfahan in 1722, and the exorbitant tribute of 70,000 *tomans* levied on the Julfans in that same year led to a greater exodus of merchants and tested the township's ability to survive the political turmoil around it. The township survived the Afghan interlude, albeit much diminished in wealth, and continued to show signs of vitality and recovery until the mid-1740s when Nadir Shah began to impose astronomical tributes on Julfa's merchants, culminating in a fine of 90,000 *tomans* during Nadir's visit to Isfahan in December–January of 1746/1747. During this period, Julfa, along with Isfahan, was plundered by Nadir Shah's army, and two of the leading members of the suburb were publicly burned alive at the stake with threats of more punishments to follow upon Nadir's return to Isfahan. The latter event caused a mass exodus of Julfa's remaining mercantile families to locations in the Mediterranean, Russia, and South Asia. The township's centralized mercantile court also appears to have ceased functioning at this time. Julfa was never able to recover from these blows, and in the decades that followed, both the township and the network it once served as the nodal center continued to deteriorate. Both eventually collapsed in the late eighteenth century due to intense monopolizing rivalry from the English East India Company in India. The near-simultaneous "hollowing out" and collapse of the two dominant Muslim empires (Safavid Iran and Mughal India) that had been crucial to the prosperity of Julfan trade only compounded the decline and collapse of Julfa and its network.

## THE MULTANI INDIANS

The Multani Indian trade network closely resembles the Julfan Armenian network on multiple levels. Like the Julfan network, the Multani network was monocentric. Its nodal center was the Northwest Indian city of Multan, one of the most important production centers for cotton and silk textiles as well as an entrepôt for indigo, sugar, and tobacco. Many Indian merchants trading in Eurasia in the early modern period seem to have hailed from Multan, "the principal dispersal point for the Indian mercantile diaspora in the seventeenth and early eighteenth century."[3] The overwhelming majority of Multani merchants were Hindus belonging to different mercantile castes, but there were Muslim Multani merchants as well.[4]

Although merchants from the region of Multan had a reputation for being savvy traders as early as the Delhi Sultanate period in the fourteenth century, their trade network began to expand only in the early modern period.[5] Whereas the Julfan network's expansion in the mid-seventeenth century was an amphibious process, expanding across both land and sea routes, the Multani expansion was predominantly across long-distance caravan routes that took them to Central Asia, Iran, and Russia. Like the Julfans, the Multanis owed their success to a "conjuncture" of several world historical events including, first, the establishment of the four Eurasian empires (Mughal, Ottoman, Safavid, and Muscovite) that also provided the foundations for Julfan expansion and, second, the concomitant state investments in the improvement of caravan routes in Safavid Iran under Shah ʿAbbas I, Afghanistan under ʿAbd Allah Khan II, and Mughal India under Akbar the Great. The European intrusion into the Indian Ocean and attempts to control the maritime routes there also contributed to the Multani network's expansion along the overland caravan routes of Eurasia. By the sixteenth century, Multani traders had branched out and established settlements in Central Asia (in Bukhara, Tashkent, Qazvin, Kashan, and Qandahar), Safavid Iran (in Isfahan, Rasht, Tabriz, Darband, Bandar 'Abbas, Kashan, Kong, and Lar),[6] Ottoman Syria (in Aleppo), and Muscovite Russia (in Astrakhan, Moscow, St. Petersburg, and Archangel). Unlike the Julfans, however, the Multanis were unable to set up a base in the Ottoman Empire (with the exception of Aleppo where they did not seem to have had a solid presence)[7] and were unable to branch out into Europe; moreover, their near-exclusive reliance on overland caravan routes, largely because the maritime routes were increasingly dominated by European powers in the seventeenth century, meant that the Multanis were relatively marginal to the Indian Ocean arena as a whole.[8] In their Eurasian-centered network, however, Multani trade settlements appear to have functioned according to a circulatory logic similar to that of the settlements in the Julfan network; they were linked to each other and to the nodal center in Multan through the circulation of merchants, credit, information, and commodities (such as textiles, for which the region around Multan was justly famous). Given the ostensible absence of proper documentation, such as mercantile correspondence, left behind by Multani merchants, it is difficult to say whether the circulation of information was as critical to the functioning of the Multani network as it was to the operation of the Julfan network, but it seems safe to conjecture that senior directors of Multani family firms would have had to correspond regularly with their agents in the field for their trade to have prospered.

Like the Julfans, the Multanis also relied on family firms and *commenda* agency as their main engines for commercial expansion. Information on Multani family firms and how they incorporated *commenda* agency into their operation is not as readily available as it is for the Julfans. Hardly any Multani commercial documents before the nineteenth century seem to have survived, and there does not seem to be any record of partnership contracts from the seventeenth and eighteenth centuries.[9] This dearth of early documentation has led scholars such as Stephen Dale, Scott Levi, and Claude Markovits to rely on archival documents stored in the Russian, Uzbeki, and British archives, many of which were written by colonial government officials and date from the nineteenth century. Data from this later period are then projected backward to the early modern period in an attempt to explain earlier mercantile customs and practices.[10] Therefore, we know considerably less about the trading practices of Multani merchants than we know about those of the Julfans and must be cautious about drawing definitive conclusions regarding the nature of Multani trading practices and how they compare to those of other mercantile communities. Despite these limitations, however, scholars of Multani trade, especially Levi, have given us a fairly detailed and reliable picture of Multani family firms, which indicates that their organization and structure were similar to the Julfan family firms of roughly the same period. In both cases, family firms were organized on a patriarchal basis with the eldest male member of the family serving as the senior director of the firm and junior members often staffing branch offices in the distant settlements. In addition to having junior family members, Multani family firms also recruited and employed agents from outside the family but based in Multan to staff their branch offices. Many of these agents were sent abroad on a contract known as the *shah-gumastha* partnership, which bore a resemblance to the *commenda* contract employed by the Julfans. "Under this system, a capitalist partner, called the *shah,* advanced the funds to one or several working partners called *gumasthas,* for a specific kind of business operation for a certain duration of time, and was remunerated by a share of the profits."[11] It is not difficult to see the parallels between the *shah* in the Multani network and the *ter* or *agha/khwaja* in the Julfan *commenda* or *enkeragir.* Both were sedentary capitalists who, in general, resided in the nodal center and, in exchange for advancing working capital or a consignment of goods (mostly silk, gems, indigo, and textiles for the Julfans, and cotton textiles and credit to be used to make loans for the Multanis), let their traveling *commenda* agents do most of the work. As we saw in chapter 6, Julfan *commenda* agents usually traveled for up to several decades before concluding their partnerships, while the Multani evidence suggests that their contracts were shorter-term with agents away from home for periods of about three years.[12] In both cases, the partnership contract seems to have originated from the same source: the Islamic prototype of the *commenda* known as the *mudaraba* contract. In both cases, profits were divided between agent and sedentary capitalists in accordance with the agreed-upon share, with agents usually receiving 30 percent of the profits. Moreover, like the Julfan agents, the Multani agents appear to all have been recruited from Multan City and its neighboring regions and to have left their families in the care of their masters. In both cases as well, potential agents appear to have undergone "rigorous training" in accounting and trade before becoming members of family firms, though there does not appear to be evidence of a centralized trade school in Multan as there was in Julfa.[13]

The mechanism for policing trust in the Multani network was also remarkably similar to that of the Julfans. As in the Julfan case, the management of trust relations was closely linked to the Indian variety of the *commenda* or the *shah-gumastha* system, wherein the traveling merchants usually left their family members behind as "detainees" with the *commenda* masters at home, who then took upon themselves the responsibility of paying for the upkeep of these families against money they would later deduct from their agents upon their return. As Levi notes, "It does not seem unreasonable to suggest that, while the firm's agents were living in distant communities in control of considerable amounts of the firm's capital, the firm directors watched over the agents' families as much to reassure the agents of their well-being as to ensure the agents' loyalty and responsible conduct."[14] In other words, the families of agents were held essentially as "hostages" under the care of the *commenda* capitalists back home while the agents circulated, thus ensuring that agents behaved in an honorable fashion. Moreover, if these extralegal control mechanisms failed, the capitalist would hold the agent's reputation hostage, ruining "his reputation and credit, leaving him unaffiliated, uncapitalized and unable to take advantage of the most profitable opportunities."[15]

For both the Julfans and the Multanis, the family firm and the *commenda* partnership were the basic organizational building blocks of long-distance trade. In both cases, the *commenda* partnership was chosen and privileged over other forms of pooling labor and capital, arguably because it was the most suitable form of partnership for long-distance trade, allowing agents to travel abroad for long stretches of time before returning home, and also because it provided a built-in mechanism for monitoring trust. In both cases, the agent who traveled abroad left behind his own family as collateral, thus ensuring that he would conduct trade in accordance with agreed-upon expectations. For both Multani and Julfan merchants, the need to monitor trust meant that agents would be recruited predominantly, if not exclusively, from inside the mercantile community and also from families residing at or near the nodal center. As we shall see later, this reduced the opportunities for both networks to engage in "cross-cultural trade" as far as partnerships were concerned. The Multani network, however, seems to have had probably more instances of short-term partnerships with non-Multanis, but this was determined by political exigencies. As Surendra Gopal and Stephen Dale have noted, when Russian authorities clamped down on Indian merchants in the 1680s by limiting their movements to Astrakhan, Multanis who had previously done business in Moscow and St. Petersburg adapted to their new circumstances by engaging in short-term partnerships with Julfan Armenians and others.[16] The Julfans, by contrast, do not seem to have engaged in short-term partnerships with non-Julfans as much as the Multanis, though there is scattered evidence that they too, on rare occasions, did rely on short-term partnerships, especially with Hindu and Muslim merchants in India as well as French *Compagnie des Indes* officials and private merchants, when the opportunity presented itself.[17]

The most significant difference between the Julfan and Multani networks has to do with the demographic base of each. The Multani network was incomparably larger than the Julfan Armenian network. Whereas the entire population of New Julfa probably never exceeded 30,000 inhabitants, of which only a fraction (probably less than 1,000) ever lived across the network of settlements from the Indian Ocean to the Mediterranean, the number of Multanis living in their settlements across Central Asia, Iran, and Russia was "perhaps in excess of" 35,000, according to one estimate.[18] Population figures for Multan City do not seem to be available, but if the figure of 35,000 Multanis residing and trading across the network is reliable, then the total population of the region of Multan could have been perhaps five to ten times larger than that of Julfa. In Iran alone, there were around 20,000 Multanis, according to Dale, and around 10,000 of them, if Jean Chardin and Engle-bert Kaempfer are to be trusted, lived in Isfahan, where they were engaged in the textile business and more importantly served as *sarrafs,* or moneylenders, some of whom loaned large sums to Julfans.[19] Population size was an important asset for the Multanis; it meant that their expansion into new markets was not curtailed by a shortage of manpower. The Julfans, as we shall see below, would have more than likely declined even if Nadir Shah had not destroyed their nodal center at Julfa in 1747 and even if they had not faced the rivalry of the monopolizing English East India Company in the 1780s and 1790s. Their preference for engaging in partnerships only with members of their own community would have imposed a demographic limit on their ability to expand to new markets, especially in places (such as the Atlantic seaboard) where their presence was negligible or nonexistent. The inherent limitations of the *commenda* partnership would not have affected the Multanis in quite the same way as the Julfans because the Multanis had a much larger pool of agents from which to recruit. In short, given the structural constraints of the *commenda* partnership in both cases, a larger population size meant the possibility of diversification, expansion, and longevity.

Perhaps the most striking parallel between the Multani and Julfan networks is their decline and collapse at roughly the same time. In both cases, the logic of decline and collapse was connected to the failure of state power and the decline of empires. Like Julfa, Multan seems to have experienced its golden age in the seventeenth and early eighteenth centuries, when its members extended into Iran and as far afield as Astrakhan, Moscow, and St. Petersburg and were poised to branch out into eastern Europe. Protectionist measures by the Russian state beginning in the 1680s and culminating in the 1730s, when more restrictions were placed on the free movement of Indian merchants in Russia, curtailed the prosperity of Russia's Multani community and prevented its members from branching out into Europe as the Julfans were able to do.[20] In Iran as well, "political events rather than competition from other merchants had eviscerated the Indian diaspora."[21] The sudden fall of the Safavids following the 1722 Afghan conquest of Isfahan had terrible consequences for the Multanis.[22] But the real causes of the decline of the Multani network were tied to events that affected the stability of the nodal center in Multan itself. Multan's woes began with the decline and disintegration of Mughal power after the death of the last great Mughal emperor, Aurangzeb, in 1707. Mughal power effectively vanished from South Asia following the 1739 sack of Delhi by the Iranian ruler Nadir Shah, leaving a vacuum that others were too eager to fill. A few years after his invasion of northwestern India in 1749, the Afghan monarch, Ahmad Shah Durrani, annexed Multan to his Afghan state. For the next three decades, Multan was ravaged by intermittent warfare between Afghan and Maratha forces, which seriously damaged Multan's textile production center. Multan never recovered from these setbacks, and many of its leading capitalist firms appear to have abandoned the city and relocated their base of operations to Shikarpur in neighboring Sind. The parallels with Julfa's continual decline after the 1722 Afghan conquest of Isfahan, the toppling of the Safavid dynasty, and the final destruction of the city under Nadir Shah in 1747 are striking. In both cases, the damage done to the nodal center led to an exodus of merchants and capital from the center that had devastating effects on the rest of the network. The Julfans were never able to recover from the collapse of their center, while the Multanis appear to have returned in the nineteenth century as Shikarpuris after relocating their base to that city.[23]

## SEPHARDIC JEWS

The Sephardic network has been described by one prominent historian as the "most flexible and widest-ranging" of the early modern period.[24] This network spanned and incorporated seven of the greatest maritime empires of the early modern age: Ottoman, Venetian, Portuguese, Spanish, Dutch, English, and French.[25] Thus, in terms of its wide geographical dispersion, the Sephardic network was very similar to the Julfan network. Two important differences in the nature and structure of the two networks, however, need to be highlighted. First, if networks have centers of gravity, that is, areas where their most decisive and largest number of commercial transactions take place, then the Sephardic network, due to its involvement in the Iberian expansion to the New World and later through the Dutch maritime expansion into the same space, was overwhelmingly centered in the Atlantic, and not the Indian Ocean arena, as was the case for the Julfans. The Julfans, as we have seen, had a spotty presence in the Atlantic, with Cadiz their only settlement whence a handful of Julfans appear to have ventured into the Atlantic. Even then, their numbers there were negligible, as were their ties to the Iberian powers. Unlike the Julfans, the Sephardim were relatively weaker in the Indian Ocean and particularly in Mughal South Asia, and they had virtually no presence in the Safavid and Russian empires.

The second difference between the Sephardic and Julfan networks was that the Sephardic network was not monocentric like the Julfan but was characterized by high levels of synchronic polycentricity. Instead of having one nodal center, the Sephardim had multiple centers—including Lisbon, Amsterdam, Livorno, Hamburg, London, Salonika, and Istanbul—that structured their global network.[26] These geographically dispersed centers acted at times synchronically and simultaneously and at times diachronically and in succession as centers of circulation. One advantage of a polycentric network was that it prevented a sudden and catastrophic collapse due to a "fatal blow" to the nodal center, like the Julfan collapse in the wake of the 1747 destruction of New Julfa and the more drawn-out collapse of Multan in the late eighteenth and early nineteenth centuries.

The Sephardic network originated in medieval Spain and Portugal but came to maturity and expanded as a result of the expulsion of Jews from Spain in 1492. As Jonathan Israel points out, unlike their Ashkenazic brethren in northern and eastern Europe, the Jews of the Iberian Peninsula, despite systematic Christian oppression, were more favorably situated than the rest of European Jewry. Until 1492, they had played a minor role in the economic life of Spain because most of the trade was in the hands of the Genoese, Flemish, and other Christians, and Spain was not a major economic or maritime power. Spanish Jewry was mostly engaged in internal trade. By the time of their expulsion from Spain in 1492, much of Spanish Jewry had forcibly converted to Christianity, thus retaining their property and right to live in their ancestral lands. They were also freed from the oppressive restrictions they had faced as Spanish Jews. The bulk of the nonconverted Jews who were expelled went to the Ottoman Empire and settled in commercial centers such as Salonika and Istanbul, where they were allowed to cultivate their Jewish identity and to live in an atmosphere of tolerance,[27] or else to Portugal where they were forcibly baptized as "New Christians" in 1497. Both Portugal and the Ottoman seaports acted as "the two most decisively situated spaces from which to respond to the new commercial opportunities and participate in the reshaping of the world's trade routes."[28] The Jews and "crypto-Jews" in Spain, Portugal, and the Ottoman Empire all shared "Iberian background, speech, culture, and were frequently linked by close social and family ties."[29]

Just as forced mass expulsion followed by resettlement and a global realignment of trade (including the rise of Safavid Iran as an important exporter in the silk trade) played a pivotal role in catapulting the Julfans to a position of relative advantage in relation to other mercantile communities, so too did the Sephardim benefit from the major realignment of early modern world trade in which the center of the global economy gravitated from the Indian Ocean and Mediterranean to the Atlantic seaboard, following the early phases of Portuguese and Spanish colonial expansion after around 1500. This Iberian expansion, coupled with the near-simultaneous Ottoman conquest of Constantinople in 1453 and the subsequent establishment of Ottoman power in the eastern Mediterranean and Black Sea region, contributed to the expansion and prosperity of the Sephardic network in the early modern period.[30]

Sephardic Jews were ideally placed to benefit from this global shift in trading patterns. By 1550, Portuguese crypto-Jews had established an important niche in the burgeoning Portuguese trade with Brazil, India, West Africa, and the Low Countries. Meanwhile, those who had been given refuge in the Ottoman Empire had began to displace the Venetians, Genoese, and Florentines in the eastern Mediterranean, primarily as a result of direct Ottoman patronage of Sephardic Jews and other Ottoman subjects, and sanctions on Italian or foreign traders.[31] However, the political union of the Spanish and Portuguese crowns in 1580 proved to be perhaps the most important cause of the expansion and consolidation of the linked Portuguese crypto-Jewish and Jewish diasporas, which prompted "the dramatic increase in Portuguese converso immigration into Spain and via Spain (and sometimes also via Brazil or Portuguese West Africa) into Spanish America."[32] With the unification of the crowns, crypto-Jews in Portugal were able to expand into the viceroyalties of New Spain and Peru. There, they formed a formidable trade network that was well situated to link the New World silver metropolis of Potosí (in present-day Bolivia) to Buenos Aires and southern Brazil. Others were established in a number of settlements in the Caribbean and New Spain (Mexico). These merchants "forged the earliest contacts between Spanish America and European countries other than Spain."[33] For instance, the Dutch first began to trade with Spanish colonies through Portuguese New Christian merchants in Puerto Rico, Cuba, and Caracas.

Similarly, when Amsterdam began to eclipse Antwerp in the 1590s as the principal center for trade,[34] and, by the early seventeenth century, had developed enduring trading connections to Iberia, Spanish America, the Indian Ocean, and the Mediterranean, many Portuguese crypto-Jews from Lisbon, Oporto, and Antwerp started to migrate to the city. By 1620, there were around 1,000 Portuguese-speaking Jews in Amsterdam. The Sephardic community of Amsterdam had established "an impressively wide ranging maritime commercial web . . . which was at the same time a social, cultural and religious network."[35]

Amsterdam's community of Sephardic Jews played an important role in Dutch trade with Portugal, Brazil, Madeira, and the Azores. They were the principal beneficiaries of the Dutch expansion across the Atlantic after the founding of the Dutch West India Company in 1621 and the conquest of northeastern Brazil in the 1630s. After the Dutch were forced to abandon their outpost of Recife in Brazil in 1654, there was an exodus of Sephardim to the Caribbean (Jamaica, Barbados, Curacao, and Surinam) and eventually to New Amsterdam (New York). Due to their presence in Amsterdam, the Sephardim were thus able to gain "a significant foothold in the Dutch trade with the Caribbean, Spain, and Italy."[36]

By the 1650s, the Sephardic network had settlements scattered across Europe, the Ottoman Empire, and, in smaller numbers, in the New World. A residual network of crypto-Jews also remained in the Iberian Peninsula and Ibero-America, including Brazil, the Caribbean, Spanish America, and North America. Some Sephardim also expanded into Portuguese, Spanish, Dutch, and British enclaves in the Indian Ocean, but their presence there appears to have been smaller than that of the Julfan Armenians.

One characteristic of the Sephardic network that emerges from this brief survey is its overwhelming, almost exclusive, maritime nature, thus distinguishing the Sephardim from the amphibious Julfans and the landlubbing Multanis. Unlike the Julfans and Multanis, who were confined to particular commodity chains, such as silk, jewels, and Indian textiles, the Sephardim engaged in a wide portfolio of commodities, including sugar, spices, bullion, diamonds, pearls, hides, cacao, and silk.[37] They were also important agents in the North African coral trade with India in exchange for diamonds.[38]

Sephardic involvement in world trade reached its high point during the second half of the seventeenth and first half of the eighteenth centuries with two principal centers, Livorno and Amsterdam, emerging as the leading commercial, religious, and cultural centers of Sephardic life. London lagged behind, despite the impressive presence of 1,700 Sephardim in the city by 1740. London was a secondary node for the Sephardim compared to Livorno, Amsterdam, Venice, Salonika, or Constantinople. London's principal importance for Sephardic trade was the city's crucial place in the corals-for-diamonds trade with Madras, a niche the Sephardim were able to use to their advantage given that the East India Company's normal monopoly privileges did not extend to the diamond trade with India.[39] Here, the Sephardim were able to rely on their network of fellow Sephardim in Livorno (an important market for Mediterranean coral) to carve out a lucrative market.

Just as economic and political realignments in the early sixteenth century were responsible for the expansion and prosperity of Sephardic networks and trade, so too did the realignments of trade in the mid-eighteenth century contribute to the decline of Sephardic fortunes. Israel sums up the decline:

> After the War of the Spanish Succession (1713), and especially during the second half of the eighteenth century, the western Sephardic trade diaspora rapidly lost its general impetus and importance in global trade. The Venetian and Dutch as well as the Ottoman maritime empires rapidly declined while the stream of crypto-Jewish emigration from Portugal and Spain dried up. Portuguese New Christians as an identifiable group ceased to play a significant or distinctive role in Spanish and Ibero-American commerce. The Sephardic community of Hamburg largely disappeared while that in London continued to stagnate. By around 1750, the western Sephardic merchant diaspora could no longer rely on a network of relatives among Portuguese New Christian merchants scattered in commercial centres dotted all over the Iberian Peninsula and Ibero-America and this, in turn, increasingly marginalized the Sephardic trans-Atlantic and international trade network as a whole. As the system lost its impetus and creative drive, and its capacity to adapt, it was increasingly deprived of its usefulness to the remaining great maritime empires, which, then, in turn, accentuated the commercial decline and added to the growing impoverishment and other social problems associated with economic deterioration.[40]

A number of important similarities also exist between the trading practices of Sephardic merchants and those of their Julfan and Multani counterparts in Eurasia. Despite the vast geographical divides separating them, all three relied on family firms and made use of communitarian institutions as well as their far-flung network of kin to structure long-distance trading ventures. According to Francesca Trivellato, the Western Sephardim operating out of their node of Livorno during the seventeenth and eighteenth centuries "used the most traditional model of a family firm: the general partnership," which had no expiration date and in which all members had mutual agency with full liability.[41]

But, unlike the Julfans and Multanis, the Sephardim did not make use of *commenda* contracts to form long-distance partnerships. Rather, they used a contract known as the commission agency. Whereas the *commenda* partnerships used by the Julfans and Multanis were typically open-ended and could last many years and even decades, commission agencies were mostly short-term contracts. Unlike salaried employees, who received fixed compensation, a commission agent normally received a percentage of the value of the transactions he conducted as a commission. A commission agent also assumed full legal responsibility, unlike both salaried employees and *commenda* agents, both of whom carried no liability. To be sure, commission-agency contracts had both advantages and serious limitations connected to trust. Unlike *commenda* partnerships, commission agencies did not normally require codified contracts enforceable in courts of law, and agents generally had wide latitude in making decisions concerning what commodities to purchase at what market rates. These factors made the commission agency a potentially risk-fraught venture. The advantages of venturing into commission-agency relations, however, become evident when the nature of long-distance trade is considered, since sending letters of instructions to distant agents and controlling their activities from a distance could make a difference between making a good investment decision on the spot or missing a valuable and time-sensitive opportunity.

Despite the risks involved in employing commission agencies for their long-distance trade, the Sephardim of Livorno appear to have made wide use of commission agents "with whom they had no personal ties."[42] Since these merchants did not specialize in a particular trade niche and "operated in markets where Jews were not dominant or from which they were personally barred from residing ... [t]hey therefore fared better when they could develop cooperative agency relations with merchants who were neither kin nor direct employees and thus expand their relations."[43] In other words, unlike the Multanis or Julfans, whose long-distance trade was for the most part confined to *commenda* agents hired from inside their communities, the Sephardim of Livorno regularly hired agents outside of their community "for the purpose of expanding their trading networks."[44]

For instance, in order to penetrate the lucrative trade of Mediterranean coral for Indian diamonds in the Portuguese empire in Asia after the mid-seventeenth century, the firm of Ergas and Silvera, based in Livorno, could no longer rely on the descendants of the Silvera family of Lisbon and sought instead to build business ties with Hindu traders residing in Goa and Christians in Lisbon.[45] In the open-ended commission-agency relations between the Sephardim of Livorno and their Hindu agents in Goa, "the only real power [the Sephardim] had to urge [their agents] to be honest and efficient was to threaten to interrupt the flow of orders; this threat too had to be credible and potentially damaging."[46] What kept their agents honest was not necessarily the threat of being hauled off to court (though this could also have been a possibility) or the immediate reward in the form of the commission, but "the prospect of future transactions" and a shared concern for maintaining their reputations.[47] Cultivating cross-cultural reputational mechanisms by generating multilateral channels of information through business correspondence allowed the Sephardim to control cases of opportunism by their overseas agents, who were neither family members nor Sephardic Jews, but strangers linked to the Sephardic network through regular business correspondence and mutual respect for shared customs of trade.

The Sephardic example brings to the fore a number of important organizational contrasts with the networks of the Julfans and Multanis. First, the Sephardic network appears to have been much more flexible in employing outsiders than were the Multani and Julfan networks. As Trivellato convincingly points out, "The Sephardim were more fully engaged in cross-cultural trade . . . than were Armenians. The less formalized and less centralized Sephardic operations relied more on non-kin and strangers as commission agents than Armenian ones did."[48] If we follow Trivellato and take "cross-cultural trade" in its strict sense to mean "prolonged credit relations and business cooperation between merchants who shared implicit and explicit agreements about rules of exchange but who, because of historical patterns beyond their control, belonged to distinct, often legally separated communities,"[49] then by this definition both the Julfans and the Multanis appear to have had rather insular mercantile networks. The overwhelming volume of both Julfan and Multani long-distance transactions appears to have been accomplished through the use of the *commenda* contract, whereby only agents belonging to their network seem to have been hired. As we have seen, both networks privileged the *commenda* over other forms of trade because of certain built-in features that enabled them effectively to monitor trust and keep cases of opportunism to a minimum. In both cases, recruited agents almost invariably came from the nodal center and would normally leave their families in the charge of their *commenda* masters as "hostages" or collateral. Moreover, in the Julfan case at least, we know that their commercial law stipulated that for a *commenda* agent to engage in future trade transactions, either as an agent wishing to work for another sedentary "capitalist" or as an independent capitalist himself, he was legally required to receive a letter of quittance (*ghatilayagir*) from his original master testifying that he had lawfully concluded his transactions. Furthermore, any legal disputes between a Julfan *commenda* agent and other Julfans, including his master, would be resolved in Julfa's centralized mercantile court (the Assembly of Merchants), which was legally empowered to adjudicate disputes between Julfans but does not seem to have had any jurisdiction over non-Julfans. The Multanis, too, appear to have relied on *panchayats* as community councils to adjudicate intra-Multani as well as intracaste disputes. The Sephardim, on the other hand, do not seem to have had a centralized community court, and this could have contributed to making them rely on cross-cultural reputational mechanisms that were part and parcel of their use of the commission agency.

The built-in checks that came with the *commenda* provided enough incentive for the Julfans as well as the Multanis to privilege the *commenda* over other forms of partnership, thus making their networks more insular than that of the Sephardim. Trivellato's groundbreaking work suggests that exclusive networks, that is, networks that depend almost exclusively on agents recruited from inside the community or "coalition," as in the case of the Multanis and Julfans, tend to have a limited ability to expand to new markets and in some cases are inclined either to stagnate due to shortages of skilled manpower or to become specialized in particular markets and commodities. Trivellato observes:

> A trading network composed only of relatives and coreligionists would be limited in its geographical scope and economic specialization. Even a global diaspora such as the one formed by Western Sephardic merchants could not count on the presence of coreligionists in every corner of the world, whether as a consequence of legal limitations or of migratory patterns.[50]

According to Trivellato's illuminating but brief comparison of Sephardic and Julfan merchants, the reason Julfan Armenians were more insular than the Sephardim has to do with the types of legal contracts they used. The implicit assumption is that the Julfans' use of *commenda* contracts over commission agencies contributed to their insularity. Trivellato also suggests that the Julfans' inability to use commission agency and, therefore, to expand into new markets had to do with "their spotty presence in European and Atlantic ports, [which] likely undermined their ability to engage in commission agency with strangers." My argument is slightly different from Trivellato's even as it takes her insights as its point of departure. My view is that the Julfans' lack of use of the commission agency has less to do with their spotty presence in Europe or the Atlantic than with their active privileging of the *commenda* over other forms of partnership; the decision to privilege the *commenda* derived from the Julfans' short-term and well-grounded (i.e., rational) concerns about monitoring trust. The long-term structural limitations of the Julfans' excessive reliance on the *commenda* and their hiring of only coalition agents for long-distance trade become particularly clear when we consider the size of Julfa's demographic base, which never exceeded 30,000 people. Given such low numbers, it should come as no surprise that Julfan settlements in the network were thinly populated, with the largest settlements in India numbering at most a few hundred individuals (Madras in the second half of the eighteenth century had less than three hundred Julfans) while those in Europe probably never exceeded a hundred at any given time. Venice, arguably one of the largest Julfan settlements in Europe, had a maximum Armenian merchant population of seventy individuals in 1750, of whom most but not all were from Julfa; and Marseilles, an important albeit small outpost in the western Mediterranean, had only about twenty to twenty-five permanent Julfan residents residing at the same time in the city between 1669 and 1695 and a total of thirty-eight Julfan merchants taken together for the same period. If we add to this the real possibility that Julfa probably could not produce more than a few hundred trained *commenda* agents at any given time, then the limitations of an insular style of trading based on the *commenda* institution become evident. From a long-term perspective, it does not seem unreasonable to suggest that even if Nadir Shah had not destroyed the nodal center of the Julfan network in 1747, and even if the English East India Company had not provided monopolistic obstacles to the continued prosperity of Julfan trade in India during the last quarter of the eighteenth century, the Julfans would have most likely encountered serious problems due to the structural flaw of their rather insular trading organization built on the *commenda* partnership. It seems unlikely that the same limitations would have applied to the Multanis, given their much larger demographic base.

We can conclude, therefore, that for both the Julfan and the Multani networks the high premium placed on tighter regulation/policing of trust through *commenda* agencies came at the cost of long-term inclusiveness and network expansion. The comparison of Julfan, Multani, and Sephardic networks suggests that a correlation might exist between network structure and choice of contract and insularity or inclusiveness in trading practices. The evidence indicates that the monocentric and centralized structure of the Julfan and Multani networks probably contributed to their insular trading habits and their privileging of the *commenda* over other types of partnerships, while the polycentric and decentralized network of the Sephardim likely contributed to their choice of the more flexible contract of commission agency, which enabled them to become more inclusive with respect to hiring outsiders and to expand their network to larger markets. That only one of the networks examined here—the Sephardic network, located in Europe—had flexible forms of trade that allowed it to be cross-cultural might lead some readers to imagine a European versus Asian pattern whereby the Sephardim incorporated the *modus commerciandi* of European merchants of the seventeenth and eighteenth centuries, while the "Asian" Julfans and Multanis were caught in a closed and insular network. My conclusion, however, is different. I argue that the patterns observed here have more to do with the organization of the different networks than with the geopolitical location of their respective nodal centers. The structure of a network, in this case monocentric (Julfan and Multani) versus polycentric (Sephardic), and not location or culture, is ultimately what accounts for different patterns of trade.

Much of the scholarship on early modern long-distance mercantile communities has relied on the "trade diaspora" paradigm first coined by Abner Cohen in the early

1970s and popularized by Philip Curtin in the mid-1980s. The popularity of this label can be explained, in part, by the rise in the 1990s of "world history," whose exponents have seen "trade diasporas" as ideal communities whose role as "cross-cultural brokers" exemplifies many of the features at the heart of world historians' challenge to nation-statist historiography. Despite its wide appeal and popular use, however, the "trade diaspora" label has yet to be rigorously defined and analyzed. In fact, most scholars who use the label to discuss merchant communities rarely take the trouble of defining it or discussing its analytical properties.[51]

In this book, I have sought, in part, to reassess the usefulness of the "trade diaspora" paradigm for the study of long-distance merchant communities by examining the history of one early modern community of long-distance merchants who hitherto have been studied using the label "trade diaspora." Following a brief examination of the theoretical assumptions underpinning the literature produced by the "trade diaspora" paradigm, I have argued that "trade diaspora" is at best a *descriptive,* and not an *analytical,* category. While it has been useful in helping us paint a broad picture of the Armenian and other merchant communities of the early modern period, its ultimate weakness has been its inability to help us understand *analytically* how this and other merchant communities actually operated. How did merchants belonging to these dispersed communities communicate with one another? What kind of institutional mechanisms did members of such merchant communities rely upon to generate networks of trust and solidarity across the great spaces covered by their communities?

In place of the "trade diaspora" paradigm, I have responded to Claude Markovits's plea for a return to the idea of a trade network and the study of the function of networks in long-distance trade in terms of what he calls the circulation of "men and things." In particular, I have argued that certain long-distance communities of merchants conventionally studied as "trade diasporas" are best understood as "circulation societies," that is, as social formations characterized by the circulation of information, capital or credit, merchants, women, and priests or religious representatives. Of these objects circulating through the networks of long-distance merchant communities, the most important is arguably information in the form of business correspondence.

This book has addressed these issues by focusing on a small community of Armenian silk merchants deported by the Safavid ruler Shah ʿAbbas I from the town of Old Julfa on the Ottoman-Safavid border and resettled on the outskirts of Isfahan in 1604–1606. These merchants managed a remarkable achievement: within a short time following their forced displacement, they came to preside over one of the greatest trade networks of the early modern era. Based upon extensive archival work in multiple languages, in thirty-one archives across twelve countries, this study reconstructs and analyzes the mercantile settlements and communities of the Julfan network, stretching from the nodal center in New Julfa, Isfahan, to London,

Amsterdam, and Cadiz in the West and Mughal India, Canton, Manila, and Acapulco in the East. In the process, it has uncovered key foundational moments in the construction and operation of the "circulation society" of Julfan merchants.

This book has examined a number of issues, including the impact of long-distance trade on the organization of community life. Armenian mercantile settlements in the Indian Ocean, Mediterranean, and northwest Europe and Russia spanned several empires, including the three most significant Muslim empires of Eurasia, namely, the Ottoman, Safavid, and Mughal, as well as several European seaborne empires, such as the British, Dutch, Portuguese, French, and Spanish. Relying on economic sociology and new economic institutionalism, this book has explored the creation of networks of trust between long-distance merchants belonging to the same closed and closely monitored trading "coalition," or socially bounded mercantile community sharing the same codes of conduct and commercial law. What has emerged with clarity from a close reading of thousands of pieces of mercantile correspondence spanning continents and decades is that these men of commerce operated within an ethos of trust and forged ties of cooperation based on an imagined mercantile community. In analyzing the nature of Julfan long-distance communities, I have sought to shed light on what I call the ethos of "transimperial cosmopolitanism," which characterizes Julfan cultural identity and business etiquette.

This study reveals the importance of information networks and communication. While it is not surprising that information sharing was important for merchants in their daily commercial affairs, what is more interesting and unexpected is the role such commercial communication played in maintaining the integrity of the Julfan network as a whole. In the context of the Julfan mercantile sphere, letter writing connected distant *commenda* agents to their masters in New Julfa and also unified the trade settlements on the periphery of the network to the nodal center of the entire network in New Julfa. Finally, this book has placed the study of the Julfan trade network within a larger context of early modern trade, comparing and contrasting the Julfan network with two other exemplary networks from the period, that of the Multani Indians and that of the Sephardic Jews. Through an examination of the structure of these networks and the types of long-distance partnership contracts they employed, this study has concluded that the privileging of the *commenda* contract by the Julfans contributed to the insularity of their network, and that in the long term this insularity, along with the Julfa's small population, would probably have prevented the Julfan network from expanding and diversifying.

# NOTES

## PREFACE

1. Hyam and Henshaw 2003, 7.
2. See Aslanian 2006c.
3. McNeill 1986, 2. I have shifted McNeill's focus on "pattern recognition" away from historical events to data contained in archival documents. Needless to say, this does not mean that the historian is free to disregard or relegate as "background noise" data that contradict or disturb the patterns that he or she discerns.
4. Steensgaard 1974, 8.

## 1. FROM TRADE DIASPORAS TO CIRCULATION SOCIETIES

1. "Forced migrations" of entire populations were a common practice of centralizing monarchs in the Safavid Empire, as in the neighboring Ottoman Empire, and did not affect the Armenians alone. Both sedentary populations (the Armenians and Caucasian Georgians) and nomadic tribes (the Qajars, Kurds, and others) were the target of such policies under 'Abbas I. See Perry 1975, 199–215; and Maeda 2002. See chapter 2 for a discussion.
2. See chapter 2 for a discussion. The original sociological treatment of the synergy between rootlessness and servants of power goes back to Georg Simmel and his treatment of the figure of the European Jew as a stranger and "pariah," qualities that Simmel argued made Jews useful to many European monarchs. For a more recent discussion, see Coser 1972, 574–581.
3. The term "service nomad" has most recently been used by Slezkine (2004), who describes service nomads as an outsider community, usually territorially mobile, with special skills that are deemed useful to a given host society. Jews, Armenians, Parsees, and others are usually referred to as service nomads.

4. Coser 1972. The practice of forcibly removing and resettling talented "outsiders" and promoting them to positions of power was also a feature of Mongol rule in Eurasia. As Allsen notes in his important study of the Mongol conquests, "'The Mongols also preferred 'outsiders' without local connections and networks. To this end, the Mongols made heavy use of foreigners as well as people from the lower strata of society. In either case, recruits with such backgrounds were more likely to remain loyal to the Chinggisids and less likely to identify with local elites" (2001, 199).

5. The terms "gunpowder empires" and "Islamicate" are associated with the pioneering work of Marshal G. H. Hodgson (1975).

6. On "early modern" as a distinct period in world history, see Bentley 2007, 13–33; 1996, 749–770. The best applications of the concept to Eurasian history are Subrahmanyam 1997; Fletcher 1995; Lieberman 2003 and 2009; and Richards 1997. See also Subrahmanyam 1992b, chap. 1.

7. Roemer 1986, 269. On roads and infrastructure in Safavid Iran, see also Floor 2000a, 35–40.

8. My brief comments here are inspired by the discussion in Dale 2002, chap. 1. See also Dale 2010.

9. On the notion of "archaic globalization," see Bayly's influential 2002 essay.

10. Schaffer et. al. 2009, xiv. See also Raj 2009 for an illuminating discussion on go-betweens in eighteenth-century Calcutta.

11. For technology transfers in the textile industry, see Raveux 2010; and Riello 2010. For art, see Landau 2007 and 2010.

12. Raj 2009, 115.

13. Ibid. On the activities of Israel di Sarhat (also written Israel Sarhad or Surhaud), see Seth 1937/1992, 420–429. Alida Metcalf's term "transactional go-between," referring to "translators, negotiators, and cultural brokers" or men and women with "complex and shifting loyalties" (Metcalf 2005, 10) who often facilitated encounters between Europeans and non-European states and cultures in an age of European expansion and "discovery" might also be an appropriate way of describing the role of Khwaja Israel di Sarhat and others like him. For the concept and its application to Portuguese expansion history in sixteenth-century Brazil, see Metcalf, 10–13.

14. On Marcara Avachintz, see Baghdiantz McCabe 1999, 309–311.

15. It should be understood that by the "Julfa dialect" here and elsewhere in the book, I mean the *mercantile* dialect used by Julfan merchants in their correspondence and other mercantile writings from the seventeenth to the mid-nineteenth century. This mercantile dialect had a larger proportion of technical and other loanwords from foreign languages than the dialect that the great linguist Hrachia Acharian studied and classified during the early years of the twentieth century. Even the nonmercantile dialect studied by Acharian was fading away under the influence of the Araratian dialect of Standard Eastern Armenian spoken today by Armenians in Iran and the Republic of Armenia. The mercantile version of the dialect used by Julfan merchants in the early modern period is largely if not entirely extinct today. The best introduction to the Julfa dialect and its grammar is the pioneering work by Acharian (1940), which has been supplemented and translated into English by Vaux (2002). See also the brief grammar, notes, and glossary in the appendices in Herzig 1991a and Aslanian 2007b,

as well as Orengo's helpful study (2000). Note that Acharian's work is not devoted to the mercantile dialect spoken and written by Julfans in the seventeenth and eighteenth centuries. Most of Acharian's texts date from the nineteenth century and almost none are from merchants, thus limiting the value of his manual for those interested in Julfan mercantile papers. According to Torgom Gushakian (1941, 261), the last two places in the Indian Ocean where the Julfa dialect was still spoken as late as the first decade of the twentieth century were Singapore and Batavia, but even there the influence of the Araratian dialect of Standard Eastern Armenian was clearly discernible.

16. Lombard and Aubin 1988, 2.

17. Ibid., 3.

18. Furber 1976, xiv.

19. Readers may consult the classic work of Ter Hovhaniants (1880), which was translated into Eastern Armenian (1980). All subsequent references to this work will provide page numbers in both editions whenever possible.

20. The authoritative account of Iran's silk trade is Matthee 1999. The Julfans' involvement in the textile trade from South Asia to the Mediterranean is explored in Raveux's trailblazing series of essays (see esp. Raveux 2010) but awaits a major systematic study, as does the Julfans' involvement in the gems and diamonds trade. For a brief discussion of the gem trade, see Kiwrtian 1945.

21. For Julfan relations with Armenian merchants from other locations in the "diaspora," see Aslanian 2006c; and Baibourtian 2004. For relations with the Safavid state, see the account in Baghdiantz McCabe 1999; Herzig 1991a; and Matthee 1999. For relations with state authorities in South Asia and the English East India Company, see Aslanian 2006c; and Ferrier 1970a and 1973.

22. Cohen 1971, 267.

23. Braudel 1972, 2: 804.

24. See Markovits 2000, 20 ff.

25. In a footnote immediately following the introduction of his term "trading diaspora," Cohen noted: "The term 'network', which has been suggested as a substitute for 'diaspora' has in recent years been used to cover different sociological phenomena and its use in this context is likely to be confusing. I think the term 'diaspora' can be relatively more easily understood to be referring to 'an ethnic group in dispersal' than the term 'network'" (1971, 267 n. 1).

26. Cohen 1971, 267.

27. Curtin 1984, 2.

28. For an excellent conceptual and genealogical history of the term "diaspora" and its intellectual career in the social sciences, see Tölölyan 1996, 3–36.

29. Three notable exceptions to this are Trivellato 2009, Levi 2002, and Mentz 2005.

30. Cohen 1997. For a critical assessment of this work, see Safran 1999, 255–291.

31. Curtin 1984, 2.

32. Ibid. (emphasis added).

33. For a critical discussion of this point, see Subrahmanyam 1992a, 340–363; also 1990, 337; 1995, 753.

34. Chaudhuri 1985, 224.

35. For the classic formulation, see Ravenstein 1885 and 1889.

36. Cohen 1997, 83–105.

37. Chaudhuri 1985, 226.

38. See Tölölyan 1996 and Safran 1999.

39. For a perceptive criticism of Curtin's work that discusses his notion of distinct cultures, see Trivellato 2003.

40. Subrahmanyam and Bayly 1988, 401–424.

41. For a discussion of "stateless power" and Julfan merchants, see Aslanian 2006c. It should be noted that the Julfans were not, in a sense, "stateless," because they sporadically relied on Safavid and other states to advance their commercial interests.

42. The peddler theory of Asian trade was first expounded by Van Leur 1955. It was popularized and given a new twist by Steensgaard 1974. Steensgaard's denigration of Asian merchants as "peddlers" bereft of economic rationality is a form of economic Orientalism and has been criticized as such by a number of scholars, including Dale 2002, 126–127; and Baghdiantz McCabe 1999, 204.

43. See essays in Baghdiantz McCabe, Harlaftis, and Pepelasis Minoglou 2005.

44. Markovits 2000; Markovits, Pouchepadass, and Subrahmanyam 2003.

45. Markovits, Pouchepadass, and Subrahmanyam 2003, 2.

46. Markovits 2000, 25.

47. Markovits, relying on earlier scholarship on Julfa, apparently does not think that his model of circulation applies to the Julfans (2007, 129).

48. Markovits, Pouchepadass, and Subrahmanyam 2003, 2.

49. Tölölyan 2005, 137.

50. I thank Khachig Tölölyan for this term.

51. Ho 2006.

52. Anderson 1991. See chapter 5 for a discussion that links Anderson's famous concept of "imagined community" to merchant correspondence.

53. Chaudhuri 1985, 204 (emphasis added).

54. Alam and Subrahmanyam 1998, 362. See also Furber 1976, xiv.

55. Alam and Subrahmanyam 1998, 362.

56. Om Prakash raised the idea of "proxy" documentation during the discussion period following his paper at the European Association for South Asian Studies Conference in Leiden, the Netherlands, in June 2006.

57. Margariti 2007, 13 ff. For a general discussion, see also Aslanian 2008a.

58. Ovington 1696, 221–222.

59. Furber 1976, 298–299. I do not mean to imply that there is no Asian "indigenous" language documentation *written by merchants* apart from those in the Julfa dialect. It could, of course, turn out that such documentation has survived in private or family collections but has yet to come historians' attention. For a sampling of several dozen Arabic script mercantile documents composed in the Persian or Arabic language, including some written by Julfan Armenians, see Lansdowne MS 1048, BL; and Sood 2007 for discussion.

60. For the trial of this ship and the background of its cargo of Julfan commercial letters and other documents, see Aslanian 2006c.

61. *Geniza* is a Hebrew word (derived from the Persian *genj,* meaning "treasure") that

refers to an antechamber of a synagogue, where, in the medieval period, documents invoking the name of God were stored before they were ritually "buried." The use of the term in historical circles was first popularized by Solomon Goitein in his 1967 groundbreaking study; see the preface to vol. 1 of Goitein 1967 for a discussion.

62.  The collection was used extensively in the 1850s by Ter Hovhaniants 1880. Since then the only other scholars working on Julfan economic history to have used documents from it are Kéram Kévonian and Michel Aghassian, who used a summary of a single accounting ledger known as a *tomar* in one of their publications. See Aghassian and Kévonian 1999; see also the trailblazing essay by Kévonian in which he transcribes and translates a long *tomar* from the Julfa archives (2007a, 283–370). Harut'iwn Kiwrtian is reported to have photographed hundreds of documents from the All Savior's Monastery Archive on a business trip there in 1937; see Kiwrtian 1944–1945, 28. Ghougassian made a more systematic use of the archives in the 1980s but mostly consulted documents (pontifical bulls, encyclicals, etc.) pertaining to the history of the diocese of the suburb; see Ghougassian 1998.

63.  I owe this information to Willem Floor. See Keyvani 1982, 5; Faroqhi 2005, 36. According to Herzig (1991a, 12), the Afghans destroyed the archives in 1723, and 'Adil Shah completed the destruction in 1748.

64.  To date, only the works of Shushanik Khachikian and Levon Khachikian, Edmund Herzig, and Kéram Kévonian have relied on Julfa dialect documentation, albeit almost exclusively confined to a single collection of three hundred documents stored at the British Library and on a significantly smaller scale than in this work. By contrast, Ina Baghdiantz McCabe and Bhaswati Bhattacharya do not work on Julfa dialect documentation and are therefore compelled to rely excessively on European language sources on the Julfans, which limits their findings.

## 2. OLD JULFA, THE GREAT DEPORTATIONS, AND THE FOUNDING OF NEW JULFA

1.  Will of Mahdasi Aghaval, 1595 (no month or day recorded), "Zanazan niwt'erov grut'iwnner—Ktakner Nor Jugha" [Documents concerning various matters—wills, New Julfa], All Savior's Monastery Archive [hereafter ASMA], folder 28/13.

2.  The other interesting aspect of this document is that, unlike similar documents drafted a few decades later in New Julfa, it contains no seals and is not witnessed by any secular authorities, such as the reigning mayor, or *kalantar,* of the town, but only by the representatives of the Armenian Church (including Bishop Azaria, who later rose to become a catholicos of the Catholicosate of Sis). The will is also written in a broken form of Classical Armenian (*grabar*) and not in the Julfa dialect, the standard vernacular of the town that was later to become the lingua franca of Armenian merchants in New Julfa, the Indian Ocean, and some Mediterranean cities. For a general survey of Julfa, see the pioneering work of Gregorian (1974).

3.  Cartwright 1611, 35–36. Cartwright spent eight days in Old Julfa sometime in the early 1580s, when the town was still "subject and tributary" to the Safavids.

4.  Herzig 1991a, 41.

5.  Chardin 1811, 2: 304: "qu'il ne se peut voir de ville située en un lieu plus sec et plus pierreux."

6. Arakelian 1911, 31.

7. Herzig 1991a, 41.

8. On Old Julfa's strategic location, see Herzig 1991a, 41; Leo 1934, 55; and Arakelian 1911, 28–29. Arakelian, without citing his evidence, states that the "the caravans coming from India would stop at the other shore of the river at the caravansary [on the outskirts of Old Julfa]." If true, this would put Old Julfa at the hub of a hemispheric commercial and information network stretching from India to the Mediterranean already in the sixteenth century.

9. The reference to Tamerlane is from a Turkish account mentioned but not named by Alishan 1893 [*Sisakan*], 410. Alishan's source for this must be Langles's editorial footnote in Chardin 1811, 2: 305, where mention is made of Katib Çelebi's (Haji Khalifa's, 1609–1657) *Gihan Numa,* translated into Latin as *Gihan Numa: Giographia Orientalis,* trans. M. Norberg, 2 vols. (London, 1818). My source for this work is Alam and Subrahmanyam 2007, 9 n. 23.

10. Newbery 1905, 468. Alishan mentions a Catholic church in Old Julfa, indicating that Catholicism had roots among some Julfans long before their resettlement in New Julfa. But the existence of a Catholic Uniate church in Old Julfa is not attested by any other source. See Alishan 1893, 413.

11. Cartwright 1611, 34–35.

12. Szuppe 1986, 93. Szuppe notes that the figure of 15,000 houses appears in some versions of Muratowics' journal as 5,000, which would still be an inflated figure but more accurate. Alishan provides population figures ranging from 12,000 to 40,000 for Old Julfa but does not cite his sources for the highest estimate (1893, 410).

13. See the letter by the Portuguese monk Juan de Rocha from Goa and dated 29 December 1605, reproduced as document 20 in Alonso 1970, 361.

14. Aivazian 1990, 38. On Chardin's figure, see Chardin 1811, 2: 303; and Arakelian 1911, 30.

15. Most English sources from the sixteenth century, including Cartwright and Newbery, use this terminology.

16. All terms except the last three are recorded in Alishan (1893, 410) and are based on his findings in the Venetian archives. Soulpha is the name Georg Tectander uses for the town in his travel account of 1602, *Iter Persicum;* Chinla is how Ortelius referred to the town in his famous world atlas (see below), and Gilgat is the term used by an anonymous English employee of the Moscovy Company (see below).

17. Herzig 1996, 308–309.

18. For a general introduction to the Ottoman-Safavid wars of the sixteenth century, see Savory 1980; Newman 2006, chap. 4.

19. On Old Julfa paying its taxes directly to the Ottoman queen mother, see Alishan 1893, 411. On the similar status of New Julfa in relation to the shah's mother, see Herzig 1991a, 385. According to Babayan 2002, 385, citing Chardin (1811, 5: 315), the tax revenues from New Julfa went to the queen mother to meet her "footwear expenditure" ("taxe de la Chaussure") in accordance with an "old Persian custom . . . [whereby] the revenue from the most famous among the cities of the realm was set aside for the wife of the sovereign as 'footwear expenditure.'"

20. Strabo is quoted in Herzig 1996, 306.

21. Cartwright 1611, 34.

22. Herzig 1996, 41.

23. Herzig 1996, 306. Alishan says that some ascribe Julfa's famous bridge to the Roman general Pompey (1893 [*Sisakan*], 423). Baltrušaitis and Kouymjian refer to an oral legend attributing the building of the bridge to Alexander the Great but discount the legend as improbable. See Baltrušaitis and Kouymjian 1986, 16.

24. This is according to an unnamed Persian historian cited by Alishan. See Alisan 1893, 410. See also Chardin 1811, 2: 305n.

25. Herzig 1996, 306.

26. Alishan raises the possibility that Julfa's prosperity could be attributed to its stone bridge, which was the main crossing of the Aras River, connecting Transcaucasia and Anatolia to Iran and the East. The Julfans also earned revenue from charging customs and transit duties at the caravansaries they had built on both sides of the river. See Alishan 1893, 411. But Alishan overlooks the importance of the Julfans' participation in the silk trade during the second half of the sixteenth century. See below.

27. Kouymjian 1994.

28. See the excellent treatment of this topic, accompanied by helpful graphs, in Kévonian 2007b, 373–376.

29. According to Alishan, the oldest tombstone in Old Julfa seems to date from 1461 (1893, 427); Arakelian testifies to having seen tombstones from 1523, 1528, and 1550 during his trip to the area in 1884 (1911, 32). Others have even suggested that there were tombstones dating back to the seventh and eighth centuries (Alishan 1893, 427). This is highly unlikely and difficult to prove one way or the other, since no such tombstone appears to have survived. Estimates of the number of tombstones that had survived until a few decades ago have ranged from 3,000 to 10,000. Azerbaijani authorities systematically destroyed most of these epigraphic witnesses to the past in the early 1990s and 2003–2004. An earlier wave of destruction occurred in the early twentieth century when Russian authorities built a railway through the region. See Herzig 1996, 319 n. 2.

30. Herzig 1996, 308–309.

31. Edwards 1905, 57.

32. See the "Letter of Master William Biddulph from Aleppo" 1625/1905, 262, 263, 274.

33. Willes 1666/1903, 147.

34. "The voyage of Arthur Edwards Agent for the Moscovy company, John Sparke, Laurence Chapman, Christopher Faucet, and Richard Pingle, servants into Persia An. 1568," in Edwards 1905, 139.

35. Surmeyan 1935, 12–13, 25.

36. Inalcik 1969, 211–213; 1994, 227.

37. Alishan 1893, 412.

38. Ibid. Alishan does not provide a reference to Alessandri's work, but it appears that the work in question is "Commissione a Vincenzo Alessandri veneto legato allo Shàh Thamasp." See Alessandri 1865, 31. Alishan even cites a will by a Julfan merchant in Venice named Shiavalat di Cubat, dated 1574, the original Armenian of which, he states, is missing in the archives. He also refers to a document in the Archivio di Stato di Venezia involving a dispute over a will left by a Julfan merchant who was said to have lived in Venice for fifteen

years. Since the will was written in 1579, the Julfan in question must have resided in Venice since 1565, five years before the first reference to Julfans in the Venetian archives.

39. Herzig 1996, 318.

40. Herzig 1991a, 43. The map to which Herzig refers was included in what is generally considered the first modern atlas in the world. See Ortelius 1570, map 49.

41. Pomeranz 2001, 4; Darwin 2008, 19; and Marks 2007, 12–13.

42. Marks 2007, 12.

43. Herzig does not use the term "Columbian exchange" but does refer to the influx of New World silver into the Mediterranean in the sixteenth century that had a world historical impact on the global economy of the period. The term "Columbian exchange" was coined by Alfred Crosby in 1972 in his pathbreaking book of that title to refer to the global exchange of European germs, bacteria, and disease that decimated the native population of the Americas, and to the New World crops that the Europeans took from their "discovery" of the Americas. The term has since become very influential in the work of many practitioners of world history and undergone some changes. Andre Gunder Frank (1998) makes use of the term, factoring in the immense quantities of silver the Europeans expropriated from South American mines such as Potosí (now in Bolivia) and discussing how they used their New World silver to gain an unfair edge in the "global casino," thus catapulting themselves into the position of dominant actors in the world economy at the expense of Asia and the rest of the world. On the role of New World silver as a global commodity, see Brook 2008, 152–184; Flynn and Giráldes 1995; 2008, 359–387; Subrahmanyam 1991; Braudel 1972, 1: 476–542.

44. Iranian silk appears to have ousted pepper as the dominant commodity for European traders in the Levant and particularly in Aleppo only at the turn of the seventeenth century, when the Dutch East India Company (VOC) and its English counterpart, the East India Company (EIC), began to consolidate the import of Asian spices via the Cape route. See Steensgaard 1974, 160; and Matthee 1999, 24. The Portuguese endeavor to "monopolize" the spice trade did not fully succeed, except for the early decades of the sixteenth century, after which there was a partial "revival" of the Red Sea and Levant routes. The classic works on the revival of these routes in the middle of the sixteenth century are Lane 1940; 1973, 285–294; Boxer 1969; Braudel 1972, 1: 543–570; and Steensgaard 1974. See also Finlay 1994; Subrahmanyam 2007; and Disney 2009, 149–153. Disney offers an important corrective to the seminal arguments first advanced by Lane (1940), who appears to have exaggerated the extent of the recovery of the Levant spice trade. According to Disney, "For most of the seventeenth century, the Portuguese were supplying 75 per cent or more of Europe's pepper imports" (2009, 152). This would seem to explain why Venetian and English Levant traders increased their purchase of Iranian silk in the second half of the sixteenth century, despite the supposed full recovery of the pepper trade on the Levant route, as claimed by Lane and his followers.

45. Herzig 1996, 318.

46. Ibid.

47. On the role of the *qizilbash* in Safavid politics, see Babayan's important book (2002, chap. 10); Savory 1980; Matthee 1999; Babai et al. 2004, 1–43; and Newman 2006, passim.

48. Babayan 2002, 361 ff.

49. Ibid., 356 ff.

50. Savory 1980; Babai et al. 2004; Matthee 2005, 20–21; Babayan 2002, 358.

51. While the comparison of the Safavid *ghulam* to the Ottoman Janissary system could be instructive, one must also be careful not to make too much of such a comparison. Babai et al., in their otherwise important contribution, model their understanding of the Safavid *ghulams* too mechanically on an outdated understanding of the Janissary system in the Ottoman Empire, thus assuming that the "slaves of the Shah" suffered "social death" once they were converted to Islam and therefore lost touch with their preconversion identities. For a good critique of Babai et al.'s work, see Maeda 2002. However, Maeda himself neglects to note that the "social death" paradigm conventionally attributed to the Janissaries has itself been subjected to considerable criticism. For a revisionist take on the Janissary system, see Kunt 1974. For the "social death" paradigm, see the classic work of Patterson 1982.

52. Asher and Talbot (2006, 125) touch upon Akbar's policies, which reorganized his nobility to centralize his power and minimize the influence of the unruly Central Asian nobility that brought his father, Humayun, to power after the brief interlude of Shah Sur's rule. Asher and Talbot refer to a revolt of the Central Asian nobles in 1564–1567 and argue that Akbar decided to replace his fractious Central Asian nobles by promoting Iranian *amirs* and Indian-born princes. The authors argue that these policies were forerunners of those pursued by 'Abbas I some twenty years later, when he was faced with a rebellion by the *qizilbash*. See also Richards 1993, 18–22.

53. Babayan 2002, chap. 10.

54. The term "infrastructural power" was coined by Michael Mann in his influential 1984 essay "The Autonomous Power of the State." Matthee refers to it in his account of 'Abbas's centralizing reforms (1999, 61). "Administrative power" is somewhat similar to Mann's notion and was developed by Giddens (1984, chap. 7).

55. For an excellent treatment of these policies, see Matthee 1999, chap. 3. See also Babayan 2002, chap. 10.

56. Matthee 1999, 70.

57. Ibid., 74 (emphasis added).

58. Savory 1980, 174.

59. Baghdiantz McCabe 1999, 37 and 38.

60. Ibid., 49.

61. Ibid., 36.

62. For the general context, see Matthee 1999, chap. 3; and Savory 1980.

63. Iskandar Beg Monshi 1978, 2: 858–860.

64. In the inscription of Khwaja Khachik's tombstone in Julfa's historic cemetery, he is described as the *k'aghak'apet,* or mayor, of Old Julfa, thus suggesting that the Safavid nomenclature of *kalantar,* later used in New Julfa, was most likely not present in Old Julfa. Khachik died in 1604 shortly before the deportations and was not resettled in New Julfa as Baghdiantz McCabe claims (1999, 52). Khwaja Khachik's two sons, *khwajas* Safar and Nazar, became the first *kalantars,* or mayors, of New Julfa, thus providing administrative continuity between Old and New Julfa. See chapter 7 below. On Khachik's family, see Kiwrtian 1975–1976.

65. Davrizhets'i 1669/1896, 24–25. See also the English translation by Bournoutian (2005, 25–26).

66. Herzig 1991a, 48. Tectander 1877, 52: "A Soulpha, ville forte habitée uniquement par

244 NOTES TO PAGES 33-34

des chrétiens arméniens, la réception fut très cordiale. Pour honorer le roi, on fit des illuminations, les maisons qui, dans ce pays, n'ont point de toits et sont garnies de balcons, furent couvertes de plus de cinquante mille lampions qui brülèrent toute la nuit. Quant à ce qui concerne les autres grandes villes de ce pays qui sont, dit-on, au nombre de cinquante-quatre, l'ambassadeur de Perse les décrira à Votre Majesté Imperiale." (At Julfa, a fortified city populated only by Armenian Christians, the reception [of the shah] was very friendly. Light was used to honor the king; the homes, which in this country have no roofs at all and are furnished with balconies, were covered with more than 50,000 oil lamps that burned all night long. As far as the other large cities of this country are concerned, which are said to number fifty-four, the ambassador of Persia will describe them to your Imperial Majesty.) Tectander was not present for the deportation of the Julfans, as he had already left the region for Europe via Russia in 1604, accompanied by a Persian ambassador. Therefore, he does not include a description of 'Abbas's scorched-earth policies.

67. Herzig 1991a, 48.

68. Sinan Pasha was one of the highest-ranking Janissaries (*yeniçeris*) in the Ottoman Empire. He was born in Messina, Sicily, into the Genoese noble house of Cigala. He was captured by corsairs in Sicily and, as a slave, converted to Islam. Sinan Pasha quickly rose through the ranks to become the grand vizier in the 1590s and then the commander of the Ottoman army sent to repel Safavid forces on the Eastern front. Portuguese sources from the period refer to him as Chigala, while in Armenian sources he is known by his Turkish name Cheghaloghlu, "son or descendant of Chigala."

69. Armenian colophon from 1608, from Hakobyan and Hovhannisyan 1974, 284–291. I have relied on Herzig's translation (1991, 64).

70. Bournoutian 2005, 51.

71. Ibid.

72. Bajets'i 1884, 6. The original passage reads: Եկաք հասաք ի գետն, որ կոչի Արասդդ, խիստ մեծ, որ մարդ առանց նաւի չէ կարիլ անցնիլ։ Ամենայն ժողովուրդն լցին ի մէջն առանց նաւի եւ առանց տաւարի. որն որ անցաւ, որն որ ջուրն տարաւ, որն որ հայրն կանչելոյ, որն որդի ճայնելոյ, որն մայրն կանչելոյ, որն եղբայր ճայնելոյ, որն որ քուր կանչելոյ, որոն որ քահանայ աղաղակելոյ՝ շատտունք ի գետ խեխստեցան։ Ես մեղաւորս այլ գետն կու տանէր. մէկ ջամշի աթի ընկաւ ձեռս, Աստուծոյ դուս եկի. I thank Vartan Mattiossian for kindly supplying me with this transcription. See Ghougassian 1998, 28-29, for a partial excerpt and translation of the original passage. Baghdiantz McCabe (1999, 49) provides a translation of the original passage by Bajets'i but refers to the French translation by Brosset (1837, 224), which is highly inaccurate, since it leaves out the phrase about the absence of boats or cattle in the crossing. Baghdiantz McCabe claims that the harrowing description provided by Bajets'i "was not the lot of the Julfan deportees. . . . The Julfans were privileged and had mounts" (1999, 49). Of course, it could be that the Julfans did not face the hardships (including drowning) described by Bajets'i and virtually every other source discussing the river crossings on the Aras, because the Aras crossing near Julfa was easier, since the river was shallow and not as wide there as in other locations. But Arakel of Tabriz makes it abundantly clear that this was not the case and that mounts were not *readily* available, thus causing many among the Julfans to be swept away by the river. See Bournoutian

2005, 52. Arakel's version is corroborated by the Portuguese monk Juan de Rocha in his letter from Goa dated 29 December 1605; see document 20 in Alonso 1970, 361. Relying on testimony from Father Belchior dos Anjos, another Portuguese monk who was at 'Abbas's camp at the time of the deportations, Juan de Rocha describes the disorderly nature of the deportations, emphasizing the role of Sinan Pasha's (called Chigalla) unexpected advance toward Yerevan, and then states: "Dalí passou a Julfai, cidade principal na das Armenias, aqual em 24 horas fez despeiar, deixando os Armenios muitas riquezas enterradas polas nao poderem levar consigo por ser a gente muita e grandes as pressas, e faltarem cavalgaduras." (From there they went to Julfa, a principal city in the Armenias, which was evacuated in twenty-four hours. The Armenians left many riches buried underground, not being able to carry them with them, being many people, and in a hurry, and lacking mounts.) The main difference between this account and Arakel's is the claim made here that the Julfans were given twenty-four hours as opposed to three days to vacate their town. Father Juan de Rocha also states that 40,000 individuals or 7,000 families were driven to Isfahan from there, which would be an exaggeration if taken as a reference to the population of Julfa, but would be sensible if seen as the total number of Armenians (including Armenians from neighboring cities such as Nakhjavan) brought to Isfahan in the 1604–1605 period. See Floristan and Gil 1986, 213.

73. Bournoutian 2005, 52–53. Alishan notes that some Julfans managed to return to Old Julfa clandestinely despite 'Abbas's attempt to prevent any repatriation. Thus in 1647 several Julfans hosted the French traveler Boulaye le Gouz while he passed through Old Julfa (Boulaye le Gouz 1657, 88). As late as the second half of the nineteenth century, Alishan notes that the town had about eighty Julfan families and five hundred souls, presumably descendants of Julfans who had evaded the deportations or who returned to their homes after the destruction of the town (1893, 420). Chardin, who visited the ruins of Old Julfa in 1673, reported about thirty Armenian families residing there (1811, 2: 304).

74. Herzig 1991b, 64.

75. Ghougassian 1998, 25; Baghdiantz McCabe 1999, 37 and 38.

76. Herzig 1991b, 66.

77. Ibid., 67.

78. Armenian colophon cited in Herzig 1991b, 67. The colophon in question is in Hakobyan and Hovhannisyan 1974, 182.

79. Herzig 1991b, 67.

80. Hakobyan and Hovhannisyan 1974, 738 (translation mine). See also du Mans 1890, 182.

81. Hakobyan and Hovhannisyan 1974, 738.

82. See the translation of this important document in Ghougassian 1998, 201.

83. Ghougassian 1998, 208.

84. See Matthee 1999, chap. 3.

85. There are few primary source accounts of the auction. The best-known account is that of the Italian traveler Pietro della Valle (1843, 1: 58).

86. Della Valle 1: 58. See also the letters sent by the East India Company officials in Baladouni and Makepeace 1998, document 4, 16–18. For a perceptive discussion, see Matthee 1999, 99–101.

87. Matthee 1999, 145. Discussing the implications of the lifting of the royal monopoly, Matthee comments: "The loosening of state control over silk benefited Iran's Armenian merchants far more than the foreign merchants" (123).

88. For "service gentry," see Matthee 1999, 6; the term "service nomad" has been most recently developed in Slezkine 2004, chap. 1.

89. For documentation from the Venetian archives on this merchant-cum-political envoy, see Berchet 1865b, 47–49.

90. Khwaja Sefer's mission to Venice was first documented by Berchet 1865b, 47–49, and discussed in Alishan 1893, 419, 443. For a recent discussion, see Zekiyan 1978b. See also the documentation, overlooked in Zekiyan's otherwise excellent essay, in Gil 1989, 97, 102, 104–105, 119–123.

91. Alishan 1893, 419, 443.

92. See the discussion in Ter Hovhaniants 1880, 40; Herzig 1991a, 68; and Karapetian 1974, 47–50.

93. Boulaye le Gouz 1657, 88.

94. Chardin 1811, 8: 105.

95. De Chinon 1671, 254. The figure of 50,000 is found in Richard 1995, 82. The original report is in Da Seggiano 1953, 316, where Father Giovanni Battista (the head of the Capuchin mission in Syria), reporting about the mission in Isfahan, states: " . . . li Armeni che sono ivi più di cinquanta mila."

96. Fryer 1698, 265. See also Herzig 1991a, 81.

97. Herzig 1991a, 81.

98. Chardin 1811, 8: 103.

99. Tavernier 1688, 157–158.

100. Fryer 1698, 265.

101. For a reliable account of the expansion of Julfa's diocese, see Ghougassian 1988, 30–34.

102. For Julfa's first printing press, see overviews in Nersessian 1980, 21–24; and Ishkhanyan 1977, 351–368; 1981, 49–52; and colophons in Voskanyan et al. 1988, 21–24. Like several other Armenian scholars, both Nersessian and Ishkhanyan mistakenly assert that printing was introduced into Iran by Khachatur Kesarats'i (Nersessian, 21; Ishkhanyan 1981, 50). They overlook the earlier printing press brought into Iran by Carmelite missionaries in 1628/1629 specifically to print in Arabic/Persian script. Not much is known about the Carmelite press, and it does not appear to have produced any books. For references to this press, see Chick 1939, 1: 305–306; and the brief note in Floor 1980, 369–370.

103. On Hovhannes Jughayets'i, see Khachatur Jughayets'i 1905, 118–120; Chiappini 1937; for the colophon of his book published in Livorno in 1644, see Kevorkian 1986, 32–34; and for the colophon of his 1647 book published in New Julfa, Voskanyan et al. 1988, 31. See also Landau 2007, 200–201.

104. Ter Hovhaniants 1880, 1: 40.

105. For a pioneering treatment of Julfa's administrative structure, see Shushanik Khachikian 1988, 37–41. See also the earlier discussion by Levon Khachikian 1966, 176 ff.

106. Coser notes: "When political rulers in absolutist states or empires or bureaucratic empires wish to shore up their autonomous powers so as not to be dependent on feudal re-

tainers, bureaucratic officials, gentry families, or guilds of commoners, they are likely to attract to their court men who have no roots in the society over which these rulers exercise
dominion. Men distant from the underlying population by virtue of alien birth are ideal servants of power. The ruler can afford to be close to them because they are so far removed from
him in the status order they can never threaten his rule" (1972, 574). In the course of his
reflections on this theme, Coser draws parallels between the sociological function of court
Jews in the Habsburg Empire and Janissaries (*yeniçeris*) in the Ottoman realm. His reflections can also easily be extended to the *ghulams* and Julfan merchants in the Safavid Empire.

107. Coser 1964, 880–885.

108. Ibid., 880.

## 3. THE JULFAN TRADE NETWORK I

1. Mauro 1990, 272.

2. The two basic survey histories of Armenian diasporic communities are Abrahamyan
1964–1967 and Alpoyachian 1941–1961. A third survey has recently been published from
an undated manuscript belonging to the great Armenian linguist and philologist Hrachia
Acharian. This posthumously published survey (2002), however, is riddled with careless ty-
pographical errors and sloppy and poor editing (or complete lack thereof), which has allowed many errors of historical fact to creep into the text. Readers should exercise extreme
caution when using this work as a reference.

3. Raynal 1804, 1: 288.

4. Braudel 1984, 490.

5. Kévonian 1998.

6. Ibid., 116.

7. In addition to the author of the itinerary mentioned above, there is an earlier tradition of the visit to southern India of an Armenian merchant known to the locals as Thomas
Cana. Cana seems to have traveled to southern India in the early ninth century and played
an active role in the revival of the Jacobite church of Christianity there. See Seth 1937/1992,
110–111; and Khojamalian, *Patmut'iwn Hndstanay* [History of Hindustan] MS 535, ASMA,
Nerses Shnorhali Library, folio 85. Khojamalian notes the date 538 for the arrival of Thomas
Cana on the southern shores of India. As far as early communities or settlements are concerned, Seth's claim that there was an "Armenian colony" at Benares during the first millen-
nium of the Common Era remains unsubstantiated.

8. Teles e Cunha 2007, 197–252 (200 ff.); and Floor 2006.

9. Van Linschoten 1885, 1: 43. See also Teles e Cunha 2007, 203.

10. Van Linschoten 1885, 1: 233. Already in 1604, an Armenian interpreter named Francisco Gonçales accompanied the Flemish merchant Jacques de Coutre to the court of Bi-
japur. See De Coutre 1990, 174, 175, 177. On De Coutre's travels, see Alam and Subrahmanyam 2007, 343–351.

11. See the accounts of Gaspar Correa and Jao De Barros quoted in Gulbenkian 1995,
103–131.

12. Martin 1931, 335–336.

13. On the Armenians in Agra, see Seth 1937/1992, 2. Seth's claim regarding Akbar's in-

vitation of Armenian merchants is not supported by any known evidence but has been taken at face value by many scholars writing in the field. See also Polatian 1963; and Hosten 1916, 115–194. Hosten does not find any proof for Akbar's "invitation" of Armenians nor for the existence of an Armenian church in Agra at such an early date, though he does provide much evidence for the presence of Armenians in Agra during that time. The *Akbarnama* notes that during Akbar's reign circa 1590 "a large number of Firhingis and Armenians arrived and brought with them China cloths and other goods of that country" (*Akbarnama of Abu-l-Fazl* 1973, 3: 874).

14. On Iskandar and Mirza Zul Qarnain, see Hosten 1916.

15. Seth 1937/1992, 2. Seth provides no references for most of the claims he makes in this work; consequently, it is difficult to assess the veracity of some of his assertions, including this one. Thus one should approach his work with care and rely on his claims only when corroborated by supporting evidence. His source in this case was most likely the appendix to Thomas Khojamalian's rare manuscript, *Patmut'iwn Hndstanay,* folios 98a-100a, where the author (probably relying on oral tradition) briefly mentions the existence of an Armenian "prayer place" in Agra in the second half of the sixteenth century (folios 98b-99a). On the Armenian presence in Agra, see also Bhattacharya's recent assessment (2005, 292).

16. *Travels of Fray Sebastian Manrique (1629-1643)* 1927, 2: 159.

17. Seth 1937/1992, 225–226. Seth does not provide a transcription of the tombstone in question.

18. Akonts 1805, 84–85. See also Richards 1993, 115–150, for background discussion on Shah Jahan.

19. Torgom Gushakian, a legate of the Armenian Patriarchate of Jerusalem, visiting the Armenian communities of South and Southeast Asia during the first decade of the twentieth century, describes the remnants of an Armenian chapel in Surat and conjectures that the first Armenian church of the city must have been built around 1668 and another church (Saint Mary's or Surb Astuatsatsin) built in 1777. Gushakian also claims to have seen at the Armenian church in Bombay an Armenian manuscript copied in Surat in 1658 and contends that in 1788 the Armenian church in Surat had four priests and four hundred parish members—a significant number, if true, for any Indo-Armenian community (1941, 36–37). Nowhere in his account does he mention any tombstones predating the seventeenth century, as does Seth.

20. I thank Elizabeth Lambourn and Asbed Kotchikian for sending me images of some of these tombstones. For an early reference to Surat's Armenian cemetery, see Fryer 1698, 100.

21. On Lahori Bandar or Lahari Bandar, see Habib 1982, maps 5A and 5B. See also the entry "Larry Bunder" in Yule and Burnell 1903.

22. See Hakobyan and Hovhannisyan 1974, 2: 587, and 3: 25.

23. Roques 1996, 116.

24. See Ferrier 1970, 438. Gushakian (1941, 37) mistakenly provides a date of 1668 for the signing of the treaty, and Baibourtyan (2004, 218) incorrectly asserts that the treaty was signed in Surat instead of London.

25. Ferrier 1970, 438.

26. Ibid., 439.

27. Ibid., 442.

28. The authenticity of this tombstone as evidence of Armenian settlement in Calcutta before the arrival of English East India Company employee Job Charnock in 1690 was disputed first by C. R. Wilson, who argued that the stone was an isolated incident and that it was probably brought to Calcutta from somewhere else at a later date (1895, 1: 137 n. 3). Gushakian (1941, 87), visiting Calcutta in 1916, also speculated that the tombstone in question could have been brought from neighboring Bihar, where the existence of Armenian tombstones from the 1640s was well attested. More recently, Bhaswati Bhattacharya, in her comprehensive account of Armenian trade in India, agrees with Wilson (2005, 292 n. 62). While there are credible grounds for doubting the authenticity of the tombstone, as some scholars have, one cannot entirely dismiss the possibility that the tombstone was actually laid there in 1630. Both Wilson and Bhattacharya ignore the fact that the Armenians in India had the habit of building their churches on sites previously used by members of their community to bury their dead. This was the case with the Armenian Church of the Holy Virgin in Madras, which, like the Church of Holy Nazareth in Calcutta, has tombstones predating its construction in the eighteenth century. Therefore, it is possible that the stone in question, dating from 1630, was on site before the church and not necessarily brought over from somewhere else. For an early account of the way the church came to be built, see Anon. 1818, 187–188. This source confirms that the grounds of the church were used as a cemetery by the Armenians in 1707 before they erected the Holy Nazareth church in 1724, but does not mention Armenian presence in the area before the 1690s, when some Armenians from Chinsura, along with some Portuguese, were first invited by the English to settle in their new settlement. The 1630 tombstone belongs to "Reeza Bibi, the wife of the deceased (voghormats) Sookias." Baghumyan's attempt to argue for its historicity is unconvincing (2007, 13–14).

29. I owe this term to Bhaswati Bhattacharya.

30. Seth 1937/1992, 304.

31. The Portuguese had a base in Bandel, a few miles from Chinsura, where they had built a church in 1595. The Dutch VOC established a factory or trade settlement in Hugli in 1635 only to abandon it a year later; they returned to Hugli between 1645 and 1647, but the "seat of the Dutch Directorate of Bengal" was in the village of Chinsura, established in 1656. See Prakash 1985, 41; 1998, 132–133. The English EIC had a factory in Hugli as early as 1651; Prakash 1998, 134. For Hugli's importance as a port town, see Chaudhury 1967, 33–68.

32. Khachikian and Papazian 1984, 281.

33. This seems to have been a custom among Armenian merchants where Armenian churches did not yet exist. For instance, the same Hovhannes mentions in his business diary that he came across an Armenian priest in Patna, where the Armenians did not have a church but were most likely using a private house to perform their religious services (Khachikian and Papazian 1984, 21–22).

34. Subrahmanyam 1990, 218.

35. See the important "legal brief" printed in Paris by one of Hovhannes's brothers, Martin Marcara Avachinz (known among the Armenians as Martiros [or] di Marcara Avakshints or Avakshinents), one of the first regional directors of the French East India Company in India, for his court case against the company in the 1670s. The document (Bibliothèque nationale de France [hereafter BnF], MS fr. 15529) is entitled *Factum contenant l'histoire tragique; pour le Sieur Martin Marcara Avachinz de la ville d'Hispahan, capitale de*

*Perse, conseiller au conseil souverain de l'isle daufine, & directeur des comptoirs de la Compagnie Françoise des Indes Orientales dans les Indes et dans la Perse, demandeur en requeste presentée au conseil de sa majesté du 6 Mars 1676. Et Michel Marcara, son fils.* See also the similar "brief" contained in BnF, MS fr. 8972. Marcara states that he had traveled to India at a young age (most likely in the 1640s) and conducted commerce there with his brothers for many years. For evidence that Martin Marcara Avachintz of Paris was in fact the brother of Hovhannes and Joseph de Marcora of India, see the will of Joseph Marcarian reproduced in Ter Hovhaniants 1880, 1: 198–201; and Richard 1995, 280 n. 389, where Richard quotes a manuscript source written by Marcara in Paris referring to his brothers as *khwajas* "Ovanès and Yusof." Seth (1937/1992, 320) seems to be mistaken when he claims that Hovhannes and Joseph Marcarian were Marcara Avachintz's sons. Seth also states (1937/1992, 304) that the Marcarian family was associated with the establishment of the Armenian community of Chinsura in 1645 but does not provide any sources for this statement. For an insightful discussion of the career of Marcara Avachintz, see Baghdiantz McCabe 1999, 295–225. For a document in the Julfa dialect concerning Marcara Avachintz, dated Paris 1680, see "Namakner—P'ariz" [Letters—Paris], ASMA, folder 289.

36. On John Demarcora, see Anderson 1890, 258–261.

37. According to Manucci (1966, 3: 88–92), the Italian traveler and longtime resident of Mughal India "Abnus" (a corruption of Hovhannes or John) acted as an agent for the East India Company at the Court of Golconda in southern India before his departure for Pegu. His name crops up on numerous occasions in the records of the East India Company's factory in Siam (roughly equivalent to present-day Thailand); see Farrington and Na Pombejra 2007, passim. John or Abnus di Marcara's departure for Pegu is attested in his brother's will (see note 38).

38. Hovsep Marcarian's will is quoted at length in Ter Hovhaniants 1880, 1: 198–201. The original copy of this valuable will was stored in the archives of All Savior's Monastery but seems to have disappeared since it was last used by Ter Hovhaniants in the 1850s. The church in Chinsura was named after Hovhannes (John) Marcarian, whose ornate tombstone was still well preserved inside the church when I visited the town in the summer of 2003.

39. Seth, for instance, dates the decline of Chinsura in the middle of the nineteenth century, arguing: "The once flourishing Armenian colony of Chinsurah . . . was deserted by the Armenians when [Chinsura] lost its commercial importance and they [i.e., the Armenians] transferred their trade to Calcutta about the middle of the last [i.e., the nineteenth] century" (1937/1992, 306).

40. For a full transcription and annotation of this letter, see Aslanian 2006a, 266. The relevant passage is in paragraph 3 of the letter. An English translation can be found in Aslanian 2008c, 379–428.

41. Seth 1937/1992, 325. Seth, as usual, does not provide any sources for this claim, but he more than likely relied on Bolts 1772, 1: 71. Gushakian (1941, 87) also refers to a Mughal *farman* by Aurangzeb as the basis for the settlement of Armenians in Saidabad in 1665, but he too provides no sources.

42. The interesting parallel with the founding of New Julfa as an Armenian suburb of Isfahan sixty years earlier through a *farman* from Shah 'Abbas was first noted by Baghdiantz McCabe 1999, 186.

43. For the Armenian presence in the French settlements, see Manning 1996, 11–12, 123–127, 178–179, 228–232, 234–236.

44. Aslanian 2007a, 165–167. For seventeenth- and eighteenth-century correspondence from Hyderabad/Bhagnagar, see "Namakner—Heydarabad, 1680, 1687, 1758" [Letters—Hyderabad, 1680, 1687, 1758], ASMA, folder 148.

45. Bombay/Mumbai was acquired by Charles II from the Portuguese in 1662 as part of the dowry of Catherine of Braganza; it was leased to the East India Company in 1668 and eventually came to displace Surat as the principal English trade settlement on the west coast of India (Furber 1976, 90).

46. Baladouni and Makepeace 1998, doc. 143, also quoted in Bhattacharya 2008b: 6. The passage comes from doc. 143, not 142 as Bhattacharya claims.

47. For the use of the Mayor's Court by Julfans, see chapter 7.

48. See Aslanian 2004b; Tölölyan 1998; Aslanian 2010; 2007b, chap. eight.

49. We do not have reliable population figures for the eighteenth and seventeenth centuries for many of the settlements in India. Most scholars to date have speculated on this issue and provided inflated and unrealistic figures. For instance, without any evidence, Oshagan (2004, 146) provides a figure of one thousand Armenians in Madras for the last quarter of the eighteenth century. Our significantly lower figure above is based on a letter by a Catholic Armenian priest named Father Manuel Emirzian dispatched to Madras from the Mkhitarist Congregation in Venice in 1771 that mentions forty houses or families of Armenians residing in Madras at the time. See the letter of 6 February 1771 by Father Manuel, in Archivio di San Lazzaro—Mkhitarist Archives, Venice [hereafter ASLaz]. Another source from 1770 (the letter of Sookias Aghamalian, dated 28 June 1770, ASLaz) gives the figure of 150 Armenian men, mostly Julfans and merchants in Madras. In the 1830s, the Armenian community of Calcutta had 505 persons, according to a census whose findings are found in Johannes Avdall, *Census of the Armenian Population of the City of Calcutta* (Calcutta: G. H. Huttmann, Military Orphan Press, 1837), which is quoted in Bhattacharya 2008b, 18 n. 92. In his travel account of a voyage to the East Indies in the 1820s, an Armenian from Constantinople named Paul Peter Lazarovich provides a slightly lower figure of sixty families or around 300 to 360 individuals during the 1820s (Lazarovich 1832, 33 and 43). The same figure of sixty families is provided by Mesrob T'aghiadian, a Calcutta-based Armenian intellectual and writer, in an essay originally published in Calcutta in 1845; see T'aghiadian 1845/1975, 300. The total number of Armenians in India seems to have reached a peak in the 1850s with more emigration from New Julfa. An official census taken by Armenian church officials in Iran and India in 1856 indicated that there were 225 Armenian families in all of India and Southeast Asia at the time, with 113 families (or 622 individuals) residing in Calcutta. See the population breakdown in Ter Hovhaniants 1980, 2: 343–344. See also Ghougassian 1999, 241–242 n. 1. Seth's figure of 20,000 is a pure guess of all the Armenians who might have set foot on Indian soil between 1600 and 1800, which may be true but gives the false and inflated impression that Armenians had large communities in India at any given point in history (Seth 1937/2002, 616). See also Alpoyachian 1961, 362 n. 1 for a figure of 18,000 to 20,000 Armenians residing in India at the height of their presence.

50. As the diocesan center for the Armenian churches in the East, the All Savior's Monastery in New Julfa periodically sent out priests not only to India, but also to the Ar-

menian communities in Pegu and Syriam (both in present-day Burma/Myanmar), as this passage from a letter from Madras dated 1711 indicates: "And I also beg from Your Eminence's generous affection, that, during this monsoon season, you send us three fine priests, two for this place at Madras and one for Pegu, for the [members of the Armenian] community of Pegu are always beseeching us [saying] that they have been left without a priest. It is necessary that you send them [priests]." "Letters—Madras, 1709–1850," ASMA, folder 104.

51. The best scholarly work on the Armenian Church diocese of New Julfa is Ghougassian 1998. However, it barely discusses the initial expansion of the diocese into India and further east.

52. Ter Hovhaniants 1880, 1: 392–393, 419. See also Khachikian 1988, 53.

53. For the colony in Tibet, see Khachikian 1966; and the introduction to Khachikian and Papazian 1984. See also Petech 1952–1956; 1950, esp. 169–170; Csoma 1833; Richardson, 1981; Manucci 1966, 2: 413.

54. Herzig 1991a, 48.

55. Petech 1950, 169.

56. Petech 1952–1956, 1: 29 and 37.

57. Ibid., 1: 4 (letter by Father Felice da Montecchio, Chandernagore, 30 September 1706).

58. Petech 1952–1956, 1: lxxxvii. According to Petech, this small book of catechism was compiled by Fathers Francesco Maria da Tours and Giuseppe da Ascoli in 1707–1708 and was translated into Tibetan by Khwaja Dawith.

59. Csoma 1833, 200–201.

60. Khachikian 1966, 161.

61. Petech 1950, 168.

62. Ibid., 169.

63. The document in question dates from 1757 and is found in Eerste Afdeling Collectie Lubbert Jan, Baron Van Eck (1719–1765), Algemeen Rijksarchief [hereafter ARA], folder 44. This is the oldest Julfa dialect document to date concerning the Julfan presence in Burma/Myanmar. It is also one of the few documents in Armenian stored in the Dutch archives. I thank Lenart Bes for bringing it to my attention. The archive of All Savior's Monastery has one Armenian will dating from 1866 ("Zanazan niwt'erov grut'iwnner" [Documents concerning various topics], ASMA, folder 28/12. It could well turn out that archives in Burma/Myanmar, especially the archive of the Armenian Church in Rangoon, might have some documentation about the community dating from the period before the nineteenth century. For treatments of the community's history, see Polatian 1959a, 169–172; Yule 1968; Sarkissian 1987, 15–19; Harvey 1925.

64. Harvey 1925, 543. Harvey's source for this information is the account of the Portuguese traveler Pinto.

65. Polatian 1959a, 170. Polatian does not provide a source for this claim. Polatian's source was most likely Varthema 1863, 112, where the author notes the presence of Christians in Bengal and in the king's army in Pegu in the second half of the sixteenth century and identifies them as Armenians. It should be noted, however, that the editor of Varthema's travels, G. P. Badger, finds this assertion to be dubious.

66. See references to wealthy and powerful Armenians in Burmese politics in Yule 1968, 141. (I thank my colleague Mana Kia for bringing this work to my attention.) As Yule points out, the Kála-woon (superintendent of Western foreigners), at the time of his visit (1855), was an influential Armenian named Makertich (most likely of Julfan origin). Makertich was also the governor of Malun, a frontier district (1). Several advisers to the king of Pegu were also Julfans. See Polatian 1959a for a list of such individuals.

67. Harvey 1925, 346.

68. Hamilton 1930, 2: 34.

69. Ibid., 22–23.

70. Ibid., 1: 203.

71. Documenti Armeni Mercantile, Archivio di Stato di Venezia [hereafter ASV], busta 2.

72. The merchant was John (Hovhannes) De Marcora (i.e., di Marcara), the brother of Marcara Avachintz. His resettlement from Hyderabad to Pegu is mentioned in his brother's will. See note 38 above.

73. Before building their own church in Syriam, Armenians financially supported the building of a Portuguese church in the city. According to Harvey, "It was an Armenian who supplied the funds for the building of the Syriam church [by the Portuguese]" (1925, 346n).

74. It is very likely that there were two Armenian churches in Syriam. The first church must have been built before 1743 because during that year, when the Mons rebelled, Syriam was ransacked for three days by the Burmese, and Armenian, French, and Portuguese churches were plundered, as were their warehouses. See Sarkissian 1987, 18; and esp. Abrahamyan 1964–1967, 2: 285–286. Abrahamyan mistakenly provides the date for the Mon rebellion and ensuing conquest and looting of Syriam as 1756 instead of the generally accepted 1743. He also states that the Armenian church was burned down at this time, which might explain the existence of another church in 1756.

75. The information on churches is from Acharian 2002, 317. See also Gasparian 1950.

76. "Letters—Madras," 1711, ASMA, folder 104.

77. See sources in note 66 for the political role played by Julfans in Burma. On portfolio capitalists, see Subrahmanyam and Bayly 1988, 401–424.

78. Lieberman 1984, 159. For scattered references to Julfans in eighteenth- and nineteenth-century Burma, see Lieberman, 156–159.

79. Bayly 1996, 122.

80. Eerste Afdeling Collectie Lubbert Jan, Baron Van Eck (1719–1765), ARA, folder 44.

81. Jughayetsi, Constant, *Vasn norahas mankants' ew yeritasartats' vacharakanats' khrat* [Concerning advice to the adolescent and to young merchants], more commonly known as *Ashkharazhoghov* [Compendium], ASMA, MS 64, folios 7–9. For literature on Armenians in maritime Southeast Asia, see Hordananian 1937; Sarkissian 1987; Colless 1969–1975; Anon., "History of the Armenian Community of the Dutch East Indies," in Bakhchinyan 2003; and the collection of documents including rare printed municipal statutes of communities in Java in "Collectie 606 Armen Joseph," invent. no. 6, ARA. For the nineteenth and twentieth centuries, see Wright 2003.

82. Jughayetsi, *Vasn norahas mankants' ew yeritasartats' vacharakanats' khrat,* ASMA, MS 64, folios 7–9.

83. Pires 1944, 2: 269.

84. Hordananian 1937, 16: and Anon., "History of the Armenian Community of the Dutch East Indies."

85. Wright 2003. For an earlier account, see Buckley 1902, 183–185.

86. Froger 1926, 92 and 143. Froger claims that Armenians stopped in Macao and Canton on their way back from Madras to Manila. For a brief discussion of the Armenian presence in Canton, see Polatian 1959b, 276–277. See also the following outstanding articles: Smith and Van Dyke 2003a and 2003b. I thank Paul Van Dyke for sharing these articles with me.

87. Morse 1926–1929, 2: 84–85.

88. Smith and Van Dyke 2003a, 29 and 35. For an excellent study of this merchant, see Smith 2003. See also Van Dyke 2008, 158–159. For the Armenian original of Matheus's will, see "Zanazan niwt'erov grut'iwnner—Cantom [sic], 1794" [Documents concerning various matters—Canton, 1794], ASMA, folder 28d. Smith and Van Dyke 2003b, 44: "After his death, the executing of Matheus's estate became a major ordeal in Macao. Because the estate involved such large amounts of money that were connected to the Macao government, Portuguese officials put many obstacles in the way of collecting the inheritance. Matheus's total receipts came to many hundreds of thousands of Spanish dollars . . . while the total receipts and expenditures of the city of Macao itself in 1797 was a mere 215,390 dollars. If all the funds in Matheus's estate were withdrawn from the treasury at the same time, it was feared that it could bankrupt the city." For further documentation on Matheus's will in Armenian, see the two letters written in 1804 by Armenian deacons at the church in Bombay: "Zanazan niwt'erov grut'iwnner—Bombay ktak" [Documents concerning various matters—Bombay will], ASMA, folder 28/3.

89. For the history of the Iranian community there and for the name's derivation, see Marcinkowski 2002, 25 ff.

90. Anderson 1890, 241. According to Chevalier de Chaumont, a seventeenth-century French traveler in Siam, there were ten to fifteen families of Armenians in Siam in 1685 (1997, 84). This figure seems exaggerated, and we should note that Chaumont is the only source to mention a significant Armenian presence in Siam.

91. "Zanazan niwt'erov grut'iwnner, Nor Jugha, 1643–1699—arevtrakan grut'iwnner vardapetneri knik'nerov" [Letters concerning various matters, New Julfa, 1643–1699—Commercial letters bearing seals of priests], ASMA, folder 5. See the brief discussion of this document in chapter 7.

92. Furber 1988, 16.

93. In his fascinating travelogue, the seventeenth-century Syrian traveler to Mexico Ilyas Hanna al-Mawsuli reports in the early 1680s: "Every year a ship sails to that island [i.e., the Philippines] from Surat; it belongs to two Armenian traders of Julfa who live on that island. . . . No permission is given to any other ship to sail there except the ship of the Julfites" (2003, 102). The reference to the Julfan ship sailing from Surat is most likely to the ship of Khwaja Minas, a resident of Surat and among the first to conduct maritime trade between India and Manila (see below). Mawsuli's claim that the two Julfan shipowners lived in Manila at this early date is unsubstantiated, and it should be remembered that Mawsuli did not visit the Philippines but reported this based on hearsay.

94. The only reliable source that discusses the settlement of Armenian merchants in

Manila is Quiason 1966. Abrahamyan 1964–1967 and Alpoyachian 1941–1961, as well as Acharian 2002, devote a few pages to Armenians in Manila, but these treatments are for the most part not only utterly useless and uninformative, but also misleading, since the authors do not provide any documentation to support their observations. The Archivo de Indias in Seville (Spain) and the Inquisition archives in the Archivo General de la Nación in Mexico City have hundreds of pages of hitherto unexplored documentation on Armenian merchants in Manila, which I am in the process of preparing for publication.

95. Chaudhuri 1985, 105; see also Bhattacharya 2008b, 14.

96. On the Armenian maritime flag used on Julfan ships in the Indian Ocean, see Terteriants 1848; and Anon. 1858, 52. See also Mauro 1990, 273 n. 24; Morse 1926–1929, 1: 174, refers to a "country ship" recorded as visiting Canton in 1723 "flying the Armenian colours." For Cochin, see Aslanian 2006c.

97. Anon. 1858; Aslanian 2006c.

98. Quiason 1966, 37; Moosvi 2007, 107; Seth 1937/1992, 294.

99. Quiason 1966, 39–42.

100. De Souza 1986, 150–151 and 154–155. See also Bhattacharya 2008b.

101. Montero y Vidal 1894, 120–121 (emphasis added).

102. Lockyer 1711, 15.

103. The best work on the Real Audiencia in the Philippines is Cunningham 1919.

104. See the voluminous *autos* from 1680 against an English pilot for the ship *San Buena Ventura* arriving from Indonesia with an Armenian (Julfan) captain: "Copia de los autos origin[al] contra Capitan Franc[is]co de Lacruz de nación Armenio . . . ," Archivo de Indias, Filipinas, 24, R.2.N. 14\4\, folios 1–378.

105. Cunningham 1919, 258; Quiason 1966, 93; and Clarence-Smith 2005, 119. Spanish authorities built the first Parián in 1581 as a ghetto "in imitation of the practice of restricting Jewish residence in European cities. The Chinese ghetto consisted of a town surrounded by a wooden palisade, in which all Chinese were to be confined at night" (Brook 2008, 166).

106. MS Ramo de Inquisición, tomo 857, "Reconciliaciones al Gremio de nuestra Santa Madre Iglesia de Minas di Elias . . . Esteban di Codidyan, todos Armenios dela Secta de cisma Armenio" [Reconciliation to the Holy Mother Church of Minas di Elias . . . Esteban di Cododyan, all Armenians of the Armenian Schismatic Sect], Archivo General de la Nación [hereafter AGN], Mexico City, folio 235. In his 1735 deposition, Nazar di Coyamal (Nazar di Cojamal/Khojamal), like several others before him, attests that in the 1730s he knew of five or six Julfan "heretics" (i.e., non-Catholics) in Manila, and gives their names as Ovan, Sarkis, Raphael, and Basilio, stating that they resided in "Binondo" (this appears to be the name for the Chinatown of Manila) and "barrio del Tulay grande" (a neighborhood close to Santa Cruz) as merchants. The number of Julfan "heretics" referred to by other Julfan converts in Manila as known to them is consistently between seven and ten in the 1730s. If we were to count those Julfans who had already "converted" to Catholicism, the number of Julfans residing in Manila in the first half of the eighteenth century would probably be around fifteen to twenty individuals.

107. Elias Isaac is mentioned as a wealthy Julfan resident and shipping tycoon in Pondicherry during the first half of the eighteenth century. According to the French docu-

ments from Pondicherry, Elias was actively involved in the Manila trade and "had already made three voyages to Manila from the Coromandel when in 1721 the Superior Council suggested that the French Company should invest in his ship" (Manning 1996, 125). According to Indrani Ray, a prominent scholar of French trade in South Asia, "Elias was accorded the title of Chevalier de l'Eperon in consideration of the important services rendered the French Company" (Subramanian 1999, 229). For French documentation on Elias, see *Procès verbaux des délibérations* 1912–1913, 1: 270–271. This Elias is most likely the same "*French Armenian*," an acquaintance of the eighteenth-century English traveler Alexander Hamilton, "who coming from Manilla had the misfortune to lose his ship on that Part of the Coast that belongs to the king of *Sambas* [i.e., on one of the islands of Southeast Asia]" (Hamilton 1930, 2: 79).

108. MS Ramo de Inquisición, tomo 857, AGN, folios 165 ff.

109. See chapter 6 for Santiago's itinerary.

110. Testimonio of Nazar di Aghamal, MS Ramo de Inquisición, tomo 857, AGN, folios 162b–163b. I thank Tatiana Seijas for her help with this document.

111. Testimonio of Gregorio de Xavier, MS Ramo de Inquisición, tomo 857, AGN, folio 220r.

112. See chapter 6 for details on the Sceriman family. Don Pedro was a Sceriman in-law, having married one of the Sceriman daughters named "Maria di Sariman" before departing for Manila and Acapulco. He was also a Catholic Julfan.

113. See the interesting proceedings from his trial, in Inq. 829, exp. 7, AGN, folios 544–560v. For a brief discussion of Don Pedro's trial, see Nunn 1979, 45–46. I am grateful to Vartan Matiossian for bringing Nunn's book to my attention. See the fascinating short study by Seijas 2007.

114. Inq. 829, exp. 7, AGN, folio 549r.

115. Binayan 1996, 59–62. I owe this information to Vartan Matiossian. For the Julfan community in Cadiz, see chapter 4.

116. Thus in an Inquisition report dated 1723 from Mexico City (Inq. 829, exp. 7, AGN, folio 548), we read the following: ". . . that the Armenians who depart from Julfa and other countries where there are more Schismatics than Catholics, upon arriving in Catholic countries, say what they must in order for them to be allowed to reside there and to conduct trade with them [i.e., the Catholics], but in returning to their lands, they declare themselves and live as Schismatics." (Dixo que a dicho en muchas conversaciones que los Armenios que salen de Chiulfa y otros payses donde ay Cismaticos y catholicos en llegando a payses de Catholicos dizen que lo son, porque los dexen contratar y viuir en ellos, pero en voluiendo a sus tierras se declaran y viuen como Cismaticos.)

117. For Khwaja Petros di Woscan, see his will: "The Last Will and Testament of Petrus Uscan," in *Madras Mayor's Court Proceedings,* P/328/60, India Office Records, British Library [hereafter BL], folios 113–289. For a smart discussion of his will, see Mentz 2004; see also Aslanian 2007b, chap. 8; and Bhattacharya 2008a.

118. For a colorful account of a Julfan merchant who converted one too many times and embraced both Sunni and Shi'a forms of Islam as well as Catholicism depending on where he happened to be residing, see Gulbenkian 1970. For *conversos* and crypto-Jews, see Israel 2002.

119. The Philippine Inquisition records, preserved in the Archivo General de la Nación

in Mexico City, contain dozens of *testimonios* by Julfan merchants throughout the seventeenth century and the first decade of the eighteenth century. These documents are extremely useful to historians of long-distance trade because they contain detailed information about trade routes and the itineraries of merchants traveling between Safavid Iran, Mughal India, the Dutch East Indies, the Spanish Philippines, and in some cases Mexico. Their existence was first publicized by Angeles (1980), who described their general contents but did not analyze them in the larger context of Julfa or Indian Ocean trade. They are being analyzed here for the first time. Bhattacharya's claim (2008b, 15) that "researches in the archives in Seville show that Armenians visiting the inquisition for such purposes had to supply their biography for the record" is not only puzzling but incorrect; the Inquisition papers are preserved in Mexico City, not Seville.

   120. The Royal Philippine Company was formed as a rival to the English and Dutch East India Companies. Unlike the other European companies, it has not been sufficiently studied. For two classic studies, see Schurz 1920; and Furber 1935.

   121. This report and the incident it covers are explored here for the first time. I have made use of two manuscript copies of Viana's report. The first is "Methodo que propongo para que la ciudad de Manilla sea el Imporio del Commercio en el Golfo chinico, Madrid, May 12, 1791," "Papeles tocantes a la Compania de Filipinas," tom. I, Egerton 518, BL, Plut. DXVIII. H, folios 217–225. A more complete version with many more accompanying documents is found in Philippine Manuscripts II, Lilly Library Collections, Indiana University [hereafter IU]. The report in question is found in documents 30 and 31 of the latter collection.

   122. Philippine Manuscripts II, IU, doc. 30.

   123. Ibid.

   124. Ibid.

   125. Ibid.

   126. Ibid., doc. 31; and Egerton 518, BL.

   127. See the footnotes appended by Viana to document 31 in "Philippine Manuscripts II," in which he mentions the diocese of the Armenian Catholic Church in Nakhichevan, then under the strict supervision of the Vatican. The same footnotes appear in Egerton 518, BL.

   128. De Zúniga 1893, 1: 264–265.

   129. See the important documents "Real Consulado de Manila," folders 28a and 28b, Bancroft Library, University of California, Berkeley.

   130. Clarence-Smith 2005, 119.

   131. Ho 2006, xxi. To be sure, as Alison Games persuasively demonstrates, English merchants during the early phase of their overseas expansion (1560–1660) did not "elbow their way in" into foreign cultures and trading markets. Unlike their descendants in the late eighteenth century, they exhibited a remarkable degree of accommodation, "cosmopolitanism and adaptability" to foreign settings, including the world of the Indian Ocean (2008, 7).

## 4. THE JULFAN TRADE NETWORK II

   1. Rothman 2006, xiv and 40–81.

   2. For the Armenian community of Aleppo, see Surmeyan 1940–1950, esp. vol. 3; Sanjian 1965, 46; Lehatsi 1936, 318 and 319; Masters 1988; Herzig 1991a, 125–127.

3. Lehatsi 1936, 318 and 319. Simeon was originally from the Armenian community of Zamosts' (Zamość) in Poland. He wrote his travelogue in the course of his pilgrimage to important Christian sites in Italy and the Ottoman Empire at the turn of the seventeenth century. See Bournoutian 2007 for an English translation; for the Turkish translation, see *Polonyalı Simeon'un seyahatnamesi* 1964. Tavernier's figure of 12,000 Armenian inhabitants in the middle of the seventeenth century seems an exaggeration (1688, 58).

4. Sanjian 1965, 46.

5. Matthee 1999, 23–25; Masters 1988; and Herzig 1991a, 125.

6. Herzig 1991a, 126.

7. Surmeyan 1940–1950, 3: 49.

8. Sanjian 1965, 48.

9. Teixeira 1902, 113.

10. Masters 1988, 84.

11. Ibid.; and Sanjian 1965, 261.

12. Sanjian 1965, 49. In addition to holding the honorific title "Khwaja," which was common among Armenian merchants from Iran, Petik was also referred to as a "Chelebi" (a roughly similar title used by the Ottoman Armenians). See Sanjian 1965, 261.

13. Sanjian 1965, 49.

14. Lehatsi 1936, 318. For reasons that remain unknown, Khwaja Petik was beheaded in 1632 on the sultan's orders. See Sanjian 1965, 331 n. 12; and Acharian 2002, 406, where Acharian provides a date of 1634.

15. P'ap'azyan 1990, 104.

16. Sanjian 1965, 49–50.

17. For the Armenian community of Izmir, see Kosian 1899; and Acharian 2002, 549–567; Goffman 1990; Herzig 1991a, 133–134. The three waves of migration are discussed in Acharian 2002, 549–551; and Kosian 1899, 1: 29 ff.

18. Lehatsi 1936, 38.

19. Tavernier 1688, 33, cited by Herzig (1991a, 113), who is reluctant to take the figure at face value. This figure is uncritically accepted by Acharian 2002, 551: and Kosian 1899, 1: 32.

20. Acharian 2002, 549–551.

21. Galland 2000, 107. I thank Olivier Raveux for bringing this work to my attention.

22. Herzig 1991a, 127. See also Matthee 1999, 144–145; and Faroqhi 1994, 505–506.

23. De Courmenin 1632, 342, quoted in Goffman 1990, 52. For the Armenian connection with Smyrna's silk trade, see also Tavernier 1688, 34.

24. P'ap'azyan 1990, 110–111.

25. Simeon Lehatsi notes the following impression about Izmir: եւ սա էր ծովու եզրն [*yal*< T: "seashore"] մեծ սկայլա [<T iskele: "port of call, wharf, seaport town,"] որ ստամպոյայ Մսրալ [<A, Misr = Egypt] Վանատիկնւ սապըզոլւ [? Sakiz/Chios] եւ այլոց կեմիք [<T, *gemi* = "ship" with *grabar* plural marker K] կոլ խաղային եւ բազում Ֆրանկ եւ հոռոմք [Greeks] կային անդ. (1936, 37). (And this was a big port of call on the edge of the sea, where ships from Istanbul, Egypt, Venice, Chios, and other places would frequent and there were numerous Europeans and Greeks there.) I have followed Bournoutian's use of the name Sakiz for Chios. See Bournoutian 2007, 61.

26. See Sarukhan 1925, 19 ff.

27. Sarukhan 1925, 56–58.

28. Lehatsi 1936, 52.

29. The Armenian community of Venice has been the subject of numerous studies thanks in large measure to the pioneering work of the Mekhitarist priest/scholar Father Ghevont Alishan. The most extensive work on the community remains Alishan 1896; see also Alishan 1893 [*L'Armeno-Veneto*]. The last volume of this valuable collection of documents relating to Armenian-Venetian relations from the fifteenth to eighteenth century remains unpublished. For more recent work, see Zekiyan's excellent monograph (1978a, 886–890), where much of the literature on Armenian relations with Italy is synthesized, as well as the essays by other contributors in Zekiyan 1996 and 1990; Zekiyan and Ferrari 2004; see also Hermet and di Desio 1993.

30. "Namakner—Izmir, 1730 [*sic*]–1861" [Letters—Izmir, 1730–1861], ASMA, folder 112. There are six documents from Izmir dating from the seventeenth century, the oldest of which is a *commenda* contract from 1666 (mistakenly catalogued as 1730) and a short accounting ledger dated 1682, also wrongly attributed to 1746.

31. ASV CZ, busta 90, fasc. 7, quoted in Gianighian 1990, 50. The original passage reads: "Nel tempo del Dominio di Ossun Cassan Rè di Persia, et Armenia, li Armeni vennero a Venezia, e fù del 1497, e ricuperarano dall'Eccell.mi Procuratori di S. Marco, la di loro casa in virtù del testamento del Ziani."

32. On the etymology of *fondaco/funduk* and the history of this fascinating institution, see Constable 2003.

33. Zekiyan 1975, 886–887.

34. See the documents in "Liti e controversi parroccia di San Zulian—Armeni," Archivio Patriarchale o Diocesano (also known as Archivio Patriarchale di Venezia) [hereafter APD], where one can find a copy of Gregorio di Geurak Mirman's petition to the patriarch of Venice for permission to transform the chapel into a church (folio 38) and a curious petition in Armenian dated November 1694 by about twenty of the community's most notable Catholics (including members of the Sceriman/Shahrimanian family) to have services performed in the church in accordance with the Catholic rite (folio 44). See also the voluminous documents in Procuratori di San Marco, ASV, busta 180 (Santa Croce); Procuratori di San Marco, ASV, misti 180/A and 180/D. The latter contains a detailed *stampa* book on the Guerak Mirman family.

35. See the colophon of this manuscript in Hakobyan and Hovhannisyan 1974, 1: 318. The donor of this manuscript, Khwaja Shirin, is described as a resident of Sebastia/Sivas in Anatolia. His name (Shirin) and title (Khwaja) suggest that he might have been a Julfan Armenian.

36. Aslanian 2004b.

37. Alishan 1896, 370 ff.

38. Vercellin 1979, 246. See also the excellent treatment of Turkish merchants in Venice in Kafadar 1996.

39. P'ap'azyan 1990, 67. Alishan (1893 [*Sisakan*], 444) suggests that the Venetian senate's decree was part of a 1614 treaty or agreement between Persia and Venice allowing Julfans low customs fees and freedom to import silk from Iran to Venice or to Spalato (Split)

on the Dalmatian coast, which was then under Venetian rule. Such agreements offering low custom dues on Persian goods were signed in 1576 and 1589 and continued later, after 1623 (Alishan, 444). Tax exemption on Iranian silk and possibly other commodities also seems to have been in place as late as the 1660s according to Constant Jughayetsi's trade manual, where the author provides the following information for his readers/students: "Whatever goods enter Venice have no taxes." Constant Jughayetsi, Matenadaran MS 8443, 165b; also quoted in P'ap'azyan 1990, 67.

40. Lehatsi 1936, 54.

41. Bonardi 1996, 230. It was not possible to locate Bonardi's source (ASV, Procuratori di Citra, Commissaria Ziani, busta 91, fasc. A, f. 3–4), since the cataloguing system (along with some of the shelf marks) appears to have changed since Bonardi consulted the document in question.

42. Procuratori di San Marco, ASV, busta 180 (Santa Croce), *stampa* folder, "Nazione degl' Armeni nella Chiesa di S. Croce di detta Nazione," 117–118. See Karapetyan 2010 for a copy of the same document preserved in the Alishan archives in San Lazzaro. The list does not include Mekhitarist monks or students on San Lazzaro, which could be another twenty to thirty people. At the most, the number of Armenians in Venice in the mid-eighteenth century appears not to have exceeded a hundred people. See also the document in the same collection entitled "Li Armeni, che sono accasiti in Venezia" [The Armenians who have become domiciled in Venice]. Alishan (1893 [*Sisakan*], 446) suggests that this census presents the low ebb of the Armenian presence in Venice and that twelve Armenian mercantile houses had left the city in the 1732–1738 period.

43. See Avogaria di Comun, ASV, busta 235, for correspondence dating from 1665 between Julfan merchants in Venice and their associates in Smyrna.

44. The history of the Armenian community of Livorno, as in the case of that of Venice, is fairly well documented thanks in great part to the pioneering book by Ughurlian in 1891. Ughurlian was the senior Armenian priest of the Armenian church in Livorno during the last quarter of the nineteenth century. For Orengo's Italian translation of this important work, with excellent annotations, see Ughurlian 1991. For other works on this community, see, among others, Paolo Castignoli's excellent essay (1979), which relies on archival sources; Paolini 1992, 73–92; and Lucia Frattarelli Fischer's outstanding studies, published in 1998, 1999, and 2006. See also Salvini's two-volume doctoral dissertation (1992–1993). I thank the author of this valuable work for granting me permission to consult her dissertation, and the Archivio di Stato di Livorno for kindly placing this work at my disposal. See also Macler 1904, where an important document by the Orientalist/Armenologist Chahan Cirbied dating from 1811 is reproduced.

45. Macler 1904. Both Cirbied and Fischer attribute the arrival of the first Armenians to a meeting in Florence between Grand Duke Cosimo I and the Armenian catholicos Stepanos V, who was attending the Council of Florence at the time. Fischer, referring to a document in the Archivio di Stato of Florence, notes that the Armenians are singled out in the 1551 privileges offered by Cosimo to Levantine traders (1999, 298).

46. The presence of Gregorio di Guerak Mirman in Livorno at such an early date is based on a letter sent by him to the archbishop of Pisa, in which Gregorio di Guerak Mirman claims to have been sent to Livorno as an agent of the shah. See Ughurlian 1891, 183, where the au-

thor provides the date 1582 instead of 1583; also Malenchini n.d., 22 and 28 (in a document reproduced in Malenchini—document 17, 31—we read that Gregorio di Guerak Mirman was also conducting trade in Venice as early as 1588); and Paolini 1992, 74. The presence of one merchant in Livorno in 1583 does not necessarily indicate the presence of a community. The Mirman family, for instance, settled in Livorno only in 1619 and continued to live both there and in Venice on a permanent basis. Like the Sceriman [Shahrimanian] family, also of New Julfa, some members of the Mirman family seem to have converted to Catholicism and were granted titles of nobility in several Italian city-states. Also like the Scerimans, the Mirmans were, on the whole, assimilated by the nineteenth century. One descendant of the family (via the female line) still resides in Livorno. On the history of this family, see Ughurlian 1891, chap. 17, 183–199; Ughurlian 1991, 166–174. See also, for the official family biography, Malenchini n.d.; although no date is given for Malenchini's work, it was certainly published after 1891, given its citation of Ughurlian's 1891 work. This Gregorio di Guerak Mirman should not be confused with his descendant who bore the same name and lived in Venice in the second half of the seventeenth century.

47. The original text of the petition is reproduced as "Privilegi che S.A.S concede a diverse nationi abitantinin Livorno del dì 10 giugno 1593 ab Inc.," in *Legislazione toscana* (1800–1808), XIV, 10–20. It is also available in the more recent work by Fischer and Castignoli 1987.

48. Ughurlian 1891, 46.

49. Fischer 1998, 26.

50. Fischer 1999, 298.

51. Ibid.

52. "Namak—Aligorna, 1659" [Letter—Livorno, 1659], ASMA, folder 6.

53. Herzig 1991a, 136.

54. "Report by Priests Basilio Barsegh and Agop to Propaganda Fide, 1669, Fondo S.C. Armeni, Vatican, vol. 1, pt. 2, folio 319 (stamped) (136 penciled). See also the later report by Cardinal Medici to the Propaganda Fide, 7 May 1688, Archivio della Propaganda Fide (AP, SOCG), vol. 223, folios 327v-328 and 331v-332; Manuela Salvini claims there were fifty Armenians in Livorno around 1630 and a maximum of seventy in 1689 out of a total population of 21,194 (Salvini 1992–1993, 71, 119). She provides no breakdown between Julfan versus non-Julfan Armenians. Salvini's considerably lower figures for Armenian residents in Livorno might be accurate, but it bears mentioning that, despite her otherwise comprehensive account of the Armenian community of Livorno and the useful collection of documents reproduced in volume 2 of her dissertation, in retelling the earlier history of the Armenians in Livorno Salvini does not appear to have consulted the documents of the archives of the Propaganda Fide. The Propaganda Fide archives are arguably the leading source of information on the Armenian community in Livorno during this period. Regrettably, Salvini has also failed to consult the vast collection of documentation regarding the Armenians of Livorno in the seventeenth century, stored in the Archivio di Stato di Firenze, which houses the bulk of documentation relating to seventeenth-century Livorno.

55. Trivellato 2009, 80 and 305 n. 56; Fischer 1998, 31–32.

56. Antoine Cheleby was the governor of Bursa in the 1650s when the famous Italian traveler Niccolau Manucci passed through the city on his way to India and was entertained by Cheleby in his "country house." Cheleby, sensing that his life and fortunes were endan-

gered in the Ottoman Empire, had taken steps to transfer his wealth to Livorno and fled there during Manucci's visit. See Manucci 1966, 10–12. See also Karnetsi, *Patmut'iwn imn karcharot,* Mekhitarist Library/Archives, Vienna, folio 165; and Karapetyan 2009, 445. Karnetsi refers to Cheleby as the "Mak'sapet" (tax collector) of Izmir and does not identify him by name as Antoine Chelebi, and neither does Karapetyan; however, the reference to his flight from Izmir to Livorno and to his opening of a *hamam* bath there make it very likely that this is the same person.

57. Carré 1947–1948, 8.

58. Chiappini 1937. See also the excellent work of Chemchemian 1989, 56–77; and Ishkhanyan 1977, 368–385.On Armenian printing in New Julfa, see Ishkhanyan 1980, 351–368.

59. Ughurlian 1891, 46.

60. The best account of the foundation of the Armenian church in Livorno is found in Ughurlian 1891; see esp. 53–64, for the constitution of the community and the initial steps in establishing the church; see also the more recent account of Fischer 1999, 300–301.

61. The church served the Armenian community until the 1940s, when it was destroyed by Allied bombing. The facade of the original building has been preserved and is now a historic monument in Livorno.

62. Discussing the transfer of calico printing knowledge by Armenians to Mediterranean port cities, Giorgio Riello notes: "In Livorno too, the birth of Calico printing is similarly attributed to two Armenians" (2010, 15).

63. Museo Civico e Raccolta Correr di Venezia, P.D. 66.c.

64. See chapter 6 for a detailed discussion of *tomars* and *roozlamas.*

65. Agha di Matus was most likely not from the city of Tabriz in Iran but from the neighborhood bearing the same name in New Julfa, Isfahan. He was also known as Agha Terterian Oghlank'eshishiants'. See Alishan 1893 [*Sisakan*], 452; and Karapetyan and Tajiryan 1998, 80. Agha di Matus appears to have resided initially in Venice before relocating to Livorno. For Venice, see the letters addressed to him in that city in the 1690s in "Documenti Armeni," Acquisti e Doni, Archivio di Stato di Firenze [hereafter ASFi], busta 123, filza 1, documents 119, 120, and 127.

66. This Minas was the founder and patriarch of the Minasian family firm active in Iran and India until the mid-eighteenth century. See Aslanian 2006c; and chapter 6 below.

67. On the life of this merchant in Livorno, see Ughurlian 1891, 64–94 passim. Agha di Matus was murdered by his own servant in Livorno in 1709. See Alishan 1893 [*Sisakan*], 452; and Karapetyan and Tajiryan 1998, 80 n. 4. He did not live to see the church for which he had spent a huge fortune. See the dozens of long letters sent to him from Julfa and Surat by Khwaja Minas di Panos (his master), as well as other members of the Minasian family firm, in "Documenti Armeni," Acquisti e Doni, ASFi, buste 123 and 124. Some of these letters date from the 1680s.

68. For works on the Armenian community of Marseilles, see Tékéian 1929; Rambert and Bergasse 1949; see also the excellent work by Raveux: 2008 and 2009; Herzig 1991a, 137–139; Macler 1920–1922.

69. Rambert and Bergasse 1949, 65; quoted in Braudel 1982, 156.

70. Séguiran 1633/1982, 306–309. I thank Olivier Raveux for alerting me to this important and overlooked source.

71. Herzig 1991a, 137.

72. See Minutier central des notaires de Paris, Archives nationales, Registre ET/VI/0198, 2 octobre 1625. There is evidence of possibly a third Julfan who visited Paris during the same period, according to the testimony of the French missionary Father Pacific de Provins. When the French father arrived in Isfahan in 1628, he recalls in his book that he went to the house of an Armenian merchant he met three or four years before in Paris. This merchant was called Khwaja "Mouchiah," and his sole son, Khwaja Lazaro, was Khwaja Nazar's (the *kalantar* of Julfa) son-in-law. The Mouchiah mentioned by the French father could also be the same person as "Alexandre, fils de Mussegen" (or Musheghian?) of the Archives nationales document cited above; Pacifique de Provins, 225. I owe this source to Olivier Raveux.

73. Herzig 1991a, 137.

74. Ibid., 138.

75. See "Quittance pour Safras Avedit contre Ovanes de Sarroian," Archives départementales des Bouches-du-Rhône (Marseille) [hereafter ADBdR], 356 E 457, acte du 7 février 1689; and "Quittance pour Honoré Guintrand contre Safras Avedit," ADBdR, 356 E 457, acte du 18 septembre 1687. I thank Olivier Raveux for kindly bringing these documents to my attention.

76. Alishan 1893 [*Sisakan*], 457; Leclant 1951/1979, 89; Braudel 1981, 257; Baghdiantz McCabe 2008, 189.

77. Matthee 2000, 241 n. 27; and Martin 1931, 2: 189 and 283–284.

78. Earlier sources (Tékéian 1929, 30) had exaggerated the number of Armenians in Marseilles to three hundred to four hundred for the same period, but Olivier Raveux's recent research into provincial archives in southern France has yielded a much smaller figure (e-mail communication, 16 February 2008). See also Raveux's 2008, 2009, and 2010 works.

79. Raveux, 2010, 5.

80. Raveux 2009, 296.

81. In addition to the important works by Raveux cited above, see also Riello 2010, 11, 14–15.

82. Raveux 2008, 45.

83. Raveux 2010, 7.

84. Herzig 1991a, 138.

85. Kevorkian 1986.

86. Cadiz is, of course, a port on the Atlantic. However, due to its commercial, political, and cultural links to the Mediterranean, it can be considered an extension of the Mediterranean zone. The literature on the Armenian community of Cadiz is very scant and consists of the following works: Ortiz 1953; Sopranis 1954; Simões 1959; Martin 2005, 44; and Ashjian 1993, 133–149.

87. According to Braudel (1982, 156), "In 1601, an Armenian, Jorge da Cruz arrived in Cádiz, claiming to have traveled there straight from Goa." Braudel's reference (617) is a document in the Simancas archives ("Estado Napoles, 1097, folio 207"), but this must surely be a mistake, because the latter document, dated December 1601, does not refer to an Armenian arriving from Goa but to a person identified simply as "Jorge de nacion Armeno," who was, for unknown reasons, incarcerated in Cadiz. It appears, however, that a certain Jorge da Cruz did travel to Cadiz from Goa in those years and has, in fact, left us a fascinating short account of one of his later voyages in Italian entitled "Relazione d'un Corriero venuto

dall'Indie Orientale partito dalla città di Goa et gionto in Genova questo giorno. li 20 Agosto 1608, da Goa parti al primo Genaro 1608." Jorge was a royal courier working for the Portuguese Estado da India and delivering sensitive mail from his native Goa to the Iberian Peninsula. His account of a later trip carried out in 1608 was discovered by the Portuguese scholar Ferreira Godofredo in the 1950s and published along with a Portuguese translation in Godofredo 1954. While the Simancas document from 1601 refers to Jorge as belonging to the "Armenian nation," the travel account does not mention whether Jorge was actually an Armenian, although it indicates that he could have been a Jacobite Indian. The ethnonym "Armenian" was frequently used by the Portuguese to refer to anyone belonging to the Syrian Church of Southern India. I thank Señor José María Mateos, in charge of the Department of References at the Archivo General de Simancas, for sending me a copy of the Simancas document cited by Braudel.

88. I have calculated these figures from the inventory of wills and other notarial documents stored in the Archivo Histórico Provincial de Cádiz [hereafter AHPC].

89. Sopranis 1954, 300–301.

90. Martin 2005, 44.

91. This appears to be the first attested case of a Julfan *commenda* agent visiting the Spanish city (known as Calis among Julfans) and dates from 1678. See "Documenti Armeni," Acquisti e Doni, ASFi, busta 123, filza 1, documents 53 and 68 (?). The latter document is missing a number but comes between docs. 67 and 69.

92. Mesrop Ashjian and Frédéric Macler have misread this merchant's name in the Armenian inscriptions as Zakarian instead of Shakarian (*shakar* means "sugar" in Armenian). The Armenian letters for *z* and *sh* look similar and are easy to confuse, particularly in worn-out inscriptions, but the inscription bearing David Shakarian's name is in very good condition and clearly reads "Shakar" rather than "Zakar." See Ashjian 1993, 138 ff. For Macler, see note 104 below.

93. Martin 2005, 44.

94. See Sopranis 1954; Ortiz 1953; Simões 1959, 103; and Ashjian 1993, 138 ff.

95. See especially Simões 1959; and Ashjian 1993, for reproductions of the Armenian inscriptions.

96. See note 105 in the section on Amsterdam.

97. Neither Sopranis (1954) nor Ortiz (1953) has fully elaborated on the nature and origin of these "popular grievances," leaving us to conclude that, as was the case in Marseilles, they were most likely fueled by local (Spanish) business interests that felt threatened by the presence of Armenians in their midst.

98. Sopranis 1954, 304.

99. Quoted in Sopranis 1954, 304; and Ortiz 1953, 195. The petition of the Armenians of Cadiz to the king is reproduced in full in Sopranis 1954, 309–314.

100. Sopranis 1954, 305–306.

101. The document in question is a will belonging to a certain Juan Zacarias Ventura, born in "Crebon [?Yerevan], Armenia" (AHPC, CA 0398).

102. By far the best work on the Armenian community of Amsterdam is still Sarukhan 1925. For other works, see Macler 1904; Alishan 1893 [*Sisakan*], 459–460; Gregorian 1966; Herzig 1991a, 139–140; and Bekius 2002 (unpublished paper). I thank Willem Floor for pro-

viding me with a copy of Bekius's paper. See also the relevant chapters in the survey histories of Abrahamyan 1964–1967 and Alpoyachian 1941–1961.

103. Herzig 1991a; 2004b, 160. The material for the latter essay is largely drawn from Herzig's dissertation.

104. Macler 1920–1922, 416; 1904, 12; see also Sarukhan 1925, 45.

105. Sarukhan 1925, 46.

106. Ibid., 48–49. See also Herzig 1991a, 139. Khwaja Sarhat was conducting business with Marseilles in 1639, as can be seen from his petition to the French Admiralty for permission to bring some bales of silk to Marseilles for commerce. See the document reproduced by Macler 1920–1922, 25. Note that Macler has mistakenly transcribed "Farat" for "Sarat."

107. Van Rooy 1966, 347. P'ap'azyan (1990, 68) citing a work by Frédéric Macler (Macler 1932, 250) states that there were about sixty Armenian "commercial houses" in Amsterdam in the seventeenth century, which might yield a higher figure than the one provided by Van Rooy.

108. Bekius (2002, 19 ff.) briefly discusses the case of Johanes di Jacob Galdar, who arrived in Amsterdam in the early 1740s, most likely to manage the trading interests of the Galdarian family firm headquartered in Julfa. In addition, we know that the Sceriman/Shahrimanian family of diamond merchants based in Julfa as well as in Venice conducted transactions in Amsterdam during the early eighteenth century. See Fortunato Seriman, *Brevie memorie sulla famiglia Seriman,* MS Cod. Cigogna 3403 [1855], Archivio della Biblioteca di Museo Correr [hereafter ABMC], folio 2.

109. The foundation stone of this church is stored in the Musée Boreli of Marseilles where it must have been taken by Armenian merchants in the second half of the seventeenth century. Herzig, who briefly refers to this stone, relying on the erroneous interpretation/translation provided by Macler (see Macler 1920–1922, 415), confuses it with a tombstone (1991a, 138). For a photograph of this stone bearing the original Armenian inscription, see Macler 1920–1922, 415–417. The existence of this stone was first publicized in Torgomian 1891. The inscription in its Armenian original reads: "I T[i]vn ṘChZhB [1112] mayisi IG [23] i k'aghak'n yamsdertam ardeampk' shakari ordwoy dawt'i chiwghayets'woy: ew entagrut'eamb karapeti bani spasawori kazmets'aw vēms ōllandioy surb karapetin."

I have corrected the transcription provided by both Torgomian and Macler based on my own reading of the inscription from the image reproduced in Macler 1920–1922, 414–415. Macler, as noted above, mistakes the Armenian word *vēm* for "tombstone" without realizing that in this context the word refers to the foundation stone of a church. More importantly, both Macler and Torgomian misread "Shakar" for "Zakar." A more accurate reading of the foundation stone reveals that the founder of the Armenian church of Amsterdam most likely was none other than the wealthy Julfan merchant residing in Cadiz, Spain, during this period, known to the Spanish as "David Zukar," who had traveled to Amsterdam to commission special ceramic tiles (*azulejos*) bearing Armenian inscriptions for the Church of Santa Maria in Cadiz where the local Armenian community was provided a small chapel inside the Catholic church to conduct their services (see the section on Cadiz). Since the tiles in Cadiz date from the early 1660s and were manufactured in Amsterdam as per David Zukar's/Shakarian's wishes, it would not be far-fetched to conjecture that the wealthy Julfan named in the foundation stone of Amsterdam's first Armenian church as the benefactor of the church and David Zukar of Cadiz are the same individual. The translation of the inscription is as follows: "In the year 1663, May 23, in the city of Amsterdam, with the support of David of Julfa, son of Shakar, and the inscription of Karapet the servant of the Lord, this foundation stone [for the Church of] Holy Karapet of Holland was built." In light of this and other evidence, Bekius's assertion that the first Armenian church in Amsterdam was built in 1714 is factually incorrect and is most likely the result of the author's failure to consult the excellent and to date unsurpassed account (in Armenian) of the Armenian community of Amsterdam found in Sarukhan 1925.

110. On Armenian printing in Amsterdam in general, and on the printing of the first Armenian Bible in particular, see Chemchemian 1989; Sarukhan 1925; Gregorian 1966; Ishkhanian 1977.

111. On the atlas, see, in addition to the works cited in note 110, the informative account in Koeman 1967, 113–114.

112. Ferrier 1970. Khwaja Panos Calander was still residing in Julfa in 1668, as his signature as a witness to a *commenda* contract drawn in the Tabriz district of Julfa on 22 Aram 1127 (6 January 1668) suggests. See "Documenti Armeni" Acquisti e Doni, ASFi, busta 123, filza 1, doc. 70. The contract is between Edigar son of Tavrizhetsi Shekhik and Avet son of Gharamelikents Hovhannes. Khwaja Panos must have permanently resettled in London sometime after 1668, but even then he was not confined to London. His seal and signature (Պայմանատրեց Փանոսու) appear in a notarized paper drawn up in Venice in 1692 involving the sale of gems and diamonds between Khwaja Minas di Panos of Julfa and his *commenda* agent Agha di Matus of Venice and Livorno (doc. 63). Khwaja Panos Calander probably died in London sometime after drafting his will and testament on 24 September 1696. See "Will of Panus Calander, Armenian Merchant of Saint Lawrence Poultrey, City of London," PROB 11/434, PRO.

113. "Quittance pour Safras Avedit contre Ovanes de Sarroian," ADBdR, 356 E 457, acte du 7 février 1689. According to this notarial document, "Safras de Avedit," described as "persien de nation en ceste ville de Londres," is responsible for procuring goods in London for Melcon de Nazar "demeurant à Marseille." The document is dated 26 September 1688 in London by notary public, Anthony Wright. I thank Olivier Raveux for obtaining this document for me.

114. Aslanian 2006c, 46.

115. Herzig 1991a, 141. The letters are stored at the British Library, Harleian MS 7013, folios 32, 112, 114, 117–120.

116. See George 2002, 23.

117. There are many accounts of the Russian agreement. The most authoritative one is Khachikian 1980; see also Herzig 1991a; and Aslanian 2009.

118. Gulbenkian 1970; see also Khachikian 1980; and Aslanian 2009.

119. Abrahamyan 1964–1967, 1: 373. The best account on the Astrakhan Armenian community and its significant Julfan population is the long introduction to Poghosyan 1967; see also the excellent treatment in Yukht 1957 as well as the documents and commentary in Bournoutian 2001.

120. Abrahamyan 1964–1967, 373.

121. De Bruyn 1738, 90.

122. Abrahamyan 1964–1967, 373; and Yukht 1957, 48.

123. Abrahamyan 1964–67, 373.

124. Ibid.; see also Bournoutian 2001, 393.

125. On the *rathaus,* see Poghosyan 1967, 50. For the administrative institutions of Astrakhan's Indian community, see the excellent treatment in Dale 2002.

126. For Kazan, see Abrahamyan 1964–1967, 372; for St. Petersburg, 377; for Moscow, see Oskanyan 1971, 25–39.

127. The best study of the Lazarian family's commercial history is Khachikian's monumental work of 2006. See the introduction to Khachikian 2006 for information on this family.

128. Ignatius Shahrimanian is mentioned on numerous occasions in a notebook of letters sent by his cousin Jacobo Sceriman/Hakob Shahrimanian preserved in Avogaria di Comun, ASV, busta 17 (see notes 61 and 65 in chapter 5 below on this notebook). For Ignatius's silk factory, see Abrahamyan 1964–1967, 382.

129. Herzig 1991a, 151.

130. Braudel 1982, 157.


5. "THE SALT IN A MERCHANT'S LETTER"

1. Barendse 2002, 164.

2. Markovits 2000, 25.

3. Barendse 1988. For an earlier use of the term "intelligence network," see Braudel 1972, 1: 566.

4. Braudel 1972, 1: 355.

5. Malynes 1622, 11, quoted in Trivellato 2009, 168; Trivellato 2006.

6. Habermas 1989, 15–16.

7. In addition to Habermas, see also the excellent essay by McCusker (2005). McCusker points out, however, that the shift from private and secretive conveyance of commercial information, the hallmark of medieval business correspondence, to a public sharing of it in commercial newspapers occurred in the 1450s in Antwerp when the first commercial newspapers or gazettes began to appear, in near simultaneity with the birth of print technology.

8. Trivellato 2009, chap. 7; 2006.

9. The idea of "print capitalism" and its corollary of "imagined communities" were famously developed by Anderson in his classic 1991 study.

10. The particle *di* found in Julfan family names is not a borrowing from Italian or Spanish, but an abbreviation of the Armenian word *ordi,* meaning "son." Before the introduction of the *-ian* suffix in the nineteenth century, Armenian family names were derived from the name of the father or patriarch of a family. Thus Pietro di Sceriman was Peter the son of Shahriman, the patriarch of the famous Sceriman/Shahrimanian family.

11. Interestingly, several letters sent from Istanbul or Diyarbakir to merchants in India have addresses in French. This was most likely because they were sent to India via Baghdad and Basra where French Capuchin monks often handled mail for Armenians. See "Spanish and Armenian [Ships Papers] 1741–1750," HCA 30/682, National Archives/Public Records Office [hereafter PRO], letter no. 1177 in the *Santa Catharina* collection.

12. Letter no. 1180 in the *Santa Catharina* collection is one of the few cases in which

Arabic is used. See "Spanish and Armenian [Ships Papers] 1741–1750," HCA 30/682, PRO, letter no. 1180.

13. On Padre Severini, see, among others, Love 1913, 2: 467–468.

14. Յաագէ զիրս ի բարեյի բ[ա]ղ[ա]քն չիսուսպւն կանթում բաղաքն պատրի սավէրափն ձեռն, որ ա հասուդարակ ի ձեռն պյուասափ խոճաֆիֆիր առաքն ի բարին, ուրէնէք բ[ա]ղ[ա]քն ա ըֆ անյապճառ հասուդարակ, ա կարձա ի Ս[ֆար]նէ առձէ ԱՄԵն:

| յՈւ ֆ Շֆարն | Ուարտֆ 12ֆ |
|---|---|
| 1747 | ի Ֆոֆւաֆ |

("Spanish and Armenian [Ships Papers] 1741–1750," HCA 30/682, PRO, letter no. 1172)

15. The merchant school in question was said to have been situated in the compound of All Savior's Monastery in Julfa and was supervised by a scribe named Constant of Julfa who wrote an exceedingly important manual of trade that was used as a textbook in his school. Many well-to-do merchants sent their young sons to be educated at Constant's school, as did others who wanted to provide their children with an opportunity for success and prosperity. The school is said to have produced over 250 graduates in the last two decades of the seventeenth century. One of the few sources on the school is Ter Hovhaniants 1980, 2: 273–274. The existence and role of this school was popularized by Khachikian's influential 1967 essay.

16. For a discussion of this dialect, see the pioneering work by Acharian 1940; Vaux 2002; the appendices of Herzig 1991a; and Aslanian 2007a. I thank Bert Vaux for sharing his manuscript with me. See also note 15 of chapter 1.

17. Anna khatun Hakobian in Julfa, Isfahan, to her husband, Davit' Sultan, in Pondicherry, 22 Ghamar 132 (9 August 1747), "Spanish and Armenian [Ships Papers] 1741–1750," HCA 30/682, PRO, letter no. 1534.

18. Sood 2007, 212. Fath Allah Mojtabai, Hashem Rajabzadeh, and Momin Mohiuddin discuss different aspects of letter writing in Safavid Iran and Mughal India in their interesting entries in the *Encyclopedia Iranica*. Mojtabai and Rajabzadeh's sample of letters does not include those written by merchants. See also Sood 2007 for a discussion of Arabic and Latin script letters, including some by merchants.

19. See Sood 2007 for an impressive examination of "epistolary structures" in Arabic script correspondence from eighteenth-century "Islamic Eurasia."

20. Sood's claim that "*all* of the mercantile groups of eighteenth-century Islamic Eurasia, no matter how they are defined, approached correspondence in a similar fashion" (2007, 212 [emphasis added]) is plausible enough, though not supported by his exclusive reliance on Arabic and Latin script documentation. As impressive as his detailed examination of correspondence in multiple languages (Arabic, Portuguese, French, and Persian) is, Sood's important study does not take note of the voluminous Julfa dialect correspondence in the Armenian script, or of Indic script documentation, as sparse as the latter might be. Therefore, his claim that the minor stylistic variations in the corpus of (Arabic and Latin script) correspondence at his disposal were caused "by the script and *not* the ethnicity or nationality—or *any other cultural trait*—of the author, *nor* the language in which the letter was composed"

(Sood, 211 [emphasis added on "any other cultural trait"]) might be sensible in the context of the binary set of Arabic versus Latin script documentation informing his study, but it is not entirely conclusive, because it fails to take into account the Julfan Armenian correspondence that makes up the bulk of the surviving mercantile documentation from "Islamic Eurasia." As my analysis in this chapter demonstrates, Julfa dialect documentation in the Armenian script bears remarkable stylistic similarities to Arabic script correspondence from the same period. These similarities do not appear to be caused or shaped by the choice of the script or by the language used but most probably by more widely shared "cultural" and linguistic norms that may be traced to "Persianate" epistolary conventions connecting Christian Armenian merchants to their Muslim or other Islamicate counterparts in Iran, Mughal India, the Indian Ocean, and beyond.

21. Herzig 2007, 65. In his authoritative Classical Armenian-English dictionary, Bedrossian offers the following definition of Է and its variants: "prefixed to a missive letter signifies the Supreme Being. Է Էս Էսն Էիս "that exists, existence, that is of itself, the Supreme Being, the Most High, God" (Bedrossian 1871/1985, 194). According to Avetikian et al.'s dictionary (1836/1979, 758), when placed at the beginning of encyclicals and letters, Է signifies God, "from the Hebrew E'hovan." See also Sebastats'i 1749, 289. We cannot be certain whether the use of Է at the beginning of mercantile letters or contracts was influenced by Persianate or Islamicate conventions; it could also have been a continuation of Classical Armenian patristic traditions influenced by the church. In any case, Armenian manuals of style for mercantile epistolary are not known to exist until the 1826 publication in Venice of Ignatios P'ap'azian's manual. See P'ap'azian 1826.

22. Sood 2007, 186.

23. *Kamin:* A/P "small, humble." This term is generally used in the Julfa dialect as a synonym for *nuast* (humble). The *ay* at the end of *kaminay* is an ablative suffix used in *grabar* as well as in the Julfa dialect. See Schröder 1711, 394 for a discussion of *kamin*, which he defines in Latin as "paucus" or "parvus," meaning "little, small, petty, puny, inconsiderable"; see Lewis 1890, 585. It should be noted that Schröder had studied Armenian (both *grabar* and dialects, especially that of Julfa) and was in close contact with many Julfan merchants in Amsterdam; thus he had plenty of opportunity to ask merchants frequenting the city about the Julfa dialect. It is not surprising, therefore, that included in his work is a chapter entitled "De Epistolographia Armenorum," in which he provides many examples of letters in the Julfa dialect with his own *scholia* in Latin.

24. *Kamtar:* P "fewer or least." The Julfa dialect has a tendency to "distort" this word by adding a *p* and changing the *a* to *o,* as in *kamptor.* The *grabar* version of this word, frequently found in clerical correspondence, is *apirat,* a self-deprecatory term meaning "roguish or base/worthless," decidedly stronger than *kamtar,* but conveying the same general meaning. Given the context and its usage, I have therefore translated *kamtar* as "menial."

25. *Aŕz:* P "petition, submission." Also used occasionally as a synonym for A *malum,* as in *malum lini,* "let it be known," or *grabar* ծանուցումն/յայտնի լինի, "let it be known or acknowledged."

26. Martiros di Sargis in Livorno to Hierapiet di Martin in Venice, 30 November 1141 (1692), Documenti Armeni Mercantile, ASV, busta 2.

27. Sood 2007, 187.

28. To Nahmat Erkani (Armenian merchant in Venice) from Julfa, in the month of Nadar Azaria year 115 (1730), Documenti Armeni Mercantile, ASV, busta 2.

29. Ovannes di Panos in Izmir to Parons Melkon, Poghos, Oskan in Venice, 22 June 1143 (1694), Documenti Armeni Mercantile, ASV, busta 2. The formal Classical Armenian form of this expression would look something like this: եւ եթէ ազնուամեծաւորութիւնն քո զձեր որպիսութիւնն հարցանիցէ . . . (And if Your Eminence/Lordship were to inquire about our well-being . . . ). See Sebastats'i 1961, letter no. 708.

30. Julfa dialect corruption of A/P *ahval* or *ahwal,* plural of *hal*: "state or condition."

31. *Auto-da-fé* literally means "a record or confession of the faith." The term is associated with the practice commonly used during the Inquisition to extort a confession from individuals by publicly burning them alive.

32. Արզ լինի որ անսմխիթաղ ծարալիս անբժշկելի տարտն յ[ա]լբ[ա]թէ լսել կնիս[կու լինիս] մսաց որ զ [6] ամիս ամէն կերպ յուսահատվելէ ամէն բանից սովրայզարուրթիւնից [<P *sovdagar:* "merchant, trader"] ձէրի վերել մինշի ողորմած ա[ստուա]ծրս իմ լուսահոգի խոր արդար արուսն որ ամ[է]նայ զար անսորէն հեր[ա]նոս նադր շայից լինք առեց որ սալէ խան համիշայ [<P *hamisha:* "continuous, always, permanent"] քէշիկի [<P *keshik:* "guard"] ս/ա/ողարն քշերով մտավ շադիրն շնայ սատակ ար[ա]ն ուր ադբոր որդի ալայ դուլի խանն դագավոր [sic] դրին էս փարավօնին տողէն թռունէրն ռիշէլ լր [35] շան սուր քաշեցին նորայ անունէրն աշխատրս վերայցուցին ա[ստուծ]յ գոյութիւն . . . թէ որդում ուտեմ [Persian construction: literally, "to eat oath," *qassam mikhoram,* i.e., "to swear"] ավատմ[ա]ն չես որ էս րթ [8,9] ամիսն յիմացել չեմ թէ աշխատրումավ ելել թէ խողում չարծում [? unknown word] թէ խելքս թադիր զնի եւ ինձ խմ[ա] ր աշխարիս վերջրնայ ըսպ[ա]հ[ա]ն իմ պարծանք խոր աշխատես զնալն եւ մեր տնեռին սոսկառելն [*song arel* <?T *son etmek:* "to put to an end, to ruin, or exterminate"; also possibly from T *süngü etmek:* "to put to the sword, to kill or finish off"] եւ կերայ կերայ քարհմէք յինք առուլն ("Spanish and Armenian letters— Santa Catharina," HCA 30/632, PRO, letter no. 1260).

33. Krusinski 1733, 2: 46–47.

34. For Adil Shah and the political situation in Julfa after Nadir's assassination, see chapter 8 below. For letters in which Adil Shah's rise to power is greeted with optimism, see letter no. 1321 and the first *post scriptum* to letter 1411 in HCA 30/682, PRO.

35. *Santa Catharina* logbook of Spanish and English translations, HCA 42/026, PRO, letter no. 49, folio 142.

36. Hovakim di Manuel to Minas di Elias, 20 Tira (6 October) 1746 in Chandernagor and received in Calcutta on 21 Tira (7 October) 1746, HCA 30/682, PRO, letter no. 1025.

37. Hakob Shahrimanian in Julfa to David Shahrimanian in Livorno, 20 Nirhan 107 (5 March 1722), Sceriman Family Papers, Archivo di Istituto Don Nicola Mazza [hereafter Don Mazza], Verona, busta 3.

38. Էս օր երկրումս բանկալու ապրանք չկայ շատ գինայ բռնել եւ հաֆալն ունեմք որ տարիս բասրայ բանկալուց նավիչ դուս եկել պատճառն էսայ որ սեհդայլյատտու նաբաբն եկել կալկաթայ ինկլիզանուն խետ կռիվ տվել ինկլիզանուն բերթն առել եւ ուրենցս դուսայ ար[ա]րէլ եւ բանկալու չօք աթթաֆն շատ խողածայ լուլմանք որ բասրուցան գրէլ թէ ինկլիզանին թադարիթան տնեսել թաքրար պիտո նաբաքին խետ կռիւ տան եւ ինկլիզի ֆրանկսիսի կռիվել դարմիան կայ աստուծ գիտի վերչն դոր զնի (Petros di Ibrahim in

Istanbul to Tadeos di Nazar Shahrimanian/Sceriman in Venice, 31 August 1757, Sceriman Family Papers, Don Mazza, Verona, busta 1). (At present, there are no goods from Bengal in this country [in Istanbul] these days, and the prices for such goods have risen [?]. And we have received news that there have been no ships in Basra from Bengal; the reason is this that the Nawab of Saidabad [Siraj-ud-daula] has gone to Calcutta, engaged the English in a fight, and taken from them the fort [Fort Saint William] and forced them out of Calcutta. Matters have become complicated in all quarters of Bengal. We have heard that [some of our community] in Basra have written that the English are taking a break from the fighting but will fight again with the Nawab, and also that the Anglo-French fighting is under way there. God [only] knows how this will end.)

39. *Santa Catharina* logbook of Spanish and English translations, HCA 42/026, PRO, letter no. 16, folio 61. Needless to say, Julfan society was built on patriarchal principles by which sons were prized over daughters.

40. Greif 1992, 530.

41. For a detailed discussion, see chapter 7.

42. Trivellato 2009, chap. 7; 2006.

43. The best-known manual in this genre was Ghukas Vanantets'i's *Gants ch'ap'oy kshroy twoy ew dramits' bolor ashkhari or ē Gitut'iwn amenayn tesak kshroy ch'ap'ots' ew dramits' orov bolor ashkhari vacharakanut'iwnn vari* [A treasury of measures, numbers, and moneys of the entire world, which is the knowledge of all types of weights, measures, and moneys with which the trade of the whole world is conducted] (Amsterdam, 1699). This manual was printed "with the expenses and at the request of Paron Petros of Julfa" for the express use of "merchants belonging to the commerce-loving Armenian nation." It was in all likelihood an amalgam of another manual of trade compiled and kept in manuscript form by Constant Jughayetsi in the 1680s (see note 43 in chapter 6). For background on the Amsterdam manual, see the excellent study by Kévonian (1975).

44. See note 39 in chapter 6 on this manuscript. Julfa MS 64 (ASMA) was copied sometime around 1694 and belonged to a number of merchants, who recorded their names and referred to various trips, mostly to Surat (India) and Izmir (Ottoman Empire), during which they seemed to have taken this manuscript with them. These inscriptions are like colophons and are found in the first seven and last two pages of the manuscript.

45. *Santa Catharina* logbook of Spanish and English translations, HCA 42/026, PRO, letter no. 52, folios 168–169 (emphasis added).

46. *Santa Catharina* logbook of Spanish and English translations, HCA 42/026, PRO, letter no. 20, folio 85. Note that the numbering system adopted for the translated letters unfortunately does not seem to correspond to the numeration scheme on the original letters written in the Julfa dialect. Despite my efforts, I was unable to locate all the originals of these translations, and therefore I am unable to corroborate their accuracy. On the whole, however, the few cases in which I succeeded in tracking down the originals indicate to me that the translations, though not word for word, remain generally faithful to the originals.

47. Պ[ա]ր[ո]ն պետրոս քն ադ[ա]մ իր [22] էս լիվոռնոյ գիրր յ[ա]մհրայ ը [8] խասակ ռ[ո]պիխունթիւնն յայտնի ելավ գիրտ տեր [?] բինամաքայ [*bi namak*<P: literally, "without salt, flavorless"] որ ոչ առֆ խաքար կայ ոչ ծախուի սոֆռագարին [<P *sovdagar*: "merchant"] գրին ադն առֆն էւ ծախսնաւ. գիր լինես գռում թէ լիվոռնոյ թէ վանատկէն ծախսի առֆի

ահվալին [<P/A *ahval,* "condition, state"] գրես մեք էլ եւելի խոշխալ կլինենք (To Parons Ohannes and Petros, 7 Ovdan 96 [21 January 1711], Documenti Armeni Mercantile, ASV, busta 2 [emphasis added]).

48. For Venetian and Genoese commercial correspondence, see Ashtor 1983, 379–382.

49. Steensgaard 1974, 57. For an insightful albeit brief attempt to criticize Steensgaard's view that Asian merchants did not possess adequate channels of information regarding market conditions, see Hussain 2005. For another critique of Steensgaard, see Baghdiantz McCabe 1999, 204. Neither of these critiques is grounded on the empirical evidence that the Julfa dialect correspondence provides.

50. Chaudhuri 1978, 74; see also Chaudhuri 1981.

51. Chaudhuri 1978, 75.

52. Ibid.

53. Echoing Chaudhuri, Philip Lawson also highlights the company's "meticulous record keeping," "attention to detail," and its "very efficient postal system" as key factors explaining its "early rise to profitability" (1993, 21–22). Similarly, Willem Kuiters, also relying on Chaudhuri, notes: "The care the Company took of its correspondence and the hierarchical organization of it reflected the importance it attached to a regular supply of dependable information from as broad a base as possible.... The carefully assembled information served to reduce such uncertainties and risks and played an essential part in the decision-making process.... The control of information was part of the Company's strategy seeking to maintain control over its proper servants" (2002, 55–57).

54. Jacobs 1991, 20; and Gaastra 2003, 149–151. According to Carlos and Nicholas (1988, 408), citing the work of a Danish historian (Glamman 1958/1981, 5), the VOC had a committee devoted to scanning data and receipts only four years after its creation in 1602, and created a special "committee of correspondence" in 1646 "as a means for relief, especially for the very time-consuming and important task of reading and answering reports and letters from India."

55. Carlos and Nicholas 1996, 921.

56. Chaudhuri 1981, 38–42. The question of whether the European-chartered companies were endowed with more "efficient" administrative/bureaucratic structures than their non-European or Asian counterparts remains to be fully explored. For a sophisticated overview touching on some of these issues, see Pomeranz 2001, chap. 4. The disparity of documentation between European-chartered firms, whose papers are readily accessible, and Asian firms, including even Julfan family firms, whose documentation is for the most part lacking, is bound to underscore the administrative sophistication of European joint-stock companies over their Asian rivals. But even if the joint-stock principle and the bureaucratic command structure of European-chartered companies represented a more "advanced" institutional innovation than the familial principle of Asian firms, these features do not, by themselves, seem to have guaranteed European supremacy over Asian firms. Julfan family firms, for instance, had the upper hand over the English East India Company and its factors in the seventeenth and early eighteenth centuries in the textile and silk trades of India and Iran because the Julfans had lower overhead costs and better "local knowledge" of markets and commodities than their European counterparts; one practice that gave the company the ultimate edge over Julfan competition was the English state's use of violence either through

privateering or through outright piracy, from which the company benefited (Aslanian 2006c). According to Pomeranz, the same applies to Chinese maritime merchants, who "competed successfully with Europeans on most routes, as long as the Europeans did not use force" (Pomeranz 2001, 171). It seems to me that the question of administrative sophistication was not ultimately a decisive factor in the long-term success of the chartered companies in Asia. As both Irfan Habib and Geoffrey Parker, among others, have noted, the ultimate success of the chartered companies had probably less to do with their commercial organization than with the superior violence at their disposal (Parker 1991, 161–162; Habib 1990, 399). Moreover, the chartered companies were institutionally sanctioned and equipped to use violence to advance trade (and vice versa) or, to use Boxer's formulation for the VOC, made "as much use of the sword as of the pen" (1965/1973, 5).

57. Steensgaard 1974, 30.

58. It seems that the Julfa dialect word for "company letter" was *sark'ari gir*. See letter to Minas di Elias in Calcutta from Aghamal, Grigor, and Minas in Julfa/Isfahan, 11 Nakha 131 (29 June 1746), HCA 32/1833, PRO, letter no. 191.

59. For a good discussion, see Sood 2007, 203–204.

60. "Ceux-la, la plus entreprenants, donnent sur tout ce qui se présente et n'ignorent rien du prix des marchandises, soit de celles de l'Europe, de l'Asie et autres parts parce qu'ils ont des correspondences partout qui las informent de la juste valeurs sur les lieux. Ainsi ils ne peuvent être trompés dans leurs achats" (Roques 1996, 147).

61. For Minas di Elias's letter book, see Santa Catherina: 14 letter books, cash books, etc. in Armenian, and loose papers, HCA 32/1832, PRO. For the letter book of Hakob di Murat, containing copies of all the letters of instruction (*barevagirs* or *ordnagirs*) he sent beginning August 16, 1731, in Moscow and continuing to St. Petersburg, Amsterdam, and Venice in 1734, see Avogaria di Comun, ASV, busta 17.

62. See Documenti Armeni Mercantile, ASV, busta 3.

63. See the introduction to a selection of Karnetsi's letters in Abrahamyan 1968, esp. xxxii–xxxxv. For a good survey of Karnetsi's life, see Karapetyan 2009, 375–382.

64. Trivellato 2006.

65. "Hierapet" di Martin's correspondence is almost exclusively with his agents Amirbek di Vardan and Martiros di Sargis, both operating in Italy. A great many of these letters are in two separate collections in ASV: Documenti Armeni Mercantile, buste 2 and 3, and the previously unknown collection in Avogaria di Comun, busta 17. These appear to be papers related to a court case in Venice, as their existence in the "Avogaria di Comun-civile" cases indicates. Another batch of letters is at the British Library: "Letters of Arapiet di Martin, Venezia, 1691–1703," BL, Oriental MS 15794. The latter, which has not been previously examined by scholars, contains seventeen letters sent by Amirbek di Vardan in Naples, Florence, and Livorno to Hierapet di Martin in Venice, most of which date from the 1690s. Almost nothing is known about the origins of this collection.

66. Lane 1944/1967. On Asian mercantile correspondence in the Indian Ocean, see Sood 2007 and 2009.

67. Documenti Armeni Mercantile, ARV, busta 2. This particular letter does not bear a date and is missing its last page.

68. See Aslanian 2006c.

69. On the *chapar* system in Safavid and post-Safavid Iran, see Floor 2001a and 2001b. I thank Rudi Matthee for the reference to the latter article.

70. For *shatirs*, see Chardin 1811, 3: 453–454; 4: 168–169. See also the brief but insightful discussion in Rochard and Chehabi 2002.

71. The Chalabies were a wealthy dynasty of Turkish merchants originally from Iraq who had migrated to Surat in the sixteenth century to become one of western India's leading merchant families. Their merchant marine fleet played a dominant role in the shipping between Surat and the Persian Gulf, especially to the port of Basra, to which they made regular runs throughout the seventeenth and the first half of the eighteenth centuries. The best accounts of this family are Das Gupta 1979, 96 and passim; and Abdullah 2001, 96–98.

72. See *Santa Catharina* logbook of Spanish and English translations, HCA 42/026, PRO, letter no. 20 folios 90–91.

73. *Bottomree* or *bottomry* and *respondentia* are technical terms for money borrowed upon a vessel or ship whereby the ship and its cargo would be held as insurance for the repayment of a loan. *Avog, awg,* and *avugge* were the Mughal equivalents. The term Julfan Armenians used was *avak.* This was "a form of speculative investment in a ship's cargo in which the investors lent money for its purchase. The money would be repaid if the ship carried the cargo safely to the stipulated port, the premium upon the principal naturally varying with the risk involved" (Habib 1990, 395).

74. *Santa Catharina* logbook of Spanish and English translations, HCA 42/026, PRO, letter no. 20, folio 91.

75. On the role of *pattamars, daks,* and mail during the Mughal period, see Chardin 1811, 4: 169; Habib 1986, 236–252; Deloche 1993, 218–225; Bayly's brief treatment: 1996, 14–15, 58–60, 164–165; Agarwal 1966; and Sood 2009.

76. See the long entry in Yule and Burnell 1903. It is interesting to note that Julfans also used this term in reference to the overland delivery of their mail in Mughal India. Thus in a letter sent by an Armenian priest in Madras to Julfa, the writer states: եւ յայտ լիցի վեհապատուութեանդ որ մեծ թիւն ՌՃԾԹ [1159 + 551 = 1710] յուլիսի մեկէն եւ ԻՔ [22] քեն գրած սուրբ օրհնունեան թուղթն սուրաթին վերայ հասաւ թիւն ՌՃԿ [1160 = 551 = 1711] յամսեանն ապրիլի ԻՁ [26] եւ մայիսի Ի [20] մէկն ձեռամբն շարիմանէնց պարոն սարհադին եւ մէկն փայեկի?/դայեկի (The Armenian priest Avet in Madras to the primate Movses in Julfa, 1160 [16 November 1711], "Namakner—Madras, 1709–1850" [Letters—Madras, 1709–1850], folder 104). (Let it be known to Your Eminence that your letters of Holy Blessing, written on July 1 and 22 of the year of the Greater Armenian Era 1159 [1710] and sent by way of Surat reached [us] in the year 1160 [1711] on April 26 and May 20. One of them [reached us] through the hands of Paron Sarhat of the Shahriman family, and the other by way of a *dayk* [or *paik*].) The word that interests us is almost certainly *day[e]k*, which would be a corruption of the Mughal term *dak* or *dawk* (see above). However, it could also be a misreading on our part (the writing is unclear here) of the Persian word *paik*, which according to Steingass means "a running footman; a carrier, messenger; a guard; a watchman; a footman, lacquey; a merchant; a traveler" (1892, 268).

77. *Santa Catharina* logbook of Spanish and English translations, HCA 42/026, PRO, letter no. 57, folio 186.

78. For a letter addressed to Manila by a Julfan merchant in Madras, see "Prize Court Papers," HCA 32/1831, PRO, box a, letter no. 67: letter to Manila, dated 29 Nakha 1739, addressed to Baron Ovanness in Manila from Grigor di Nazar in Madras.

79. See Goitein 1967–1993, 1: 276–277. As Goitein points out, "The word mawsim designated both the caravan and the fair or business season connected with its arrival." The term was only later associated exclusively with the oceanic seasons dependent on the wind patterns of the Indian Ocean. The Julfa dialect word was most likely a direct borrowing from Arabic or its Persian variant *mausim*.

80. I have drawn information on the monsoon seasons from Tibbetts 1971, esp. 360–382; Chaudhuri 1985, 127; and Abu-Lughod 1989, 251–260 and chap. 8. Hourani's 1995 classic, *Arab Seafaring in the Indian Ocean in Ancient and Early Medieval Times,* also has a useful discussion on the monsoon system, as does Arasaratnam 1994, 1–7.

81. Tavernier noted the peculiar nature of traveling on the Indian Ocean (1688, pt. 2, 15–16).

82. Braudel, 1972, 1: 355.

83. Pearson 2003, 20.

84. The habit of writing down information concerning the date of departure and arrival of letters was also widespread among Italian merchants in the Mediterranean, as Melis's work demonstrates (1983, 16).

85. See the third paragraph of the Julfan letter annotated and reproduced in full in Aslanian 2006c. For an English version, see Aslanian 2008c.

86. In a letter mailed from Isfahan to India, the author apologizes to his correspondent for the delay in writing him and explains the reasons why: "After having delivered this letter for those eight days to the Post, the same was returned to us because the man was robbed on the road." See *Santa Catharina* logbook of Spanish and English translations, HCA 42/026, PRO, letter no. 16, folio 56.

87. According to Kuiters, "Letters between Europe and India were always sent in duplicate or even triplicate to avoid loss of important information by shipwreck" (2002, 55).

88. Letter from Pegu addressed to a certain Paron Hovhannes either in Julfa or in Livorno, stored in folder 2 in Documenti Armeni Mercantile, ASV, busta 2. Since the letter was originally part of the Sceriman family papers before it was deposited in the ASV in the nineteenth century, it is safe to assume that it was a family letter addressed to one of its members. The verso side of the letter has the following notation in Italian: "Lettera familiare scritta dalle Indie nell'anno 1676" (Family letter written from the Indies in the year 1676). The letter does not contain the author's name. The opening lines read, in the Julfa dialect: Մայլու լինի վալխնսամաթ դու ժՁ [16] տարիա գնացել աս ինչ կասեն ապա քո սիրտն ղռախմ [<A *rahim:* "pity, compassion"] չկայ խալալոր [<A dialect *halevor:* "old man, father"] խերու [<JD: "last year"] գարուղարդու ձեղտեսուն կարոտ մեռաւ մեր ուլայու քօռացել: տան խիզանն [<P: "family, children," also "housewife"] գամաքել պյրղրկձած.

89. Ի սոյն գրովս սիրելի իմ հհնզ գիր եղել գողգրեցից եւ յղեցի՝ ծովով եւ գամաքով եւ ն'չ մի ամենեւին գպատտասխան գրեանցն իմոց ընկալայ ն'չգխտեմ թէ էսա գանց արադեր եւ թէ ոչ էսա այլ գայս դուգխտես եւ ոչ ես (HCA 30/682, PRO, letter no. 1172). The irony here is that this letter did not reach its destination either, since the ship it was traveling on (the *Santa Catharina*) was captured as a "prize" in 1748 by the British fleet off the coast of

southern India and all the ship's paper cargo of 2,000 letters, including this letter, was shipped to London to be presented as "exhibits" in a high-stakes trial at the High Court of Admiralty, after which they were deposited in the archives. See Aslanian 2006c.

90. *Barovagir* seems to be one of the technical terms in the Julfa dialect, along with *ordnagir*, that refers to letters that a "master" sent to his overseas factor containing specific instructions that the factor was, according to Julfan commercial law, compelled to carry out. Unfortunately, this term is not mentioned in the Astrakhan Code of Laws, which contains the precepts of commercial law used by Julfans (see Poghosyan 1967), and no other work known to me discusses this term. However, an important petition addressed to Julfa's Assembly of Merchants in the 1730s mentions the dispatch of several *Barovagir* in the context of a legal dispute between the Khwaja Minasian family firm and one of its factors in India who had apparently refused to return home, despite the *Barovagir* written to him by the senior members of the Minasian firm. According to this document, it seems that *barovagir* was another word for *ordnagir*. See chapter 7 below for a discussion of this document. The document in question is the following: Petition to the Assembly of Merchants, 30 Nirhan 116 (15 March 1731), "Arevtrakan grut'iwnner vardapetneri knik'nerov, zanazan niwt'erov grut'iwnner, 1726–1738" [Commercial documents bearing priests' seals, documents concerning various matters, 1726–1738], ASMA, folder 5b.

91. The term *ordnagir* appears throughout most Julfan correspondence. It is discussed in the Astrakhan Code of Laws (chapter 14, article 10), where the authors equate it to a *gir khratoy*, or "letter of advice." For an etymology of this term, see Herzig 1991a, 434.

92. We can presume that the choice between Tabriz-Aleppo and Tabriz-Izmir would depend on how urgent the letter was and whether the letter was sent via a merchant traveling by trade caravan. If the latter, the longer route to Izmir would probably be chosen due to lower customs and road fees. For a comparison of road fees on these two routes, see P'ap'azyan 1990, 111; and my brief discussion in chapter 4 above.

93. The only known case of an excommunication issued from Julfa concerns the case of an Armenian priest in Madras, Ter Ohannes Khachikian, accused of having poisoned a newly arrived senior priest, Harut'iwn Vardapet, in 1741. The case was overturned when twenty-one of Madras's leading merchants complained to the clerical hierarchy in Julfa and defended the accused priest. See letter of 11 Tira 1743, "Namakner—Madras," ASMA, folder 104.

94. This is probably a reference to an Ottoman embassy that arrived in Isfahan on December 7, 1724, and left eleven days later (December 18) totally dissatisfied, because Mahmud Khan had not even received it. The envoy had been sent by Ahmad Pasha, governor of Baghdad, in reaction to the earlier Afghan embassy under Sayyed Sadeq. See Floor 1998, 191. The Armenian identified in this passage as Hagobjan seems to have been in the embassy's suit, possibly as a translator. Unfortunately the word used in the passage to describe his role in the embassy is unknown to me (see note 95 for the original passage).

95. "Մէք Գ [3] գիր թարերեցս յառէջ ամք աղարկել միՃս պ[ա] ր[ո]ն մարտիրոսիՃ եւ Բ [2] գիր միՃ մազբուՃ [*mazbun*<A/P *mazmun*, "content, meaning, purpose"; the writer uses a standard Julfa phrase to indicate that two identical copies of the letter were written, or in his words: "two letters, one content"] խորոմաց [<JD *horom*: Ottoman, *Rumi*] էլչիՃ [<P/T, old Turcic, *ilchi*: "ambassador or envoy"] տեղէս յետ դառմաՃ ճառակատարեցց յակրբջաՃՃ խոտուրն [<JD, contraction of *khet ur, grabar, het iur*: i.e., "with him"] արեւ [JD, past tense

of "to take"] զսամանէր պատրա [this is most certainly a scribal error; the writer probably had Hamadan or Tabriz or any other Ottoman city to the north in mind, but mistakenly wrote Basra instead; Basra is in the south, so it would not make sense to give mail to someone going there with the goal of remitting it to Istanbul or Izmir in the north] տվ̀ինք մինն թողաթա ադարկեն իզմիր կամ յալապ միւսն ըստանբոլայ վ[ե]ր[ա]յ ադարկեն ումիդ ա[ստուծ]մէ սահ[ա]բնւս դուլունն լինի խասել (Documenti Armeni Mercantile, ASV, busta 2, letter dated 1725).

96. See note 100 below.

97. Unfortunately, Melis provides no data for postal delivery times from Venice or Livorno to Izmir, but his data indicate that the delivery time from Venice to Istanbul in the fifteenth century was thirty-eight days (1983, 43).

98. եթէ մեր ո[ր]պ[իս]ութիւնն հարցանեք թարեդէս յառէչ յակրբ դի դավիթ̀ոփս եւ խալդարէնց մարգարին չաբրոփս եւ հալապալ կապուչինին չաբրոփս մեր ահվալնգրելանք մինչի գրուս խասանելն վերոյգրերն խասել կո լինի (Sceriman family letter, written from Isfahan, 30 Shabat 98 [18 June 1713], Documenti Armeni Mercantile, ASV, busta 2). (And if you ask us how we are, we wrote about it last year [and sent the letters] through the couriers of Hakob di David, of the Margar Khaldarian family and of the Capuchin [monks] of Aleppo. Until the arrival of this letter, the above-mentioned letters should have reached you.) See also the letter dated 1Ghamar 98 (19 July 1713), in the same folder.

99. եւս տեղս էլի ադարկեցինդէլ յամադան որ տեղէն զնալ ըստանբոլ պարոն մանվէլ էլչուս խեռ հուքմ արադինգոյ արեկ մերգրերն տվ̀ինք ուրն (Dados [Tadeo di Nazar Sceriman], Bartoghomeos, and Hakob to Petros and Ohannis, 15 Tira Azaria year 110 [1 October 1725], Documenti Armeni Mercantile, ASV, busta 2).

On Manuel Shahrimanian's role in the Persian embassy to the Sublime Porte in 1725, see, among others, Bellingeri 2004, 93–124; Lockhart 1958, 282; and especially Krusinski 1733, 2: 185 ff. Concerning the embassy, Krusinski writes: "The Person he [Shah Ashraf] made choice of for this Embassy, was an *Aghvan* [i.e., Afghan], who from a mule driver, was advanc'd to be a Colonel. But because a Man of that Stamp was not very proper to manage a Negotiation, he gave him only the Title of Ambassador, and joyn'd with him *Manuel-Cheriman,* Head of the Family of that Name, the most noble and considerable of all the *Armenian* Families at *Zulfa,* to act and negotiate according to his Intentions, with the *Grand-Signior's* Ministers" (2: 185). On the failure of the embassy in Constantinople, see Krusinski 1733, 2: 190 ff.

100. Sceriman letter of 16 Shams 96 (5 April 1711), Documenti Armeni Mercantile, ASV, busta 2.

101. Hovhannes (Giovanni/Gianbattista?) di Zaccaria Sceriman is said to have lived in Malacca in the 1720s, where he copied a manuscript that is now stored in the library of the Armenian Convent of Saint James in Jerusalem. See Khachikian 1988, 75.

102. Letter to Paron Ohanes and Paron Petros, 16 Shams 96 (5 April 1711), Documenti Armeni Mercantile, ASV, busta 2. This letter contains an obscure reference to a certain Mr. Abraham (one of the Sceriman factors in India) receiving a letter from "Brazil" and making investments there (պարոն աբրահամ̀ գրելէր թէ բրագելոյ գիր արեկ բրագիլ ծախսայ արարէլ). The writer hopes that this will prove to be profitable. If true, this would imply that the Scerimans were conducting commerce with Brazil, most likely through Portuguese Goa.

In the same paragraph in which Brazil is mentioned, there is discussion of maintaining factors (whose names are also given) in Surat and in Bengal, as well as in Istanbul and Izmir, and of investing family capital in those places.

103. There are, however, two letters in Documenti Armeni Mercantile, ASV, busta 2, from Paron Abraham, a Sceriman agent in Surat, sent directly to Pietro (Petros) and Gianbattista (Ohannes) Sceriman in Venice. Unfortunately, these letters do not bear the date of their arrival in Venice, so it is not possible to calculate how long it took for them to travel from Surat to Venice.

104. Headrick 1980, chap. 8 and esp. 130–131.

105. Furber 1959, 112, 117–118. The Portuguese *Estado da India* seems to have had a faster overland messenger service in the early seventeenth century, and "four months was considered to be the maximum time reasonably allowable for a courier on urgent business to get from Madrid to Goa, or vice versa" (Disney 1983, 59; see also Disney 1996). It should go without saying that my reliance on these seventeenth century–based studies does not pose any problems for my eighteenth century–based discussion in these pages, because there was no revolution in transportation between the seventeenth and eighteenth centuries.

106. Barendse 2002, 188.

## 6. THE CIRCULATION OF MEN AND CREDIT

1. Nshanian 1915, 457–458.

2. See De Roover 1963, 50.

3. Udovitch 1970, 170.

4. See De Roover 1963, 49–53; Lopez 1971, 76; and Lopez and Raymond 2001, 174–176.

5. Udovitch 1970, 170.

6. On the role of the East India Companies as forerunners of modern multinational firms, see Carlos and Nicholas 1988; for the English East India Company, see Chaudhuri 1981.

7. De Roover 1963, 49–53.

8. Ibid., 49–50.

9. Lopez and Raymond 2001, 174.

10. Udovitch 1962. This seminal essay was later revised and expanded as a chapter in Udovitch 1970. For a survey of the *commenda*'s origin and spread, see Harris 2009.

11. Udovitch 1970, 172. See also the recent work by Heck 2006. Heck devotes considerable space to the Islamic *qirad/mudaraba* and concurs with Udovitch that all the circumstantial evidence points in the direction of an Islamic origin for the Mediterranean *commenda*. For the role of Islamic commercial and legal instruments in fueling the recovery of the European economy after its stagnation during the period of "Dark Age Economics," see Heck, 235–248. For a good discussion, based on primary sources, of the place of the *qirad/mudaraba* in Islamic law, see Heck, 301–304. Heck notes that not only was the Prophet Muhammad a *commenda* agent for Khadija, but several of his close associates, including the future caliphs Umar and Uthman, "likewise reportedly were parties to such contracts" (105).

12. For the spread of other Islamic/Arab business practices and their adoption in Europe, see Lieber 1967.

13. For a brief discussion of the Astrakhan Code of Laws, see chapter 7 below.

14. Poghosyan 1967, 130.

15. Herzig 1991a, 213.

16. Khachikian 1988, 121–139. The importance of the Julfan *enkeragir* was noted earlier, though not identified as a variety of *commenda*, by Levon Khachikian in his groundbreaking 1966 essay, "The Ledger of the Merchant Hovhannes Joughayetsi."

17. Khachikian 1988, 121–122.

18. Herzig 1991a, chap. 3.

19. Ibid.

20. For a history of Armenia during this period, see Ter-Ghewondyan 1976 and Garsoïan 1997, 117–143.

21. If the Julfan *commenda* was indeed a later borrowing from the Iranian *mudaraba*, it could have been adopted in the second half of the sixteenth century, when the trade of Old Julfa experienced a sudden growth. All this, of course, is pure speculation because no primary sources on the trade of Old Julfa seem to have survived, and neither the history of Old Julfa nor the history of the Iranian *mudaraba* has been studied properly.

22. For instance, in his otherwise informative work on the history of Islamic partnerships, Murad Çizakça seems too eager to ascribe an Islamic genealogy to the Julfan *commenda*. Ignoring Herzig's carefully worded discussion on *possible* Islamic origins, Çizakça treats matters as though the Islamic derivation of the *commenda* is a demonstrated fact. He does the same with regard to Udovitch's excellent work on the Islamic precedents for the *commenda*, giving the reader the impression that the debate over the Islamic or Byzantine prehistory of the Mediterranean *commenda* had ended in favor of Islam. See Çizakça 1996, 19–20, for the author's views on the Julfans based as they are on a rather careless reading of Herzig, and pp. 10–19 for his eager endorsement of Udovitch's carefully reasoned account of the possible Islamic origins of the Western *commenda*. Çizakça's rendition of these debates is devoid of the qualifying phrases with which both Herzig and Udovitch articulate their controversial views.

23. There is also a remote possibility that aspects of the Julfan *commenda* may have been related to a Mediterranean prototype that could have entered Armenian usage via the Cilician kingdom of Armenia during the Crusades. A surviving Armenian translation of a French code of laws for the principality of Antioch includes a chapter on commercial arrangements that vaguely resemble the *commenda*. Even if this were the case, it still remains true that the European *commenda* was most likely of Islamic origin. It is possible, therefore, that Armenians could have borrowed the *commenda* from the Europeans and introduced further Islamic elements, including terminology such as "muzarbay," later. See Alishan 1876, 82–85.

24. Weber 1947, 201, quoted in Goody 1996, 50. Weber, of course, argued that "rationality," which he saw as historically emanating from double-entry accounting and other related economic practices, was a peculiarly European invention, along with the *commenda* contract. This blatantly Eurocentric view of history has been denounced and comprehensively refuted by most scholars writing on these topics today. For an insightful overview of the debates on the role of "rationality" and double accounting in the histories of the East and West, and a good discussion of the *commenda* in this debate, see Goody, 49–89.

25. The *kata ruznama* is one of two Julfa dialect designations for a daily accounting ledger. The other term is *kata ruzlama*. Both are "corruptions" of the Hindi word *khata* (account-

ing ledger) and the Persian *ruzname*. For a surviving copy of such a ledger, see Khachikian and Papazian 1984. Several other ledgers, including at least one belonging to the Sceriman/ Shahrimanian family and a multivolume ledger belonging to the Minasian family, have survived in the archives but remain unpublished.

26. Poghosyan 1967, 132–133.

27. Khachikian 1988, 123–126. It should be noted here that the agent's share also increased if he invested his own capital in a bilateral *commenda*.

28. This etymology is suggested by Herzig 1991a, 434.

29. Poghosyan 1967, 132.

30. Ibid., 133–134. The binding nature of the *ordnagirs* (also referred to as *barova-girs/barevagirs*) is revealed in a petition to Julfa's Assembly of Merchants in a dispute concerning the refusal of a *commenda* agent in India to return immediately to his masters in Julfa, as instructed in an *ordnagir/barovagir*. See document 17 in the appendix in Aslanian 2007b.

31. Lansdowne MS 1047, BL, folio 78.

32. Poghosyan 1967, 133.

33. Ibid., 134.

34. Ibid.

35. For translations of *tomars*, see the appendix in Aslanian 2007b.

36. Agha di Matus, "Tomar Book," ABMC, P.D. 66.c. This *tomar* was concluded between an agent named Agha di Matus and Khwaja Minas and covers the agent's transactions from the 1670s to the 1680s, most of which involve diamonds. In terms of format and style, it differs from all other *tomars* I have examined in that it is not a roll, as most *tomars* are, but a series of long sheets of paper folded and accommodated in a rectangular leather notebook. For a discussion of this *tomar*, see the section on Livorno in chapter 4.

37. Lansdowne MS 1047, BL, folio 76. See the appendix in Aslanian 2007b for full transcription, translation, and gloss for this and other *commenda* contracts.

38. "Coja Zecharia de Avettde v. Cooja Tentasu, Coja Avetlake and Coja Sarad, brothers and partners, 19 April 1735, *Mayor's Court Proceedings*, P 328/70, India Office Records, BL, folios 45–47 (45).

39. See the very brief and unsatisfactory attempt in Baghdiantz McCabe 1999, 217.

40. This point is made by Baghdiantz McCabe 1999, 217. See *The Journal of Zak'aria of Agulis*, annotated and translated in Bournoutian 2003, 161–162. For the original in Armenian, see Zak'aria of Agulis 1938, 159–160. Like most of the agents we encounter in Manila, Zakaria was very young (only seventeen years old) when he embarked on his first *commenda* mission.

41. Khachikian 1966, 155.

42. Ter Hovhaniants 1880, 2: 273–274.

43. Constant Jughayetsi, *Vasn norahas mankants' ew yeritasartats' vacharakanats' khrat* [Concerning advice to the adolescent and to young merchants), more commonly known as *Ashkharazhoghov* [Compendium], Bodleian MS F14, folios 10, 31, 34 and 59, for references to Constant's school in New Julfa. There are a few surviving copies of this trade manual. The Bodleian copy of this manuscript seems to have been copied in the late 1680s. MS 64 of the Nerses Shnorhali Library collection at the All Savior's Monastery in Julfa is the

best and oldest surviving copy. Two other copies are stored at the Mashtots Matenadaran in Yerevan (Armenia): MS 10704 dates from the first decade of the eighteenth century and was copied in Baghdad; MS 5994 also dates from a later period. The Bodleian copy seems to have escaped the attention of scholars. I am grateful to Bert Vaux for bringing it to my attention.

44. This is especially the case with MS 64, stored in New Julfa.

45. Vanantets'i 1699. This manual was largely based on Constant's earlier manual. See Kévonian 1975.

46. As the title page and preface of the Amsterdam manual indicate, the merchant who commissioned the printing of this manual was a certain Khwaja Petros of Julfa.

47. Villotte 1730, 425.

48. Tavernier 1688, 160.

49. Fryer 1698, 269; also quoted in Raveux 2011. I thank Olivier Raveux for sharing his work with me.

50. See Orengo 1993.

51. For the sociological impact of the *commenda* on Julfan women who were left alone in their suburb to tend their families while their men circulated throughout the Julfan trading settlements in the Indian Ocean and the Mediterranean, see Aslanian 2007b, 343–350. I discuss there the paradoxical role of the *commenda* in helping to undermine the patriarchal foundations of Julfan society. For a perceptive and pioneering discussion of the role of women in Julfan society, see Berberian 2010.

52. Fryer 1698, 263–264 (emphasis added).

53. Francisco Pelsaert's denunciation of their indigo-buying techniques in India in the early 1600s is one of the harshest appraisals of the greedy attributes associated with Julfan *commenda* agents. Pelsaert describes them as "racing over the country from village to village, with greedy eyes like guests who think there is not enough food on the table to go around, reaching for every dish, and jostling the other guests" (Pelsaert's passage is from Moreland 1923/1990, as quoted in Boxer 1976, 85).

54. Tavernier 1688, 159.

55. Fryer 1698, 268.

56. Santiago or Ohannes had become a wealthy merchant in his own right twenty years after his deposition in Manila, for we come across him in Basra in 1755 in a document testifying that he had loaned a large sum of rupees to Gevorg Vardapet, the primate of the All Savior's Monastery in New Julfa. See the *avak,* or promissory note, dated 30 Aram 1755, in "Zanazan niwt'erov grut'iwnner 1700–1800" [Documents concerning various matters, 1700–1800], ASMA, folder 3. The will of one of his relatives, Grigor di Barakial, dated 1684, is located in "Zanazan niwt'erov grut'iwnner—Ktakner Nor Jugha" [Documents concerning various matters—wills, New Julfa], ASMA, folder 28/12.

57. MS Ramo de Inquisición, tomo 857, "Reconciliaciones al Gremio de nuestra Santa Madre Iglesia de Minas di Elias . . . Esteban di Codidyan, todos Armenios dela Secta de cisma Armenio" [Reconciliation to the Holy Mother Church of Minas di Elias . . . Esteban di Cododyan, all Armenians of the Armenian Schismatic Sect], AGN, Mexico City, folio 213b.

58. Ibid., folios 213b–215a.

59. Ibid., folios 207b–208b.

60. See deposition of Constantino di Lazzaro in MS Ramo de Inquisición, tomo 857, AGN, Mexico City, folio 419a.

61. There are at least three or four cases of Julfan merchants traveling to Acapulco in the 1730s for a seasonal visit before returning to Manila on the Manila galleon. In one case, at least, we have a Julfan merchant, a certain "Don Pedro di Zarate" [Agha Petros di Sarhat?], who traveled and lived in New Spain in the 1720s. We know about Don Pedro's life in Mexico because he was accused of heresy by the Inquisition in Mexico City and was put on trial in 1731. See the interesting proceedings from his trial, in MS Ramo Inquisición, tomo 829, exp. 7, AGN, folios 544–560v. For a brief discussion of Don Pedro's trial, see Nunn 1979, 45–46. See also Seijas 2007. I am grateful to Vartan Matossian for bringing Nunn's book to my attention. Given the illegible quality of the microfilm at my disposal, I relied on a transcription of the original document by Tatiana Seijas, to whom I am grateful.

62. This document from the municipal archives of Amsterdam is reproduced and translated in Van Rooy 1966, 353. Herzig, relying on the Astrakhan Code of Laws, cites the age of twenty-five for maturity among the Julfans (1991a, 163).

63. In a long passage describing Julfan merchants, and especially *commenda* agents, and their dispersal across vast spaces, Roques (1996, 149) suggests that these agents married locally and possibly outside their official religion: "Although Christian, they did as the other factors and married women in all the places where they traded in order to have a home there." (Quoique chretien, de meme que les autres facteurs font, ils prennent des femmes dans tous les lieux ou ils commercent afin d'y avoir un chez soi.)

64. Herzig 1991a, chap. 4. As Herzig notes, commission agency was referred to in Julfan sources as *amanatkar*. The Astrakhan Code refers to commission agency as one of the four forms of conducting commerce (Poghosyan 1967, 130).

65. For a brief discussion of these partnerships, see Lopez's 1971 classic, *The Commercial Revolution of the Middle Ages, 950–1350,* 74–76; see also Lane's vintage essay, published in 1944, "Family Partnerships and Joint Ventures in the Venetian Republic." For a helpful overview, see Hickson and Turner.

66. Lopez 1971, 174.

67. The role of the family firm in Islamicate societies has not received the attention it deserves. For a broad survey of the available literature regarding family business in India and further east, see Goody 1996, 138–162.

68. Herzig 1991a, 321; and Enthoven 2006, 433.

69. Lane 1944, 178.

70. See Goody 1996, 138–162.

71. The treaty was first published in its Russian translation in Parsamyan 1953, 1: 72. A photostat copy of the original in the Julfa dialect was appended to the Russian translation. For an English translation of the Russian text, see Bournoutian 2001, 25. Bournoutian's translations here as elsewhere are not from the Armenian text but from the *flawed* Russian translation.

72. Hovhannisyan 1957, 441–442. For a list of other Soviet Armenian historians who propagated the view that the Julfans had a centralized trading company, see Khachikian 1980, 260 n. 3.

73. See the photostat of the original text of the treaty reproduced by Parsamyan 1953,

72, but ignored by scholars until Shushanik Khachikian pointed out the glaring differences in the wording. See Khachikian 1988, 27; 1980, 271.

74. See Khachikian 1988, chap. 1; 1980, passim.

75. Baghdiantz McCabe 1999, 244. Most reviewers of Baghdiantz McCabe's book have noted the deeply problematic nature of her assertions regarding the "Trading Company of the Julfans." For a measured asssessment, see in particular Herzig's review 2004a, 174.

76. Baghdiantz McCabe 1999, 244.

77. Ibid.

78. See Baghdiantz McCabe, Harlaftis, and Minoglou 2005.

79. Baghdiantz McCabe 1999, 244.

80. Ibid., 245.

81. "The Respondents Case," in *Prize Appeals* (London, 1752?), 16. *Prize Appeals* is a collection of printed cases relating to ships confiscated during the War of Austrian Succession, originally belonging to Sir George Lee and now held at the New York Public Library, call no. KC+++p.v. 20–21. For background on this document, see Aslanian 2006c.

82. Herzig 1991a, chap. 3, is the only solid English-language study of the Julfan family firm to date. See also the earlier work by Khachikian 1988, chap. 1 and passim.

83. Cartwright 1611, 24, quoted in Herzig 1991a, 159.

84. Chardin 1811, 178: "Les familles des chrétiens orientaux sont très-nombreuses; il y en a d'Arméniens à Ispahan, qui comptent plus de cinq cents personnes dans leur parenté." (The families of Eastern Christians are very large; there are some [families] among the Armenians at Isfahan that count more than five hundred persons among their relatives.) Chardin discusses the importance Armenians placed on having large families and describes how celibacy and sterility were held in horror.

85. See Herzig 1993 for an excellent discussion.

86. See the classic works of Carlos and Nicholas: 1988 and 1996.

87. For instance, both the Sceriman/Shahrimanian and Guerak-Mirman families, originally from Julfa but resettled in Venice and Livorno beginning in the seventeenth century, claimed aristocratic ancestry. For the Scerimans, see Monsignor Basilio Sceriman's "Libro di Memorie di Monsignor Basilio Sceriman" [Book of memoirs of Monsignor Basilio Sceriman], Avogaria di Comun 348 Processi di Nobiltà—Sceriman (unpaginated court proceedings), ASV. For the Guerak-Mirmans, see P. Malenchini, *Brevi cenni storici sull' antichissima familglia Mirman de Ghirach* (Livorno, n.d. [but certainly published after 1891]).

88. Villotte 1730, 154–155.

89. The family's name is also given as Shehrimanian. I shall refer to them as either the Shahrimanian family or the Sceriman, which is how they identified themselves in most of the Italian cities where they lived, except Venice, where they used the Venetianized spelling "Seriman." They are not to be confused with the Shahamirian family of Madras who were members of the Armenian Gregorian church. Bhattacharya appears to be conflating the two names when she calls the family the "Shahmirians" and identifies them as "followers of the Catholic Church" (2008a, 84).

90. The literature on the Sceriman family is sparse and of uneven quality. One of the first historians to write about them was Ter Hovhaniants, who devoted a chapter to the family in his classic work on Julfan history (1880, 1: 123–142). Khachikian also has a useful discus-

sion of the family (1988, 69–89). Both authors make a number of factual errors about the family's history largely stemming from their lack of access or inability to consult the family's private papers stored in Venice. The first wide-ranging biographical study of the family, relying on previously ignored archival documents in Italian from the Venetian archives, was White 1961 (see esp. his introduction). There are also several studies of the Scerimans in Venice and Livorno. For Livorno, see the excellent study by Sanacore 1988, 127–161; for Venice, see Bonardi 1990 and 1996. While they broach a number of fascinating and previously ignored issues, Bonardi's essays contain some inaccuracies and errors probably arising from her failure to consult Armenian-language work on the family and especially the family correspondence written in the Julfa dialect and preserved in the Archivio di Stato of Venice, the Alishan archives in San Lazzaro, and the Don Mazza archives in Verona. See also the excellent study by Gugerotti 1990.

91. Khachikian 1988, 70. See also Fortunato Seriman, *Brevie memorie sulla famiglia Seriman* [Brief memoirs of the Seriman family], MS Cod. Cigogna 3403 [1855], ABMC, folio 4.

92. See the English translation of a Russian document in Bournoutian 2001, 9.

93. Seriman, *Brevie memorie,* ABMC, folio 2; and Anon. 1843, 13 ff.

94. Seriman, *Brevie memorie,* ABMC, folios 1–2, where the author writes: "The oldest notion to be had about this family is that eighty years prior to 1693, they maintained a house in Venice in the Corte dei Pignoli [in the parish of] San Giulian inhabited in that year [i.e., 1693] by Nazar the grandfather of Nazar and before him by other relatives. Thus it is stated in the memoirs of Monsignor Basilio Sceriman. . . . But the house of Venice could not have been maintained for reasons other than commerce albeit intermittently by individuals of the family and their agents." Both Maxwell White and, following him, Bonardi note that though the Sceriman presence in Venice goes back to the house of 1612 or 1613, the family did not reside there but kept it for the use of family members or agents/factors occasionally visiting the city. Bonardi draws our attention to an interesting fact not frequently mentioned in the literature. She points to a document in the Archivio di Stato of Venice containing the names of some seventy or so Armenians associated with the *Santa Croce* Armenian church and dating from 1653, and notes that the Scerimans are conspicuously missing from this list. She also points out that the majority of individuals on the list were originally from New Julfa (1996, 230–231).

95. Both Ter Hovhaniants (1880) and Khachikian (1988) confuse the brothers Nazar and Shahriman with the sons of the family's patriarch, Agha Murat, which would place their loan to the Venetian republic in the 1630s or 1640s. However, the documents in the Venetian archives make it abundantly clear that these two brothers were sons of Khwaja Murat the son of Sarhat and were thus separated by a generation from Agha Murat's sons.

96. Chick 1939, 2: 1358.

97. The letter of conversion is written in the Julfa dialect and preserved in the Archives of the Propaganda Fide in the Vatican, SOCG, vol. 495, folios 247r–261v. This document has been reproduced in Karapetyan and Tajiryan 1998, 87–88.

98. White 1961, 12; and Seriman, *Brevie memorie,* ABMC, folio 7. For the family's generous patronage of the Vatican, including the erection of several Catholic churches in Isfahan and Julfa and the establishment of a Catholic parish there, see White, 10–11; and Fortunato Seriman, folios 2–4.

99. Seriman, *Brevie memorie,* ABMC, folio 8.

100. See the eighteenth-century manuscript *Resultato del processo per la verificazione de requisiti alla N.V. nella famiglia de Co. Co: Fr[ate]lli Sceriman,* MS Cod. Cigogna 3428/9, ABMC, Venice (no pagination).

101. White 1961, 12.

102. Chick 1939, 2: 1358.

103. For a detailed and excellent analysis of the sectarian situation in Julfa in the 1680s and 1690s, see Karapetyan and Tajiryan 1998.

104. White 1961, 12.

105. Chick 1939, 2: 1358. Marcara's lengthy will in Armenian (dated 1700) is reproduced in Ter Hovhaniants 1880, 1: 111–127; 1980, 124–142.

106. By the early eighteenth century, the Shahrimanians were well integrated into Venice's ruling class through marriage alliances with several Venetian noble families. The Shahrimanians were also well integrated into the hierarchy of the Catholic Church, which further increased their prestige as foreigners in Venice. For instance, Basilio son of Gaspar Shahrimanian, was ordained a monsignor and later became governor of a number of regions, including Perugia, while Stefano Domenico Sceriman was elected bishop of several regions subordinate to Venice. Another prominent Sceriman from Venice was Zaccaria di Seriman, who became a celebrated writer and satirist in Venice in the 1760s.

107. This is puzzling because the eldest brother was Zacaria, and he appears to have been still alive in 1684, since his signature is on the document confessing the Catholic faith. If this is the case, how is one to explain Khachikian's assertion (1988, 27 and 31) that the 1667 trade agreement bore Marcara's and not Zacaria's name as the representative of the family?

108. Bonardi 1990, 110. Bonardi does not provide any evidence for this controversial claim.

109. The letter book of Hakob di Murat contained copies of all the letters of instruction (*barevagirs* or *ordnagirs*) he sent beginning August 16, 1731, in Moscow and continuing to 1734, in St. Petersburg, Amsterdam, and Venice. This valuable book is stored in the Avogaria di Comun, ASV, busta 17. Hakob di Murat, unlike his "aristocratic" cousins in Venice and Livorno, was normally based in Isfahan/Julfa but continued to correspond with them on business matters in the Julfa dialect—an indication that even if the family firm was liquidated in 1717, as Bonardi suggests, the separate branches could have been cooperating until the 1730s. In short, the breakup of the family firm into independent units did not necessarily mean an end to family cooperation. I thank Edmund Herzig for bringing this possibility to my attention in an e-mail communication on 12 June 2006.

110. "Documenti Armeni," Acquisti e Doni, ASFi, busta 123, filza 1, document 61. The document in question is a notarized letter by Canaan di Minas (Khwaja Minas di Panos's son) stating that the latter sent Melkum di Matos to Venice on 12 Aram, Azaria year 77 (27 December 1692), with precious stones to be delivered to Agha di Matos. Other letters sent by the Minasians to Agha di Matos in this folder are also addressed to Melkum as well as other known Minasian agents, such as a certain Vanjale and Herapet, who must have been either relatives of Agha di Matus or very closely associated with him. See "Documenti Armeni," Acquisti e Doni, ASFi, busta 123, filza 1, doc. 131.

111. See the *commenda* contract between Grigor son of Kaluts/Galuts and Nazar di Murat Sceriman/Shahrimanian dated 15 Nirhan 1711, Azaria year 95 (Don Mazza, busta 2). See

also several legal papers, including a *ghatilayagir,* or letter of quittance, in the same busta, and a *tomar* of Grigor son of Kaluts/Galuts made with Nazar di Murat Sceriman in Venice on 7 Tira (23 September), Azaria year 90 (1705).

112. Unpaginated account book of Hakob di Murat, July 1728, Documenti Armeni Mercantile, ASV, busta 1.

113. Chick 1939, 1: 485. According to a Carmelite letter from 1689, paraphrased by Karapetyan and Tajiryan (1988, 89), the Shahrimanian family (and *not* the family firm) had over a hundred members, including servants and women.

114. The Sceriman family papers in the Don Mazza archives in Verona (especially busta 1) contain numerous documents, including at least half a dozen *tomars* and many business letters involving the family's agents operating from various places in the Ottoman Empire.

115. For Sarhat di Emmanuel in Calcutta, see the discussion in Seth 1922, 303 n. 1, where the author provides a transcript of the inscription on Sarhat's tombstone in a Catholic church in Calcutta. For his cousin Marcara's life between Madras and Livorno, see Sanacore 1988, 147–150.

116. Khachikian 1988, 74–75. There are several letters to Ignatius Shahriman in Hakob di Murat's letter book (Avogaria di Comun, ASV, busta 217).

117. See the letter addressed to a certain Ohanis Shahrimanian from Pegu (Burma) dated 1676 in Documenti Armeni Mercantile, ASV, busta 2. The verso side of the letter has a note in Italian stating that this is a "family letter sent from the Indies."

118. Khachikian 1988, 100; see also Collectie 606 Armen Joseph, ARA, invent. no. 6. This Hovhannes son of Zacaria does not appear on any known family trees.

119. "Libro di memorie di Monsignor Basilio Sceriman," Avogaria di Comun 348 Processi di Nobiltà—Sceriman, ASV (unpaginated court proceedings). It is possible that there were several wealthy Khwaja Minases during the same period, as Aghassian and Kévonian sensibly maintain (1999, 77–78 n. 11), and that the Minas mentioned in Monsignor Basilio's memoirs and active in Surat is not Minas di Panos. It is impossible to say one way or the other. The only evidence that suggests that the Minas mentioned in Monsignor Basilio's memoir is Minas di Panos is the name given for Minas's daughter (Nanajan) in both the *Libro di memorie* and Minas di Panos's last will.

120. "Libro di memorie di Monsignor Basilio Sceriman," Avogaria di Comun 348 Processi di Nobiltà—Sceriman, ASV (unpaginated court proceedings).

121. Boxer 1976. Boxer's essay is the only available treatment of Khwaja Minas. However, see the important documentation from the India Office Records reproduced in Baladouni and Makepeace 1998. The Minas mentioned in Boxer's essay, as well as in the East India Company documents, is said to have died in Diu (northwestern India) in 1687, whereas Minas di Panos died in New Julfa in 1702. It could well turn out that Aghassian and Kévonian (1999, 77–78 n. 11) are correct in concluding that Minas di Panos of the Minasian family firm is not the same person as the famous Minas of Surat.

122. Baladouni and Makepeace 1998, 54.

123. Ibid., 71.

124. Boxer 1976, 83.

125. Baladouni and Makepeace 1998, 59.

126. Gopal 1971, 204.

127. Khachikian 1988, 24–28.

128. The original will is in "Zanazan niwt'erov grut'iwnner—Ktakner Nor Jugha," ASMA, folder 28/13; for a transcription see Ter Hovhaniants 1880, 1: 159–161; and for an English translation, see Herzig 1991a, 289–290. See figure 15 for a reproduction of the will.

129. Seth 1937/1992, 484.

130. Wright 2003, 309.

131. Document 102 in Lansdowne MS 1048, BL, is a *commenda* contract between Minas di Elias and senior members of the Minasian firm, including Emniaz di Minas, Grigor di Sethagha, and Aghamal di Sarfras, dated 25 Ovtan (8 February) 1744, Julfa, Isfahan. The ratio of profits seems to be 33.33 percent for Minas di Elias as tractator and the rest to the senior members of the firm. For background on Minas di Elias's ill-fated investments in India, see Aslanian 2006c.

132. Minas di Elias visited the Inquisition office in Manila and left a *testimonio* in 1735. See MS Ramo de Inquisición, tomo 857, AGN, folio 201. The testimony indicates that, despite his family's reputation as staunch defenders of the Armenian Church, Minas di Elias had no qualms about converting to Catholicism when it was in his self-interest to do so.

133. Many of these documents are stored in the Documenti Armeni Mercantile, ASV, buste 1 and 2; and Avogaria di Comun, ASV, busta 217.

## 7. TRUST, SOCIAL CAPITAL, AND NETWORKS

1. Tilly 2005, 12 (emphasis added).

2. Coleman 1988, S-101.

3. Seabright 2004, 48.

4. Greif 2006, 313–314.

5. According to Greif, the contractual problem that gives rise to risk and malfeasance stems from "the need to commit ex ante not to breach contractual obligations ex post despite the separation between the *quid* and the *quo*" (2006, 314).

6. Trivellato 2005, 101–103. For the notion of "communities of mercantile trust," see Bayly 2002, 59.

7. Trivellato 2005, 102.

8. Trivellato 2009, 12.

9. Mauro 1990, 273.

10. Braudel 1982, 164.

11. Baladouni and Makepeace 1998, xxxiv.

12. Chaudhury 2005, 68 (emphasis added).

13. Baghdiantz McCabe, Harlaftis, and Pepelasis Minoglou 2005.

14. The literature on trust is too extensive to be listed here. For an excellent and well-known essay, see Dasgupta 1998. See also the contributions of Gambetta and Luhmann in the same volume (Gambetta 1988b), as well as Cook 2001; and Hardin 2002. For discussions critical of the concept, see Guinnane 2005; Sosis 2005; and esp. Williamson 1993. A good early survey on trust can be found in Barber 1983. For an excellent discussion of some of these sources and an application of "trust" as defined in some of this literature to the Sephardic merchant network in the early modern period, see the important contribution by Trivellato

2005 and 2009. My own approach to trust is less concerned with definitional issues explored in the rather abstract treatment of the topic by some of the theorists of trust listed above than with its place in the context of social networks, norms, and monitoring/policing practices used in some networks to create and maintain trust among long-distant merchants.

15. The only work known to me that employs the social capital concept to examine trust among merchants before the twentieth century is Ogilvie 2005, which focuses on the nineteenth century. Steven Shapin's classic work (1991) on early modern science in England also has an illuminating discussion on trust but does not discuss long-distance trade or social capital.

16. Gambetta 1988b, ix.

17. See Trivellato 2009.

18. Though research needs to be done on this topic, it is likely that Julfan-Indian credit relations in Isfahan would have been predicated on recourse to Safavid legal institutions, as they apparently were with Dutch-Indian relations. I owe this information to Willem Floor.

19. Barber 1983, 8. For a good survey of definitions of "trust," see Barber, chap. 2.

20. Gambetta 1988b, 217 (emphasis added).

21. Ibid.

22. Dasgupta 1998, 54.

23. For Smith and Hume, see Bruni and Sugden 2000.

24. Bourdieu first discussed social capital in his 1980 essay, "Le capital social: Notes provisoires," 2–3. It was translated into English much later (2001) as "The Forms of Capital." The neoclassical notion of capital refers to physical and financial resources accumulated as a result of human labor and investments. This kind of capital, as Bourdieu points out in his essay, represents only one species of capital, the others being "cultural" and "social" capital. A fourth form of capital, invented by economists in the 1960s, is "human capital," or investments in the education of individuals that promise dividends later both for the individual and for society.

25. The best introduction to the literature of social capital is Halpern 2005, especially his introduction. For other surveys, see Portes 2000 and Woolcock 1988.

26. Putnam 1995, 664–665.

27. Cited in Cohen and Prusak 2001, 3.

28. My definition here and the ideas in the rest of this paragraph heavily rely on Ogilvie 2005, 15.

29. Bourdieu's notion of *habitus* is famously developed in his *Outline of a Theory of Practice* (1977, chap. 2).

30. North 1991, 24 (emphasis added). For a clear and rigorous introduction to the literature on transaction costs, see North 1990, chap. 4.

31. Coleman 1988, S-99 ff.

32. Ogilvie 2005, 17.

33. One of the most influential accounts of reputation effects is found in Greif 1989.

34. Coleman 1988, S-108–S-109. The idea of multiplexity or denseness in network ties is also developed in Granovetter's classic 1973 essay, "The Strength of Weak Ties," and in his influential 1985 work, "Economic Action and Social Structure: The Problem of Embedded-

ness." See also the earlier treatment of multiplex ties in Boissevain 1974, 34 ff., where Boissevain also refers to "many-stranded relations."

35. Bruni and Sugden 2000, 33–34.

36. Ogilvie 2005, 17.

37. Diamond merchants are used as a case study by Coleman 1988, S-98–S-99 and passim; and Putnam 2000; as well as by Cohen and Prusak 2001, chap. 1; and Halpern 2005, introduction. Sosis, who does not work within the social capital paradigm, also has a concise and insightful discussion of the diamond industry (2005, 11–12).

38. Bernstein 1992, 121.

39. Ibid.

40. The figure 95 percent is from Sosis 2005, 11 n. 8, where Sosis cites R. Shields, *Diamond Stories* (Ithaca, NY: Cornell University Press, 2002) as his source. It may not hold for today.

41. Bernstein 1992, 128.

42. Ibid.

43. Coleman 1988, S-99.

44. One of the unexpected drawbacks of a network in which the conclusion of substantial transactions is based on trust is that it can also be "hacked" and exploited by clever outsiders, as a recent high-stakes heist reported in the *Los Angeles Times* demonstrates. See the interesting account "As Scams Go, This Is a Gem," *Los Angeles Times,* 29 March 2006. In this case, a Geneva-based diamond dealer advanced $14 million worth of gems to a woman claiming to be the wife of deposed Congolese dictator Mobutu Sese Seko without receiving a penny in return. Such cases of outside manipulation, however, are extremely rare.

45. See chapter 4 for a discussion of Astrakhan's Julfan Armenian community.

46. The best account of the Astrakhan Armenian community and its significant Julfan population is the long introduction to Poghosyan 1967; see also the excellent treatment in Yukht 1957; and the documents and commentary in Bournoutian 2001.

47. Poghosyan 1967, 7.

48. Ibid., 6.

49. Ibid.

50. Hodgson 1974, 1: 59.

51. Herzig 2007, 71–77.

52. Poghosyan 1967, 132. Chapter 14, article 10 states that the agent is obliged to obey the instructions contained in his master's *ordnagir,* or letter of advice/instruction. Article 14 of the same chapter states that if a master writes an *ordnagir* to his agent and commands him to immediately return home without conducting further commerce, the agent is naturally obliged to follow his master's instructions (Poghosyan 1967, 133–134). In this connection, it is interesting to note that this same matter was addressed in a petition to the Assembly of Merchants by the Khwaja Minasian family firm dated 12 Nadar 112 (29 October 1727) in "Arevtrakan grut'iwnner vardapetneri knik'nerov, zanazan niwt'erov grut'iwnner—1726–1738" [Commercial documents bearing priests' seals, documents concerning various matters, 1726–1738], ASMA, folder 5b. In this case, the assembly voted in favor of the plaintiffs, thus affirming the right of the master in a *commenda* contract to have his instructions concerning the immediate return home of his agent(s) in accordance with his *ordnagir.*

53. Poghosyan 1967, 132–133. My translation is slightly different than that offered in Khachikian 1966, 153.

54. Tavernier 1688, 159. Elsewhere (202), Tavernier notes that "drubbing" was a common punishment in Safavid Iran for merchants who had defaulted on their commitments.

55. To trace the development of his seminal theory of the Maghribi coalition, see Greif 1989, 1991, and 1992. These essays have been republished with certain modifications in Greif's 2006 magnum opus, *Institutions and the Path to the Modern Economy: Lessons from Medieval Trade*. Greif's use of the concept of a coalition assumes that members apply "multilateral reputational mechanisms" *collectively* to punish members who are caught breaking the coalition's norms. Such punishment for Greif takes the form of banishment or ostracism of the guilty party from the coalition. Greif's theory of the Maghribi coalition and its emphasis on collective punishment by *all* coalition members of the guilty party have been taken to task by Edwards and Ogilvie (2008) on empirical grounds. See Greif's compelling response (2008). Unlike Greif, I do not assume that the Julfan "coalition" collectively banished guilty parties or imposed sanctions as a collective. Evidence of collective sanctions in the Julfan case is lacking, though there is evidence of multilateral reputational mechanisms involving more than two parties.

56. Israel 2002.

57. The figure is cited in Richard 1995, 82; it derives from a missionary report of 1672 that points out that the Catholic missionaries give Mass in Julfa for three hundred attendees. Karapetyan and Tajiryan (1998, 89) state that there were about twenty Catholic families in Julfa in 1689, not counting the Sceriman/Shahrimanian family.

58. Quoted in Kaplan 2002, 51.

59. The coffeehouse venture was a local partnership between the Julfan Paul de Serquis and the Ottoman Armenian Harut'iwn or Pascal from Aleppo. It dates from the 1670s and lasted at least twelve years. I owe this information to Olivier Raveux.

60. North 1991, 31.

61. As noted in chapter 2, there are no reliable population figures for Julfa in the seventeenth or eighteenth century and none at all for the "coalition" of merchants. My rough calculation here is based on a conservative estimate of the number of Julfan *commenda* agents and other business employees operating in the coalition at any given time in the late seventeenth and early eighteenth centuries. Commenting on Julfan *commenda* agents in his important manual of trade concerning India, Georges Roques writes: "All these factors are dependents of those big merchants of Julfa, some with eighty, others a hundred, some more some less, some of them relatives, others servants or lads whom they groom to become merchants" (1996, 148). Ter Hovhaniants (1880, 1: 161–162; 1980, 1: 177–178) notes that the Ghaldarents family had at least twenty-seven factors whose names are recorded in the archives. Similarly, the Shahrimanian/Sceriman family firm of Julfa is said to have had a hundred employees in 1699. The Mirman family of Julfa operating out of Italy in the late seventeenth and early eighteenth centuries had twenty-two factors whose names have come down to us. See the list of factors in a *stampa* book on the Mirmans in Procuratori di San Marco, ASV, busta 180/D, folios 21–22. If we assume that the average family firm in Julfa had thirty business employees, including *commenda* agents and lower-level employees such as couriers and so on whose names are not recorded in the surviving papers, and accept Ter

Hovhaniants's conventional figure of twenty to thirty leading family firms as operating in Julfa at the peak of the township's commerce, then the number of Julfans involved in long-distance trade and active in the coalition would be between six hundred and nine hundred, and possibly more. Bhattacharya offers a lower estimate of three hundred to four hundred, without providing evidence or documentation for her figure (2008b, 18).

62. See letter of Minas di Elias, 14 Ovdan 129 (28 January 1744), "High Court of Appeals for Prizes: Papers," HCA 42/026, PRO, letter no. 24, folio 103. It seems that on some occasions, Julfan merchants knew when a debt could not be repaid due to extenuating circumstances, in which case they preferred not to apply to the court system. The example of Mr. Nerses is a case in point. One of the Minasian letters states: "Mr. Nierses [sic] the debtor is not in any manner whatever able to satisfy and Pay his Debt; And if we should ask him to pay his Debt, the very thing could occasion to us more Detriment than the value of the same, so it is better for us to leave the whole to providence" (HCA 42/026, PRO, letter no. 24, folios 109–110).

63. Greif 1992, 530.

64. "High Court of Appeals for Prizes: Papers," HCA 42/026, PRO, letter no. 49, folio 146.

65. Studnicki-Gizbert 2007, 84.

66. Ibid.

67. Mentz 2005, 68.

68. Steingass 1892, 72.

69. As Jessica Goldberg points out in her impressive Geniza-based study of Maghribi Jewish merchants, the exact term for "reputation" did not exist in Geniza documents. When twelfth-century Jewish merchants wanted to refer to reputation, they most frequently used the Arabic term *'ird,* "whose semantic field includes honor and dignity," or *jāh,* "whose primary semantic range includes rank, standing and prestige" (Goldberg 2007, 123; see also Goldberg 2005). Goldberg 2005, 99–104, contains an interesting discussion of "the management of commercial correspondence," which is remarkably parallel to Julfan usage. I thank Jessica Goldberg for sharing her important work with me.

70. Steingass 1892, 1180.

71. Bedrossian 1871/1985.

72. See Hakob Sceriman/Shahrimanian in Amsterdam to Parons Stepan and Astuatsatur in Venice, 19 December 1732, Avogaria di Comun, ASV, busta 17.

73. Fenster and Smail 2003, 2. As Fenster and Smail point out, *fama* became identified with gossip (i.e., idle chatter) only in the eighteenth and nineteenth centuries.

74. Hovanjan di Tahmaz in Basra to Aghazar son of Tsatur in Pondicherry or Madras, 21 Aram 132 (5 January 1747), HCA 32/1833, PRO, box 1, letter no. 181.

75. "Documenti Armeni," Acquisti e Doni, ASFi, busta 123, filza 1, document 34: Իսկ թէպէտ երեսունք զիրաւանքդ չէմ տեսեր բայց անուամբ զհտեմ ո[րպէ]ս անուն քո է պ[այ]ծ[ա]ռ եւ ճրագ ի մէջ հայոց ազգիս: զի ամէն ուրեք տարածեալ է քո բարհամբաւդ եւ մեծութիւնդ:

76. Burt 2001.

77. See Herzig 1991a, 192; Chardin 1811, 8: 105.

78. See "Namakner—Bangala, 1712–1800" [Letters—Bengal, 1712–1800], ASMA, folder 48. For a transcription and translation, see Aslanian 2008c and 2006a.

79. Անփորձ մարդի [մարդոյ, different genitive construction in the Matenadaran copy (MS 10704, folio 100) of this manuscript] փոխս [փոխ—according to Matenadaran MS 10704] եւ ամանաթ [<P amanat: "consignment, deposit"] մի տալ [տար, different infinitive in the Oxford Bodleian copy, MS F17, folio 84] եթէ դու ըստունքիւ գիտենաս թէ լել ախտիբարի մարդայ ա. բ. գ. [1,2,3] հոբիէլ հաշց եւ փորձ թախիֆս [<P tahqiq: "examination, interrogation"] արայ. Ապայ թէ եայ փոխս [փոխ—according to MS 10704] տուր եայ ամանաթ թամամրկոդ եւ վկայիւ. Բայց գամ[ենայն] առդու եւ տուրտո գրեայ գրեայ եւ գրեայ. Եսորէն վառն մի ձգեր (Constant Jughayetsi, *Vasn norahas mankants'ew yeritasartats'vacharakanats' khrat* [Concerning advice to the adolescent and to young merchants], more commonly known as *Ashkharhazhoghov* [Compendium], MS 64, ASMA, folio 6 [emphasis added]).

80. Khachikian 1988, 122–123. For the original source, see Zak'aria of Agulis 1938, 160–161. An English translation is available in Bournoutian 2003, 162–163.

81. See Greif 1989, 1991, 1992, and 2006.

82. *Santa Catharina* logbook of Spanish and English translations, HCA 42/026, PRO, letter no. 147, folios 369–370. It should be noted that the discussion about "blotting out" names does not seem to be connected to dishonesty in business, but rather to the refusal of a prominent Julfan merchant, a certain Johannes Savahi di Canan, who was residing in India during the unstable years of Nadir Shah's reign in the 1740s, to pay the taxes ascribed to him by the *kalantar* and the Assembly of Merchants in Julfa. Since I have not located the original Julfa dialect version of this letter, it is difficult to conjecture about how the assembly had decided upon Mr. Savahi di Canan's share of the tax, or whether the "list" of names the writer refers to in connection with the blotting out of names was a real list kept at the township, or a metaphorical expression. It could be a vague reference to a list of Julfa's twenty leading district heads, or *kadkhudas* (see below for discussion). The author of this letter seems to refer to the Assembly of Merchants as "the Gentlemen of Hispahan."

83. Mentz 2005, 42.

84. Trivellato 2006.

85. The standard works on this office are Lambton 1963, 206–207; 1992; and Floor 1999 and 2000b, 45–48.

86. Lambton 1963, 206; see also Keyvani 1982, 65–66.

87. The most comprehensive study of this famous family is Kiwrtian 1975–1976.

88. For a partial list of Julfa's *kalantars,* see Ghougassian 1988, 294. Ghougassian also has a good discussion of Julfa's administrative autonomy.

89. See Herzig 2007, 67.

90. "Arevtrakan grut'yunner vacharakannneri yev mayrapetneri Amenap'rkich ev kusakan vank'eri veraberogh, zanazan niwt'erov grut'iwnner—1700–1800" [Commercial papers belonging to merchants and nuns and concerning the All Savior's Monastery and the convent of the nuns, documents concerning various matters, 1700–1800], ASMA, folder 3.

91. The English traveler Thomas Herbert refers to Khwaja Nazar as "the Armenian prince" (1677, chap. 2). Robert Stodart, in the same embassy suite, also refers to Khwaja Nazar as a "prince" (1935, 71 and 73).

92. Thus Adam Olearus, the secretary to the Duke of Holstein's embassy to the Safavid court in the mid-seventeenth century, refers to *kalantar* Safraz beg as an "Armenian Lord" (1662, 265).

93. Tavernier 1688, 159. See also Bembo 2007, 356.

94. *Tadhkirat al-Muluk* 1943, 148.

95. On the role of *kadkhudas* in Isfahan, see Keyvani 1982, 85–87.

96. Khachikian 1988, 37–41; Baghdiantz McCabe 1999, 93–97.

97. Baghdiantz McCabe alternates between *tasnakavak* and *kadkhuda* without realizing that both terms designated the same official (1999, 97–98). Evidence that the Julfans themselves referred to the *tasnakavaks* as *kadkhudas* in both Persian and the Julfa dialect is provided in the petitions discussed below, in which *kadkhudas* is used to designate the district heads of New Julfa who simultaneously acted as judges in the township.

98. The Assembly of Merchants was never known as the Jumiyat, as Bhattacharya (2008a, 74), misinterpreting my work, seems to think.

99. Khachikian 1988, 37–41. See also the earlier discussion in Khachikian 1966, 176 ff.

100. Ter Hovhaniants 1880, 1: 183; 1980, 201.

101. Khachikian 1966, 176.

102. Herzig 2007, 68.

103. I photographed most of the available commercial documents (including petitions to the Assembly of Merchants) dating from 1595 to 1800, while on a research trip to Isfahan in the spring of 2005.

104. Herzig 2007, 70. The catalogue in question is Minasian 1983. Minasian was not aware that many of the documents in the Julfa archives were originally part of the records of New Julfa's administrative bodies and were therefore preserved for a long period. Most petitions to the Assembly of Merchants or the Municipal Assembly (see below) are stored in folders along with commercial contracts and sundry letters and are not identified in the catalogue as being connected to either body. Many of the dates ascribed to these documents by Minasian and his assistant(s) are also incorrect.

105. De Bruyn 1738, 232.

106. A comparison of two petitions to the Assembly of Merchants, dated 1727 and 1731 and both written by the Khwaja Minasian family, indicate an overlap of ten signatories in four years with an additional five names introduced in the interval. The petition dated 1731 has only fifteen merchant seals in addition to that of the *kalantar*, while the petition dated 1731 has twenty or possibly twenty-one seals (some seals are difficult to decipher, and therefore the twenty-first seal could be a mistake in reading on my part). Both documents are found in "Arevtrakan grut'iwnner vardapetneri knik'nerov, zanazan niwt'erov grut'iwnner—1726–1738," ASMA, folder 5b.

107. Herzig also makes this point (2007, 68).

108. Herzig 2007, 68.

109. Willem Floor has made one of the few preliminary studies of Safavid administrative and legal history; see Floor 2000a, passim; and 2000b, 42–44.

110. See petitions dated 1727 and 1731 in "Arevtrakan grut'iwnner vardapetneri knik'nerov, zanazan niwt'erov grut'iwnner—1726–1738," ASMA, folder 5b.

111. This point is also noted by Khachikian 1988, 54.

112. The formulaic judgment is recorded on a petition dated 12 Nadar 112 (29 October 1727) in "Arevtrakan grut'iwnner vardapetneri knik'nerov, zanazan niwt'erov grut'iwnner—1726–1738," ASMA, folder 5b. The verdict in another petition, dated 30 Nirhan 116 (15 March

1731), in the same folder at ASMA contains a slightly different wording: "mer shinin tujjari dasturn ēsay vor . . . " (The verdict of our community of merchants is this, that . . . ). Both petitions were sent to the assembly by the Khwaja Minasian family.

113.  A sample phrase containing this formulaic statement is found in a petition dated 30 Nadar 123 (16 September 1728) in "Arevtrakan grut'iwnner vardapetneri knik'nerov, zanazan niwt'erov grut'iwnner—1726–1738," ASMA, folder 5b." The petition ends with the following phrase, immediately preceding the date: "veroy greloys jaht'an sēghay asats'i farsi arapi ew hayerēn hayr mern" (While writing concerning the latter [matter], I said the oath and pronounced the formula in Persian [*farsi*], Arabic, and in the Lord's Prayer in Armenian). This same phrase is found at the conclusion of almost all the petitions addressed to the Municipal Assembly in Julfa (see below for a discussion of Julfa's Municipal Assembly). Many such petitions in the Archivio di Stato di Venezia also have the same expression.

114.  See the several powers of attorney sent from Julfa to Venice by Ovsana Sharimanean, giving full power to her representative to appeal to the Julfan *jumiat* in Venice as well as to the *cinque savi* to contest family inheritance from her cousin "Conte" Stefano Sceriman, then residing in Venice. The documents are in Documenti Armeni Mercantile, ASV, busta 2.

115.  On Marcara's famous trial in Paris, see the insightful discussion in Baghdiantz McCabe 1999, chap. 10. See also the earlier account, Cole 1939, 1: 511–514, which was not consulted by Baghdiantz McCabe.

116.  Baghdiantz McCabe (1999) reproduces this certificate; however, she mistakenly traces its origin to the Armenian Church hierarchy of the suburb. Even a cursory reading suffices to convince one that it was certified by the Municipal Assembly. In addition to the *kalantar's* name, the names of Julfa's leading merchants, some of whom were also the *kadkhudas* of the twenty districts, are also listed. For background on the certificate, see Richard 1995, 279–281. The trial papers of Marcara's lawsuit in Paris indicate that two other certificates were sent to Paris, one from the Julfan community of Amsterdam, the other from Venice. On the Venice certificate, see Baghdiantz McCabe's brief mention, as well as the much earlier reference in Alishan 1893 [*Sisakan*], 457, overlooked by Baghdiantz McCabe. Alishan states that ten Julfans in Venice testified before a notary public that Marcara was indeed of noble birth. Since Alishan does not provide his source for this information, it is reasonable to conclude that he had seen the Armenian original of this certificate in the Archives of the Armenian Church of *Santa Croce* in Venice, which were moved into the archives of the Mkhitarist Congregation on San Lazzaro in the 1740s, and thus must have been accessible to Alishan.

117.  The document is in *Protocolo de Cádiz,* AHPC, pr. 3.586 (Notary Juan Antonio de Torres). For accompanying notarial papers, including a translation of this document into Spanish, see the same manuscript, folios 765–773. I am grateful to the director of the Archivo Histórico Provincial de Cádiz, Manuel Ravina Martín, for bringing this precious document to my attention.

118.  Khachikian 1966, 176.

119.  Khachikian 1988, 52. The notarial document referring to this dispute and its resolution was originally translated and discussed in Sarukhan 1925, 104–105; and, following him, in Gregorian 1966, 48–49.

120.  Audiences du tribunal de commerce de Marseille, séances des 26 février et 6 août

1682, 13 B 43, Archives départementales des Bouches-du-Rhône (Marseille), folios 156 v°
et 281. The case involved a dispute between Paul de Serquis, a native of Julfa, and Marcara
de Caripgian (Gharipjian), a merchant from Shorot, concerning the sale of coral, woolen
cloths, turbans, and knives. The judges of the tribunal of trade in Marseilles ordered that the
dispute be resolved by Melchion de Nazard. Once again, I thank Olivier Raveux for sharing
this information with me.

121.   The document is in Documenti Armeni Mercantile, ASV, busta 1 and dated 15 April
1697; it is briefly discussed in Herzig 2007, 71. Only a page long, the document does not
contain many details regarding the resolution of the dispute except that the final verdict, as
well as supporting documentation (account books, petitions, and so on) brought by the disputing parties, was stored in the books (*defter*) of Venice's Armenian church (Surb Khach/
Santa Croce), which was frequented by Julfan merchants. The *Santa Croce* archives are stored
in the larger archival collection of the Mkhitarist Congregation in Venice on San Lazzaro
and have been off-limits to researchers for many decades now. It is very likely that when permission is finally granted to consult these archives, many documents directly connected to
the Julfan merchant community of Venice will be found there and will shed important light
on various aspects of the workings of the *jumiat*'s portable court in the city.

122.   Khachikian 1966, 177.

123.   Steingass 1892, 1187.

124.   Shushanik Khachikian was the first scholar to notice this link between the portable
courts in the settlements and the Assembly of Merchants in Julfa. For references to *manzaras* being sent back by the portable courts to the assembly in Julfa, see Khachikian 1988,
177. Herzig has also commented on bills being sent from the settlements for final resolution in Julfa. In this connection, Herzig makes the astute observation that "the mother
colony acted as a sort of court of appeal if local efforts at judgment and arbitration failed"
(2007, 70).

125.   For a case of "shaming," see letter no. 1428 in "Spanish and Armenian [Ships Pa-
pers] 1741–1750," HCA 30/682, PRO. The letter is written by a priest in New Julfa to a merchant in Madras, literally begging for money to cover his rising debts: "And one brother of
mine whose name is Grigor, who has left his mother, sister, and brothers in much suffering
and difficulties for the past fifteen years has come to your blessed city of Madras. It has been
five or six years now that he has not written a single letter. His poor mother is with saddened
heart and crying eyes filled with bitter tears. Moreover, we have been afflicted with much
sorrow and borne difficulties and sufferings on account of the fact that five years ago we took
a bill of exchange [*barat/berat*] of 105 rupees from Paron Simon, the son of the deceased
Hovan, so that Grigor, the brother of this servant [i.e., the author's brother], would give the
above-mentioned 105 rupees to Sahap Mukel, the son of the deceased Grigor [another mer-
chant] in Madras. Now the latter had come to Madras, but my brother Grigor had not paid
him for reasons that we are not aware of. The bill of exchange was thus returned to Julfa with
a notarized document [*manzara*], and they [the Assembly of Merchants?] caused us many
difficulties, much grief, disrespect to my [religious order?], and have poured insults, scorn,
and shame on me [*Yeresis tuk mur tal* means, literally, "to spit and throw soot on my face,"
but the metaphoric meaning of "to pour scorn, to disparage, to insult, and to shame" is in-

tended here; see Malkhaseants 1944, 2: 126]. . . . Now the amount of this loan [i.e., from five years ago] has risen to seven tomans, and we have an additional debt of twenty-seven tomans here, and we are in grave difficulties."

It is interesting to note that shaming tactics and harassment also applied to (lower-level) religious officials if they failed to honor a bill and became indebted to a merchant.

126. On the *Orfi* courts, see Floor 2000b.

127. *Santa Catharina* logbook of Spanish and English translations, HCA 42/026, PRO, letter no. 55, folio 180.

128. See the document in "Arevtrakan grut'iwnner vardapetneri knik'nerov, zanazan niwt'erov grut'iwnner—Nor Jugha, 1643–1699" [Commercial letters bearing seals of priests, documents concerning various matters—New Julfa, 1643–1699], ASMA, folder 5. As with other folders in the ASMA, the documents are not paginated but identified by date and place of writing.

129. Sharinov is a reference to the medieval Siamese or Thai city of Ayutya, 920 km north of present-day Bangkok. For a discussion of this city and the role of Muslim Persian immigrants there, see Marcinkowski 2002, 25 ff.; and Ibrahim 1972, 42 ff. For Sharinov's identification in Arabic travel manuals from the fifteenth century, see Tibbetts 1971, 488.

130. See the document in "Arevtrakan grut'iwnner vardapetneri knik'nerov, zanazan niwt'erov grut'iwnner—Nor Jugha, 1643–1699," ASMA, folder 5. For a transcription and translation of this document, along with commentary, see Aslanian 2007b, 605–615 (document 18).

131. This document was originally stored at the Armenian church in Livorno and was sold along with other documents to the state archives in Florence in 1861 by an Armenian priest in Livorno. See "Documenti Armeni," Acquisti e Doni, ASFi, busta 123, filza 1, document 49.

 Է

Թիվս առ66ր [1152] հոգտեմբերի իզ [23] վանայտկունմ: Պատ6առ գրոյս այսէ որ 2ուղեցի առագելի որդի պողորն որ ապր2ծով եկելալ լիվօռնալ. Մասկուր պողոսին խետ եղեալ ապրանքրն ումայ եւ ում կունբթայ. եւ կամ պողոսն ումայ ընկեր. Ովբք որ էս հաղեղաթա գիտակայ. Աստունօնյ համար բ [2] քալամայ ուր վկայութիւնն ներքոյ գրի եւ մհրի. "In the year 1152 [1703] October 23. The purpose of this document [concerns] the Julfan, Poghos son of Arakel, who has arrived in Livorno with silk. Those who know the truth about whose goods or on whose account the above-mentioned Poghos is trading or whose commenda agent he is are asked, for God's sake, to testify below and to seal their testimony." A short note at the back of the document, evidently written in Livorno, states that this is the "mazar" that has arrived from Venice about the merchant Poghos di Arakel. The document has three sealed testimonies one of which reads: "Ես փարվանէ որդի մրկրտումս գիտակամ որ րսպահանալ առաքելի որդի պողոսին խետ վէրկացինք մին2ի գիլան ուր բերանoվս կասէլ էս փողրն մարգարէ որդի մարտէիինալ ուր համ[ա]ր գնամանամ գիլան ապի2ում առում: Ես մարտէին դոնլունov նբարամ: Եւ էս մվրտումս իգմիրուն ի քան վէրոյ պողոսն արէկ իգմիր ուրիխետ բերած ապրի2ունմ նալունս երաոց ինքէլ նէ մտավ գնագ ալիկոռնալ ես մկրտումս գիր չէի գիրէլ գրել սունյթանունմի որդի պապ2անին ագ գրեց եսմ մrptgի իմ միրնալ

Փարվանէ որդի մկրրտում"

"I Mkrtum son of Parvaneh know [or testify] that I traveled together with Poghos son of Arakel of Isfahan from Isfahan to Gilan [and that] I heard him say with his own mouth that his money belonged to Martin son of Marcar and he was going to Gilan on his [Martin's] account to purchase silk and that he was serving as an agent or retainer [naukar/nokar] for Martin. And when I Mkrtum was in Izmir the above named Poghos came to Izmir and loaded the silk he had brought with him on a ship and went to Livorno. I Mkrtum did not know how to write and asked Papajan son of Sultanum and he wrote this [on my behalf] and I sealed this with my own seal.

Mkrtum son of Parvaneh"

The merchant named as Martin son of Marcara is most likely Marcara Avachints discussed above. He is mentioned in at least one other document from the period in the same collection. See Ibid., doc. 54.

132. The documents about this fleeced merchant are preserved in "Namakner—Ch'ini P'atan, 1696–1761" [Letters—Chinipatan, 1696–1761], ASMA, folder 233; see the document dated 20 Nadar 1146 (6 September 1697). For a translation with commentary of this document, see Aslanian 2007b, 579–590 (document 16).

133. The document is in "Arevtrakan grut'iwnner yev Namakner—P'ariz, 1666–1939" [Commercial correspondence and letters—Paris, 1666–1939], ASMA, folder 289. This document is dated and classified as 1666 by the archivist, although it seems, in all likelihood, to have been written in 1682. It is very poorly written and therefore extremely difficult to understand.

134. Khachikian 1966, 276.

135. On the Mayor's Court of Madras, see Arasaratnam 1986, chap. 7, esp. 274–279 and 281–292; Brimnes 2003, 513–550, esp. 523 ff.; and Mines 2001. On the use made of this court by Armenian merchants, see Bhattacharya 2008a and b. Bhattacharya's essays provide a useful and empirically grounded discussion of Armenian cases brought before the Mayor's Court in Madras; however, due to her one-sided reliance on English-language documentation for the study of Julfan trade, which often leads her to commit historical blunders, Bhattacharya offers little if any explicit discussion of how Julfans used the Mayor's Court in Madras in conjunction with the legal system in place in Julfa.

136. For a contemporary account of the Mayor's Court in Madras, see Fenning 1771. According to Fenning, a court was held by the mayor and aldermen twice a week at the town hall, "where the Asiatic inhabitants sue for their debts and implead each other" (207).

137. See, among others, the case of Coja Melcum D'Hierapiet against Coja Poguze, in "Madras: Mayor's Court Proceedings, Pro Anno 1743," India Office Records, range 328/77, folios 204 ff. For the court's attempts to take into account Julfan commercial law, referred to as "the custom among Armenian merchants" or "Armenian law," while deliberating on cases involving Julfan merchants, see the case of Coja Pogose de Cauchick vs. Coja Murzam de Muckerton, 2nd October 1744, in *Pleadings in the Mayor's Court, 1745*, 1939, 49–73. For another case in which Julfan commercial law was taken into account in deliberating on a dispute, see "Coja Zecharia de Avettde v. Cooja Tentasu, Coja Avetlake and Coja Sarad, brothers and partners, 19 April 1735," *Mayor's Court Proceedings*, P 328/70, India Office Records, folios 45–47.

138. As previously mentioned, many of these documents are powers of attorney sent by Ovsanna Shahrimanian. Several of these powers of attorney are found in Documenti Armeni Mercantile, ASV, busta 2. Another batch of similar documents is stored in various fold-

ers in the Avogaria di Comun series of the ASV. See in particular the petition to New Julfa's Municipal Assembly submitted by Ovsanna Shahrimanian and others in her family, dated 5 Tira 1734, in Avogaria di Comun, ASV, busta 198.

139. See chapter 9 below.

140. Arasaratnam 1986, 298. For the court case, see "Coja Zecharia de Avettde v. Cooja Tentasu, Coja Avetlake and Coja Sarad, brothers and partners, 19 April 1735," *Mayor's Court Proceedings,* P 328/70, India Office Records, folios 45–47. The Astrakhan Code of Laws indicates that it was possible for a Julfan *commenda* agent to serve more than one master but that doing so required the express permission of the first master (Poghosyan 1967, 139).

141. Examination of hundreds of wills stored in the Julfa archives has revealed only one Portuguese executor for a Julfan will drawn up in Canton and one Spaniard for a will written in Manila. The Canton will is found in "Zanazan nyuterov grutʻiwnner—Cantom *[sic]*, 1794" [Documents concerning various matters—Canton, 1794], ASMA, folder 28d, and is dated 1794. For the Manila will, see the reference in a commercial letter stored in *Santa Catharina* logbook of Spanish and English translations, HCA 42/026, PRO, letter no. 9, folio 26. There are also two seemingly isolated cases (exceptions rather than the rule) from Madras in which Julfans appointed non-Julfans as executors. See Bhattacharya 2008a, 82.

142. For an attempt to criticize my conception of the Julfan network, one that is not always well informed of the particularities of my arguments and is based on a selective and partial reading of my work, see Bhattacharya 2008a.

143. My comments here are inspired by a passage from Greif's 2006 work (59).

## 8. THE CENTER CANNOT HOLD

1. Braudel 1982, 163–164.

2. For the polycentric nature of Sephardic networks, see the excellent account in Israel 2002; and Trivellato 2009. See also chapter 9 below.

3. For the origins of Julfa's decline and collapse during the rule of Shah Sultan Hussein, see Ter Hovhaniants 1880, 1: 277; 1980, 1: 299.

4. Ghougassian 1998, 164.

5. Baghdiantz McCabe 1999, 353.

6. Ibid.

7. Ibid.355.

8. Gilanentz 1988, 35. The figure provided by the Dutch reports from Iran during the same period is slightly lower. According to the entry of 25 March 1722 in Floor's collection of translated documents on the Afghan occupation of Isfahan, Mahmud Ghalzai forced the Armenian merchants of Julfa to "sign an obligation of 60,000 tomans or Dfl. 2,550,00, which will have to be paid shortly" (1998, 105). There is much useful information on the situation in Julfa in the Dutch reports; see Floor, 105–107.

9. Herzig 1991a, 104.

10. Ibid.

11. Ibid.

12. Ibid., 107.

13. Ibid., 106–107.

14. For a rarely consulted source on Nadir's reign and its implications for Julfan Armenians, see Stepanos Yerets, *Girk' vor koch'i hangitagirk' or ē mtatsmunk' zhamanakats' ants'elots' ew nerkayits'* [Book called book of treasures which contains reflections on times past and the present], ASMA, MS 654, 1786, folios 109–118, 126–134.

15. There is much confusion about the *kalantars* of this period. Ter Hovhaniants (1880 and 1980, 1: chap. 41) seems to think that the *kalantar* during most of Nadir's reign was a man named Sargis, whom he accuses of colluding with Nadir in mercilessly exploiting and extorting his own people. In light of the evidence provided by this letter, it now appears that there were several *kalantars* during the turbulent 1740s, one of whom, whose name we do not know, as this letter indicates, was replaced by Nadir in 1745. Sargis must have been appointed immediately afterward. Herzig is also suspicious of Ter Hovhaniants's identification of Sargis as the ruling *kalantar* throughout Nadir's rule (1991a, 107 n. 402).

16. "High Court of Appeals for Prizes: Papers," HCA 42/026, PRO, folios 78–79 (emphasis added).

17. Ibid., folio 85.

18. "Spanish and Armenian [Ships Papers] 1741–1750," HCA 30/682, PRO, letter no. 933.

19. Ibid.

20. Bazin 1780, 300.

21. Ibid.

22. Hanway1753, 4: 258.

23. Bazin 1780, 300–301. Laurence Lockhart skirts Nadir's second visit to Isfahan and its disastrous consequences for Julfans and Isfahanis in general in his pioneering study of the despot (1938, 257–258). The most recent assessment of Nadir Shah's life and reign also contains very little information on Nadir's stay in Isfahan and even less on his relations with the Julfans: see Axworthy 2006.

24. Bazin 1780, 301–302.

25. Chick 1939, 1: 652. See also the brief mention of this gruesome episode in Ter Hovhaniants 1880, 1: 256; 1980, 1: 278–279. See also Jughayets'i 1905, 269.

26. One of the few Armenians of the period who portrayed Nadir Shah in a positive light was Joseph Émïn, whose dislike of Julfa and its mercantile community is as intense as his account of Nadir's rule is laudatory, making his statements on both equally suspect. Consider, for instance, the following veiled reference to the auto-da-fé incident: "Nadir, in all his reign, never hurt an Armenian, except two of the chief merchants of Julpha, who had sworn falsely by his head, and were burnt alive in the grand square of Ispahan, in the year 1746 [*sic*]" (1792, 30).

27. Chick 1939, 1: 652.

28. Ibid.

29. Ibid., 631 and 653. In a fascinating letter by a Mkhitarist monk, Father Poghos Vardaped, in Istanbul, dated 28 May 1743, to Abbot Mkhitar in Venice, we learn that a Capuchin physician who attended Nadir Shah's illness and cured him asked Nadir to have the Capuchin church in Tiflis restored. Nadir inquired as to who had ordered it to be shut down or destroyed, to which the physician responded that it was the Armenian catholicos at Ejmiatsin (Ghazar Chahgetsi). According to the letter, this prompted Nadir to order the catholicos to be sent to him and pay an exorbitant fine to help rebuild the church. Although the letter is reprinted in

exerpted form, it sheds some light on Nadir's hostility toward Ejmiatsin. The physician in question must be the Jesuit Pere Bazin mentioned above; see Tayean 1930, 111. In another letter from Istanbul, dated 9 January 1747, Father Mikayel Chamchian writes to the abbot in Venice that he has heard that Nadir Shah had forcibly brought Catholicos Chahgetsi naked before him (probably in 1743) in a humiliating fashion before sending him back to Ejmiatsin. The same monk writing again from Istanbul on 23 March 1747 relays rumors that Catholicos Chahgetsi has fled Ejmiatsin for Erzerum. See Tayean 1930, 308 and 309.

30. See HCA 30/682, PRO, letter no. 933; and "High Court of Appeals for Prizes: Papers," HCA 42/026 PRO, letter no. 20, folio 79.

31. "High Court of Appeals for Prizes: Papers," HCA 42/026, PRO, letter no. 162, folios 414–415.

32. Ibid., folio 415.

33. For Julfa's history during this turbulent period, see Perry 1979, 2–4, 239–240; Ter Hovhaniants 1880, 1: 279–285; 1980, 1: 301–307; and Yerets, *Girkʻ vor kochʻi hangitagirkʻ,* MS 654, ASMA, folios 134–173.

34. Ter Hovhaniants 1880, 1: 284; 1980, 1: 306.

35. On Hasan Khan's unsuccessful attempt to extort money from the Julfans, see Ter Hovhaniants 1880, 1: 288; 1980, 1: 311; Yerets, *Girkʻ vor kochʻi hangitagirkʻ,* MS 654, ASMA, folio 158. See also Herzig 1991a, 108.

36. Quoted in Herzig 1991a, 109.

37. The census report uses the term "souls," indicating that the reference here is to the number of surviving individuals. Herzig believes the reference is to houses or families, which would still make the number of individuals significantly small compared to a population of 15,000 to 20,000 residents or roughly 4,000 families in the pre-1748 period. Joseph Émïn, writing at about the same time, states in his memoirs: "The fine suburb of Julpha, once inhabited by 12,000 rich families, contain[s] at present hardly 500 houses, and may soon be deserted and left for the Musulmans of Ispahan" (1792, 618).

38. Herzig 1991a, 109.

39. HCA 30/682, PRO, letter no. 1380.

40. Letter of Padri Raymond Dominican, Julfa, 4 April 1750, Sceriman Family Papers, Don Mazza, busta 1. This letter is written in the Julfa dialect and reads as follows: Այլենց թունիր թէ էլ շուլդայ չէկայ քանդվաւ եւ օրէզօր քանդվումայ. իրէք տուն մաացէլէն ունեւոր ա. ըմմիասին, սեվ ծաղուրին, եւ յոհաննեսին տի կաաթ/ա/ր տէնէրն *[sic].*

41. "ըստ բէրմանէ չար պատահանց դոլվաթաւորք փող տալով նեղութեան մէջ ընկան ումանք էլ փրա [<A/P, A رارف *farār, firār, furār:* "running away, absconding; flight, escape"] արարին գնացին շէսս դատտակէ *[sic]*." The document is dated 24 Tira 136 (10 October 1751) and is found in "Arevtrakan grutʻiwnner vacharakanneri yev mayrapetneri Amenapʻrkich ev kusakan vankʻeri veraberogh, Zanazan niwtʻerov grutʻiwnner—1700–1800" [Commercial documents concerning the All Savior's Monastery and the Convents of the Nuns, documents concerning various matters—1700–1800], ASMA, folder 3.

42. Ter Hovhaniants 1880, 1: 297; I have followed Ghougassian's translation. See also Ter Hovhaniants 1880, 1: 295–298; 1980, 1: 319–322. This letter is partially quoted in Herzig 1991a, 109; and in Khachikian 1988, 96 n. 153; and in full in Ghougassian 1998, 164.

43. Նոր եկողացէ յիմացայ մեր երկրին ողորմէլիութիւնն. էլ յոյս չկայ ապա 4 մեծ տունսիցս միայն յովանջանին խիզանական մացէլ. Աստուած նոցայ էլ ազատի (Ter Astuatsatur in Moscow to Tadeo and Nazar Shahrimanian in Venice, 11 July 1755, Sceriman Family Papers, Don Mazza, busta 1). Another Sceriman/Shahrimanian correspondent, Avetik di Ibrahim, writing from Basra in 1753, states: եւս իսպահանայ հափայն էսայ որ բարբարոսաց երկիրայ դառցէլ օրն մին թագաւորայ դու գլման թայանում բաց թողունման փախման զնամման (Avetik di Ibrahim in Basra to Dateos di Nazar Sceriman/Shahrimanian and Nazar di Dateo Sceriman/Shahrimanian, 31 December 1753, Sceriman Family Papers, Don Mazza, busta 1). (And the situation in Isfahan is this, that it has become a country of barbarians. Every day a new king appears and plunders [the land]. People are abandoning [the city] and fleeing.)

44. Bhattacharya takes a different view of the Julfan network and raises some legitimate questions about the overall importance of Julfa as the nodal center, as argued in my work; however, she misstates my position in order to argue that nodes of the Julfan network in India, especially Madras, should be viewed as having more autonomy: "The hypothesis that nodes such as Madras were not peripheries of New Julfa but major links in a chain of multiple nodes is supported by the fact that some of the Armenians settling down in Manila were undoubtedly agents/family members of merchants settled in Madras" (2008b, 15). Bhattacharya posits an "either/or" dichotomy that does not exist in my work, according to which a "node" such as Madras is either a "periphery" of New Julfa or a "major link . . . in a chain of multiple nodes." Such a simplistic view fails to take into account that an important settlement like Madras in the first half of the eighteenth century could in fact be both a subordinate node linked to the nodal center of Julfa *and* what I have called a "regional center" for other subsidiary nodes in its orbit, such as Calcutta, Pegu, Battavia, and most importantly Manila. The more important question raised in my work is why a peripheral node such as Madras did not become a surrogate nodal center for a reinvented Julfan network after the collapse of Julfa as the nodal center in the years following 1747, a question Bhattacharya does not examine or even raise. One is almost tempted to conclude that Bhattacharya's attempts to make Madras and Calcutta into their own centers independent of Julfa during the first half of the eighteenth century, when Julfa was still functioning as a nodal center, are not so much attempts to restructure the Julfan network as an "archival restructuring" and valorizing of English-language East India Company documentation at the expense of thousands of previously unconsulted Julfa dialect documents stored at the nodal center and for reasons of language inaccessible to her. For her attempts to devalorize documents that she is unable to read or understand, see Bhattacharya 2008a, 69–70. Bhattacharya's contention that Madras was an autonomous entity is in part informed by her work on a single will (available in English translation) belonging to one Julfan merchant, Petrus Uscan (Khwaja Petros Woskan), who lived in Madras for several decades in the first half of the eighteenth century and whose trading ventures exhibit relative autonomy from Julfa. But even in the case of this merchant, the English-language documentation does not fully indicate the extent to which this merchant's *commenda* contracts with fellow Julfan agents were dependent on their notarization or ratification in Julfa by the Municipal Assembly. Among many documents pertaining to Petrus di Uscan's business ventures, see "Prize Court Papers," HCA 32/1831, PRO, no. 387,

box b, for the concluding part of a *tomar* between Petros di Woskan and one of his agents, Petros di Grigor, dated 10 Shebat 126 (30 May 1741). The document was drafted in Madras but notarized in Julfa.

45.  See Das Gupta's astute analysis of the decline of Surat in the eighteenth century: 2004, 7-8 and chaps. 3 and 5.

46.  The best work on the decline of the Muslim empires in the eighteenth century is Bayly 1989, 16-74; 1988; see also Marshall 2005. For the Mughals and Safavids, see also Gommans 1999; for an earlier and dated account, see Hodgson 1974.

47.  Bayly 1989, 35 ff.

48.  Braudel 1982, 164.

49.  See Aslanian 2007b, chap. 8, where I argue that this transformation from a regional Julfan identity to a national Armenian one did not occur until the Julfan network, along with the *hayrenik* (homeland/patria) of the Julfans in Julfa, had collapsed in the second half of the eighteenth century, compelling the Julfans to reinvent themselves as members of a larger and modern Armenian "nation."

## 9. CONCLUSION

1.  Pomeranz and Topik 2006, 7.

2.  Israel 2005, 3. The most significant attempts at comparative work on "trade diaspora" communities have been Israel's 2005 essay and Trivellato 2009. Other attempts, which discuss different merchant communities in different chapters of a book (e.g., Curtin 1984; Lombard and Aubin 1988; Subrahmanyam 1996; Baghdiantz McCabe, Harlaftis, and Pepelasis Minoglou 2005), have offered empirical observations and rich description but little explicit comparison. To date only Trivellato has provided an analytical comparison of the economic practices (use of contracts, etc.) of different communities and how they dealt with the problem of trust. This chapter is inspired by Trivellato's work and attempts to broaden her framework by incorporating the often-neglected merchant community of the Multani Indians; unlike Trivellato and others, I also attempt to examine the role of trade networks and their structural properties in my comparison.

3.  Dale 2002, 130.

4.  Levi 1999, 488-489; on references to Multanis in the Delhi Sultanate period, see Alam 1994, 202-227 (211); Habib 1964, 406; and Ray 1995, 460.

5.  See Levi 2002, 99-100; 2008, 31-65.

6.  Floor 2000a, 21.

7.  Masters 1988, 81 and 82. According to Masters, the Indians in Aleppo "were exclusively Muslim" (81).

8.  The main exception here concerns Multani trade with Iran, which was both overland and maritime, relying on the Surat-Bandar 'Abbas corridor (Floor 2000a, 21). According to Chardin, there were about five thousand families of Hindu Indians in Bandar 'Abbas alone, constituting about one-third of the population of this port town at the mouth of the Persian Gulf. Note, however, that Chardin does not specify that these Indians were from Multan (1811, 8: 508).

9. According to Levi (2002, 174 n. 189), however, Russian translations of some *commenda* contracts from the seventeenth century have survived in the Astrakhan archives.

10. Levi 1999, 496. According to Dale (2002, 65), "no record of [*commenda* contracts] is known to have survived from the Mughul [*sic*] period, but hints of commenda-like arrangements occur in nineteenth and twentieth century studies of powindah tribes."

11. Markovits 2000, 85. It should be noted that the *shah-gumastha* contract that Markovits discusses is based on evidence from the nineteenth century. Levi's and Dale's arguments that this type of *commenda* partnership also existed in the seventeenth and eighteenth centuries seem compelling but are not based on hard evidence.

12. Levi 2002, 85 and 94.

13. For a brief mention of the training of Multani agents, see Levi 1999, 496; and 2002, 211.

14. Levi 1999, 491; see also 2002, 210–211.

15. Levi 1999, 491.

16. Gopal 1986, 207–208. See also Dale 2002, 118–119, for Indian-Armenian contracts; and 96–98, for Russian protectionist measures against foreign merchants and especially Indians. "The Armenians were the most sought after partners [for the Indians in Russia]," according to Surendra Gopal (208) One reason for this was their privileged status in Russia (where they were exempt from protectionist measures). They also had solid connections in Iran. In addition, the Armenians were quite familiar to the Indians because of their networks in India and their ongoing relations with Indians in Isfahan. Most importantly, the Armenians were not restricted to Astrakhan, as the Indians were after 1689. Armenians were also favored because they had ready capital to invest in partnerships with Indians.

17. For sporadic Julfan partnerships with the French in India, see Manning 1996, 124–126. Manning does not discuss the nature of the "partnerships" between the Julfans and French company officials or what kind of legal paperwork was involved in such partnership ventures, but her evidence suggests that these joint ventures involved mostly the shipping sector of Indian Ocean trade, such as freighting of French ships or French-Julfan maritime trade with Manila.

18. Levi 1999, 551; and 2002, 112, 182.

19. For Chardin's estimate of Indians in Isfahan, see Dale 2002, 67. For Kaempfer's estimate, see Levi 2002, 99. Tavernier estimated "ten or twelve thousand *Banians* in *Ispahan* . . . all Bankers, and very knowing in Money." Projecting his anti-Semitic stereotypes onto the Indian moneylenders in Isfahan, Tavernier found them to be "worse Userers than the *Jews*" and compared them to "Pests and Vipers" as well as "Vermin" (1688, 168 and 202). The figure of 12,000 Indians is also found in Ambrosio Bembo's account of his stay in Isfahan (2007, 329), as well as in Olearius (1662, 269). See also Matthee 2000, 247, for a calculation of 12,000 to 15,000 Indian "banians," not necessarily Multanis. It should be noted that Isfahan also had a community of Marwari merchants, originally from Rajasthan, who also played an important role as *sarrafs* in the Iranian capital and from whom the Julfans also appear to have regularly borrowed large sums of money. Cross-cultural economic relations between Julfans and Indians in Isfahan is a fascinating topic that awaits serious study. In the absence of previous work on this topic, one can only speculate that "trust relations" between Julfan borrowers and In-

dian moneylenders would be managed by recourse to Safavid courts and on the basis of shared commercial norms and cross-cultural reputational mechanisms. A number of letters of credit or bills of exchange between Julfans and most likely Marwaris or Sindis have been preserved in various collections of Julfan documents bearing writing in Indic script alongside the Julfa dialect. See documents in the Sceriman Family Papers, Don Mazza: *awag/avak* document, dated 10 Ovdan 111 (24 January 1727) in Isfahan, between Dateos and Bartoghomeos di Nazar Shahriman and Khwaja J'nsu (Jinsu or Jishnu?) and Kimchand, busta 3; *awag/avak,* dated 5 Ovdan 111 (19 January 1727) in Isfahan, between Dateos di Nazar Shahriman and Khwaja J'i[n]su and Cheleram Hayachand [Harichand?], busta 2; see also the long accounting documents nos. 1489 and 1492 in HCA 30/682, PRO, both of which appear to be from Bengal, and a smaller fragment also from Bengal in document no. 1617 of the same source. The Verona documents appear to be written in the Landa script used by Marwaris, Sindis, and Punjabis, according to Anshuman Pandey (personal communication, 19 September 2008). For a brief discussion of Isfahan's Marwari community, see Dale 2002, 59.

20. Dale 2002, 98 and 99.

21. Ibid., 128.

22. According to a contemporary witness of the Afghan conquest of Isfahan, the Multanis, like the Julfans and others, were targeted by the Afghan warlord Mahmud Khan to pay a special fine of 20,000 *tumans,* which they had trouble raising; see Gilanentz 1988, 36.

23. On the Shikarpuri network, see Markovits 2000, 57–109. The notion that Multanis returned in the nineteenth century as Shikarpuris is upheld by both Dale (2002) and especially Levi (2002), who argue that a significant shift of capital and merchants occurred in the early nineteenth century from Multan in the Punjab to Shikarpur in Sindh. But Markovits advises caution about seeing the Shikarpuri network as a reincarnation of that of Multan. In his view, "There will always remain a certain amount of uncertainty regarding the nature of the transition between 'Multani' and a 'Shikarpuri' network, and it is most probable that there was at the same time some basic continuity and a certain amount of significant change. . . . To sum up, Shikarpuris appear to have been at the same time a new avatar of the Multanis, and a network which had some new characteristics, different from those of the Multani network as the latter operated in the seventeenth century" (2007, 131).

24. Israel 2005, 3.

25. Israel 2005, 5; also 2002, 4.

26. On the multiple centers of the Sephardic network, see the essays in Israel's magisterial 2002 collection, as well as Trivellato 2009. For an excellent discussion of Sephardic trans-Atlantic settlements, see Studnicki-Gizbert 2007; and the collection of essays in Kagan and Morgan 2007.

27. For the Ottoman Sephardim, see Rodrigue 1992; and Rodrigue and Bembassa 2000.

28. Israel 2005, 13.

29. Ibid.

30. Ibid., 12.

31. Ibid.

32. Israel 2002, 18.

33. Ibid.

34. Israel 1998, 307 ff.

35. Israel 2002, 22.
36. Israel 2005, 20.
37. Israel 2002, 11.
38. Trivellato 2009, 224–250.
39. Ibid., 132 and 244 ff.
40. Israel 2005, 23–24.
41. Trivellato 2009, 132.
42. Ibid.
43. Ibid., 145.
44. Ibid., 133.
45. Ibid., 156.
46. Ibid., 169.
47. Ibid.
48. Ibid., 152.
49. Ibid., 1–2.
50. Ibid., 156.
51. Curtin 1984.

# BIBLIOGRAPHY

## ARCHIVAL SOURCES

### Armenia

*MATENADARAN STATE REPOSITORY OF ANCIENT MANUSCRIPTS*

Jughayetsi, Constant. *Vasn norahas mankants' ew yeritasartats' vacharakanats' khrat* [Concerning advice to the adolescent and to young merchants]. More commonly known as *Ashkharhazhoghov* [Compendium]. MSS 10704 and 8443.

### Austria

*MKHITARIST LIBRARY/ARCHIVES, VIENNA*

Karnetsi, Yeghia. *Patmut'iwn imn karcharot i vera antskuteants' Yeghiayis Astuatsaturian Mushegheants' zors krets'i i azgen frankats', manavand i khabeba kronavorats'n ev i sut ekhpayrts' ev barekam kochetselots'* [A short history concerning the sufferings that I Yeghia Astuatsaturian Musheghian bore from the nation of Catholic Europeans and especially from the deceitful clergy and those known as the false brothers and friends]. MS 980.

*ÖSTERREICHISCHE NATIONALBIBLIOTHEK*

Evdokiatsi, Gabriel. "Oragrut'iwn" [Diary]. Cod. Arm. 21.

### France

*ARCHIVES COLONIALES (AIX EN PROVENCE)*

*Colonies: Inde—Correspondance générale, 1744–1746* [Colonies: India—General correspondence, 1744–1746]. Archives Colonial Fonds Ministériels C/2/81.

*ARCHIVES DÉPARTEMENTALES DES BOUCHES-DU-RHÔNE (MARSEILLE)*

Audiences du tribunal de commerce de Marseille, séances des 26 février et 6 août 1682. 13 B 43. Fol. 156 v° et 281.

*ARCHIVES NATIONALES (PARIS)*
Minutier central des notaires de Paris. Registre ET/VI/0198, 2 octobre 1625.

*BIBLIOTHÈQUE NATIONALE DE FRANCE (BNF)*
*Factum contenant l'histoire tragique; pour le Sieur Martin Marcara Avachinz de la ville d'His-pahan, capitale de Perse, conseiller au conseil souverain de l'isle daufine, & directeur des comptoirs de la Compagnie Françoise des Indes Orientales dans les Indes et dans la Perse, demandeur en requeste presentée au conseil de sa majesté du 6 Mars 1676. Et Michel Marcara, son fils.* MS fr. 15529.

## Great Britain

*BRITISH LIBRARY (BL)*
"Coja Zecharia de Avettde v. Cooja Tentasu, Coja Avetlake and Coja Sarad, brothers and partners, 19 April 1735. *Mayor's Court Proceedings.* P 328/70. India Office Records. Folios 45–47.
Harleian MS 7013. Folios 32, 112, 114, 117–120.
L-L7. India Office Records.
Lansdowne MSS 1047 and 1048.
"'The Last Will and Testament of Petrus Uscan." *Madras Mayor's Court Proceedings.* P 328/60. India Office Records. Folios 113–289.
Letter no. 96. "Miscellaneous Letters Received [by the Court of Directors], 1752–1753." E/1/37. India Office Records.
"Letters of Arapiet di Martin, Venezia, 1691–1703." Oriental MS 15794.
LMAR/C/324. India Office Records. Folios 49–62.
"Madras: Mayor's Court Proceedings, Pro Anno 1734." India Office Records. Range 328/69.
"Madras: Mayor's Court Proceedings, Pro Anno 1735." India Office Records. Range 328/71.
"Madras: Mayor's Court Proceedings, Pro Anno 1738." India Office Records. Range 328/73.
"Madras: Mayor's Court Proceedings, Pro Anno 1743." India Office Records. Range 328/77.
"Methodo que propongo para que la ciudad de Manilla sea el Imporio del Commercio en el Golfo chinico. Madrid, May 12, 1791." *Papeles tocantes a la Compania de Filipinas,* tom. I. Egerton 518. Plut. DXVIII. H. Folios 217–225.

*THE NATIONAL ARCHIVES/PUBLIC RECORDS OFFICE (PRO)*
"High Court of Admiralty: Instance and Prize Courts." HCA 24/127.
"High Court of Admiralty: Prize Court: Papers." HCA 32/440/14.
"High Court of Appeals for Prizes: Papers." HCA 42/026.
"High Court of Appeals for Prizes: Papers." HCA 42/47.
"Prize Court Papers." HCA 32/1831.
"Prize Court Papers." HCA 32/1832.
"Spanish and Armenian [Ships Papers] 1741–1750." HCA 30/682.
"Will of Panus Calander, Armenian Merchant of Saint Lawrence Poultrey, City of London," 24 September 1696. PROB 11/434. Records of the Prerogative Court of Canterbury.

*OXFORD UNIVERSITY BODLEIAN MANUSCRIPTS*

Jughayetsi, Constant. *Vasn norahas mankants' ew yeritasartats' vacharakanats' khrat* [Concerning advice to the adolescent and to young merchants]. More commonly known as *Ashkharazhoghov* [Compendium]. Bodleian MS F14.

*STAFFORDSHIRE RECORDS OFFICE*

"Letter of Babajan di Avedik."Anson Papers. D615/PA/2. (The letter is included in a bundle of correspondence with John Dick, Thomas Anson's agent in Livorno.)

*India*

*HOLY NAZARETH CHURCH*

"Orinakk'hayeren yev anglieren ktakats'vor paheal havandatan nazaretay surb yekeghets'woy sgseal 1786 minch 1862" [Copies of Armenian and English wills preserved in the Vestry Room of the Holy Church beginning in 1786 until 1862]. Vestry Room.

*SAINT MARY'S ARMENIAN CHURCH (MADRAS/CHENNAI)*

Book of Minutes, 1804–1840. 4 vols. Vestry Room.

*Iran*

*ALL SAVIOR'S MONASTERY ARCHIVE (ASMA)*

"Arevtrakan grut'iwnner vardapetneri knik'nerov, zanazan niwt'erov grut'iwnner—1726–1738" [Commercial documents bearing priests' seals, documents concerning various matters, 1726–1738]. Folder 5b.

"Arevtrakan grut'iwnner yev Namakner—P'ariz, 1666–1939" [Commercial correspondence and letters—Paris, 1666–1939]. Folder 289.

"Hashvetghter anhatakan, 1703–1729" [Individual accounting papers, 1703–1729]. Box no. 35/2.

Jughayetsi, Constant. *Vasn norahas mankants' ew yeritasartats' vacharakanats' khrat* [Concerning advice to the adolescent and to young merchants]. More commonly known as *Ashkharazhoghov* [Compendium]. MS 64.

Khojamalian, Thomas. *Patmut'iwn Hndstanay* [History of Hindustan]. MS 535, 1769.

"Namak—Aligorna, 1659" [Letter—Livorno, 1659]. Folder 6.

"Namakner—Bangala, 1712–1800" [Letters—Bengal, 1712–1800]. Folder 48.

"Namakner—Ch'ichra, 1701–1876" [Letters—Chichra, 1701–1876]. Folder 234.

"Namakner—Ch'ini P'atan, 1696–1761" [Letters—Chinipatan, 1696–1761]. Folder 233.

"Namakner—Halēb, 1715–1880" [Letters—Aleppo, 1715–1880]. Folder 141.

"Namakner—Heydarabad, 1680, 1687, 1758" [Letters—Hyderabad, 1680, 1687, 1758]. Folder 148.

"Namakner—Hukli Bandar, 1708–1715" [Letters—Hugli Bandar, 1708–1715]. Folder 152.

"Namakner—Izmir, 1730 *[sic]*–1861" [Letters—Izmir, 1730–1861]. Folder 112.

"Namakner—Madras, 1709–1850" [Letters—Madras, 1709–1850]. Folder 104.

"Namakner—Nor Jugha, 1685–1800" [Letters—New Julfa, 1685–1800]. Folder 217.

Yerets, Stepanos. *Girk' vor koch'i hangitagirk' or ē mtatsmunk' zhamanakats' ants'elots' ew nerkayits'* [Book called book of treasures which contains reflections on times past and the present]. MS 654, 1786.

"Zanazan niwt'erov grut'iwnner—1700–1800" [Documents concerning various matters—1700–1800]. Folder 3.

"Zanazan niwt'erov grut'iwnner—1751–1775" [Documents concerning various matters—1751–1775]. Folder 6/1.

"Zanazan niwt'erov grut'iwnner—Bombay ktak" [Documents concerning various matters—Bombay will]. Folder 28/3.

"Zanazan niwt'erov grut'iwnner—Cantom *[sic]*, 1794" [Documents concerning various matters—Canton, 1794]. Folder 28d.

"Zanazan niwt'erov grut'iwnner—Kalkata, 1807–1897" [Documents concerning various matters—Calcutta, 1807–1897]. Folder 28/10.

"Zanazan niwt'erov grut'iwnner—Ktakner Nor Jugha" [Documents concerning various matters—Wills, New Julfa]. Folder 28/13.

"Zanazan niwt'erov grut'iwnner—Madras, 1763–1820" [Documents concerning various matters—Madras, 1763–1820]. Folder 28/11.

"Zanazan niwt'erov grut'iwnner—Muchlibandar, 1814" [Documents concerning various matters—Muchlibandar, 1814]. Folder 28/12.

"Zanazan niwt'erov grut'iwnner—Nor Jugha, 1643–1699. Arevtrakan grut'iwnner vardapetneri knik'nerov" [Documents concerning various matters—New Julfa, 1643–1699. Commercial letters bearing seals of priests]. Folder 5.

"Zanazan niwt'erov grut'iwnner—Nor Jugha, Peria ew ayln: Yandsnararagrer, Liazoragrer 1706–1888–1931" [Documents concerning various matters—New Julfa, Peria, etc.: Letters of recommendation, powers of attorney, 1706–1888–1931]. Folder 44.

"Zanazan niwt'erov grut'iwnner—Surat, 1682–1816" [Documents concerning various matters—Surat, 1682–1816]. Folder 28/19.

*Italy*

ARCHIVIO DELLA BIBLIOTECA DI MUSEO CORRER (ABMC)
Agha di Matus. "Tomar Book." P.D. 66.c.

*Resultato del processo per la verificazione dei requisiti alla N.V. nella famiglia de Co. Co: Fr[ate]lli Sceriman.* MS Cod. Cigogna 3428/9 (unpaginated manuscript).

Seriman, Fortunato. *Brevie memorie sulla famiglia Seriman* [Brief memoirs of the Seriman family]. MS Cod. Cigogna 3403 [1855].

ARCHIVIO DI ISTITUTO DON NICOLA MAZZA (DON MAZZA)
Sceriman Family Papers. Buste 1–4.

ARCHIVIO DI SAN LAZZARO—MKHITARIST ARCHIVES, VENICE (ASLAZ)
Accounting Ledger. Manuscript of Gasparo Sceriman. MS 1800.

"Letter of Father Manuel Emirzian, dated February 6, 1771."

"Letter of Father Sookias Aghamalian from Madras to Abbot Melkonian in Venice, 28 June 1770."

Sceriman Papers. Alishan Collection. Busta 1.

*Vark' ew patmut'iwn Tovmachanean Mahtesi Tēr Hovhannisi Konstandnupōlsets'woy oroy ĕnd eresun tĕrut'iwns shrjeal vacharakanut'eamb ew husk hetoy verstin darts'arareal i bnik k'aghak' iwr kostandnupōlis dseṙnadri and k'ahanay hIgnatios yepiskoposĕ yotanasnerort ami hasaki iwroy apa ekeal dadarē i vans rabunapeti metsi Mkhitaray abbay hōr i Venetik* [The life and history of Mahtesi Ter Hovhannes Tovmachanian of Constantinople, who, after wondering through thirty states conducting commerce, once again returns to his native city of Constantinople where he is anointed a celibate priest by Bishop Ignatius at the age of seventy and then comes to repose at the monastery of the great master, Abbot Mkhitar, in Venice]. MS 1688.

*ARCHIVIO DI STATO DI FIRENZE (ASFI)*
"Documenti Armeni," Acquisti e Doni. Buste 123 and 124.

*ARCHIVIO DI STATO DI LIVORNO (ASL)*
"Supplica della nazione armena di Livorno al Granduca, risalente al 1646" [Request of the Armenian nation resident in Livorno to the Grand Duke, 1646]. *Capitano* . . . 2603, c.519.

*ARCHIVIO DI STATO DI VENEZIA (ASV)*
Avogaria di Comun. Buste 17, 85, 217, 198, 210, 235, 286, 393.
Documenti Armeni Mercantile. Buste 1, 2, and 3.
Inquisitori di Stato, 876 and 181.
"Libro di memorie di Monsignor Basilio Sceriman" [Book of memoirs of Monsignor Basilio Sceriman]. Avogaria di Comun 348 Processi di Nobiltà—Sceriman (unpaginated court proceedings).
Notarile, 487.
Procuratori di San Marco. Busta 180.
Procuratori di San Marco. Misti, buste 180/A and 180/D.

*ARCHIVIO DI STATO PADUA (ASP)*
Sceriman Family Papers. Buste 1, 2, 3, 4, 10, 12, 14, 15, 27, 28, 34, 35, 41, 45, 56–57.

*ARCHIVIO PATRIARCHALE O DIOCESANO (APD)*
"Curia Patriarchale—Examinorium matrimonium" [Historical records of the Venetian Ecclesiastical Patriarchate—Marriage examinations]. Busta 51, folios 99–105.
"Liti e controversi parroccia di San Zulian—Armeni" [Disputes and controversies of the parish of San Zulian].

*ARCHIVIO STORICO, CONGREGAZIONE PER L'EVANGELIZZAZIONE DEI POPOLI O "DE PROPAGANDA FIDE" (PROP FIDE)*
Report by Cardinal Medici to the Propaganda Fide. 7 May 1688. Archivio della Propaganda Fide (AP, SOCG). Vol. 223, folios 327v-328 and 331v-332.
Report by Priests Basilio Barsegh and Agop to Propaganda Fide. 1669. Fondo S.C. Armeni, Vatican. Vol. 1, folios 319v–323r.

"Sceriman Family Letter of Confession and Loyalty to the Catholic Church." Fondo SOCG. Vol. 495, folios 241b-262a.

### Mexico

ARCHIVO GENERAL DE LA NACIÓN, MEXICO CITY (AGN)

MS Ramo Inquisición, tomo 829, exp. 7, folios 544–560v. "Proceso Contra Pedro De Zarate Por Sospechas De Ser Cismatico." [Proceeding against Pedro De Zarate for suspicions of being a Schismatic]

MS Ramo de Inquisición, tomo 857, "Reconciliaciones al Gremio de nuestra Santa Madre Iglesia de Minas di Elias . . . Esteban di Codidyan, todos Armenios dela Secta de cisma Armenio" [Reconciliation to the Holy Mother Church of Minas di Elias . . . Esteban di Cododyan, all Armenians of the Armenian Schismatic Sect].

MS Ramo de Inquisición, tomo 861, "Reconciliaciones al Gremio de nuestra Santa Madre Iglesia de Constantino de Lazaro, Phelipe Agapiri, Jachic de Obanes, Abraham de Luis . . . "

### The Netherlands

ALGEMEEN RIJKSARCHIEF, THE HAGUE (ARA)

Collectie 606 Armen Joseph.

Eerste Afdeling Collectie Lubbert Jan, Baron Van Eck (1719–1765). Folder 44.

Petition from Aga Mal Sarfras, Sarquis Nicknolar, Babtista Pirataam, Errapiet Vanos, Sadier Kaluta at Bender Ricq to Mossel, GG of the VOC at Batavia. VOC 2824 (20/02/1753). Nationaal Archief, The Hague. Folios 78–80.

### Spain

ARCHIVO DE INDIAS (SEVILLE)

Contratación, 452, N.1, R. 11\11\. Folios 1–15 (recto and verso).

"Copia de los autos origin[al] contra Capitan Franc[is]co de Lacruz de nación Armenio" [Copy of legal documents against Captain Francisco de Lacruz of the Armenian nation]. Filipinas, 24, R.2.N. 14\4\. Folios 1–378.

ARCHIVO GENERAL DE SIMANCAS (AGS)

"Estado Napoles, 1097." Folio 207.

ARCHIVO HISTÓRICO PROVINCIAL DE CÁDIZ (AHPC)

Protocolos de Cádiz, pr. 3.586 (Notary Juan Antonio de Torres).

Wills and notarial documents: CA 5073, fol. 305; CA 0012, fols. 75–76, 703–704; CA 5088, fols. 458–459; CA 5168, fols. 312–313; CA 2528, fols. 10–12; CA 1815, fols. 65–66; CA 2363, fols. 1265–1267; CA 5556, fols. 325–326; CA 1152, fols. 3–7; CA 1801, fols. 61–63, 116–117; CA 2528, fols. 192–193; CA 5088, fols. 458–459; CA 5168, fols. 312–313; CA 2528, fols. 10–12; CA 1815, fols. 85–88; CA 2363, fols. 1265–1267; CA 5556, fols. 325–326; CA 0012, fols. 703–704; CA 0012, fols. 703–704; CA 1152, fols. 3–7; CA 1801, fols. 116–117; CA 2528, fols. 192–193; CA 3573, fols. 246–249; CA 3123, fols. 15–15; CA 0011, fols. 78–79.

*United States*

THE BANCROFT COLLECTION OF WESTERN AND LATIN AMERICANA,
BANCROFT LIBRARY, UNIVERSITY OF CALIFORNIA, BERKELEY
"Real Consulado de Manila." Folders 28a and 28b.

LILLY LIBRARY COLLECTIONS, INDIANA UNIVERSITY (IU)
Philippine Manuscripts II.

UCLA LIBRARY
"Caro Minasian Collection of Armenian Material, ca. 1800–1968." Boxes 3, 6, 10, 15–17, 21–23.

PRINTED PRIMARY SOURCES AND REFERENCE BOOKS

Abrahamyan, A. G. 1968. *Eghia Karnets'u divanĕ; nyut'er Merdzavor Arevelk'i ev Andrkovkasi patmut'yan* [The Archive of Yeghia Karnetsi: Materials for the history of the Near East and Transcaucasia]. Yerevan: Mitk Hratakch'ut'yun.

*The Akbarnama of Abu-l-Fazl* [History of the reign of Akbar including an account of his predecessors]. 1973. Trans. H. Beveridge. Vol. 3. Delhi: ESS Publications.

Alessandri, Vincenzo. 1865. "Commisione a Vincenzo Alessandri veneto legato allo Shàh Thamasp." In *Bolletino consolare: Pubblicato per cura del Ministero degli affari esteri di S. M Il re d'Italia,* ed. Guglielmo Berchet, 3: 29–37. Turin.

Alishan, Ghevont, ed. 1876. *Assises d'Antioche: Reproduites en français et publiées au sixième centenaire de la mort de Sempad le Connétable.* Venice: Imprimerie Armeniénne Médaillée.

———. 1893. *L'Armeno-Veneto: Compendio storico e documenti delle relazioni degli Armeni coi Veneziani; Primo periodo, secoli XIII-XIV.* Venice: Stab. Tip. Armeno, S. Lazzaro.

Al-Mawsuli, Ilyas Hanna. 2003. "The Book of Travels of the Priest Ilyas, Son of the Cleric Hanna al-Mawsuli." In *In the Lands of the Christians: Arabic Travel Writing in the Seventeenth Century,* ed. and trans. Nabil I. Matar. New York and London: Routledge.

Alonso, C. 1970. "Nueva documentación inédita sobre las misiones agustinianas en la India y en Persia (1571–1609)." *Analecta Augustiniana* 33: 309–394.

"The Appellants' Case." 1752? In *Prize Appeals* [A collection of printed cases relating to ships confiscated during the War of Austrian Succession, originally belonging to Sir George Lee]. New York Public Library collection, call no. KC+++p.v. 20–21.

Avetikian, H. Gabriel, H. Khachatur Surmelian, and Mkrtich Avgerian. 1836/1979. *Nor Bargirk' Haykazean Lezui, hator arajin A-K.* Venice: Tparani srboyn Ghazaru. Facsimile ed. Yerevan: Yerevani Hamarsarani Hratarakch'ut'yun.

Bajets'i, Awgostinos. 1884. "Chanaparordut'iwn Yevropa." In *Nshkhark' matenagrut'ean hayots',* ed. K. Patkanian. St. Petersburg.

Bakhchinyan, Artsvi, ed. 2003. "An Unpublished Research about the Armenians in Indonesia." *Haigazian Armenological Review* 23: 399–422.

Baladouni, Vahé, and Margaret Makepeace. 1998. *Armenian Merchants of the Seventeenth and Early Eighteenth Centuries: English East India Company Sources.* Philadelphia: American Philosophical Society.

Bazin, Frère. 1780. "Sur les dernières années du règne de Thamas Kouli-Kan, & sur sa mort tragique, contenus dans une lettre du Frère Bazin, de la Compagnie the Jésus, au Père Roger, Procurateur général des Missions du Levant." In *Lettres édifiantes et curieuses, écrites des missions étrangères.* New ed. Paris.

Bedrossian, Rev. Matthias. 1871/1985. *New Dictionary: Armenian-English.* 1st ed. San Lazzaro, Venice. Facsimile ed. Beirut: Librairi du Liban.

Bembo, Ambrosio. 2007. *The Travels and Journal of Ambrosio Bembo.* Trans. Clara Bargellini and ed. Anthony Welch. Berkeley: University of California Press.

Berchet, Guglielmo, ed. 1865a. *Bolletino consolare: Pubblicato per cura del Ministero degli affari esteri di S. M Il re d'Italia.* Vol. 3. Turin.

———. 1865b. *La repubblica di Venezia e la Persia.* Turin.

Bolts, William. 1772. *Considerations on India affairs; particularly respecting the present state of Bengal and its dependencies. . . . The second edition, with additions.* Vol. 1. London.

Boulaye le Gouz. 1657. *Les Voyages et observations du sieur de Boulaye le Gouz Gentil-Homme Angevin, où sont décrites les Religions, Governemens, (et) situations des Estats (et) Royaume d'Italie, Grèce, Natolie, Syrie, Perse, Palestine, Karamenie, Kaldée, Assyrie, grand Mogol.* Paris.

Bournoutian, George, trans. 2001. *Armenians and Russia, 1626–1796: A Documentary Record.* Annotated translation and commentary by George A. Bournoutian. Costa Mesa, CA: Mazda Publishers.

———, trans. 2003. *The Journal of Zak'aria of Agulis.* Annotated and translated by George Bournoutian. Costa Mesa, CA: Mazda Publishers.

———, trans. 2005. *Arakel of Tabriz: The History of Vardapet Arakel of Tabriz.* Vol. 1. Costa Mesa, CA: Mazda Publishers.

———, trans. 2007. *The Travel Accounts of Simeon of Poland.* Costa Mesa, CA: Mazda Publishers.

Brosset, Marie-Félicité. 1837. "Itinéraire du très-révérend frère Augustin Badjélsi, évêque arménien de Nakbidchévan, de l'ordre des Frères-Prêcheurs, à travers l'Europe; écrit, en langue arménienne." *Journal Asiatique* 3.3: 209–245, 401–421.

Carré, Abbé. 1947–1948. *The Travels of Abbé Carré in India and the Near East, 1672 to 1674.* Trans. from the Ms. Journal of His Travels in the India Office by Lady Fawcett and ed. by Sir Charles Fawcett. 3 vols. paginated as one. London: Hakluyt Society.

Cartwright, John. 1611. *The Preacher's Travels: Wherein is Set downe a True Journall to the Confines of the East Indies, through the Great Countries of Syria, Mesopotamia, Armenia, Media, Hircania, and Parthia.* London: T. Thorppe.

Chardin, Jean. 1811. *Voyages du Chevalier Chardin en Perse, et autres lieux de l'Orient.* Ed. L. Langles. 10 vols. Paris: Le Normant, Imprimeur-Libraire.

Chaumont, Alexandre, Choisy, abbé de, and Michael Smithies. 1997. *Aspects of the Embassy to Siam, 1685: The Chevalier de Chaumont and the Abbé de Choisy: being Alexandre de Chaumont, Relation of the embassy to Siam 1685, and, François-Timoléon de Choisy, Memoranda on religion and commerce in Siam and reflections on the embassy to Siam.* Chiang Mai: Silkworm Books.

Chick, H., ed. 1939. *Chronicles of the Carmelites in Persia and the Papal Mission of the XVIIth and XVIIIth Centuries.* 2 vols. London: Eyre & Spottiswoode.

Da Seggiano, Ignazio Padre. 1953. "Documenti inediti sull'Apostolico dei Minori Capuccini nel vicino oriente (1623–1683)." *Collectanea Franciscana* 13: 297–338.

Datta, K. K., ed. 1958. *Fort William–India House Correspondence and Other Contemporary Papers Relating Thereto (Public Series)*. Vol. 1. Delhi: Civil Lines.

Davrizhets'i, Arakel. 1669/1896. *Girk' patmut'eants'* [Book of histories]. Amsterdam. 2nd ed. Vagharshapat.

De Bruyn, Cornelius. 1738. *Travels into Muscovy, Persia and Part of the East Indies* . . . Translated from the original French. Vol. 1. London.

De Chinon, Père Gabriel. 1671. *Relations nouvelles du Levant ou traités de la religion, du gouvernement et des coutumes des Perses, des Arméniens et des Gaures. Avec une description particulière de l'établissement et des progréz que y font les missionaries et diverses disputes qu'ils ont eu avec les Orientaux . . . Compozés par le P. G. D.C. C. (Père théologie)*. Lyon.

De Courmenin, Baron Louis Deshayes. 1632. *Voyage de Levant fait par le Commandement du Roy en l'année 1621 par le Sr. D. C.* 2nd ed. Paris.

De Coutre, Jacques. 1990. *Andanzas Asiáticas*. Ed. Eddy Stols, B. Teensma, and J. Werberckmoes. Madrid: Historia 16.

Della Valle, Pietro. 1843. *Viaggi di Pietro della Valle, il pellegrino, descritti da lui medesimo in lettere familiari all'erudito suo amico Mario Schipano, divisi in tre parti cioè: La Turchia, la Persia, e l'India, colla vita e ritratto dell'autore*. 2 vols. Brighton.

Desvignes, Père. 1750/1780. "Lettre écrite de Julfa près d'Ispahan, par le Père Desvignes, Missionaire Jésuite, au Père Roger, Procureur des Missions du Levant." In *Lettres édifiantes et curieuses, écrites des missions étrangères*. New ed. Paris.

Du Mans, Raphaël. 1890. *Estat de la Perse en 1660*. Ed. Charles Henri Auguste Schefer. Paris: E. Leroux, Farnborough, Gregg.

Edwards, Arthur. 1905. "Certaine Letters of Arthur Edwards written out of Russia, Media and Persia, to the Company of the Moscovie Merchants in London." In *The Principal Navigations, Voyages, Traffiques and Discoveries of the English Nation*, by Richard Hakluyt. Vol. 3. Glasgow: James MacLehose and Sons.

Émïn, Joseph. 1792. *The Life and Adventures of Joseph Émïn, an Armenian. Written in English by Himself*. London.

———. 1918. *Life and Adventures of Joseph Emin, 1726–1809, Written by Himself*. 2nd ed. Ed. Amy Apcar. Calcutta: Baptist Mission Press.

Ērzrumets'i, Khachatur. 1713. *Chartasanut'iwn arareal ew sharadrets'eal i Khachatroy Ērzrumets'woy* [Rhetoric, compiled and composed by Khachatur of Ērzrum]. Venice: Antonio Bortoli.

Farrington, Anthony, and Na Pombejra, Dhiravat. 2007. *The English Factory in Siam, 1612–1685*. 2 vols. London: The British Library.

Fenning, Daniel. 1771. *A new system of geography: or a general description of the world. . . . Embellished with a new and accurate set of maps, . . . The third edition, revised, corrected, and much improved*. London.

Floor, Willem. 1998. *The Afghan Occupation of Safavid Persia, 1771–1729*. Compiled, annotated, and translated by Willem Floor. Les Cahiers de Studia Iranica 19. Paris: Association pour L'Avancement des Études.

Froger, François. 1926. *Relation du premier voyage des François à la Chine fait en 1698, 1699 et sur le vaisseau 'L'Amphitrite'.* Leipzig: Verlag der Asia Major.

Fryer, John. 1698. *A New Account of East India and Persia, in Eight Letters Being Nine Years Travels, Begun 1672 and Finished 1681.* London.

Galland, Antoine. 2000. *Le voyage à Smyrne: Un manuscrit d'Antoine Galland (1678).* Introduction, transcription, and notes by Frédéric Bauden. Paris: Chandeigne.

Gil, Luis. 1989. *Garcia de Silca y Figueroa: Epistolario diplomatico.* Madrid: Institucion cultural 'El Brocense.'

Gilanentz, Petros di Sarkis. 1988. *The Chronicle of Petros Di Sarkis Gilanentz concerning the Afghan Invasion of Persia in 1722, the Siege of Isfahan, and the Repercussions in Northern Persia, Russia, and Turkey.* Trans. Caro Owen Minasian. Lisbon: Calouste Gulbenkian Foundation.

Godofredo, F. 1954. *Relaçao da viagem de um correio do Vice Rei as Indias orientais a sua majestade expedido de Goa, no primeiro de Janeiro de 1608.* Lisbon.

Gosh, Mkhitar. 2000. *The Lawcode [Datastanagirk '] of Mxit'ar Goš.* Trans. with commentary and indices by Robert W. Thomson. Amsterdam: Rodopi.

Hakluyt, Richard. 1666/1903. *The Principal Navigations, Voyages, Traffiques and Discoveries of the English Nation.* Vol. 3. 1st ed. Glasgow: J. MacLehose and Sons.

Hakobyan, A., and V. Hovhannisyan. 1974. *Hayeren dseragreri ZhĒdari hishatakaranner* [Colophons of Armenian manuscripts from the seventeenth century]. Vol. 1. Yerevan: Haykakan SSH Gitut'yunneri Akademiayi Hratarakch'ut'yun.

Hamilton, Alexander. 1930. *A New Account of the East Indies.* 2 vols. London: Argonaut Press.

Hanway, Jonas. 1753. *An historical account of the British trade over the Caspian Sea: with a journal of travels from London through Russia into Persia; and back again through Russia, Germany and Holland. To which are added, the revolutions of Persia during the present century, with the particular history of the great Usurper Nadir Kouli.* Vol. 4. London.

Herbert, Thomas. 1677. *Some Yeares Travels into Africa and Asia the Great Especially Describing the Famous Empires of Persia and Industani as also divers other kingdoms in the Oriental Indies.* London.

Ibrahim, Muhammad. 1972. *The Ship of Suleiman.* Trans. John O'Kane. New York: Columbia University Press.

Jughayets'i, Khachatur. 1905. *Khachatur Abeghayi Jughayets'woh Patmut'iwn Parsits'* [History of Persia by Deacon Khachatur of Julfa]. Vagharshapat: Holy Ejmiatsin Press.

Krusinski, Judasz, Tadeus. 1733. *The History of the Late Revolutions of Persia: Taken from the Memoirs of Father Krusinski, Procurator of the Jesuits at Ispahan . . . done into English from the Original . . . by Father Du Cerceau.* Vol. 2. London: J. Pemberton.

Lazarovich, Poghos Petros. 1832. *Storagrut'iwn kalkat'ay k'aghak 'i zor arar paron Poghos Petros Lazarovich konstandnupolsets'i' i chanaparhortel iwrum yarewelean hndiks* [A description of the city of Calcutta made by Mister Paul Peter Lazarovitch from Constantinople during his voyage to the East Indies]. Venice: San Lazzaro.

Lehatsi, Simeon. 1936. *Simeon dpri lehatswoy ughegrut'iwn, taregrut'iwn ew Hishatakarank'* [The travel diary, chronicle, and colophons of Simeon from Poland]. Ed. N. Akinian. Vienna: Mkhitarist Press.

"Letter of Master William Biddulph from Aleppo." 1625/1905. In *Hakluytus Posthumus or Purchas His Pilgrimes* . . . Vol. 8. Glasgow: James MacLehose and Sons.

Lewis, Charlton T. 1890. *An Elementary Latin Dictionary*. New York: Harper and Brothers.

Lockyer, Charles. 1711. *An Account of the Trade in India*. London.

Malkhaseants, S. 1944. *Hayeren Bats'atrakan Bararan* [Explanatory dictionary of Armenian]. Vol. 2. 1st ed. Yerevan: Haykakan SSR Petakan hratarakch'ut'yun.

Malynes, Gerard. 1622. *Consuetudo, vel, Lex Mercatoria; or, The Ancient Law-Merchant*. London: Adam Islip.

Manucci, Niccolao. 1966. *Storia do Mogor; or Mogul India, 1653–1708, by Niccolao Manucci*. Trans and introd. William Irvine. 4 vols. Calcutta: Editions Indian.

Martin, François. 1931. *Mémoires de François Martin Fondateur de Pondichery (1665–1696)*. Ed. A. Martineau. 3 vols. Paris: Soc. d'Éd. Géographiques, Maritimes et Coloniales.

Monshi, Iskandar Beg. 1978. *The History of Shah 'Abbas the Great*. Trans. Roger Savory. Vol. 2. Boulder, CO: Westview Press.

Morse, Hosea Ballou. 1926–1929. *The Chronicles of the East India Company Trading to China 1635–1834*. 5 vols. Oxford: Oxford University Press.

Newbery, John. 1625/1905. "Two Voyages by Master John Newberie . . . " In *Hakluytus Posthumus: or Purchas his Pilgrimes: Contayning a History of the World in Sea Voyages*, by Samuel Purchase. Vol. 8. Glasgow: James MacLehose and Sons.

Nshanian, Mesrop, comp. and ed. 1915. *Zhamanakagrut'iwn Grigor vardapeti kamakhets'wo kam daranaghts'wo* [Chronicle of the Vardapet Grigor Kamakhetsi or Daranaghtsi]. Jerusalem: Saint James Monastery Press.

Olearius, Adam. 1662. *The Voyages and Travels of the Ambassadors Sent by Frederich Duke of Holstein to the Great Duke of Muscovy, and the King of Persia* . . . London.

Ortelius, Abraham. 1570. *Theatrum orbis terrarum*. Antwerp.

Ovington, John. 1696. *A Voyage to Surat in the Year 1689*. London.

P'ap'azian, Ignatios. 1826. *Patchēnk' namakats vacharakanut'ean*. Venice: San Lazzaro.

Parsamyan, Vahan. 1953. *Armiano-russkie otnosheniia v XVIII veke* [Documents on Armenian-Russian relations in the seventeenth century]. Vol. 1. Yerevan.

Patkanian, R. 1884. *Nshkhark' matenagrut'ean hayots'* [Relics of Armenian literature]. St. Petersburg.

Père Pacifique de Provins. 1645/1939. *Relation du voyage de Perse*. Paris. Reprint. Assisi: Collegio s. Lorenzo da Brindisi dei minori cappuccini.

Petech, Luciano. 1950. "Un itinirario della Persia alla Cina." *Bolletino della Società Geografica Italiana* 8th ser., 3.2/3 (Mar.–June): 163–170.

———, ed. 1952–1956. *I missionari italiani nel Tibet e nel Nepal*. 7 vols. Rome: Libreria delo Stato.

Pires, Tome. 1944. *The Suma Oriental of Tome Pires: An Account of the East, from the Red Sea to Japan, Written in Malacca and India in 1512–1515*. Trans. and ed. Armando Cortesao. Vol. 2. London: Hakluyt Society.

*Pleadings in the Mayor's Court, 1745*. 1939. Records of Fort St. George Series, vol. 5. Madras: Government Press.

Poghosyan, F. G., ed. 1967. *Datastanagirk' Astrakhani Hayots'* [Code of Laws of the Armenians of Astrakhan]. Yerevan: Haykakan SSH Gitut'yunneri Akademiayi Hratarakch'ut 'yun.

*Prize Appeals*. A collection of printed cases relating to ships confiscated during the War of Austrian Succession, originally belonging to Sir George Lee. New York Public Library collection, call no. KC+++p.v. 20–21.

*Procès-verbaux des délibérations du Conseil Supérieur de Pondichéry, 1701–39*. 1912–1913. Ed. E. Gaudart and A. Martineau. Pondicherry: Société d'histoire de l'Inde française.

Rambert, Gaston, and Louis Bergasse. 1949–. *Histoire du Commerce de Marseille . . .* Vol. 4. Paris: Lib. Plon.

Raynal, abbé, Guillaume Thomas François. 1804 [orig. ed. 1770s]. *A philosophical and political history of the settlements and trade of the Europeans in the East and West Indies.* Vol. 1. Edinburgh: Bundell and Sons.

Redhouse, James Sir. 1890/1997. *Redhouse Turkish/Ottoman-English Dictionary.* Istanbul: SEV Matbaacilik ve yayincilik A.Ş.

"'The Respondents Case.'" 1752? In *Prize Appeals*. [A collection of printed cases relating to ships confiscated during the War of Austrian Succession, originally belonging to Sir George Lee]. New York Public Library collection, call no. KC+++p.v. 20–21.

Richard, Francis, ed. 1995. *Raphaël du Mans: Missionnaire en Perse au XVIIe siècle.* Vol. 1, *Biographie, Correspondance.* Paris: Édition L'Harmattan.

Roques, Georges. 1996. *La manière de négocier aux Indes 1676–1691: La compagnie des Indes et l'art du commerce.* Ed. and annotated by Valérie Bérinstain. Paris: École Française d'Extrême Orient.

Schröder, Joachim. 1711. *Thesaurus linguae armenicae.* Amsterdam: Vanandetsi.

Sebastats'i, Mkhitar. 1749. *Baṙgirk' haykazean lezowi: Bazhaneal 2 hators 1* [Dictionary of the Armenian language comprising two volumes]. Venice: Antonio Bortoli.

———. 1961. *Namakani Tsarayin Astutsoy Tearn Mkhitaray Abbayi eranashnorh himnadri Mkhitarean Miabanut'ean* [Letterbook of the Servant of God, Abbot Mkhitar, the blessed founder of the Mkhitarist Congregation]. Venice: San Lazzaro.

Séguiran, Henry de. 1633/1982. "Rapport Séguiran sur le commerce et la défense des côtes de Provence" (April 1633). In *Abrégé de l'histoire de Provence et autres textes inédits,* by Nicolas Claude Fabri de Peiresc, Jacques Ferrier, and Michel Feuillas. Avignon: Aubanel.

Shahrimanian, Marcara. 1788. *Patmut'iwn Metsin Gengizkhani arajin kayser nakhni mghulats' ev t'at'arats', bazhaneal i chors girs* [A history of the Great Genghiz Khan, the first emperor of the former Mongols and Tatars, comprising four letters)]. Trieste: Mekhitarist Press.

Steingass, Francis Joseph. 1892. *A Comprehensive Persian-English Dictionary, including the Arabic Words and Phrases to Be Met with in Persian Literature.* London: Routledge & K. Paul.

Stodart, Robert. 1935. *The Journal of Robert Stodart being an account of his experiences as a member of Sir Dodmore Cotton's Mission in Persia in 1628–29.* Ed. Sir Dennison Ross. London: Luzac & Co.

*Tadhkirat al-Muluk: A Manual of Safavid Administration (circa 1137/1725), Persian Text in Facsimile BM, Or. 9496.* 1943. Trans. and expl. V. Minorsky. London: E. J. W. Gibb Memorial Series, Luzac & Co.

T'aghiadian, Mesrop. 1845/1975. "Hndkastan ew Jugha" [India and Julfa]. In *Grakan Zharangut'yun, 9, Mesrop T'aghiadyan: ughegrutyunner, hodvatsner, namakner, vaveragrer* [Literary heritage, 9, Mesrop T'aghiadyan, travelogues, essays, letters, documents], ed. Ruzan Nanumyan. Yerevan.

Tavernier, Jean Baptiste. 1688. *Collection of Travels Through Turky into Persia and the East Indies Giving an Account of the Present State of those Countries . . .* London.

Tayean, Ghewond. 1930. *Mayr Diwan mkhit'ariants' venetko i Surb ghazar, 1707–1773* [Grand Archives of the Mkhitarists of Venice at San Lazzaro, 1707–1773]. Venice: San Lazzaro.

Tectander, Georg. 1877. *Iter Persicum ou description du Voyage en Perse enterpris en 1602.* Paris.

Teixeira, Pedro. 1902. *The travels of Pedro Teixeira; with His "Kings of Harmuz," and Extracts from His "Kings of Persia."* Trans. and annotated by William F. Sinclair. London: Printed for the Hakluyt Society.

Tibbetts, G. R., trans. 1971. *Arab Navigation in the Indian Ocean before the Coming of the Portuguese, Being a Translation of Kitab al-fawaidfi usul al-bahr wa'l-qawa'id of Ahmad b. Majid al-Najdi.* London: Royal Asiatic Society of Great Britain and Ireland.

*Travels of Fray Sebastian Manrique (1629–1643).* 1927. Trans. C. E. Luard. Vol. 2. London: Hakluyt Society.

Vanantets'i, Ghukas. 1699. *Gants ch'ap 'oy kshroy twoy ew dramits' bolor ashkhari or ē Gitut'iwn amenayn tesak kshroy ch'ap 'ots 'ew dramits' orov bolor ashkhari vacharakanut'iwnn vari* [A treasury of measures, numbers, and moneys of the entire world, which is the knowledge of all types of weights, measures, and moneys with which the trade of the whole world is conducted]. Amsterdam.

Van Linschoten, John Huyghen. 1885. *The Voyage of John Huyghen van Linschoten to the East Indies.* 2 vols. Trans. A. C. Burnell; Pieter Anton Tiele. London: Hakluyt Society.

Varthema, Ludovico. 1863. *Travels (The Travels of Ludovico di Varthema in Egypt, Syria, Deserta and Arabia Felix, Persia, India, and Ethiopia, A.D. 1503 to 1508).* Trans. from the original Italian edition of 1510. London: Hakluyt Society.

Villotte, Jacques. 1730. *Voyages d'un missionaire de la compagnie de Jésus en Turquie, en Perse, en Arménie, en Arabie et en Barbarie.* Paris.

Voskanyan, Ninel, Korkotyan, K'narik, and Savalyan, Ant'aram, eds. 1988. *Hay Girk'ĕ, 1512–1800 tvakannerin: hay hnatip grk'i matenagitut'yun* [The Armenian book, in the years 1512-1800: A bibliography of old Armenian books]. Erevan: Al. Myasnikyani Anvan HSSH Petakan Gradaran.

Willes, Richard. 1666/1903. "Notes Concerning this fourth voyage into Persia, begun in the Moneth of July 1568. gathered by M. Richard Willes from the mouth of Master Arthur Edwards, which was Agent of the same." In *The Principal Navigations, Voyages, Traffiques and Discoveries of the English Nation,* by Richard Hakluyt. Vol. 3. Glasgow: J. MacLehose and sons.

Wilson, C. R. 1895. *Early Annals of the English in Bengal: Being the Bengal Public Consultations for the First Half of the 18th Century.* Vol. 1. London: W. Thacker.

Yule, Henry. 1968. *A Narrative of the Mission to the Court of Ava in 1855, compiled by Henry Yule, together with the Journal of Arthur Phayre, Envoy to the Court of Ava.* New York: Oxford University Press.

———, and Arthur Coke Burnell, comps. 1903. *Hobson-Jobson: A Glossary of Colloquial*

*Anglo-Indian Words and Phrases, and of Kindred Terms, Etymological, Historical, Geographical, and Discursive*, ed. William Crooke. 2nd ed. London: J. Murray.
Zak'aria of Agulis. 1938. *Zak'aria Agulets'u Oragrut'yunĕ* ['The diary of Zak'aria of Agulis]. Yerevan.


## SECONDARY SOURCES

Abdullah, 'Thabit A. J. 2001. *Merchants, Mamluks, and Murder: The Political Economy of Trade in Eighteenth-Century Basra*. Albany: State University of New York Press.
Abrahamyan, A. G. 1964–1967. *Hamarot urvagits hay gaghtavayreri patmut'yan* [A concise overview of the history of Armenian settlements]. 2 vols. Yerevan: Haypethrat.
———. 1972. *Hayots Gir yev Grch'ut'yun* [Armenian writing and literature]. Yerevan: Erevani hamalsarani hratarakch'ut'yun.
Abu-Lughod, Janet L. 1989. *Before European Hegemony: The World System, A.D. 1250–1350*. New York: Oxford University Press.
Acharian, Hrachia. 1940. *K'nnut 'iwn Nor Jughayi Barbari* [A study of the New Julfa dialect]. Yerevan.
———. 2002. *Hay gaghtakanut'yan patmut'yun* [History of Armenian emigration]. Yerevan: Zangak-97.
Agarwal, Usha. 1966. "An Account of the Postal System in India from 1650 to 1750." *Bengal Past and Present*: 40–57.
Aghassian, Michel, and Kéram Kévonian. 1988. "Le commerce arménien dans l'océan Indien aux 17e et 18e siècles." In *Marchands et hommes d'affaires asiatiques dans l'océan Indien et la mer de Chine, 13e–20e siècles*, ed. D. Lombard and J. Aubin. Paris: Éd. De L'Ehess.
———. 1999. "The Armenian Merchant Network: Overall Autonomy and Local Integration." In *Merchants, Companies, and Trade: Europe and Asia in the Early Modern Era*, ed. Sushil Chaudhury and Michel Morineau. Cambridge: Cambridge University Press.
———. 2000. "Armenian Trade in the Indian Ocean in the Seventeenth and Eighteenth Centuries." In *Asian Merchants and Businessmen in the Indian Ocean and the China Sea*, ed. Denys Lombard and Jean Aubin. New York: Oxford University Press.
Aivazian, Argam. 1990. *Djugha* [Julfa]. Yerevan.
———. 2004. *Nakhijewani Vimagrakan Zhaṙangut'iwnĕ, hator A, Jugha* ['The epigraphical patrimony of Nakhijewan, vol. 1, Julfa]. Yerevan.
Akonts, Stepanos Giuver. 1805. *Ashkharagrut'iwn chorits' masants', hator 4, hndik's* [Geography of the four parts of the world, vol. 4, 'The Indies]. Venice: San Lazzaro.
Alam, Muzaffar. 1994. "Trade, State Policy, and Regional Change: Aspects of Mughal-Uzbek Commercial Relations (1550–1750)." *Journal of the Economic and Social History of the Orient* 37.3: 202–227.
Alam, Muzaffar, and Sanjay Subrahmanyam, eds. 1998. *The Mughal State, 1526–1750*. Delhi: Oxford University Press.
———. 2007. *Indo-Persian Travels in the Age of Discoveries, 1400–1800*. Cambridge: Cambridge University Press.
Ali, M. Atthar. 1997. *The Mughal Nobility under Aurangzeb*. New Delhi.

Alishan, Gh. 1893. *Sisakan: Teghagrut'iwn siwneats' ashkhari* [Sisakan: A topography of the land of Siwnik]. Venice.

———. 1896. *Hay-Venet* [Armenian-Veneto]. Venice: San Lazzaro.

Allsen, Thomas T. 2001. *Culture and Conquest in Mongol Eurasia.* Cambridge: Cambridge University Press.

Alpoyachian, Arshak. 1941–1961. *Patmut'iwn Hay gaghtakanut'ean: Hayeru tsrvumĕ ashkharhi zanazan Maserĕ*[History of Armenian emigration: The dispersal of the Armenians to various parts of the world]. 3 vols. Cairo: Tp. Sahak Mesrop.

Anderson, Benedict. 1991. *Imagined Communities: Reflections on the Origin and Spread of Nationalism.* Rev. and extended ed. 2nd ed. London and New York: Verso.

Anderson, John. 1890. *English Intercourse with Siam in the Seventeenth Century.* London: Kegan Paul Trench, Trubner & Company.

Angeles, F. Delor. 1980. "Armenians before the Philippine Inquisition." *Silliman Journal:* 113–121.

Anon. 1818. *A Compendious Ecclesiastical, Chronological and Historical Sketches of Bengal since the Foundation of Calcutta.* Calcutta.

Arakelian, H. 1911. *Parskastani Hayerĕ, nrants' ants'ealĕ, nerkan ew apagan, masn a* ['The Armenians of Persia, their past, present, and future, pt. 1]. Vienna: Mkhitarean tparan.

Arasaratnam, Sinnappah. 1986. *Merchants, Companies, and Commerce on the Coromandel Coast, 1650–1740.* Delhi: Oxford University Press.

———. 1994. *Maritime India in the Seventeenth Century.* Delhi: Oxford University Press.

Asher, Catherine Ella Blanshard, and Cynthia Talbot. 2006. *India before Europe.* Cambridge: Cambridge University Press.

Ashjian, Mesrop Srbazan. 1993. *Handipumner* [Encounters]. New York: The Armenian Prelacy.

———. 2001. "Nor Jughayetsi mĕ . . . Cadizi Mej" [A New Julfan in Cadiz]. In *Handipumner* [Encounters]. New York: Armenian Prelacy.

Ashtor, Eliyahu. 1983. *Levant Trade in the Later Middle Ages.* Princeton, NJ: Princeton University Press.

Aslanian, Sebouh. 2002. "The 'Treason of the Intellectuals'? Reflections on the Uses of Revisionism and Nationalism in Armenian Historiography." *Armenian Forum* 2.4: 1–37.

———. 2004a. *Dispersion History and the Polycentric Nation: The Role of Simeon Yerevantsi's Girk' or Koch'i Partavjar in the Armenian National Revival of the 18th Century.* Venice: San Lazzaro.

———. 2004b. "European Piracy and Armenian Maritime Merchants in the Indian Ocean: Captain Kidd and the *Quedah Merchant.*" Unpublished essay.

———. 2006a. "Hndkahay vacharakanut'ean patmutyunits' (XVIII d.skizb)" [From the history of Indo-Armenian trade (beginning of the eighteenth century)]. *Patma-Banasirakan Handēs* 1.171: 254–271.

———. 2006b. "Social Capital, 'Trust,' and the Role of Networks in Julfan Trade: Informal and Semiformal Institutions at Work." *Journal of Global History* 1.3: 383–402.

———. 2006c. "Trade Diaspora versus Colonial State: Armenian Merchants, the East India Company, and the High Court of Admiralty in London, 1748–1752." *Diaspora: A Journal of Transnational Studies* 13.1: 37–100.

———. 2007a. "Circulating Credit and Merchants in the Indian Ocean: The Role and Influence of the *Commenda* Contract in Julfan Trade." *Journal of the Economic and Social History of the Orient* 50.2: 124–171.

———. 2007b. "From the Indian Ocean to the Mediterranean: Circulation and the Global Trade Networks of Armenian Merchants from New Julfa/Isfahan, 1606–1747." PhD diss., Columbia University.

———. 2008a. "Aden, Geniza, and the Indian Ocean during the Middle Ages." *Journal of Global History* 3: 451–457.

———. 2008b. "'The Salt in a Merchant's Letter': The Culture of Julfan Correspondence in the Indian Ocean and Mediterranean." *Journal of World History* 19.2: 127–188.

———. 2008c. "Some Notes on a Letter Sent by an Armenian Priest in Bengal in 1727." In *Between Paris and Fresno: Armenian Studies in Honor of Dickran Kouymjian*, ed. Barlow Der Mugrdechian. Costa Mesa, CA: Mazda Publishers.

———. 2009. "Julfan Agreements with Foreign States and Chartered Companies: Exploring the Limits of Julfan Collective Self-Representation in the Early Modern Age." Unpublished paper.

———. 2010. "Silver, Missionaries, and Print: A Global Microhistory of Early Modern Networks of Circulation and the Armenian Translation of Charles Rollin's History of Rome." *Diaspora: A Journal of Transnational Studies*, forthcoming.

"As Scams Go, This Is a Gem." *Los Angeles Times*, March 29, 2006.

Axworthy, Michael. 2006. *Sword of Persia: Nader Shah, from Tribal Warrior to Conquering Tyrant*. London: I. B. Tauris.

Babai, Sussan, et al. 2004. *Slaves of the Shah: New Elites in Safavid Iran*. London: I. B. Tauris.

Babayan, Kathryn. 2002. *Mystics, Monarchs, and Messiahs: Cultural Landscapes of Early Modern Iran*. Cambridge, MA: Harvard University Press.

Baghdiantz McCabe, Ina. 1998. "Merchant Capital and Knowledge: The Financing of Early Printing Presses by the Eurasian Silk Trade of New Julfa." In *Treasures in Heaven: Armenian Art, Religion, and Society*, ed. T. F. Mathews and R. S. Wieck. New York: Pierpont Morgan.

———. 1999. *The Shah's Silk for Europe's Silver: The Eurasian Trade of the Julfa Armenians in Safavid Iran and India, 1530–1750*. Atlanta: University of Pennsylvania Armenian Texts Series/Scholars Press.

———. 2008. *Orientalism in Early Modern France: Eurasian Trade, Exoticism, and the Ancien Régime*. Oxford and New York: Berg.

Baghdiantz McCabe, Ina, Gelina Harlaftis, and Ioanna Pepelasis Minoglou, eds. 2005. *Diaspora Entrepreneurial Networks: Four Centuries of History*. Oxford and New York: Berg.

Baghumyan, Tigran Sarkavag. 2007. *Arevmtyan Bengaliayum Taghvats Hay Hogeworakannerě* [Armenian clergymen buried in West Bengal]. Yerevan-Calcutta.

Baibourtyan, Vahan. 2004. *International Trade and the Armenian Merchants in the Seventeenth Century*. New Delhi: Sterling.

Baltrušaitis, Jurgis, and Dickran Kouymjian. 1986. "Julfa on the Arax and Its Funerary Monuments." In *Armenian Studies/Études Arméniennes in Memoriam Haig Berberian*, ed. Dickran Kouymjian. Lisbon: Calouste Gulbenkian Foundation.

Barber, Bernard. 1983. *The Logic and Limits of Trust*. New Brunswick, NJ: Rutgers University Press.

Barendse, Rene. 1988. "The Long Road to Livorno: The Overland Messenger Service of the Dutch East India Company in the Seventeenth Century." *Itinirario* 12: 25–45.

———. 2000. "Trade and State in the Arabian Seas: A Survey from the Fifteenth to the Eighteenth Century." *Journal of World History* 11.2: 173–225.

———. 2002. *The Arabian Seas: The Indian Ocean World of the Seventeenth Century.* Armonk, NY: M. E. Sharpe.

Bayly, Christopher. 1988. *Indian Society and the Making of the British Empire.* Cambridge: Cambridge University Press.

———. 1989. *Imperial Meridian: The British Empire and the World, 1780–1830.* London and New York: Longman.

———. 1996. *Empire and Information: Intelligence Gathering and Social Communication in India, 1780–1870.* Cambridge and New York: Cambridge University Press.

———. 2002. "'Archaic' and 'Modern' Globalization in the Eurasian and African Arena, c. 1750–1850." In *Globalization in World History,* ed. A. G. Hopkins. London: W. W. Norton.

Bekius, Rene. 2002. "The Armenian Colony in Amsterdam in the 17th and 18th Century: Armenian Merchants from Julfa before and after the Fall of the Safavid Empire." Paper presented at the conference "Iran and the World in the Safavid Age," London.

Bellingeri, Gian Pierro. 2004. "Sugli Sceriman rimasti a Giulfa: Devozione agli ultimi Safavidi?" In *Gli Armeni e Venezia: Dagli Sceriman a Mechitar; Il momento culminante di una consuetudine millenaria,* ed. Boghos Levon Zekiyan and Aldo Ferrari. Venice: Istituto Veneto di Scienze, Lettere ed Arti.

Bentley, Jerry. 1996. "Cross-Cultural Interaction and Periodization in World History." *American Historical Review* 101 (June): 749–770.

———. 2007. "Early Modern Europe and the Early Modern World." In *Between the Middle Ages and Modernity: Individual and Community in the Early Modern World,* ed. Jerry Bentley and Charles Parker. Lanham, MD: Rowman and Littlefield.

Berberian, Houri. 2010. "'Unequivocal Sole Ruler': The Lives of Julfan Armenian Women and Early Modern Laws." Unpublished paper.

Bernstein, Lisa. 1992. "Opting Out of the Legal System: Extra Legal Contractual Relations in the Diamond Industry." *The Journal of Legal Studies* 21.1 (January): 115–157.

Bhattacharya, Bhaswati. 2005. "Armenian European Relationship in India, 1500–1800: No Armenian Foundation to a European Empire?" *Journal of the Economic and Social History of the Orient* 48: 277–322.

———. 2008a. "The 'Book of Will' of Petrus Woskan (1680–1751): Some Insights into the Global Commercial Network of the Armenians in the Indian Ocean." *Journal of the Economic and Social History of the Orient* 52: 67–98.

———. 2008b. "Making Money at the Blessed Place of Manila: Armenians in the Madras-Manila Trade in the Eighteenth Century." *The Journal of Global History* 3: 1–20.

Binayán, Narciso. 1996. *Entre el pasado y el futuro: Los armenios en la Argentina.* Buenos Aires.

Boissevain, Jeremy. 1974. *Friends of Friends: Networks, Manipulators, and Coalitions.* Oxford: Blackwell.

Bonardi, Claudia. 1990. "Il commercio dei preziosi." In *Gli Armeni in Italia,* ed. Boghos Levon Zekiyan. Rome: De Luca.

————. 1996. "Gli Sceriman di Venezia da mercanti a possidenti." In *Ad limina Italiae Ar Druns Italioy: In viaggio per L'Italia con mercanti e monaci armeni,* ed. Boghos Levon Zekiyan. Padua: Editoriale Programma.

Bourdieu, Pierre. 1977. *Outline of a Theory of Practice.* Cambridge: Cambridge University Press.

————. 1980. "Le capital social: Notes provisoires." *Actes de la Recherche en Sciences Sociales* 31 (January): 2–3.

————. 2001. "The Forms of Capital." In *The Sociology of Economic Life.* ed. Mark Granovetter and Richard Swedberg. 2nd ed. Boulder, CO: Westview Press.

Boxer, C. R. 1965/1973. *The Dutch Seaborne Empire, 1600–1800.* Harmondsworth, UK: Penguin.

————. 1969. "A Note on Portuguese Reactions to the Revival of the Red Sea Spice Trade and the Rise of Atjeh, 1540–1600." *Journal of Southeast Asian History* 10.3: 415–428.

————. 1976. "A Portuguese Document of 1670 concerning Khwaja Minaz." *Indica* 13.1–2: 83–92.

Braude, Benjamin. 1999. "The Nexus of Diaspora, Enlightenment, and Nation: Thoughts on Comparative History." In *Enlightenment and Diaspora, the Armenian and Jewish Cases,* ed. Richard Hovannisian and David Myers, 5–44. Atlanta: Scholars Press.

Braudel, Fernand. 1972. *The Mediterranean and the Mediterranean World in the Age of Philip II.* Trans. Siân Reynolds. 2 vols. 2nd ed. New York: Harper & Row.

————. 1981. *The Structures of Everyday Life.* Vol. 1 of *Civilization and Capitalism, 15th–18th Century.* Trans. Siân Reynolds. New York: Harper.

————. 1982. *The Wheels of Commerce.* Vol. 2 of *Civilization and Capitalism, 15th–18th Century.* Trans. Siân Reynolds. New York: Harper.

————. 1984. *The Perspective of the World.* Vol. 3 of *Civilization and Capitalism, 15th–18th Century.* Trans. Siân Reynolds. New York: Harper.

Brimnes, Niels. 2003. "Beyond Colonial Law: Indigenous Litigation and the Contestation of Property in the Mayor's Court in Late Eighteenth-Century Madras." *Modern Asian Studies* 37.3: 513–550.

Brook, Timothy. 2008. *Vermeer's Hat: The Seventeenth Century and the Dawn of the Global World.* New York: Bloomsbury Press.

Brubaker, Rogers. 2005. "The 'Diaspora' Diaspora." *Ethnic and Racial Studies* 28.1 (January): 1–19.

Bruni, Luigino, and Robert Sugden. 2000. "Moral Canals: Trust and Social Capital in the Works of Smith, Hume, and Genovesi." *Economics and Philosophy* 16: 21–45.

Buckley, Charles Burton. 1902. *An Anecdotal History of Old Times in Singapore . . . from the Foundation of the Settlement . . . on February 6th 1819, to the Transfer to the Colonial Office as Part of the Colonial Possessions of the Crown on April 1st, 1867.* Singapore: Fraser & Neave.

Burt, Ronald S. 2001. "Bandwidth and Echo: Trust, Information, and Gossip in Social Networks." In *Networks and Markets,* ed. James E. Rauch and Alessandra Casella. New York: Russell Sage Foundation.

Carlos, Ann M., and Stephen Nicholas. 1988. "'Giants of an Earlier Capitalism': The Chartered Trading Companies as Modern Multinationals." *The Business History Review* 62.3: 398–419.

———. 1996. "Theory and History: Seventeenth-Century Joint-Stock Chartered Trading Companies." *The Journal of Economic History* 56.4: 916–924.

Carswell, John. 1968. *New Julfa: The Armenian Churches and Other Buildings*. Oxford: Clarendon Press.

Castignoli, Paolo. 1979. "Gli Armeni a Livorno nel seicento: Notizie sul loro primo insediamento." *Studi Storici e Geografici* 3: 27–61.

Chatterjee, Kumkum. 1992. "Trade and Darbar Politics in the Bengal Subah, 1733–1757." *Modern Asian Studies* 26: 233–273.

Chaudhuri, K. N. 1965. *The English East India Company: A Study of an Early Joint-Stock Company, 1600–1640*. Cambridge: Cambridge University Press.

———. 1978. *The Trading World of Asia and the English East India Company, 1660–1760*. London and New York: Cambridge University Press.

———. 1981. "The English East India Company in the Seventeenth Century." In *Companies and Trade: Essays on Overseas Trading Companies during the Ancien Régime*, ed. Leonard Blussé and Femme Gaastra. The Hague: Leiden University Press.

———. 1985. *Trade and Civilisation in the Indian Ocean: An Economic History from the Rise of Islam to 1750*. Cambridge and New York: Cambridge University Press.

Chaudhury, Sushil. 1967. "The Rise and Decline of Hugli: A Port in Medieval Bengal." *Bengal Past and Present: A Journal of Modern Indian and Asian History* (January–June): 33–68.

———. 1990. "Khwaja Wazid in Bengal Trade and Politics, c1740–60." *The Indian Historical Review* 26: 137–148.

———. 2005. "Trading Networks in a Traditional Diaspora: Armenians in India, c. 1600–1800." In *Diaspora Entrepreneurial Networks: Four Centuries of History*, ed. Ina Baghdiantz McCabe, Gelina Harlaftis, and Ioanna Pepelasis Minoglou. Oxford: Berg.

Chemchemian, Sahak. 1989. *Hay tpagrut'iwně ew Hrom (ZhE. dar)* [Armenian printing and Rome in the seventeenth century]. Venice: San Lazzaro.

Chiappini, Guido. 1937. "Il primo tipografo di Livorno fu un sacerdote armeno." *Liburni Civitas* 15: 33–47. Also translated and annotated by Eghia Pēchik'ian, in *Bazmavep* 95: 227–237.

Çizakça, Murat. 1996. *A Comparative Evolution of Business Partnerships: The Islamic World and Europe, with Specific Reference to the Ottoman Archives*. London, New York, and Cologne: E. J. Brill.

Clarence-Smith, William Gervase. 2005. "Lebanese and Other Middle Eastern Migrants in the Philippines." In *Population Movement beyond the Middle East: Migration, Diaspora, and Network*, ed. Akira Usuki, Omar Farouk Bajunid, and Tomoko Yamagishi. JCAS Symposium Series 17. Osaka: Japan Center for Area Studies, National Museum of Ethnology.

Cohen, Abner. 1971. "Cultural Strategies in the Organization of Trading Diasporas." In *The Development of Indigenous Trade and Markets in West Africa*, ed. Claude Meillassoux. Oxford: Oxford University Press.

Cohen, Dan, and Laurence Prusak. 2001. *In Good Company: How Social Capital Makes Organizations Work*. Cambridge, MA: Harvard Business School Press.

Cohen, Robin. 1997. *Global Diasporas: An Introduction.* Seattle: University of Washington Press.

Cole, Charles Woolsey. 1939. *Colbert and a Century of French Mercantilism.* Vol. 1. New York: Columbia University Press.

Coleman, James. 1988. "Social Capital in the Creation of Human Capital." *The American Journal of Sociology* 94 (Supplement): S-95–S-120.

Colless, B.C. 1969–1975. "The Traders of the Pearl: The Mercantile Activities of Nestorian Christians and Armenians." *Abr Nahrain* 9 (1969–1970): 17–38; 10 (1970–1971): 102–121; 11 (1971): 1–21; 13 (1972–1973): 115–135; 14 (1973–1974): 1–16; 15 (1974–1975): 6–17.

Constable, Olivia Remie. 2003. *Housing the Stranger in the Mediterranean World: Lodging, Trade, and Travel in Late Antiquity and the Middle Ages.* Cambridge: Cambridge University Press.

Conybeare, Frederick Cornwallis. 1913. *A Catalogue of Armenian Manuscripts at the British Museum.* London: British Museum.

Cook, Karen S., ed. 2001. *Trust in Society.* New York: Russell Sage Foundation.

Coser, Lewis A. 1964. "The Political Functions of Eunuchism." *American Sociological Review* 29.6 (December): 880–885.

———. 1972. "The Alien as a Servant of Power: Court Jews and Christian Renegades." *American Sociological Review* 37 (October): 574–581.

Csoma, Körösi. 1833. "A Tibetan Passport Dated 1688 A.D." *The Journal of the Asiatic Society of Bengal* 2: 201–202.

Cunningham, Charles Henry. 1919. *The Audiencia in the Spanish Colonies as Illustrated by the Audiencia of Manila (1583–1800).* Berkeley: University of California Press.

Curiel, Carlo L. 1930. *La fondazione della colonia armena in Trieste.* Trieste: Typographia del Lloyd Triestino.

Curtin, Philip. 1984. *Cross-Cultural Trade in World History.* Cambridge: Cambridge University Press.

Dale, Stephen. 2002. *Indian Merchants and Eurasian Trade, 1600–1750.* Cambridge: Cambridge University Press.

———. 2010. *The Muslim Empires of the Ottomans, Safavids, and Mughals.* Cambridge: Cambridge University Press.

Darwin, John. 2008. *After Tamerlane: Global History of Empire since 1405.* New York: Bloomsbury Press.

Das Gupta, Ashin. 1979. *Indian Merchants and the Decline of Surat: c. 1700–1750.* Wiesbaden: Steiner.

———. 2004. *India and the Indian Ocean World: Trade and Politics.* New Delhi: Oxford.

Dasgupta, Partha. 1998. "Trust as a Commodity." In *Trust: Making and Breaking Cooperative Relations,* ed. Diego Gambetta. Oxford and New York: Basil Blackwell.

Datta, K.K. 1963. *Alivardi and His Times.* Calcutta: The University of Calcutta.

Deloche, Jean. 1993. *Transport and Communications in India prior to Steam Locomotion.* Vol. 1. Oxford and Delhi: Oxford University Press.

De Roover, Raymond. 1963. "The Organization of Trade." In *The Cambridge Economic History of Europe,* vol. 3. Cambridge: Cambridge University Press.

De Souza, George Bryan. 1986. *Survival of Empire: Portuguese Trade and Society in China and the South China Sea, 1630–1754.* Cambridge: Cambridge University Press.

De Zúniga, Fr. Joaquin Martinez. 1893. *Estadismo de las islas filipinas o mis viajes por este pais.* Ed. and annotated by W. E. Retana. 2 vols. Madrid: Impr. de la viuda de M. Minuesa de los Rios.

Disney, Anthony. 1983. "The Portuguese Overland Courier Network from India to Portugal." In *Don Peter Felicitation Volume,* ed. E. C. T. Candappa and M. S. S. Fernandopulle. Colombo, Sri Lanka: D. P. F. Committee.

———. 1998. "The Gulf Route from India to Portugal in the Sixteenth and Seventeenth Centuries: Couriers, Traders, and Image-makers." In *A Carreira da India e as rotas dos estreitos: Actas do VIII Seminario Internacional de Historia Indo-Portuguesa,* ed. Artur Teodoro de Matos and Luís Filipe F.R. Thomaz. Angra do Heroísmo: O Seminario.

———. 2009. *A History of Portugal and the Portuguese Empire.* Vol. 2, *The Portuguese Empire.* Cambridge: Cambridge University Press.

Edwards, Jeremy, and Sheilagh Ogilvie. 2008. "Contract Enforcement, Institutions, and Social Capital: The Maghribi Traders Reappraised." CESifo Working Paper 2254. http://SSRN .com/abstract1/41107801 (accessed 3 September 2008).

Enthoven, Victor. 2006. "Joint-Stock Company." In *History of World Trade since 1450,* ed. John J. McCusker. Detroit: Macmillan Reference USA.

Faroqhi, Suraiya. 1994. "Trade: Regional, Inter-regional, and International." In *An Economic and Social History of the Ottoman Empire,* vol. 2, ed. Suraiya Foroqhi, Bruce McGowan, Donald Quataert, and Şevket Pamuk. Cambridge: Cambridge University Press.

———. 2005. *The Ottoman Empire and the World around It.* London: I. B. Tauris.

Fenster, Thelma, and Daniel Lord Smail, eds. 2003. *Fama: The Politics of Talk and Reputation in Medieval Europe.* Ithaca, NY, and London: Cornell University Press.

Ferrier, Ronald. 1970. "The *Agreement of the East India Company with the Armenian Nation,* 22nd June 1688." *Revue des Études Arméniennes* n.s. 7: 427–443.

———. 1973. "The Armenians and the East India Company in Persia in the Seventeenth and Eighteenth Century." *Economic History Review* 2nd ser., 26: 38–62.

———. 1986. "The Terms and Conditions under Which English Trade Was Transacted with Safavid Persia." *Bulletin of the School of Oriental and African Studies* 49.1: 48–66.

Finlay, Robert. 1994. "Crisis and Crusade in the Mediterranean: Venice, Portugal, and the Cape Route to India (1498–1509)." *Studi Veneziani* 28: 45–90.

Fischer, Lucia Frattarelli. 1998. "Per la storia dell'insediamento degli Armeni a Livorno nel seicento." In *Gli Armeni lungo le strade d'Italia: Atti del Convegno Internazionale (Torino, Genova, Livorno, 8–11 Marzo 1997),* ed. Claudia Bonardi. Pisa and Rome: Ist. Editoriali e Poligrafici Internazionali.

———. 1999. "Gli Armeni a Livorno." In *Roma-Armenia,* ed. Claude Mutafian. Rome: De Luca.

———. 2006. " 'Pro Armenis unitis cum conditionibus': La costruzione della Chiesa degli Armeni a Livorno; Un iter lungo e accidentato." In *Gli Armeni a Livorno: L'intercultura di una diaspora,* ed. Giangiacomo Panessa and Massimo Sanacore. Livorno: Debatte Otello.

Fischer, Lucia Frattarelli, and P. Castignoli. 1987. *Le "Livornine" del 1591 e del 1593.* Livorno: Cooperativa Risorgimento.

Fletcher, Joseph. 1995. "Integrative History: Parallels and Interconnections in the Early Modern Period, 1500–1800." In *Studies on Chinese and Islamic Inner Asia,* by Joseph Fletcher, ed. Beatrice Forbes Manz. Aldershot, Hampshire, UK, and Brookfield, VT: Variorum.

Floor, Willem. 1980. "The First Printing-Press in Iran." *Zeitschrift der Deutschen Morgen-ländischen Gesellschaft*: 361–371.

———. 1999. "Kalantar." *Encyclopedia of Islam* (Supplement).

———. 2000a. *The Economy of Safavid Persia*. Wiesbaden: Reichert Verlag.

———. 2000b. "The Secular Judicial System in Safavid Persia." *Studia Iranica* 29.1: 9–60.

———. 2001a. "Chapar." *Encyclopedia Iranica* 39. http://www.iranica.com/articles/capar-or-capar-turk.

———. 2001b. "The Chapar-khana System in Qajar Iran." *Iran* 39: 257–291.

———. 2006. *The Persian Gulf: A Political and Economic History of Five Port Cities, 1500–1730*. Washington, DC: Mage.

Floristan, J. M., and Luis Gil. 1986. "Las misiones luso-españolas en Persia y la cristianidad Armenia (1600–1614)." *Sefarad* 46.1–2: 207–218.

Flynn, Dennis, and Giráldes, Arturo. 1995. "'Born with a Silver Spoon': The Origin of World Trade in 1571." *Journal of World History* 6.2: 201–221.

———. 2008. "Born Again: Globalization's Sixteenth-Century Origins (Asian/Global versus European Dynamics)." *Pacific Economic History Review* 13.3: 359–387.

Frank, Andre Gunder. 1998. *Re-Orient: Global Economy in the Asian Age*. Los Angeles and Berkeley: University of California Press.

Furber, Holden. 1935. "An Abortive Attempt at Anglo-Spanish Commercial Cooperation in the Far East in 1793." *The Hispanic American Historical Review* 15.4 (Nov.): 448–463.

———. 1959. "The Overland Route to India in the Seventeenth and Eighteenth Centuries." *Journal of Indian History* 29.2: 105–133.

———. 1976. *Rival Empires of Trade in the Orient, 1600–1800*. Oxford: Oxford University Press.

———. 1988. "The History of East India Companies: General Problems." *The Indian Ocean Review* 1.1 (March): 13–16.

Gaastra, Femme. 2003. *The Dutch East India Company: Expansion and Decline*. Zutphen: The Walburg Pers.

Gambetta, Diego. 1988a. "Can We Trust Trust?" In *Trust: Making and Breaking of Cooperative Relations*, by Diego Gambetta. Oxford: Basil Blackwell.

———. 1988b. *Trust: Making and Breaking Cooperative Relations*. Oxford: Basil and Blackwell.

Games, Alison. 2008. *The Web of Empire: English Cosmopolitans in an Age of Expansion, 1560–1660*. Oxford and New York: Oxford University Press.

Garsoïan, Nina G. 1997. "The Arab Invasions and the Rise of the Bagratuni." In *The Armenian People from Ancient to Modern Times*, vol. 1, ed. Richard G. Hovannisian. New York: St. Martin's.

Gasparian, Mikayel. 1950. "Brmastani Hay Gaghutě" [The Armenian colony of Burma]. *Nor Azdarar* 1: 15–19.

George, Joan. 2002. *Merchants in Exile: The Armenians of Manchester, England, 1835–1935*. London: Gomidas Institute Press.

Ghougassian, Vazken. 1998. *The Emergence of the Armenian Diocese of New Julfa in the Seventeenth Century*. Atlanta: Scholars Press.

———. 1999. "The Quest for Enlightenment and Liberation: The Case of the Armenian Community of India in the Late Eighteenth Century." In *Enlightenment and Diaspora*:

*The Armenian and Jewish Cases*, ed. Richard G. Hovannisian and David N. Myers. Atlanta: Scholars Press.

Gianighian, Giorgio. 1984. "L'ospitio della nazione armena a San Zulian, Venezia." In *Atti del Terzo Simposio Internazionale di Arte Armena, 1981*. Venice: San Lazzaro.

———. 1990. "La Chiesa di Santa Croce e l'ospizio degli Armeni a Venezia." In *Gli Armeni in Italia: Hayere Italyo mej*, ed. Boghos Levon Zekiyan. Rome: De Luca Edizione d'Arte.

Giddens, Anthony. 1984. *A Contemporary Critique of Historical Materialism*. Berkeley and Los Angeles: University of California Press.

Glamman, Kristof. 1958. *Dutch-Asiatic Trade, 1620–1740*. Copenhagen: Nijhoff.

Goffman, Daniel. 1990. *Izmir and the Levantine World, 1550–1650*. Seattle: University of Washington Press.

Goitein, Solomon D. 1967–1993. *A Mediterranean Society: The Jewish Communities of the Arab World as Portrayed in the Documents of the Cairo Geniza*. 5 vols. Berkeley: University of California Press.

Goldberg, Jessica. 2005. "'The Geographies of Trade and Traders in the Eastern Mediterranean, 1000–1150: A Geniza Study." PhD diss., Columbia University.

———. 2007. "Back-Biting and Self-Promotion: The Work of Merchants of the Cairo Geniza." In *History in the Comic Mode: Medieval Communities and the Matter of Person*, ed. Rachel Fulton and Bruce W. Holsinger. New York: Columbia University Press.

Gommans, J. J. L. 1999. *The Rise of the Indo-Afghan Empire, c. 1710–1780*. Oxford: Oxford University Press.

Goody, Jack. 1996. *The East in the West*. Cambridge: Cambridge University Press.

Gopal, Surendra. 1971. "Armenian Traders in India in the Seventeenth Century." In *Central Asia: The Movement of Peoples and Ideas from Times Prehistoric to Modern*, ed. A. Guha. New York: Barnes and Noble.

———. 1986. "A Brief Note on Business Organisation of Indian Merchants in Russia in the 17th Century." *Journal of the Economic and Social History of the Orient* 29.2 (June): 207–208.

Granovetter, Mark S. 1973. "'The Strength of Weak Ties." *American Journal of Sociology* 78.6 (May): 1360–1380.

———. 1985. "Economic Action and Social Structure: The Problem of Embeddedness." *American Journal of Sociology* 91.3 (Nov.): 481–510.

Gregorian, Mesrop. 1966. *Nor Niwt'er ew ditoghut'iwnner hratarakich Vanantets'woh masin* [New materials and observations on the Vanantetsi family of publishers]. Vienna: Mkhitarist Press.

Gregorian, Vartan. 1974. "Minorities of Isfahan: The Armenian Community of Isfahan 1587–1722."*Iranian Studies* 7, 3/4 (Summer–Autumn): 652–80.

Gregory, S. M. 1923. "Haykakan hin dseragirner, Londoni Britanakan Tangaranum" [Old Armenian manuscripts in the British Museum of London]. *Bazmavep* 21: 5–7.

———. 1925. "Armenians in Southern India." *The Asiatic Review* 21: 113–123.

Greif, Avner. 1989. "Reputation and Coalition in Medieval Trade: Evidence on the Maghribi Traders." *Journal of Economic History* 49.4: 857–882.

———. 1991. "'The Organization of Long-Distance Trade: Reputation and Coalitions in the

Geniza Documents and Genoa during the Eleventh and Twelfth Centuries." *Journal of Economic History* 51.2 (June): 459–462.

———. 1992. "Contract Enforceability and Economic Institutions in Early Trade: The Maghribi Traders' Coalition." *American Economic Review* 133.3: 525–548.

———. 2006. *Institutions and the Path to the Modern Economy: Lessons from Medieval Trade.* Cambridge: Cambridge University Press.

———. 2008. "Contract Enforcement and Institutions among the Maghribi Traders: Refuting Edwards and Ogilvie." CESifo Working Paper 2350. http://ssrn. com/abstract1/41159681 (accessed 3 September 2008).

Gugerotti, C. 1990. "Una famiglia emblematica: Gli Sceriman tra Isfahan e Venezia." In *Gli Armeni in Italia,* ed. Boghos Levon Zekiyan. Rome: De Luca.

Guinnane, Timothy. 2005. "Trust: A Concept Too Many." *Jahrbuch für Wirtschaftsgeschichte* 1: 77–92.

Gulbenkian, Roberto. 1970. "Philippe de Zagly, marchand arménien de Julfa, et l'établissement du commerce persan en Courland en 1696." *Revue des Études Arméniennes* 7: 361–426.

———. 1995. *Estudos Históricos: Relaçoes entre Portugal, Armenia e Medio Oriente.* 3 vols. Lisbon: Acad. Portuguesa da História.

Gushakian, Torgom. 1941. *Hndkahayk': Tpavorut'iwnner ev teghekut'iwnner* [Indo-Armenians: Impressions and information]. Jerusalem: Saint James.

Habermas, Jurgen. 1989. *The Structural Transformation of the Public Sphere: An Inquiry into a Category of Bourgeois Society.* Cambridge, MA: MIT Press.

Habib, Irfan. 1964. "Usury in Medieval India." *Comparative Studies in Society and History* 6.4 (July): 393–419.

———. 1982. *An Atlas of the Mughal Empire: Political and Economic Maps with Detailed Notes.* Oxford: Oxford University Press.

———. 1986. "The Postal Communications in Mughal India." In *Proceedings of the Indian Historical Congress, 46th Session.* Delhi.

———. 1990. "Merchant Communities in Precolonial India." In *The Rise of Merchant Empires: Long-Distance Trade in the Early Modern World, 1350–1750,* ed. James Tracy. Cambridge: Cambridge University Press.

Hall, R. 1996. *Empires of the Monsoon: A History of the Indian Ocean and Its Invaders.* London: Harper Collins Publishers.

Halpern, David. 2005. *Social Capital.* Cambridge, UK, and Malden, MA: Polity.

Hardin, Russell. 2002. *Trust and Trustworthiness.* New York: Russell Sage Foundation.

Harris, Philip Rowland. 1998. *A History of the British Museum Library, 1753–1973.* London: British Library.

Harris, Ron. 2009. "The Institutional Dynamics of Early Modern Eurasian trade: The Commenda and the Corporation." *Journal of Economic Behavior & Organization* 71: 606–622.

Harvey, G. E. 1925. *History of Burma: From the Earliest Times to 10 March 1824, the Beginning of the English Conquest.* London: Longmans.

Headrick, Daniel R. 1980. *The Tools of Empire: Technology and European Imperialism in the Nineteenth Century.* Oxford: Oxford University Press.

Heck, Gene W. 2006. *Charlemagne, Muhammad, and the Arab Roots of Capitalism.* Berlin and New York: Walter de Gruyter.

Hermet, Alaremo, and P. Cogni Ratti di Desio. 1993. *La Venezia degli Armeni: Sedici secoli tra storia e leggenda.* Milan: Mursia.

Herzig, Edmund. 1991a. "The Armenian Merchants from New Julfa: A Study in Premodern Trade." Diss., St. Antony's College, Oxford University.

———. 1991b. "The Deportation of the Armenians in 1604–05 and Europe's Myth of Shah 'Abbas I." In *Persian and Islamic Studies in Honor of P. W. Avery,* ed. Charles Melville. Cambridge: Cambridge University Center for Middle Eastern Studies.

———. 1993. "The Family Firm in the Commercial Organization of the Julfa Armenians." In *Études safavides,* ed. L. Calmard. Paris and Tehran: Institut Français de Recherche en Iran.

———. 1996. "The Rise of the Julfa Merchants in the Late Sixteenth Century." *Pembroke Papers* 4: 305–322.

———. 2004a. Review of *The Shah's Silk For Europe's Silver,* by Ina Baghdiantz McCabe. *Iranian Studies* 37.3: 170–175.

———. 2004b. "Venice and the Julfa Merchants." In *Gli Armeni e Venezia: Dagli Sceriman a Mechitar; Il momento culminante di una consuetudine millenaria,* ed. Boghos Levon Zekiyan and Aldo Ferrari. Venice: Ist. Veneto di Scienze, Lettere ed Arti.

———. 2006. "Borrowed Terminology and Techniques of the New Julfa Armenian Merchants: A Study in Cultural Transmission." Paper presented at the Sixth Biennial Conference on Iranian Studies, London (3–5 August).

———. 2007. "Commercial Law of the New Julfa Armenians." In *Les Arméniens dans le commerce asiatique au début de l'ère moderne,* ed. Sushil Chaudhury and Kéram Kévonian, 63–81. Paris: Éditions de la Maison des Sciences de l'Homme.

Hickson, Charles R., and John D. Turner. 2006. "Partnership." In *History of World Trade since 1450,* ed. John J. McCusker. Detroit: Macmillan Reference USA.

Ho, Engseng. 2002. "Names beyond Nations: The Making of Cosmopolitans." *Études Rurales* 164.4 (July–December): 215–232.

———. 2006. *The Graves of Tarim: Genealogy and Mobility across the Indian Ocean.* Berkeley: University of California Press.

Hodgson, Marshal H. 1974. *The Venture of Islam.* 3 vols. Chicago: University of Chicago Press.

Hordananian, Hordanan. 1937. *Netrlandakan Arewelean Hndkastanay hay gaghuti patmut'iwně skzbēn minch mer Ōrerē* [The history of the Armenian diaspora in the Dutch East Indies, from the beginning to our times]. Jerusalem: Tparan Srbots Hakovbeants.

Hosten, Rev. H., SJ. 1916. "Mirza Zul Qarnain, A Christan Grandee of Three Great Moghuls, with Notes on Akbar's Christian Wife and the Indian Bourbons." In *Memoirs of the Asiatic Society of Bengal.* Calcutta: Asiatic Society of Bengal.

Hourani, George F. 1995. *Arab Seafaring in the Indian Ocean in Ancient and Early Medieval Times.* Revised and expanded by John Carswell. Princeton, NJ: Princeton University Press.

Hovhannisyan, Ashot. 1957. *Druagner Hay Azatagrakan Mtk'i Patmut'ean* [Episodes of the history of Armenian liberation thought]. Vol. 1. Yerevan.

Hussain, Ruquia. 2005. "Communication and Commerce: The Armenian World Trade in the Seventeenth Century." In *Webs of History: Information, Communication, and Technology from Early to Post-Colonial India,* ed. Amiya Kumar et al. New Delhi: Manohar.

Hyam, Ronald, and Peter Henshaw. 2003. *The Lion and the Springbok: Britain and South Africa since the Boer War.* Cambridge: Cambridge University Press.

Inalcik, Halil. 1969. "Harir" [Silk]. *Encyclopedia of Islam,* 2nd ed., 3: 211–213.

———. 1994. "Bursa and the Silk Trade." In *An Economic and Social History of the Ottoman Empire,* vol. 1, *1300–1600,* by Inalcik Halil. Cambridge: Cambridge University Press.

Ishkhanyan, Raffael. 1977. *Hay Girk'i Patmut'yun* [History of the Armenian book]. Yerevan: Hayastan Hratarakch'ut'yun.

———. 1981. *Hay Girk'ě, 1512–1920.* [The Armenian book, 1512–1920]. Yerevan: SSH GA hratarakch'ut'yun.

Israel, Jonathan. 1998. *The Dutch Republic: Its Rise, Greatness, and Fall, 1477–1806.* Oxford: Oxford University Press.

———. 2002. *Diasporas within a Diaspora: Jews, Crypto-Jews, and the World of Maritime Empires, 1540–1740.* Leiden: Brill Series in Jewish Studies.

———. 2005. "Diasporas Jewish and Non-Jewish and the World Maritime Empires." In *Diaspora Entrepreneurial Networks: Four Centuries of History,* ed. Ina Baghdiantz McCabe, Gelina Harlaftis, and Ioanna Pepelasis Minoglou. Oxford: Berg.

Jacobs, E. M. 1991. *In Pursuit of Pepper and Tea: The Story of the Dutch East India Company.* Amsterdam: Netherlands Maritime Museum.

Kafadar, Cemal. 1996. "A Death in Venice (1575): Anatolian Muslim Merchants Trading in the Serenissima." Chapter 5 in *Merchant Networks in the Early Modern World,* ed. Sanjay Subrahmanyam. Aldershot, UK: Variorum.

Kagan, Richard L., and Philip Morgan, eds. 2007. *Atlantic Diasporas: Jews and Crypto-Jews in the Age of Mercantilism, 1500–1800.* Baltimore: Johns Hopkins University Press.

Kaplan, Josef. 2002. *An Alternative Path to Modernity: The Sephardi Diaspora in Western Europe.* Leiden, Boston, and Cologne: Brill Series in Jewish Studies.

Karapetian, K. 1974. *Isfahan, New Julfa: Le case degli armeni/The Houses of Armenians; Una raccolta di rilevamenti architettonici/A Collection of Architectural Surveys.* Rome: Ismeo.

Karapetyan, Meroujan. 2009. "Zhĕ Dari Aṙajin K'aṙordi Mi Erkkhosut'iwn" [A dialogue from the first quarter of the eighteenth century]. *Handēs amsōreay: Baroyakan, usumnakan, aruestgitakan:* 375–476.

———. 2010. "Hayerě Venetikum 1750 Tuin (a)" [The Armenians in Venice, in 1750 (a)]. *Handēs amsōreay: Baroyakan, usumnakan, aruestgitakan:* 211–226.

Karapetyan, Meroujan, and E. Tajiryan. 1998. "Ejer XVII dari verji nor Jughayi patmut'yunits '" [Pages from the late seventeenth-century history of New Julfa]. *Banber Yerevani Hamalsarani, hasarakakan gitut'yunner* 2.95: 80–96.

Kévonian, Kéram. 1975. "Marchands arméniens au XVIIe siècle, à propos d'un livre arménien publié à Amsterdam en 1699." *Cahiers du Monde Russe et Sovietique* 16: 199–244.

———. 1998. "Un itinéraire arménien de la Mer de Chine." In *Histoire de Barus: Sumatra Le site de Lobu Tua; Études et Documents,* ed. Claude Guilllot. Cahiers d'Archipel 30. Paris.

———. 2007a. "Numération, calcul, comptabilite et commerce." In *Les Arméniens dans le commerce asiatique au début de l'ère moderne,* ed. Sushil Chaudhury and Kéram Kévonian. Paris: Éditions de la Maison des Sciences de l'Homme.

———. 2007b. "La société reconstituée." In *Les Arméniens dans le commerce asiatique au début de l'ère moderne,* ed. Sushil Chaudhury and Kéram Kévonian. Paris: Éditions de la Maison des Sciences de l'Homme.

Kevorkian, Raymond H. 1986. *Catalogue des 'incunables' arméniens (1511–1965) ou chronique de l'imprimerie arménienne.* Geneva: Patrick Cramer.

Keyvani, Mehdi. 1982. *Artisans and Guild Life in the Later Safavid Period: Contributions to the Social-Economic History of Persia.* Berlin: Klaus Schwarz Verlag.

Khachikian, Levon. 1966. "The Ledger of the Merchant Hovhannes Joughayetsi." *Journal of the Asiatic Society* 8.3: 153–186.

Khachikian, Levon, and Hakob Papazian. 1984. *Hovhannes Tēr Davt'yan Jughayets'u Hashvetumarĕ* [The accounting ledger of Hovhannes Tēr Davt'yan of Julfa]. Yerevan: Haykakan SSH GA Hratarakch'ut'yun.

Khachikian, Shushanik. 1980. "Hay-rusakan arevtrakan paymanagirĕ ev Nor Jughayi ink'navar marminnerĕ" [The Armenian–Russian commercial agreement and the autonomous organizations of New Julfa]. *Haykazean Hayagitakan Handēs:* 259–288.

———. 1988. *Nor Jughayi hay vacharakanut'iwnĕ ev nra arrevtratntesakan kaperĕ Rusastani het XVII–XVIII darerum* [The Armenian commerce of New Julfa and its commercial and economic ties with Russia in the seventeenth and eighteenth centuries]. Yerevan: Haykakan SSH GA Hratarakch'ut'yun.

———. 2006. *Lazarean Arevtrakan ĕnkerut'ean hashuemateanĕ (1741–1759 t't')* [The accounting ledger of the Lazarian Commercial Company, 1741–1759]. Yerevan: Matenadaran—Mashtots Institute of Ancient Manuscripts.

Kiwrtian, H. 1944–1945. "Niwt'er Hay Vacharakanut'ean Patmut'ean Hamar: Hum Metak'si Vacharakanut'iwnĕ ew Hayerĕ" [Materials for Armenian mercantile history: The trade of raw silk and the Armenians]. *Hayrenik Amsagir,* 1944, nos. 1–6; and 1945, nos. 1–2.

———. 1945. "Niwt'er Hay Vacharakanut'ean Patmut'ean Hamar: Goharneru Patmut'iwnĕ Hayots' Mot" [Materials for Armenian merchantile history: The history of gems among the Armenians]. *Hayrenik Amsagir* 3: 67–81.

———. 1975–1976. "Jughayetsi Khoja Safar u Khoja Nazar ew irents gerdastanĕ" [Khwaja Safar and Khwaja Nazar of Julfa and their extended families]. *Bazmavep* 3–4 (1975): 379–396; 1–2 (1976): 52–73; 3–4 (1976): 375–395.

Koeman, C. 1967. "A World-Map in Armenian Printed at Amsterdam in 1695." *Imago Mundi* 21: 113–114.

Kosian, Hakob. 1899. "Hayk' i zmyurna ew i shrjakays' " [Armenians in Smyrna and its vicinity]. In *Zmyurna ev hayk* [Smyrna and Armenians]. 2 vols. Vienna: Mkhitarist Press.

Kouymjian, Dickran. 1994. "From Disintegration to Reintegration: Armenians at the Start of the Modern Era." *Revue du Monde Arménien* 1: 9–18.

Kuiters, Willem G. J. 2002. *The British in Bengal, 1756–1773: A Society in Transition Seen through the Biography of a Rebel, William Bolts (1739–1808).* Paris: Indes savantes.

Kulbenkian, Roberto. 1986. *Hay Portugalakan Haraberut'yunner* [Armenian-Portuguese relations]. Yerevan: HSSH GA Hratarakch'ut'yun.

Kunt, Metin Ibrahim. 1974. "Ethnic-Regional (Cins) Solidarity in the Seventeenth-Century Ottoman Establishment." *International Journal of Middle East Studies* 5.3 (June): 233–239.

Lambton, A. K. S. 1963. "The Office of Kalantar under the Safavids and Afshars." In *Mélanges d'orientalisme offerts à Henri Massé.* Tehran: Impr. de l'université.

———. 1992. "Cities i.-iii: Administration and Social Organization." *Encyclopedia Iranica* 5: 611–613.

Landau, Amy. 2007. "Farangī-Sazī at Isfahan: The Court Painter Muḥammad Zamān, the Armenians of New Julfa, and Shāh Sulaymān (1666–1694)." PhD diss., Oxford University.

———. 2010. "From the Workshops of Julfa to the Court of Tsar Aleksei Mikhailovich: Armenian Networks and the Mobility of Visual Culture." Paper presented at the 124th annual meeting of the American Historical Association, San Diego, January 8, 2010.

Lane, Frederic. 1940. "The Mediterranean Spice Trade: Further Evidence of Its Revival in the Sixteenth Century." *American Historical Review* 45.3: 581–590.

———. 1944. "Family Partnerships and Joint Ventures in the Venetian Republic." *The Journal of Economic History* 4.2 (Nov.): 178–196.

———. 1944/1967. *Andrea Barbarigo, Merchant of Venice, 1418–1449.* New York: Octagon Books.

———. 1973. *Venice: A Maritime Republic.* Baltimore: John Hopkins University Press.

Lawson, Philip. 1993. *The East India Company: A History.* London and New York: Longman.

Leclant, Jean. 1951/1979. "Coffee and Cafés in Paris, 1644–1693." In *Food and Drink in History,* ed. R. Forster and O. Ranum. Baltimore: Johns Hopkins University Press.

Leo [Arakel Babakhanian]. 1934. *Khojayakan kapitalĕ ev nra kʻaghakʻakan-hasarakakan derĕ hayeri mej* [Khoja capital and its socio-political role among the Armenians]. Yerevan: Petakan Hratarakchʻutʻyun.

Levi, Scott, C. 1999. "The Indian Merchant Diaspora in Early Modern Central Asia and Iran." *Iranian Studies* 32.4: 483–512.

———. 2002. *The Indian Diaspora in Central Asia.* Leiden and Boston: Brill.

———, ed. 2007. *India and Central Asia: Commerce and Culture, 1500–1800.* Debates in Indian History and Society. New Delhi: Oxford University Press.

———. 2008. "Multanis and Shikarpuris: Indian Diasporas in Historical Perspective." *Global Indian Diasporas: Exploring Trajectories of Migration and Theory,* ed. Gijsbert Oonk. Amsterdam: Amsterdam University Press.

Levonian, Garegin. 1946. *Hay girkʻĕ ev tpagrutʻyan arvestĕ: patmakan tesutʻyun skzbitsʻ minchev XX dare* [The Armenian book and art of printing: A historical survey from the beginning until the twentieth century]. Yerevan: HSSR GA Hratarakchʻutʻyun.

Lieber, A. E. 1968. "Eastern Business Practices and Medieval European Commerce." *Economic History Review* 21: 230–243.

Lieberman, Victor. 1984. *Burmese Administrative Cycles: Anarchy and Conquest, c. 1580–1760.* Princeton, NJ: Princeton University Press.

———. 2003. *Strange Parallels: Southeast Asia in Global Context, c. 800–1830.* Vol. 1, *Integration on the Mainland.* Cambridge: Cambridge University Press.

———. 2009. *Strange Parallels: Southeast Asia in Global Context, c. 800–1830.* Vol. 2, *Mainland Mirrors: Europe, Japan, China, South Asia, and the Islands.* Cambridge: Cambridge University Press.

Lockhart, Laurence. 1938. *Nadir Shah: A Critical Study Based Mainly upon Contemporary Sources.* London: Luzac.

———. 1958. *The Fall of the Safavi Dynasty and the Afghan Occupation of Persia.* Cambridge: Cambridge University Press.

Lombard, Denys, and Jean Aubin, eds. 1988. *Asian Merchants and Businessmen in the Indian*

*Ocean and the China Sea from the Thirteenth to the Twentieth Centuries.* New Delhi and New York: Oxford University Press.

Lopez, Robert S. 1971. *The Commercial Revolution of the Middle Ages, 950–1350.* Englewood Cliffs, NJ: Prentice-Hall.

Lopez, Robert S., and Irving W. Raymond. 2001. *Medieval Trade in the Mediterranean World: Illustrative Documents.* New York: Columbia University Press.

Love, Henry Davison. 1913. *Vestiges of Old Madras, 1640–1800: Traced from the East India Company's Records . . .* 4 vols. London: J. Murray.

Macler, Frédéric. 1904. "Notes de Chahan de Cirbied sur les Arméniens d'Amsterdam et de Livourne." *Anahit* (Paris) 1: 12–13, 43–44.

———. 1920–1922. "Notices de manuscrits arméniens ou relatifs aux Arméniens vus dans quelques bibliothèques de la Péninsule Ibérique et du sud-est de la France." *Revue des Études Arméniennes* 1 (1920–1921): 63–80, 85–116, 237–272, 411–417; 2 (1922): 7–64, 235–291.

———. 1932. *Quatre conférences sur l'Arménie, faites en Hollande.* Paris: Adrien-Maisonneuve.

Maeda, Hirotake. 2002. "Exploitation of the Frontier: Shah 'Abbas I's Policy towards the Caucasus." Paper presented at the conference "Iran and the World in the Safavid Age." London.

Malenchini, P. N.d. *Brevi cenni storici sull' antichissima familglia Mirman de Ghirach.* Livorno.

Mann, Michael. 1984. "The Autonomous Power of the State." *Archives Européennes de Sociologie* 25: 185–213.

Manning, Catherine. 1996. *Fortunes à Faire: The French in Asian Trade, 1719–1748.* Aldershot, UK: Variorum.

Marcinkowski, M. Ismail. 2002. "The Iran-Siamese Connection: An Iranian Community in the Thai Kingdom of Ayutthaya." *Iranian Studies* 35.1–3 (Winter/Summer): 23–47.

Margariti, Roxani. 2007. *Aden and the Indian Ocean Trade: 150 Years in the Life of a Medieval Arabian Port.* Chapel Hill: University of North Carolina Press.

Markovits, Claude. 2000. *The Global World of Indian Merchants, 1750–1947: Traders of Sind from Bukhara to Panama.* New York: Cambridge University Press.

———. 2007. "Indian Merchants in Central Asia: The Debate." In *India and Central Asia: Commerce and Culture, 1500–1800,* ed. Scott Levi. New Delhi: Oxford University Press.

Markovits, Claude, Jacques Pouchepadass, and Sanjay Subrahmanyam, eds. 2003. *Society and Circulation: Mobile Peoples and Itinerant Cultures in South Asia, 1750–1950.* Delhi: Permanent Black.

Marks, Robert. 2007. *The Origins of the Modern World: A Global and Ecological Narrative from the Fifteenth to the Twenty-first Century.* 2nd ed. Lanham, MD: Rowman & Littlefield.

Marshall, Peter J. 2005. *The Making and Unmaking of Empire: Britain, India, and America, c. 1750–1783.* Oxford: Oxford University Press.

Martín, Manuel Ravina. 2005. Untitled catalogue entry. In *Pasaron por Cádiz, personas y cosas.* Cadiz: Archivo Histórico Provincial de Cádiz, Catálogo de la Exposición.

Masters, Bruce. 1988. *The Origins of Western Economic Dominance in the Middle East: Mercantilism and the Islamic Economy of Aleppo, 1600–1750.* New York: New York University Press.

Matthee, Rudolph. 1999. *The Politics of Trade in Safavid Iran: Silk for Silver, 1600–1730.* Cambridge: Cambridge University Press.

———. 2000. "Merchants in Safavid Iran: Participants and Perceptions." *Journal of Early Modern History* 4: 233–268.

———. 2005. *The Pursuit of Pleasure: Drugs and Stimulants in Iranian History, 1500–1900.* Princeton, NJ: Princeton Univrsity Press.

Mauro, Frédéric. 1990. "Merchant Communities, 1350–1750." In *The Rise of Merchant Empires: Long-Distance Trade in the Early Modern World, 1350–1750,* ed. James D. Tracy. Cambridge: Cambridge University Press.

McCusker, John J. 2005. "'The Demise of Distance: 'The Business Press and the Origins of the Information Revolution in the Early Modern Atlantic World." *American Historical Review* 60.2: 295–321.

McNeill, William H. 1986. "Mythistory, or Truth, Myth, History, and Historians." *American Historical Review* 91.1: 1–10.

Melis, Frederigo. 1983. "Intensità e regolarità nella diffusione dell'informazione economica generale nel Mediterraneo e in Occidente alla fine del Medioevo." *Quaderni di Storia Postale* 2 (June).

Mentz, Søren. 2004. "'The Commercial Culture of the Armenian Merchant: Diaspora and Social Behaviour." *Itinerario* 28.1: 16–28.

———. 2005. *The English Gentleman Merchant at Work: Madras and the City of London, 1660–1740.* Nordea, Denmark: Museum Tusculanum Press.

Metcalf, Alida C. 2005. *Go-Betweens and the Colonization of Brazil, 1500–1600.* Austin: University of Texas Press.

Minasian, Levon G. 1983. *Diwan N. Jughayi S. Amenap'rkich 'vank'i, 1600–1900: Ughets'oyts' grguyk* [Archive of the All Savior's Monastery of New Julfa, 1600–1900: Guidebook]. New Julfa: All Savior's Press.

Mines, Mattison. 2001. "Courts of Law and Styles of Self in Eighteenth-Century Madras: From Hybrid to Colonial Self." *Modern Asian Studies* 35.1: 33–74.

Montero y Vidal, José. 1894. *Historia general de Filipinas desde el descubrimiento de dichas islas hasta nuestros días.* Vol. 2. Madrid: M. Tello.

Moosvi, Shireen. 2007. "Armenians in Asian Trade, 16th and 17th centuries." In *Les Arméniens dans le commerce asiatique au début de l'ère moderne,* ed. Kéram Kévonian and Sushil Chaudhury. Paris: Éditions de la Maison des Sciences de l'Homme.

Moreland, William Harrison. 1923/1990. *From Akbar to Aurangzeb: A Study in Indian Economic History.* Delhi: Low Price Publications.

Nadel-Golobich, Eleanora. 1979. "Armenians and Jews in Medieval Lvov: 'Their Role in Oriental Trade, 1400–1600." *Cahiers du Monde Russe et Soviétique* 20: 345–88.

Nersessian, Vrej. 1980. *Catalogue of Early Armenian Books.* London: British Library.

Newman, Andrew J. 2006. *Safavid Iran: Rebirth of a Persian Empire.* I. B. Tauris.

North, Douglas C. 1990. *Institutions, Institutional Change, and Economic Performance.* Cambridge: Cambridge University Press.

———. 1991. "Institutions, Transaction Costs, and the Rise of Merchant Empires." In *The Political Economy of Merchant Empires: State Power and World Trade,* ed. James Tracy. Cambridge: Cambridge University Press.

Nunn, Charles F. 1979. *Foreign Immigrants to Early Bourbon Mexico, 1700–1760*. Cambridge: Cambridge University Press.

Ogilvie, Sheilagh. 2005. "The Use and Abuse of Trust: Social Capital and Its Development by Early Modern Guilds." *Jahrbuch für Wirtschaftsgeschichte* 1: 15–52.

Orengo, Alessandro. 1993. "I principi di grammatica italiana stampati a Marsiglia nel 1675." *Studi e Saggi Linguistici* 33: 25–72.

———. 2000. "Una lettera del XVII secolo, scritta nell' 'Armeno dei Mercanti.'" *Ashtanak: Hayagitakan barberagirk'* [Ashtanak: Armenological periodical] 3: 24–35.

Ortiz, Antonio Domíngues. 1953. "Armenios en Sevilla." *Archivo Hispalense: Revista Histórica, Literaria y Artística* 19: 189–196.

Oshagan, Vahé. 1997. "Modern Armenian Literature and Intellectual History." In *The Armenian People from Ancient to Modern Times: Foreign Dominion to Statehood, the Fifteenth Century to the Twentieth Century*, vol. 2. New York: Palgrave Macmillan.

Oskanyan, V. K. 1971. "Hayerě Moskvayum, XV–XVII darerum" [Armenians in Moscow: Fifteenth–seventeenth centuries]. *Patma-Banasirakan Handes* 1: 25–39.

Panossian, Razmik. 2006. *The Armenians: From Kings and Priests to Merchants and Commissars*. New York: Columbia University Press.

Paolini, Luca. 1992. "La communità armena." In *Livorno crocevia di culture ed etnie diverse: Razzismi ed incontri possibili*, ed. R. Mastinu. Livorno: Casa Editrice San Benedetto.

P'ap'azyan, V. H. 1990. *Hayastani Aṛevtrakan Ughinerē mijazgayin aṛevtri olortum XVI–XVII darerum* [Trade routes of Armenia in the sphere of international trade from the sixteenth–seventeenth centuries]. Yerevan.

Parker, Geoffrey. 1991. "Europe and the Wider World, 1550–1750: The Military Balance." In *The Political Economy of Merchant Empires: State Power and World Trade, 1350–1750*, ed. James Tracy. Cambridge: Cambridge University Press.

"Patmut'iwn Hay Vacharakanut'ean'" [History of Armenian commerce]. 1858. *Yevropa* 2: 44–46; 7: 52–54.

Patterson, Orlando. 1982. *Slavery and Social Death: A Comparative Study*. Cambridge, MA: Harvard University Press.

Pearson, Michael. 2003. *The Indian Ocean*. Seas in History. London and New York: Routledge.

Perry, John R. 1975. "Forced Migrations in Iran during the Seventeenth and Eighteenth Century." *Iranian Studies* 8.4: 199–215.

———. 1979. *Karim Khan Zand: A History of Iran, 1747–1779*. Chicago: University of Chicago Press.

Polatian, Derenik. 1959a. "Brmahayk" [Burmese Armenians]. *Sion: Amsagir Kronakan, Grakan, Banasirakan* 7–8: 169–172; 9–10: 228–231.

———. 1959b. "Chinastani Hay vacharakannerě ew Hovhannes Ghazarean" [The Armenian merchants of China and Hovhannes Ghazarian]. *Sion: Amsagir Kronakan, Grakan, Banasirakan* 11–12: 276–277.

———. 1963. *Agrayi Hayerě* [The Armenians of Agra]. Beirut: Tparan Tonikean.

*Polonyalı Simeon'un seyahatnamesi, 1608–1619*. 1964. Trans. and prep. Hrand D. Andreasian. Istanbul: Baha Matbaası.

Pomeranz, Kenneth. 2001. *The Great Divergence: China, Europe, and the Making of the Modern World Economy*. Princeton, NJ: Princeton University Press.

Pomeranz, Kenneth, and Steve Topik. 2006. *The World That Trade Created: Society, Culture, and the World Economy, 1400 to the Present*. New York and London: M. E. Sharpe.

Portes, Alejandro. 1998. "Social Capital: Its Origins and Application in Modern Sociology." *Annual Review of Sociology*: 1–24.

———. 2000. "The Two Meanings of Social Capital." *Sociological Forum* 15.1 (March): 1–12.

Prakash, Om. 1985. *The Dutch East India Company and the Economy of Bengal, 1630–1720*. Princeton, NJ: Princeton University Press.

———. 1998. *European Commercial Enterprise in Pre-Colonial India*. Cambridge: Cambridge University Press.

Putnam, Robert. 1995. "Tuning In, Tuning Out: The Strange Disappearance of Social Capital in America." *PS: Political Science and Politics* 28.4 (Dec.): 664–683.

———. 2000. *Bowling Alone: The Collapse and Revival of American Community*. New York: Simon and Schuster.

Quiason, Serafin D. 1966. *English Country Trade with the Philippines, 1644–1765*. Quezon City: University of the Philippines Press.

Raj, Kapil. 2009. "Mapping Knowledge Go-Betweens in Calcutta, 1770–1820." In *The Brokered World: Go-Betweens and Global Intelligence, 1770-1820*, ed. Simon Schaffer, Linda Roberts, Kapil Raj, and James Delbourgo. Sagamore Beach, MA: Science History Publications.

Ravenstein, E. 1885. "The Laws of Migration." *Journal of the Royal Statistical Society* 46: 167–235.

———. 1889. "The Laws of Migration: Second Paper." *Journal of the Royal Statistical Society* 52: 241–305.

Raveux, Olivier. 2008. "'À la façon du Levant et de Perse': Marseille et la naissance de l'indiennage européen (1648–1689)." *Rives Nord-Méditerranéennes* 29: 37–51.

———. 2009. "The Birth of a New European Industry: L'Indiennage in Seventeenth-Century Marseilles." *The Spinning World: A Global History of Cotton Textiles, 1200–1850*, ed. Giorgio Riello and Prasannan Parthasarathi. Oxford: Oxford University Press.

———. 2010. "Armenian Networks in the Trade and Production of Calicoes in the Mediterranean during the Last Third of the 17th Century." Paper presented at the 124th annual meeting of the American Historical Association, San Diego, January 8, 2010.

———. 2011. "Orientaux en Occident: Les marchands choffelins de Marseille et les langues durant le dernier tiers du XVIIᵉ siècle." In *Langues et langages du commerce en Méditerranée (XVIe–XIXe siècle)*.

Ray, Rajat Kanta. 1995. "Asian Capital in the Age of European Domination: The Rise of the Bazaar, 1800–1914." *Modern Asian Studies* 29.3 (July): 449–554.

Richards, John F. 1993. *The Mughal Empire*. Cambridge: Cambridge University Press.

———. 1997. "Early Modern India and World History." *Journal of World History* 8.2: 197–209.

Richardson, H. E. 1981. "Armenians in India and Tibet." *Journal of the Tibet Society* 1: 63–67.

Richie, Robert C. 1986. *Captain Kidd and the War against the Pirates*. Cambridge, MA: Harvard University Press.

Riello, Giorgio. 2010. "Asian Knowledge and the Development of Calico Printing in Europe in the Seventeenth and Eighteenth Centuries." *Journal of Global History* 5.1: 1–28.

Rochard, Philippe, and H. E. Chehabi. 2002. "The Identities of the Zūrkhanah." *Iranian Studies* 35.4 (Fall): 313–340.

Rodrigue, Aron. 1992. "The Sephardim in the Ottoman Empire." In *Spain and the Jews: The Sephardi Experience, 1492 and After,* ed. Elie Kedourie. London: Thames and Hudson.

Rodrigue, Aron, and Esther Bembassa. 2000. *Sephardi Jewry: A History of the Judeo-Spanish Community, 14th-20th Centuries.* Berkeley: University of California Press.

Roemer, H. R. 1986. "The Safavid Period." In *The Cambridge History of Iran,* vol. 6, *The Timurid and Safavid Periods,* ed. Peter Jackson and Laurence Lockhart. Cambridge: Cambridge University Press.

Rothman, Ella-Nathalie. 2006. "Between Venice and Istanbul: Trans-Imperial Subjects and Cultural Mediation in the Early Modern Mediterranean." PhD diss., University of Michigan.

Safran, William. 1991. "Diasporas in Modern Societies: Myths of Homeland and Return." *Diaspora* 1.1 (Spring): 83–99.

———. 1999. "Comparing Diasporas: A Review Essay." *Diaspora: A Journal of Transnational Studies* 8.3 (Winter): 255–291.

Salvini, Manuela. 1992–1993. "Cenni storici, Identità etnica e culturale della nazione Armena di Livorno (Sec. XVI–XX)." Diss., Università di Pisa.

Sanacore, M. 1988. "Splendore e decadenza degli Sceriman a Livorno." In *Gli Armeni lungo le strade d'Italia: Atti del Convegno Internazionale (Torino, Genova, Livorno, 8–11 Marzo 1997),* ed. Claudia Bonardi. Pisa and Rome: Ist. Editoriali e Poligrafici Internazionali.

Sanjian, Avedis K. 1965. *The Armenian Communities in Syria under Ottoman Dominion.* Cambridge, MA: Harvard University Press.

Sarkissian, Margaret. 1987. "Armenians in South-East Asia." *Crossroads: An Interdisciplinary Journal of Southeast Asian Studies* 3.2–3: 1–33.

Sarukhan, Arakel. 1925. *Holandan ew Hayer* [Holland and the Armenians]. Vienna: Mkhitarist Press.

Savory, Roger. 1980. *Iran under the Safavids.* Cambridge: Cambridge University Press.

Schaffer, Simon, Linda Roberts, Kapil Raj, and James Delbourgo, eds. 2009. *The Brokered World: Go-Betweens and Global Intelligence, 1770–1820.* Sagamore Beach, MA: Science History Publications.

Schopp, Susan E. 1999. "L'épave trouvée près du récif Thitu." *Monuments et mémoires publiés par L'Académie des Inscriptions et Belles-Lettres* 77: 41–72.

Schurhammer, Georg. 1973–1982. *Francis Xavier: His Life, His Times.* Trans. M. Joseph Costelloe. 4 vols. Rome: Jesuit Historical Institute.

Schurz, William Lytle. 1920. "The Royal Philippine Company." *The Hispanic American Historical Review* 3.4 (Nov.): 491–508.

Seabright, Paul. 2004. *The Company of Strangers: A Natural History of Economic Life.* Princeton, NJ: Princeton University Press.

Seijas, Tatiana. 2007. "Don Pedro de Zarate: A Julfan Armenian in Mexico City, 1723–31." Paper presented at the UCLA conference "Armenian Communities in the Indian Ocean."

Seth, Mesrovb. 1922–1923. "Haykaban mi vardapet hisusean" [A Jesuit priest Armenologist]. *Bazmavep* (October 1922): 299–303, 326–328; (December 1922): 354–357; (January 1923): 3–5.

———. 1937/1992. *History of the Armenians in India from the Earliest Times to the Present.* New Delhi: Asian Ed. Services.

Shapin, Steven. 1991. *A Social History of Truth: Civility and Science in Seventeenth-Century England*. Chicago and London: University of Chicago Press, 1991.

Simões, João Miguel dos Santos. 1959. *Carreaux céramiques hollandais au Portugal et en Espagne*. The Hague: Nijhoff.

Slezkine, Yuri. 2004. *The Jewish Century*. Princeton, NJ: Princeton University Press.

Smith, Carl T. 2003. "An Eighteenth-Century Macao Armenian Merchant Prince." *Revista de Cultura* 6: 120–129.

Smith, Carl T., and Paul A. Van Dyke. 2003a. "Armenian Footprints in Macao." *Revista de Cultura* 8: 20–39.

———. 2003b. "Four Armenian Families." *Revista de Cultura* 8: 40–50.

Sood, Gagan. 2007. "'Correspondence Is Equal to Half a Meeting': The Composition and Comprehension of Letters in Eighteenth-Century Islamic Eurasia." *Journal of the Economic and Social History of the Orient* 50.2: 172–214.

———. 2009. "The Informational Fabric of Eighteenth-Century India and the Middle East: Couriers, Intermediaries, and Postal Communication." *Modern Asian Studies*: 1–32.

Sopranis, Hipólito Sancho de. 1954. "Los Armenios en Cádiz." *Sefarad: Revista de la Escuela de Estudios Hebraicos* 14: 295–314.

Sosis, Richard. 2005. "Does Religion Promote Trust? The Role of Signaling, Reputation, and Punishment." *Interdisciplinary Journal of Research on Religion* 1: 1–30.

Steensgaard, Niels. 1974. *The Asian Trade Revolution of the Seventeenth Century: The East India Company and the Decline of the Caravan Trade*. Chicago: University of Chicago Press.

Studnicki-Gizbert, Daviken. 2007. *A Nation upon the Ocean Sea: Portugal's Atlantic Diaspora and the Crisis of the Spanish Empire, 1492–1640*. Oxford: Oxford University Press.

Subrahmanyam, Sanjay. 1990. *The Political Economy of Commerce: Southern India, 1500–1650*. Cambridge: Cambridge University Press.

———. 1991. "Precious Metal Flows and Prices in Western and Southern Asia, 1500–1750: Some Comparative and Conjunctural Aspects." *Studies in History* n.s. 7.1: 79–105.

———. 1992a. "Iranians Abroad: Intra-Asian Elite Migration and Early Modern State Formation." *Journal of Asian Studies* 51 (May): 340–363.

———. 1992b. *The Portuguese Empire in Asia, 1500–1700*. London: Longman.

———. 1995. "Of Imarat and Tijjarat: Asian Merchants and State Power in the Western Indian Ocean, 1400–1750." *Comparative Studies in Society and History* 37.4: 750–780.

———, ed. 1996. *Merchant Networks in the Early Modern World*. An Expanding World 8. Aldershot, UK: Variorum.

———. 1997. "Connected Histories: Notes towards a Reconfiguration of Islamic Eurasia." In "The Eurasian Context of the Early Modern History of Mainland South East Asia, 1400–1800." Special issue, *Modern Asian Studies* 31.3 (Jul.): 735–762.

———. 2007. "Birth-Pangs of Portuguese Asia: Revisiting the Fateful 'Long Decade,' 1498–1509." *Journal of Global History* 2: 261–280.

Subrahmanyam, Sanjay, and C. A. Bayly. 1988. "Portfolio Capitalists and the Political Economy of Early Modern India." *The Indian Economic and Social History Review* 25.4: 401–424.

Subramanian, Lakshmi, ed. 1999. *The French East India Company and the Trade of the Indian Ocean: A Collection of Essays,* by Indrani Ray. Calcutta: Munishiram Manoharlal.

Surmeyan, Artavazd. 1935. *Patmut'iwn Halepi azgayin gerezmanatants' yev ardsanagir hayeren tapanak'arern* [History of Aleppo's Armenian cemeteries and Armenian inscribed tombstones]. Aleppo: Tparan A. Tēr Sahakean.

——. 1940–1950. *Patmut'iwn Halepi Hayots* [History of the Aleppo Armenians]. 3 vols. Paris: Araxes.

Szuppe, Maria. 1986. "Un marchand du Roi de Pologne en Perse, 1601–1602." *Moyen Orient & Ocean Indien, XVI–XIX siècles* 3: 81–110.

Tékéian, Charles-Diran. 1929. *Marseille, la Provence, et les Armeniens.* Marseilles: Inst. Historique de Provence.

Teles e Cunha, João. 2007. "Armenian Merchants in Portuguese Trade Networks in the Western Indian Ocean in the Early Modern Age." In *Les Arméniens dans le commerce asiatique au début de l'ère moderne,* ed. Sushil Chaudhury and Kéram Kévonian. Paris: Éditions de la Maison des Sciences de l'Homme.

Ter-Ghewondyan, Aram. 1976. *The Arab Emirates in Bagratid Armenia.* Trans. Nina G. Garsoïan. Lisbon: Livraria Bertrand i distr.

Ter Hovhaniants', Harut'iwn T. 1880. *Patmut'iwn Nor Jughayu vor yAspahan* [History of New Julfa which is at Isfahan]. 2 vols. Nor Jugha: Tparan Sb. Amenap'rkich' Vank'i.

——. 1980. *Patmut'iwn Nor Jughayi (Spahan)* [History of New Julfa (Isfahan)]. Trans. from Classical Armenian into Eastern Armenian by Poghos Petrossian. 2nd ed. Nor Jugha: Tparan Sb. Amenap'rkich ' Vank'i.

Terteriants, Ghukas. 1848. *Gitut'iwn vacharakanut'ean* [The science of commerce]. Vienna: Mkhitarist Press.

Tilly, Charles. 2005. *Trust and Rule.* New York: Cambridge University Press.

Tölölyan, Khachig. 1996. "Rethinking Diasporas: Stateless Power in the Transnational Moment." *Diaspora* 5: 3–36.

——. 1998. "Textual Nation: Poetry and Nationalism in Armenian Political Culture." In *Intellectuals and the Articulation of the Nation,* ed. Ronald G. Suny and Michael D. Kennedy. Ann Arbor: University of Michigan Press.

——. 2005. "Restoring the Logic of the Sedentary." In *Les diasporas: 2000 ans d'histoire,* ed. Lisa Anteby-Yemina, William Berthomière, and Gabriel Sheffer. Rennes: Presses Universitaires de Rennes.

Torgomian, Vahram. 1891. "Hay ardsanagrut'iwn mě i Marseyl" [An Armenian inscription in Marseilles]. *Handēs amsōreay: Baroyakan, usumnakan, aruestgitakan* 9: 272–273.

Trivellato, Francesca. 2003. "Juifs de Livourne, Italiens de Lisbonne, Hindous de Goa: Réseaux marchands et échanges interculturels à l'époque moderne." *Annales* (May-June): 581–603.

——. 2005. "Sephardic Merchants in the Early Modern Atlantic and Beyond: Toward a Comparative Historical Approach to Business Cooperation." In *Atlantic Diasporas: Jews and Crypto-Jews in the Age of Mercantilism, 1500–1800,* ed. Richard L. Kagan and Philip Morgan. Baltimore: Johns Hopkins University Press.

——. 2006. "Merchant Letters across Geographical and Social Boundaries." In *Corre-*

*spondence and Cultural Exchange in Europe, 1400–1700*, ed. Francisco Bethencourt and Florike Egmond. Cambridge: Cambridge University Press.

———. 2009. *The Familiarity of Strangers: The Sephardic Diaspora, Livorno, and Cross-Cultural Trade in the Early Modern Period*. New Haven, CT: Yale University Press.

Udovitch, Abraham L. 1962. "At the Origins of the Western *Commenda*: Islam, Israel, or Byzantium?" *Speculum* 37: 198–207.

———. 1970. *Partnership and Profit in Medieval Islam*. Princeton, NJ: Princeton University Press.

Ughurlian, Mesrop Vardapet. 1891. *Patmutʻiwn Hayotsʻ Gaghtakanutʻean ew shinutʻean ekeghetsʻwoy notsa i Livorno kʻaghakʻi handertsʻ yhavelwatsovkʻ* [History of the Armenian colony of Livorno and the construction of their church there, accompanied with appendices]. Venice: Mechitaris Press.

———. 1991. *Storia della colonia armena di Livorno della costruzione della sua chiesa (con appendici)*. Trans. Alessandro Orengo. Livorno: Tipografia O. Debatte.

Van der Cruysse, Dirk. 1998. *Chardin le Persan*. Paris: Fayard.

Van Dyke, Paul A. 2008. *The Canton Trade: Life and Enterprise on the China Coast, 1700–1845*. Hong Kong: Hong Kong University Press.

Van Leur, Jacob Cornelius. 1955. *Indonesian Trade and Society: Essays in Asian Social and Economic History*. The Hague: J. Van Hoeve.

Van Rooy, Sylvio. 1966. "Armenian Merchant Habits as Mirrored in 17th–18th Century Amsterdam Documents." *Revue des Études Arméniennes* 3: 347–357.

Vaux, Bert. 2002. *The Armenian Dialect of New Julfa*. Unpublished manuscript. [An annotated and modified translation of Acharian's original text.]

Vercellin, Giorgio. 1979. "Mercanti Turchi a Venezia alla fine dell Cinquecento." *Il Veltro* 23: 243–276.

Weber, Max. 1947. *Theory of Social and Economic Organization*. Edinburgh.

White, Maxwell. 1961. *Zaccaria Seriman, 1704–1784, and the "Viaggi di Enrico di Wanton": A Contribution to the Study of the Enlightenment in Italy*. Manchester, UK: Manchester University Press.

Williamson, Oliver E. 1993. "Calculativeness, Trust, and Economic Organization." *Journal of Law and Economics* 36.1, pt. 2: 453–486.

Woolcock, Michael. 1988. "Social Capital and Economic Development: Toward a Theoretical Synthesis and Social Policy Formation." *Theory and Society* 27.2 (April): 151–208.

Wright, Nadia H. 2003. *Respected Citizens: The History of Armenians in Singapore and Malaysia*. Victoria, Australia: Amasia Publishing.

Yukht, A. I. 1957. "Astrakhani Haykakan gaghuti bnakchʻutʻean sotsʻialakan kazmĕ18rt dari arachin kesum" [The social formation of the Armenian population of Astrakhan in the first half of the 18th century]. *Haykakan SSR Gitutʻyunneri Academyayi Teghekagir* 7: 47–60.

Zacks, Richard. 2002. *The Pirate Hunter: The True Story of Captain Kidd*. London: Hyperion.

Zekiyan, Boghos Levon. 1978a. *Le colonie Armene del Medio Evo in Italia e le relazioni culturali italo-armene*. Venice: San Lazzaro.

———. 1978b. "Xoga Safar ambasciatore di Shah ʻAbbas a Venezia." *Oriente Moderno* 58: 357–367.

————, ed. 1990. *Gli Armeni in Italia.* Rome: De Luca.

————, ed. 1996. *Ad limina Italiae, Ar druns Italioy: In viaggio per l'Italia con mercanti e monaci armeni.* Padua: Editoriale Programma.

————. 1999. "The Armenian Way to Modernity: The Diaspora and Its Role." In *Enlightenment and Diaspora: The Armenian and Jewish Cases,* ed. Richard G. Hovannisian and David N. Myers. Atlanta: Scholars Press.

Zekiyan, Boghos Levon, and Aldo Ferrari, eds. 2004. *Gli Armeni e Venezia: Dagli Sceriman a Mechitar; Il momento culminante di una consuetudine millenaria.* Venice: Ist. Veneto di Scienze, Lettere ed Arti.

# INDEX

Page numbers in italics refer to illustrations.

345

Alexei Mikhaylovich, Czar: Julfan gift to, 82, 83, 150

Alexevich (czar of Russia), agreement with Julfans, 145

Ali Qoli Khan. *See* Adil Shah

Alishan, Ghevont, 240nn9–10, 259n29; on Old Julfa, 241nn23,26, 244n73; on Venice, 28, 259n39, 260n42, 294n116

All Savior's Monastery (New Julfa): architecture of, 175; Archive of, xvii–xviii, 21, 102, 187, 189, 293n104; construction of, 40; information flow from, 182; merchant school at, 136–37, 268n15; missions of, 182; religious jurisdiction of, 52, 55, 212, 251n49, 252n51

Alpoyachian, Arshak, 247n2

*amanatkars* (commission agencies), 282n64

Amasya, treaty of (1555), 26

Amirbek di Vardan, 102, 273n65

Amsterdam: commercial importance of, 227; connection to New Julfa, 80; dissident minorities in, 79; Julfan community in, 79–80, 264n102, 265nn107–8, 269n21, 294n116; *jumiat* of, 192, 295n119; as regional center, 211; Sephardic community of, 227

Anderson, Benedict, 17

Angeles, F. Delor, 257n119

Arakelian, H., 241n29

Arakel of Tabriz, 32–33, 34, 36

Arasaratnam, Sinnappah, 198

Aras River, at Old Julfa, 26, 29, 35

architecture, Julfan, 175

Archivio di Stato di Firenze (ASFi), xvii, 21, 73, 261n54

Archivio di Stato di Venezia (ASV), xvii, 21, 157, 190

Arithmetic, merchants' training in, 137. *See also* accounting

Armenia, Cicilian: collapse of, 68; relations with Venice, 71, 125, 259n29

Armenia, classical: aristocracy of, 148

Armenian Gregorian Church: correspondence of, 110; diocesan headquarters of, 40, 52, 177, 182, 246n101; East India Company and, 49; excommunication from, 110, 276n93; marriage restrictions of, 155n15; merchants' relationship with, 75; relations with Roman Catholics, 62–63, 151; role in information flow, 181, 182–83; sanctions by, 182; services in private homes, 50, 249n33. *See also* All Savior's Monastery; churches, Armenian

Armenian language: alphabet of, 269n21; dialects

of, 236n15; transliteration of, xix–xx. *See also* Julfan dialect

Armenians: in Burmese politics, 253n66; converts to Islam, 30, 42, 203; *ghulam*, 30, 34, 38, 42; Ottoman subjects, 73, 76, 77, 178; of Umayyad dynasty, 125. *See also* Julfans; merchants, Armenian; merchants, Julfan

Armenis, Antoine, 75

Ascoli, Giuseppe da, 252n58

Asher, Catherine Ella Blanshard, 243n52

Ashraf, Shah: embassy to Ottomans (1725), 118, 204, 277n99

Ashul Khan, government of New Julfa, 208–9

Assembly of Merchants (New Julfa), 18, 41, 148, 212; adjudication of commercial disputes, 176, 194–95, 219, 230; information flow from, 182, 193; *jumiats* and, 193, 194–95, 196, 197, 199; Minasian family and, 290n52; petitions to, 188–90, 276n90, 280n30, 293nn104,106; ratification of documents, 189–90, 193, 196–97; regulation of *commenda* agents, 289n52; sanctions by, 196; Scerimans in, 164; taxation decisions of, 292n82; treaties of, 145–46; workings of, 187, 188–91

Assembly of Merchants and Portable Courts (AMPC), 193, 196, 197, 199, 295n124

Astrakhan: Armenian community in, 82–83, 174–76, 266n119, 289n46; Indian community of, 267n125; *rathaus* of, 83, 267n125

Astrakhan Code of Laws. *See Datastanagirk' Astrakhani Hayots'*

Aurangzeb (Mughal emperor), 224

Austro-Hungarian Empire, Sceriman family in, 150–51

*autos-da-fé*, 270n31. *See also* Nadir Shah Afshar, burnings under

Avachintz, Marcara, 191; dispute with Hakob, 197; trial of, 294nn115–16

Avachintz, Martin di Marcara, 4, 249n35

*avaks* (mercantile investments), 274n73

Avetik di Ibrahim, 300n43

Avet of the Khaldarents, 206–7

Aviet (son of Sarat), 154n10

Azaria (catholicos of Cilicia), 68

Azaria (catholicos of Sis), 239n2

*Azdarar* (newspaper), 51, 87–88

Babai, Sussan, 243n51

Babakhanian, Arakel, 145

Babayan, Kathryn, 31

Badger, G. P., 252n65

UNIVERSITY OF CALIFORNIA PRESS GRATEFULLY ACKNOWLEDGES THE
FOLLOWING GENEROUS DONORS TO THE AUTHORS IMPRINT ENDOW-
MENT FUND OF THE UNIVERSITY OF CALIFORNIA PRESS FOUNDATION.

Wendy Ashmore
Clarence & Jacqueline Avant
Diana & Ehrhard Bahr
Robert Borofsky
Beverly Bouwsma
Prof. Daniel Boyarin
Gene A. Brucker
William K. Coblentz
Joe & Wanda Corn
Liza Dalby
Sam Davis
William Deverell
Frances Dinkelspiel & Gary Wayne
Ross E. Dunn
Carol & John Field
Phyllis Gebauer
Walter S. Gibson
Jennifer A. González
Prof. Mary-Jo DelVecchio Good
    & Prof. Byron Good
The John Randolph Haynes & Dora Haynes
    Foundation / Gilbert Garcetti
Daniel Heartz
Leo & Florence Helzel / Helzel Family
    Foundation
Prof. & Mrs. D. Kern Holoman
Stephen & Gail Humphreys
Mark Juergensmeyer
Lawrence Kramer

Mary Gibbons Landor
Constance Lewallen
Raymond Lifchez
David & Sheila Littlejohn
Dianne Sachko Macleod
Thomas & Barbara Metcalf
Robert & Beverly Middlekauff
Jack & Jacqueline Miles
The Estate of David H. Miller
William & Sheila Nolan
Dale Peterson
Sheldon Pollock
Stephen P. Rice
Robert C. Ritchie
The Rosenthal Family Foundation /
    Jamie & David Wolf
Rémy & Nicole Saisselin
Carolyn See
Lisa See & Richard Kendall
Ruth A. Solie
Michael Sullivan
Patricia Trenton
Roy Wagner
J. Samuel Walker
John & Priscilla Walton
Kären Wigen & Martin Lewis
Lynne Withey
Stanley & Dorothy Wolpert

TEXT
10/12.5 Minion Pro

DISPLAY
Minion Pro

COMPOSITOR
Integrated Composition Systems

INDEXER
Roberta Engleman

CARTOGRAPHER
Bill Nelson

PRINTER AND BINDER
Maple-Vail Book Manufacturing Group